Adolescence in Literature

ENGLISH AND HUMANITIES SERIES

ADVISORY EDITOR: Lee A. Jacobus
University of Connecticut, Storrs

Adolescence in Literature
Thomas West Gregory

Business in Literature
Charles A. Burden, Elke Burden, Lynn Ganim, and Sterling Eisiminger

Fifty Contemporary Poets: The Creative Process
Alberta T. Turner

Medicine in Literature
Joseph F. Ceccio

Sharing Literature with Children: A Thematic Anthology
Francelia Butler

Short Stories from Around the World
Lee A. Jacobus

Sports in Literature
Henry B. Chapin

Writing in the Margin: From Annotation to Critical Essay
Ronald Primeau

Adolescence in Literature

Thomas West Gregory
University of Richmond

Longman

New York and London

ADOLESCENCE IN LITERATURE

Longman Inc., New York
Associated companies, branches, and representatives
throughout the world.

Developmental Editor: Gordon T. R. Anderson
Interior Design: Angela Foote
Cover Design: Copyright © by Abner Graboff
Manufacturing and Production Supervisor: Kris Becker
Composition: Maryland Linotype Composition Co., Inc.
Printing and Binding: The Maple Press, Inc.

Library of Congress Cataloging in Publication Data

Main entry under title:

Adolescence in literature.

    (English and humanities series)
    Bibliography: p.
    Includes index.
    1. Adolescence—Fiction.   2. Short stories,
American.   I. Gregory, Thomas West.
PZ1.A2294   [PS648.A34]   813'.01   77-17719
ISBN 0-582-228045-1

Manufactured in the United States of America
2 4 6 8 9 7 5 3

For G. Robert Carlsen

Acknowledgments

"A Temple of the Holy Ghost" by Flannery O'Connor. Copyright, 1954, by Flannery O'Connor. Reprinted from her volume, *A Good Man Is Hard to Find and Other Stories*, by permission of Harcourt Brace Jovanovich, Inc.

"The Thumping of the Grass" by Philip F. O'Connor. From *Old Morals, Small Continents, Darker Times* by Philip F. O'Connor. Copyright © 1971 by the University of Iowa Press. Reprinted by permission of the University of Iowa Press and the author.

"Barred" by John O'Hara. Copyright © 1967 by John O'Hara. Reprinted from *And Other Stories*, by John O'Hara, by permission of Random House, Inc.

"Sentimental Education" by Harold Brodkey. Reprinted by permission of International Creative Management. Copyright © 1958 by Harold Brodkey. First published in *The New Yorker*.

"Cecelia Rosas" by Amado Muro. First appeared in the *New Mexico Quarterly*, volume xxxiv:4 (Winter 1964–65), Copyright © 1965 by the University of New Mexico Press. Reprinted by permission of Mrs. Chester Seltzer.

"The White Circle" by John Bell Clayton. Reprinted with permission of Macmillan Publishing Co., Inc. from *The Strangers Were There* by John Bell Clayton. Copyright 1947 by Harper & Brothers. Copyright renewed 1975 by John Bell Clayton III.

"Waiting for Jim" by Vera Randall. Reprinted by permission from *The Colorado Quarterly*. Copyright © 1963 by the University of Colorado, Boulder, Colorado.

"The Lesson" by James Purdy. James Purdy, *Children Is All*. Copyright © 1959 by James Purdy. Reprinted by permission of New Directions Publishing Corporation.

"Mr. Princeton" by Marvin Schiller. Copyright 1958 by Epoch Associates. Reprinted by permission.

"The Potato Baron and the Line" by Stephen Tracy. Reprinted by permission; © 1972 The New Yorker Magazine, Inc.

"A Kind of Savage" by James Baker Hall. Reprint from *The Saturday Evening Post* © 1968 The Curtis Publishing Company.

"The Outing" by James Baldwin. "The Outing" excerpted from *Going to Meet the Man* by James Baldwin. Copyright © 1951 By James Baldwin. Originally published in *New Story*. Reprinted by permission of The Dial Press.

"Like a Piece of Blues" by George Davis. Copyright © 1967 by George Davis. From *Black World*, July 1967. Reprinted by permission of the author.

"If They Knew Yvonne" by Andre Dubus. Copyright © 1969 by Andre Dubus. From *North American Review*, volume 6, number 3, 1969. Reprinted by permission of the author.

"Point of Conversion" by Starkey Flythe. Copyright © 1971 by the Antioch Review, Inc. Reprinted from *The Antioch Review*, Vol. XXXI, No. 1, by permission of the editors.

"The Conversion of the Jews" by Philip Roth. From *Goodbye, Columbus and Five Stories*. Copyright © 1959 by Philip Roth. Reprinted by permission of Houghton Mifflin Company.

"The Law" by Hugh Nissenson. From *A Pile of Stones* by Hugh Nissenson. Reprinted by permission of William Morris Agency, Inc. Copyright © 1965 by Hugh Nissenson.

"Phineas" by John Knowles. Copyright © 1956 by John Knowles. Reprinted from *Phineas*, John Knowles, by permission of Random House, Inc.

"The Somebody" by Danny Santiago. Copyright © 1970 by Danny Santiago. First published in *Redbook Magazine*. Reprinted by permission of Brandt & Brandt.

"The Sorcerer's Eye" by Howard Nemerov. From *A Commodity of Dreams* by Howard Nemerov. Copyright © 1947, 1948, 1953, 1955, 1956, 1957, 1958, 1959 by Howard Nemerov. Reprinted by permission of Simon & Schuster, Inc.

"The Grey Bird" by Hannah Green. Reprinted by permission of Russell & Volkening, Inc. as agents for the author. Copyright © 1954 by Hannah Green.

Contents

Preface

In recent years a great deal of critical and popular attention has been devoted to adolescents as heroes of important novels, yet, surprisingly, no one has systematically examined the short story as it portrays adolescence. This anthology offers the reader a representative selection of stories about adolescents living in modern America. In keeping with recent scholarly trends (psychosociological criticism, contextualism, phenomenology, structuralism, neo-historianism), it is concerned with literature existing in time and relating to its immediate cultural context. For many years the editors of *Prize Stories: The O. Henry Awards* and *The Best American Short Stories* have observed that of the different genres the short story, with its quality of on-the-spot reportage, most immediately reflects society. These stories are by American authors about American adolescence from World War II to the present and serve as a psychosociological document of the period.

Adolescents have been fascinating personalities in American literature ever since Mark Twain set Huck Finn on his odyssey down the Mississippi a little over ninety years ago. Like Huck, his literary descendants in modern fiction also have to discover that the journey to maturity requires an exquisite struggle. It is this struggle that is the heart of the universal fascination with literature about adolescence. Twain's portrayal of Huck was well ahead of the times, for its realism and lack of moralizing contrasted with the sentimental, didactic literature of his day, a trend that prevailed until World War I.

Much of the prewar fiction concerning adolescence was formulaic and based on stereotypes. Most notable of these were the gawky, mischievous boy and the virtuous, simpering girl. Both characters were without guilt, doubt, and complexity of character; both were laughably innocent. Booth Tarkington, Gene Stratton-Porter, and Burt L. Standish were among the most popular writers of the time who established their reputations by creating variations of these stock characters. It is noteworthy that Standish wrote more than 200 novels about his hero Frank Merriwell, an extraordinary athlete who always won the game at the last minute while never deviating from his code of fair play; over 25,000,000 copies of Standish's novels were sold. The poor literary quality and great number of popular novels of adolescence caused most critics and readers to shy away from it as a subject worthy of serious consideration. For the most part, a patronizing humor and naïve sentimentality predominated in the novels and short stories about adolescence before World War I.

During the prewar period there was also the growth of naturalism in American fiction and the development of psychology and sociology. These came together in serious fiction to help create a more realistic portrait of adolescence than the facile one found in popular fiction. Stephen Crane's *The Red Badge of Courage* and Sherwood Anderson's *Windy McPherson's Son* are fine examples of frank, probing considerations of the thoughts, motives, and actions of young people. The short fiction and novels of the "Jazz Age" characterized a rebellion against the naïveté and optimism of prewar times; and F. Scott Fitzgerald's *This Side of Paradise* was one of many novels that created this mood of disenchantment. With the Great Depression of the thirties, a strong current of social criticism joined with the rebellious attitude of the preceding decade. A documentation of the American proletariat predominated in literature, with the novels and stories of John Dos Passos, James T. Farrell, and John Steinbeck best illustrating the trend. The best writers of the period, William Faulkner and Thomas Wolfe, showed little interest in the proletarian cause. However, all of them created a number of enduring adolescent personalities: Henry Fleming, George Willard, Studs Lonigan, Ike McCaslin, and Eugene Gant, to mention only a few.

The end of World War II was used as the beginning of this survey because it marks the start of a trend in which adolescence is generally treated with candor. As an aftermath of the war there was a revival among popular writers of the innocent, often ridiculous, but ever-lovable adolescent. On the other hand, the better postwar writers stressed the probing of the conscious and subconscious, the interaction of complex personalities, and the use of symbols and depth psychology. By the end of the forties prudery and censorship were overcome to the point that there were few phases of human activity that were not explored in fiction. Richard Wright's *Native Son* and Truman Capote's *Other Voices, Other Rooms* exemplify the honesty with which writers could examine their themes.

During the fifties, depth psychology and the use of symbolism were used extensively. Naturalism was in decline but not yet dead. The psychological problems of adolescents had become a focus of interest, with J. D. Salinger's

Holden Caulfield summing up the disillusionment of many adolescents of the early fifties as he soliloquized about adolescent troubles. Later in the decade the "beat generation" created a literature that expressed its rage and despair in the age of the atomic bomb. This existentialistic attitude was expressed in a rejection of all inhibitions and found release in sex, drugs, jazz, and aimless wandering. Jack Kerouac's *On the Road* became the philosophical handbook for many young people of the late fifties. America's involvement in Vietnam further aggravated the pessimism of the sixties and continued it to the present. Since the end of World War II, with all these social and historical developments, the growing trend in American short fiction about adolescents has been characterized by a candid, honest treatment of adolescents and their society.

The major criterion in selecting the stories in this anthology was that they had to deal with the experiences of adolescents. Arriving at a working definition of adolescence was problematic. Definitions currently in use by experts in the disciplines of psychology, sociology, anthropology, medicine, and education are based on differing considerations. Adolescence has been defined variously in terms of psychological maturity, emotional development, familial dependence, physical growth, chronological age, and grade placement in school. All experts are somewhat in agreement, though, that chronological age is an adequate definition of adolescence in contemporary American society. The ages of twelve to twenty-one have been used as outside limits because they include most definitions and sufficiently describe the transition from late childhood dependence to the early maturity of adulthood. However, almost all of the main characters in this collection fall between the somewhat narrower limits of ages thirteen and eighteen.

The anthology emphasizes a psychosociological approach to the study of adolescence through literature. Its seven section headings identify themes that represent the most important stages of adolescent development. These are sexual awakening and experience; emotional development; family relationships; social adjustment and delinquency; schools, students, and teachers; religions and values; and initiation and identity. In actuality the stages of adolescent development are not so clearly divided, overlapping and paralleling each other in many ways. Sometimes one stage may predominate, as in the case of youngsters who are completely absorbed in establishing their social status within a group. At other times a stage may seem quiescent— for example, when adolescents' value systems evolve imperceptibly over a long period of time. All of the stages are important. All occur in different intensities and combinations depending on individual circumstances.

Only a handful of books has used a psychosociological approach to literature about adolescence. The design of the books is one in which psychological and sociological facts are defined and then illustrated by excerpts from novels, and the range of literature referred to is impressive. Nevertheless, they suffer from a minor fault: for most readers the quotations lack context and are difficult to place in their proper literary perspective. By using short fiction to illustrate important psychosociological stages, this anthology can present the reader with five complete stories about each stage and can present the material on adolescence without the literary distortion of missing context.

The stories are arranged to illustrate the various stages of adolescent development as literary themes, though no one story is solely restricted to a single category. Many overlap or fit equally well into more than one section. While it appears in section one, "Sexual Awakening and Experience," Harold Brodkey's "Sentimental Education" could easily be placed in some of the other sections: it says a great deal about the emotional development of two people experiencing their first serious love; it gives a penetrating view of student life away from the classroom; and it reveals a rite of passage into the adult world. Its placement in "Sexual Awakening and Experience" is appropriate because it works well with the other four stories of that section to develop the theme adequately. Each section is intended to offer representative points of view on its theme that will stir provocative discussions and carry over to the other stories of the book. Of course, the arrangement does not preclude reading at random, for each story offers its own distinctive insight into the lives of modern adolescents. Because most stories can illustrate the themes of more than one section, introductions to the seven sections contain interpretive comments, not only on the five stories of the particular section but also on related stories in other sections.

The collection is the outcome of a four-year survey of approximately 100,000 short stories. The primary sources examined were the *Short Story Index* and its five supplements and the more widely adopted college anthologies in use since 1945; the stories included in these primary sources were drawn from the full range of publications in which short fiction appears: "little magazines," college and university quarterlies, popular magazines with national circulations, authors' collections, and yearly compilations of "best" and "prize" short fiction, to catalogue the most common secondary sources. Of the 1,000 or so short stories published in America each year, roughly 200 have real literary merit, and of these only about twenty to thirty deal in some way with adolescence; from the end of World War II this number has been fairly consistent and indicates a theme that has continually interested writers. The reason seems self-evident in light of the growing economic power, political sophistication, social conscience, and educational attainments of adolescents over the past thirty years.

There are several reasons why the stories were collected. Most important, all of them have been used in class as a basis for discussions and writing assignments, and the response to them has been enthusiastic and positive. Certainly students were pleased in being able to identify with familiar situations and personalities, but their main delight was experienced in reading first-rate modern fiction. As a teacher with an interest in the social sciences as they relate to literature, this editor after much searching could not find an anthology such as this one. And so the book was conceived and compiled with several audiences in mind: students and teachers of English realizing the need to use short stories together with novels in teaching literature for the adolescent; students in psychology and sociology courses dealing with adolescence wanting to correlate a casebook of fiction with their texts; students of reading instruction and library science needing a more thorough knowledge of the literature they will be recommending to young readers; special-topics courses in the modern short story; and, most important, adolescents, for this is a book for and about them.

The final selections represent two groups of writers: those with firmly established reputations and those emerging as artists of stature. All, however, might well be called the "new voices" since World War II. The writings demonstrate the technical mastery of form that has characterized the American short story since its inception. They range in length from the vignette of several pages to the long-short story that is nearly a novelette and offer the reader a typical cross section of contemporary techniques of narration, characterization, plotting, style, and tone. They are enjoyable and provocative and serve as a case study in the developments that have taken place in modern American short fiction.

1
Sexual Awakening and Experience

BECAUSE IT IS SO READILY APPARENT, the onset of puberty is a dramatic occurrence in the lives of young people and their parents. Both notice and comment on the rapid physical changes that are taking place in the adolescent: the increase in height and weight, the alteration of voice, the appearance of facial and pubic hair, the growth of the sex organs, the broadening of shoulders for boys and the rounding of hips for girls. All these changes cause adolescents to become intensely aware of their bodies and to spend much time appraising them as the outward symbols of self.

At the same time as adolescents are beginning to consolidate their biological and psychological dimensions, they are also having to grapple with strong social forces. Their interest in the opposite sex intensifies as they become sexually mature, yet their need for sexual fulfillment is discouraged by the restraints and taboos set by society. Further aggravating the situation is the prolongation of adolescent dependence, very often through the college years and into adulthood. Society's expectations of sexual abstinence, especially at a time when adolescent sexual drives are so powerful, creates a great deal of anxiety. Within the last decade or two the revolution in the United States regarding sexual mores has had as its most important features a sexually titillating media, secularism, female emancipation, safe contraception, legalized abortion, and some medical guarantee against the fear of venereal disease. By and large, however, the permissiveness promised by the sexual revolution is an invitation from which adolescents are excluded.

A large number of stories about adolescence deal with sex and cover the full range of sexual expression. These stories may be divided into two general categories: those that explore "normal" heterosexual relationships, from hand holding and kissing to petting and sexual intercourse; and those that explore sexual activity traditionally considered "abnormal," such as voyeurism, fetishism, masturbation, homosexuality, incest, and prostitution. Certain shifts in these classifications reflect society's changing attitude toward sexual practice. At present, for instance, the "abnormality" of masturbation and homosexuality are much debated issues. At any rate, stories in the first category have been continually published since the turn of the century; stories in the second have been published with increasing frequency since World War II as censorship has been relaxed. Both categories include a number of themes that appear regularly and deserve close examination. All the stories help to explain the powerful role sex plays in the lives of adolescents.

The theme concerning adolescent sexual experience that has been written about most and for the longest period of time deals with adolescent crushes. The censors never seem to have been bothered by these stories, and the general public has steadily demanded them—and for obvious reasons. They are only indirectly concerned with sexual issues or bypass them altogether, and they are usually narrated in a humorous vein. They are safe reading for anyone. "Cecilia Rosas" and "The Four Sides of a Triangle" (section 3) are typical examples of the crush theme, particularly as they show younger persons being attracted to someone older and inevitably discovering the impossibility of their infatuations. The humorous element injected into this type of story provides laughter for the reader; however, it seldom lessens the sting felt by rejected young lovers. Still, the perceptive reader also senses that these adolescents, with their hard-earned knowledge about the opposite sex, will move on to more realistic and successful romances in the future. A variation on the crush theme is found in "Waiting for Jim" (section 2). This story examines a growing attraction between two adolescents and ends by broadly hinting at what the sexual consequences of that attraction will be. In the crush story there is little or no physical contact but merely an idealized worshiping from afar.

Typifying the theme of first sexual experience are "The Thumping of the Grass," "A Temple of the Holy Ghost," and "The Vault" (section 3). Most stories of this kind deal with autoeroticism or mutual masturbation and for the most part are not concerned with affection. The customary sequence of emotions is one in which fear is overcome by sexual curiosity, which in turn gives way to apprehension. In "The Vault," written in the late forties, the habit of masturbation is alluded to by the father as the cause of his son's pimples. The boy is so stricken with guilt he has written "in his algebra book on every other page to the last page of the book 'It will drive you crazy.'" In contrast, the explicit description of masturbation and petting in "The Thumping of the Grass," written in the late sixties, confronts the issues forthrightly and in a way few writers of the forties would have attempted. Nevertheless, a feeling of guilt also pervades this story. In "A Temple of the Holy Ghost" Susan and Joanne, convent-schooled and naïve, go to a country fair with their dates. There they see and listen to a hermaphrodite in a side show. Though the encounter is grotesque, it piques their curiosity more than it disturbs them. In fact, Susan later tells her younger cousin in a matter-of-fact fashion that "it was a man and woman both. It pulled up its dress and showed us. It had on a blue dress." Bizarre as the incident is, it seems not to cause the girls much concern, yet it marks the beginning of their sexual awakening.

"Barred" is a period piece on the theme of prostitution. Stories of adolescents losing their virginity in whorehouses are seldom written any more except as reminiscenses. Because of the sexual revolution of the sixties and seventies, allowing male and female adolescents more freedom to experiment with sex, few houses of prostitution now thrive as they used to on the clientele supplied by colleges and universities. Another type of story that receives little attention today concerns unwed mothers. Again, modern contraception and legalized abortion make "Point of Conversion" (section 6) more a story of historical interest than one of pressing current concern.

A type of story that has become very popular in the last fifteen years is about college couples living as husband and wife. Sometimes in these stories they are able to live together openly with the implicit approval of society, as is "The Potato Baron and the Line" (section 5), and sometimes they must be furtive about their relationship because of restrictive parietals, as in "Sentimental Education." The protagonists in these stories are generally drawn together by love, mutual interests, and a genuine concern for each other. There is a merging of one personality with another and a commitment of self that rises above childish sexual curiosity and experimentation. Even so, most of these experimental marriages do not last long.

Until recently the subject of homosexuality has been generally ignored in short fiction. "The Outing" (section 6) is a fine example of a growing body of stories that explore this theme with compassion, insight, and sensitivity. However, most of the stories published on this theme are about adult, not adolescent, homosexuality.

Flannery O'Connor
A Temple of
the Holy Ghost

ALL WEEK END THE TWO GIRLS were calling each other Temple One and
Temple Two, shaking with laughter and getting so red and hot that they
were positively ugly, particularly Joanne, who had spots on her face anyway. They came in the brown convent uniforms they had to wear at Mount
St. Scholastica but as soon as they opened their suitcases, they took off the
uniforms and put on red skirts and loud blouses. They put on lipstick and
their Sunday shoes and walked around in the high heels all over the house,
always passing the long mirror in the hall slowly to get a look at their legs.
None of their ways were lost on the child. If only one of them had come,
that one would have played with her, but since there were two of them,
she was out of it and watched them suspiciously from a distance.

They were fourteen—two years older than she was—but neither of them
was bright, which was why they had been sent to the convent. If they had
gone to a regular school, they wouldn't have done anything but think about
boys; at the convent the sisters, her mother said, would keep a grip on their
necks. The child decided, after observing them for a few hours, that they
were practically morons and she was glad to think that they were only
second cousins and she couldn't have inherited any of their stupidity. Susan
called herself Su-zan. She was very skinny but she had a pretty pointed face
and red hair. Joanne had yellow hair that was naturally curly but she talked
through her nose and when she laughed, she turned purple in patches.
Neither one of them could say an intelligent thing and all their sentences
began, "You know this boy I know well one time he . . ."

They were to stay all week end and her mother said she didn't see how
she would entertain them since she didn't know any boys their age. At this,
the child, struck suddenly with genius, shouted, "There's Cheat! Get Cheat
to come! Ask Miss Kirby to get Cheat to come show them around!" and

she nearly choked on the food she had in her mouth. She doubled over laughing and hit the table with her fist and looked at the two bewildered girls while water started in her eyes and rolled down her fat cheeks and the braces she had in her mouth glared like tin. She had never thought of anything so funny before.

Her mother laughed in a guarded way and Miss Kirby blushed and carried her fork delicately to her mouth with one pea on it. She was a long-faced blonde schoolteacher who boarded with them and Mr. Cheatam was her admirer, a rich old farmer who arrived every Saturday afternoon in a fifteen-year-old baby-blue Pontiac powdered with red clay dust and black inside with Negroes that he charged ten cents apiece to bring into town on Saturday afternoons. After he dumped them he came to see Miss Kirby, always bringing a little gift—a bag of boiled peanuts or a watermelon or a stalk of sugar cane and once a wholesale box of Baby Ruth candy bars. He was bald-headed except for a little fringe of rust-colored hair and his face was nearly the same color as the unpaved roads and washed like them with ruts and gulleys. He wore a pale green shirt with a thin black stripe in it and blue galluses and his trousers cut across a protruding stomach that he pressed tenderly from time to time with his big flat thumb. All his teeth were backed with gold and he would roll his eyes at Miss Kirby in an impish way and say, "Haw haw," sitting in their porch swing with his legs spread apart and his hightopped shoes pointing in opposite directions on the floor.

"I don't think Cheat is going to be in town this week end," Miss Kirby said, not in the least understanding that this was a joke, and the child was convulsed afresh, threw herself backward in her chair, fell out of it, rolled on the floor and lay there heaving. Her mother told her if she didn't stop this foolishness she would have to leave the table.

Yesterday her mother had arranged with Alonzo Myers to drive them the forty-five miles to Mayville, where the convent was, to get the girls for the week end and Sunday afternoon he was hired to drive them back again. He was an eighteen-year-old boy who weighed two hundred and fifty pounds and worked for the taxi company and he was all you could get to drive you anywhere. He smoked or rather chewed a short black cigar and he had a round sweaty chest that showed through the yellow nylon shirt he wore. When he drove all the windows of the car had to be open.

"Well there's Alonzo!" the child roared from the floor. "Get Alonzo to show em around! Get Alonzo!"

The two girls, who had seen Alonzo, began to scream their indignation.

Her mother thought this was funny too but she said, "That'll be about enough out of you," and changed the subject. She asked them why they called each other Temple One and Temple Two and this sent them off into gales of giggles. Finally they managed to explain. Sister Perpetua, the oldest nun at the Sisters of Mercy in Mayville, had given them a lecture on what to do if a young man should—here they laughed so hard they were not able to go on without going back to the beginning—on what to do if a young man should—they put their heads in their laps—on what to do if—they finally managed to shout it out—if he should "behave in an ungentlemanly manner with them in the back of an automobile." Sister Perpetua said they were to say, "Stop sir! I am a Temple of the Holy Ghost!" and that would put an end to it. The child sat up off the floor with a blank face. She didn't see anything so funny in this. What was really funny was the idea of Mr. Cheatam or Alonzo Myers beauing them around. That killed her.

Her mother didn't laugh at what they had said. "I think you girls are pretty silly," she said. "After all, that's what you are—Temples of the Holy Ghost."

The two of them looked up at her, politely concealing their giggles, but with astonished faces as if they were beginning to realize that she was made of the same stuff as Sister Perpetua.

Miss Kirby preserved her set expression and the child thought, it's all over her head anyhow. I am a Temple of the Holy Ghost, she said to herself, and was pleased with the phrase. It made her feel as if somebody had given her a present.

After dinner, her mother collapsed on the bed and said, "Those girls are going to drive me crazy if I don't get some entertainment for them. They're awful."

"I bet I know who you could get," the child started.

"Now listen. I don't want to hear any more about Mr. Cheatam," her mother said. "You embarrass Miss Kirby. He's her only friend. Oh my Lord," and she sat up and looked mournfully out the window, "that poor soul is so lonesome she'll even ride in that car that smells like the last circle in hell."

And she's a Temple of the Holy Ghost too, the child reflected. "I wasn't thinking of him," she said. "I was thinking of those two Wilkinses, Wendell and Cory, that visit old lady Buchell out on her farm. They're her grandsons. They work for her."

"Now that's an idea," her mother murmured and gave her an appreciative look. But then she slumped again. "They're only farm boys. These girls would turn up their noses at them."

"Huh," the child said. "They wear pants. They're sixteen and they got a car. Somebody said they were both going to be Church of God preachers because you don't have to know nothing to be one."

"They would be perfectly safe with those boys all right," her mother said and in a minute she got up and called their grandmother on the telephone and after she had talked to the old woman a half an hour, it was arranged that Wendell and Cory would come to supper and afterwards take the girls to the fair.

Susan and Joanne were so pleased that they washed their hair and rolled it up on aluminum curlers. Hah, thought the child, sitting cross-legged on the bed to watch them undo the curlers, wait'll you get a load of Wendell and Cory! "You'll like these boys," she said. "Wendell is six feet tall ands got red hair. Cory is six feet six inches talls got black hair and wears a sport jacket and they gottem this car with a squirrel tail on the front."

"How does a child like you know so much about these men?" Susan asked and pushed her face up close to the mirror to watch the pupils in her eyes dilate.

The child lay back on the bed and began to count the narrow boards in the ceiling until she lost her place. I know them all right, she said to someone. We fought in the world war together. They were under me and I saved them five times from Japanese suicide divers and Wendell said I am going to marry that kid and the other said oh no you ain't I am and I said neither one of you is because I will court marshall you all before you can bat an eye. "I've seen them around is all," she said.

When they came the girls stared at them a second and then began to giggle and talk to each other about the convent. They sat in the swing together and Wendell and Cory sat on the banisters together. They sat like monkeys, their knees on a level with their shoulders and their arms hanging down between. They were short thin boys with red faces and high cheekbones and pale seed-like eyes. They had brought a harmonica and a guitar. One of them began to blow softly on the mouth organ, watching the girls over it, and the other started strumming the guitar and then began to sing, not watching them but keeping his head tilted upward as if he were only interested in hearing himself. He was singing a hillbilly song that sounded half like a love song and half like a hymn.

The child was standing on a barrel pushed into some bushes at the side of the house, her face on a level with the porch floor. The sun was going down and the sky was turning a bruised violet color that seemed to be connected with the sweet mournful sound of the music. Wendell began to smile as he sang and to look at the girls. He looked at Susan with a dog-like loving look and sang,

> "I've found a friend in Jesus,
> He's everything to me,
> He's the lily of the valley,
> He's the One who's set me free!"

Then he turned the same look on Joanne and sang,

> "A wall of fire about me,
> I've nothing now to fear,
> He's the lily of the valley,
> And I'll always have Him near!"

The girls looked at each other and held their lips stiff so as not to giggle but Susan let out one anyway and clapped her hand on her mouth. The singer frowned and for a few seconds only strummed the guitar. Then he began "The Old Rugged Cross" and they listened politely but when he had finished they said, "Let us sing one!" and before he could start another, they began to sing with their convent-trained voices,

> "Tantum ergo Sacramentum
>   Veneremur Cernui:
> Et antiquum documentum
>   Novo cedat ritui:"

The child watched the boys' solemn faces turn with perplexed frowning stares at each other as if they were uncertain whether they were being made fun of.

> "Praestet fides supplementum
>   Sensuum defectui.
> Genitori, Genitoque
>   Laus et jubilatio
>
> Salus, honor, virtus quoque . . ."

The boys' faces were dark red in the gray-purple light. They looked fierce and startled.

> "Sit et benedictio;
> Procedenti ab utroque
>   Compar sit laudatio.
>   Amen."

The girls dragged out the Amen and then there was a silence.

"That must be Jew singing," Wendell said and began to tune the guitar.

The girls giggled idiotically but the child stamped her foot on the barrel. "You big dumb ox!" she shouted. "You big dumb Church of God ox!" she roared and fell off the barrel and scrambled up and shot around the corner of the house as they jumped from the banister to see who was shouting.

Her mother had arranged for them to have supper in the back yard and she had a table laid out there under some Japanese lanterns that she pulled out for garden parties. "I ain't eating with them," the child said and snatched her plate off the table and carried it to the kitchen and sat down with the thin blue-gummed cook and ate her supper.

"Howcome you be so ugly sometime?" the cook asked.

"Those stupid idiots," the child said.

The lanterns gilded the leaves of the trees orange on the level where they hung and above them was black-green and below them were different dim muted colors that made the girls sitting at the table look prettier than they were. From time to time, the child turned her head and glared out the kitchen window at the scene below.

"God could strike you deaf dumb and blind," the cook said, "and then you wouldn't be as smart as you is."

"I would still be smarter than some," the child said.

After supper they left for the fair. She wanted to go to the fair but not with them so even if they had asked her she wouldn't have gone. She went upstairs and paced the long bedroom with her hands locked together behind her back and her head thrust forward and an expression, fierce and dreamy both, on her face. She didn't turn on the electric light but let the darkness collect and make the room smaller and more private. At regular intervals a light crossed the open window and threw shadows on the wall. She stopped and stood looking out over the dark slopes, past where the pond glinted silver, past the wall of woods to the speckled sky where a long finger of light was revolving up and around and away, searching the air as if it were hunting for the lost sun. It was the beacon light from the fair.

She could hear the distant sound of the calliope and she saw in her head all the tents raised up in a kind of gold sawdust light and the diamond ring of the ferris wheel going around and around up in the air and down again and the screeking merry-go-round going around and around on the ground. A fair lasted five or six days and there was a special afternoon for school children and a special night for niggers. She had gone last year on the afternoon for school children and had seen the monkeys and the fat man and had ridden on the ferris wheel. Certain tents were closed then because they contained things that would be known only to grown people but she had looked with interest at the advertising on the closed tents, at the faded-looking pictures on the canvas of people in tights, with stiff stretched composed faces like the faces of the martyrs waiting to have their tongues cut out by the Roman soldier. She had imagined that what was inside these tents concerned medicine and she had made up her mind to be a doctor when she grew up.

She had since changed and decided to be an engineer but as she looked out the window and followed the revolving searchlight as it widened and shortened and wheeled in its arc, she felt that she would have to be much more than just a doctor or an engineer. She would have to be a saint because that was the occupation that included everything you could know; and yet she knew she would never be a saint. She did not steal or murder but she was a born liar and slothful and she sassed her mother and was deliberately ugly to almost everybody. She was eaten up also with the sin of Pride, the worst one. She made fun of the Baptist preacher who came to the school at commencement to give the devotional. She would pull down her mouth and hold her forehead as if she were in agony and groan, "Fawther, we thank Thee," exactly the way he did and she had been told many times not to do it. She could never be a saint, but she thought she could be a martyr if they killed her quick.

She could stand to be shot but not to be burned in oil. She didn't know if she could stand to be torn to pieces by lions or not. She began to prepare her martyrdom, seeing herself in a pair of tights in a great arena, lit by the early Christians hanging in cages of fire, making a gold dusty light that fell on her and the lions. The first lion charged forward and fell at her feet, converted. A whole series of lions did the same. The lions liked her so much she even slept with them and finally the Romans were obliged to burn her but to their astonishment she would not burn down and finding she was so hard to kill, they finally cut off her head very quickly with a sword and she went immediately to heaven. She rehearsed this several times, returning each time at the entrance of Paradise to the lions.

Finally she got up from the window and got ready for bed and got in without saying her prayers. There were two heavy double beds in the room. The girls were occupying the other one and she tried to think of something cold and clammy that she could hide in their bed but her thought was fruitless. She didn't have anything she could think of, like a chicken carcass or a piece of beef liver. The sound of the calliope coming through the window kept her awake and she remembered that she hadn't said her prayers and got up and knelt down and began them. She took a running start and went through to the other side of the Apostle's Creed and then hung by her chin on the side of the bed, empty-minded. Her prayers, when she remembered to say them, were usually perfunctory but sometimes when she had done something wrong or heard music or lost something, or sometimes for no reason at all, she would be moved to fervor and would think of Christ on the long journey to Calvary, crushed three times under the rough cross. Her mind would stay on this awhile and then get empty and when something roused her, she would find that she was thinking of a different thing entirely, of some dog or some girl or something she was going to do some day. Tonight, remembering Wendell and Cory, she was filled with thanksgiving and almost weeping with delight, she said, "Lord, Lord, thank You that I'm not in the Church of God, thank You, Lord, thank You!" and got back in bed and kept repeating it until she went to sleep.

The girls came in at a quarter to twelve and waked her up with their giggling. They turned on the small blue-shaded lamp to see to get undressed by and their skinny shadows climbed up the wall and broke and continued moving about softly on the ceiling. The child sat up to hear what all they had seen at the fair. Susan had a plastic pistol full of cheap candy and Joanne a pasteboard cat with red polka dots in it. "Did you see the monkeys dance?" the child asked. "Did you see that fat man and those midgets?"

"All kinds of freaks," Joanne said. And then she said to Susan, "I enjoyed it all but the you-know-what," and her face assumed a peculiar expression as if she had bit into something that she didn't know if she liked or not.

The other stood still and shook her head once and nodded slightly at the child. "Little pitchers," she said in a low voice but the child heard it and her heart began to beat very fast.

She got out of her bed and climbed onto the footboard of theirs. They turned off the light and got in but she didn't move. She sat there, looking hard at them until their faces were well defined in the dark. "I'm not as old as you all," she said, "but I'm about a million times smarter."

"There are some things," Susan said, "that a child of your age doesn't know," and they both began to giggle.

"Go back to your own bed," Joanne said.

The child didn't move. "One time," she said, her voice hollow-sounding in the dark, "I saw this rabbit have rabbits."

There was a silence. Then Susan said, "How?" in an indifferent tone and she knew that she had them. She said she wouldn't tell until they told about the you-know-what. Actually she had never seen a rabbit have rabbits but she forgot this as they began to tell what they had seen in the tent.

It had been a freak with a particular name but they couldn't remember the name. The tent where it was had been divided into two parts by a black curtain, one side for men and one for women. The freak went from one side to the other, talking first to the men and then to the women, but everyone could hear. The stage ran all the way across the front. The girls heard the freak say to the men, "I'm going to show you this and if you laugh, God may strike you the same way." The freak had a country voice, slow and nasal and neither high nor low, just flat. "God made me thisaway and if you laugh He may strike you the same way. This is the way He wanted me to be and I ain't disputing His way. I'm showing you because I got to make the best of it. I expect you to act like ladies and gentlemen. I never done it to myself nor had a thing to do with it but I'm making the best of it. I don't dispute hit." Then there was a long silence on the other side of the tent and finally the freak left the men and came over onto the women's side and said the same thing.

The child felt every muscle strained as if she were hearing the answer to a riddle that was more puzzling than the riddle itself. "You mean it had two heads?" she said.

"No," Susan said, "it was a man and woman both. It pulled up its dress and showed us. It had on a blue dress."

The child wanted to ask how it could be a man and woman both without two heads but she did not. She wanted to get back into her own bed and think it out and she began to climb down off the footboard.

"What about the rabbit?" Joanne asked.

The child stopped and only her face appeared over the footboard, abstracted, absent. "It spit them out of its mouth," she said, "six of them."

She lay in bed trying to picture the tent with the freak walking from side to side but she was too sleepy to figure it out. She was better able to see the faces of the country people watching, the men more solemn than they were in church, and the women stern and polite, with painted-looking eyes, standing as if they were waiting for the first note of the piano to begin the hymn. She could hear the freak saying, "God made me thisaway and I don't dispute hit," and the people saying, "Amen. Amen."

"God done this to me and I praise Him."

"Amen. Amen."

"He could strike you thisaway."

"Amen. Amen."

"But he has not."

"Amen."

"Raise yourself up. A temple of the Holy Ghost. You! You are God's temple, don't you know? Don't you know? God's Spirit has a dwelling in you, don't you know?"

"Amen. Amen."

"If anybody desecrates the temple of God, God will bring him to ruin and if you laugh, He may strike you thisaway. A temple of God is a holy thing. Amen. Amen."

"I am a temple of the Holy Ghost."

"Amen."

The people began to slap their hands without making a loud noise and with a regular beat between the Amens, more and more softly, as if they knew there was a child near, half asleep.

The next afternoon the girls put on their brown convent uniforms again and the child and her mother took them back to Mount St. Scholastica. "Oh glory, oh Pete!" they said. "Back to the salt mines." Alonzo Myers drove them and the child sat in front with him and her mother sat in back between the two girls, telling them such things as how pleased she was to have had them and how they must come back again and then about the good times she and their mothers had had when they were girls at the convent. The child didn't listen to any of this twaddle but kept as close to the locked door as she could get and held her head out the window. They had thought Alonzo would smell better on Sunday but he did not. With her hair blowing over her face she could look directly into the ivory sun which was framed in the middle of the blue afternoon but when she pulled it away from her eyes she had to squint.

Mount St. Scholastica was a red brick house set back in a garden in the center of town. There was a filling station on one side of it and a firehouse on the other. It had a high black grillework fence around it and narrow bricked walks between old trees and japonica bushes that were heavy with blooms. A big moon-faced nun came bustling to the door to let them in and embraced her mother and would have done the same to her but that she stuck out her hand and preserved a frigid frown, looking just past the sister's shoes at the wainscoting. They had a tendency to kiss even homely children, but the nun shook her hand vigorously and even cracked her knuckles a little and said they must come to the chapel, that benediction was just beginning. You put your foot in their door and they got you praying, the child thought as they hurried down the polished corridor.

You'd think she had to catch a train, she continued in the same ugly vein as they entered the chapel where the sisters were kneeling on one side and the girls, all in brown uniforms, on the other. The chapel smelled of incense. It was light green and gold, a series of springing arches that ended with the one over the altar where the priest was kneeling in front of the monstrance, bowed low. A small boy in a surplice was standing behind him, swinging the censer. The child knelt down between her mother and the nun and they were well into the *"Tantum Ergo"* before her ugly thoughts stopped and she began to realize that she was in the presence of God. Hep me not to be so mean, she began mechanically. Hep me not to give her so much sass. Hep me not to talk like I do. Her mind began to get quiet and then empty but when the priest raised the monstrance with the Host shining ivory-colored in the center of it, she was thinking of the tent at the fair that had the freak in it. The freak was saying, "I don't dispute hit. This is the way He wanted me to be."

As they were leaving the convent door, the big nun swooped down on her mischievously and nearly smothered her in the black habit, mashing the side of her face into the crucifix hitched onto her belt and then holding her off and looking at her with little periwinkle eyes.

On the way home she and her mother sat in the back and Alonzo drove by himself in the front. The child observed three folds of fat in the back of his neck and noted that his ears were pointed almost like a pig's. Her mother, making conversation, asked him if he had gone to the fair.

"Gone," he said, "and never missed a thing and it was good I gone when I did because they ain't going to have it next week like they said they was."

"Why?" asked her mother.

"They shut it on down," he said. "Some of the preachers from town gone out and inspected it and got the police to shut it on down."

Her mother let the conversation drop and the child's round face was lost in thought. She turned it toward the window and looked out over a stretch of pasture land that rose and fell with a gathering greenness until it touched the dark woods. The sun was a huge red ball like an elevated Host drenched in blood and when it sank out of sight, it left a line in the sky like a red clay road hanging over the trees.

Philip F. O'Connor
The Thumping of the Grass

IT WAS A VACANT LOT, I remember that, and they used to burn it out every summer. My brother and I watched from our bedroom window, afraid to go up by the trucks or the firemen. What keeps coming back has to do with the lot and it comes back in dreams, the ones I remember, the ones I have just before waking, and I am in the lot with a girl only the girl is my brother which in the dream seems natural but not natural now that I say it.

There was a real girl and she lived in a dirty yellow house beyond our back fence and after my brother died I saw her kissing a big boy in the vacant lot and it embarrassed me but I watched. It was like somebody getting beaten the way he came down over her with his heavy arms and brought her hard to the ground and made her whimper.

Her name was Sylvia and one day I rode my bike around the block and saw her sitting on one of the three steps in front of the yellow house's screened-in porch reading comic books and maybe waiting for the big boy and I looked away, afraid my eyes would tell her what I knew about her in the lot but she saw me and said "Come here" and I did.

Her knees were up so high I could see part of her thick white thighs under her skirt and she said will you go to Holman's and buy me a candy bar and I said nothing but took the money and went and brought it back and she said want to help me eat it and I didn't but I didn't know what to do so I nodded and she took me into the house and it was empty and she sat on the sofa just by the window and ate most of the candy bar herself, slowly, and said why are you looking at my legs, smiling at me and saying it, and then I spoke for the first time saying I don't know but I was looking at them and she held out the candy bar and nodded and then again until I came over and took a little bite and she said wasn't that good and I said yes very softly and she took my forefinger and said touch right here.

My brother and I used to lie under the weeping willow tree and rub ourselves against the grass until one day our mother saw us and called us inside and said what were you doing and we told her rubbing ourselves and she said that is a naughty trick and we must never do it again and if she caught us she would have to tell the priest. So we didn't do it again because we were afraid of the priest who had a voice like the thunder that came in from the ocean but we did talk about it, at night we talked about it, and I said what did it feel like to you and he said I don't know, what did it feel like to you, and I said it felt sweet and he said yes it felt sweet and we didn't question why we shouldn't do it but just talked about the sweetness, remembered it, and wanted to tell, at least I did, everyone about the sweetness, except the priest, but didn't.

There was a swimming pool at the far end of town and in the summer, his last summer, we started going there on our scooters even though it was far and our mother forbade us to swim and the girls wore bright swimming suits and lay on their backs and stomachs and we stood outside the fence and watched them, for hours we watched them with our eyes against the fence, and then we went home. It was going home from the swimming pool that my brother got hit by a car and run over and killed.

"Now here," Sylvia said, "and now here," and I did it and did it wherever she said and the sweetness came over me and I squatted between her big legs while I did it and the room got hot and my clothes grew sticky and Sylvia leaned back against the curtain and wiggled and made soft sounds and finally she said, "That's enough. You better go home," and I did.

"Jesus came to save mankind which are serpents in the surrounding darkness and He has redeemed us from that darkness because He cast upon himself the flesh of man . . . ."

Sylvia went to Mass and wore a wide-brimmed white hat and sat up in front right next to the nun and when the priest's words began to frighten me I looked at her for she, her hat, never moved in the slightest as though she knew what he was going to say and lived by it and had nothing to fear, just looked upward saying yes with her eyes and that was all. I looked up too but was still afraid.

I was playing around the willow tree and my mother was hanging up the wash and Sylvia said over the back fence, "I'll make him lunch," and my mother said do you hear Sylvia and I said yes and she turned to Sylvia and said, "I think it's the best thing for him. He misses his brother." So I went.

She said I'm going to take a bath, do you want to watch, and I said I don't care but I did, I wanted to watch, and she filled the tub and took off her clothes and got in and the suds came up to her breasts and she told me to soap them, easy, and she put her head back on the rim and closed her eyes and said all over them, all over, and I did it all over until the sweetness came out of me, burst out of me, and flooded the room and the house and the neighborhood and the town. I fell forward into the tub and held her very tight my face between those enormous breasts. When it was over I cried.

She pushed me away and got up and dried very fast and said if you tell your mother I'll kill you and made me take off my clothes and put them in the oven until they were dry and hard and made me put them on and said, "Did you hear me what I said?" and I said yes and she said you're a little brat, I should have known, you acted crazy jumping in there on me, I should have known, don't come back. She was frightened more than angry. For once I seemed to understand her. But I didn't go back.

I went out by the willow tree one evening after supper to think about my brother because out there I remembered him happy as I didn't when I thought of him at other places. And then I heard Sylvia.

I crept over to the fence bordering her yard and listened but the sound was coming from someplace else so I went along the fence to the other fence, the one bordering the lot with the tall grass, and I heard her and she was saying, "You're too rough. You're too rough, David. Be easier." I listened and heard the grass swishing and her talking, chiding David, and after a while she stopped talking and the grass stopped swishing and I became frightened as though they were lying right in front of me, the two of them, staring back at me and waiting, waiting for something to happen to me, maybe doing something to me.

I crawled across our yard and slipped into our basement and sat in the blackness on the cold wet floor for a long time and feeling Sylvia and David in there with me, hanging from nails on the wall, one in front of me and one in back, leering at me with shiny teeth and panting, waiting, waiting for something, and then David growled and Sylvia came down off the wall and floated over to me, I was so sure of it I put my foot out to feel for her, she wasn't there, but still she was, pressing her great body down on me, crushing me into the concrete, saying "DON'T TELL! DON'T TELL! DON'T TELL!" Screaming it against my ears.

And I grew older and forgot or thought I forgot the sweetness but I was in a department store in the city and there were a lot of school girls around a counter where sweaters were on sale and my mother was someplace else in the store and I was waiting for her, I guess that was it. I got closer and closer to the girls and their skirts were short and when the girls moved about the skirts seemed alive with those bottoms dancing so softly beneath them and I had to do it and I did, I touched one of the bottoms so very gently but the girl spun about and then she screamed. The man came. My mother didn't believe him when he told her but all the way home from the city on the Greyhound she kept asking me, did I? did I? I didn't want to hurt her, she seemed so frightened. I said no.

My brother and I are rolling together in the tall grass of the lot through dream after dream and magically sinking into the earth when the big kitchen window opens and my mother shouts at us. And then we go flying invisibly, clinging together, up into the oak tree at the back of the lot when Sylvia and David lumber toward us making the ground shake. We hold each other and don't listen to the obscenities my mother roars from the big window and don't look as Sylvia and David kick and beat at each other on the grass until the oak tree trembles. We know there is something lovely in us holding, caressing, each other up here where no one can know us or touch us.

John O'Hara
Barred

IT WAS A FACT THAT JIMMY BRESNAHAN got so mad at Nora Muldoon that he was ready to kill her. He went to her house that night and her mother answered the door. "Good evening, Jimmy," said Mrs. Muldoon, showing polite surprise. "Would you like to come in?"

"Why, yes, or I'll wait on the porch," said Jimmy. "That is, Nora's expecting me."

"Oh, I don't think so," said Mrs. Muldoon. "She went to the movies right after supper."

"That's funny," said Jimmy. "She was supposed to go to the Lake with me."

"You must have the wrong evening," said Mrs. Muldoon.

"Thursday. That's the night for the big orchestras. George Olsen is playing tonight. We made the date over a week ago."

"Then it must have slipped her mind. She and Isabel and Mary went uptown soon after supper," said Mrs. Muldoon.

"I was supposed to call for her at ha' past eight."

"Well, it's that now, but the movie won't be over till after nine. Then they go for a soda. I don't expect her much before ha' past nine. If then. Sometimes they go to Isabel's after the picture show, and Bud walks her home."

"Is it all right if I wait a little while?" said Jimmy. "I'll just sit out here on the porch."

"Well, I wouldn't count on her," said Mrs. Muldoon. "Knowing her, she wasn't dressed to go to the dance, and she's liable to stay at Isabel's till quite late. I think the whole thing must have slipped her mind."

"Are you sure she's not standing me up, Mrs. Muldoon?" said Jimmy.

"Well, I couldn't be sure of that either," said Mrs. Muldoon. "You wouldn't be the first one, and you've never had a date with her before. Nora's as changeable as the weather. I tell her time and again, if she wants to remain popular she has to start thinking of other people's feelings."

"She is standing me up, isn't she?" said Jimmy.

"Now I didn't say that, Jimmy. But it looks that way. I don't say she's standing you up, but I'm positive she isn't going to the Lake tonight."

"Why are you so positive?"

"Why am I so positive? Well, I just remembered, they *are* going back to Isabel's from the picture show. Yes, Isabel has a new Victrola, the table model to take to school with her. Yes, now I remember."

"Then there's no use my waiting," said Jimmy.

"No, I honestly don't think there is. I'll tell Nora you were here promptly at ha' past eight."

"Why is she standing me up? You know why, Mrs. Muldoon," said Jimmy.

"No, I can't exactly say I do, *if she is.*"

"You know she is, and you know why. Maybe you told her to break the date with me."

"Now, Jimmy, I don't intend to stand here letting the flies in while we discuss Nora. If you have anything to say to Nora it'd be better to say it to her."

"I'm right, though. You told her to break the date with me. You won't let her go out with me, is that it?"

"She made that decision without any help from me, Jimmy. Not many mothers—"

"That's it. It was you."

"No, it wasn't. Nora thought it over and then she thought better of it."

"With a little help from you."

"Don't get personal, Jimmy. Have more respect for your elders."

"It was you. Nora wanted to go out with me, but you wouldn't let her."

"I didn't have to say a word. Nora made up her own mind. And it's against the law to leave your car there with the motor running."

"You! You and those mothers!" said Jimmy. He heard her say something about a good thing some mothers—but he missed the rest in his angry haste to his car. He drove away noisily and recklessly, hating Mrs. Muldoon but even more so hating Nora for her treachery. For a week he had been saying that Nora Muldoon was the only one of the so-called nice girls who had the courage to make a date with him. She was the prettiest one of them all, the only one worth taking to a dog fight. He had taken George McLoughlin's two-dollar bet that Nora would back out at the last minute. "That shows you how much you know about girls," he had said to George. "The real pretty ones are sure of themselves."

"Maybe I don't know so much about girls, but I'm related to those Muldoons and I know Nora better than you do."

"Two bucks, two bucks," Jimmy had said.

Now, driving through the streets of town, he recognized cars and couples in them, off to an early start for the Lake. They would all know that he had a date with Nora Muldoon—and some of them would already know that Nora had stood him up. They would have seen Nora and Isabel Murphy and Mary McCorkindale—sometimes known as Faith, Hope, and Charity—marching together to the movies. It was bad enough that Nora had broken the date, bad enough if she had broken it and stayed home; but she had made it worse by going to the movies with Isabel and Mary, passing the homes of their friends who knew she had made the date with Jimmy. She did not even pretend she was sick or something. In a way it was worse than if she had gone to the Lake with someone else. At least then she could have pretended there was a mix-up on the dates. Or he could have pretended it.

He had almost twelve dollars in his pocket, the family Nash, his good white linen suit—the man in the saying: all dressed up and no place to go. It was too early for the Busy Bee. Nobody went there this early. George McLoughlin would be shooting pool at the Olympic, but one of the last people he wanted to see was George McLoughlin right now. Not that George would give him the razz, but he did not want any kind of sympathy from George. Or from anybody. He would like to get Nora Muldoon by the throat and throttle her, to tear the clothes off her and make her walk down Main Street half naked. He would like to disgrace her, the dirty little double-crosser. Why not? It was what they all expected of him.

One bad thing, one really bad thing that he had told in confession and got absolution for, that had brought shame and disgrace on his mother and father and cost his father a lot of money. The whole town knew it even if it never got in the papers. Jimmy Bresnahan caught in a raid on Sally Minzer's roadhouse by the state police. Taken to the county jail and held as a material witness because he offered resistance. The older men were let go, but he had taken a swing at a statie and they put him in the truck with the whores and locked him up overnight. Lawyers. Politics. Money. Disgrace. New Year's Day in the county jail. Hysterical mother. Angry father. Embarrassed sister. Pompous priest. Condescending neighbors. Hesitant friends. Leering acquaintances. The delayed return to college escorted by his father, and the interview with the prefect of discipline. "Yes, we heard all about James," said the prefect of discipline. "A truism that bad news travels fast, and there always seem to be volunteer informers in cases like this. Well, Mr. Bresnahan, you did the honorable thing coming here. Father Rector put it entirely in my hands when he heard you were coming with James. I will say parenthetically, Father Rector recommended clemency in recognition of your honorable behavior, and I was inclined that way myself, but I don't say the rector's attitude hurt any. Now then, Mr. Bresnahan, the university has no *official* knowledge of James's peccadillo, misconduct, whatever you wish to call it. It took place during the vacation, hundreds of miles from here. And according to our information, James's name doesn't even appear on the county records of your home county. How fortunate indeed. Because regardless of official record or no official record, I doubt very much whether James would have been admitted as a freshman if he had such a mark on his record. You wouldn't say such a mark testified to his good character. But when a boy is home on vacation he's supposed to be out of our jurisdiction, so to speak. Back in the jurisdiction of his parents, you might say, and in view of the fact that the university got no official report on the unfortunate episode, we decided to look the other way. Taking into consideration, of course, the fact that James has a record here that's about average—not as good as some, not as bad as others. Average."

So they let him back in the university, never officially having put him out. His father reduced his allowance. "None of my money goes for prostitutes," said Mr. Bresnahan. His mother sent him five dollars a week, or he would have had little money for cigarettes and movies. That second semester he did penance, but when he got home in June it was soon apparent that the mothers and fathers of the so-called nice girls deemed the penance inadequate. He was not fully ostracized; they nodded to him when they could not avoid it. But he was no longer welcome on their porches, he was not invited to picnics, he was left out of several birthday parties. His father had got him a job, not a soft job in a law office where he might learn something about the profession he expected to follow, but a three-dollar-a-day job cutting brush for a surveying party with the power company. He chopped away a lot of brush and killed a dozen rattlesnakes, got browned by the sun and learned just enough about civil engineering to confirm his preference for the law. In the evenings he played pool with George McLoughlin and spoke often of Nora Muldoon. "Why don't you ask her for a date?" said George. "All she can do is say no."

"If she says that," said Jimmy. "I haven't said two words to her all year."

"She didn't stop talking to you, did she?"

"No, but she never did say much to me," said Jimmy.

"Does she look at you with those big brown eyes?"

"Boy, those big brown eyes," said Jimmy.

"I'd like to dip my socks in her coffee, all right," said George. "Cousin or no cousin Go ahead and ask her for a date, see what she says."

Jimmy discussed the problem with an older man, the chief of the surveying party, who had lived all over the world and had what he called his own personal League of Nations—his recollections of the women he had slept with. "Well, if she's as pretty as you say," said McDowell, "you can ask her anything, provided you ask her in the right way. The pretty ones you don't have to worry about. The homely mutts are the ones that sic the dogs on you. Now this kid knows you were pinched in a whorehouse, so she isn't expecting any saint. If it was me, I'd go right up to her and say, 'What about it?' But I don't live here, and you do. I can afford to put it all on one roll of the dice, because I'll be getting out of here after Labor Day. Don't be shy. One time in Mexico City I made a play for my boss's wife, expecting to get fired and sent home. It turned out quite the opposite. She said if I hadn't made my play when I did, she was going to make the first move herself. You never know what's in their minds."

Thus encouraged, Jimmy Bresnahan blocked Nora Muldoon's progress on the sidewalk one afternoon. "I'll treat you to a malted," he said.

"Thanks, but I'm on my way to the hairdresser," said Nora Muldoon.

"How long'll you be?"

"Two hours, maybe more," she said.

"What I wanted to say was, would you care to go hear George Olsen, at the Lake?"

"You mean on a date with you?"

"Or with another couple?"

"It's next Thursday, isn't it?"

"Yes."

"All right."

"I'll stop for you at eight-thirty," said Jimmy.

"I have to be home by one," she said.

"Whatever you say," he said.

"All right," she said.

"Thanks, Nora," he said. He was grateful to her for making the transaction so simple. As he said later to George McLoughlin, she did not make him get a letter from his pastor, or promise to behave like a gentleman.

"We'll see," said George, and his skepticism led to the two-dollar bet. McDowell, the civil engineer, provided a piece of advice. "Get her away from that dance," said McDowell. "Otherwise she'll be bored to death and you'll never get another chance at her. She's ripe for plucking. If you don't get anywhere maybe I'll have a go at her myself—or even if you do."

"She's not that kind of a girl," said Jimmy.

"My boy, they all are," said McDowell. "Take it from a man that's been everywhere, seen everything, and done everything, and ready to start all over again. If she's a she, she's a she."

Now, driving up and down the streets of the town while this particular she sat watching a movie, Jimmy Bresnahan fully agreed with McDowell's opinion of the female sex. He hated her, he hated them all. In the morning McDowell would want to know all about his date with Nora, and he would have nothing to tell. He hated McDowell for having raised his hopes, and hated him in advance for the glib explanation he would have for her having stood him up. But the only explanation worth a damn was that Nora Muldoon had wanted to humiliate him publicly, and he tried to think of a way to humiliate her that would not get him arrested.

Well, everybody expected him to show up at the Lake with Nora Muldoon. What if he showed up, not with her but with the worst tart in the county? They would all be looking for Nora Muldoon, but what if he showed up with Sally Minzer instead? And if not Sally herself—who was nothing to look at—one of Sally's girls.

He swung around in the middle of the block and headed for Sally Minzer's joint.

It was early for Sally Minzer's, but that meant that the girls would not be busy. They would have no objection to going to the Lake for a couple of hours. On the way to Sally's he imagined Nora's friends when he showed up with one of Sally's girls. Nora's girl friends would not recognize any of

Sally's girls, but some of the boys would. He could imagine the whispers. "That's one of Sally Minzer's you-know-what. What happened to Nora Muldoon?"

That would be the cream of the jest, his bringing one of Sally Minzer's girls to the Lake instead of Nora. It would get back to Nora before the night was over. Some of Nora's friends were quite likely to telephone her from the Lake. As the prefect of discipline had said, there was always some volunteer informant.

It was early for Sally Minzer's place, but there were a few cars in front of the entrance and all the lights were on inside the house and in the driveway. Obviously the authorities had given Sally permission to open up. Jimmy parked his car and walked to the barroom, where two men were sitting at a table, having drinks. They were strangers to Jimmy and they paid little attention to him. The bartender was likewise a stranger. "What'll it be?"

"Rye and ginger ale," said Jimmy. "Is Sally in?"

"Sally? Do you know her?"

"Sure I know her."

"Does she know you?"

"Sure she knows me. You're new here," said Jimmy.

"Not so new. Who will I say wants to see Sally?"

"The name is Bresnahan."

"I'll go see if she's in," said the bartender. He left the barroom, but he was not gone long. Sally Minzer came in, stared at Jimmy and shouted, "Get him the hell out of here! Get him out! Who the hell let him in? This kid is poison. He hits cops. You, Bresnahan, get out of here and I never want to see your face again. You cost me plenty, you young punk."

"He owes for the rye," said the bartender.

"The hell with that, just get him out of here," said Sally Minzer. "And you, if you ever show your face in here again, I'll put them to work on you. *You're barred*, you understand that? *Barred.*"

The men at the table had got to their feet. "You heard what she said," said one of them. "You're barred."

Harold Brodkey
Sentimental Education

IT WAS EIGHT O'CLOCK ON A WARM SEPTEMBER evening, and all the bells of Harvard were striking the hour. Elgin Smith, tired of studying, was standing on the steps of the Widener Library—those wide, Roman, inconvenient steps—blinking his eyes and staring into the distance, because that was supposed to refresh the corneas and the retina. He was thinking, but not of his schoolwork. He was thinking of what it would be like to fall in love, to worship a girl and to put his life at her feet. He despised himself, because he feared he was incapable of passion and he believed that only passionate people were worth while and all other kinds were shallow. He was taking courses in English Literature, in German Literature, in Italian Literature, in History, ancient and medieval, and every one of them was full of incidents that he thought mocked him, since they seemed to say that the meaning of life, the peak of existence, the core of events was one certain emotion, to which he was a stranger, and for which he was very likely too rational. Therefore, he stood on the steps of Widener, so cracked by longing that it seemed only gravity held him together.

He was very tall, six feet three, and gangling. He had a small head, curiously shaped (his roommate, Dimitri, sometimes accused him of looking like a wedge of cheese), and a hooked nose. He wanted to be a professor in the field of comparative philology, and he believed in Beauty. He studied all the time, and there were moments when he was appalled by how hard he worked. He was known for his crying in movies. He was not unathletic.

Somehow, he had become convinced that he was odd and that only odd girls liked him, pitiable girls who couldn't do any better, and this singed his pride.

It was his fate that this particular night he should see a girl walking up the steps of Widener Library. She was of medium height and had black hair cut short; she was wearing a light-colored coat that floated behind her because she was walking so fast, nearly running, but not quite; and the curve of her forehead and the way her eyes were set took Elgin's breath away. She was so pretty and carried herself so well and had a look of such healthy and arrogant self-satisfaction that Elgin sighed and thought here was the sort of not odd girl who could bestow indescribable benefits on any young man she liked—and on his confidence. She was that very kind of girl, that far from unhappy, that world-contented kind, he believed would never fall for him.

She carried her books next to her bosom. Elgin's eyes followed her up the steps; and then his head turned, his nostrils distended with emotion; and she was gone, vanished into Widener.

"Surely this year," he thought, looking up at the sky. "Now that I'm almost nineteen." He stretched out his arms, and the leaves on the trees, already growing dry at the approach of autumn, rustled in the breezes.

He thought about that girl once or twice in the days that followed, but the longing for her didn't really take root until he saw her again, two weeks later, at a Radcliffe Jolly-Up in Cabot Hall. It was in one of the dimly lit common rooms, where couples were indefatigably dancing in almost total darkness. Elgin was swaying in place (he was not a good dancer) with a girl who helped him on his German when he caught sight of his Widener Library vision. When the next dance began, he wound through the couples looking for her, to cut in on her, but when he drew near her, he turned and walked over to the wall, where he caught his breath and realized he was frightened.

This was the stroke that fatally wounded him. Knowing he was frightened of that girl, he longed for her, the way men who think they are cowards long for war so they can prove they're not. Or perhaps it was some other reason. The girl had a striking appearance; there was her youth and her proud, clean look to recommend her.

But whatever the reason, he did begin to think about her in earnest. She rose up in clouds of brilliant light in his head whenever he came across certain words in his reading. ("Mistress" was one, "beautiful" another; you can guess the rest.) He did a paper on "The Unpossessable Loved One in Troubadour Poetry." When he walked through the Yard on his way to classes, his eyes revolved nervously and never rested, searching all the faces on all the walks in the hope of seeing her. In fact, on his walks to classes he looked so disordered that a number of his friends asked him if he was feeling ill, and it pleased Elgin, after the first two times this happened, to reply that he was. He was ill with longing.

At night, before going to the dining hall for supper, he would put on his bathrobe and slip down to the pool in the basement of Adams House. There, under the wooden beams, he would swim angrily from one end of the pool to the other, faster and faster, until his arms ached. Then he would take a cold shower.

When he slept, he dreamed of carnage, horses, and speeding automobiles. He went to French movies and ground his knees against the seat in front of him. He laughed at himself, and decided to break this absurd habit he had got into of thinking all the time about this girl he had never met, but he didn't quite succeed. At last, he admitted to himself that he was in love with her; and one night, sleeping in his lower bunk while Dimitri breathed heavily over his head, he had tears in his eyes because he was so foolish and did desire that girl whom he had seen the two times mentioned and only twice more besides.

Having resigned himself—in imitation of Dante—to a state of perpetual longing, he felt calmer and looked at the world with sad, scholarly eyes. But his equilibrium was delicate, and in December Dimitri began having an affair with a Radcliffe girl named Felicia. Upperclassmen could have girls in their room in the afternoon if they signed them in with the campus policeman who sat in a little room near the main entrance of their house, and signed them out when they left. There was always the chance the policeman would come to the room and check up, but even so on gray December afternoons Dimitri, all bundled up, would come searching through Widener for Elgin and ask him not to come home until after six o'clock because Dimitri was taking Felicia to the room. Then Elgin would sit in front of his books, numbed, unable to read, with fine beads of sweat standing out on his upper lip and forehead.

Once he came back to the room and found Dimitri lying in front of a fire in the fireplace; the fire was being fed by Dimitri's lecture notes. "Oh God, it's you. How I hate your ugly face!" Dimitri said, but Elgin knew what he meant; at that moment, being Elgin and not Felicia was a blasphemy. He tiptoed through the room to hang up his coat and tiptoed out again.

In January, immediately after exams, Elgin came down with flu. He was exhausted. When he was well again, it seemed to him that he had been washed clean and purified. He hardly thought about that girl at all.

But one sunny, cold morning in February Elgin saw her standing in front of Sever Hall. She was wearing long blue woollen socks, and she was talking to a pock-marked boy in a raccoon overcoat. Elgin suddenly turned and went into Sever and waited in the hall until the bell rang. The girl came in, and Elgin followed her upstairs and into a classroom; he sat three rows in back of her. It was a course given by Professor Bush on Metaphysical Poets of the Seventeenth Century. And that afternoon Elgin went and got permission to transfer from The Victorian Novel to that class.

The girl's name was Caroline Hedges and she came from Baltimore. She was a horsewoman of considerable ability. She spent a good deal of her time on clothes, not ever being quite sure where true elegance lay. She was inclined to buy pale colors, blouses one size too large for her, and tweeds. She was easily embarrassed. She read a good deal, her favorite books being *The Charterhouse of Parma*, *Anna Karenina*, and *Madame Bovary*.

She was very proud and easily moved by appeals to her courage. She considered she'd had a happy childhood, and she liked her family (although she could not help looking down on them a little because their name was not famous in the history of America). When she was ten, she had briefly loved a cousin of hers, who was twelve, and who had taken her to the National Museum of Art in Washington and told her the names of the great painters.

At Radcliffe, her freshman year, she discovered that she had been sheltered, compared to most of the other girls, and she felt young and slightly ashamed of herself. This gave her a look of great purity, and she was something of a belle. But late in the spring of her freshman year she stayed up all one night, obsessed and genuinely moved by the fact that she was intelligent and hadn't really known it before. She had just found it out by noticing that section men and assistant professors and sometimes full professors liked to hear her talk in class. From that night on, she limited her dating and threw herself into studying.

"It is poetry that I love," she wrote in her diary. "It is hard for me to explain why. Once when I was staying with Aunt Kitty in New York I went for a walk in Central Park when it was snowing. In the zoo I saw the Bactrian camel standing in the middle of its pen. It was holding its head straight up in the air with its mouth open and its tongue out and the snowflakes were falling on it. Perhaps he never saw snow before. I'm not exactly sure where Bactria is or what its climate is like—perhaps it was remembering snow. That is how I feel about poetry."

Another entry read, "My mother writes and asks me if I still see Louis Du Pont whom she thought such a charming boy. How can Mother think anyone so plump is charming?"

Early in April of her junior year, she wrote, "Today in Metaphysical Poetry, we discussed the tradition of Platonic Love in Jacobean England. A boy named Elgin Smith spoke brilliantly, I thought. He described the winters the young people spent in those vast country houses, twenty or so young people visiting in one house, with two or three chaperons, and snow everywhere. They sang and gave masques and such things. Because young people are so hot-blooded, it was necessary to devise a code of courtship to restrain them, for marriages of alliance had to be made later. Needless to say, it didn't work, Platonic Love, I mean, and it was much more often written about than observed. I do so admire brilliance and wish that I had some. This young man had the oddest voice, it is positively nasal and twangs and twangs. I wanted to put my hand over his mouth and tell him 'Sh-h-h.' He is terribly intense and nervous. He has borrowed a pencil from me several times, and he asked me to have coffee with him once. I said I couldn't, but next time he asks, I will accept. I long for some really intelligent friends."

When you consider the combustibility of the emotions of these two young people, it is hardly surprising that within two weeks of their first long conversation together they were trembling when they talked, and found themselves oppressed whenever silences fell. The impulse to discuss this state of affairs with each other kept recurring, but they fought it, until one afternoon when they were sitting in the Cambridge Common and having a cigarette together before separating for dinner.

All through the Common, young mothers were sitting, bored, by baby carriages, and beneath the trees, newly come to leaf, children were climbing on the old cannon. Abraham Lincoln was brooding under his canopy, and trolleys clanged on Massachusetts Avenue.

"Elgin," Caroline said, "we've talked about a hundred things, a thousand things, I bet."

"Yes."

"But we've never talked about what we think of each other."

"No," he said, twisting his fingers together. "I guess we never have."

"I—I don't approve of it, actually," Caroline said. "Analyzing things and all. Some things are better left unsaid."

"I agree," Elgin said. The words seemed to explode on his lips, leaving a faintly surprised look on his face.

"Do you?" Caroline said. For her part, she was having difficulty hanging on to her poise.

"There isn't much people can say that hasn't been said before," Elgin said with finality. Then he added, "It's my reading. I've read so much I guess I'm a little jaded."

"I see," said Caroline. "Well, it's a fascinating subject."

"Yes," said Elgin, "it is."

They sat in silence for several seconds, both of them on the verge of speaking, but Elgin was frightened and Caroline was disconcerted, as if her ideas of what could happen had been trampled on and left for dead.

"Let's get started back," Elgin said, and Caroline agreed. She rose and the two of them walked on toward Radcliffe, past the Hotel Continental. At the corner, Caroline said, "You coming by this evening?"

Elgin nodded.

Caroline reached out and shook Elgin's hand, which was a strange thing for her to do.

"Caroline!" Elgin said sharply.

"Yes."

"Let's go have dinner together."

"Where? I thought you were broke."

"The Chinese restaurant."

"All right, if I have enough money." She opened her purse and looked; she and Elgin went Dutch most places. "I've got two dollars and some change." They linked arms and walked back to the Common.

"I think Vaughan is a little bit of a bore," Caroline said. "Really, the language has deteriorated so much since Donne."

They sat down on the same bench where they had sat before.

Elgin said, "I assume since our conversation fifteen minutes ago it would be terrible if I talked about the way I feel about you."

"Oh, no," said Caroline. "Go right ahead."

"Well, they're very strong."

"I'd more or less guessed that," Caroline said, unable to make her voice sound normal.

"But I never mentioned it before," Elgin said, "because I didn't want anything to come up that might make you want to stop seeing me."

"I understand," Caroline said. "That was very subtle of you."

"Please shut up," Elgin said. "I'm trying to get some words out and it's very hard. I want you to know I'm not just chasing you or anything like that."

"Oh?"

"I saw you last fall. You were going into Widener. It was—you know— at first sight."

"Elgin!"

"It was. I only took Metaphysical Poetry because you were taking it. Caroline, I have deep feelings about you."

Caroline felt an intense sense of relief. "Well, I always thought so," she said. "But I wasn't sure." Then she realized Elgin was trembling. "Elgin, what's wrong?"

A child ran by with a red disintegrator pistol. "You're not angry?" Elgin asked.

"Of course not!" she said ringingly.

"You're not going to tell me that the most I can expect is your friendship? And if I expect more we oughtn't to see each other any more?"

There was silence. "I hadn't thought this far," Caroline said. She thought it was much more decent if she didn't have to mention her feelings; she felt trapped. "Well, Elgin, I'll tell you, I certainly don't want to stop seeing you." She moved her legs until they were spread ungracefully. "But, really, I think . . . we ought to be careful and not get, oh, I don't know, sloppy, if you know what I mean."

"I don't mind that," Elgin said. He swallowed. "But is it all right—is it all right, Caroline, if I show how I feel a little more?" His voice rose and quivered with longing.

"I don't know what you mean."

"You do."

"Honestly, Elgin, I—"

"You do!"

"I suppose so. . . . Yes. Do show it. Let's be honest. For God's sake, who can it hurt? Yes, let's not be priggish."

To her astonishment and delight, Elgin caught her hand and pressed it to his lips.

They hadn't kissed then, nor did they kiss each other for several days afterward. It was a tacit confession that they suspected the presence of passion, and in such cases, if one is at all practical, one stands back, one dawdles, one doesn't rush in to confront the beast in its lair. Or to put it another way, one doesn't go tampering with the floodgates. What they did, after this conversation, was suddenly to become lighthearted. They made jokes; Caroline stole Elgin's notebook from his hands and made him chase her; they discussed Metaphysical Poetry. And when this lightness and gaiety had eased their suspicion and their fright was in abeyance, Caroline decided she wanted Elgin to kiss her.

She was walking up Garden Street in late afternoon, and the sunlight was clear and golden. There was a light wind that ruffled her hair, and she was striding along, passing any number of couples, Harvard boys and Radcliffe girls, some with their arms around each other's waist, some holding hands, some just walking side by side. Caroline decided then, in a single flash; and the next minute her cheeks began to glow and she pushed happily at her hair, which kept blowing across her eyes.

At seven o'clock that evening, Elgin arrived at Cabot Hall to pick her up. He was wearing his shabby tweed jacket and khaki pants and striped tie. Caroline came downstairs wearing her prettiest sweater, a pink cashmere. Her hair was carefully brushed and she wore lipstick, so Elgin knew something was up.

"I'd sort of like to go to a movie tonight," she said. "I've got enough money for both of us if you're flat."

Elgin told her he had a little cash. They settled on the U.T.—the University Theatre in Harvard Square.

"I'm in the mood for gangsters," Caroline said as they emerged from Cabot into the spring evening.

The sky between the trees was purple, a deep, stirring plum color. Caroline put her arm through Elgin's, and they strode briskly through the Quad toward Garden Street, and then through the Common—one of a number of couples, in a long, irregular procession stretching from the Radcliffe dormitories to Harvard Square.

"I finished my paper on Donne," Elgin said.

Caroline laughed inconsequently, and Elgin laughed, too, for no good reason.

They passed through the middle of the Common, by Lincoln's statue, where a lamp cast a ghostly white glare on leaves and benches and the surface of the walk. Caroline's charming face swam into the light, shadows fell across it, and Elgin closed his eyes.

Caroline pressed his hand. They hurried.

All during the movie, they sat holding both of each other's hands, and their shoulders touching. Entwined and tangled like that, they giggled together whenever the movie became particularly violent. They couldn't stop giggling after a while, as the death toll in the movie mounted. When the movie ended, they left and Elgin bought Caroline a chocolate ice-cream cone at St. Clair's and they walked down to the Charles River.

The Charles looked placid, and glimmered as it quietly flowed under the bridge; the lights of Eliot House were reflected in its surface. Caroline put her head on Elgin's shoulder. They breathed in unison, the two of them, standing on the bank of the river, and then Elgin said, "It's clumsy to ask, but Caroline, do you really . . . or . . . would I . . ." He missed her lips, kissing her cheek instead, and he was holding her so tightly that she couldn't move and correct his mistake. But a minute later he corrected his error himself. They both had difficulty breathing. "I love, I love you, I love you," he whispered.

It sounded beautiful in the moonlight, the river ran quietly beneath the bridge, and Caroline was glad she had let him kiss her.

After that they took to kissing each other a good deal. They met every afternoon at Widener. When one of them broke off work, the other would break off, too, and they would both go downstairs. Along either side of the steps rose large stone arms, which looked as if they should be surmounted by statues, but they were bare, and in spring, in the afternoons, on both of them there would usually be people sitting, sometimes alone, sometimes in pairs. Here Elgin and Caroline would sit and look out over the Yard toward the Chapel.

At four-thirty, they would go to Massachusetts Avenue and have a cup of coffee in one of the luncheonettes. Usually they separated then, Caroline to go to Cabot Hall, Elgin to Adams House, for supper, but some evenings, when they had the money, they had dinner together at a Chinese restaurant near the Square, where the food was very cheap. (Elgin didn't like taking her to Adams House on the nights when girls were allowed in the dining hall, because it reminded him that he was young and ineffectual and under the control of an institution.) In the evenings, they studied, either in the library or in one of the common rooms at Cabot, and at nine o'clock when the library closed, they would walk down to the riverbank. Elgin had an old raincoat that he wore, and they used that to spread on the grass, to sit on. They sat side by side and shared long, rather tender kisses. At first on these expeditions they talked about poetry, but after a while conversation began to seem disagreeable, and they sat in silence.

Then they began to leave off studying at Widener earlier in the afternoon, at three-thirty, or even three. Caroline liked going with Elgin to the Boston Museum of Fine Arts, and they would look at the pictures and, when their feet were tired, go and sit in the Fens, the park just behind the Museum, which has a rose garden at one end of it. Caroline wanted Elgin to lose his Middle Western pronunciation, and the excuse they used for these jaunts was that this was time spent in teaching Elgin how to speak. He would bring a book, Bacon's *Essays*, or Montaigne's, or Jeremy Taylor's *Sermons*, or Johnson's *Rasselas*—good, sturdy books, with sentences so rich that sometimes Elgin's voice grew fuzzy with the pleasure he felt reading them.

"Always, all-ways, not oll-wez," Caroline would say.

"Wait, Caroline, just wait a bit, listen to this," and he would read another rolling, rhetorical period. "Isn't that gorgeous?"

"Not gorgeous," Caroline would say. "That's not the right word somehow."

"Oh, it is in this case," Elgin would say. "It's absolutely exact."

And Caroline, struggling not to be moved, would say, "I suppose. I suppose, just barely."

Then Elgin started reading Colette and Boccaccio. Now, when silence fell, something seemed to be lying beside them on the grass, breathing softly. Glances, trees, the movements of people in the park suddenly split off from the commonsensical, taken-for-granted world and became strange. Caroline frowned more and more often, turned into something very like a nag. She made Elgin buy new ties and have his shoes reheeled. Often, in the afternoons, she would take him to St. Clair's and make him drink freshly squeezed orange juice. When it was raining, she still insisted they go for walks because it was good for Elgin. She took to proofreading all his papers and typing them over for him because he was a poor and careless typist. One day, Elgin read to her the story in Boccaccio of the young girl who used to tell her mother that she wanted to sleep in the garden in order to hear the nightingale sing, but the girl met her lover in the garden—*he* was the nightingale. Elgin read this story to Caroline in an intense and quavering voice. For a week afterward, Caroline walked back and forth to classes hearing in her head the phrase "listening to the nightingale." Finally, the phrase came to stand for so much, it aroused such deep tumult in her and made her feel so lonely and deprived, that one night Elgin came back to his room, woke Dimitri from a sound sleep, and asked him to stay away from the room the next afternoon.

It turned out that Elgin and Caroline were both virgins.

Their first dip into sensual waters left them nonplussed. They didn't know what to make of it. They tried to persuade themselves that something had really happened, but the minute it was over, they couldn't believe they had ever done such a thing. They rushed into further experiences; they broke off in the middle of embraces and looked at each other, stunned and delighted. "Is this really happening?" they both asked at different times, and each time the other said, "No," and they would laugh. They knew that nothing they did was real, was actual. They had received a blow on the head and were prey to erotic imaginings, that was all. But at the same time they half realized it was true, they *were* doing these things and then the fact that they, Caroline and Elgin, shared such intimacy dazed and fascinated them; and when they were together, they tried to conceal it, but this indescribable attraction they felt for each other kept making itself known and draining all the strength from their bodies. They tried to make jokes about themselves and this odd little passion they felt. "We're unskilled labor," Elgin said. "You know, I'm just giving in because you're irresistible," Caroline said. She always pretended that she was completely dispassionate about sex. It just happened that she was susceptible to Elgin's entreaties. But he was too shy to entreat unless she encouraged him, and Caroline often felt like the worst kind of hypocrite. The truth of the matter is, they were caught up in a fever of their senses.

Caroline would have her lunch in Cabot Hall, locked in an impenetrable haze of daydreaming, not even hearing the girls chattering around her. She would walk to Widener, and if boys she knew stopped her to talk, she would stare at them stonily, afraid the boy might guess her feelings for Elgin and think they applied to him. She would run up the stairs of Widener, past the Sargent murals, petrified that Elgin might not be waiting for her. Every day this fear grew worse; but every day he was there, sitting at one of the long wooden tables in the reading room, beneath the great coffered ceiling, and the look on his face when he caught sight of her would make Caroline smile giddily, because she had never known before what a miraculous power she had over men.

They managed a wry stiffness when they were in public. They spoke to each other in tones of the crudest good-fellowship. Elgin called her "Girl." "Girl, you finished with that book?" Caroline called Elgin "Cheese." "No, Cheese. Don't rush me." They didn't hold hands or touch. They thought they fooled everyone, but everyone who knew them guessed, and they both told their roommates. In fact, they wanted to talk about what was happening to them to everyone; this news was always on the tip of their tongues; and so they got into the habit of suddenly breaking off conversations with their friends when the impulse to confess grew too strong to be contained a moment longer, and all their friends thought they were becoming very queer and difficult indeed.

Each afternoon that they met in Widener started on this high level of confusion and rapidly ran downhill. The minute hand of the clock over the door of the reading room jerked every sixty seconds, marking off a whole minute in one movement, and at two-thirty they were no longer capable of speech. Elgin would be pale or flushed. He would draw breath irregularly through a mouth he couldn't quite close, or through distended nostrils, and this phenomenon would fascinate Caroline, except that she couldn't look at him for too long without feeling the most awful pain in her head. Finally, Elgin would gasp, "Well?"

"I'm finished," Caroline would say in the weakest voice imaginable.

They would walk in silence to Adams House, and Elgin would sign Caroline in at the policeman's room. In silence they would mount the stairs, and Elgin would unlock the door of his room, and then they would fall into each other's arms, sometimes giggling with relief, sometimes somber, sometimes almost crying with the joy of this privacy and this embrace.

Then, later, both of them dressed and their faces scrubbed, Caroline, like an addict, would descend on Elgin's bureau and haul out his torn and buttonless shirts. She didn't know how to sew, but she thought she did, and she sat on Elgin's couch, smiling to herself, softly humming, and sewed buttons on wrong. Elgin tried to study, but his moods whirled and spun him around so that one minute he'd be reading quietly and the next minute he'd be striding up and down the room on the worn carpet, wringing his hands or else waving them aloft and denouncing the College and the

American Educational System, full of rage, but not knowing with what or why, and forced to let it out any way he could, while Caroline, faintly bored, ignored him mostly and sewed.

Every once in a while, Caroline would cry. Then she would be unable to dress properly, and she'd drag around the room with her hair badly combed, her shoes off, looking slatternly, and say, "I don't know what's wrong with me. Actually, nothing's wrong with me." But every few minutes tears would course down her cheeks. Nor did she know why she cried; she was as innocent of understanding herself as she was of understanding Elgin.

Sometimes they quarreled. Once, it was because Caroline wouldn't use Elgin's towel.

"If you loved me, you'd use it."

"I'd adore to use *your* towel," Caroline said, "but *this* towel is dirty."

Elgin thought her preposterous; she called Elgin a boor and slammed out of the room. She reached the bottom of the stairs and started back up and heard Elgin coming down. Neither of them said a word; they didn't apologize or mention this episode again. They went for a walk along the riverbank and talked about Metaphysical Poetry.

On Saturdays, Elgin took Caroline to the Harvard courts to play tennis. Caroline had fine ankles and legs, and while they walked to the courts, Elgin kept stealing glances at them, which made Caroline nervous. She was a good tennis player, as good as Elgin, but he could throw her off her game by charging the net and yelling at her, "I've got you now!" This would rattle her so she'd completely miss the ball, and then she would laugh with exasperation.

When he served, he made a point of calling the score in a loud, cheerful, teasing voice: "Thirty-love!" He'd say the "love" in such a way that Caroline would blush, and then she would try to drive the ball directly at him, and most of the time it went out of bounds.

One afternoon, they were in each other's arms in Elgin's room. Elgin was whispering, "I love you, Caroline. I love you so much," and someone knocked on the door. The sound seemed to blind Elgin, who squeezed his eyes closed, as tightly as he could. The knock was repeated a second time, and a third, echoing in the small room. Then the footsteps retreated.

Elgin got up and fetched cigarettes and towels for them both. They leaned back on the couch, at opposite ends, wrapped in towels, and smoked. They didn't mention the fact that they were afraid it had been the campus policeman and they would be expelled. They discussed whether or not they were depraved.

"We are," Caroline said. "Otherwise, we wouldn't be so ashamed."

"We don't have to be ashamed," Elgin said. "We only pretend we are anyway, to be polite."

"You're a rebel," Caroline said gloomily. "You can say that. But I'm a conformist. I'm basically a nice girl. I *am* ashamed."

The pressure of details, the maze of buttons, hooks, and zippers that they had to make their way through to that condition which pleased them best, kept forcing them to be self-conscious. They couldn't believe that what they were doing was real, and yet it was real, as they well knew the minute they separated, when the memory of their last encounter would descend on both of them, occupying their minds, and unfitting them for any occupation except dreaming of the next encounter. At night, lying in his bunk, Elgin would try to sleep, but he'd think of Caroline, and slowly, like a leaf curling in a salt solution, he would twist under his covers until his knees were even with his chest, and this was a tortured, involuntary movement of longing he could no more control than he could control his thoughts. He would try to do his reading for his courses: "In the early years of this century, I moved to London, feeling that Ireland and my love for Ireland were too distracting for my poetry." And then right on the printed page would appear "CAROLINE," in capital letters, and Elgin would rub his face foolishly with both hands, twisting his mouth and his cheeks and his nose.

He didn't believe that Caroline loved him as much as he loved her, or at least that she desired him as much as he did her, and this made him sullen. He picked on her. He told her she wasn't as smart as she thought she was; people treated her as if she were intelligent only because she was pretty. He would accuse her of pettiness, and she would agree with him, confess that she had an awful character, and while he was consoling her, their embraces would begin.

Elgin would be hurt whenever Caroline was the first to point out that it was time to go and have dinner. Caroline would eye the clock, but Elgin would pretend he was so entranced with Caroline he didn't know what time it was. The minutes would tick by, and Caroline would grow gayer and gayer, trying to ignore the time, while Elgin, beetling, thin, and sardonic, refused to say the words that would release her.

Elgin became frightened. He was so frightened he couldn't eat. He was afraid of losing Caroline, of failing his courses because he couldn't study unless she was sitting beside him where he could reach out and touch her every few minutes. The thought of what it would be like if any of the quarrels they had should turn serious worried him until he was sick. Finally, looking gray and haggard, he suggested to her one afternoon that the two of them should run off and get married.

"Elgin, don't. Don't let's talk about that. You know we can't."

Elgin shrugged and looked disheartened. "I dont like self-pity," he said. "But I admit I have some. Oh, yes. I pity myself a lot. Imagine, here I am, in love with a common, ordinary, conventional girl like you."

Caroline supported her head with her hands. "Oh, Elgin," she said, "you're being cruel. You know we're awfully young. And just because we got carried away—there's no need, really, to . . . It's our animal appetites mostly, you know. . . ."

Elgin wanted to say something bitter but her last remark stopped him. "*Your* animal appetites, too?"

"Yes."

He was so happy he forgot his feelings had been hurt.

Sometimes, she and Elgin went out with Felicia and Dimitri. Caroline could not now bear girls she thought were virgins; they made her uneasy, and she would not double with Dimitri and Felicia until Elgin swore they were lovers, too. Elgin spent more than one afternoon telling her that almost all the girls at Radcliffe and all other colleges had slept with somebody. "The percentage is very high," he said.

They went boating twice at Marblehead. Dimitri had a car, which Elgin borrowed—an old, weak-lunged Ford—and they would wheeze up to Marblehead and rent a dinghy and be blown around the bay, with the sunlight bright on Caroline's hair and the salt air making them hungry and the wind whipping up small whitecaps to make the day exciting.

Caroline wrote in her diary, "His back is so beautiful. It has such a lovely shape. It's so defenseless. I like to put my ear against his back and listen to his heart—I think it's his heart I hear. It's funny he is not more handsome in his clothes, but that only makes him seem more beautiful to me, I think. I feel I would like to give birth to him. Sometimes, I want to crawl into his pocket and be carried like a pencil. I never let him see how strongly I feel. I am a dreadful person, dreadful. . . ."

Elgin wrote her a letter.

"Dear Caroline, Isn't it funny to have me writing a letter to you when I see you every day? But just imagine how it would seem later if we looked back and saw that we had never written each other how we felt.

"You, Caroline Hedges, are the greatest love of my life, just as you are the first.

"I don't suppose, you being a girl, that you know what it's like to love a girl like you, but if you knew how dependent men are on women, you might understand. Not that men can't survive alone, but they don't seem to really amount to anything until they have a woman they love.

"Reading over what I have just written, I see that everything I've said applies only to the selfish side of love. I guess that's a dead giveaway about me. But as for you, kid, just knowing you is rather awe-inspiring."

Sometimes, there would be birds singing in the ivy outside the window of Elgin's room. Sometimes, Elgin would sing to Caroline; he had a sweet, insecurely pitched voice, and his singing would give them both pleasure. Sometimes, seeing Elgin walk across the room unclothed would make all the breath leave Caroline's body, and she would not even be conscious of her gasp or that he heard her. One afternoon, Elgin went into the bathroom to get Caroline a glass of water. She was lying in the lower bunk, lapped in shadows, and she saw him come back into the room and she said weakly, "I love you, Elgin." It was the first time she had said it, that proud, stubborn girl. Elgin heard her; he stopped in his tracks and he put his head back. "God," he said. "This is the happiest moment I ever had."

Now there was no bar to their intimacy, and they talked. Elgin was relentless about asking questions: "What do you think about money? What is your father like? Are you fond of him?"

At first, Caroline was cautious. "Well, I think there's a minimum amount of money people should have. . . . My father is sort of nice. He's shallow, I guess. He doesn't seem to have very strong emotions. He works for an insurance company. I used to like him a lot; I still do. . . . I think I feel sorry for him."

"What do you mean by that?" Elgin asked. He handed her a cigarette and lit it for her. "Tell me everything about yourself. Be honest. I've never known anyone as well as I know you."

Caroline cupped her hands over her mouth. "I think he loves me, and now I love you, and I think that's sad. That he's older . . . Should we be talking like this, Elgin?"

"Why not? Who else can we talk to?"

Then it all began to come out, her feelings toward her father, toward her mother, toward money. Caroline wanted a nice house and a large family; she looked down a little on people who weren't well off. When she felt exhausted from telling Elgin these things, she asked him questions.

"My mother's very possessive," he said. "If we got married, I think we'd have in-law problems. I want to be a famous scholar. I don't disapprove of campus politics. I know I should, but I don't. Isn't that shameful?"

"This isn't dignified, talking like this," Caroline said. "I don't want to do it any more."

She was frightened. Having admitted she loved Elgin, she felt naked, and these conversations only made her feel worse. She kept hoping she and Elgin would reach some stability together, but it never came. She still was frightened when she ran up the stairs of Widener that he wouldn't be waiting for her. She wondered why she couldn't get used to this situation, why the pleasures she was drawn into didn't lose their elements of pain— indeed, why the elements of pain grew steadily worse, until she dreaded seeing Elgin and had to force herself to get out of bed in the morning and go through her day. She couldn't help thinking that what she was with comparative strangers was much pleasanter than what she was with Elgin. With him she was capricious, untruthful, often sharp-tongued, giddy with emotions that came and went, and while one emotion might be ennobling, having six or seven in the space of an hour was undignified and not decent at all. She had always believed that a woman ought to walk very straight, write a firm hand, keep house and entertain well—in short, be like those friends of her mother's whom she admired. The fact that she was young didn't seem any excuse at all for her not being like those women, and now she said to herself, "I'm wild. That's all there is to that."

She decided she was inordinately sexual. Elgin caught her in Widener reading a book describing the great courtesans of the nineteenth century, La Belle Otero and Lola Montez. She believed that Elgin would inevitably forsake her because she had lost all her dignity and mystery, and she boasted to him that he would never forget her, even if he married some pasty-faced virgin. Elgin couldn't calm her; in fact, he was more than half persuaded that she *was* unusually passionate when she said she was, and he became uneasy with her. Caroline began to wear a little too much lipstick and to walk not in her habitual erect fashion but slouching and swaying her hips. She drank and smoked more, and when she got high, she would look at Elgin through lowered eyelids and kiss him in a knowing—a childishly knowing—way. And all of this humbled Elgin, who felt Caroline was a great enigma and that she was drawing away from him. One night, they were sitting on the riverbank and Caroline put her hands on Elgin's head and drew him to her, and Elgin pulled away desperately. "I don't want you to kiss me like that!"

"What's wrong?" Caroline asked haughtily. "Am I too much woman for you?"

Elgin's eyes grew moist. "I don't know what you do to me," he said miserably. "I'm ready to cry. I didn't think we were having *that* kind of an affair."

In the darkness, he saw Caroline's eyelids descend. Then a shudder passed over her face. He decided to stake everything rather than have Caroline frighten him into helplessness.

He grabbed her arm. "Listen, you've got to get hold of yourself. You're acting like an ass."

Caroline was motionless.

"You're ruining everything," Elgin said.

"You have too many illusions about me," Caroline said coldly. She pulled away from his grasp and lay down on his old, battered raincoat and put her hands under her head. "There are a lot of things you don't know about me. I didn't want to tell you I loved you because I wanted to hold you. There, what do you think of that?"

Elgin hit himself on the chest. "You think that's bad? Well, I always intended to seduce you, right from the beginning. God!" He lay down, too, on the damp grass, two feet away from her, and he put his hands under his head.

Lying like that, they quarreled in this peculiar way, libelling themselves, lowering the object of love in the other's eyes.

"I think it's loathsome that we sleep together," Caroline said. "I feel like a you-know-what."

"I hate seeing you every day," Elgin said. "Not because of you but because I'm always afraid you'll see through me. Also, I miss having free time to study—that's how cold-blooded I am."

There was a full moon that night, and its light was no chillier than what these two young people said about themselves. But after a while Elgin rolled over and took Caroline in his arms. "Please don't hate me."

"I don't hate you. I love you."

"I love you, too. God, it's hell!"

They decided to be more sensible. The next day they didn't meet in Widener. Elgin stayed in his room, and at three o'clock the phone rang.

"It's me—Caroline."

"Oh God, you called. I was praying you would. Where are you?"

"In the drugstore on the corner." There was silence. "Elgin," she said at last, "did you have any orange juice today?"

He ran, down the stairs, along the sidewalk, to the drugstore, to have his orange juice.

One day, Elgin told Caroline he was going to stay home and play poker with some of the boys in his entry. Caroline said that was a good idea. She had to write her mother; for some reason, her letters home had got her mother all upset, and she wanted to take some time and calm the old biddy down. "Poor thing," said Caroline. "She's had such an empty life, and I'm so important to her." Then she smiled a thin, nervous smile. "Of course, when I think how stupid she is, I wonder what I'll find to say to her."

Elgin played poker. He lost four dollars and sixty cents. At eleven-thirty, he excused himself from the game and went out on the street. He walked hurriedly, jogging part of the distance, until he stood on the sidewalk across from Cabot Hall, looking up at the light in Caroline's room. Finally, a shadow passed over the window, and Elgin felt what he could only describe as anguish.

He looked in the gutter until he found a pebble, and then he hurled it at Caroline's window. It struck. The shadow appeared again, standing quite still. At that moment, a policeman rounded the corner. Elgin thrust his hands in his pockets and walked up the street. The policeman stopped him.

"Hey, buddy, did you just throw something at that building?"

"No, Officer." Elgin was sweating and looked so pitiable the officer said, "I guess it was a trick of the light."

When Caroline asked him if he had come by Cabot the night before, he denied it.

The next day, he and Caroline went up to his room. As Elgin closed the door, Caroline threw herself onto the couch. She looked pale and unhappy, and she was making a face, preparing herself for what was coming. But Elgin walked over and stood next to the couch and said, "Caroline, we've got to be chaste. God!" he cried. "It's not easy to say this, and if your feelings get hurt, I don't know what I'll do!"

"They're not hurt."

"I want you to be happy," he said, looking down at her. "I think we ought to get married."

"We're under age, Elgin—you know that. Our parents won't let us."

"We'll tell them you're pregnant. We'll do something."

Caroline jumped up. "But I don't want to marry you! You won't make me happy. I'm scared of you. You don't have any respect for me. I don't know how to be a good wife."

"Listen, Caroline, we haven't done the right thing. You want to have children?"

A pink, piteous flush covered Caroline's face. "Oh," she said.

"We ought to get married," he said doggedly. "It won't be easy, but otherwise we'll never be happy. You see, what we didn't figure out is the teleology of the thing. We don't have a goal. We have to have a goal, do you see?"

"Elgin, we can't be foolish. If we really love each other, we have to be very practical or else we'll just cause each other very needless pain."

They looked at each other, pure at last, haloed by an urge to sacrifice. "I may not be right for you," Caroline whispered. "We'll wait. We'll wait until fall. We'll have the summer to think things over."

Elgin frowned, not liking to have his sacrifice ignored. "I'm willing to marry you," he said.

"No, it's not right," said Caroline. "We're too young. We couldn't have children now. We're too ignorant. We'd be terrible parents." How it pained her to say this!

"If you feel that way," Elgin said, "I think we ought to plan to break up. Nothing sudden," he added, to ease the sudden twinge that was twisting his stomach. "When school's over."

Caroline hesitated, but it seemed to her dreamlike and wonderful to be free of this febrile emotion. And atonement would be so wonderful. . . . At the same time, she was hurt. "All right," she said with dignity. "If you want."

Elgin turned away from her. "Caroline, tell me one thing," he said with his back to her. "Emotionally, would you like to marry me?"

"Yes."

"God!" he said. "You're so practical!"

"I'm not!" she cried. "I can't help it." She wrung her hands. "If you tried to carry me off, I wouldn't resist," she said. "But if you ask me, I think— I think—"

He didn't have to marry her; he wouldn't have to worry about supporting her; he hadn't lost his career. Elgin felt irrepressible relief welling up in him. "God, how we love each other."

Caroline laughed. "It's true." She laughed a little more. "It's so true!" She threw her arms around his neck and kissed him.

Of course, they didn't stick to Elgin's plan of breaking up when school ended. They decided they would take a vacation from each other, and meet in the fall, when college began again, as friends. This agreement seemed to remove a great weight from them. They had only two weeks of the reading period and three weeks of exams left to be together, but they resumed some of their old habits—the walks between classes, for instance, and the trips to the Boston Museum of Fine Arts—and they even took to reading stories aloud again, preferring Chekhov and Colette. The sweetness and the sadness of their predicament were what they loved, and they threw themselves into the role of well-disciplined lovers with all their energy. Hardly a day passed without their thinking of some new gesture toward each other. Elgin gave flowers to Caroline; she bought him cuff links and books of poetry. Elgin left off suspecting that he was being made a fool of, and was actually gentlemanly, opening doors for Caroline and lighting her cigarettes. Caroline was ladylike and concealed her moods. They engaged in rough-house; Elgin pulled her hair and she pummeled him when they sat on the riverbank. They were chaste. They referred sometimes to the times when they had listened to the nightingale, and while the chastity didn't come easily to them, the act of sacrifice did. Elgin put on weight, and his face regained its color. "My goodness," Caroline said. "I think knowing me has improved your looks." It seemed they had found the secret of being happy together, in the imminence of separation, and while they didn't understand the paradox, they knew it was true.

But as their five last weeks passed, they discovered why it was true. All the pain of the relationship was now bound up with the parting and not with the things they did to each other. "It's dreadful," Caroline said. "I have feelings. They're like heavy mice that come out of holes and sit in my stomach and weigh me down."

They had been so proud of themselves, so free and relaxed and peaceful together, and now, when they saw what this parting was going to be like, all their vivacity and happiness flagged, they lost interest in talking to each other, and all they wanted was to get it over with.

On the last day of exams, they went up to Elgin's room at six o'clock. Elgin had bought a bottle of champagne and rented two glasses. Caroline was all dressed up because she was going to catch a train for Baltimore at nine o'clock. She had on a small hat, which she kept eying in the mirror. Poor Elgin was nervous about opening the champagne. "It's imported," he said. "I don't want to sound tight, but if half of it explodes or comes out in foam, I won't be happy." Caroline laughed, but when the cork popped, she turned very serious. She was afraid of what Elgin would toast; she was afraid it would ruin her self-possession.

Elgin slowly poured the champagne into the two glasses. Then the two young people, alone in the room, picked up their glasses and held them together. "To our reunion in the fall," Elgin said. "God knows what it will be like." They drank.

Caroline put her glass down. "Let's play a record and dance," she said. Elgin put on a Cole Porter L.P., and he and Caroline circled around the room, dodging the furniture, pausing to take occasional sips of their champagne. At six-thirty, they went downstairs and ate in the dining hall.

By seven-fifteen, they were back upstairs in Elgin's room, sitting on the bunk, kissing each other with a dry, intense helplessness. At quarter of eight, Caroline said she had to go. Elgin pulled away from her; she had taken off her hat, and her dress, made of some pretty gray-blue material, was hopelessly rumpled. With his hands, he set her just so on the bunk. Then he took out his pocket comb and combed her hair. "There," he said.

"Do I look prettier now?" Caroline asked.

"Yes," Elgin said.

They walked downstairs and out the door of Adams House. When they reached the sidewalk, Caroline said, "I don't want you to come with me. I want to go back to the dorm alone. All right?"

Elgin nodded.

"I'll write you from Europe," Caroline said. "Goodbye," she said and walked away, up the sidewalk; she tried to walk crisply but her feet dragged because she felt tired. Slowly, the hoped-for sense of relief was coming; she was free of Elgin, she had herself back, but not all of herself. Elgin still held some of her, and she would never get it back except when he was beside her.

Elgin sat on the steps in front of Adams House and buried his face in his hands. "God!" he said to himself. "I love her." And he wondered what would become of them now.

Amado Muro
Cecilia Rosas

*"Since I was only fourteen and in love for
the first time, I looked at her more chastely
than most."*

WHEN I WAS IN THE NINTH GRADE at Bowie High School in El Paso, I got a
job hanging up women's coats at La Feria Department Store on Saturdays.
It wasn't the kind of a job that had much appeal for a Mexican boy or for
boys of any other nationality either. But the work wasn't hard, only boring.
Wearing a smock, I stood around the Ladies' Wear Department all day
long waiting for women customers to finish trying on coats so I coud hang
them up.

Having to wear a smock was worse than the work itself. It was an agonizing ordeal. To me it was a loathsome stigma of unmanly toil that made an
already degrading job even more so. The work itself I looked on as onerous
and effeminate for a boy from a family of miners, shepherds, and ditch-
diggers. But working in Ladies' Wear had two compensations: earning three
dollars every Saturday was one; being close to the Señorita Cecilia Rosas
was the other.

This alluring young woman, the most beautiful I had ever seen, more
than made up for my mollycoddle labor and the smock that symbolized it.
My chances of looking at her were almost limitless. And like a good Mexican,
I made the most of them. But I was only too painfully aware that I wasn't
the only one who thought this saleslady gorgeous.

La Feria had water fountains on every one of its eight floors. But men
liked best the one on the floor where Miss Rosas worked. So they made
special trips to Ladies' Wear all day long to drink water and look at her.

Since I was only fourteen and in love for the first time, I looked at her
more chastely than most. The way her romantic lashes fringed her obsidian
eyes was especially enthralling to me. Then, too, I never tired of admiring
her shining raven hair, her Cupid's-bow lips, the warmth of her gleaming
white smile. Her rich olive skin was almost as dark as mine. Sometimes she
wore a San Juan rose in her hair. When she did, she looked so very lovely

I forgot all about what La Feria was paying me to do and stood gaping at her instead. My admiration was decorous but complete. I admired her hourglass figure as well as her wonderfully radiant face.

Other men admired her too. They inspected her from the water fountain. Some stared at her boldly, watching her trimly rhythmic hips sway. Others, less frank and open, gazed furtively at her swelling bosom or her shapely calves. This effrontery made me indignant. I too, looked at these details of Miss Rosas. But I prided myself on doing so more romantically, far more poetically than they did, with much more love than desire.

Then, too, Miss Rosas was the friendliest as well as the most beautiful saleslady in Ladies' Wear. But the other salesladies, Mexican girls all, didn't like her. She was so nice to them all they were hard put to justify their dislike. They couldn't very well admit they disliked her because she was pretty. So they all said she was haughty and imperious. Their claim was partly true. Her beauty was Miss Rosas' only obvious vanity. But she had still another. She prided herself on being more American than Mexican because she was born in El Paso. And she did her best to act, dress, and talk the way Americans do. She hated to speak Spanish, disliked her Mexican name. She called herself Cecile Roses instead of Cecilia Rosas. This made the other salesladies smile derisively. They called her La Americana or the Gringa from Xochimilco every time they mentioned her name.

Looking at this beautiful girl was more important than money to me. It was my greatest compensation for doing work that I hated. She was so lovely that a glance at her sweetly expressive face was enough to make me forget my shame at wearing a smock and my dislike for my job with its eternal waiting around.

Miss Rosas was an exemplary saleslady. She could be frivolous, serious or demure, primly efficient too, molding herself to each customer's personality. Her voice matched her exotically mysterious eyes. It was the richest, the softest I had ever heard. Her husky whisper, gentle as a rain breeze, was like a tender caress. Hearing it made me want to dream and I did. Romantic thoughts burgeoned up in my mind like rosy billows of hope scented with Miss Rosas' perfume. These thoughts made me so languid at my work that the floor manager, Joe Apple, warned me to show more enthusiasm for it or else suffer the consequences.

But my dreams sapped my will to struggle, making me oblivious to admonitions. I had neither the desire nor the energy to respond to Joe Apple's warnings. Looking at Miss Rosas used up so much of my energy that I had little left for my work. Miss Rosas was twenty, much too old for me, everyone said. But what everyone said didn't matter. So I soldiered on the job and watched her, entranced by her beauty, her grace. While I watched I dreamed of being a hero. It hurt me to have her see me doing such menial work. But there was no escape from it. I needed the job to stay in school. So more and more I took refuge in dreams.

When I had watched her as much, if not more, than I could safely do without attracting the attention of other alert Mexican salesladies, I slipped out of Ladies' Wear and walked up the stairs to the top floor. There I sat on a window ledge smoking Faro cigarettes, looking down at the city's canyons, and best of all, thinking about Miss Rosas and myself.

They say Chihuahua Mexicans are good at dreaming because the mountains are so gigantic and the horizons so vast in Mexico's biggest state that men don't think pygmy thoughts there. I was no exception. Lolling on the ledge, I became what I wanted to be. And what I wanted to be was a handsome American Miss Rosas could love and marry. The dreams I dreamed were imaginative masterpieces, or so I thought. They transcended the insipid realities of a casual relationship, making it vibrantly thrilling and infinitely more romantic. They transformed me from a colorless Mexican boy who put women's coats away into the debonair American, handsome, dashing and worldly, that I longed to be for her sake. For the first time in my life I reveled in the magic of fantasy. It brought happiness. Reality didn't.

But my window-ledge reveries left me bewildered and shaken. They had a narcotic quality. The more thrillingly romantic fantasies I created, the more I needed to create. It got so I couldn't get enough dreaming time in Ladies' Wear. My kind of dreaming demanded disciplined concentration. And there was just too much hubbub, too much gossiping, too many coats to be put away there.

So I spent less time in Ladies' Wear. My flights to the window ledge became more recklessly frequent. Sometimes I got tired sitting there. When I did, I took the freight elevator down to the street floor and brazenly walked out of the store without so much as punching a time clock. Walking the streets quickened my imagination, gave form and color to my thoughts. It made my brain glow with impossible hopes that seemed incredibly easy to realize. So absorbed was I in thoughts of Miss Rosas and myself that I bumped into Americans, apologizing mechanically in Spanish instead of English, and wandered down South El Paso Street like a somnambulist, without really seeing the street vendors, cafes and arcades, tattoo shops, and shooting galleries at all.

But if there was confusion in these walks there was some serenity too. Something good did come from the dreams that prompted them. I found I could tramp the streets with a newly won tranquillity, no longer troubled by, or even aware of, girls in tight skirts, overflowing blouses, and drop-stitch stockings. My love for Miss Rosas was my shield against the furtive thoughts and indiscriminate desires that had made me so uneasy for a year or more before I met her.

Then, too, because of her, I no longer looked at the pictures of voluptuous women in the *Vea* and *Vodevil* magazines at Zamora's newsstand. The piquant thoughts Mexicans call *malos deseos* were gone from my mind. I no longer thought about women as I did before I fell in love with Miss Rosas. Instead, I thought about a woman, only one. This clear-cut objective and the serenity that went with it made me understand something of one of the nicest things about love.

I treasured the walks, the window-ledge sittings, and the dreams that I had then. I clung to them just as long as I could. Drab realities closed in on me chokingly just as soon as I gave them up. My future was a time clock with an American Mister telling me what to do and this I knew only too well. A career as an ice-dock laborer stretched ahead of me. Better said, it dangled over me like a Veracruz machete. My uncle, Rodolfo Avitia, a straw boss on the ice docks, was already training me for it. Every night he took me to the mile-long docks overhanging the Southern Pacific freight yards. There he handed me tongs and made me practice tripping three-hundred-pound ice blocks so I could learn how to unload an entire boxcar of ice blocks myself.

Thinking of this bleak future drove me back into my fantasies, made me want to prolong them forever. My imagination was taxed to the breaking point by the heavy strain I put on it.

I thought about every word Miss Rosas had ever said to me, making myself believe she looked at me with unmistakable tenderness when she said them. When she said: "Amado, please hang up this fur coat," I found special meaning in her tone. It was as though she had said: "Amadito, I love you."

When she gave these orders, I pushed into action like a man blazing with a desire to perform especially heroic feats. At such times I felt capable of putting away not one but a thousand fur coats, and would have done so joyously.

Sometimes on the street I caught myself murmuring: "Cecilia, *linda amorcita*, I love you." When these surges swept over me, I walked down empty street so I could whisper: "Cecilia, *te quiero con toda mi alma*" as much as I wanted to and mumble everything else that I felt. And so I emptied my heart on the streets and window ledge while women's coats piled up in Ladies' Wear.

But my absences didn't go unnoticed. Once an executive-looking man, portly, gray, and efficiently brusque, confronted me while I sat on the window ledge with a Faro cigarette pasted to my lips, a cloud of tobacco smoke hanging over my head, and many perfumed dreams inside it. He had a no-nonsense approach that jibed with his austere mien. He asked me what my name was, jotted down my work number, and went off to make a report on what he called "sordid malingering."

Other reports followed this. Gruff warnings, stern admonitions, and blustery tirades developed from them. They came from both major and minor executives. These I was already inured to. They didn't matter anyway. My condition was far too advanced, already much too complex to be cleared up by mere lectures, fatherly or otherwise. All the threats and rebukes in the world couldn't have made me give up my window-ledge reveries or keep me from roaming city streets with Cecilia Rosas' name on my lips like a prayer.

The reports merely made me more cunning, more doggedly determined to city-slick La Feria out of work hours I owed it. The net result was that I timed my absences more precisely and contrived better lies to explain them. Sometimes I went to the men's room and looked at myself in the mirror for as long as ten minutes at a time. Such self-studies filled me with gloom. The mirror reflected an ordinary Mexican face, more homely than comely. Only my hair gave me hope. It was thick and wavy, deserving a better face to go with it. So I did the best I could with what I had, and combed it over my temples in ringlets just like the poets back in my hometown of Parral, Chihuahua, used to do.

My inefficiency, my dreams, my general lassitude could have gone on indefinitely, it seemed. My life at the store wavered between bright hope and leaden despair, unrelieved by Miss Rosas' acceptance or rejection of me. Then one day something happened that almost made my overstrained heart stop beating.

It happened on the day Miss Rosas stood behind me while I put a fur coat away. Her heady perfume, the fragrance of her warm healthy body, made me feel faint. She was so close to me I thought about putting my hands around her lissome waist and hugging her as hard as I could. But thoughts of subsequent disgrace deterred me, so instead of hugging her I smiled wanly and asked her in Spanish how she was feeling.

"Amado, speak English," she told me. "And pronounce the words slowly and carefully so you won't sound like a country Mexican."

Then she looked at me in a way that made me the happiest employee who ever punched La Feria's time clock.

"Amadito," she whispered the way I had always dreamed she would.

"Yes, Señorita Cecilia," I said expectantly.

Her smile was warmly intimate. "Amadito, when are you going to take me to the movies?" she asked.

Other salesladies watched us, all smiling. They made me so nervous I couldn't answer.

"Amadito, you haven't answered me," Miss Rosas said teasingly. "Either you're bashful as a village sweetheart or else you don't like me at all."

In voluble Spanish, I quickly assured her the latter wasn't the case. I was just getting ready to say "Señorita Cecilia, I more than like you, I love you" when she frowned and told me to speak English. So I slowed down and tried to smooth out my ruffled thoughts.

"Señorita Cecilia," I said. "I'd love to take you to the movies any time."

Miss Rosas smiled and patted my cheek. "Will you buy me candy and popcorn?" she said.

I nodded, putting my hand against the imprint her warm palm had left on my face.

"And hold my hand?"

I said "yes" so enthusiastically it made her laugh. Other salesladies laughed too. Dazed and numb with happiness, I watched Miss Rosas walk away. How proud and confident she was, how wholesomely clean and feminine. Other salesladies were looking at me and laughing.

Miss Sandoval came over to me, "*Ay papacito,*" she said. "With women you're the divine tortilla."

Miss de la Rosa came over too. "When you take the Americana to the movies, remember not to speak Christian," she said. "And be sure you wear the pants that don't have any patches on them."

What they said made me blush and wonder how they knew what we had been talking about. Miss Arroyo came over to join them. So did Miss Torres.

"Amado, remember women are weak and men aren't made of sweet bread," Miss Arroyo said.

This embarrassed me but it wasn't altogether unpleasant. Miss Sandoval winked at Miss de la Rosa, then looked back at me.

"Don't go too fast with the Americana, Amado," she said. "Remember the procession is long and the candles are small."

They laughed and slapped me on the back. They all wanted to know when I was going to take Miss Rosas to the movies. "She didn't say," I blurted out without thinking.

This brought another burst of laughter. It drove me back up to the window ledge where I got out my package of Faros and thought about the wonderful thing that had happened. But I was too nervous to stay there. So I went to the men's room and looked at myself in the mirror again, wondering why Miss Rosas liked me so well. The mirror made it brutally clear that my looks hadn't influenced her. So it must have been something else, perhaps character. But that didn't seem likely either. Joe Apple had told me I didn't have much of that. And other store officials had bulwarked his opinion. Still, I had seen homely men walking the streets of El Paso's Little Chihuahua quarter with beautiful Mexican women and no one could explain that either. Anyway it was time for another walk. So I took one.

This time I trudged through Little Chihuahua, where both Miss Rosas and I lived. Little Chihuahua looked different to me that day. It was a broken-down Mexican quarter honeycombed with tenements, Mom and Pop groceries, herb shops, and spindly salt-cedar trees; with howling children running its streets and old Mexican revolutionaries sunning themselves on its curbs like iguanas. But on that clear frosty day it was the world's most romantic place because Cecilia Rosas lived there.

While walking, I reasoned that Miss Rosas might want to go dancing after the movies. So I went to Professor Toribio Ortega's dance studio and made arrangements to take my first lesson. Some neighborhood boys saw me when I came out. They bawled "*Mariquita*" and made flutteringly effeminate motions, all vulgar if not obscene. It didn't matter. On my lunch hour I went back and took my first lesson anyway. Professor Ortega danced with me. Softened by weeks of dreaming, I went limp in his arms imagining he was Miss Rosas.

The rest of the day was the same as many others before it. As usual I spent most of it stealing glances at Miss Rosas and slipping up to the window ledge. She looked busy, efficient, not like a woman in love. Her many other admirers trooped to the water fountain to look at the way her black silk dress fitted her curves. Their profane admiration made me scowl even more than I usually did at such times.

When the day's work was done, I plodded home from the store just as dreamily as I had gone to it. Since I had no one else to confide in, I invited my oldest sister, Dulce Nombre de María, to go to the movies with me. They were showing Jorge Negrete and María Felix in *El Rapto* at the Colon Theater. It was a romantic movie, just the kind I wanted to see.

After it was over, I bought Dulce Nombre *churros* and hot *champurrado* at the Golden Taco Cafe. And I told my sister all about what had happened to me. She looked at me thoughtfully, then combed my hair back with her fingertips as though trying to soothe me. "Manito," she said, softly. "I wouldn't. . . ." Then she looked away and shrugged her shoulders.

On Monday I borrowed three dollars from my Uncle Rodolfo without telling him what it was for. Miss Rosas hadn't told me what night she wanted me to take her to the movies. But the way she had looked at me made me think that almost any night would do. So I decided on Friday. Waiting for it to come was hard. But I had to keep my mind occupied. So I went to Zamora's newsstand to get the Alma Norteña songbook. Pouring through it for the most romantic song I could find, I decided on *La Cecilia*.

All week long I practiced singing it on my way to school and in the shower after basketball practice with the Little Chihuahua Tigers at the Sagrado Corazón gym. But, except for singing this song, I tried not to speak Spanish at all. At home I made my mother mad by saying in English, "Please pass the sugar."

My mother looked at me as though she couldn't believe what she had heard. Since my Uncle Rodolfo couldn't say anything more than "hello" and "goodbye" in English, he couldn't tell what I had said. So my sister Consuelo did.

"May the Dark Virgin with the benign look make this boy well enough to speak Christian again," my mother whispered.

This I refused to do. I went on speaking English even though my mother and uncle didn't understand it. This shocked my sisters as well. When they asked me to explain my behavior, I parroted Miss Rosas, saying, "We're living in the United States now."

My rebellion against being a Mexican created an uproar. Such conduct was unorthodox, if not scandalous, in a neighborhood where names like Burciaga, Rodriguez, and Castillo predominated. But it wasn't only the Spanish language that I lashed out against.

"Mother, why do we always have to eat *sopa, frijoles, refritos, mondongo,* and *pozole?*" I complained. "Can't we ever eat roast beef or ham and eggs like Americans do?"

My mother didn't speak to me for two days after that. My Uncle Rodolfo grimaced and mumbled something about renegade Mexicans who want to eat ham and eggs even though the Montes Packing Company turned out the best *chorizo* this side of Toluca. My sister Consuelo giggled and called me a Rio Grande Irishman, an American Mister, a gringo, and a *bolillo*. Dulce Nombre looked at me worriedly.

Life at home was almost intolerable. Cruel jokes and mocking laughter made it so. I moped around looking sad as a day without bread. My sister Consuelo suggested I go to the courthouse and change my name to Beloved Wall which is English for Amado Muro. My mother didn't agree. "If *Nuestro Señor* had meant for Amadito to be an American he would have given him a name like Smeeth or Jonesy," she said. My family was unsympathetic. With a family like mine, how could I ever hope to become an American and win Miss Rosas?

Friday came at last. I put on my only suit, slicked my hair down with liquid vaseline, and doused myself with Dulce Nombre's perfume.

"Amado's going to serenade that pretty girl everyone calls La Americana," my sister Consuelo told my mother and uncle when I sat down to eat. "Then he's going to take her to the movies."

This made my uncle laugh and my mother scowl.

"*Qué pantalones tiene* [what nerve that boy's got]," my uncle said, "to serenade a twenty-year-old woman."

"La Americana," my mother said derisively. "That one's Mexican as pulque cured with celery."

They made me so nervous I forgot to take off my cap when I sat down to eat.

"Amado, take off your cap," my mother said. "You're not in La Lagunilla Market."

My uncle frowned. "All this boy thinks about is kissing girls," he said gruffly.

"But my boy's never kissed one," my mother said proudly.

My sister Consuelo laughed. "That's because they won't let him," she said.

This wasn't true. But I couldn't say so in front of my mother. I had already kissed Emaline Uribe from Porfirio Díaz Street not once but twice. Both times I'd kissed her in a darkened doorway less than a block from her home. But the kisses were over so soon we hardly had time to enjoy them. This was because Ema was afraid her big brother, the husky one nicknamed Toro, would see us. But if we'd had more time it would have been better, I knew.

Along about six o'clock the three musicians who called themselves the Mariachis of Tecalitlán came by and whistled for me, just as they said they would do. They never looked better than they did on that night. They had on black and silver charro uniforms and big, black, Zapata sombreros.

My mother shook her head when she saw them. "Son, who ever heard of serenading a girl at six o'clock in the evening," she said. "When your father had the mariachis sing for me it was always at two o'clock in the morning—the only proper time for a six-song *gallo*."

But I got out my Ramírez guitar anyway. I put on my cap and rushed out to give the mariachis the money without even kissing my mother's hand or waiting for her to bless me. Then we headed for Miss Rosas' home. Some boys and girls I knew were out in the street. This made me uncomfortable. They looked at me wonderingly as I led the mariachi band to Miss Rosas' home.

A block away from Miss Rosas' home I could see her father, a grizzled veteran who fought for Pancho Villa, sitting on the curb reading the Juárez newspaper, *El Fronterizo*.

The sight of him made me slow down for a moment. But I got back in stride when I saw Miss Rosas herself.

She smiled and waved at me. "Hello, Amadito," she said.

"Hello, Señorita Cecilia," I said.

She looked at the mariachis, then back at me.

"Ay, Amado, you're going to serenade your girl," she said. I didn't reply right away. Then when I was getting ready to say "Señorita Cecilia, I came to serenade you," I saw the American man sitting in the sports roadster at the curb.

Miss Rosas turned to him. "I'll be right there, Johnny," she said.

She patted my cheek. "I've got to run now, Amado," she said. "Have a real nice time, darling."

I looked at her silken legs as she got into the car. Everything had happened so fast I was dazed. Broken dreams made my head spin. The contrast between myself and the poised American in the sports roadster was so cruel it made me wince.

She was happy with him. That was obvious. She was smiling and laughing, looking forward to a good time. Why had she asked me to take her to the movies if she already had a boyfriend? Then I remembered how the other salesladies had laughed, how I had wondered why they were laughing when they couldn't even hear what we were saying. And I realized it had all been a joke, everyone had known it but me. Neither Miss Rosas nor the other salesladies had ever dreamed I would think she was serious about wanting me to take her to the movies.

The American and Miss Rosas drove off. Gloomy thoughts oppressed me. They made me want to cry. To get rid of them I thought of going to one of the "bad death" cantinas in Juárez where tequila starts fights and knives finish them—to one of the cantinas where the panders, whom Mexicans call *burros*, stand outside shouting "It's just like Paris, only not so many people" was where I wanted to go. There I could forget her in Jalisco-state style with mariachis, tequila, and night-life women. Then I remembered I was so young that night-life women would shun me and *cantineros* wouldn't serve me tequila.

So I thought some more. Emalina Uribe was the only other alternative. If we went over to Porfirio Díaz Street and serenaded her I could go back to being a Mexican again. She was just as Mexican as I was, Mexican as *chicarrones*. I thought about smiling, freckle-faced Ema.

Ema wasn't like the Americana at all. She wore wash dresses that fitted loosely and even ate the *melocha* candies Mexicans like so well on the street. On Sundays she wore a Zamora shawl to church and her mother wouldn't let her use lipstick or let her put on high heels.

But with a brother like Toro who didn't like me anyway, such a serenade might be more dangerous than romantic. Besides that, my faith in my looks, my character, or whatever it was that made women fall in love with men, was so undermined I could already picture her getting into a car with a handsome American just like Miss Rosas had done.

The Mariachis of Tecalitlán were getting impatient. They had been paid to sing six songs and they wanted to sing them. But they were all sympathetic. None of them laughed at me.

"Amado, don't look sad as I did the day I learned I'd never be a millionaire," the mariachi captain said, putting his arm around me. "If not that girl, then another."

But without Miss Rosas there was no one we could sing *La Cecilia* to. The street seemed bleak and empty now that she was gone. And I didn't want to serenade Ema Uribe even though she hadn't been faithless as Miss Rosas had been. It was true she hadn't been faithless, but only lack of opportunity would keep her from getting into a car with an American, I reasoned cynically.

Just about then Miss Rosas' father looked up from his newspaper. He asked the mariachis if they knew how to sing *Cananea Jail*. They told him they did. Then they looked at me. I thought it over for a moment. Then I nodded and started strumming the bass strings of my guitar. What had happened made it only too plain I could never trust Miss Rosas again. So we serenaded her father instead.

2
Emotional Development

ADOLESCENCE IS NOT ONLY A TIME of rapid physical growth, it is also one of heightened emotionality. Arthur T. Jersild offers this definition of the subject in *The Psychology of Adolescence*: "To be emotional means to be 'moved.' An emotional experience usually involves *feeling* (such as the feeling of fear), *impulse* (such as an impulse to flee), and a *perception* of what it is that gives rise or seems to give rise to the emotion. Sometimes these elements of the experience are so vague that a person cannot clearly identify them. . . . we shall notice that the impulses, feelings, and perceptions may be so clouded and ambiguous (as under some conditions of anxiety) that a person has no distinct notion of what is happening to him or why he feels as he does."[1] The emotions which are most powerfully felt by adolescents of all ages are those that undercut their self-image, pride, expectations, and security.

From their earliest training American children are taught how to control, hide, or disguise the way they feel. These early lessons in social conduct strongly influence later behavior. By the time children become adolescents, they have little difficulty knowing when and how to tailor their emotions so that they are socially acceptable. This knowledge is rewarded when adolescents win approval for their actions by those who are important to them; yet there are disadvantages when too tight control leads to repression and concealing feelings from themselves, either consciously or unconsciously.

1. Arthur T. Jersild, *The Psychology of Adolescence*, 2nd ed. (New York: Macmillan, 1963), pp. 177–178.

Much conflict results when adolescents habitually smother valid emotions and impulses because they may be unsuitable to the occasion. Cultural norms and expectations, especially those relating to sexual roles, are important in dictating "acceptable" behavior. A high-school quarterback must deny himself the natural impulse to cry after having fumbled the ball one yard from a touchdown, though he can swear profusely to himself and his team-mates. Likewise, an adolescent would be ostracized by many groups if she physically attacked the girl who had been spreading malicious rumors about her, yet none of her peers would be disturbed over her catty retaliatory remarks—and more than likely would take great delight in them. In both cases immediate and natural impulses to vent anger have been socially modified into different forms of behavior.

In short fiction about adolescents, love, anger, fear, and anxiety are the emotions that require the most effort to cope with and understand—and it is a truism that these continue to vex and puzzle people throughout their lives.

"The White Circle," "The Lesson," and "The Death of Horatio Alger" (section 4) are typical short stories about the volcanic hatred and anger of younger adolescents, commonly between the ages of twelve and fifteen. In most such stories, the anger is aroused by a situation that threatens self-esteem or physical safety. In almost all, the protagonists vent their wrath in fighting, swearing, fantasizing some diabolical revenge, or victimizing a scapegoat if their tormentors are too formidable to be confronted success-fully. What makes these stories remarkable is the extreme degree of hatred and violence to be found in them, sometimes, as in "The White Circle," even reaching a fevered decision to murder. And, without doubt, it would be difficult to find a story with as much unleashed spleen and frustration as in "The Death of Horatio Alger." "The Lesson" is a case study of how two strong, conflicting wills can precipitate an explosive emotional situation. Mr. Diehl, an adult swimming instructor, tries to coerce sixteen-year-old Polly to do something she does not want to do. Her obstinant refusal in the face of his mounting insistence results in her physically attacking him by "pushing into his chest, rushing him with a strength he had seldom felt before." Given the reasonable nature of Mr. Diehl's request, Polly's reaction to it is excessive—though it is explained in part by her unconscious sexual confusion regarding Mr. Diehl.

"Waiting for Jim" is a fine example of a story that explores the anxiety of adolescents standing on the threshold of adulthood and wanting to be autonomous, yet being reluctant to give up the easy dependence of child-hood. In this story, after much painful hesitation, Nancy takes the difficult step into the world of adults by swimming under "the rope that marked off the outermost limit for children." Stories about adolescent anxiety often show that once adolescents have committed themselves to some action, often unconsciously, their anxieties are greatly reduced or disappear altogether.

Since the late forties, stories about adolescents with serious emotional problems have been in vogue. These are notable for stressing psychological fact and archetypal symbolism. Joyce Carol Oates's "Boy and Girl," like so many of her stories, explores the emotional lives of adolescents who are badly in need of psychiatric care. Like many other writers who probe the adolescent psyche, she often uses the jargon of psychiatry to diagnose what is wrong with the protagonist. It is almost as if readers are allowed a quick glimpse at the psychiatrist's notebook when they are told that Alex has a "neurosis induced by Oedipal aggression further stimulated by a sense of inferiority and frustration." Alex's poor self-image is due, in part, to his acne, but mainly it is due to his inability to fulfill the unrealistic expectations implicitly demanded by his parents and himself.

In contrast to stories of psychic dysfunction are those that explore the world of adolescents who are at peace with themselves and the world. These might well be called "vacation stories," for often it is away from the irritations of classroom and home somewhere in nature that their protagonists feel a childlike joy in being alive, in anticipating the possibilities that life offers. The adolescents in both "Fireflies" and "The Grey Bird" (section 7) experience an idyllic summer, an almost mystical communion with nature, although at the end of "Fireflies" the unnamed girl is brought back to reality by a death and her responsibility to attend a funeral.

John Bell Clayton
The White Circle

AS SOON AS I SAW ANVIL squatting up in the tree like some hateful creature that belonged in trees I knew I had to take a beating and I knew the kind of beating it would be. But still I had to let it be that way because this went beyond any matter of courage or shame.

The tree was *mine*. I want no doubt about that. It was a seedling that grew out of the slaty bank beside the dry creek-mark across the road from the house, and the thirteen small apples it had borne that year were the thirteen most beautiful things on this beautiful earth.

The day I was twelve Father took me up to the barn to look at the colts—Saturn, Jupiter, Devil, and Moonkissed, the white-face. Father took a cigar out of his vest pocket and put one foot on the bottom plank of the fence and leaned both elbows on the top of the fence and his face looked quiet and pleased and proud and I liked the way he looked because it was as if he had a little joke or surprise that would turn out nice for me.

"Tucker," Father said presently, "I am not unaware of the momentousness of this day. Now there are four of the finest colts in Augusta County; if there are four any finer anywhere in Virginia I don't know where you'd find them unless Arthur Hancock over in Albemarle would have them." Father took one elbow off the fence and looked at me. "Now do you suppose," he asked, in that fine, free, good humor, "that if I were to offer you a little token to commemorate this occasion you could make a choice?"

"Yes sir," I said.

"Which one?" Father asked. "Devil? He's wild."

"No sir," I said. "I would like to have the apple tree below the gate."

Father looked at me for at least a minute. You would have to understand his pride in his colts to understand the way he looked. But at twelve how could I express how *I* felt? My setting such store in having the tree as my own had something to do with the coloring of the apples as they hung among the green leaves; it had something also to do with their ripening, not in autumn when the world was full of apples, but in midsummer when you *wanted* them; but it had more to do with a way of life that had come down through the generations. I would have given one of the apples to Janie. I would have made of it a ceremony. While I would not have said the words, because at twelve you have no such words, I would have handed over the apple with something like this in mind: "Janie, I want to give you this apple. It came from my tree. The tree stands on my father's land. Before my father had the land it belonged to his father, and before that it belonged to my great-grandfather. It's the English family land. It's almost sacred. My possession of this tree forges of me a link in this owning ancestry that must go back clear beyond Moses and all the old Bible folks."

Father looked at me for that slow, peculiar minute in our lives. "All right, sir," he said. "The tree is yours in fee simple to bargain, sell, and convey or to keep and nurture and eventually hand down to your heirs or assigns forever unto eternity. You have a touch of poetry in your soul and that fierce, proud love of the land in your heart; when you grow up I hope you don't drink too much."

I didn't know what he meant by that but the tree was mine and now there perched Anvil, callously munching one of my thirteen apples and stowing the rest inside his ragged shirt until it bulged out in ugly lumps. I knew the apples pressed cold against his hateful belly and to me the coldness was a sickening evil.

I picked a rock up out of the dust of the road and tore across the creek bed and said, "All right, Anvil—climb down!"

Anvil's milky eyes batted at me under the strangely fair eyebrows. There was not much expression on his face. "Yaannh!" he said. "You stuck-up little priss, you hit me with that rock. You just do!"

"Anvil," I said again, "climb down. They're my apples."

Anvil quit munching for a minute and grinned at me. "You want an apple? I'll give you one. Yaannh!" He suddenly cocked back his right arm and cracked me on the temple with the half-eaten apple.

I let go with the rock and it hit a limb with a dull chub sound and Anvil said, "You're fixin' to git it—you're real-ly fixin' to git it."

"I'll shake you down," I said. "I'll shake you clear down."

"Clear down?" Anvil chortled. "Where do you think I'm at? Up on top of Walker Mountain? It wouldn't hurt none if I was to fall out of this runty bush on my head."

I grabbed one of his bare feet and pulled backwards, and down Anvil came amidst a flutter of broken twigs and leaves. We both hit the ground. I hopped up and Anvil arose with a faintly vexed expression.

He hooked a leg in back of my knees and shoved a paw against my chin. I went down in the slate. He got down and pinioned my arms with his knees. I tried to kick him in the back of the head but could only flail my feet helplessly in the air.

"You might as well quit kickin'," he said.

He took one of my apples from his shirt and began eating it, almost absent-mindedly.

"You dirty filthy stinkin' sow," I said.

He snorted. "I couldn't be a sow, but you take that back."

"I wish you were fryin' in the middle of hell right this minute."

"Take back the stinkin' part," Anvil said thoughtfully. "I don't stink."

He pressed his knees down harder, pinching and squeezing the flesh of my arms.

I sobbed, "I take back the stinkin' part."

"That's better," Anvil said.

He ran a finger back into his jaw to dislodge a fragment of apple from his teeth. For a moment he examined the fragment and then wiped it on my cheek.

"I'm goin' to tell Father," I said desperately.

" 'Father,' " Anvil said with falsetto mimicry. " 'Father.' Say 'Old Man.' You think your old man is some stuff on a stick, don't you? You think he don't walk on the ground, don't you? You think you and your whole stuck-up family don't walk on the ground. Say 'Old Man.' "

"Go to hell!"

"Shut up your blubberin'. Say 'Old Man.' "

"Old Man. I wish you were dead."

"Yaannh!" Anvil said. "Stop blubberin'. Now call me 'Uncle Anvil.' Say 'Uncle Sweetie Peetie Tweetie Beg-Your-Pardon Uncle Anvil.' Say it!"

"Uncle Sweetie . . . Uncle Peetie, Tweetie Son-of-a-Bitch Anvil."

He caught my hair in his hands and wallowed my head against the ground until I said every bitter word of it. Three times.

Anvil tossed away a spent, maltreated core that had been my apple. He gave my head one final thump upon the ground and said "Yaannh!" again in a satisfied way.

He released me and got up. I lay there with my face muscles twitching in outrage.

Anvil looked down at me. "Stop blubberin'," he commanded.

"I'm not cryin'," I said.

I was lying there with a towering, homicidal detestation, planning to kill Anvil—and the thought of it had a sweetness like summer fruit.

There were times when I had no desire to kill Anvil. I remember the day his father showed up at the school. He was a dirty, half crazy, itinerant knickknack peddler. He had a club and he told the principal he was going to beat the meanness out of Anvil or beat him to death. Anvil scudded under a desk and lay there trembling and whimpering until the principal finally drove the ragged old man away. I had no hatred for Anvil then.

But another day, just for the sheer filthy meanness of it, he crawled through a classroom window after school hours and befouled the floor. And the number of times he pushed over smaller boys, just to see them hit the packed hard earth of the school yard and to watch the fright on their faces as they ran away, was more than I could count.

And still another day he walked up to me as I leaned against the warmth of the school-hack shed in the sunlight, feeling the nice warmth of the weatherbeaten boards.

"They hate me," he said dismally. "They hate me because my old man's crazy."

As I looked at Anvil I felt that in the background I was seeing that demented, bitter father trudging his lonely, vicious way through the world.

"They don't hate you," I lied. "Anyway I don't hate you." That was true. At that moment I didn't hate him. "How about comin' home and stayin' all night with me?"

So after school Anvil went along with me—and threw rocks at me all the way home.

Now I had for him no soft feeling of any kind. I passionately hated him as he stood there before me commanding me to stop blubbering.

"Shut up now," Anvil said. "I never hurt you. Stop blubberin'."

"I'm not cryin'," I said again.

"You're still mad though." He looked at me appraisingly.

"No, I'm not," I lied. "I'm not even mad. I was a little bit mad, but not now."

"Well, whattaya look so funny for?"

"I don't know. Let's go up to the barn and play."

"Play what?" Anvil looked at me truculently. He didn't know whether to be suspicious or flattered. "I'm gettin' too big to play. To play much, anyway," he added undecidedly. "I might play a little bit if it ain't some sissy game."

"We'll play anything," I said eagerly.

"All right," he said. "Race you to the barn. You start."

I started running toward the wire fence and at the third step he stuck his feet between my legs and I fell forward on my face.

"Yaannh!" he croaked. "That'll learn you."

"Learn me what?" I asked as I got up. "Learn me what?" It seemed important to know. Maybe it would make some difference in what I planned to do. It seemed very important to know what it was that Anvil wanted to, and never could, teach me and the world.

"It'll just learn you," he said doggedly. "Go ahead, I won't trip you any more."

So we climbed the wire fence and raced across the burned field the hogs ranged in.

We squeezed through the heavy sliding doors onto the barn floor, and the first thing that caught Anvil's eye was the irregular circle that father had painted there. He wanted to know what it was and I said "nothing" because I wasn't yet quite ready, and Anvil forgot about it for the moment and wanted to play jumping from the barn floor out to the top of the fresh rick of golden straw.

I said, "No. Who wants to do that, anyway?"

"I do," said Anvil. "Jump, you puke. Go ahead and jump!"

I didn't want to jump. The barn had been built on a hill. In front the ground came up level with the barn floor, but in back the floor was even with the top of the straw rick, with four wide, terrible yawning feet between.

I said, "Nawh, there's nothin' to jumpin'."

"Oh, there ain't, hanh!" said Anvil. "Well, try it—"

He gave me a shove and I went out into terrifying space. He leaped after and upon me and hit the pillowy side of the straw rick and tumbled to the ground in a smothering slide.

"That's no fun," I said, getting up and brushing the chaff from my face and hair.

Anvil himself had lost interest in it by now and was idly munching another of my apples.

"I know somethin'," I said. "I know a good game. Come on, I'll show you."

Anvil stung me on the leg with the apple as I raced through the door of the cutting room. When we reached the barn floor his eyes again fell on the peculiar white circle. "That's to play prisoner's base with," I said. "That's the base."

"That's a funny-lookin' base," he said suspiciously. "I never saw any base that looked like that."

I could feel my muscles tensing, but I wasn't particularly excited. I didn't trust myself to look up toward the roof where the big mechanical hayfork hung suspended from the long metal track that ran back over the steaming mows of alfalfa and red clover. The fork had vicious sharp prongs that had never descended to the floor except on one occasion Anvil knew nothing about.

I think Father had been drinking the day he bought the hayfork in Colonial Springs. It was an unwieldy, involved contraption of ropes, triggers and pulleys which took four men to operate. A man came out to install the fork and for several days he climbed up and down ladders, bolting the track in place and arranging the various gadgets. Finally, when he said it was ready, Father had a load of hay pulled into the barn and called the men in from the fields to watch and assist in the demonstration.

I don't remember the details. I just remember that something went very badly wrong. The fork suddenly plunged down with a peculiar ripping noise and embedded itself in the back of one of the work horses. Father said very little. He simply painted the big white circle on the barn floor, had the fork hauled back up to the top, and fastened the trigger around the rung of a stationary ladder eight feet off the floor, where no one could inadvertently pull it.

Then he said quietly, "I don't ever want anyone to touch this trip rope or to have occasion to step inside this circle."

So that was why I didn't now look up toward the fork.

"I don't want to play no sissy prisoner's base," Anvil said. "Let's find a nest of young pigeons."

"All right," I lied. "I know where there's a nest. But one game of prisoner's base first."

"You don't know where there's any pigeon nest," Anvil said. "You wouldn't have the nerve to throw them up against the barn if you did."

"Yes, I would too," I protested. "Now let's play one game of prisoner's base. Get in the circle and shut your eyes and start countin'."

"Oh, all right," Anvil agreed wearily. "Let's get it over with and find the pigeons. Ten, ten, double ten, forty-five—"

"Right in the middle of the circle," I told him. "And count slow. How'm I goin' to hide if you count that way?"

Anvil now counted more slowly. "Five, ten, fifteen—"

I gave Anvil one last vindictive look and sprang up the stationary ladder and swung out on the trip rope of the unpredictable hayfork with all my puny might.

The fork's whizzing descent was accompanied by that peculiar ripping noise. Anvil must have jumped instinctively. The fork missed him by several feet.

For a moment Anvil stood absolutely still. He turned around and saw the fork, still shimmering from its impact with the floor. His face became exactly the pale green of the carbide we burned in our acetylene lighting plant at the house. Then he looked at me, at the expression on my face, and his Adam's apple bobbed queerly up and down, and a little stream of water trickled down his right trouser leg and over his bare foot.

"You tried to kill me," he said thickly.

He did not come toward me. Instead, he sat down. He shook his head sickly. After a few sullen, bewildered moments he reached into his shirt and began hauling out my apples one by one.

"You can have your stinkin' old apples," he said. "You'd do that for a few dried-up little apples. Your old man owns everything in sight. I ain't got nothin'. Go ahead and keep your stinkin' old apples."

He got to his feet and slowly walked out of the door.

Since swinging off the trip rope I had neither moved nor spoken. For a moment more I stood motionless and voiceless and then I ran over and grabbed up the nine apples that were left and called, "Anvil! Anvil!" He continued across the field without even pausing.

I yelled, "Anvil! Wait, I'll give them to you."

Anvil climbed the fence without looking back and set off down the road toward the store. Every few steps he kicked his wet trouser leg.

Three sparrows flew out of the door in a dusty, chattering spiral. Then there was only the image of the hayfork shimmering and terrible in the great and growing and accusing silence and emptiness of the barn.

Vera Randall
Waiting for Jim

"NANCY, HONEY, WOULD YOU DO MY BACK NOW?" Mrs. Hanna said.

Her mother's voice blended with the steady, incoming roar of the ocean, yet reached her clearly enough. In a minute, Nancy thought. In just a minute. And she stood motionless, her slim, still boyish flat back turned toward the bright splash of blanket, her feet set slightly apart, half buried in sand, and her bony, sharp-planed face untilted on its slender stalk of neck.

The small section of beach belonging to the summer colony was empty except for the two of them. The lifeguard stand rose dead white and skeletal from the sand, but Jim, the lifeguard, had been there earlier to plant the giant stakes in the ocean floor and tie the ropes that marked off the outer limits for the children. It was, Nancy told herself, like being at a play long anticipated. The stage was set and soon the curtain would go up. The mothers and children would come, the beach chairs, the pails and shovels, the swimming tubes, the gaily colored beach balls. And Jim would climb on his stand to watch over this safe little world. For a moment, almost as if she were a thing apart, Nancy could see herself, blade lean against the flat stretch of beach, with the sun burning on her square, fleshless, winter-pale shoulders, awaiting her cue. "The fourteenth summer," she whispered. "This is my fourteenth summer."

"Nancy, honey, my back." Nancy turned slowly. "The oil's right there, honey, on the edge of the blanket, next to my books."

The beach and the ocean were gone, and there was only the blanket now, blood red as though the earth itself were wounded, and its liquid life had trickled up through the immaculate white of the sand. "Perhaps I shall be sick." Nancy formed the words soundlessly and bent from the waist, knees straight, to pick up the bottle. "Copper Glow," she read aloud in a thin, precise voice. "Promotes even tanning without burn."

"Promotes even tanning without burn," Mrs. Hanna echoed complacently. "A good tan, and perhaps a couple of pounds off around the middle." She reached out a scarlet-tipped hand to pinch at the flesh around her waist. "Just a pound or two should do it," she said cheerfully, rolling over on her stomach and exposing the naked, blue-white expanse of her back.

Nancy knelt and cupped her hand to hold the amber oil. "I'm a little sandy." She held her hand poised. Beneath the back was the great swell of hips, fleshy like soft, overripe fruit, and then the thighs with their tiny purple lines, broken veins under skin gone slack. "I'm a little sandy," she repeated, waiting.

"You should have wiped your hands, darling." Mrs. Hanna propped herself on an elbow and half turned her head, her eyes dark circles of glass framed in gold. "We have dozens of towels. But go ahead anyhow."

The tiny purple lines of her mother's thighs interconnected like rivers on a map, lost themselves in seas of bluish discoloration. Nancy remained motionless, at once fascinated and repelled.

"Well, dear?"

Abruptly Nancy bent her head and spread the oil, her hand moving swiftly in long strokes from shoulder to waist, neck to waist. The heat of her mother's body reached her through the palm of her hand, and she jerked her hand away, rubbing it against the gray wool of her bathing suit. "It's warm," she said. "It's getting pretty warm."

Mrs. Hanna nodded. "It is warm. You're going to roast in those wool things you insisted on wearing." The green lenses moved downward from Nancy's face. "They're too tight, anyway. You've . . ." Mrs. Hanna paused, and the glasses moved upward. "You've grown a good deal since last summer."

Nancy raised her arms with what had become an automatic gesture, folding them across the round, hard, alien lumps on her chest. "They're not tight," she said sullenly. "And you can't swim in ruffles and frills." She moved away from her mother and settled herself on the blanket, clutching her knees tight against herself.

"There are other things besides swimming, Nancy, honey. There are lots of things."

There were lots of things, things like the hard lumps on her chest and the damp matted hair under her arms. "I like to swim," she said. "That's the only thing I like to do. Swim."

"Now, Nancy, honey. You like to read." Mrs. Hanna pushed herself up onto hands and knees and turned clumsily to sit beside her.

"I like to read all right." The waves were breaking against the shore, creeping upward over the dark dampness of the sand, sliding back. Turning her head slightly, Nancy could see the deep cleft between her mother's breasts, the loose hanging ovals of flesh under rosebud cotton. "You gave me a book to read." The book was at home in the city, hidden in the closet, buried under toys she no longer played with but couldn't bear to part with: a worn, eyeless plush elephant, a red-haired rag doll with a rent in its side roughly sewn, a music box with scenes of Switzerland painted on the sides, the little handle broken off, the music gone. The book was there too, as though somehow contact with this innocence could wipe its pages clean. "You gave me a book," Nancy said with a kind of finality. "I read it."

"I try to talk to you. There are things. Things a girl has to know. Things a mother . . ." Mrs. Hanna stopped, silent, waiting.

"I read it."

"It's a stage you're going through, honey," Mrs. Hanna said wearily. "Another year or two." Her voice drifted off, and she reached for one of the thick books on the blanket, opened it at random, and closed it again. "It's just a stage you're going through."

"All the world's a stage." Nancy looked at her mother contemptuously. "Shakespeare said that. Did you know?"

"No. I didn't know. Your father would know."

Father would know of course. Father knew more than anyone, even more than her English teacher, and sometimes in the evenings they would make a game of guessing quotations. And all the time Mother would sit beneath a pink-shaded lamp, mending, or turning the pages of those huge, thick books she never managed to read. "One day I'm going to be as smart as you two," Mother would say, sighing a little. Then Father would reach out a scrubbed, short-nailed hand with fine golden hairs curling along the back, curling along his hand and up on his wrist and his muscle-knotted forearm, and move his hand, slowly, slowly, over Mother's knee. And Mother would smile, a soft-eyed, contented smile.

Nancy scooped up a handful of sand, and, spreading her fingers, watched it fall in fine, swift streams. She looked over to the lifeguard stand. "I wish Jim would come so I could swim."

"He'll be along. It's not eleven yet." Mrs. Hanna pulled off her sunglasses and looked at Nancy with mild, pale brown eyes. "I do believe you have a crush, honey."

"All I said was I wanted to swim." Her mother was smiling, the terrible, mocking smile of adulthood, and she could feel the heat rising to her cheeks, spreading upward over her forehead, and down to the soft hollow at the base of her throat. "I haven't even seen Jim since last summer. I don't even remember what he looks like, hardly."

"All right," Mrs. Hanna said. "All right, then."

Sand spattered as John and Timmy Royce raced past, lifting their feet high, their young boy bodies smooth and hard above brief navy shorts. "Hi," they shouted. "Hi, Mrs. Hanna. Hi, Nancy."

"Hi," Nancy said. Turning her head, she could see Mrs. Royce, a circus creature in the distance, jutting pails and shovels, sinking heavily into the sand as she walked.

"Hello, Margaret." Mrs. Royce stopped beside the blanket, thick legs set apart, eyes black slits in a flat biscuit of a face. "It's a fine day."

"Fine," Mrs. Hanna said.

"Did you have a good winter?"

"Good enough. Colds and such. The usual."

"Nancy's grown so. She doesn't look like the same child." Mrs. Royce tittered, and the black slits of eyes widened slightly. Nancy raised her arms to cover her chest. "I guess she's not the same child, is she?"

"She has grown, hasn't she?" Mrs. Hanna said.

"Mummy," one of the boys shrieked. They were kneeling in the damp sand near the water, digging, their hands scoop-shaped.

"My master's call." The biscuit face split into a nicotine-stained smile, and Mrs. Royce walked on, pails clanking, narrow shoulders widening to broad hips and heavy, shapeless legs, feet plodding.

"Bridge tonight at my place," Mrs. Hanna called after her.

Mrs. Royce turned her head. "Good," she said. "That'll be fine."

The beach was filling now, splattered here and there with bits of red and yellow and orange, children's swimsuits vivid against the sand. "I'm going to dig. I'm going to dig all the way to China. Anyone wanna help me?" a little girl shouted.

That was I, Nancy thought, and the sadness rose in her, wavelike. Once that was I. Mrs. Royce's buttocks were quivering, jellylike, under violet silk as she walked. "I won't be," Nancy said softly to herself. "I just won't."

"What won't you be, honey?" Mrs. Hanna reached for a multicolored towel to mop at the thin stream of sweat that trickled between her breasts. "What is it you won't be?"

"Like her." Nancy spat out the words, her head jerking forward on its reed neck, in line with Mrs. Royce's retreating back.

"She's a perfectly nice woman," Mrs. Hanna said. "She's a lovely woman."

Mrs. Royce was squatting near her sons, cautiously lowering her huge, quivering rear to the sand. Beyond her, way out where the ocean met the sky, a boat, tiny, a child's toy, hung against the vastness. "Lovely," Nancy said flatly. Turning her head she could see the tiny balls of moisture clinging to the oiled surface above her mother's upper lip.

"All the way to China," the little girl shouted again. "All the way. Anyone wanna help me?" She had come quite close to the blanket, and stood there, a brightly painted pail in one hand, a tiny tin shovel in the other, her elf face eager, and her compact little body golden in the sun.

Nancy turned around and flung herself face down on the blanket. "I won't be," she whispered into the fuzz. "I won't be," and nausea, like a cold damp hand, twisted in her stomach.

"Hello, baby," Mrs. Hanna said. "You go dig a nice hole. A nice deep hole."

"To China," the child said, half questioning.

Mrs. Hanna laughed. "Of course to China. Nancy, honey, you're going to burn. You'd better let me put some oil on you."

"No." Nancy's voice was muffled by the blanket.

"You'll blister, honey. It's the first day out. You know you have to be careful the first few days, or you'll blister."

"I don't care." She would blister, then. All over her back there would be pale raised bumps, with colorless liquid beneath. And she would burn. She would burn right through her skin and her flesh, right through all those unspeakable things her mother told her she had inside her, that the little book said she had inside her. And finally there would be nothing left, nothing but bones to be washed clean by the rising tide, bleached white by the summer sun. "I don't care," she cried into the sand-flecked wool of the blanket. "I don't care."

"Here's Mrs. Henderson to join us," her mother said brightly.

"I don't care."

"It's Mrs. Henderson, honey."

Hearing the annoyance in her mother's voice she sat up, out of old habit, and then rose to help Mrs. Henderson unfold her beach chair and settle herself in it. Mrs. Henderson kissed her with white, chapped lips. "You're a good girl," she said. "A sweet child. She's a sweet child, Margaret."

"Yes." Mrs. Hanna said.

The mole on the tip of Mrs. Henderson's nose was like a giant fly. If I just flick it with my little finger, Nancy thought, just ever so gently. And she giggled.

"Is something funny?" Mrs. Henderson asked, taking her knitting from the straw basket at her side.

"No," Nancy said. Mrs. Henderson was older than her mother, maybe forty-five or even fifty. Mrs. Henderson had raised blue veins on the sides of her legs, and bony, yellow knees, and her face was thin except for the cheeks that looked like they had tiny, plump cushions inserted under the skin. Mrs. Henderson was flatter in front than her mother or Mrs. Royce, but not really flat. More like the brown paper bags that Nancy used to blow up when she was little, and then punch, so that they would make a loud banging sound, and then collapse, wrinkled, empty. "No," she said. "Nothing's funny. Nothing at all."

"Nancy's bored," Mrs. Hanna said. "I'm afraid she's going to be very bored here."

Mrs. Henderson nodded over her clicking needles. "This is a good place for children," she said. "Children and old ladies like me. She needs to be with young people her own age."

"I'm not bored." Nancy sat again, arms wrapped around her knees, face turned to the ocean. "I'm not a bit bored."

Mrs. Hanna plucked idly at a corner of the blanket. "I know, Emily. Bill and I felt that way. There was a tour to the coast some of the girls in her class were going on. And there are camps. But she wanted this. She wanted to come back here."

"We've always come here," Nancy said. She tried to recapture her morning vision, the vision that had comforted her through the cold confused winter. The mothers, the children. And above it all Jim, sitting in his high chair, watching, making the world small and safe. Staring out she could see that the toy boat had moved a bit. Its smoke stacks were matched sticks in the distance, scarcely visible. Near her the little girl sat, her smooth blond head bent, her lower lip beaded with tiny pearls of teeth, her shovel moving busily in and out of the hole she was digging between her widespread legs.

When Jim comes, Nancy thought. Then it will be all right, when Jim comes.

"I hardly know what to do with her," Mrs. Hanna said. "Sometimes I hardly know what I'm supposed to do with her. She's so difficult. So— different."

"They're all difficult." Mrs. Henderson reached the end of her line, swung the long brown mass of knitting about, and settled it again in her lap. "And they're all different. I've raised a couple of them."

"Boys," Mrs. Hanna said. "Boys are easier."

"I suppose so. I suppose boys are easier."

"She's growing so fast," Mrs. Hanna said. "She's sprouting like a weed."

"Give her another year or two. She'll be just like the rest of them. It's a stage." Mrs. Henderson paused, staring thoughtfully out over the sand, then bobbed her head down once and up again. "That's what it is, Margaret. The child's going through a stage."

Nancy rested her chin on her raised knees. When Jim comes, she thought. "What time is it? It must be eleven by now."

"Eleven?" Mrs. Henderson peered at her wristwatch. "It's almost eleven. What's happening at eleven?"

"She's waiting for Jim," Mrs. Hanna said. "We've been here since half past nine, waiting for Jim."

"Jim?"

"You know. The lifeguard." Her mother's voice rose teasingly, making an alliance with Mrs. Henderson, excluding her. "I think my daughter has a crush."

"Well now, Nancy. What did I tell you, Margaret?" Mrs. Henderson's voice was mock serious. Nancy sat rigidly, tense, silent. "Well, tell us all about it, Nancy." Mrs. Henderson's fingers moved swiftly, spiders in the yarn.

"She's been waiting for him since half past nine," Mrs. Hanna laughed. "Surely that must mean something."

"A beachcomber is an interesting first choice for a young girl," Mrs. Henderson said. "Mine, as far as I can recall, was a riding instructor, but that is, after all, rather more conventional. A beachcomber, now." Her knitting rested in her lap, her hands were momentarily idle, and she waited, watching the girl.

Nancy turned to them, thin-faced, thin-lipped, feeling herself shrunken to smallness. "He's not a beachcomber." She spoke quietly, spacing her words. "He's not."

"He's a knight," Mrs. Hanna said. "They're all knights, Emily, complete with shining armor. The riding instructors, the music instructors, the life-guards on the beach."

"You don't know everything," Nancy said to her mother. "You don't know anything."

"Nancy," Mrs. Hanna turned the name into a reproach.

But Mrs. Henderson stuck out a bony hand to touch Nancy on the cheek. "Perhaps your mother has forgotten," she said. "Perhaps she never knew a riding instructor, or a music teacher, or a lifeguard. Or perhaps she's just forgotten."

Nancy pulled her head back and rubbed at her cheek, feeling the heat of her face, knowing that she was reddening. It's not like that, she wanted to scream. It's not like you think. It's not any of it like you think. "It's getting awfully hot," she said.

"It is hot." Mrs. Hanna's voice was again warm with concern. "I wish you'd let me put some oil on you, honey. I'm afraid you're going to burn."

Timmy Royce had walked back from the water's edge. He stood over Nancy, snub-nosed, frowning. "Our tunnel keeps busting. Would you help us with our tunnel? Mummy said maybe you would help us with our tunnel."

"I'm too big to make tunnels, Timmy," Nancy said. "I don't make tunnels any more."

"Mummy said you make the best tunnels. Our tunnel keeps busting."

"Maybe later she'll help you," Mrs. Hanna said. "Maybe after a bit, Timmy."

"Okay, Nancy? Later will you? Because ours keeps busting."

"Maybe. Maybe later." Too big to make tunnels any more. She was too big.

Mrs. Hanna looked across the sand. "There's your fellow," she said. "There he is now, finally."

Jim was standing near the lifeguard stand, dwarfed by its skeletal height, with his navy canvas bag in one hand, the bag that would be full of sandwiches and soda to last him through the day. He lowered the bag to the sand and raised his arms to pull off his sweat shirt. "Yes," Nancy said. "There he is."

"Well," Mrs. Henderson said. "After all this waiting about, are you just going to sit there?" The teasing tone had returned. "The poor man may have been counting the minutes until he would see you again. He may have pined all summer. He may—"

"You see what I mean, Emily," Mrs. Hanna said. "We've been here since nine-thirty this morning. She can be difficult sometimes."

"I just wanted to swim." Nancy remained where she was, arms around her knees, waiting. "All I ever said was I wanted to swim." Jim's sweat shirt was off now, and he was looking out over the water, one hand lifted to shade his eyes, his skin dark against the white of his swimming trunks.

"You see what I mean, Emily," Mrs. Hanna said. Mrs. Henderson bent over her knitting, nodding slightly. "That's the way she is, Emily. We've been here for hours waiting. And now he's come, and she sits. Just sits." Mrs. Hanna sighed lengthily. "I find her very difficult to understand."

Nancy's hands had grown cold, and she felt herself trembling slightly, despite the heat of the morning. It wasn't like they thought, not any of it. If only he would climb onto his high white seat and sit watching over the safe little summertime world of the children. Didn't they understand that this was what he was, not a man at all really, but just this? Didn't her mother understand? Alone, lost, she looked to her mother, plumpness encased in rosebud cotton, and thought briefly, fleetingly, who is she? And pushed the thought from her in panic. This was her mother. "Mother," she said softly, almost questioningly.

Mrs. Hanna jerked erect from the waist, removed her sunglasses, frowned. "What is it, Nancy, honey? Is something wrong?" And, after a pause, her voice worried, "Did you get too much sun?"

"No," Nancy said. Did you get too much sun? Did you brush your teeth? You're a bit hoarse, honey. Does your throat hurt? "No. It's nothing."

"Are you sure?"

"Yes. Yes, I'm sure."

"Then go along, honey. All this fuss about Jim and swimming." Mrs. Hanna slouched backward on the blanket. "It will be time to go back for lunch before you know it."

Nancy rose reluctantly. The ocean air seemed poisoned with words, and the small, weather-beaten summer cottage up the road from the beach was suddenly a haven to her. She was starved, for hamburgers, hot dogs, milk, coke, a sandwich—anything. Her dog Sambo would be waiting for her, eager after his long morning's confinement, leaping at the screen door when he heard her footsteps, his long black ears flopping forward, his plume tail high. She could go to her tiny cell of a room with its high old painted chest of drawers, its iron cot, its little nighttable with her books. *David Copper-field*, and *Oliver Twist*, and *Great Expectations*. She was going to read straight through Dickens this summer, just the way Father had when he was a boy. What if she said she wanted to leave? She did want to. She wanted to turn and run, to lock herself away.

"We're leaving in an hour, honey," Mrs. Hanna said.

"An hour?"

"That's right, honey. Go along now."

Nancy nodded, mute. She stooped and picked up her terry cloth robe, slipped her arms through the sleeves, belted it loosely.

Mrs. Henderson smiled slyly over her clicking needles. "If I had a fine young body like yours, I wouldn't hide myself. I'd strut."

Nancy turned away, walking slowly toward the lifeguard stand. I hate them, she thought. God, how I hate them. And then, realizing she had included her mother in her hatred, she whispered softly, experimentally, "I hate my mother." But children didn't hate their mothers. It was wrong, like stealing and telling lies. "I hate my mother," she whispered again.

"Run along, honey."

Nancy looked back, startled, and saw that she had not moved more than half a dozen steps from the blanket. "Yes, Mother," she said.

"Have a good swim."

"Yes, Mother."

"And be careful."

"Yes, Mother. I'll be careful."

The sand was hot, fire against the bottoms of her feet, glinting gold, with here and there the sharp jut of a broken fragment of shell. She picked her way around the clusters of women, and paused to let a tiny creature in red and black plaid dart in front of her, and walked on as voices greeted her, heads lifted or twisted to look at her. But why were they looking at her like that? Did her front jiggle like Mrs. Royce and Mrs. Henderson and her mother? Surely not, she reassured herself. The robe was so loose. But she flushed, painfully self-conscious, feeling herself stripped naked by prying eyes.

The sun was almost directly overhead, pouring molten gold on the women, the heavy thighs, the loose-fleshed upper arms, the flaccid breasts, the layers of fat, broken veins, bodies stretched shapeless from child-bearing. Almost Nancy thought she could smell them, a smell heavy and sweetish with oil and stale lipstick, perspiring armpits, caked face powder, decay— a smell penetrating and overpowering the clean salt smell of the ocean. Voices reached after her, poked and pawed at her. "Nancy, you've grown so. How you've grown, dear. Peggy, lamb, come let Mummy wipe your nose. It's dripping. See, here's Nancy. Hasn't she grown? You have grown incredibly, Nancy. Almost a little woman, really."

Almost a little woman. Almost a woman. Nancy ran, arms bent, hands fisted, the loose ends of her belt flapping back between her thighs, ran feeling her small breasts quivering and the nausea twisting snakelike in her stomach. The sand was cool and damp against her feet now, and the water lapped icily at her toes. She pulled off her robe and tossed it backward, away from the ocean edge. Glancing sideward she could see Jim, standing at the foot of his high seat, idle, quiet, as if waiting. She shut her eyes. Let him climb up and sit as he always has, she willed. Let him climb up and sit and watch. Let it be as it was.

But he was walking toward her, and she knew without looking that he was coming. "Hi, Nancy," he said. "How's the girl?"

The feet next to her own were slender, with long, almost fingerlike toes and purplish-blue nails. She raised her eyes slowly, seeing the hairy legs, the heavily muscled thighs, the trunks white against sunbrowned skin, the skin taut over the ribs, the neck, surprisingly short and thick. "Hi, Jim." His eyes were greenish and bloodshot, and his brown hair was clipped short. "I'm okay, I guess." He was a stranger to her, lost between summer and summer. "I guess I'm okay."

"Gonna swim the ocean this year?"

He was smiling at her. He had deep wrinkles like bloodless cuts in his leathery cheeks, but the eyes were familiar now, laughing somehow along with the full-lipped mouth. It was their private joke, continued from one summer to the next for as far back as she could remember. "Gonna swim the ocean this year?" And suddenly it was all right. Here was the safe little world of her childhood, the beach, the ocean, the children digging their holes and tunnels, the pails, the shovels, the mothers stretched on their blankets. She laughed, a high-pitched childish giggle that seemed, as she heard it, to belong to another, earlier self. "Yep," she said. "This is the year." She waited, a small girl again, for the swift, silly exchange of banter before he climbed on his stand to watch.

"Surprised you're back, Nancy," he said. "Mostly they stop coming when they get your size."

She was sullen, disappointed. "I just wanted to come back." She looked down at the sand, at the feet in a row, his long and brown, hers pale, narrow, pink-toed.

"I'm glad you did. It's nice to have someone to talk to besides mamas and babies. And someone to look at. Someone cute."

Someone cute? Bewildered, she groped for something to say. "Are you a beachcomber, Jim? Mrs. Henderson says you're a beachcomber."

"A beachcomber?" He touched her arm lightly.

"A person who hangs around a beach and doesn't do anything much. They have them in South Sea stories." She stared at the hand resting on her arm. It was a long brown hand, hot against her skin, covered with curling, golden hairs. Like Father's, she thought. Golden hairs like Father's. But what was Father's hand—Jim's hand doing on her arm?

"Sure," he said. "Your folks pay me a couple of hundred to watch their kids summers. And I maybe pick up an odd job or two during the winter. I guess that's what I am all right. A beachcomber." He laughed, a thick throaty sound. "I never had a name for what I was before. You're a cute girl, Nancy."

She was sharply aware of the slight pressure of his hand on her arm, of the naked upper half of his body so close to her own. "Don't you work any?" Her breath was coming in hard little gasps. "I mean don't you have a regular kind of job?"

"Don't need to," he said. "Got enough to eat on. Got a little shack up there, back away. Its a good enough little place. I'll show it to you one day if you like."

"No," she said nervously. "I mean Mother wouldn't let me."

"Mother wouldn't let me," he mimicked, and his teeth glistened whitely against the brown of his skin. "What a baby you are, Nancy."

He was squeezing her arm. Glancing sideways, she watched a fat pink worm of a tongue crawl from between his lips. She stood motionless an instant. Then, shaking her head frantically, she jerked away from his hand and darted forward. She lifted her feet high, running, with the water splashing against her legs, pushed forward against an oncoming breaker, half fell, and stood again, holding the thick wet rope with one hand.

Looking back, she could see the beach, the mothers on their blankets, the children playing in the sand. Off to the left was her own mother, with the tiny blond girl, very close, still digging. She watched Jim climb to the top of his stand and sit, brown and still and watchful. It was for this that she had waited, all through the winter. She turned away, and the ocean stretched vast and terrifying before her. "Mother," she said. And her lips sought and found an earlier name. "Mama, mama." She hesitated briefly, her eyes burning with unshed tears. Taking a deep breath, she ducked under the rope that marked off the outermost limit for children.

James Purdy
The Lesson

"THIS IS NOT LADY'S DAY AT THE POOL," Mr. Diehl said. "I can't admit her."

"But she pleaded so."

Mr. Diehl was about to give his lesson to a young man and wanted no women in the pool. He knew that if a woman entered the pool during the lesson she would distract the young man, who was already nervous about learning to swim. The young man was quite upset already, as he was going to have to go to a country house where there was lots of swimming and boating, and if he didn't know how, his hosts would be very put out with him. They might never invite him again. At any rate that was his story, and besides, he was the commander's son.

"But my grandmother always wants as many people to come into the pool as possible," the girl said. Her grandmother owned the pool.

"I have worked for your grandmother for a long time," Mr. Diehl, the swimming instructor said, "and I'm sure that she would not want a woman in the pool at this hour who does not belong to the club and so far as I know doesn't even know how to swim."

"Well, I asked her that," the girl said.

"And what did she say?" the swimming instructor wanted to know.

"She said she could swim."

"Just the same she can wait until the lesson is over. It takes only half an hour."

"I told her that, but she wanted to go in the pool right away. She has gone downstairs to change."

"For Christ's sake," Mr. Diehl said.

His pupil, the commander's son, was already splashing around in the shallow water, waiting for the lesson.

"Go and tell her in a half hour."

The girl looked as though she was not going to tell the woman.

72

"If your grandmother were here she would back me up on this," Mr. Diehl said.

"But she's not here and my instructions were to do as best I thought."

"As best you thought," Mr. Diehl considered this, looking at the girl. She was sixteen, but he knew she had a slow mind and he wondered what had ever made Mrs. Schuck leave the pool in the hands of such an immature person.

"Look," Mr. Diehl said. "Just go and tell the woman that I can't have her in the pool while I am giving this special lesson."

"Well, I can't forbid her the pool very well, now, can I. If she wants to come in! This club isn't that exclusive and she knows one of the members."

"I don't care if she knows the man who invented swimming, she can't come in. Is that clear?"

"Mr. Diehl, you forget that I am the granddaughter of the owner of the pool."

"I am responsible for what goes on in the water, am I not?"

"Yes, I'll go along with you there."

"All right then," Mr. Diehl said, as though having made his point. "Go tell her I can't have her in the water until after the lesson. Can't you do that?"

"No," the girl said. "I can't tell that to a perfectly good customer."

"You have this pool mixed up with a public dance hall or something. This is not exactly a money-making organization, as your grandmother must have told you. It is a club. Not open to everybody. And this unknown woman should not have been allowed in here anyhow. Not at all."

"I know better," the girl said. "Many nice people come here just for an occasional swim."

"Not unless they are known," Mr. Diehl said.

"But she knows a member," the girl pointed out.

"Who is the member?" Mr. Diehl wanted to know.

"Oh, I can't remember," the girl told him.

"But I know every member by name." Mr. Diehl was insistent. "I've been swimming instructor here now for nine years."

"I know, I know," the girl said. "But this woman has every right to come in here."

"She's not coming in the water."

"Well, I don't know what to tell her. She's already putting on her suit."

"Then she can take it right off again," Mr. Diehl said.

"But not here, though," the girl tried a joke. Mr. Diehl did not laugh.

"What I'm trying to get you to see, Polly," Mr. Diehl said, and it was the first time he had ever called her by name, "is that this is a pretty high-class place. Do you know by chance who that boy is who is waiting for the lesson?"

Mr. Diehl waited for the girl to answer.

"I don't know who he is," she replied.

"That is Commander Jackson's son."

"And he doesn't know how to swim?"

"What has that got to do with it?" the swimming instructor said.

"Well, I'm surprised is all."

"Look, time is slipping away. I don't want to have any more argument with you, Polly. But I'm sure your grandmother would back me up on this all the way if she were here. Is there any way we can reach her by telephone?"

"I have no idea where she went."

"Well, this strange woman cannot come into the pool now."

"I am not going down to the locker room and tell her to put her clothes back on, so there," Polly said.

She was very angry, but she had also gotten a little scared.

"Then I'm going to have to tell your grandmother how nasty you've been."

"How nasty *I've* been?"

Mr. Diehl went up to the girl and put his hands on her shoulder as he often did to his students. "Look here now," he said. He did not realize how he was affecting the girl and how the water fell from him on her blouse. She looked at his biceps as they moved almost over her mouth and the way his chest rose and fell. She had always lowered her eyes when she met him in the hall, avoiding the sight of his wet, dripping quality, the many keys held in his hand, his whistle for the days when they practiced champion swimming. He had seemed to her like something that should always remain splashing about and breathing heavily in water.

"Polly, will you please cooperate with me," Mr. Diehl said.

"I don't think I can," she said.

He put down his arms in a gesture of despair. "Will you please, please just this once go down to the ladies' dressing room and tell that woman that you've made a mistake and that she can't come into the pool just now?"

Polly looked out now into the water where the commander's son was floating around by holding on to a rubber tire.

"I just can't tell her," Polly said, turning red.

"You can't tell her," Mr. Diehl observed. Then: "Look, do you know who the commander is?"

"Well, doesn't everybody?" Polly answered.

"Do you know or don't you?" Mr. Diehl wanted to know. Some more water fell from him as he gesticulated, wetting her blouse and her arms a little, and she was sure that water continued to fall from him no matter how long he had been out of the pool. She could hear him breathing and she could not help noticing his chest rise and fall as though he were doing a special swimming feat just for her in this room.

"Polly!" he said.

"I can't! I can't!" she cried.

He could see now that there was something else here, perhaps fear of something, he could not tell, he did not want to know.

"You're not going to run into any difficulty in just telling her, are you, that you didn't know the rules and that she will have to wait until the lesson is over."

"I can't and I won't," Polly said, and she refused to look at him.

The commander's son was watching them from the middle of the shallow part of the pool, but he did not act as though he was impatient for the lesson to begin, and Polly remembered what a severe instructor Mr. Diehl was said to be. Sometimes while she had sat outside in the reception room she had heard Mr. Diehl shout all the way from the pool.

"Look, do we have to go all over this again?" Mr. Diehl said. "You know the commander."

"I know the commander, of course," she said.

"Do you know he is the most influential member of the club here?"

Polly did not say anything.

"He built this pool, Polly. Not your grandmother. Did you know that?"

She felt that she might weep now, so she did not say anything.

"Are you hearing me?" Mr. Diehl wanted to know.

"*Hearing* you!" she cried, distracted.

"All right now," he said, and he put his hand on her again and she thought some more drops of water fell from him.

"I can't see how anybody would know," she said. "How would the commander know if a young woman went into his pool. And what would his son out there care."

"His son doesn't like people in the pool when he is taking a lesson," Mr. Diehl explained. "He wants it strictly private, and the commander wants it that way too."

"And the commander pays you to want it that way also."

"Polly, I'm trying to be patient."

"I'm not going to tell her she can't come in," Polly said.

She stood nearer now to the edge of the pool away from his moving arms and chest and the dripping water that she felt still came off them.

"Step away from the edge, please, Polly," he said, and he took hold of her arm, drawing her firmly over to him, in his old manner with special pupils when he was about to impart to them some special secret of swimming.

"Don't always touch me," she said, but so faintly that it was hardly a reproach.

"Polly, listen to me," Mr. Diehl was saying to her. "I've known you since you were a little girl. Right?"

"Known me?" Polly said, and she felt the words only come vaguely toward her now.

"Been a friend of your family, haven't I, for a good long time. Your grandmother knew me when I was only a boy. She paid for some of my tuition in college."

"College." Polly nodded to the last word she had heard, so that he would think she was listening.

"You'll feel all right about this, Polly, and you will, I know, help me now that I've explained it to you."

"No, I can't," she said, awake again.

"You can't what?" Mr. Diehl said.

"I can't is all," she said but she spoke, as she herself recognized, like a girl talking in her sleep.

The hothouse heat of the swimming pool and the close presence of Mr. Diehl, a man she had always instinctively avoided, had made her forget in a sense why they were standing here before the water. Somewhere in a dressing room, she remembered, there was a woman who in a little while was going to do something wrong that would displease Mr. Diehl, and suddenly she felt glad this was so.

"Mr. Diehl, I am going," she said, but she made no motion to leave, and he knew from her words that she was not going. They were going on talking, he knew. It was like his students, some of them said they could never be champions, but they always were. He made them so. Some of the timid ones said they could never swim, the water was terror to them, but they always did swim. Mr. Diehl had never known failure with anything. He never said this but he showed it.

"Now you listen to me," Mr. Diehl said. "All you have to do is go and tell her. She can sit outside with you and watch television."

"The set isn't working," Polly said, and she walked over close to the edge of the pool.

"Please come over here now," Mr. Diehl said, and he took hold of her and brought her over to where he had been standing. "Polly, I would never have believed this of you."

"Believed what?" she said, and her mind could not remember now again why exactly they were together here. She kept looking around as though perhaps she had duties she had forgotten somewhere. Then as she felt more and more unlike herself, she put her hand on Mr. Diehl's arm.

"Believed," he was saying, and she saw his white teeth near her as though the explanation of everything were in the teeth themselves—"believed you would act so incorrigible. So bad, Polly. Yes, that's the word. Bad."

"Incorrigible," she repeated, and she wondered what exactly that had always meant. It was a word that had passed before her eyes a few times but nobody had ever pronounced it to her.

"I would never want your grandmother to even know we had to have this long argument. I will never tell her."

"I will never tell her," Polly said, expressionless, drowsily echoing his words.

"Thank you, Polly, and of course I didn't mean to tell you you didn't have to. But listen to me."

She put her hand now very heavily on his arm and leaned there.

"Are you all right, Polly," he said, and she realized suddenly that it was the first time he had ever really been aware of her being anything at all, and now when it was too late, when she felt too bad to even tell him, he had begun to grow aware.

"Polly," he said.

"Yes, Mr. Diehl," she answered and suddenly he looked down at her hand on her arm, it was pressing there, and he had become, of course, conscious of it.

He did not know what to do, she realized, and ill as she felt, the pleasure of having made him uncomfortable soothed her. She knew she was going to be very ill, but she had had at least, then, this triumph, the champion was also uncomfortable.

"You'll go and tell her then," Mr. Diehl said, but she knew now that he was not thinking about the woman anymore. The woman, the lesson, the pool had all lost their meaning and importance now.

"Polly," he said.

"I will tell her," she managed to say, still holding him tight.

"Polly, what is it?" he exclaimed.

He took her arm off him roughly, and his eyes moved about the room as though he were looking for somebody to help. His eyes fell cursorily upon the commander's son, and then back to her, but it was already too late, she had begun to topple toward him, her hands closed over his arms, and her head went pushing into his chest, rushing him with a strength he had seldom felt before.

When they fell into the water it was very difficult for him to get hold of her at all. She had swallowed so much water, and she had struck at him so hard, and had said words all the time nobody could have understood or believed but him. It was her speaking and struggling, as he said later, which had caused her to swallow so much water.

He had had to give her partial artificial respiration, a thing he had not done really in all his life, although he had taken all the courses in it as befitted a champion swimmer.

"Get out of the pool for God's sake and call somebody," Mr. Diehl yelled to the commander's son, and the boy left off hanging to the rubber tire, and slowly began to climb out of the shallow water.

"Get some speed on there, for Christ's sake," he said.

"Yes, sir," the commander's son replied.

"I can't be responsible for this whole goddamn thing," he shouted after the retreating boy.

"Now see here, Polly, for Christ's sake," Mr. Diehl began, looking down at her.

She opened her eyes and looked at him.

"You certainly pulled one over me!" he cried looking at her, rage and fear on his mouth.

She lay there watching his chest move, feeling the drops of water falling over her from his body, and smelling behind the strong chemical odor of the pool the strong smell that must be Mr. Diehl himself, the champion.

"I'll go tell her now," Polly said.

Mr. Diehl stared at her.

"She must never come here at all," Polly said. 'I think I see that now."

Mr. Diehl stretched out his hand to her to lift her up.

"Go away, please," she said. "Don't lean over me, please, and let the water fall from you on me. Please, please go back into the pool. I don't want you close now. Go back into the pool."

Joyce Carol Oates
Boy and Girl

THE BOY WAS LOOSE AND GANGLING and looked about fifteen instead of eighteen; it was embarrassing that his father was so handsome. The girl was slight and had the frail powdery look of a moth, a colorless fluttering insect of some sort. It was embarrassing that her mother was so solid and horsey; in fact the girl, Doris, called her mother "the horse" behind her back with a kind of smirking, satisfied affection. The boy, Alexander Jr., spoke of his father as "my father" and to his father's face he said, "Father . . ."

They kept meeting all their lives, in and around Lakeshore Point. He went to a boys' school and she to a girls' school and their friends overlapped, though neither of them really had "friends"; they had new and old acquaintances. It was an achievement that they had both lived for so long in Lakeshore Point, because it was a suburb people moved in and out of constantly; it was a surprise, in April, how all the "For Sale" signs went up before houses, in time for a quick deft selling in a day or two, a few weeks of arrangements, and the move to the next city and the next suburb as soon as school ended. So, in the midst of all this coming and going, the loading and unloading of great Allied Vans that proudly conquered the continent, sooner or later Doris and Alex would have fixed upon each other, at least for a while. As Doris grew older—she was now sixteen—it occurred to her that the atmosphere of a typical school dance was the atmosphere of life itself. Partners went out to dance, the music changed, partners came back, switched around, danced again, and the gymnasium would be filled beneath its fluttering strips of crepe paper with the shuffling of legs and feet and the movements of arms: so many bodies. It was like this in Lakeshore Point itself, with strangers always moving in and strangers moving out.

They were different types: Doris was popular and had a nervous irritating laugh, the laugh of girls in crowds who are sure of being overheard. Alex was faintly stereotyped, liking chess and astronomy and complicated crossword puzzles his mother could not understand. Prepared for Harvard, he had been deeply wounded in his senior year at Lakepoint Boys' Academy when his application at Harvard had been rejected. He had the usual extraordinary grades, and his hobbies—chess and astronomy and, at an adviser's suggestion, ice hockey—had seemed good enough. It was a mystery, his rejection. So he would be going to the University of Michigan in the fall, and he walked about with his stoop more pronounced than usual, muttering in reply to greetings, casting away imagined slurs with a nervous wave of his hand. When the other boys bothered to think about him, they thought he was rather queer. Everyone had an opinion of Doris Moss, even at distant high schools, but Alex wasn't up on any recent news; he and Doris had gone to the same orthodontist several years before and he remembered her as a slight, shy child, perpetually twelve.

Alex had decided firmly to become a doctor and to go into medical research, and somehow his rejection from Harvard was not believable. He carried this rejection about with him everywhere, anxious to drag it out and admit it, humble, questioning, nervous in the hope that it had all been a mistake and he was accepted after all. He was the kind of boy adults believed they could talk to, until they talked to him. His parents' friends approached him with stiff, helpful smiles.

He had decided to go into medical research because his father, a doctor, was in a kind of medical research himself. One evening when his parents were having a dinner party Alex had heard something that impressed him strangely and changed his life. He had come in from a movie—he always went alone—and used the downstairs guest bathroom, in the back of the house. There was something about this bathroom he liked. It was done in black and gold, with decanters of scented soap and lovely scented tissue and toilet paper, also gold, and small exquisite guest towels that were white linen with gold embroidering. On the dressing table was a delicate mirror, balanced for the fine-lashed eyes of his parents' lady guests; underfoot was a black, black rug. Alex liked to use this bathroom because he felt very special in it. He felt like one of his parents' guests. Before parties he cautiously checked this bathroom, by himself, since the maid was always harassed and could not be trusted to see whether the soap was clean or not. The special soap in this bathroom was ball-shaped, gold and white, and it gave off a lovely sweet scent. But sometimes the soap balls grew dusty because they were never used.

This feeling for the bathroom was important, because it might have had to do with Alex's decision. He was in there when he heard his father and another man come into the kitchen, and his father's grave words were somehow mixed in with the scent of the toilet paper and the soap. His father was saying, "It's a hell of a complex operation. You don't have a neat laboratory situation, of course. You must consider the environmental factors—the humidity, the wind, the area, the particle size, the amount of saturation, the method of ejaculation. You can imagine the variability there." The other man, unknown to Alex, said something about computers. "Yes, computers are certainly helpful," Alex's father said in his kind, serious voice, "but beyond a certain point only the existential fact is real. Nothing else is real. An event happens only once and that's the difficult thing about life— it isn't a laboratory experiment."

Alex was strangely agitated. He admired his father and feared him a little and it seemed that each of his father's words was valuable. His father worked for the government now on classified projects and it was sometimes necessary for him to be gone for weeks at a time. Perhaps these long trips or the isolation of the laboratory had made Alex's father rather remote about most things, as if holding them out at arm's length; so it was intimate, hearing his father talk like this. Above the clinking of ice cubes his father said, "The biological cloud agent is a totally new frontier. It's fascinating work. You have to think of it as disease control in reverse, breeding patho- genic organisms that we've usually thought of in rather negative terms. And then, apart from the physical reality, there is a totally unexplored area of psychological reaction—what the bonus effect in terms of enemy panic might be, we don't know. We have some ideas, that's all."

Alex remained in the bathroom after they left. He kept hearing his father talk about "reality." His father's other words rose and circled in Alex's brain, and he could not quite understand them, but again and again the word "reality" returned to him. What was real? What was real? "Beyond a certain point only the existential fact is real," his father had said solemnly, and Alex tried to understand that concept. It was strange that he could be so quick at school and so slow, even dense, around the house. It was as if his father gave off a kind of glimmering cloud that fogged up Alex's glasses and also fogged up his brain.

Inspired, he wrote a theme for his English teacher, Mr. Godwin, called "Precisely What is Real?" Mr. Godwin was very pleased with it and read it to the class, embarrassing Alex immensely. Mr. Godwin, though not so tall and handsome as Alex's father, was a minor, substantial hero in Alex's life. He was a raspy, enthusiastic man with nicotine-stained fingers.

Though Doris was younger, she was more experienced than Alex. For years she had been a child and she recalled those years with a kind of dis- belief. Then, one summer, she had stayed with a girl friend at Cape Cod and met a boy who was supposed to be a television actor, or had hopes of being one. He told her about the television business and the people who ran it that you never saw and had no idea existed; they were the people who really counted, he said. He had a narrow, darkly handsome face and might have been fifteen or twenty-three. There was something indeterminate about him, as if he were waiting to be instructed about himself. "The people that run things are off to the side. Hidden. You don't see them, you stupid guys at home," he said with a sneer. When they were together on the beach it was like a television scene. He was always close to her, with the head-on, slightly myopic look of actors on television; he seemed also to be saying words he had used before. Doris had a fragile, freckled look and a rather thin body. He had forced her to take an icy cold shower with him on the first night they met, and since then her body felt faintly unreal, tingling and numb at the same time. Her body held this sensation for some time. She could not get over it, her mind wanted to break free but couldn't, her body retained this daze—it was nothing she could explain. She didn't talk about it. What she remembered about the boy was his face and body and hands and especially his words, which were strange. "On television there's all these people running around you never see, and cameras and stuff. You stupid bastards at home don't know anything. You don't know how things really are and even the people on television, that work for it, they don't know either. It's too big."

Though what he did to her was no different from what other boys were to do to her when she returned to Lakeshore Point, she could not get over his words. There was something forlorn and angry in them, something violent. She kept hearing the violence in them, replaying the words in her head, and her body had that vague, suspended feeling about it, numb and excited at the same time.

Doris' mother insisted upon a Saturday-morning ritual of shopping. Doris shrank from anyone seeing her with her mother, and her small, closed, sleek face and her rather pigeon-toed, arrogant step quite clearly distinguished her from her mother. Her mother had a long, kindly face; it was unfortunate that her two front teeth were prominent Doris' parents were both rather homely and sturdy; Doris was lithe and quite a surprise. While her mother chattered about nonsense in the stores, Doris dreamed of what she would be doing that evening on her date, and about whether she gave a damn if the boy called her again.

Alex's mother knew Doris' mother slightly. Both belonged to the Village Women's Club. Doris' mother had inherited quite a lot of money and seemed to apologize for it with her big, toothy, hesitant smile; Alex's mother, coming from a less wealthy background, was therefore sharper and knew whom to befriend and whom to slight; she always avoided Doris' mother. Sometimes she saw the mother and daughter out shopping on Saturday— the mother galloping along enthusiastically in short, squat, thick-heeled shoes, and the girl dressed like a little slut in a short skirt. At such times Alex's mother called out, "Why, hello, Edith!" and breezed on by.

Yes, she thought with an involuntary satisfaction, that girl what's-her-name did look like a slut.

She had her own problems with Alex. Though he was eighteen, his skin was still awful; it was a pity to look at him. Every Saturday she packed him in the car and drove him all the way into the city—and she hated the city— to a really superb dermatologist who played squash with her husband at the Athletic Club and who administered to poor Alex X-ray treatments, dried-ice treatments, a variety of pills and hormones, and numerous salves. Poor Alex had to wash his face with a white sponge and work the lather up and then rinse it away, using only lukewarm water. Not hot water. Acne was caused by overexcitation of the oil glands, his mother had learned to her distaste, and so he must not make things worse. She thought the word *acne* was at least as ugly as the problem itself. It always startled her to see her own son—such a tall, gangling boy!—come out of the doctor's inner office and into the waiting room, with that apologetic stoop to his shoulders, that half-chagrined, half-challenging smirk, and that terrible bluish-violet acne all over his face— It fascinated her in a way. It was lumpy and flaky at once. Some pimples were very hard, like berries; other were ripe and soft and draining. Sometimes it was all she could do to keep her hands off his face, but no, no, one never squeezes these problems away; nothing so violent. After a good lathering and a good tepid rinsing, Alex applied a special ointment to his poor bumpy face, and it was also a shock to come upon him late in the evening—that tall, thin boy in his pajamas looking for food downstairs, his face covered with a ghostly white film of medicine that flaked off as he walked.

Poor Alex.

In the spring of his senior year in high school, something began to happen to him. He lost his appetite. He walked about mumbling to himself, arguing over something. His father was in Washington for most of April. His mother had a number of teas and luncheons; Alex felt vaguely protective, knowing that his mother dreaded to be alone and that loneliness was increased by this constant round of parties, and yet he was uneasy with such knowledge and did not know what to do with it. Should he have such an understanding of his own mother? Was it proper? Though he was forbidden by Dr. Lurch to eat chocolates, he ate them secretly, like a twelve-year-old. When his father called, every evening at eight, he made sure he was not around, though he would have liked nothing better than to talk to him. He felt dizzily as if he were becoming a child again. . . .

His mother began to plead with him. Wasn't he an intelligent boy, at the head of his class? Then what was wrong? Why was he so argumentative? Why did he so hate to change his clothes? His underwear? Ah, his mother pleaded with him! Alex knew that he was becoming strange but he did not understand it. He felt a peculiar resistance to taking showers or baths and he disliked brushing his teeth because . . . because in this way wasn't he stirring up germs . . . ? But he did not want to think about it.

"What will your father say about this?" his mother cried.

She was a pretty, dismayed woman. Every day she rose at seven-thirty and showered and put on excellent clothes, all the required paraphernalia of a woman, including high-heeled shoes; every day she went out at about noon or twelve-thirty to have luncheon somewhere or to play bridge or to do something, Alex wasn't sure what—she was tremendously and wonderfully busy. On the other days her friends visited her and she served luncheon—chicken or shrimp or crab in some kind of cream dish, usually, with a delicate icy fruit dessert—and Alex loved the very odor of such days, the rich promise of his mother's happy life. He did not want to disturb her. It would be a disgrace for any son to disturb so happy and busy a woman, and yet . . . he felt that there was indeed something wrong with him, some dissociation from his body, a fear and a distrust of his own skin.

For Mr. Godwin he wrote an unassigned essay called "The Limits of Reality." It was long, rambling, and feverish. He wrote it late at night and was quite proud of certain sentences: "The nature of disease may well be the ultimate reality, and the method of survival in adjustment. Isolation and adaptation. Living with disease. Nothing can be repeated. History comes and goes. There is nothing but the Existential Fact. My skin is a dense, swarming sea of maggots invisible to the eye. . . ."

He handed the essay in with great excitement on a Friday morning, and that evening he went to a party against his wishes, at his mother's wishes. She was concerned about his "social life." It was a party for high-school kids at the big Payne house, and he was probably invited only because his mother played bridge with Mrs. Payne, no other reason. He spent most of his time eating, scooping up dip with his finger. He ate a lot of shrimp. In the recreation room—which was long, with a low, stucco ceiling and a great fireplace at one end, without a fire—couples were dancing in the darkness. Alex half knew everyone there and disdained them. Betty Payne had been rude to him, which meant she had been forced to invite him. So he stayed by himself and his face was fixed with a knowing, philosophical smirk as he ate shrimp.

There was a commotion in the recreation room. One girl, dressed in white, stamped on the floor and threw herself about in what was either a new dance or a tantrum. She thrashed her body, flung her arms around violently, let her long hair fly out about her face—from the way others were watching her, Alex decided it must be a tantrum. The girl had a thin, delicate body and her legs were quite thin; it was Doris Moss. She was associated with a crowd Alex had been aware of for years, without taking any real interest, having heard of their perpetual adventures and daring every Monday throughout high school. He had heard a number of things about them but did not exactly believe everything he heard. The girl Doris continued stamping the floor in her shiny white low-heeled shoes, exactly like a child, and a boy shouted something in her face.

She whirled around and stalked out of the room and came right to Alex. "Hi, Alex, how are you," she said in a taunting voice. "Let's go for a ride and get out of here. Do you have a car?"

"I walked over."

"I've got a car. Come on."

Her face was wet with perspiration and strands of hair stuck to it. A few kids were watching her, but Alex ignored them. "Come on, come on," she said in a husky, flirtatious voice, tugging at Alex's hands. "Let's get out of this place before I suffocate."

He followed along with her, both surprised and pleased. She kept touching him with her small, darting, nervous hands and he wondered if perhaps a new self might rise out of him, a new Alex, popular and assured. But she said as they left the house, "Why don't you have a girl friend?" This hurt him a little and he did not reply. "Are you queer?" she said with a happy stamp of her foot. She leaned around and laughed up into his face. "There's my car. It's boxed in," she said, pulling at him. "No, don't look in that car, leave them alone! You really are queer, aren't you?"

They got into her car and she managed to get out by driving over the lawn. She had to back up and drive forward a few times, impatiently turning the wheel, and she finally managed to get out. Alex watched the doorway of the house for someone to appear and shout at them, but no one came.

"Why don't you have a car? Why don't you have a girl friend?"

"I don't know. Don't want them."

Her brisk, brassy manner was good because it expected nothing of him. She talked so fast and so loudly that she hardly listened to him. "No, really, tell the truth for once," she said, poking him in the ribs, "is it some religious thing or something? The way you act?"

He had been drinking at the party, but it had not released a freer, bolder Alex. Instead he felt hot and nervous. As Doris drove along the boulevard, she kept laughing in a strange, mocking way. "Alexander Junior!" she said with a snicker. Then her mockery changed to a kind of fake sugary concern. "Your father's kind of cute though. I like your father. Why didn't your father come to this lousy party tonight?"

She drove carelessly and kept jabbing at him and teasing him, and Alex wondered if this was the usual way for girls to behave with boys; he didn't know if he liked it or resented it. "Tell me what you're doing these days," Doris commanded. "Are the braces off your teeth? What's wrong with your skin? Tell me about your father. Tell me something, say something," she laughed. She let her head fall back and her mouth opened blankly. On her delicate ears tiny earrings glinted; Alex liked them. He was glad he had found something about her to like.

"My boy friend pierced my ears for me. This was someone you don't know, some bastard. I don't go out with him any more. First you get it clean and then you put a piece of cotton behind the ear, you know, to protect that—you know—that vein or artery or something that's there—but anyway it bled a lot. My mother gave me these earrings for Christmas."

"They're very nice."

She reached over and seized his hand. "Do you like me, do you think I'm beautiful? What are you thinking right now?"

"I have sort of a headache. . . ."

"I've got this crazy idea, it's a great idea, there's this little kid I'm going to take for a ride. Let's take him for a ride. On Sundays people drive up and down the lake shore with kids on rides, looking at the lake, so let's go get him, all right?" There were flecks of saliva around her mouth. Alex, staring at her, felt his head begin to ache seriously and wondered how he would get out of this situation. She was driving fast and carelessly. She turned off onto a darker street and raced along it, not stopping at intersections, and after a while she braked the car to a fast stop before a ranch house. Alex sat in the car, bewildered, and she ran out.

A few minutes later she appeared at the door of the house, backing out, and then she turned and ran down the walk with something in her arms. It was a baby. "Look. This is my brother Dorsey's baby. Look at it. It's my nephew. What do you think, I'm an aunt. No, let me drive, I want to drive," she said rudely, though he had only slid over to look out at what she held. It was a baby, yes.

"What's that?"

"What's it look like?" she laughed. "I told the kid inside, she's in seventh grade at Cooley, I told her we'd be right back, we wanted to take the baby for a ride. It's sort of a nice baby. Here."

Alex did not want to hold the baby, thinking he was not good enough for it, wouldn't know how to hold it, would frighten it. But she thrust it at him and started the car again.

"But maybe we shouldn't—"

"Oh, shut up," she said. The baby began to whimper and Doris snapped on the radio. "This is a lousy car. This isn't my car. This is Fred's car, Fred Smith, do you know him? Of course you don't."

"Fred Smith?"

"You don't know him and you don't know anybody. Can't you stop that baby crying? What kind of a father are you?"

Alex rocked the baby experimentally and it did stop. He felt a kind of numbness move over him, as if he were indeed a father, and the frantic perspiring Doris who sat beside him were his wife, a mother. He stared down at the baby in awe. "Fred's this guy I have kind of a thing with, he's real wild. He's real strange, he's from Olcott. He doesn't hang around with any bunch. This is Fred's car that he lent me for tonight, I was at his place and drove it over, my mother thought I was at Toni Sargant's. There's a slumber party there tonight. She thinks I'm going there but I'm not."

"Where are you going, then?" Alex asked suspiciously.

He held the baby as if in accusation of her, rocking it gently. The girl cast a sideways glance at him. He could not figure out her wild chatter, and then he remembered suddenly talk at school about certain kids who took pills; Doris had been mentioned. He saw at once that of course she was high. She had a strange waxen look beneath the perspiration, a dummy's look. Seen in ordinary light, she would have been a girl of about sixteen with a slightly snubbed nose; in the changing, disruptive lights from the drive-in restaurants and gas stations they were passing she looked as if her skin had been painfully tightened around the blunt hollows and ridges of her face. "We'd better go back," Alex said.

"This Fred is awfully strange. He lives by himself," Doris went on. A car approaching them flicked its lights and finally blew its horn to urge her back onto her own side of the street. "I said I'd be back around twelve but I got hung up with someone, that Tommy, but he made me mad . . . and Fred will get mad, but . . . but I don't know if I'll go back to his place. . . . I don't know. I should get his car back or he'll be mad. I took a bus over to his place but that was during the day . . . but if I go back he'll make me stay . . . he's sort of strange. . . . He's twenty-four."

"Doris, we'd better go back. Let's take the baby back."

He felt a little sick. Doris had driven out quite far and was in a dark, dinky suburb now, rushing along the main street. "I want to get to the country," she said angrily. "I'm so sick of all this, I could puke. We've got a cottage up north we could go to, nobody'd know. My brother Dorsey, he's a goddamn show-off, he's really my stepbrother and he's an awful lot older than I am. I don't remember him, really. That might not have been his house. I think it was. I told the babysitter my sister-in-law wanted the baby and she believed me, and I'm pretty sure it's the right baby, my nephew. His name should be Walter. . . . Isn't that a stupid name for a baby?" she said angrily.

The baby began to cry again, as if startled by her remark. Alex stared helplessly down at it and felt, once again, a magical sensation of being its father: the two of them besieged by the cruel, crazy words of its mother. He wondered suddenly if there might not be some danger of their infecting the baby. His hands were very large, holding it; his skin looked dangerous and flaky in the mottled light.

"I know what, let's play a trick on Dorsey. Let's fix him," Doris whispered.

"What?"

"Lets kill it."

"What?"

"The baby here," Doris said. "Isn't that a wild idea? Huh? What do you think?"

She stopped the car. She leaned over to Alex and stared down at the baby's face; Alex leaned away from her. "We could let it drop out of the car by accident. We could say it got out by itself. Some other car would hit it, not us. We could watch. . . . We could stuff that blanket in its mouth, what do you think, isn't that wild? What do you think?"

Alex's head was pounding violently. "You're crazy," he said.

"Who's crazy?"

"You, you're crazy. Why do you want to do a thing like that?"

Doris laughed and laughed at him. Oh, he was absurdly intelligent; he'd never get over it any more than he'd get over his acne. Doris lay back against the seat laughing until she began to sob angrily. Alex stared at her. "You want me to drive back?" he said cautiously.

"Stupid bastard like you don't know how to drive," she muttered.

She said nothing more. Her stare was fixed upon something before her, on the dashboard, maybe. Or on nothing. Her mouth opened upon rapid, jagged gasps. Once in a while she giggled convulsively and Alex waited, frightened, but she did not speak. He said shyly, "I'll drive back," and Doris made no resistance when he squeezed over her and got behind the wheel.

He drove back to the Payne's house and parked in the circle driveway and walked home by himself, terribly frightened. His fear was a kind of intoxication, and he could not think straight. Later he was to hear that the police had been called, that the baby did belong to Doris' brother, and that

Doris had been found unconscious in the car; the baby was crying on the seat beside her.

And who was to know that Alex had been involved?

He told no one about it, no one. His father returned from Washington and had a talk with him. He was a serious, handsome, busy man and it was a serious matter that he take time to talk so lengthily with Alex. He talked about being normal. "Do you think it's normal," he said, "to hoard your dirty clothes? Not to change your socks, to wear them in bed?"

"I'm not bothering anybody," Alex muttered.

"Your mother says this is getting worse. It's getting worse. And what about this essay you wrote?"

Mr. Godwin had called Alex's father about the essay. It was no surprise; Alex should have known better than to write such a thing. *What is reality? Reality is germs and microbes and infectious scum. . . .*

As he listened to his father read these strange, angry words, he was torn between a knowledge of their insanity and a hope, a terrible hope, that his father would glance up at him with respect. But his father held the paper at some distance, reading, his mouth working the peculiar words as if they themselves were infectious. Finally he said, "Do you think this is the work of a *normal* mind?"

Alex broke down at that point. He confessed to his father about the terrible odor of his skin, the infection of his skin, the sensation of crawling and gnawing and fluttering. . . . Oh, it was terrible, it was terrible, and his voice rose to hysteria; he began to claw himself. "It's all over me, I tried to keep it secret but it got worse. I don't want it to fly off or anything . . . the X-ray treatments help, it isn't on my face . . . it needs to be burned off, not stirred up, that's the danger if I fool around, I don't want it to get stirred up and go off on other people. . . ."

"What's wrong with you? What are you talking about?" his father demanded. His father showed no fear; he was calm and logical, and Alex tried to imitate him, though his skin became cancerous with germs as he spoke; so active, so restless! His very skin crept upon his bones and his scalp moved of its own accord. "I think it could be treated but I don't want to miss school," he said sorrowfully. "I know something's wrong with me, I know it isn't normal, and I'm sorry. I'm sorry. Please don't tell Mother or she'll worry about it. . . ."

So he was taken by his father to Dr. Mate, a friend of his father's from Harvard Medical School. Dr. Mate was a psychiatrist whose practice consisted entirely of disturbed adolescent boys. Alex's problem was judged not a serious one because it did not threaten violence, and it was not even an uncommon one: a neurosis induced by feelings of Oedipal aggression further stimulated by a sense of inferiority and frustration. He clawed at himself, in the opinion of Dr. Mate, because he could not claw at his father. Still his "problem" did not go away. After many sessions with this doctor, who reminded Alex of his own father, Alex was made to understand that it was his mind that was sick and not his skin. They arranged for him to spend some time in a hospital called Oakridge Manor, about twenty miles from home, and he was cautioned not to tell the other patients his secret about his skin being infected and seething with germs. Oakridge Manor cost sixty dollars a day but was worth it, everyone said. After a while Alex's father transferred him to another private hospital, Foxridge Manor. He was allowed to come home on weekends. He liked these visits home but he was unable to relax; he carried himself about cautiously and stiffly through the familiar rooms, his own former room, the lovely guest bathroom downstairs, and when he spoke, it was in a cautious, stiff voice. His mother talked to him about the way the living room was going to look when it was painted and the drapes changed.

"But why are you sitting like that? You can let your arms rest on the table, please, Alex, don't sit there like that—you know you're perfectly all right, please," his mother said.

"Yes, I know. That's right," Alex said.

"Then why are you sitting like that? You look so strange."

"I'm sorry. I know there's nothing wrong with me."

She rushed on to talk about the painters' union and the terrible fight a friend of hers had had with a painter. First he had painted her friend's dining-room walls white, and then apparently he had leaned on them with his dirty hands—and so the walls were blotched and smudged—and what did he think? What did Alex think happened next?

Alex said vaguely, "Out at the hospital the other day there was a girl I thought I knew. She was sitting in the reading room. She was leafing through magazines very fast. There were little scabs on her fingers, it looked like, as if she bit her fingernails, but . . . maybe there weren't scabs, I didn't get that close. . . . I thought it might be Doris Moss."

"Was it?"

"I don't know."

His mother said slowly, avoiding his eyes, "Well, it was awfully sad about Doris. Of course I don't know anything about it. But some boy beat her up. Some man. He beat her up very badly a few weeks ago in some awful place downtown. It was such a shock."

"Then what happened?"

"To her, you mean? I don't know." She was staring at Alex with her blank, flattened-out look, a pretty, dismayed mother who had seen too much and thought about too much, who had been destined for a life of luncheons and dinners and the fulfillment of a good marriage and the enjoyment of a successful son . . . and instead, this had happened. She stared at him.

"She didn't die or anything?" Alex said.

"I don't think so, no, she didn't die. I don't know what happened to her," his mother said. The telephone began ringing in the next room. "That's the contractor with the estimate," she said apologetically and with a rush of mild enthusiasm; after a decent moment she rose and went to answer it and Alex heard her in the next room talking about the living-room walls. They were to be painted either white or oyster. That was the conclusion of their talk about Doris Moss, and the subject never came up again.

Miriam Goldman
Fireflies

THE OTHER DAY I READ A CHAPTER CALLED "The Firefly Hunt" by the Japanese writer, Tanizaki Junichirō. Reading, I stumbled on my own thirteenth summer. And though I know our memories return to us at once both maimed and magnified, it seemed to me those weeks were given back intact, an object not only lost and found, but darkened and gleaming with the special radiance that surrounds a green tract of childhood suddenly recovered.

My mother and I were spending the summer in Hightstown, New Jersey, farm country as flat as the palm of one's hand. We were staying with old school chums of my mother's, two childless couples, who migrated from Trenton to Hightstown every June until September. I see their house, white clapboard and small as a postage stamp, with a tiny porch tacked onto half of the front of it, like an unimportant second thought. After a late supper, when the three women had finished washing up, we all sat there, crowded together as in a theatre box, to watch the summer night come down; and when the last rim of light had finally faded away below the horizon and it grew too dark to see the fields, we went for a long and leisurely walk before sleep.

The grownups, even the women, had talked themselves out. Now they sang. I followed a short distance behind, catching fireflies. Above the open fields the sky hung brilliant and close, but on either side of the narrow road, at eye level and lower down, trains of sparks meandered and curved, starparticles one could reach out for and hold. They gleamed by the dozens in the tall dusty grass, and I could hear, more with my nerves than with my ears, the faint continuous swish they made as they flickered past. Not only were the fireflies magical, the adults too, as if under their spell, behaved miraculously, identifiably human. For once, I was able not only to understand their occupation but even to approve it. They sang. And since they were singing they must be happy, and since they were happy could be happily dismissed.

One of the men, Emanuel Speer, was a cantor, with a flexible, unnaturally powerful *heldentenor*. He lived his secret life passionately waiting to be discovered by the Metropolitan, a second Richard Tucker. Just by closing its eyes during the High Holiday services, his congregation was able to imagine itself at the opera, while a contrary process stained evey aria he sang with the fast unalterable color of woe. Now, walking along under cover of darkness, he indulged his frustrated dreams to the hilt; denied his ambition, he gave of himself in our nightly walks without stinting—threw back his head, opened his arms, and assaulted the night. *Quell' amor ch'e palpito . . . dell' universo intero . . . misterioso altero . . .* he lamented, with the rhythmic thrust of a courante or gigue. In his pauses, my mother's soprano rose lightly, singing the songs of her girlhood in three-quarter time. I caught fireflies, held them enclosed in my hands to tire them, then set them on my blouse and in my hair to sparkle and gleam. Urged, I too sang.

> *Hold the wind, hold the wind,*
> *Hold the wind, don't let it blow.*
> *Hold the wind, hold the wind,*
> *Hold the wind, don't let it blow.*
> *My soul got lost in the midnight dew,*
> *Hold the wind, don't let it blow.*
> *The Morning Star was a witness too,*
> *Hold the wind, don't let it blow.*

No, my soul wasn't lost that summer, though the fireflies did lend themselves to that conceit; metaphysical insects, they glowed without fire or heat—off and on—between the darkness and the light. Holding them in my hands, I sometimes forgot what I was holding, and asked myself whether these could be the flickering souls of the dead, those who had been both mild and good in life. Still, I caught them nightly, dropped them into a milk bottle stuffed with grass, and carried them back to the narrow bare room my mother and I shared.

Happy nights . . . because my childhood was corroded by an insane terror of the dark, these were my first happy nights. For me the darkness was a swamp, inhabited by murderers, maniacs, stealthy gray ravening wolves, and the rotting dead. If I was lucky, I saw my assassins, screamed, and was saved. But mostly, lying rigid in the ticking darkness, wiping my wet palms on the woolen blanket, I just knew that they were there. Now here was my mother within arm's reach; she slept restlessly too, as if contriving how best to soothe me, turning and turning to try and find a more comfortable position. She coughed softly. She sighed. All night long I could hear her breathe. Beside me on a stool, my night light, a milk bottle stuffed with fireflies and grass. One night we accidentally knocked the bottle over and stayed awake for a long while watching the fireflies dim and glow in the room; stayed awake so long, we heard the cry of a bird that we had never heard before whose name we didn't know: its call, a three times repeated descending trill, furry, mournful and strangely near. "How sad it sounds," my mother whispered, unable to stifle her sighs. Perhaps I sighed, but if I did, it was only to keep her company and from a welling up of joy.

That summer I was allowed to sleep as late as I liked and woke often close to noon. I ate my breakfast standing barefoot in my nightgown with my hair unbrushed, in one hand, a thick black buttered slice of bread sticky with honey, and in the other, a ripe and dripping peach. Still dazed from sleep, I wandered from the overheated kitchen where the women were preparing a hot midday meal, on out to the tiny porch where both men sat in the sun reading their newspapers, or doing what they called their "paper work." Neither hearing nor answering when spoken to, I remained unmolested, for I had learned early how to protect myself: spinning secret webs, I appeared weighed down with worries, but alert. Dreaming, eating, frowning. I planned the pleasures of the day; my few chores completed, and lunch for two in a brown paper bag, I ran half a mile down the track that cut through the corn to the farm where my summer friend lived.

We shared the same first name and believed this set a seal on our friendship as mystical as a blood-pact would have between us. And we shared, as well, the purest form of happiness—hour after hour of summer idleness, acres of idleness, untainted by guilt or evil pangs of conscience.

We swam in a pond ringed by tall grass and low growing sumac and starred over all its surface with water lilies. The bottom, as in all such ponds, was oozingly slimy and a tangle of rubbery smooth stems. When we stripped in our rowboat and jumped in, we looked modestly away—just one good hard stare, then backs chastely turned. My friend was a year older than I, but names aside, we were very much alike, both blue-eyed, with skin darker from the summer than our light streaked hair. She was sturdier, steadier, and sunnier than I, of Polish descent, with their characteristic tilt of the cheekbones and the eyes. Today I no longer remember her last name.

Once while we were swimming, we watched a strange man walk halfway round the pond and disappear. We held him in sight for a long minute, standing in the water up to our noses. The sun burned down; the boat drifted imperceptibly with the current; a twig snapped under his foot; the dragonflies flashed as they pierced and stitched the surface of the pond. Then how we roared, took a few strokes and threw ourselves gasping into the boat convulsed with laughter. A man—a man and we naked!—and we laughed until we had to sit doubled over with our knees drawn up to our chins to relieve the strain on our aching bellies. Then fell to thinking about love.

At thirteen, I was still in my heroic age, dreaming not so much about love itself but more how I could prove my worth. My lover was featureless, a silhouette cast for the role of He Who Is Saved: Saint without a halo, I sat nursing him, day and night, without food or sleep, a wan specter of tenderness; carrying my burden, I ran out of flaming buildings, held raging mobs at bay, from how many bridges crazily leaped! My motto: brave as a lion, strong as a horse. And when we swam again that day after our hysterical laughter, what a rescue I made then, down down down to the very bottom of the shallow pond. That afternoon, I anticipated Lawrence Durrell and his "Clea" as did many another such adventurer before me. Hacking away and hacking away, I twisted, turned, persisted, until lungs bursting I burst through the surface of the pond, and laid my water lilies gently down on the bottom of the boat, inhaling with pleasure their honeyed licorice scent. After such a triumph, I was content to wait and see, alas, whether love would venture anything half so glorious for me. Letting the boat drift, we lay back and gazed through half-closed eyes at the summer sky. It arched over us hazily in the distance, like our future, but unlike the future, we were able to make the clouds take on any shape we wished. We remembered lunch when it was time to go home for supper, and though we were suddenly ravenous, we forced ourselves to eat slowly in order to stretch our few remaining minutes together.

We saw each other at night once, after my father had come to take my mother and me home. I spilled my bottle of fireflies above her head; we were sentimental and tried to cry. Arms around each other's neck, we walked together part way down the road, promised very much, and kissed. Running the rest of the way alone in the dark, I forgot to listen for padding footsteps and to watch out for escaped lunatics crouching in the corn. I was already shaping the phrases of my first letter, and for the coming months, my every thought and sensation existed only to be stripped bare and shared in ink. And the next morning, all the long ride home from New Jersey to Boston over the ugly highway, I was composing a letter describing the long ride home over the ugly highway. When absentmindedly I happened to look up, I saw my mother's face contorted with silent weeping.

My father had just finished telling her that an old and beloved friend had been murdered—robbed and shot in his drugstore as he was getting ready to go home for the night.

"But why did you have to tell her now?" I demanded. "Couldn't you wait until we got back?"

"And what about me?" my father retorted. "Or don't you think I'm human, is that it? Still, that's what it means to be a duchess! Do you think you were left on the doorstep? Well, we didn't find you there, I can tell you that for certain. But now I'd like you to tell me something. Will I ever live to see the day when you think of anyone except yourself?"

Not very logical, my father, but along the way he often hit it and this time too he happened to be right. It wasn't my poor mother I was worrying about. As always, it was myself. I couldn't bear to think of the visit of condolence I knew I should be forced to make. What could I say? Where would I look?

"Well I won't go," I said, bringing their fury down on me.

But I did go and I remember that house of mourning: the living room rug rolled up and the furniture shoved back against the walls for some mysterious reason, as if for a dancing party; while through the curtainless windows, the later afternoon end-of-August sun blazed on the varnished floor scattered with cookies and toys and a soiled baby's diaper that saturated the air with its smell of ammonia and heated iron. And Mrs. Walther, whom I liked so much, her bony freckled face as grief-stricken as I had imagined a face of grief should be, but with an ecstatic light in her eyes, disquieting to preconceived notions—like a horse about to bolt. Her face, white, yes, as I had known it would be, yet not so much drained bloodless from prolonged weeping, as it was pale and luminous, polished by her tears.

3
Family
Relationships

THE FAMILY LIFE OF CONTEMPORARY ADOLESCENTS is a delicate interrelationship among different personalities, customs, and points of view. Until children reach adolescence, their roles and those of their parents are well defined, and for the most part a state of equilibrium exists in the home. The parents are largely responsible for their children's social development, feeling of worth, and sense of belonging. They may in fact seem omnipotent to their children, who themselves exercise little power within the family circle; for it is from the parents that all authority and control and protection come.

This situation is often turned topsy-turvy when the sudden change from childhood to adolescence occurs with its many ambiguities. Adolescents become unpredictable. They begin to respond to new forces within themselves and outside the family circle. They strive for more power and the freedom to exercise it at their discretion. As new emotional and physical needs are awakened, new patterns of interaction within the family are inevitable. Parents have to face the often difficult realization that their adolescents must be psychologically weaned from the dependency of childhood if they are to become self-sufficient adults. Consciously or unconsciously many parents are themselves made insecure wondering about how they will be regarded in the future by their offspring, in whom they have invested so much love and attention.

Oftentimes parents, in trying to overcome their own insecurities, interfere with the normal process of allowing their children to become what their inclinations and talents dictate. Parents motivated by the best intentions—

affection, concern, ambition—may try to spare their children the pains and sorrows they experienced during their own adolescence. Some may try to prescribe "proper" behavior or attempt to compensate for their thwarted aspirations by wrongheadedly directing their children's lives into inappropriate entertainment, schooling, and the like. These unrealistic expectations cause a great deal of stress in adolescents who fail to live up to them. Nevertheless, the great majority of parents have better sense and not only allow but rather encourage their children to develop according to their talents and interests.

Adolescents' conceptions of their families and their relations to them change considerably as they strive toward self-sufficiency. At times they are confused by their simultaneous attraction toward and hostility against their parents. They become sensitive to the appearance of their homes and the mannerisms of their family, especially as these might enhance or detract from peer-group prestige. Some older adolescents show a reformist attitude that is intolerant and difficult to live with if they feel their families are lacking in some way.

Younger adolescents, in making a bid for independence, often attempt to repudiate their parents. Such attempts rarely succeed but only point up how dependent they really are. With growing insight they discover that true independence develops over a long period of time as they gradually assume responsibility for their own decisions, thoughts, and feelings. Without a feeling of disloyalty they question their parents' political and religious beliefs—and as much research shows, they more often than not adopt them in early adulthood after doubting or rejecting them so thoroughly in adolescence. More and more their decisions are based on what they, not their parents, feel is right. They pursue interests that may be quite different from those enjoyed by their parents and begin to develop their individuality in the process.

In defining their families and their changing relationships with them, older adolescents arrive at a new conception of who their parents are. While no longer omnipotent as decision-makers, parents are sometimes discovered to be important sources of valuable experience. The problems of their parents are seen more realistically by adolescents as they start to grapple with similar ones. At this stage, many parents become models to be imitated by adolescents, while, without rejecting their parents, other adolescents find more appropriate models outside the family. Before full maturity is reached, most adolescents have imitated the behavior of a number of admired adults. Though it may be difficult for parents to relinquish their accustomed roles, they do so as they see their children acquiring the maturity to do many things that formerly had to be done for them.

Parental love and acceptance are vitally important to the healthy emotional development of young people. Nevertheless, this form of love has its limitations. It cannot cure many deeply felt disappointments, or correct inherent weaknesses of body and mind, or protect adolescents from errors of judgment. On the other hand, adolescents who are rejected and unloved have a difficult time; they receive little aid, support, or guidance during a period in their lives when these are most needed. The insecurity, frustration, and rejection they feel over this absence of love too often carry over into their adult lives, with predictably sad results.

As adolescents become young adults, the friction between parents and adolescents in time transforms itself into a new understanding. These new adults are likely to recognize the sacrifices their parents have made for them. And parents usually take satisfaction in the accomplishments of the young adults who were once their children.

"A Young Person with Get-Up-and-Go" epitomizes the theme of adolescents developing a keen awareness of themselves in relation to their home environment, particularly as it reflects family status. The reformist attitude customarily associated with the theme is lacking in this story. Walter senses that his parents are set in their slovenly ways and beyond being changed. His principal wish is to have a presentable place where he can entertain his friends without embarrassment. Though their intentions are noble, reforming adolescents in stories on this theme are usually depicted as naïve gadflies who have yet to learn that much of humanity is imperfect and not likely to be changed.

In an opposing but related type of story adolescents have homes that are attractive, as in "Louisa, Please Come Home," yet they lack parental love and understanding. Unloving parents are often rejected by their children. For Louisa the solution is to run away from home and establish her independence elsewhere; in so doing she finds in Mrs. Peacock an affectionate substitute for her family. The story is unusual because of the success of Louisa's bid for independence. The cause of her running away is to be found in large measure at the end of the story where her parents fail to recognize her when she returns. In most stories of this kind, however, adolescents find they are not capable of self-sufficiency and must return home, as painful as the return may be, in order to mature a little more.

A typical father-son conflict is found in "The Vault." The father thinks his son will become a "sissy" if he continues to practice the piano. The boy has talent and wants to continue playing, yet he doesn't want to displease his father. He also has a compulsion to pay his father for the lessons he has already taken. His unique attempt at payment, to appease instead of to revolt, leaves the boy at the end of the story crying out "Papa, Papa, accept all happiness from me." In stories with older adolescents, however, confrontation rather than conciliation is the norm in similar situations. There is little doubt about the impending break in "The Outing" (section 6), for instance, or the finality of it in "The Sorcerer's Eye" (section 7). Father-son stories of conflict are more numerous than those between mother and daughter. "Homecoming" exemplifies the frequent predicament in which mothers and daughters fail to interpret an event in the same way. When Harold, a young soldier Susan hardly knows, is killed in Vietnam, her mother creates a melodramatic scene of mourning, one completely inappropriate to the situation. Failing to understand the relationship between Susan and

Harold, the mother projects the circumstances of her husband's death in Korea years before into those associated with the death of Susan's acquaintance. Harold's death serves only for the mother to relive vicariously a tragic moment in her own life through an event that hardly troubles her daughter. Susan's feelings about the death are unemotional: "There just isn't anything, she thought. I'm sorry, Harold. I hope it wasn't too bad and I hope it didn't hurt much. . . . 'Good-bye,' she said in a very light whisper. 'You poor bastard.' " The different reactions to Harold's death expose the inability of mother and daughter to communicate effectively.

A good number of stories have been written about new members entering a family circle. Predictably, they are a handsome uncle or aunt or an unlucky niece, nephew, or cousin in need of a home. "The Four Sides of a Triangle" illustrates the attraction that develops between the adolescent and the new member. Adolescents in this situation with an older relative inevitably realize the impossibility of their infatuation while still continuing to admire the older relative. Many of these stories are narrated as fond remembrances and lack the bitterness of thwarted romance that is found in similar stories of young lovers whose romances have gone sour. On the other hand when new members intrude into the family who are about the same age as the adolescent protagonist, a sibling rivalry is almost bound to result—sometimes after a close friendship has developed.

Fewer stories of broken homes have been written in recent years, perhaps because they have become such a predictable condition of American society. The effect, not the process, is the frequent focus in these stories, which often take place well after the divorce itself. Some stories show adolescents rising above their unhappy domestic situation and excelling—or perhaps over-compensating—in some way to establish their integrity; most stories, however, spell out a grimmer picture, one of emotional maladjustment or juvenile delinquency. Both "Stealing Cars" (section 4) and "The Boats" (section 4), though dealing with adolescents from different socioeconomic levels, describe what is generally the same antisocial, destructive behavior.

It is well established how important the home is in molding adolescent values. "Debut" (section 4) demonstrates that what is taught—in this case selfish manipulation—is not always the best for healthy social development. The harmony and security that permeate "The Grey Bird" (section 7) create a contrasting, affirmative counterpoint to the many short stories that thrive on the bleaker aspects of family life. Without being sentimental, it contains most of the elements of a very popular type of story written during the forties and fifties, one emphasizing an idealized vision of American home life.

Ann Parsons
A Young Person with
Get-Up-and-Go

EVERY DAY WALTER GOT OFF the school bus at the stop before his own, where an asphalt street cut up the hill to the left and out of sight into a thicket of pin oaks. By then, no other riders from the neighborhood remained on the bus to look from the windows and ask questions about his roundabout homecoming. The houses up here among the trees were carefully tended, fussed over.

If he stayed aboard, as he had the first day of school the bus stopped next some distance down the road, right in front of his own driveway—what there was of it. When the town had widened this road, even the narrow flower bed in front had been erased. He remembered that he had been in the third grade when his mother had bought flower seeds from some Girl Scouts who came to the front door. She had worked for most of a week, rooting out the stones from the patch between the driveway and the front steps. Gardening was tough going, as the mailman had remarked each day when he saw his mother stooped over in the sun. It was no wonder she had given up the garden almost before the acid soil had poisoned and turned yellow the first young shoots. Then they'd widened the road, and the bare patch of ground went, too.

When the bus had stopped that first day, people sitting in their seats could look right through the gaping Venetian blinds into the sunporch. One of the blinds was stuck and had been since his father had first installed it a long time ago. The slats in the others had warped and split with the dampness of the climate, so that it might as well have been bare glass sitting there, face to face with the bare glass of the bus windows. He bet they could see the dirty old daybed his brother slept in and probably the pin-up pictures brought home from the garage where his brother worked. His brother's bed was never made, and the only other furniture on the porch was an old metal lawn chair that had spent some winters in the backyard.

Today there would probably be a scummy milk bottle on the chair, and the jockstrap his brother wore to practice on the trampoline.

He'd not paid too much attention when he'd been in grade school. He'd left the house on his bicycle every morning in the fall and spring, and come home when he felt like it. Winters he had walked or hitched. And never bringing people around, not having any reason, he'd not minded the crazy look of the house. But the day the bus had stopped right where the flower bed used to be, he'd been gagged by the sight. The house had no roof to speak of, just a flat top, like a box. That's how his house had looked, like a box. Nothing about the house ran straight beside anything else; not the line of a sill, not the edge of a shingle, not the set of a doorjamb, and especially not one slat of one Venetian blind. Worst of all, though, was the truck his father had sitting on blocks in the side yard, a forty Chevy with the words *Norwalk Volunteer Rescue Corps* painted on the door. The old man enjoyed what flash was left over from the war effort. He'd bought the truck from a wrecker, and said he wanted to fix it up for the lawn maintenance business he ran, but the carcass had sat undisturbed in the side yard for several years now.

Standing by the strangers' mailboxes, he waited until the blinker light stopped flashing, and the bus moved on out of sight before he turned and walked down the road after it. He'd always followed this road home from grade school—years ago it seemed now—but it was only this fall he'd gone to junior high. When he was small, all along here it had been open country.

Home now, he found the mail was still in the box by the driveway. His father hadn't picked it up at lunchtime. Walter hoped that didn't mean it had been one of his mother's bad days. It could be simply that his father had been in a hurry to get going after lunch. He left it alone himself; probably most of it was the usual Rural Box Holder envelopes filled with penny coupons and news of some sale at a hardware store. He didn't get much mail anymore since he had quit the "Y" downtown. They had always sent him quite a bit. *"Hi fellas! Another of our very popular Lad 'n' Dad Nites is on the calendar. Just a reminder. Sign up pronto."* He'd heard what they were like: a bottle of Dr. Pepper and some show-off guys in ladies' makeup doing a dance.

He adjusted his face into the expression he favored for entering a strange classroom at school, and eased his body through the front door, still screened, though it was growing chilly with the autumn weather. His mother was asleep on the studio couch in the front room. She was a large woman with no special shape to her face or her body either. Some of her hair was black and some of it gray. She wore a knit cotton T-shirt, taut across her heavy breasts, and a lint-covered skirt was bunched about her thighs and buttocks as she slept.

He decided against getting something to eat in the kitchen. The noise of the icebox door closing might waken her. He would have a hot dog later at the golf range where he sometimes worked after school. He picked his way out again through the breezeway to the garage, and there among the mowers and spray guns—the tools of his father's trade—among the broken furniture and dried whitewash in cans, he found his bicycle. He slung one leg across the leatherette seat, and hopped and wobbled on his other the short length of the driveway to the road.

As he had yanked his bike from the tangle in the garage, his eye had fallen upon the spavined old sofa he could remember standing in the front room when he was small. That was all lots of people he knew had to sit on in their playrooms, just old couches, no good anymore for upstairs. Their mothers called such places the family room—often just a corner of the basement, the walls nothing but cement, dressed up with peach-colored paint. They weren't such nice places really. It was a matter of what they were named—in those same houses Walter was asked if he wanted to "wash his hands."

If he were to ask anyone over after supper, after dark, they wouldn't see the outside of his house, not even its shape. He could do it before it grew really cold. He could fix up the garage to be as good as a family room any day. He might even paint it, the inside, anyway.

The driving range was always busy late in the day, jammed with high-school boys from Darien (money to burn), and women shagging balls after their lesson with the pro. Walter made seventy-five cents an hour walking back and forth at the end of the lot and gathering up the balls in a bucket. As he walked, he wheeled along a square shield of wire mesh, keeping it always between himself and the flying balls. It wasn't bad work when the weather was clear, and on rainy days he didn't show up. It gave him a good feeling, spying out and gathering the white balls that lay hidden in the frost-puffed meadow. He crossed the field on the diagonal and slowly wobbled back again. The creaky wire cage was heavy, and he advanced at a deliberate speed. It was actually not necessary to push it quite so slowly as he did, but he found the pace right for thinking.

Castagna, the proprietor of the range, had manners that made even Brown-Nose Boske, the biggest patsy in the ninth grade, want to cheat him. Walter took his time, stooping, taking up the balls, feeling their impact make his pail ring and vibrate in his hands. He felt bound to walk even slower, finally, as he approached the counter where Castagna sat on a high stool, doling out scarred balls and shabby drivers.

"Enjoying your stroll, kid? Maybe you got this operation mixed with a Easter egg hunt, huh?"

"Mr. Castagna, I got to go now. I got homework my mother says I got to get done, or I can't work at all anymore."

Castagna didn't answer, but continued arranging putters in their notched rack. He wiped the phony trophies with which he decorated his cubbyhole, fitted two pretty women with irons, and finally, still not speaking, shied some coins down the counter in payment, since he already had the cash drawer open to receive the women's money. Otherwise he'd have made Walter wait even longer. That's how he was.

Walter wheeled his bike through the parking lot, one tire screeching against the paintless fender, and took off, pedaling fast, and not caring if Castagna noticed that he wasn't headed toward home at all, but toward the shopping center. It stood by the railroad right-of-way, a flinty horseshoe of brick storefronts with painted white gables and posts like those on the Congregational Church up the road.

He took out the famous-make steerhide wallet that had caught his eye at the discount house, and counted out the bills there. He selected a brush and a lamb's wool roller of the best quality, its softness sheathed in a plastic wrapper. The paint samples were pasted in books the size of the dictionary in the school library, the pages rich and heavy with the shining squares, all colors. He finally settled on a lightish tan, with nothing fruity about it.

He waited while a lady tried some collars on a poodle, and when the man behind the counter was free, he ordered three quarts of Sandalwood Buff. Who'd have guessed paint would cost so much?

"Better be sure that's the shade your mother has in mind, Sonny. We can't take it back, once I got it mixed, after all." The man thought he was some little kid.

"My mother said I could pick one all by myself."

"Oh, fixing up your room, huh? That's get-up-and-go. I'd like to see more young people today take such interest in their home surroundings. Most of 'em won't pick up their dirty drawers off the carpet on their way out the door. For you, friend, I throw in a brand-new stick to stir with, on the house."

They all sounded alike, once they got old.

He bought a sack of jelly doughnuts in the bakery next door. He ate them as he pedaled slowly home along the Post Road, keeping an eye out for wild-driving commuters who swarmed out of the station parking lot, in those beat-up cars they thought were so great for getting to work.

His father's truck was parked in the driveway, beaded with the mist of dried insecticide that pocked the underlying veil of lime. There was no point in washing the truck, his father often said; a sensible man confined his attention to the windshield. The truck's dull hide caused his brother's Ford, parked alongside, to shine all the brighter, with the glow of true enamel, rich and deep. Even the mudguards hanging at rest now glowed as if they had been rubbed with shoe polish.

Walter squeezed between the truck and the car, and wheeled his bicycle into the shadowy garage. He hauled open the screen door, nearly opaque with a haze of dust, and padded on noiseless sneakers into the back hallway.

The house smelled of rust; and this smell settled upon you most heavily in the dark hall.

The three others sat at the kitchen table where they always ate. The table had a white enamel top, and years of serving plates from heavy pans balanced on the edge had chiseled and gnawed at the rim until it was a wobbly scallop of dark blue chips.

"I'd like to think people who come home for their dinner at 7 P.M. has got a good reason," his father said, rising from the table. He was on his way out. "But I'd be surprised a person I knew *did* have a good reason. I've never seen him *work* more than a half hour at a time, so which was it tonight, movies or the roller rink?" His father had a very loud voice from shouting over the roar of lawn mowers and power saws all day long. He did a lot of talking, too, without really expecting to hear an answer. Silence, Walter knew, was the best reply at these times, but someday he'd tell old Lardass what he could do.

Walter slid half a can of ravioli out into his plate and replaced the can in the saucepan of simmering water. They all came in at different times, so each helped himself, and left the rest of the can for the next person. If he ran out, he just opened a new one. Ravioli was one thing Walter couldn't get enough of. Even after the jelly doughnuts, he ate a whole can. His father had just finished, and was, as usual, in a big hurry to get down to the rowboat owned by a friend while it was still light enough to coast out into the harbor for crappies. Then he'd spend the evening drinking beer at the Polish American Yacht Club right next to the dock where the oyster boats came in. What a stink! His father usually gave the crappies to the man who owned the boat, since he didn't like cleaning them. "You feel like fish," his father said, "you can buy fishburgers all over town."

Tonight it was a help that the old man was in such a rush. He could count on his brother to take off any minute, too. Lately his brother had been hanging around at the airport. Some fool who was trying to set an altitude record for a flyweight Piper Cub needed another man riding along as a witness. They hadn't made it yet, but his father told him not to worry— they'd make the headlines one way or another any day now.

"So long, Shithead," his brother said, in a voice that was not unfriendly, and, moving his arm in a throwaway salute, headed out. In a minute he heard the roar of revved-up carburetors, and then he was gone.

His mother sat pushing a piece of bread around and around her plate with one finger, making stripes in the tomato sauce.

"Come on, Mama, finish your supper so I can clean up."

The last one out washed her stuff—that was the rule—or it just got hard as cement sitting in the sink until they ran short of plates. She didn't eat much, and she left most of the food on her plate. She liked to play with it and mix it all up together: jelly, canned macaroni salad, and stew, for instance. Try to get *that* off when it's stood a couple of days in a dish.

She gave him one of her smiles, or rather, he thought, gave it to the sleeve of his shirt. (Her smiles were like the smile of a lady at the grocery store when she saw her cart had you blocked—very polite.) She gave her plate a little nudge toward him to show him how sorry she was that she'd held him up, and attended to the circle she was making on the table with her finger. After a while, he knew she'd sit in the other room until he went to bed, when he would guide her by the arm, and she would get the idea, and go upstairs by herself. One thing he didn't have to worry about was that she'd go out into the road or anyplace outside. It made her afraid to go out of the house. Big tears would run along her nose, past the corners of her mouth, and fall like those in comic books, several drops at a time, raining down.

He rinsed their plates and forks, poured out the hot water from the pan on the stove, and wiped up the circle of tomato sauce from the white table. Then, very gently, he wiped the fingers lying beside it. If you were careful when you touched her, she didn't cry.

He was free after that to get to work in the garage. Beyond the screen door was off limits for her, and he returned to his planning when he heard it slam behind him. Even the trip through the breezeway was too far for his mother. He never need worry that she'd come out here and be laughed at, or make people afraid, either. Out here, people would be left strictly alone. Anybody wanted a smoke, he could go right ahead. A person could say what he pleased, too—anything that came to mind, without stopping first to look in the other room or listen for footsteps. He had a friend whose mother was a pest whenever they fooled around over there. Always running off about an electric train that had cost so much and now nobody played with it. *Played* with it. Christ!

He started moving it out, all of it—a broken lawn mower, the old couch that stank of mice, garden tools and the electric edger, newspapers sticky with dampness, the hose in wild, unyielding loops that angled about every heavy object in the place. He dragged and shoved it all out into the drive-way where he sorted it by destination. He'd need to have the driveway cleared so the cars could park when they came home. Some of his father's stuff he could pile in the old shed at the rear of the lot where the cow had been kept for a while. (She'd had an actually pretty face, that cow, but when her milk had been tested they said she had Bang's disease, and she'd been sold for dog food.)

He got most of the things stashed away, and the rest he piled by the side of the house in the darkness. The couch he planned to move back inside after he finished painting.

As it got late, he hurried, sweating even in the October coolness. It was a mess to move in the dark, all sharp edges and splinters. He kicked the hose out of the way finally, and threw his weight against the open garage door, but it wouldn't budge. The track had long ago been forced out of shape by the bulging mess within. Just having that door closed would make quite a difference in the looks of the place. He could work something out tomorrow. He turned out the light and left the garage, surprisingly black in its emptiness.

He was awakened as usual next day by the sound of the toilet's flushing. His father was sullen and slow in the morning and made certain with his racket that no one in the family outslept him. He stood in the kitchen this morning, leaning over the stove as if it were a roaring fire, and warmed himself as he fried an egg.

"Who's been stirring up trouble outside? Those are valuable supplies, worth a lot of money. People who got so much energy could put it to use helping their father, who, I might add, works a twelve-hour day many a time." Then he buttered the toast for his wife and put it on the table before her. He stroked her coarse hair, like wire. "How's Mama today? If you behave yourself, act like a good girl for me, when I get home noontime, I'll turn on the movie, and you can watch all afternoon."

When would his father quit kidding himself? She'd as soon watch the burner on the stove, or the drip from the faucet, as TV or anything else.

They dealt with breakfast as they dealt with other meals, substituting a skillet of bacon grease for a pan of water. You dropped in whatever you felt like: bacon, bread soaked in milk, or eggs, removed them when done, and left the pan for the next man. The last one out washed up. If he didn't wash his face until he was leaving, he could cut out after breakfast ahead of his brother. His mother was always awake early, too. The first one in gave her a piece of bread and jelly. She'd sit there watching the flame on the gas stove until the last one finished, and turned it off. Then she'd go sit in the front room until his father came home for lunch. Why she was the first one up mornings, Walter couldn't say. She had all the time in the world.

He, on the other hand, was pushed for time, if he planned to catch the bus up the road. Missing it meant a long bike ride to school, so he'd better get it out right away—the thing he had on his mind. He'd better cut out the stalling and say it.

"Listen, Daddy, I thought I might fix up the garage, and have a few kids over some night before it gets too cold out. We wouldn't be in anybody's way or scare Mama. Just mess around and listen to the radio, or play some cards. I got lots of friends, people who been nice to me, and I'd like to pay them back."

His father flipped the egg, breaking the yolk, and the flame sputtered with the grease that flew in a fine hot spray from the pan. He hadn't yet, in all these years, learned to cook his breakfast egg for himself, and when he answered, the volume of his voice caused his wife to turn her eyes from the flame.

"Worries me enough, you hanging around with trash, without you don't bring them here. That's all this house needs is a bunch of free-loading bums on the premises. Between you and your brother, I'd come home some night and find we was living in a roadhouse."

Walter slammed out the front door, along the cement walk, and stood still, looking at the empty driveway. Only two round stains, side by side on the pavement, gave a sign that the truck and the Ford had ever stood there. The old pickup loomed up, dull within the shadowy garage. The gloss on the beet-red convertible, and its chrome, gleamed undiminished in the rusty-smelling dark.

After a time, he crossed the driveway, turned the corner into the side yard, and made his way over the hard-packed cinders of the place to the old blue truck sitting on its blocks. He opened the doors that worked so easily and silently, and climbed in, shutting them behind him. He heard the school bus lumber past, and shortly thereafter the wheeze of the lawn-maintenance service departing, then the roar of the special carburetors.

When they had gone, there was no sound in the morning darkness.

Samuel Yellen
The Four Sides
of a Triangle

I WAS SIXTEEN YEARS OLD when I first learned that a triangle has four sides. Of course, I don't mean the triangle of Euclid, but the triangle of human passions. And when I say *I*, I don't mean the middle-aged man now to be seen irresolutely buying a pair of comfortable shoes, but an adolescent stranger, a character in the fiction of the past, seen through the warped, scratched, dusty pane of memory. Actually, this story concerns one of my mother's seven sisters, my favorite among them, whom I shall call Esther. Although she was then in her early thirties, she exercised for me that strong attraction which an adolescent boy often discovers in a young aunt, or in a schoolteacher, without the sexual taboo surrounding his mother, and yet not demanding decision and action as would a girl his own age—a state of having his cake, but not having to eat it. Taller and slenderer than my mother, who was an inch over five feet in height and was turning plump, Esther had the same wavy, bobbed, purple-black hair, the vivacious black eyes and warm dusky skin, the quickness and lightness of movement. And like my mother, she laughed easily. However, at the time I am speaking of, she would break off with a deep sigh, shake her head, and exclaim: "Oh, Becky, Becky, Becky!" And my mother would know, as I would, that she was paying toll to the trouble she was having with Boris, her husband.

What made Esther my favorite, aside from the physical attraction, was that very shadow darkening her laughter, that intimation of sadness and uncertainty. She was kind as well as kin. But it was more than that. By some magic in her manner, she persuaded me into considering myself an adult, and a man. I desperately needed such persuasion. The usual difficulties of adolescence were compounded in me. For, at an age when I should have been in the second year of high school, I was struggling with the freshman year at Western Reserve University. And while I was trying, with small success, to fill the role of college man, the friends of my parents would twitter (as if I were not present) the Yiddish equivalents of "My goodness, how he has shot up!" or (this by the wags) "I'll bet he's a regular lady-killer!" Whereas Esther, when we were out walking, would quietly take my arm, press it warmly to her body, and look up to me as a manly support, not an ungainly shoot. Or she would make me believe, contrary to all the evidence, in the possibility of ladies even for me to kill, by saying in an intimate tone: "Sam, I hope you will still be fond of me after I'm an old ugly divorced woman."

Which brings me to why Esther closed down her home in Boston one December and came to Cleveland to live with us for many weeks. After nine years of marriage, she was seeking a divorce. The full picture was not clear to me, since I had to put the details together out of those infrequent moments when I emerged from my thicket of anxieties and nameless longings. Very likely Esther and her husband (who had preceded her to Cleveland and was staying with friends of his named Kaplan) were establishing residence in Ohio to escape some inflexibility in the divorce laws of Massachusetts. It may well be, however, that she had at last caught up with her "slippery" Boris, who had several times before this deserted her and their two little daughters. There was even a strong probability that she still yearned for a reconciliation. My mother would scold: "Esther, don't be a fool! You'll be well rid of him! What good is he to you? It'll always be the same story. As soon as you take him back he'll start throwing his money around again. And you know he's never going to stop chasing the women!"

"But, Becky, how will I get along without him? He's my man!"

In exasperation my mother would cry out: "Your man! Your man! What good is he? What do you want him for?" And I can see those two sisters confronting each other like two angry blackbirds, their voices throbbing, their dark skin flushed, their black eyes flashing. And my mother, thrusting out her arms in indignation from her short plump body, and yet suggesting the smugness of a woman sure of her own husband and intolerant of others' waywardness, would go on: "What do you want him for, Esther? What are you worried about? You know you can always make a living for yourself and the girls."

To which Esther would turn abruptly and pace the room, burying her hands in her hair and biting her lip, while her eyes would possess a face gone strained and waxen. "Oh, that's not it, Becky! Sure I can always make a living. But you've got your Selig, and you just don't understand. A woman needs a man, Becky! What kind of a life will I have without a man?"

Not that I credited the despair and the anguished desire in her voice. Such passion belonged to the beautiful ladies and the handsome gentlemen who moved about languidly and agelessly in the slick magazines and movies, not to men and women with haggard faces and disheveled hair, with children to bring up, livings to make, and gross physiological needs to satisfy. Enveloped thus in my adolescent romanticism. I was only remotely aware of Esther's dealings with her husband, just as I was remotely aware of the shifts in our sleeping and eating arrangements to accommodate

Esther and my two little cousins (aged eight and five, and contemporaries of my sister and brother) in our cramped apartment of five small, boxlike rooms; of the to-do every night as sofa and extra cot were made up; of the crowded, noisy kitchen table at meals. Somewhere the legal mill was grinding out a divorce for Esther, a divorce from a legendary Uncle Boris whom I had never met, but whom I knew to be an expert carpenter able to earn good money whenever caprice prompted, and whom I distinctly visualized (thanks to my mother's observations) as a selfish, sullen, spiteful, slippery, unscrupulous monster resembling Lon Chaney made up as the Hunchback of Notre Dame.

To me the machinery of the law seemed to creak along by fits and starts. However, that impression may merely have arisen from my own life, which was itself then all skips and jumps. Each morning I would ride the streetcars to the university to attend a hodgepodge of classes; at regular hours day and night I would hurry off to whatever odd job was paying my way through school; and I would then return home to attempt to study my assignments or to write my weekly theme amid the antics, giggles, and screeches of my sister and brother, now amplified by my two cousins. No wonder that I was blind to signs. And no wonder that my remembrance of those days is a succession of startling *tableaux vivants* separated by long blank stretches. Thus one evening, climbing the flight of stairs to our apartment after a typically checkered and confused day, I heard the door above open and my mother say: "No, it's not Selig, it's Sam."

I entered an unwonted silence to discover Esther walking round and round the center table of our front room, halting now and then to stare distraught into space. Finally she said: "Becky, I just can't wait any longer! I must go there! Please come with me!" Then with pleading eyes she turned to me, and for the first time I took note of gray glints in her hair. "Sam, maybe *you* would come with us too?"

Within a few minutes we were hurrying along Eddy Road to Arlington, and up 123rd Street toward Superior Avenue. I had assumed the defender's position on the outside; and Esther, who had in her trusting and affectionate manner taken my arm, was between my mother and me. It was already past seven o'clock, and the street lights, swaying on their suspension wires, cast yellow splotches down upon the settled dark. A cold, wet February wind from Lake Erie cut into our backs and whipped us on our way. We had our coats buttoned up to the throat. And as I lengthened my stride to keep up with Esther and my mother, whose high heels were tapping out their urgency on the stone slabs of the sidewalk, my heart beat fast with apprehension.

We scuttled along for several blocks before I was able to piece together what had happened and where we were headed. Through his lawyer, my Uncle Boris had requested to be allowed to enjoy the company of his two little daughters for the day. Esther had agreed, with the stipulation that the girls were to be back by five o'clock, in time for their supper; and she had delivered them to within a short distance of the Kaplan apartment, had pointed out the building, and had watched them enter it safely. But five o'clock had come, and no girls. Since in those days neither the Kaplans nor my family had a phone, there was no way of calling to learn what the trouble might be. My cousins had not gone prepared to spend the night; and as twilight had deepened into evening, Esther had grown more and more worried. Reluctant to come face to face with Boris and the Kaplans (a reluctance I was later to understand), and also fearful of unforeseen difficulties, she had waited from minute to minute in the hope that my father might come home to accompany her. When I had arrived instead, she had seized upon me as her knight-errant.

To my ears, however, there was one equivocal note in the account I had been given. Clearly something else chafed Esther besides the fact that Boris had broken his word and that her daughters, sans nightgown and toothbrush, might be spending the night in a strange house. For at one point she had interrupted my mother vehemently: "I know Boris would never think of doing anything like this. It's not like him. *She* must have put him up to it. Yes, *she's* the one behind the whole business!"

I had no time to ponder the mysterious *she*, nor the vehemence that shook Esther's voice. We had turned into one of the side streets leading east from 123rd. That neighborhood was then much more prosperous than now; and the Jews who dwelt there had climbed several rungs above us on the socioeconomic ladder. I was only slightly acquainted with those streets, the well-kept one-family houses perched on small, neat rectangles of lawn, the occasional new apartment building extravagantly named Waverly Arms, Kenilworth Arms, or Lancaster Arms. As we slowed down before one such bourgeois stronghold, Esther indicated a front apartment on the second floor. We entered a hallway paneled in marble veneer except for a brass inset of mail slots and buzzers, and there we consulted in whispers as though planning a surprise attack. "Now don't make any trouble," Esther cautioned me. "I don't want to have any trouble. Just go in there and tell them you've come to get the girls."

Luckily, someone had left the inner door unlocked, and there was no need to press the buzzer. Leaving Esther and my mother below, I went up the stairs and came to a door, the upper half of which had set into it a large square of glass with an elaborate fleur-de-lis in frostwork. I knocked, and the door opened. There before me stood a scrawny man of medium height, with a gray bony face, silver-rimmed glasses, and sloping shoulders, inconsequential figure in drooping trousers and rumpled shirt with the sleeves partly rolled up and the collar unbuttoned. I guessed instantly that this could not be my Uncle Boris and must be Mr. Kaplan. With a spurious boldness, I pushed past him and announced: "I have come for my two little cousins!"

I doubt that I would ever have got beyond the door if anyone else had answered my knock. But Mr. Kaplan was an emblem of indecision, a cipher with two blank circles of glass where his eyes should have been. His very clothes lacked spine, had no distinct pattern, shape, or color. Once I stepped into the room, however, I *was* abashed by the furnishings, which were of a degree of middle-class wealth I was not accustomed to. Underfoot was a thick rug, not the worn linoleum covering our floors. A plum-colored plush davenport was balanced by two squat matching armchairs. And wherever I glanced, small mahogany tables supported ornate lamps, all of them lavishly lighted. I record these details as a measure of my adolescent bravado while I struck a pose in the middle of that luxurious room, rigid with the determination not to disgrace myself by turning and running. Mr. Kaplan, I must add, standing there irresolutely and clasping his thin hairy hands, also seemed out of his natural habitat in the affluence of that room. Before he could summon up enough presence to speak, a woman (Mrs. Kaplan, I surmised) bustled in from a hallway that led to the other rooms of the apartment. She had a hard, fair-skinned face, decisively rouged; her blond hair was enameled into permanently fixed waves; and her opulent flesh overflowed a tight corset. In contrast to her husband, she was all dressed up (*ausgeputzt*, my mother would scornfully have said) in a dark-green satin dress, as if ready to go out for the evening. There was no irresolution about *her.* She walked directly to me, with a cold stare, and demanded in a harsh voice: "Who are you? What are you doing in my house?"

"I have come to get my cousins and take them home."

"They're asleep already," she said. "You can tell their mother we'll send them back in the morning." And she placed her hands flat against my chest and pushed me rudely toward the open door, which by chance my elbow caught and slammed shut, trapping me inside and forcing heroism upon me.

"I'm not going to leave without my cousins!" I declared in a high voice which I was unable to keep from quavering.

At that, I heard a deep basso say jocularly: "Aha! Aha! This must be my illustrious nephew."

I must confess that my Uncle Boris, who had come in from the hallway and whom I now saw for the first time, did not at all appear the sullen monster I had been led to expect. Legend and fact were plainly at odds. I realized suddenly how much I wanted to have a look at this man whom Esther still desired, this rival of mine for her attentions. To my discomfiture, he seemed jovial and pleasant, indeed, as I recognized, a good sport, the kind a woman might easily be taken with. A short, swarthy man with powerful chest and shoulders, he had a big head, almost bald, and heavy bluish jowls. His dark-brown eyes gave a sardonic cast to his face. His thick stubby hands bore the bruises and cuts of his work with hammer and chisel. What I had least expected, I think, was his smart dress. He was wearing trousers of a fine, flowing tan gabardine and a shirt of tan striped silk with a figured, expensive four-in-hand held in place by a gold tie-clip. All in all, he gave off the air of a man of the world, an air that thrust all my gauche and shabby adolescence back upon me. And as he rocked there on his feet and regarded me with amusement, he had the assurance not of a guest but of one completely at home. To this impression Mrs. Kaplan gave countenance by the softening of her voice and the possessive familiarity with which she turned to him. "Boris, I *told* him the girls are already in bed and we'll bring them back in the morning."

"But the agreement you made was to bring them back today!"

Boris laughed easily and said: "What's the rush, illustrious nephew? Where's the fire? Today? Tomorrow? What difference does it make?"

Just then my two cousins, having heard the disturbance, ran down the hallway and huddled in the entrance, their arms about each other, their frightened eyes staring at us. In their long winter woolens and barefooted, they appeared touchingly defenseless, like two little orphans in a sentimental calendar illustration.

"Go back and put your clothes on," I ordered them gently. "We're going home."

"They'll do nothing of the sort!" said Mrs. Kaplan, and again pushed me toward the door.

That push maddened me. Even more maddening was the sight of Boris standing there like a superior and unconcerned onlooker, smiling mockingly and seeming to enjoy the spectacle. Losing all sense for the chivalric, I pushed the offending woman away from me. Instantly, her husband intervened. "Now, young man, you ought not to do that," he said, and gave me a reproving shove. I shoved him in return, and for a minute we shoved each other back and forth, like two boys loath to begin with their fists. All the while I sensed (perhaps Mr. Kaplan did too) that we were both absurdly misdirecting our resentment. Finally, one shove caught me off balance. I stumbled against one of the small tables, overturning it and sending the lamp on it smashing to the floor. We halted in dismay and gazed down at the scattered shards of the pottery base. Then Mrs. Kaplan cried out angrily: "This really is too much! What a nerve! If you don't leave my house this minute, I'll call the police!"

When she once more put her hands on me and I slapped them away, a melee developed. A floor lamp toppled over with a crash, and my two cousins began to scream. Immediately there was a pounding at the door, and I heard my mother's voice: "Sam! Sam!" She banged her fists furiously at the ornamental pane and shattered it. For a moment we could see her anxious face framed in the jagged glass. Then the door swung open, and my mother rushed in, blood flowing from one wrist. Behind her came Esther. As soon as my cousins saw their mother, they ran to her with a cry of "Mamma! Mamma!" and she stooped and clutched them to her.

Facing the invading group theatrically, with arms akimbo, Mrs. Kaplan shouted: "What kind of hoodlums are these!"

But there was a false tonal quality to her outcry. Despite the invasion of her home, despite the overturned lamps and broken glass, she did not seem displeased. And now she sprang with a flourish at Esther and tried to tear the girls from her. They shrieked again and clung to their mother, who straightened up and glared at Mrs. Kaplan, while Boris stood off to one side and looked upon those two women, his silk shirt and gabardine trousers glowing sleekly in the lamplight, his lips relishing a complacent smile. At that moment a triangle outlined itself before my eyes, as if heavy pencil strokes had been drawn from one corner to another, pencil strokes that quaked with an intense emotion. The rest of us receded and faded into the background. I realized that I was an intruder in a relationship which I did not fully comprehend and in which (to my mortification) I did not count. At last Mr. Kaplan, whose dim presence I had forgotten, said in a sick voice: "Oh, let them go, Anna! Let them go!"

"Well, they can't go like that," Boris said dryly, and he went back down the hallway, soon to return carrying a pile of dresses, stockings, shoes, coats, and hats. Esther grabbed the jumble of clothes from him, and our party ran out, with me holding up the rear. Mrs. Kaplan kept pushing at me gratuitously and clamoring a counterfeit alarm: "Hoodlums! Hoodlums!" As we plunged down the stairs, I could hear doors opening elsewhere in the building. The brazen stagy voice pursued us out into the street: "Hoodlums! Hoodlums! Hoodlums!"

As I strode along that dark side street back toward 123rd at the head of my little troop, I was the victorious knight-errant, carrying off my two cousins from their wicked captivity. What wrenched me back to actuality was the appalled look on the face of a passer-by fixed momentarily in the light from a house. I stopped short, and glanced back. It was no triumphant troop I was leading. On the contrary, it was a demoralized little band that straggled in and out of the patches of light. Esther was hurrying frantically, with the jumble of clothes clutched under her arm, and hauling the five-year-old behind her by one hand. My small cousin was still in her long woolen underwear and barefooted, as was her older sister, who ran whimpering after them. And far to the rear trailed my mother, pressing a handkerchief to her wrist, and pausing to examine it at each patch of light.

The shocked face of the passer-by must have brought the same realization to Esther. For she halted abruptly in her flight and turned up one of the walks leading to the steps of a front porch. She sat both of the girls on the bottom step and, kneeling on the cold stone before them, wiped their bare feet with her handkerchief. Then while I stood by and watched, she quickly began to dress the younger girl, leaving the older to dress herself. By the faint light flowing from the windows of the house, I could see that the girls were shivering in the damp night air. It was a most haphazard putting on of clothes, accomplished with impatient tugs, slaps, and yanks. The long black ribbon cotton stockings were drawn up over lumps and bunchings of the woolen underwear, so that my cousins appeared to be suffering from some malformation of the leg bones. The dresses, slipped on hastily over their heads, were left to hang wrinkled and awry. Shoes, coats, and hats clumsily jerked on completed the scarecrow silhouettes. But at least the shivering girls had some shield against the sharp wind. And all the while, Esther talked nervously and distractedly: "Here, let me have the other foot. Just imagine, trying to keep the girls there all night! And after he gave his word! No, wait a minute, we've got this backwards. What a fool that Boris is! What an absolute fool! How can he see anything in her? That *ausgeputzte* cow! Becky, did you see her dyed hair? Oh my, there's a knot in this shoelace. Did you see her, Becky? That woman *wanted* to make trouble. Here, give me your arm. Where's the sleeve? Well, if she's so anxious to have that prize package of a Boris, she's welcome to him!"

Whatever Esther may have felt, my own feeling at that moment, I recall, was one of chagrin at the renewed revelation that very likely I had been an unwitting pawn in the hands of Mrs. Kaplan. Apparently she had premeditated detaining the girls beyond the agreed hour and had deliberately provoked the fracas, even as she was pretending outrage. But then, I realized, she could not have known about *me*. It was Esther whose reactions she had foreseen step by step, in fact, had probably *counted* on. And with a pang I remembered how inadequate, even paltry, Esther had looked in her drab gray coat facing that rouged, enameled, determined woman sheathed in green satin. Certainly chagrin now vibrated in her voice as she went on: "Yes, Becky, she wanted it this way! She had it all worked out! Well, she needn't be afraid that I'm going to have a change of heart! She can keep that gift to the ladies for all I care! Oh, Becky, Becky, what am I going to *do* now?" Only then was it that she, and I too, became aware of how silent my mother had been; and looking around, we saw her standing off in the outer darkness. Esther sprang up. "Becky, what's the matter?"

"There's something wrong with my wrist."

"Oh, Becky, Becky!" Esther cried. "All I'm good for is to bring trouble! Come over here in the light."

My mother obeyed, and we clustered around her as she removed the blood-soaked handkerchief, to uncover a ragged wound just above the wrist bones. Even in that dim light we could see the blackish pulp of torn bloody flesh out of which fresh blood oozed. I suppose that my mother and I might have stood there forever in helpless paralyzed fascination. But Esther said: "We've got to get home right away and take care of this." And grasping my mother's arm, she led the way quickly to 123rd Street, while I hastened after them with my whimpering cousins, tugging each along by a hand. We were a subdued little band as, leaning into the wind, we retraced our steps back home. Esther's words of self-reproach were carried back to me: "Why did I have to do this to you, Becky? All my life I've been a *schlimmazel*. I shouldn't bring my troubles and my bad luck into other people's lives. Oh, let that woman have her way! Tomorrow I'm going to see the lawyer and have him get it all over with. Why should I keep on with that Boris! I'll just pack my girls and my troubles and go back to Boston, and you won't have to have me around your neck."

And as I hurried along, my heart ached for Esther in her admission of defeat. Yes, perhaps she was a *schlimmazel*, the kind of person who never gets the breaks. But what exactly were the breaks? Were they crumbs thrown to you by the Great God Chance? Or was it a matter of pressing ahead recklessly? Obviously, Esther had not been equal to the struggle, and

"that woman" was having her way. I saw again, and vividly, the three sides
of the triangle—Boris, standing complacent, confident, knowing he couldn't
lose; Esther, already lost in the resolution of forces, bent out of her direct
path by irrelevant concerns; and Mrs. Kaplan, like a sword thrust, feinting to
expose the vulnerability of others, pitiless in satisfying her desires. That
woman's boldness, her blond polish, and a quality of ripeness in her at once
repelled and attracted me. Clearly she exerted a pull on men. (Or was it
that she simply enforced her demands?) And clearly, whether it was a driving appetite or a philosophy of life (this is it, there will be no other, while
the heedless earth bowls down the ecliptic), she seized upon every advantage with the ruthlessness that we generally reserve for games like poker
or handball. No doubt about it. She was playing at life for keeps.

This rudimentary ethical speculation actually was then a mere jumble
in my head. Before I could do much disentangling, we were back at last
in our apartment, where we were greeted anxiously by my father, who had
already sent my sister and brother to bed. Somehow, with many interrup-
tions, and much backing and filling, the story of the night's adventures got
itself told, while my mother's wrist was washed out and bandaged, and my
cousins were undressed, bathed, and put to bed. By then it was past ten
o'clock. It seemed to me not three hours but three lifetimes since we had
set out for the Kaplans'. I felt as though I were awakening from a series of
nightmares which I still had to quell and reduce to normalcy. However, I
was allowed no time for such putting of my emotions into order. A shock
was yet in store. My parents, Esther, and I had settled around the kitchen
table to drink some coffee and rehash the night's events, when the bell rang
and we heard heavy footsteps climbing the stairs. My father and I went to
the door together. There stood a policeman, in a navy-blue overcoat, and
officer's cap. "Does Sam Yellen live here?" he asked.

My father replied: "Yes, he does. What's the trouble, Officer?"

"I have a summons for him. Breaking and entering and assault and
battery."

"Well," said my father. Then he waved a hand toward me and assumed
a jocose tone. "Well, here is your dangerous criminal."

The policeman handed me a folded official-looking paper and, probably
in deference to my scared face, said rather gently: "You're to be at the
Prosecutor's office in the Central Police Station at nine in the morning.
Now, you be sure to show up."

I took the paper, and the policeman started back down the stairs. The
summons lay like a brittle object in the palm of my hand. I turned to find
Esther staring at me with stricken eyes from the kitchen doorway. My attempt at a smile of reassurance must have been dismaying. For my father
spoke up, trying to make light of the affair: "What's there to be so upset
about? All right, so we have a criminal in the family! So what?"

"That woman just won't let us alone!" cried Esther. And her eyes held me,
begging forgiveness. And somewhere within me, underneath the layers of

apprehension, stirred a sense of triumph over Boris, triumph at having pushed him out of her heart, if only for a moment.

The next morning, with an inner quaking, and pale for lack of sleep, I found myself at the Central Police Station in a large waiting room with three small offices opening off one end. Despite the sun at the grimy scraps of window, the room was gloomy and depressing. The walls were painted a dark brown, the wooden floor was worn and splintered, and the furniture consisted of many straight wooden chairs and a battered table at which presided a uniformed policeman. I was facing my ordeal by myself. My mother, her hand having throbbed all night, was off to see our family doctor. My father had had to go about his usual business of earning the daily bread. The children were left at home under the supervision of a neighbor, while Esther was to join me as soon as possible with her lawyer. In fact, my sole immediate support was a French grammar which I carried partly to review for an examination scheduled for the next day but more to suggest nonchalance (unconvincing, I am sure).

Even though it was not yet nine o'clock, about two dozen persons were already sitting in chairs backed against the walls. Clearly, like me, these were ordinary people wondering at finding themselves in this place. However, after nine o'clock, others came in, the more hardened pickings of the previous night's scrapes, men and women accompanied by lawyers carrying briefcases and greeted familiarly by the policeman at the table. It was nine thirty before the presiding officer began to call out the names of persons who were directed into one or another of the three small offices, where apparently they were dealt with by the assistant prosecutors. Just about that time I was startled to see Boris enter the waiting room together with the Kaplans. Again I was struck by the smart appearance my uncle made in a dark-blue cashmere overcoat with a black-velvet collar. Mrs. Kaplan, also very smart in a fashionable coat of black caracul, walked into the room with an assured air. But Mr. Kaplan still seemed as rumpled and as inconsequential dressed up as the night before in his shirtsleeves. All three recognized me, and Boris half greeted me with a sardonic nod. Making an elaborate play of ignoring them, I opened my French grammar.

I was not permitted to grow weary of my self-imposed dumb show. In a few minutes I heard my name called, coupled with that of Anna Kaplan. Starting up, I followed the Kaplans and Boris into the office toward which the policeman motioned us. Behind an old desk, its varnish peeling and its top littered with papers, sat a middle-aged man with a tired, lined face, who, continuing to study a sheet of notations before him, indicated chairs for us. Then he looked up and, without preliminaries, asked: "Sam Yellen?" I raised my hand like a schoolboy.

"Anna Kaplan?"

Mrs. Kaplan said: "Yes."

"And these others?"

"My husband and a friend. They're my witnesses."

The prosecutor nodded. "I see there was a little trouble last night. Now, Mrs. Kaplan, suppose you tell me what happened."

"Well," she began, "we were quietly at home when for no reason at all this young hoodlum broke into our apartment and started fighting and knocking over my furniture and smashing my lamps and—"

Almost involuntarily I cried out: "Why, that's a lie!"

The prosecutor silenced me with an expression of great weariness. "Just let her tell her story, son. You'll get your turn later."

Fortunately, at that moment Esther came in, accompanied by her lawyer. "Good morning, Jim," he said.

"Why, hello, Jake," said the prosecutor.

"Can I see you a minute about this case?"

"Sure thing." And the prosecutor got up and walked out with the lawyer into the waiting room, where I could see them consulting.

Esther took a chair next to mine. In the bleak morning light she looked haggard and untidy, and I recall noticing that there was a snarl in her hair and that her slip was showing unevenly below her dress. She appeared bruised in spirit and avoided looking at anyone but me. For a full minute Mrs. Kaplan stared at her with a provoking disdain, and then turned ostentatiously to Boris: "Think of dragging those two sweet little girls out into the street barefooted like gypsies! What kind of a mother would do that!"

A shadow of pain fell across Esther's face, and I was ready to reply to that taunt. But Esther put a restraining hand on my arm. "Let her talk, Sam. It doesn't matter." And then she lifted her eyes to Boris with a look of reproach that brought the blood to his swarthy face. Again, as on the preceding night, I had the sensation of fading into the background while Esther, Boris, and Mrs. Kaplan came forward into bold relief, joined as if with steel cables in a triangle of concealed passions.

Before anything further could be said, the prosecutor approached the door and beckoned to Mrs. Kaplan and to Esther. "I'd like to have you come into this next office for a minute," he said. Then as an afterthought, he turned to Boris. "I guess you'd better come along too." Mr. Kaplan also started up, but the prosecutor motioned him back. "No, no, we won't need you."

I was left alone in that small office with Mr. Kaplan, who sat hunched forward in his chair, his tiny hairy hands between his knees, his eyes invisible behind the reflection of the silver-rimmed glasses. However, occupied with my own welter of thoughts, I was hardly conscious of him. Even though I knew that I should have been boning up on my French, I was unable to put my mind to it. Suddenly I became aware that Mr. Kaplan was speaking, and in fact was speaking to *me*. "Did you hear him, young man? *No, no, we won't need you.* They won't need me. You think maybe I don't know it?"

1 thought to myself, Why, he's in it too! He's another one! The *fourth* side of the triangle! And as I looked at him closely, he moved into focus

out of a flat vague background. He was wearing an Oxford-gray overcoat in need of pressing. He had placed his hat on a nearby chair, and his dry sparse hair fell upon a furrowed and veined forehead. But the chief impression I got was of a face as gray as a face in an etching.

"Yes, young man, you see one of God's unfortunates before you. You think I don't know what has been going on right under my nose? But what can I do? That woman! I love her and I'm afraid of her. Can you believe that, young man? But at your age, how little you understand of what goes on in the heart! And I've been a good husband. I've made a good living. No wife could complain. You saw that fur coat she was wearing? Persian lamb. That cost a pretty penny. What kind of a man is that uncle of yours? To walk right into a house and take away your wife! If only she would stay here with me. But I know she's going to run away with him. Something has got into her, and she won't listen to anything. They're just waiting for this divorce. And she's got all our savings in her name. More than five thousand dollars! Can you believe that, young man? But I would gladly give him the money if he would go away and leave me my Anna. You think maybe I don't know how people laugh at me? But what will I do without her? Tell me, what will I do? I might just as well stick my head in the kitchen stove and turn on the gas."

As I listened to his grotesque mixture of Yiddish and English, I stared at him, horribly embarrassed, and yet compelled by a binding spell. He took his glasses off, and groped under his overcoat in his trousers pocket for a handkerchief. He had eyes after all, faded blue eyes, weak and misty. And, held motionless, I observed two big tears roll down over the lower lids and course along the lines deeply etched in that face. He looked into my eyes and shook his head. "Yes, young man, I've lost her. I don't know how I'm going to get along. I've lost her. I've lost her."

His cry of finality echoed in my head. And sitting in that dingy office, I was shaken out of my self-centered adolescence. Suddenly I knew he was speaking for me too, and for everyone. All of life was loss. Remembering the look of reproach which Esther had given Boris and the flush it had raised in his face, I knew that I too had lost, that she would certainly leave Cleveland, and me, now that she no longer had her Boris. Yes, I too had been cast aside. Did I say a triangle has *four* sides? I should have said *five*.

Thomas Dabney Mabry
The Vault

WE NEVER DROVE OUT TO THE OLD City Graveyard except to Memorial Day
Exercises. It was down by the river on the edge of town where the niggers
lived and nobody was buried there any more. The soldiers were buried
there, and Indian Bill, and a parcel of babies they found on the Court House
steps, but nobody else.

It's a right pretty old place, Mamma said. I wish we drove out here
oftener.

Papa was already waiting in the car. Mamma handed me the empty
flower basket and turned round for a minute, shading her eyes with her
handkerchief. Then I opened the door for her and she got in the back seat.
I got in front with Papa and held the basket.

Wait for Sister, Mamma said.

Papa backed over on the grass to let some of the other cars get by, and
waited for Sister.

You can't compare it to Shady Grove Cemetery, he said.

The flat graves were on a steep hillside, covered mostly with pines that
had been planted. There weren't many tombstones, just metal markers, and
the scattered little flags that our class had stuck in the ground that morning
before the Exercises began looked like they'd been lost in the grass by somebody on a picnic.

It couldn't have been a nicer day for it, Mamma said.

Sister got in and Papa coasted slow down to the entrance gate, by the
river. At the gate we turned left, out around the Confederate Monument.
It was a tall column with some piled-up cannonballs at the foot. On top of
the column was a stone soldier.

Lean your head out the car, said Papa, and holler up and ask him what
he's doing up there. He'll answer you and say Nothing at all.

I wouldn't lean out but Sister did. She leaned out and hollered up. Papa laughed but Mamma and I didn't.

We drove on back along the dusty River Road toward town. On the right was a line of nigger houses, their yards lower than the road. The river was close behind the houses and the glisten hurt your eyes as it came and went between them. I looked out the left side. It was still the Graveyard but there wasn't any fence along here, and not many graves, just weeds. In the corner, next to the old Hackett place, was the vault. I had seen it lots of times before on my bicycle. It was right next to the road. It had its own gate to the road.

What's that little stone house, Mamma, said Sister.

That's the vault, I said.

What's it for, Sister said.

For dead people, I said. A rich lady is buried there right now.

I'll bet she's not, said Sister.

Isn't she, Mamma, I said.

I don't know about the rich part, Mamma said. Old Patrick Henry Smith was supposed to have built it for his wife who died soon after they were married. The story when I was a young girl was that when he put her in there he locked the door and threw the key in Clinch River. Then he left town and never did come back.

Slayden Dinwiddie says he buried her with rings on her fingers, I said.

Why did he do that, Sister said.

People are often buried with their wedding rings, said Mamma. It's a matter of sentiment.

Slayden says there were lots of rings, I said.

How can you believe such a story, Papa said.

Whereabouts did he throw the key in, I said.

Right along here somewhere I guess, Mamma said.

Didn't anybody ever find it, I said.

It's just some trumped-up story, Papa said.

There must have been another key, said Sister.

Slayden Dinwiddie says there wasn't but that one key, I said.

I looked out the car again at the nigger houses on the right. From the road it looked like their back steps were sticking in the water.

You suppose he threw it in from here, I said.

He could have, Mamma said. Anywhere along here. It was a long time ago.

At the corner we turned sharp left up the long hill away from the river.

That nicotine factory smells terribly, said Mamma. It's totally ruined this end of town.

It was ruined before they built the nicotine factory, Papa said. You know as well as I do there's been nothing but nigger cabins and white trash along here since we were children.

We went into second up the hill and passed the old Hackett place. One of the front-porch columns was propped up with a beam. There were cracks in the unpainted rusty brick you could see from the road. A little girl with white hair sat on the top porch step holding a baby. She looked at us as we drove by.

It was not quite ruined, Mamma said. The old Hackett place used to be lovely. I can remember going to parties there, and in the halls the walls had Italian scenes painted on them. Mrs. Hackett was supposed to have blue carnations in her garden.

Nobody ever heard of blue carnations, Papa said.

Let's stop, Mamma, said Sister, and go in the garden. Maybe they're still there.

Certainly not, Papa said.

We drove on home.

After dinner I went into the sitting room and started reading *Raffles* where I'd had to leave off that morning before school. Mamma came in. She came over and put her arm around me.

Don't you think you'd better do a little practising, Son, since you don't have to go back to school this afternoon? You have your lesson tomorrow.

I went into the parlor and started practising. It was the *andante cantabile* from the Pathétique Sonata. I couldn't play the fast movement. After a while I heard Papa come out into the hall and take his hat off the hatrack. I played softer but I knew he was going to stop. The folding doors were almost closed, but he pushed one side open.

Why don't you get out of the house some time, Papa said. You're going to grow to that piano stool.

Mamma said for me to practise, I said.

No boy ought to want to stay in the house all the time, Papa said.

I looked at the music on the music rack. You said you wouldn't mind if I took music lessons, I said. I remember you said you wouldn't mind when Mamma asked you last winter.

Papa stepped inside the parlor. He stood there like the parlor was the wrong place to be in.

It's not a question of minding, he said.

Right next to the end of the piano was a window. There was a little torn place in one of the lace curtains and I could see through it clear down the street as far as the Catholic Church.

All you do is sit at that piano, Papa said. Either that or stay up there in your room. Any other boy would want to get out. You know why you've got all those pimples.

I didn't look at Papa, and he walked back to the door.

If you don't want me to take piano lessons, I said. If you mean it costs too much and you don't want to spend the money.

You know what I mean, Papa said.

He went out and shut the door, and then I heard him open the front door and shut it behind him. It was cool in the house because most of the windows were closed and the blinds pulled to. I couldn't practise any more. It was like Papa was still standing there, and the piano was different from what it had been. I went up to my room and lay down on the bed. I knew what he meant but it wasn't true because I hadn't been doing it for a long time. Because I had tried to stop. Six months ago I had written in my Algebra book on every other page to the last page in the book "It will drive you crazy," and I hadn't been doing it for a long time.

He said I could take piano lessons. I remember when Mamma asked him. If I just had some money I would give it to him. I would say Here's a lot more money than my piano lessons ever cost. If I had a thousand dollars I'd take it out of my pocket and give it to him and say It isn't true what you said, I haven't been doing it for a long time. I know it isn't true.

I got up and looked at my face in the window pane. It looked better than it did in the mirror. I began thinking: If old Patrick Henry Smith had gone away and never come back. There wasn't but that one key, but even if he'd had another key he had gone away and never come back. If there was jewelry and rings inside they'd still be there. Because the river was deep behind the nigger houses and that key would never come up. It was down on the bottom lost in the thick bottom mud. All those rings and jewelry would still be inside that vault. They'd still be shining, locked away in there.

I went downstairs and out into the back yard. From our back fence I could see them playing ball in the vacant lot over on Madison Street. Slayden Dinwiddie was getting all wound up to throw one of his curves, and everybody was standing around with their mouth open so a fly could fly in, except me. I was down behind our fence where they couldn't see me and I was thinking of a vault full of rings and jewelry, and about something else that would just about have scared Slayden Dinwiddie to death.

I climbed up onto the roof of the chicken house and from there climbed up into the apple tree. All the petals had dropped off and the little apples were starting to grow, about as big as shoe buttons. I sat there a long time.

When I came back in the house it was almost supper time. Mamma was in the sitting room. She had on her nice pair of glasses and smelled sweet. She was playing Russian Bank with Sister. I went over and put my hand on the back of her chair.

I've been wondering where you were, said Mamma. Your father will be home pretty soon and he's bringing company to supper. You'd better go wash your face and brush your hair. Then go in the parlor and play me something I like to hear.

Who's Papa bringing to supper, Mamma, said Sister.

I think he's some nice man from Europe who wants to buy some tobacco from your father, said Mamma.

After I had finished doing what she said I went into the parlor. I played some things by ear and then I played the piece I'd made up. I called it The Sand Storm. I had got to the loud part and didn't hear Papa. He switched on the lights. There was a man with him.

You can't see in the dark. Come in Mr. Wooters. This is my son, Papa said.

He's quite a musician, the man said.

Son go tell your mother Mr. Wooters is here, Papa said.

I went to the sitting room to tell Mamma. She was already smoothing her hair. I'll be right in, she said.

I stayed in the sitting room.

Mamma says he is a foreigner, said Sister. What does he look like?

He looks like a foreigner, I said. Sort of short, and bald. He was smiling and he had a yellow moustache.

I'll bet he talks funny. I won't be able to stand it if he talks funny, she said.

He said I was a musician, I said.

I was thinking that maybe if he thought I was a musician he might want to hear me play some more. He had come in the parlor when I was right in the middle of The Sand Storm, and Papa didn't let me finish.

We played Russian Bank until supper.

I knew it was going to be a company supper because I had seen Ulus freezing ice cream out the back. He had on a clean white coat now, but the sleeves were too long for him. His right sleeve came halfway down over his thumb as he waited on the table. He called each of our names as he passed the biscuits, and it always did sound funny. He'd start with Mamma and say Will you have a biscuit Miss Edith? And then go all the way around the table. Sister was sitting next to Mr. Wooters, and Ulus said Will you have a biscuit Sister, but he didn't know Mr. Wooters' name so he just said Will you have a biscuit Mister.

I touched Sister's foot with my foot under the table and she started laughing. Papa looked at me.

Will you have some more meat Mr. Wooters, he said.

Oh no thank you, Mr. Wooters said.

Let me give you some more potatoes Mr. Wooters, Mamma said.

Oh no thank you, I have a great deal, a great deal, Mr. Wooters said.

I don't believe you Belgiums eat as much as we do over here, said Papa.

I am afraid you are right, sir, said Mr. Wooters, but I really have still a great deal on my plate.

Won't you have some more butter then, Mamma said.

Thank you I will have a little more butter, Mr. Wooters said. Then he looked at the wall over my head. I am admiring that very pretty picture, he said. I have seen the original in the museum in Paris.

You have? I said. Is it bigger than this one?

My son gave me this one on my last birthday, Mamma said, smiling at me. Only last month.

He shows very good taste, Mr. Wooters said. It is much bigger than this one, he said turning to me. Do you like pictures?

Yes sir, I said.

You are a very talented boy, he said. You like pictures and you play the piano.

I tried to take a bite but I couldn't. Maybe if I played some more for Mr. Wooters he might take me with him to a foreign country and I could learn to be a musician like Beethoven and I would pay Papa a thousand dollars. I would send him a thousand-dollar check. I took a bite. Then I said, if you want me to, I'll play for you after supper.

Mr. Wooters would rather play a game of cards, said Papa, than hear you play the piano. You better change your mind Mr. Wooters and let me give you another helping of meat.

Mr. Wooters wouldn't take another helping of meat so we had the ice cream. Then he wouldn't take any more ice cream so we got up from the table. They walked down the hall toward the parlor.

You better go get your lessons, Papa said to Sister and me. We were standing in the hall by the parlor doors.

Let him play one piece for Mr. Wooters, Mamma said.

They sat down in the parlor. Sister came in too and went over to the window and pressed her nose against the pane. The bright lights from the chandelier made the keys fly up at me. I played the *andante cantabile*. I was hot and I felt my pants sticking to the varnish on the piano stool. Sometimes it came off in damp weather. My fingers were slippery and wet. When I finished Mr. Wooters said, You are a very talented boy.

Now you better go get your lessons, said Papa, unfolding a card table. You too, Sister.

We went into the sitting room. Sister sat down on the floor with her books. I didn't have any English and Latin to get, just Algebra, and Spelling. Tomorrow's lesson was on an even-numbered page. "It will drive you crazy" it said on top in pencil. Papa was wrong, I thought, to say what he said. It isn't true because I haven't been, not for a long time. But he had pushed open the parlor door that afternoon and said that about my face. He had stood there with his straw hat in his hand, his nose tight at the sides and his mouth tight, and he acted like he didn't want to be in the parlor or anywhere near the parlor. I didn't dare think it but I thought it, he hates me, I thought, I know he hates me. He said I could take piano lessons last winter. I remember when he said it.

I finished my Algebra and Spelling. When Sister was finished too, we played a game of Dominoes.

I know what would be fun, she said. Let's scare them.

You mean put a tic-tac on the house? That wouldn't scare them, I said. They've heard that before. Slayden Dinwiddie put one on the house last week.

I don't mean that or anything like that, she said. I've thought of something a hundred times better than that.

What is it, I said.

Well, she said, let's tell them goodnight like we always do, and then go on up stairs. Then we'll turn out the light in our rooms. Then you go in and get under their bed before they come up stairs. Then when they get in bed you make a noise and I'll yell and we'll both scare them at the same time.

All right, I said. I didn't think it would scare them much but maybe if I could make Mamma laugh and holler the way I could every now and then,

Papa would stop hating me. But I didn't think he would. I really didn't think that would make him stop hating me at all. But I wanted to make her laugh once more before I went to get the jewelry and rings. Because Mr. Wooters was not going to take me to Belgium with him to study music so I could send Papa a thousand-dollar check. I'd have to pay him back the other way.

So we told them goodnight and went up stairs. And after I had stood around a few minutes I turned out the light in my room and went in and got under their bed in the dark. I lay there and thought it would be fun to scare them if it did scare them and maybe Mamma would laugh and I could see her laughing.

A long time passed and nothing happened. Then all of a sudden the light was on and I was awake and I saw Papa's bare feet moving near the bed. Papa was talking.

But didn't you see the way he acted in front of Mr. Wooters tonight? I was downright embarrassed, I heard Papa say. Every time I come in the house he's sitting on that blame piano stool. Why don't he get out and play like an ordinary boy? Hasn't he got any friends?

He doesn't seem to know very many boys of his own age, Mamma said, but Mrs. Pickering told me yesterday that he was her most talented pupil. You remember agreeing last winter to let him take lessons.

I felt the blood rushing to my head and I couldn't breathe.

Well it's making a damn sissy out of him, I heard Papa say. He'll grow up into another Henry Harrison and be making doll clothes next.

Oh we can't let him do that. He won't do that, Mamma said, and I wasn't sure if she was crying.

What's that noise, Papa said.

It's under the bed, Mamma said. Aren't you going to look and see what it is?

I tried not to make any noise. I could feel Papa leaning over but I couldn't see his face from where I lay. Then, after what seemed like a long time I heard Papa say, No, I'm going to wait and see what it is.

I couldn't stand it there any longer. I crawled and sort of wriggled out from under the bed, and when I got out I felt like I was naked but I had all my clothes on, even my shoes. I couldn't look at Papa. I looked at Mamma. She was sitting far off, over by the window on the shoe box, and I was kneeling in the middle of the room under the electric light.

You ought to know better than to crawl under your mother's bed like a two-year-old child, Papa said. Stand up.

He was in his underwear and standing very close to me, holding his pants on his arm. I looked over at Mamma. But I couldn't get over there. It was too far. The electric light held me in the middle of the rug. If I fell down I couldn't fall that far. Then her hand was on my head, and the light wasn't shining in my face any more, and my head was in her lap.

There now, Mamma said. Hush. It'll be all right. Hush now.

I didn't know what to do. I couldn't look at Papa. I wanted to tell Mamma he hated me. I had to tell her that he hated me, but I couldn't tell her.

I'll try to do better, I remember saying.

Of course you will, Mamma said. Hush now.

I felt her hands on my shoulders, and then in a minute my hand was in her warm dry hands and I felt her ring, her round gold ring and the other hard rings that stood up from her fingers.

Of course you will, Mamma said again.

Here, Papa said, get up and stand up. There's no sense in crying about it.

He'll be all right, won't you Son, Mamma said, and she looked at Papa. Your father didn't mean to hurt your feelings.

Papa went over to the bureau where his watch and watch fob and his money and collar were. Here, take this, he said.

He handed me a dollar. It felt heavy in my hand.

Kiss me goodnight again Son, said Mamma.

I went over and kissed her.

Now go on to your room and go to bed, said Papa, and don't ever do a fool thing like crawling under your mother's bed again.

I went to my room.

I went to my room and my legs stood up like sticks and my hands kept twitching. My lips felt hot but I couldn't feel them when I touched them with my fingers. My tongue and my mouth were dry but I was wet all over. I stood in the middle of my room with the light on, and I filled it to the corners, I squeezed out against the bureau, against my desk, against my initials carved on the desk, against the window pane and my initials I had cut in the pane with a glass cutter. I thought, I've got to do it now. I've got to. Then my knees could move again and I sat down on the bed. My hand was hanging open and the dollar glinted in my palm so I stood up and put the dollar on my desk, and I sat down at my desk. I took my flashlight out of the letters pigeonhole and my roll of tape out of the little drawer. I fixed some of the tape over the glass so all the beam wouldn't show when I turned the flashlight on. I went over to my bed and took the pillow out of the pillow slip and laid the pillow on the floor by the window. I got the hammer and screwdriver out of my tool chest in the closet and I put the flashlight and hammer and screwdriver on the pillow by the window. I opened the window and leaned my head out: I heard the darkness humming but I couldn't see anything through the soft black air. Then I turned out the light and went back to my desk and sat down again and looked at my radium dial watch propped against the brick I used for a paperweight. I wanted to sleep more than anything else but I had to go now. There wasn't anything else I could do, I had to. I rested my head on my arms.

I thought maybe I ought to go tell Sister that I hadn't been able to make the noise. I opened my door and listened. The light was out in the hall and there wasn't any light shining from under Mamma's door. I pulled off my shoes and tiptoed across the hall to Sister's open door. She must have been asleep because I heard her slow breathing. I guess she must have fallen asleep even before they'd come upstairs. But I didn't want her to think I had forgotten all about her and making the noise. I tiptoed back to my room and got my radium dial watch, and brought it back to Sister's room and put it on her dress in the chair. It was eleven-thirty.

The floor of the hall, over near the stairs, creaked when you stepped on it, so I had to go close to Mamma and Papa's door each time. I kept thinking that Papa must feel me passing their door. It wasn't true what he said. I hadn't been, not for a long time, not for six months, not since I wrote in my Algebra book. But he wouldn't believe me. I knew he wouldn't believe me.

I strapped the pillow and screwdriver and hammer on with my belt, and put the flashlight in my pocket. Its beam would flash up those jewels and rings hidden away safe where old Patrick Henry Smith had locked them up and left them, and gone away and never come back. They'd been safe inside that vault all these years.

I stepped out the window onto the flat tin roof over the back porch. It was easy climbing down because I had done it before. I slid down over the edge at the corner where the gutter went down and the back porch lattice braced my feet. Then I let go and dropped down on the walk that went along the side of the house. I went around to the front porch and got my bicycle. I left the dollar Papa had given me in the middle of the top step. Then I pushed my bicycle out the drive to the street.

I felt the night air in my armpits and against my ribs as I coasted down Main, cut over on Seventh and hit Delafield heading toward the river. It was black dark and the hanging corner lights scarcely came through the new branched leaves of the trees overhead. It seemed like my bicycle slid through the air, invisible and noiseless, except in the brief hanging dome of light as Delafield hit Sixth, then Fifth, then Fourth on down, always down, to the River Road.

I coasted across First and stood on my brake all the way down the long hill past the old Hackett place. The nicotine factory was black and silent, and the shadows on the narrow porches of the nigger houses were so black deep I couldn't tell whether anybody was up and sitting there or not.

I got off my bicycle in front of the vault and walked up the path to the gate. A dog barked from one of the nigger houses, and then another started up, and that made me feel better. They sounded sort of scared, and I knew they were lifting their heads and sniffing my smell and the night, but not getting up, not curious enough to get up and walk out into the road and sniff, just curious enough to raise their heads and then drop them back down under the edge of the house and stretch out in the dust to go back to sleep. All the time I walked up the path I kept thinking about that morning when we drove back to town and how the puffy dust rose in the sunlight to settle back down on the niggers' flower beds. I could see those daylight ruts in the road as I pushed open the gate and walked the few steps through the tall weeds to the vault door. It was smooth and cool and I could barely see some bars that made a small window. A little coolness came out from be-

hind the bars. I felt the doorhandle and a chain, so I flashed on my flashlight. It made a small thread of light and I saw that the chain was loose
and the lock was broken. I pushed open the door.

I couldn't see anything until I pulled off the tape I had stuck on the
flashlight. The stone walls glistened like they were wet. The stone ceiling
was right on top of me. On one side was a long stone table and on that was
a long-locking box. I went over and touched it: it was iron.

But I couldn't get the top off. It was screwed on. I took the screwdriver
and unscrewed all the screws around the edge. It took a good while. Then
I dragged the top off and rested it on the ground against the table. I was
afraid I'd made some noise so I went to the door and listened, but I didn't
hear anything.

I flashed on the flashlight and looked at the box: I had taken off only
the first top, because what I saw then was another top. Half of it was glass.
I rubbed off the dirt with my arm and tried to look in: I couldn't see very
well but I could see that something was inside.

I leaned over and picked my pillow up. I put it on the glass and hit it
as hard as I could, but it wouldn't break. I didn't know what to do. My
knees ached and the air was oozing up from the damp ground like in a
cave. The air was full of damp and smelled like an old cellar. I flashed my
flashlight over my head and it seemed like the ceiling was getting closer. If
Papa hadn't said that to Mamma, if he hadn't told all that to her maybe I
could have forgotten what he said to me even though it wasn't true and he
said himself I could take piano lessons. But he said that to Mamma and I
had to know. I leaned over and studied the glass. It was screwed down with
a metal rim. I took my screwdriver again and unscrewed all those screws.
I thought my fingers were going to come off: they kept slipping and sliding
on the screwdriver. I counted ten screws but there was more than that. I
kept on unscrewing them. I'd pay him back for those piano lessons. I'd
pay him back twice as much, three times as much.

I unscrewed the last screw, and lifted the glass off. It wasn't like the
skeleton they had in the case in biology class. The bones were sort of separated and half covered up in a lot of dust and trash. I could make out
where the head was though. I tried to figure out where the hands would be
if they'd been folded like I'd heard they always folded dead people's
hands, and I dug my own fingers down in that place; but it didn't feel like
bones, it felt like it did when I raked the yard and gathered up armfuls of
leaves and sticks to carry round back. My fingers pushed down and I was
scared I'd pushed the rings and jewelry farther down and I wouldn't be
able to find them. Then the bones got all mixed up and I couldn't tell where
I was. I began to feel down along the sides thinking maybe I was wrong
about the hands. It was dry and powdery but my sweating fingers got all
stuck together. I bent over and shined my flashlight down under the iron
half of the top, toward the foot. I didn't see anything that looked like
jewelry. All I saw was the eyelets off her shoes that had stayed on top in
four little rows after the shoes themselves had rotted away.

I stood up, sort of sick, wondering if I ought to take out all those bones and trash to see if the rings had sunk underneath. I didn't know whether I could do it. I went over to the door and put my head out. A little air floated up from the river and touched me in the face. My pants pockets was heavy with all those screws. It would take me more than an hour to screw them all back. I put my hand up. My shirt was wet: a drop of water had fallen from the ceiling. The box hadn't better stay open much longer. I thought of all those rings but it was no sense hunting any more. I'd have to find some other way to pay Papa back.

From somewhere over behind the nigger houses a rooster gave a long, drawn-out crow; it was a good bit past midnight. I pushed the door open. After the black of the vault the air looked chalky blue. Across the river, mist blurred the hills. I stood there in the path. But behind me the vault was still open. The cavernous door drew me backward. To sink backward into the black vault. To fall forever deeper. To sleep the deep sleep of revenge where Papa could never reach me, where he could never, never reach me. My feet were at the edge. I stood at the vault's dark edge. The rooster crowed again. The sky was lightening. I saw my bicycle leaning against the tree.

I went over and touched the worn and narrow seat, the hard coiled springs. I shut my eyes. The night came to me from everywhere. From everywhere the soft quick sound of speed, the wheels spinning beneath me. And beyond the night were the speeding mornings and I awake, the thousand speeding mornings and I always awake.

I pulled the handlebars forward. The hard rubber wheel, pressing my leg, gave off its dusty familiar smell. The air from the river was fresh and warm. In the weeds the crickets started. A million miles away the Big Dipper had almost moved to the other side of the North Star. Over my head the freckled sky shifted towards morning. I would speak to Papa. I will go to him and take his hand. I will look into his eyes. I will stand in the doorway in the morning light. Then I will be gone through the endless speeding miles, saying Papa, Papa, accept all happiness from me.

Shirley Jackson
Louisa, Please Come Home

"LOUISA," MY MOTHER'S VOICE CAME OVER THE RADIO; it frightened me badly for a minute. "Louisa," she said, "please come home. It's been three long long years since we saw you last; Louisa, I promise you that everything will be all right. We all miss you so. We want you back again. Louisa, please come home."

Once a year. On the anniversary of the day I ran away. Each time I heard it I was frightened again, because between one year and the next I would forget what my mother's voice sounded like, so soft and yet strange with that pleading note. I listened every year. I read the stories in the newspapers—"Louisa Tether vanished one year ago"—or two years ago, or three; I used to wait for the twentieth of June as though it were my birthday. I kept all the clippings at first, but secretly; with my picture on all the front pages I would have looked kind of strange if anyone had seen me cutting it out. Chandler, where I was hiding, was close enough to my old home so that the papers made a big fuss about all of it, but of course the reason I picked Chandler in the first place was because it was a big enough city for me to hide in.

I didn't just up and leave on the spur of the moment, you know. I always knew that I was going to run away sooner or later, and I had made plans ahead of time, for whenever I decided to go. Everything had to go right the first time, because they don't usually give you a second chance on that kind of thing and anyway if it had gone wrong I would have looked like an awful fool, and my sister Carol was never one for letting people forget it when they made fools of themselves. I admit I planned it for the day before Carol's wedding on purpose, and for a long time afterward I used to try and imagine Carol's face when she finally realized that my running away was going to leave her one bridesmaid short. The papers said that the wedding went ahead as scheduled, though, and Carol told one newspaper reporter that her sister Louisa would have wanted it that way; "She would never have meant to spoil my wedding," Carol said, knowing perfectly well that that would be exactly what I'd meant. I'm pretty sure that the first thing Carol did when they knew I was missing was go and count the wedding presents to see what I'd taken with me.

Anyway, Carol's wedding may have been fouled up, but *my* plans went fine—better, as a matter of fact, than I had ever expected. Everyone was hurrying around the house putting up flowers and asking each other if the wedding gown had been delivered, and opening up cases of champagne and wondering what they were going to do if it rained and they couldn't use the garden, and I just closed the front door behind me and started off. There was only one bad minute when Paul saw me; Paul has always lived next door and Carol hates him worse than she does me. My mother always used to say that every time I did something to make the family ashamed of me Paul was sure to be in it somewhere. For a long time they thought he had something to do with my running away, even though he told over and over again how hard I tried to duck away from him that afternoon when he met me going down the driveway. The papers kept calling him "a close friend of the family," which must have overjoyed my mother, and saying that he was being questioned about possible clues to my whereabouts. Of course he never even knew that I was running away; I told him just what I told my mother before I left—that I was going to get away from all the confusion and excitement for a while; I was going downtown and would probably have a sandwich somewhere for supper and go to a movie. He bothered me for a minute there, because of course he wanted to come too. I hadn't meant to take the bus right there on the corner but with Paul tagging after me and wanting me to wait while he got the car so we could drive out and have dinner at the Inn, I had to get away fast on the first thing that came along, so I just ran for the bus and left Paul standing there; that was the only part of my plan I had to change.

I took the bus all the way downtown, although my first plan had been to walk. It turned out much better, actually, since it didn't matter at all if anyone saw me on the bus going downtown in my own home town, and I managed to get an earlier train out. I bought a round-trip ticket; that was important, because it would make them think I was coming back; that was always the way they thought about things. If you did something you had to have a reason for it, because my mother and my father and Carol never did anything unless *they* had a reason for it, so if I bought a round-trip ticket the only possible reason would be that I was coming back. Besides, if they thought I was coming back they would not be frightened so quickly and I might have more time to hide before they came looking for me. As it happened, Carol found out I was gone that same night when she couldn't sleep and came into my room for some aspirin, so all the time I had less of a head start than I thought.

I knew that they would find out about my buying the ticket; I was not silly enough to suppose that I could steal off and not leave any traces. All my plans were based on the fact that the people who get caught are the ones who attract attention by doing something strange or noticeable, and what I intended all along was to fade into some background where they would never see me. I knew they would find out about the round-trip ticket, because it was an odd thing to do in a town where you've lived all your life, but it was the last unusual thing I did. I thought when I bought it that knowing about that round-trip ticket would be some consolation to my mother and father. They would know that no matter how long I stayed away at least I always had a ticket home. I did keep the return-trip ticket quite a while, as a matter of fact. I used to carry it in my wallet as a kind of lucky charm.

I followed everything in the papers. Mrs. Peacock and I used to read them at the breakfast table over our second cup of coffee before I went off to work.

"What do you think about this girl disappeared over in Rockville?" Mrs. Peacock would say to me, and I'd shake my head sorrowfully and say that a girl must be really crazy to leave a handsome, luxurious home like that, or that I had kind of a notion that maybe she didn't leave at all—maybe the family had her locked up somewhere because she was a homicidal maniac. Mrs. Peacock always loved anything about homicidal maniacs.

Once I picked up the paper and looked hard at the picture. "Do you think she looks something like me?" I asked Mrs. Peacock, and Mrs. Peacock leaned back and looked at me and then at the picture and then at me again and finally she shook her head and said, "No. If you wore your hair longer, and curlier, and your face was maybe a little fuller, there might be a little resemblance, but then if you looked like a homicidal maniac I wouldn't ever of let you in my house."

"I think she kind of looks like me," I said.

"You get along to work and stop being vain," Mrs. Peacock told me.

Of course when I got on the train with my round-trip ticket I had no idea how soon they'd be following me, and I suppose it was just as well, because it might have made me nervous and I might have done something wrong and spoiled everything. I knew that as soon as they gave up the notion that I was coming back to Rockville with my round-trip ticket they would think of Crain, which is the largest city that train went to, so I only stayed in Crain part of one day. I went to a big department store where they were having a store-wide sale; I figured that would land me in a crowd of shoppers and I was right; for a while there was a good chance that I'd never get any farther away from home than the ground floor of that department store in Crain. I had to fight my way through the crowd until I found the counter where they were having a sale of raincoats, and then I had to push and elbow down the counter and finally grab the raincoat I wanted right out of the hands of some old monster who couldn't have used it anyway because she was much too fat. You would have thought she had already paid for it, the way she howled. I was smart enough to have the exact change, all six dollars and eighty-nine cents, right in my hand, and

I gave it to the salesgirl, grabbed the raincoat and the bag she wanted to put it in, and fought my way out again before I got crushed to death.

That raincoat was worth every cent of the six dollars and eighty-nine cents; I wore it right through until winter that year and not even a button ever came off it. I finally lost it the next spring when I left it somewhere and never got it back. It was tan, and the minute I put it on in the ladies' room of the store I began thinking of it as my "old" raincoat; that was good. I had never before owned a raincoat like that and my mother would have fainted dead away. One thing I did that I thought was kind of clever. I had left home wearing a light short coat; almost a jacket, and when I put on the raincoat of course I took off my light coat. Then all I had to do was empty the pockets of the light coat into the raincoat and carry the light coat casually over to a counter where they were having a sale of jackets and drop it on the counter as though I'd taken it off a little way to look at it and had decided against it. As far as I ever knew no one paid the slightest attention to me, and before I left the counter I saw a woman pick up my jacket and look it over; I could have told her she was getting a bargain for three ninety-eight.

It made me feel good to know that I had gotten rid of the light coat. My mother picked it out for me and even though I liked it and it was expensive it was also recognizable and I had to change it somehow. I was sure that if I put it in a bag and dropped it into a river or into a garbage truck or something like that sooner or later it would be found and even if no one saw me doing it, it would almost certainly be found, and then they would know I had changed my clothes in Crain.

That light coat never turned up. The last they ever found of me was someone in Rockville who caught a glimpse of me in the train station in Crain, and she recognized me by the light coat. They never found out where I went after that; it was partly luck and partly my clever planning. Two or three days later the papers were still reporting that I was in Crain; people thought they saw me on the streets and one girl who went into a store to buy a dress was picked up by the police and held until she could get someone to identify her. They were really looking, but they were looking for Louisa Tether, and I had stopped being Louisa Tether the minute I got rid of that light coat my mother bought me.

One thing I was relying on: there must be thousands of girls in the country on any given day who are nineteen years old, fair-haired, five feet four inches tall, and weighing one hundred and twenty-six pounds. And if there are thousands of girls like that, there must be, among those thousands, a good number who are wearing shapeless tan raincoats; I started counting tan raincoats in Crain after I left the department store and I passed four in one block, so I felt well hidden. After that I made myself even more invisible by doing just what I told my mother I was going to—I stopped in and had a sandwich in a little coffee shop, and then I went to a movie. I wasn't in any hurry at all, and rather than try to find a place to sleep that night I thought I would sleep on the train.

It's funny how no one pays any attention to you at all. There were hundreds of people who saw me that day, and even a sailor who tried to pick me up in the movie, and yet no one really *saw* me. If I had tried to check into a hotel the desk clerk might have noticed me, or if I had tried to get dinner in some fancy restaurant in that cheap raincoat I would have been conspicuous, but I was doing what any other girl looking like me and dressed like me might be doing that day. The only person who might be apt to remember me would be the man selling tickets in the railroad station, because girls looking like me in old raincoats didn't buy train tickets, usually, at eleven at night, but I had thought of that, too, of course; I bought a ticket to Amityville, sixty miles away, and what made Amityville a perfectly reasonable disguise is that at Amityville there is a college, not a little fancy place like the one I had left so recently with nobody's blessing, but a big sprawling friendly affair, where my raincoat would look perfectly at home. I told myself I was a student coming back to the college after a week end at home. We got to Amityville after midnight, but it still didn't look odd when I left the train and went into the station, because while I was in the station, having a cup of coffee and killing time, seven other girls—I counted —wearing raincoats like mine came in or went out, not seeming to think it the least bit odd to be getting on or off trains at that hour of the night. Some of them had suitcases, and I wished that I had had some way of getting a suitcase in Crain, but it would have made me noticeable in the movie, and college girls going home for week ends often don't bother; they have pajamas and an extra pair of stockings at home, and they drop a toothbrush into one of the pockets of those invaluable raincoats. So I didn't worry about the suitcase then, although I knew I would need one soon. While I was having my coffee I made my own mind change from the idea that I was a college girl coming back after a week end at home to the idea that I was a college girl who was on her way home for a few days; all the time I tried to think as much as possible like what I was pretending to be, and after all, I *had* been a college girl for a while. I was thinking that even now the letter was in the mail, traveling as fast as the U.S. Government could make it go, right to my father to tell him why I wasn't a college student any more; I suppose that was what finally decided me to run away, the thought of what my father would think and say and do when he got that letter from the college.

That was in the paper, too. They decided that the college business was the reason for my running away, but if that had been all, I don't think I would have left. No, I had been wanting to leave for so long, ever since I can remember, making plans till I was sure they were foolproof, and that's the way they turned out to be.

Sitting here in the station at Amityville, I tried to think myself into a good reason why I was leaving college to go home on a Monday night late, when I would hardly be going home for the week end. As I say, I always tried to think as hard as I could the way that suited whatever I wanted to be, and I liked to have a good reason for what I was doing. Nobody ever asked me, but it was good to know that I could answer them if they did. I finally decided that my sister was getting married the next day and I was going home at the beginning of the week to be one of her bridesmaids. I thought that was funny. I didn't want to be going home for any sad or frightening reason, like my mother being sick, or my father being hurt in a car accident, because I would have to look sad, and that might attract attention. So I was going home for my sister's wedding. I wandered around the station as though I had nothing to do, and just happened to pass the door when another girl was going out; she had on a raincoat just like mine and anyone who happened to notice would have thought that it was me who went out. Before I bought my ticket I went into the ladies' room and got another twenty dollars out of my shoe. I had nearly three hundred dollars left of the money I had taken from my father's desk and I had most of it in my shoes because I honestly couldn't think of another safe place to carry it. All I kept in my pocketbook was just enough for whatever I had to spend next. It's uncomfortable walking around all day on a wad of bills in your shoe, but they were good solid shoes, the kind of comfortable old shoes you wear whenever you don't really care how you look, and I had put new shoelaces in them before I left home so I could tie them good and tight. You can see, I planned pretty carefully, and no little detail got left out. If they had let me plan my sister's wedding there would have been a lot less of that running around and screaming and hysterics.

I bought a ticket to Chandler, which is the biggest city in this part of the state, and the place I'd been heading for all along. It was a good place to hide because people from Rockville tended to bypass it unless they had some special reason for going there—if they couldn't find the doctors or orthodontists or psychoanalysts or dress material they wanted in Rockville or Crain, they went directly to one of the really big cities, like the state capital; Chandler was big enough to hide in, but not big enough to look like a metropolis to people from Rockville. The ticket seller in the Amityville station must have seen a good many college girls buying tickets for Chandler at all hours of the day or night because he took my money and shoved the ticket at me without even looking up.

Funny. They must have come looking for me in Chandler at some time or other, because it's not likely they would have neglected any possible place I might be, but maybe Rockville people never seriously believed that anyone would go to Chandler from choice, because I never felt for a minute that anyone was looking for me there. My picture was in the Chandler papers, of course, but as far as I ever knew no one ever looked at me twice, and I got up every morning and went to work and went shopping in the stores and went to movies with Mrs. Peacock and went out to the beach all that summer without ever being afraid of being recognized. I behaved just like everyone else, and dressed just like everyone else, and even *thought* just like everyone else, and the only person I ever saw from Rockville in three years was a friend of my mother's, and I knew *she* only came to Chandler to get her poodle bred at the kennels there. She didn't look as if she was in a state to recognize anybody but another poodle-fancier, anyway, and all I had to do was step into a doorway as she went by, and she never looked at me.

Two other college girls got on the train to Chandler when I did; maybe both of them were going home for their sisters' weddings. Neither of them was wearing a tan raincoat, but one of them had on an old blue jacket that gave the same general effect. I fell asleep as soon as the train started, and once I woke up and for a minute I wondered where I was and then I realized that I was doing it, I was actually carrying out my careful plan and had gotten better than halfway with it, and I almost laughed, there in the train with everyone asleep around me. Then I went back to sleep and didn't wake up until we got into Chandler about seven in the morning.

So there I was. I had left home just after lunch the day before, and now at seven in the morning of my sister's wedding day I was so far away, in every sense, that I *knew* they would never find me. I had all day to get myself settled in Chandler, so I started off by having breakfast in a restaurant near the station, and then went off to find a place to live, and a job. The first thing I did was buy a suitcase, and it's funny how people don't really notice you if you're buying a suitcase near a railroad station. Suitcases look *natural* near railroad stations, and I picked out one of those stores that sell a little bit of everything, and bought a cheap suitcase and a pair of stockings and some handkerchiefs and a little traveling clock, and I put everything into the suitcase and carried that. Nothing is hard to do unless you get upset or excited about it.

Later on, when Mrs. Peacock and I used to read in the papers about my disappearing, I asked her once if she thought that Louisa Tether had gotten as far as Chandler and she didn't.

"They're saying now she was kidnapped." Mrs. Peacock told me, "and that's what *I* think happened. Kidnapped, and murdered, and they do *terrible* things to young girls they kidnap."

"But the papers say there wasn't any ransom note."

"That's what they *say*." Mrs. Peacock shook her head at me. "How do we know what the family is keeping secret? Or if she was kidnapped by a homicidal maniac, why should *he* send a ransom note? Young girls like you don't know a lot of the things that go on, *I* can tell you."

"I feel kind of sorry for the girl," I said.

"You can't ever tell," Mrs. Peacock said. "Maybe she went with him willingly."

I didn't know, that first morning in Chandler, that Mrs. Peacock was going to turn up that first day, the luckiest thing that ever happened to me. I decided while I was having breakfast that I was going to be a nineteen-year-old girl from upstate with a nice family and a good background who had been saving money to come to Chandler and take a secretarial course in the business school there. I was going to have to find some kind of a job to keep on earning money while I went to school; courses at the business school wouldn't start until fall, so I would have the summer to work and save money and decide if I really wanted to take secretarial training. If I decided not to stay in Chandler I could easily go somewhere else after the fuss about my running away had died down. The raincoat looked wrong for the kind of conscientious young girl I was going to be, so I took it off and carried it over my arm. I think I did a pretty good job on my clothes, altogether. Before I left home I decided that I would have to wear a suit, as quiet and unobtrusive as I could find, and I picked out a gray suit, with a white blouse, so with just one or two small changes like a different blouse or some kind of a pin on the lapel, I could look like whoever I decided to be. Now the suit looked absolutely right for a young girl planning to take a secretarial course, and I looked like a thousand other people when I walked down the street carrying my suitcase and my raincoat over my arm; people get off trains every minute looking just like that. I bought a morning paper and stopped in a drugstore for a cup of coffee and a look to see the rooms for rent. It was all so usual—suitcase, coat, rooms for rent—that when I asked the soda clerk how to get to Primrose Street he never even looked at me. He certainly didn't care whether I ever got to Primrose Street or not, but he told me very politely where it was and what bus to take. I didn't really need to take the bus for economy, but it would have looked funny for a girl who was saving money to arrive in a taxi.

"I'll never forget how you looked that first morning," Mrs. Peacock told me once, much later. "I knew right away you were the kind of girl I like to rent rooms to—quiet, and well-mannered. But you looked almighty scared of the big city."

"I wasn't scared," I said. "I was worried about finding a nice room. My mother told me so many things to be careful about I was afraid I'd never find anything to suit her."

"*Any*body's mother could come into my house at any time and know that her daughter was in good hands," Mrs. Peacock said, a little huffy.

But it was true. When I walked into Mrs. Peacock's rooming house on Primrose Street, and met Mrs. Peacock, I knew that I couldn't have done this part better if I'd been able to plan it. The house was old, and comfortable, and my room was nice, and Mrs. Peacock and I hit it off right away. She was very pleased with me when she heard that my mother had told me to be sure the room I found was clean and that the neighborhood was good, with no chance of rowdies following a girl if she came home after dark, and she was even more pleased when she heard that I wanted to save money and take a secretarial course so I could get a really good job and earn enough to be able to send a little home every week; Mrs. Peacock believed that children owed it to their parents to pay back some of what had been spent on them while they were growing up. By the time I had been in the house an hour Mrs. Peacock knew all about my imaginary family upstate: my mother, who was a widow, and my sister, who had just gotten married and still lived at my mother's home with her husband, and my young brother Paul, who worried my mother a good deal because he didn't seem to want to settle down. My name was Lois Taylor, I told her. By that

time, I think I could have told her my real name and she would never have
connected it with the girl in the paper, because by then she was feeling that
she almost knew my family, and she wanted me to be sure and tell my
mother when I wrote home that Mrs. Peacock would make herself personally
responsible for me while I was in the city and take as good care of me as
my own mother would. On top of everything else, she told me that a stationery store in the neighborhood was looking for a girl assistant, and there
I was. Before I had been away from home for twenty-four hours I was an
entirely new person. I was a girl named Lois Taylor who lived on Primrose
Street and worked down at the stationery store.

I read in the papers one day about how a famous fortuneteller wrote to
my father offering to find me and said that astral signs had convinced him
that I would be found near flowers. That gave me a jolt, because of Primrose
Street, but my father and Mrs. Peacock and the rest of the world thought
that it meant that my body was buried somewhere. They dug up a vacant
lot near the railroad station where I was last seen, and Mrs. Peacock was
very disappointed when nothing turned up. Mrs. Peacock and I could not
decide whether I had run away with a gangster to be a gun moll, or whether
my body had been cut up and sent somewhere in a trunk. After a while
they stopped looking for me, except for an occasional false clue that would
turn up in a small story on the back pages of the paper, and Mrs. Peacock
and I got interested in the stories about a daring daylight bank robbery in
Chicago. When the anniversary of my running away came around, and I
realized that I had really been gone for a year, I treated myself to a new
hat and dinner downtown, and came home just in time for the evening news
broadcast and my mother's voice over the radio.

"Louisa," she was saying, "please come home."

"That poor poor woman," Mrs. Peacock said. "Imagine how she must feel.
They say she's never given up hope of finding her little girl alive someday."

"Do you like my new hat?" I asked her.

I had given up all idea of the secretarial course because the stationery
store had decided to expand and include a lending library and a gift shop,
and I was now the manager of the gift shop and if things kept on well
would someday be running the whole thing; Mrs. Peacock and I talked
it over, just as if she had been my mother, and we decided that I would be
foolish to leave a good job to start over somewhere else. The money that I
had been saving was in the bank, and Mrs. Peacock and I thought that one
of these days we might pool our savings and buy a little car, or go on a
trip somewhere, or even a cruise.

What I am saying is that I was free, and getting along fine, with never a
thought that I knew about ever going back. It was just plain rotten bad
luck that I had to meet Paul. I had gotten so I hardly ever thought about
any of them any more, and never wondered what they were doing unless
I happened to see some item in the papers, but there must have been something in the back of my mind remembering them all the time because I
never even stopped to think; I just stood there on the street with my mouth

open, and said, *"Paul!"* He turned around and then of course I realized what I had done, but it was too late. He stared at me for a minute, and then frowned, and then looked puzzled; I could see him first trying to remember, and then trying to believe what he remembered; at last he said, "Is it possible?"

He said I had to go back. He said if I didn't go back he would tell them where to come and get me. He also patted me on the head and told me that there was still a reward waiting there in the bank for anyone who turned up with conclusive news of me, and he said that after he had collected the reward I was perfectly welcome to run away again, as far and as often as I liked.

Maybe I did want to go home. Maybe all that time I had been secretly waiting for a chance to get back; maybe that's why I recognized Paul on the street, in a coincidence that wouldn't have happened once in a million years —he had never even *been* to Chandler before, and was only there for a few minutes between trains; he had stepped out of the station for a minute, and found me. If I had not been passing at that minute, if he had stayed in the station where he belonged, I would never have gone back. I told Mrs. Peacock I was going home to visit my family upstate. I thought that was funny.

Paul sent a telegram to my mother and father, saying that he had found me, and we took a plane back; Paul said he was still afraid that I'd try to get away again and the safest place for me was high up in the air where he knew I couldn't get off and run.

I began to get nervous, looking out the taxi window on the way from the Rockville airport; I would have sworn that for three years I hadn't given a thought to that town, to those streets and stores and houses I used to know so well, but here I found that I remembered it all, as though I hadn't ever seen Chandler and *its* houses and streets; it was almost as though I had never been away at all. When the taxi finally turned the corner into my own street, and I saw the big old white house again, I almost cried.

"Of course I wanted to come back," I said, and Paul laughed. I thought of the return-trip ticket I had kept as a lucky charm for so long, and how I had thrown it away one day when I was emptying my pocketbook; I wondered when I threw it away whether I would ever want to go back and regret throwing away my ticket. "Everything looks just the same," I said. "I caught the bus right there on the corner; I came down the driveway that day and met you."

"If I had managed to stop you that day," Paul said, "you would probably never have tried again."

Then the taxi stopped in front of the house and my knees were shaking when I got out. I grabbed Paul's arm and said, "Paul . . . wait a minute," and he gave me a look I used to know very well, a look that said "If you back out on me now I'll see that you never forget it," and put his arm around me because I was shivering and we went up the walk to the front door.

I wondered if they were watching us from the window. It was hard for me to imagine how my mother and father would behave in a situation like this, because they always made such a point of being quiet and dignified and proper; I thought that Mrs. Peacock would have been halfway down the walk to meet us, but here the front door ahead was still tight shut. I wondered if we would have to ring the doorbell; I never had to ring this doorbell before. I was still wondering when Carol opened the door for us. "Carol!" I said. I was shocked because she looked so old, and then I thought that of course it had been three years since I had seen her and she probably thought that *I* looked older, too. "Carol," I said, "Oh, Carol!" I was honestly glad to see her.

She looked at me hard and then stepped back and my mother and father were standing there, waiting for me to come in. If I had not stopped to think I would have run to them, but I hesitated, not quite sure what to do, or whether they were angry with me, or hurt, or only just happy that I was back, and of course once I stopped to think about it all I could find to do was just stand there and say "Mother?" kind of uncertainly.

She came over to me and put her hands on my shoulders and looked into my face for a long time. There were tears running down her cheeks and I thought that before, when it didn't matter, I had been ready enough to cry, but now, when crying would make me look better, all I wanted to do was giggle. She looked old, and sad, and I felt simply foolish. Then she turned to Paul and said, "Oh, *Paul*—how can you do this to me again?"

Paul was frightened; I could see it. "Mrs. Tether—" he said.

"What is your name, dear?" my mother asked me.

"Louisa Tether," I said stupidly.

"No, dear," she said, very gently, "your *real* name?"

Now I could cry, but now I did not think it was going to help matters any. "Louisa Tether," I said. "That's my name."

"Why don't you people leave us alone?" Carol said; she was white, and shaking, and almost screaming because she was so angry. "We've spent years and years trying to find my lost sister and all people like you see in it is a chance to cheat us out of the reward—doesn't it mean *any*thing to you that *you* may think you have a chance for some easy money, but *we* just get hurt and heartbroken all over again? Why don't you leave us *alone?*"

"Carol," my father said, "you're frightening the poor child. Young lady," he said to me, "I honestly believe that you did not realize the cruelty of what you tried to do. You look like a nice girl; try to imagine your own mother—"

I tried to imagine my own mother; I looked straight at her.

"—if someone took advantage of her like this. I am sure you were not told that twice before, this young man—" I stopped looking at my mother and looked at Paul— "has brought us young girls who pretended to be our lost daughter; each time he protested that he had been genuinely deceived and had no thought of profit, and each time we hoped desperately that it would be the right girl. The first time we were taken in for several days.

The girl *looked* like our Louisa, she *acted* like our Louisa, she knew all kinds of small family jokes and happenings it seemed impossible that anyone *but* Louisa could know, and yet she was an imposter. And the girl's mother— my wife—has suffered more each time her hopes have been raised." He put his arm around my mother—his wife—and with Carol they stood all together looking at me.

"Look," Paul said wildly, "give her a *chance*—she *knows* she's Louisa. At least give her a chance to *prove* it."

"How?" Carol asked. "I'm sure if I asked her something like—well—like what was the color of the dress she was supposed to wear at my wedding—"

"It was pink," I said. "I wanted blue but you said it had to be pink."

"I'm sure she'd know the answer," Carol went on as though I hadn't said anything. "The other girls you brought here, Paul—*they* both knew."

It wasn't going to be any good. I ought to have known it. Maybe they were so used to looking for me by now that they would rather keep on looking than have me home; maybe once my mother had looked in my face and seen there nothing of Louisa, but only the long careful concentration I had put into being Lois Taylor, there was never any chance of my looking like Louisa again.

I felt kind of sorry for Paul; he had never understood them as well as I did and he clearly felt there was still some chance of talking them into opening their arms and crying out, "Louisa! Our long-lost daughter!" and then turning around and handing him the reward; after that, we could all live happily ever after. While Paul was still trying to argue with my father I walked over a little way and looked into the living room again; I figured I wasn't going to have much time to look around and I wanted one last glimpse to take away with me; sister Carol kept a good eye on me all the time, too. I wondered what the two girls before me had tried to steal, and I wanted to tell her that if *I* ever planned to steal anything from that house I was three years too late; I could have taken whatever I wanted when I left the first time. There was nothing there I could take now, any more than there had been before. I realized that all I wanted was to stay—I wanted to stay so much that I felt like hanging onto the stair rail and screaming, but even though a temper tantrum might bring them some fleeting recollection of their dear lost Louisa I hardly thought it would persuade them to invite me to stay. I could just picture myself being dragged kicking and screaming out of my own house.

"Such a lovely old house," I said politely to my sister Carol, who was hovering around me.

"Our family has lived here for generations," she said, just as politely.

"Such beautiful furniture," I said.

"My mother is fond of antiques."

"Fingerprints," Paul was shouting. We were going to get a lawyer, I gathered, or at least Paul thought we were going to get a lawyer and I wondered how he was going to feel when he found out that we weren't. I couldn't imagine any lawyer in the world who could get my mother and my father and my sister Carol to take me back when they had made up their minds that I was not Louisa; could the law make my mother look into my face and recognize me?

I thought that there ought to be some way I could make Paul see that there was nothing we could do, and I came over and stood next to him. "Paul," I said, "can't you see that you're only making Mr. Tether angry?"

"Correct, young woman," my father said, and nodded at me to show that he thought I was being a sensible creature. "He's not doing himself any good by threatening me."

"Paul," I said, "these people don't want us here."

Paul started to say something and then for the first time in his life thought better of it and stamped off toward the door. When I turned to follow him —thinking that we'd never gotten past the front hall in my great home-coming—my father—excuse me, Mr. Tether—came up behind me and took my hand. "My daughter was younger than you are," he said to me very kindly, "but I'm sure you have a family somewhere who love you and want you to be happy. Go back to them, young lady. Let me advise you as though I were really your father—stay away from that fellow, he's wicked and he's worthless. Go back home where you belong."

"We know what it's like for a family to worry and wonder about a daughter," my mother said. "Go back to the people who love you."

That meant Mrs. Peacock, I guess.

"Just to make sure you get there," my father said, "let us help toward your fare." I tried to take my hand away, but he put a folded bill into it and I had to take it. "I hope someday," he said, "that someone will do as much for our Louisa."

"Good-by, my dear," my mother said, and she reached up and patted my cheek. "Very good luck to you."

"I hope your daughter comes back someday," I told them. "Good-by."

The bill was a twenty, and I gave it to Paul. It seemed little enough for all the trouble he had taken and, after all, I could go back to my job in the stationery store. My mother still talks to me on the radio, once a year, on the anniversary of the day I ran away.

"Louisa," she says, "please come home. We all want our dear girl back, and we need you and miss you so much. Your mother and father love you and will never forget you. Louisa, please come home."

Shirley Ann Grau
Homecoming

THE TELEGRAM WAS IN THE MIDDLE OF THE dining-room table. It was leaning against the cutglass bowl that sometimes held oranges, only this week nobody had bought any. There was just the empty bowl, lightly dust coated and flecked with orange oil. And the telegram.

"Did you have to put it there?" Susan asked her mother.

"It's nothing to be ashamed of," her mother said.

"I'm not ashamed," she said, "but why did you put it there?"

"It's something to be proud of."

"It looks just like a sign."

"People will want to see it," her mother said.

"Yes," Susan said, "I guess they will."

She took her time dressing, deliberately. Twice her mother called up the stairs, "Susan, hurry. I told people any time after three o'clock."

And they were prompt, some of them anyway. (How many had her mother asked? She'd been such a long time on the phone this morning . . .) Susan heard them come, heard their voices echo in the high-ceilinged hall, heard the boards creak with unaccustomed weight. She could follow their movements in the sounds of the old boards. As clearly as if she were looking at them, she knew that the women had stayed inside and the men had moved to the porches.

Wide porches ran completely around two sides of the house, south and west. "Porches are best in old houses like this," her mother often said. "Good, useful porches."

The west porch was the morning porch. Its deep overhang kept off the sun even in these July afternoons. There was a little fringe of moonflower vine too, across the eaves, like lace on a doily. The big white moonflowers opened each night like white stars and each morning, like squashed bugs, dropped to the ground. They were trained so carefully on little concealed wires up there that they never once littered the porch. . . . The south porch was the winter porch. The slanted winter sun always reached that side, bare and clear no vines, no planting. A porch for old people. Where the winter sun could warm their thin blood, and send it pumping through knotty blue veins. Her grandmother sat out there, sightless in the sun, all one winter. Every good day, every afternoon until she died. . . .

Susan always thought one porch was much bigger until she measured them—carefully, on hands and knees, with a tape measure. How funny, she thought; they seemed so different to be just the same.

On this particular afternoon, as Susan came downstairs—slowly, reluctantly, hesitating at each step—she glanced toward the sound of men's voices on the south porch. Looking through the screen into the light, she saw no faces, just the glaring dazzle of white shirts. She heard the little rattle of ice in their glasses and she smelled the faint musty sweet odor of bourbon.

Like a wake, she thought. Exactly like a wake.

Her mother called: "In the dining room, dear."

There was coffee on the table, and an ice bucket and a bottle of sherry and two bottles of bourbon. "Come in, Susan," her mother said. "The girls are here to see you."

Of course, Susan thought. They had to be first, her mother's best friends, Mrs. Benson and Mrs. Watkins, each holding a sherry glass. Each kissed her, each with a puff of faint flower scent from the folds of their flowered dresses. "We are so sorry, Susan," they said one after the other.

Susan started to say thank you and then decided to say nothing.

Mrs. Benson peered over her sherry glass at the telegram propped on the table next to the good silver coffeepot. "I thought the Defense Department sent them," she said, "that's what I always heard."

Susan's mother said emphatically, her light voice straining over the words, just the way it always did: "They sent me one for my husband."

"That's right." Mrs. Watkins nodded. "I saw it just now when I came in. Right under the steps in the hall. In that little gold frame."

"When I read that telegram," Susan's mother said, "I got a pain in my heart that I never got rid of. I carried that pain in my heart from that day to this."

And Susan said, patiently explaining: "The army told Harold's parents."

"And the Carters sent word to you," her mother said firmly. Her hand with its broad wedding band flapped in the air. "There on the table, that's the word they sent."

All of a sudden Susan's black dress was too hot and too tight. She was perspiring all over it. She would ruin it, and it was her good dress.

"I'm so hot," she said. "I've got to change to something lighter."

Her mother followed her upstairs. "You're upset," she said, "but you've got to control yourself."

"The way you controlled yourself," Susan said.

"You're mocking now, but that's what I mean, I had to control myself, and I've learned."

"I've nothing to control," Susan said. She stripped off the black dress. The wet fabric stuck and she jerked it free. Close to her ear, a couple of threads gave a little screeching rip. "I've got to find something lighter. It's god-awfully hot down there."

"White," her mother said. "White would be correct."

Susan looked at her, shrugged, and took a white piqué out of the closet. "Are you all right?"

"I'm fine," Susan said, "I'm great."

She put the white piqué dress across a chair and sat down on her bed. Its springs squeaked gently. She stretched out and stared up at the crocheted tester and felt her sweat-moistened skin turn cool in the air. She pulled her slip and her bra down to her waist and lay perfectly still.

Abruptly she thought: If there were a camera right over me, it would take a picture of five eyes: the two in my head, the one in my navel, and the two on my breasts. Five eyes staring up at the ceiling.

She rolled over on her stomach.

It was a foolish thing to think. Very foolish. She never seemed to have the proper thoughts or feelings. Her mother now, she had the right thoughts, everybody knew they were right. But Susan didn't. . . .

Like now. She ought to be more upset now. She ought to be in tears over the telegram. She'd found it stuck in the crack of the door this morning. "Have been informed Harold was killed at Quang Tri last Thursday." She should have felt something. When her mother got the news of her father's death in Korea, the neighbors said you could hear her scream for a block; they found her huddled on the floor, stretched out flat and small as she could be with the bulging womb that held an almost completed baby named Susan.

Susan lifed her head and looked at the picture on her night table. It was a colored photograph of her father, the same one her mother had painted into a portrait to hang over the living-room fireplace. Susan used to spend hours staring into that small frame, trying to sharpen the fuzzy colored lines into the shape of a man. She'd never been quite able to do that; the only definite thing she knew about him was the sharp white lines of his grave marker in Arlington.

"That picture looks just exactly like him," her mother would say. "I almost think he'll speak to me. I'm so glad you can know what your father looked like."

And Susan never said: I still don't know. I never will.

And this whole thing now, her mourning for Harold, it was wrong. All wrong. She hadn't even known him very well. He was just a nice boy from school, a tall thin boy who worked in the A & P on Saturdays and liked to play pool on Sundays, who had a clear light tenor and sang solo parts with her in the glee club. His father worked for the telephone company and they lived on the other side of town on Millwood Street—she knew that much. He'd finished high school a year ago and he'd asked her to his senior prom, though she hadn't expected him to. On the way home, he offered her his class ring. "You can take it," he said. She could see his long narrow head in the light from the porch. "Till I get out of the army."

"Or some other girl wants it."

"Yeah."

Because she couldn't think of anything else, she said: "Okay, I'll keep it for you. If you want it, just write and I'll send it to you."

That was how she got the ring. She never wore it, and he didn't ask for it back. She didn't even see him again. His family moved away to the north part of the state, to Laurel, and Harold went there on his leaves. He didn't come back to town and he didn't call her. He did send a chain to wear the ring on—it was far too big for her finger—from California. She wrote him a thank-you note the very same day. But he didn't answer, and the ring and the chain hung on the back of her dresser mirror. He was just a boy she knew who went in the army. He was just a boy whose ring she was keeping.

Maybe he'd told his parents something more. Why else would they wire her? And what had he told them? All of a sudden there were things she couldn't ask. The world had changed while she wasn't looking.

And Harold Carter was killed. Harold was the name of an English king, and he was killed somewhere too. Now there was another Harold dead. How many had there been in between? Thousands of Harolds, thousands of different battles . . .

Her mother opened the door so quickly it slipped from her hand and smashed into the wall. The dresser mirror shivered and the class ring swung gently on its chain. "Susan, I thought, I just thought of something . . ."

What, Susan asked silently. Did you forget the extra ice? Something like that? Will people have to have warm drinks?

"You're acting very strangely. I've never seen you act like this. . . . Did something go on that shouldn't have? Tell me."

Susan tossed a hairbrush from hand to hand. "Maybe it's me," she said, "but I just don't know what people are talking about any more."

"All right," her mother said, "you make me put it this way. Are you going to have a baby?"

Susan stared at the broken edges of the bristles, and she began to giggle. "Harold left a year ago, Mother."

"Oh," her mother said, "oh oh oh." And she backed out the door.

Susan said after her, sending her words along the empty hall where there was nobody to hear them: "That was you who was pregnant. And it was another war."

She put on some more perfume; her flushed skin burned at its touch. She glanced again at the photograph of her father.

You look kind of frozen there. But then I guess you really are. Frozen at twenty-three. Smile and crooked cap and all.

And Susan remembered her grandmother sitting on the porch in the sun, eyes hooded like a bird's, fingers like birds' claws. Senility that came and went, like a shade going up and down. "He don't look nothing like the pictures," she said. She always called her dead son-in-law he, never used his name. "Never looked like that, not dead, not alive." The one hand that was not paralyzed waved at an invisible fly. "Died and went to glory, that boy. Those pictures your mother likes, they're pictures of him in glory. Nothing more nor less than glory."

The old woman was dead now too. There weren't any pictures of her. She'd gone on so long she fell apart, inch by inch of skin. All the dissolution visible outside the grave . . .

Susan breathed on the glass front of her father's picture and polished it with the hem of her slip. The young glorious dead . . . like Harold. Only she didn't have a picture of Harold. And she didn't really remember what he looked like.

She could hear the creak of cane rockers on the porch, the soft mumbling of men's talk. She stood by the screen to listen.

"I'll tell you." Harry Benson, the druggist, was sitting in the big chair, the one with the fancy scrolled back. "They called us an amphibious unit and put us ashore and they forgot about us. Two weeks with nothing to do but keep alive on that beach."

That would be Okinawa. She had heard about his Okinawa.

"And after a while some of the guys got nervous. If they found a Jap still alive they'd work him over good, shoot him seven or eight times, just to see him jump. They kind of thought it was fun, I guess."

"Hold it a minute, Harry," Ed Watkins, who was the railroad agent, said. "Here's Susan."

They both stood up. They'd never done that before.

"We were talking about our wars, honey," Mr. Benson said. "I'm afraid we were."

"That's all right," Susan said. "I don't mind."

"It was crazy, plain crazy," Mr. Watkins said. "Like that guy, must have been '51 or '52."

"Ed, look," Mr. Benson said. "Maybe we ought to stop talking about this."

"Nothing so bad . . . This guy, I don't think I ever knew his name, he was just another guy. And in those days you remember how they came down in waves from the North. You could hear them miles away, yelling and blowing horns. So, this time, you could hear them like always, and this guy, the one I didn't know a name for, he puts a pistol right under his jaw and blows the top of his head off. The sergeant just looked at him, and all he can say is, 'Jesus Christ, that son of a bitch bled all over my gun.'"

"Hard to believe things like that now," Mr. Benson said.

"I believe them," Susan said. "Excuse me, I have something to do in the kitchen."

She had to pass through the dining room. Mrs. Benson still had a sherry glass in her hand, her cheeks were getting flushed and her eyes were very bright. Mrs. Watkins had switched from sherry to whiskey and was putting more ice in her highball. Susan's mother poured herself coffee.

Susan thought: Mrs. Benson's going to have an awful sherry hangover and Mrs. Watkins' ulcer is going to start hurting from the whiskey and my mother's drunk about twenty cups of coffee today and that's going to make her sick. . . .

She only said, "I'm just passing through."

But she found herself stopping to look at the telegram. At the shape of the letters and the way they went on the page. At the way it was signed: "Mr. and Mrs. Carter." She thought again how strange that was. They were both big hearty people—"Call me Mike," Mr. Carter said to all the kids. "We're Mike and Ida here." Now all of a sudden they were formal.

Like a wedding invitation, Susan thought suddenly. Only just the opposite.

She reached out and touched the paper. It crackled slightly under her fingers. She went on rubbing her thumb across the almost smooth surface, watching the sweat of her skin begin to stain the yellow paper. A little stain, a little mark, but one that would grow if she kept at it.

That was the end of Harold Carter, she thought. He ended in the crisp, crunchy feel of a piece of paper. A tall thin boy who'd taken her to a dance and given her a ring that was too big for her. All that was left of him was a piece of paper.

She'd send the ring back to his parents. Maybe they'd like to have it.

Or maybe they'd rather she kept it. But keeping it would be keeping him. All of a sudden she saw the ring hanging on the side of her dresser mirror, and she looked into its blue stone and way down in its synthetic depths she saw a tiny little Harold, germ-sized and far away. As she looked he winked out.

She put the telegram down. "I really was just going to the kitchen."

"You're not wearing your ring," Mrs. Watkins said.

"No," she said, "no, I never did wear it."

"You must be so upset." Mrs. Benson sipped delicately at the edge of the yellow sherry. "Just like your poor mother."

"I wasn't married to him," Susan said, "it's different."

Her mother was standing next to her, hand on her shoulder. "You would have married him."

"No," Susan said, "no, I don't think so."

"Of course you would have." Her mother was firm. "Why else would he have given you the ring?"

Susan started to say: Because he didn't have anybody else to give it to and he couldn't give it to his mother.

Her mother went on patting her shoulder. "We should be proud of them, Susan. Harold was a fine young man."

Was he? She didn't have the heart to say that aloud either. Did he shoot people to see them squirm? Did he pull the trigger against his own head with fear?

"The young men are so heroic," her mother said. The two women murmured consent. Her mother would know; her mother had lost a husband in a war, she would know.

All the brave young men that die in their glory, Susan thought. And leave rings to girls they hardly knew, and pictures on mantels in houses where they never lived. Rings that don't fit and pictures that don't resemble them.

"Harold was an English king," she said aloud.

"Yes, dear," her mother said patiently. "That's history."

Harold Carter didn't get to sit on porches and remember, the way Watkins and Benson were doing now. He hadn't got to do anything, except go to high school and die. But then, you didn't really know that either, Susan thought. You really didn't know what he did out there, what memories he might have brought back inside his head.

Mrs. Watkins repeated, "All the young men are so brave."

"No," Susan said abruptly. "Not my father, and not Harold. They weren't brave, they just got caught."

In the silence she could hear the soft wheeze of their astonished breaths, and, as she turned, the creak of old boards under her heel. "They don't die in glory." The words came out sounding like her speech at the Senior Debating Society. "They just die dead. Anyway, I was on my way to fix a cup of tea."

Nobody followed her to the kitchen, just the little ribbon of sound from her high heels on the bare boards and the linoleum. She flipped on the fire under the kettle, decided it would take too long and began to heat some water in a pan. Her feet hurt; she kicked off her shoes. The water warmed and she poured it over the instant tea. There were no lemons in the refrigerator; she remembered suddenly that there weren't any oranges on the dining-room table either, that today had been marketing day and nobody had gone.

She put sugar in the tea and tasted it. It was barely warm and nasty, salty almost. She'd forgotten to rinse the dishes again. She would drink it anyway, while she made another proper cup. She put the flame back under the kettle. She pushed open the screen door and went out on the kitchen porch.

It was very small, just wide enough for one person to pass between the railing and the garbage can that always stood there. She'd often argued with her mother over that. "Put it in the yard, it just brings flies into the house." "A clean can," her mother said, "does not attract flies." And the can stayed.

She sat down on the railing, wondering if it would leave a stripe on her white dress. She decided she didn't care. She sipped the cold tea and stared out into the back yard, at the sweet peas growing along the wire fence, at the yellow painted boards on the house next door.

She was still staring over there, not seeing anything in particular, not thinking anything at all, when Mr. Benson came around the corner of the house. He walked across the back yard and stopped, finally, one foot on the bottom step.

"You left the girls in quite a state back there," he said.

So they had rushed to the porch to tell the men . . . Susan didn't take her eyes off the sweet peas, the soft gentle colors of the sweet peas. "They get upset real easy."

"I reckon they do," he said, "and they quiet down real easy too."

She began to swing her leg slowly. I shouldn't have left my shoes in the kitchen, she thought. I'll ruin my stockings out here.

"I take it he wasn't even a very good friend of yours," Mr. Benson said.

"You'd take it right." Because that sounded rude, she added quickly: "Nobody understands that. He was just a boy I knew."

"Shouldn't be so hard to understand."

"It's like a wake in there, and that's silly."

"Well," Mr. Benson said, "he was nineteen and maybe when it's somebody that young you don't even have to know him to mourn after him."

"He was twenty." Susan looked at Mr. Benson then, the short stocky man, with a fringe of black hair around his ears and a sweaty pink skull shining in the heat. His eyes, buried in folds of puffy skin, were small sharp points of blue. My father might have looked like that, she thought.

"Twenty's still pretty young," he said.

"This whole thing is my mother. The minute she saw the telegram all she could think of is how history is repeating itself. She's called everybody, even people she doesn't like."

"I knew your mother," Mr. Benson said.

"And that dying in glory talk." Susan hopped off the railing and leaned against it, palms pressing the rough wood. "That's all I ever hear. My mother knows those stories—the ones you were telling on the porch—she knows it's awful and stupid and terrible."

"No," Mr. Benson said, "it isn't awful." He pulled a cigarette holder from his pocket and began to suck it. "I gave up smoking and this is all I got left. . . . You're wrong, child, but maybe the stories don't say it clear enough."

Susan said slowly, "You talk about it all the time, any time."

He nodded slowly and the empty cigarette holder whistled in the hot afternoon air. "Because it was the most glorious thing ever happened to us."

"Too bad you can't tell Harold," she said.

"Take Harold now." Mr. Benson's voice was dull and monotonous, singsonging in the heat. "He didn't have to join up right out of high school. Draft calls been pretty low around here lately."

"He knew he was going to have to, that's why."

"It don't happen like that." He blew through the cigarette holder again, then tapped it on his palm. "Always seemed to me like men have got to have their war. I had to have mine twenty-five years ago. When you're in it maybe it's different, but you got to go. Once you hear about it, you got to go to it."

"That doesn't make any sense to me," Susan said. "None."

"Even when you're in it, you know that if you live, you're going to remember it all the rest of your life. And you know that if there was another war and you were young enough, you'd go again."

"That's stupid," Susan said.

"Maybe. You forget places you've been and you forget women you had, but you don't forget fighting."

Behind her the tea kettle gave a shriek. He glanced up. "Sounds like your water is boiling."

"Yes," she said, "I'll see to it."

He nodded and walked away, leaving a light smell of bourbon behind him. He turned once, lifted his hands, palms up in a little shrugging gesture.

She made her tea. As if she were obeying a set of rules. Things were beginning to feel less strange to her. Even the talk about Harold didn't seem as silly as it had.

I'm beginning not to mind, she thought, but it's still all mixed up. He was the sort of boy I could have married, but I didn't even know him. And that's lucky for me. Otherwise I might be like my mother. His being dead doesn't really change anything for me. I'll get married after a while to somebody as good as him or even better. . . .

She drank her tea slowly; she was sad and happy at once. Harold was a young man who had died. He didn't leave a memory behind, he didn't leave anything. He was just gone and there wasn't even a mark at the place where he had been.

Her mother stood in the door. "Do you feel well enough to come back in, child?"

Susan chuckled, a quiet little self-contented chuckle.

"Whatever is funny, child?"

"You're having such a good time, Mother, you haven't had such a good time in ages."

"Well, really."

"You're alive and I'm alive and Harold's not alive."

"That's horrible."

"Sure."

She followed her mother across the waxed linoleum. "Wait, I've got to put my shoes on."

There just isn't anything, she thought. I'm sorry, Harold. I hope it wasn't too bad and I hope it didn't hurt too much. You and my father. I bet your parents have your picture on the mantel too.

Her shoes were on now and she straightened up.

"Good-by," she said in a very light whisper. "You poor bastard."

And she went inside to join the people.

4
Social
Adjustment
and Delinquency

IMPORTANT AS THE FAMILY IS, it serves mainly to prepare adolescents for a larger society outside its small circle. Being accepted in some capacity by peers is vitally important to adolescents, and there are few experiences more ego-deflating to them than being rejected. For the most part, the way adolescents feel about themselves and the way they measure their self-worth are largely based on the status they have within a group. Within any group both leader and follower are part of a well-defined social structure, and there is little doubt in the mind of either whose company is prized and whose is not. Nevertheless, in greater or lesser degree, they feel a sense of belonging, and this is what is significant. Both leader and follower have a relatively clear concept of what their roles are. But since their concept of self is only partially formed, both may feel threatened when their roles change and they are unable to fill them. Being rejected is an even more traumatic experience. Most adolescents do not have the ego strength at this stage in their psycho-sociological development to accept a radical reduction in their social prestige. Even dull adolescents are able to intuit quickly how others make important value judgments about them based on their rank within a group.

Although there are many different types of adolescent groups, their structure is similar: a leader initiates and directs activities, gives them some meaning, and establishes an appropriate hierarchy of roles; the members lend their talents and energies in varying degrees. Leaders possess the ability to make their followers feel they are doing things because they want to, not because they have to. The company of these leaders is enjoyable for other adolescents, yet the leaders command respect. Those who have more to offer to the group are correspondingly high in its hierarchy; those with little else to offer except a desire to belong and share in its activities rank near the bottom.

Many interrelated traits are responsible for social acceptance or rejection among adolescents. Those highly valued by contemporary adolescents are physical attractiveness, social prominence, athletic talent, leadership ability, intelligence, a quick wit, and a distinctive "personality." The number and types of friendships adolescents have serve as the primary index of their acceptability. Additionally, there is a close relationship between social activity and social approval. Those who do not have the desired qualities to be members of a group often find themselves as outcasts. When this happens, they may band together into social structures that have their own, often rigid, entrance requirements and evaluation systems. Individually and as groups these rejected adolescents often resort to delinquent behavior, sometimes to draw attention to themselves, sometimes to strike back at a society that does not value their participation. A growing feeling of adolescent alienation from peers and adult society has resulted in a significant increase in juvenile delinquency since World War II. Many of these antisocial actions help juvenile delinquents to establish some sense of identity.

There are many cases for antisocial behavior, but the interrelationship among personality, intelligence, and community values is the most important. For example, rambunctious students with modest intellectual gifts can hardly be expected to develop a sense of self-esteem in an academically oriented high school that values cool, restrained behavior. For unknown reasons, many students facing such a predicament manage to muddle through without becoming delinquent, while a few do not and find themselves in serious trouble. Petty stealing and chronic truancy, which are common in early adolescent delinquency, not infrequently give way to armed robbery, auto theft, drunkenness, drug abuse, or homicide in later adolescence.

While every story in this anthology deals in some way with adolescents adjusting to society, those contained in the following section mirror the growing emphasis in short fiction since World War II on the adjustment problems encountered by adolescents, particularly those resulting in juvenile delinquency.

Stories about fistfights among young adolescent males, age twelve to fifteen, are quite common. These are usually precipitated by a casual remark that is misunderstood. A lack of practice in controlling anger and placing statements in their proper social context are behind most early adolescent confrontations. Emotions invariably mount as fights progress, and those emotions end in relief for both loser and winner. The hard blows that are exchanged are often responsible for significant epiphanies; for instance, "the short skinny kid with the bubble eyes" in "The Death of Horatio Alger" learns that the rags-to-riches dreams of young Alger are not to be found by a young black in a slum. Fight stories are mainly told from the point of view of protagonists who are in the very process of learning about their strengths and weaknesses, as well as about the social dynamics that have brought them into conflict with an opponent. After a fight has started, they feel unable to back out because they might be called "chicken" by the onlookers, a fate worse than the blows they are exchanging. Cut lips and blackened eyes are remembered well past their healing and no doubt account for older adolescents' being more cautious about getting involved in a fight; their fights are more premeditated and often are contests to determine who is to assume the leadership of a group.

"Debut" represents a type of story that features explicit parental instruction about social conduct. On the night of Judy's first formal dance, her mother describes the occasion as a "battle that starts tonight and it goes on for the rest of your life." As in the case of Judy's mother, such direct information is usually offered by parents who have been thwarted socially and are trying to save their children from the same fate. Further frustration is experienced by parents when adolescents reject the heavy-handed advice—though Judy does not. Much, if not the greatest part, of adolescent social instruction actually comes from peers. Numerous stories have been written, for example, concerning the problems of learning the subtle shibboleths and codes of conduct in private boys' and girls' schools. In "Phineas" (section 7) it is the ways of adolescent, not adult, society that are important to learn—and the lessons are frequently subtle and difficult to grasp. Stories about private schools have fallen out of favor with most writers since the mid-sixties and have been replaced by stories set in public schools, which, drawing from diversified social strata, offer more interesting possibilities for writers to explore.

"Stealing Cars" unfolds the dilemma of sixteen-year-old Alex Housman, who is caught after stealing his fourteenth car. As in many stories about theft, the motivation behind the act is uncertain. Alex "knew no answer" when asked by his interrogator why he had become a thief. A desire for the thrill of a joyride is the motivation of many car-theft stories of the fifties; stories from the sixties and seventies usually go deeper, intimating that the quest for excitement is a symptom of underlying psychological and societal problems. Delinquency stories of younger adolescent boys focus on stealing from parents, shoplifting, or purse snatching; most end with reformed but conscience-stricken adolescents who see the error of their ways. Delinquency stories of younger and older adolescent girls often show them involved in shoplifting, with the older girls sometimes presented as sexually delinquent. Generally, females are less violent and direct in their delinquency than males. For example, when in "The Boats" Joan and her mother are ignored by the vacation social set, Joan expresses her resentment in a roundabout way.

During the past fifteen years the concern in short fiction over adolescent drunkenness has been replaced by an investigation of drug abuse. Some writers narrate the kaleidoscopic hallucinations of LSD users. Others—frequently in the documentary fashion of "Hector Rodriguez"—report the pitfalls of marijuana, cocaine, and heroin. Most stories in this category probe the environmental factors that cause adolescents to take drugs and the psychological state they produce when used. Older stories about the drunken fraternity parties that caused a prewar generation to lament the perils of alcohol seem naïve when compared to those that spell out the dangers of heavy drug use. Like juvenile delinquency in general, drug addiction exists at all levels of adolescent society.

LeRoi Jones
(Imamu Amiri Baraka)
The Death of Horatio Alger

THE COLD RED BUILDING BURNED MY EYES. The bricks hung together, like the city, the nation, under the dubious cement of rationalism and need. A need so controlled, it only erupted out of the used-car lots, or sat parked, Saturdays, in front of our orange house, for Orlando, or Algernon, or Danny, or J.D. to polish. There was silence, or summers, noise. But this was a few days after Christmas, and the ice melted from the roofs and the almost frozen water knocked lethargically against windows, tar roofs and slow dogs moping through the yards. The building was Central Avenue School. And its tired red sat on the corner of Central Avenue and Dey (pronounced *die* by the natives, *day* by the teachers, or any non-resident whites) Street. Then, on Dey, halfway up the block, the playground took over. A tarred-over yard, though once there had been gravel, surrounded by cement and a wire metal fence.

The snow was dirty as it sat dull and melting near the Greek restaurants, and the dimly lit "grocery" stores of the Negroes. The rich boys had metal wagons, the poor rode in. The poor made up games, the rich played them. The poor won the games, or as an emergency measure, the fights. No one thought of the snow except Mr. Feld, the playground director, who was in charge of it, or Miss Martin, the husky gym teacher Matthew Stodges had pushed into the cloakroom, who had no chains on her car. Grey slush ran over the curbs, and our dogs drank it out of boredom, shaking their heads and snorting.

I had said something about J.D.'s father, as to who he was, or had he ever been. And J., usually a confederate, and private strong arm, broke bad because Augie, Norman, and white Johnny were there, and laughed, misunderstanding simple "dozens" with ugly insult, in that curious scholarship the white man affects when he suspects a stronger link than sociology, or the tired cultural lies of Harcourt, Brace sixth-grade histories. And under their naïveté he grabbed my shirt and pushed me in the snow. I got up, brushing dead ice from my ears, and he pushed me down again, this time dumping a couple of pounds of cold dirty slush down my neck, calmly hysterical at his act.

J. moved away and stood on an icy garbage hamper, sullenly throwing wet snow at the trucks on Central Avenue. I pushed myself into a sitting position, shaking my head. Tears full in my eyes, and the cold slicing minutes from my life. I wasn't making a sound. I wasn't thinking any thought I could make someone else understand. Just the rush of young fear and anger and disgust. I could have murdered God, in that simple practical way we kick dogs off the bottom step.

Augie (my best white friend), fat Norman, whose hook shots usually hit the rim, and were good for easy tip-ins by our big men, and useless white Johnny who had some weird disease that made him stare, even in the middle of a game, he'd freeze, and sometimes line drives almost knocked his head off while he shuddered slightly, cracking and recracking his huge knuckles. They were howling and hopping, they thought it was so funny that J. and I had come to blows. And especially, I guess, that I had got my lumps. "Hey, wiseass, somebody's gonna break your nose!" fat Norman would say over and over whenever I did something to him. Hold his pants when he tried his jump shot; spike him sliding into home (he was a lousy catcher); talk about his brother who hung out under the El and got naked in alleyways.

(The clucks of Autumn could have, right at that moment, easily seduced me. Away, and into school. To masquerade as a half-rich nigra with shiny feet. Back through the clean station, and up the street. Stopping to talk on the way. One beer gets you drunk and you stand in an empty corridor, lined with Italian paintings, talking about the glamours of sodomy.)

Rise and Slay.

I hurt so bad, and inside without bleeding I realized the filthy grey scratches my blood would carry to my heart. John walked off staring, and Augie and Norman disappeared, so easily there in the snow. And J.D. too, my first love, drifted against the easy sky. Weeping at what he'd done. No one there but me. THE SHORT SKINNY BOY WITH THE BUBBLE EYES.

Could leap up and slay them. Could hammer my fist and misery through their faces. Could strangle and bake them in the crude jungle of my feeling. Could stuff them in the sewie hole with the collected garbage of children's guilt. Could elevate them into heroic images of my own despair. A righteous messenger from the wrong side of the tracks. Gym teachers, cutthroats, aging pickets, ease by in the cold. The same lyric chart, exchange of particulars, that held me in my minutes, the time "Brownie" rammed the glass door down and ate up my suit. Even my mother, in a desperate fit of rhythm, was not equal to the task. Which was simple economics. I.e., a white man's dog cannot bite your son if he has been taught that something very ugly will happen to him if he does. He might pace stupidly in his ugly fur, but he will never never bite.

But what really stays to be found completely out, except stupid enterprises like art? The word on the page, the paint on the canvas (Marzette dragging in used-up canvases to revive their hopeless correspondence with the times), stone clinging to air, as if it were real. Or something a Deacon would admit was beautiful. The conscience rules against ideas. The point was to be where you wanted to, and do what you wanted to. After all is "said and done," what is left but those sheepish constructions. "I've got to go to the toilet" is no less pressing than the Puritans taking off for Massachusetts, and dragging their devils with them. (There is in those parts, even now, the peculiar smell of roasted sex organs. And when a good New Englander leaves his house in the earnestly moral sub-towns to go into the smoking hells of soon to be destroyed Yankee Gomorrahs, you watch him pull very firmly at his tie, or strapping on very tightly his evil watch.) The penitence there. The masochism. So complete and conscious a phenomenon. Like a standard of beauty; for instance, the bespectacled, soft-breasted, gently pigeon-toed maidens of America. Neither rich nor poor, with intelligent smiles and straight lovely noses. No one would think of them as beautiful but these mysterious scions of the puritans. They value health and devotion, and their good women, the lefty power of all our nation, are unpresuming subtle beauties, who could even live with poets (if they are from the right stock), if pushed to that. But mostly they are where they should be, reading good books and opening windows to air out their bedrooms. And it is a useful memory here, because such things as these were the vague images that had even so early, helped shape me. Light freckles, sandy hair, narrow clean bodies. Though none lived where I lived then. And I don't remember a direct look at them even, with clear knowledge of my desire, until one afternoon I gave a speech at East Orange High, as sports editor of our high-school paper, which should have been printed in Italian, and I saw there, in the auditorium, young American girls, for the first time. And have loved them as flesh things emanating from real life, that is, in contrast to my own, a scraping and floating through the last three red and blue stripes of the flag, that settles the hash of the lower middle class. So that even sprawled there in the snow, with my blood and pompous isolation, I vaguely knew of a glamorous world and was mistaken into thinking it could be gotten from books. Negroes and Italians beat and shaped me, and my allegiance is there. But the triumph of romanticism was parquet floors, yellow dresses, gardens and sandy hair. I must have felt the loss and could not rise against a cardboard world of dark hair and linoleum. Reality was something I was convinced I could not have.

And thus to be flogged or put to the rack. For all our secret energies. The first leap over the barrier: when the victim finds he can no longer stomach his own "group." Politics whinnies, but is still correct, and asleep in a windy barn. The beautiful statue of victory, whose arms were called duty. And they curdle in her snatch thrust there by angry minorities, along with their own consciences. Poets climb, briefly, off their motorcycles, to find out who owns their words. We are named by all the things we will never understand. Whether we can fight or not, or even at the moment of our hugest triumph we stare off into space remembering the snow melting in our cuts, and all the pimps of reason who've ever conquered us. It is the hardest form of love.

I could not see when I "chased" Norman and Augie. Chased in quotes because, they really did not have to run. They could have turned, and myth aside, calmly whipped my ass. But they ran, laughing and keeping warm. and J.D. kicked snow from around a fire hydrant flatly into the gutter. Smiling and broken, with his head hung just slanted towards the yellow dog ice running down a hole. I took six or seven long running steps and tripped. I couldn't have been less interested, but the whole project had gotten out of hand. I was crying, and my hands were freezing, and the two white boys leaned against the pointed metal fence and laughed and slapped their knees. I threw snow stupidly in their direction. It fell short and was not even noticed as it dropped.

(All of it rings in your ears for a long time. But the payback . . . in simple terms against such actual sin as supposing quite confidently that the big sweating purple whore staring from her peed up hall very casually at your whipping has *never* been loved . . . is hard. We used to say.)

Then I pushed to my knees and could only see J. leaning there against the hydrant looking just over my head. I called to him, for help really. But the words rang full of dead venom. I screamed his mother a purple nigger with alligator titties. His father a bilious white man with sores on his jowls. I was screaming for help in my hatred and loss, and only the hatred would show. And he came over shouting for me to shut up. Shut Up skinny bastard. I'll break your ass if you don't. Norman had both hands on his stomach, his laugh was getting so violent, and he danced awkwardly toward us howling to agitate J. to beat me some more. But J. whirled on him perfectly and rapped him hard under his second chin. Norman was going to say, "Hey me-an," in that hated twist of our speech, and J. hit him again, between his shoulder and chest, and almost dropped him to his knees. Augie cooled his howl to a giggle of concern and backed up until Norman turned and they both went shouting up the street.

I got to my feet, wiping my freezing hands on my jacket. J. was looking at me hard, like country boys do, when their language, or the new tone they need to take on once they come to this cold climate (1940's New Jersey) fails, and they are left with only the old Southern tongue, which cruel farts like me used to deride their lack of interest in America. I turned to walk away. Both my eyes were nothing but water, though it held at their rims, stoically refusing to blink and thus begin to sob uncontrollably. And to keep from breaking down I wheeled and hid the weeping by screaming at that boy. You nigger without a father. You eat your mother's pussy. And he wheeled me around and started to hit me again.

Someone called my house and my mother and father and grandmother and sister were strung along Dey street, in some odd order. (They couldn't have come out of the house "together.") And I was conscious first of my father saying, "Go on Mickey, hit him. Fight back." And for a few seconds, under the weight of that plea for my dignity, I tried. I feinted and danced, but I couldn't even roll up my fists. The whole street was blurred and hot as my eyes. I swung and swung, but J.D. bashed me when he wanted to.

My mother stopped the fight finally, shuddering at the thing she'd made. "His hands are frozen, Michael. His hands are frozen." And my father looks at me even now, wondering if they'll ever thaw.

Kristin Hunter
Debut

"HOLD STILL, JUDY," MRS. SIMMONS SAID around the spray of pins that protruded dangerously from her mouth. She gave the thirtieth tug to the tight sash at the waist of the dress. "Now walk over there and turn around slowly."

The dress, Judy's first long one, was white organdy over taffeta, with spaghetti straps that bared her round brown shoulders and a floating skirt and a wide sash that cascaded in a butterfly effect behind. It was a dream, but Judy was sick and tired of the endless fittings she had endured so that she might wear it at the Debutantes' Ball. Her thoughts leaped ahead to the Ball itself. . . .

"*Slowly*, I said!" Mrs. Simmons' dark, angular face was always grim, but now it was screwed into an expression resembling a prune. Judy, starting nervously, began to revolve by moving her feet an inch at a time.

Her mother watched her critically. "No, it's still not right. I'll just have to rip out that waistline seam again."

"Oh, Mother!" Judy's impatience slipped out at last. "Nobody's going to notice all those little details."

"They will too. They'll be watching you every minute, hoping to see something wrong. You've got to be the *best*. Can't you get that through your head?" Mrs. Simmons gave a sigh of despair. "You better start noticin' 'all those little details' yourself. I can't do it for you all your life. Now turn around and stand up straight."

"Oh, Mother," Judy said, close to tears from being made to turn and pose while her feet itched to be dancing, "I can't stand it any more!"

"You can't stand it, huh? How do you think *I* feel?" Mrs. Simmons said in her harshest tone.

Judy was immediately ashamed, remembering the weeks her mother had spent at the sewing machine, pricking her already tattered fingers with needles and pins, and the great weight of sacrifice that had been borne on Mrs. Simmons' shoulders for the past two years so that Judy might bare hers at the Ball.

"All right, take it off," her mother said. "I'm going to take it up the street to Mrs. Luby and let her help me. It's got to be right or I won't let you leave the house."

"Can't we just leave it the way it is, Mother?" Judy pleaded without hope of success. "I think it's perfect."

"You would," Mrs. Simmons said tartly as she folded the dress and prepared to bear it out of the room. "Sometimes I think I'll never get it through your head. You got to look just right and act just right. That Rose Griffin and those other girls can afford to be careless, maybe, but you can't. You're gonna be the darkest, poorest one there."

Judy shivered in her new lace strapless bra and her old, childish knit snuggies. "You make it sound like a battle I'm going to instead of just a dance."

"It is a battle," her mother said firmly. "It starts tonight and it goes on for the rest of your life. The battle to hold your head up and get someplace and be somebody. We've done all we can for you, your father and I. Now you've got to start fighting some on your own." She gave Judy a slight smile; her voice softened a little. "You'll do all right, don't worry. Try and get some rest this afternoon. Just don't mess up your hair."

"All right, Mother," Judy said listlessly.

She did not really think her father had much to do with anything that happened to her. It was her mother who had ingratiated her way into the Gay Charmers two years ago, taking all sorts of humiliation from better-dressed, better-off, lighter-skinned women, humbly making and mending their dresses, fixing food for their meetings, addressing more mail and selling more tickets than anyone else. The club had put it off as long as they could, but finally they had to admit Mrs. Simmons to membership because she worked so hard. And that meant, of course, that Judy would be on the list for this year's Ball.

Her father, a quiet carpenter who had given up any other ambitions years ago, did not think much of Negro society or his wife's fierce determination to launch Judy into it. "Just keep clean and be decent," he would say. "That's all anybody has to do."

Her mother always answered, "If that's all *I* did we'd still be on relief," and he would shut up with shame over the years when he had been laid off repeatedly and her days' work and sewing had kept them going. Now he had steady work but she refused to quit, as if she expected it to end at any moment. The intense energy that burned in Mrs. Simmons' large dark eyes had scorched her features into permanent irony. She worked day and night and spent her spare time scheming and planning. Whatever her personal ambitions had been, Judy knew she blamed Mr. Simmons for their failure; now all her schemes revolved around their only child.

Judy went to her mother's window and watched her stride down the street with the dress until she was hidden by the high brick wall that went around two sides of their house. Then she returned to her own room. She did not get dressed because she was afraid of pulling a sweater over her hair—her mother would notice the difference even if it looked all right to Judy—and because she was afraid that doing anything, even getting dressed, might precipitate her into the battle. She drew a stool up to her window and looked out. She had no real view, but she liked her room. The wall hid the crowded tenement houses beyond the alley, and from its cracks and bumps and depressions she could construct any imaginary landscape she chose. It was how she had spent most of the free hours of her dreamy adolescence.

"Hey, can I go?"

It was the voice of an invisible boy in the alley. As another boy chuckled, Judy recognized the familiar ritual; if you said yes, they said, "Can I go with you?" It had been tried on her dozens of times. She always walked past, head in the air, as if she had not heard. Her mother said that was the only thing to do; if they knew she was a lady, they wouldn't dare bother her. But this time a girl's voice, cool and assured, answered.

"If you think you're big enough," it said.

It was Lucy Mae Watkins; Judy could picture her standing there in a tight dress with bright, brazen eyes.

"I'm big enough to give you a baby," the boy answered.

Judy would die if a boy ever spoke to her like that, but she knew Lucy Mae could handle it. Lucy Mae could handle all the boys, even if they ganged up on her, because she had been born knowing something other girls had to learn.

"Aw, you ain't big enough to give me a shoeshine," she told him.

"Come here and I'll show you how big I am," the boy said.

"Yeah, Lucy Mae, what's happenin'?" another boy said. "Come here and tell us."

Lucy Mae laughed. "What I'm puttin' down is too strong for little boys like you."

"Come here a minute, baby," the first boy said. "I got a cigarette for you."

"Aw, I ain't studyin' your cigarettes," Lucy Mae answered. But her voice was closer, directly below Judy. There were the sounds of a scuffle and Lucy Mae's muffled laughter. When she spoke her voice sounded raw and cross. "Come on now, boy. Cut it out and give me the damn cigarette." There was more scuffling, and the sharp crack of a slap, and then Lucy Mae said, "Cut it out, I said. Just for that I'm gonna take 'em all." The clack of high heels rang down the sidewalk with a boy's clumsy shoes in pursuit.

Judy realized that there were three of them down there. "Let her go, Buster," one said. "You can't catch her now."

"Aw, hell, man, she took the whole damn pack," the one called Buster complained.

"That'll learn you!" Lucy Mae's voice mocked from down the street. "Don't mess with nothin' you can't handle."

"Hey, Lucy Mae. Hey, I heard Rudy Grant already gave you a baby," a second boy called out.

"Yeah. Is that true, Lucy Mae?" the youngest one yelled.

There was no answer. She must be a block away by now.

For a moment the hidden boys were silent; then one of them guffawed directly below Judy, and the other two joined in the secret male laughter that was oddly high-pitched and feminine.

"Aw man, I don't know what you all laughin' about," Buster finally grumbled. "That girl took all my cigarettes. You got some, Leroy?"

"Naw," the second boy said.

"Me neither," the third one said.

"What we gonna do? I ain't got but fifteen cent. Hell, man, I want more than a feel for a pack of cigarettes." There was an unpleasant whine in Buster's voice. "Hell, for a pack of cigarettes I want a bitch to come across."

"She will next time, man," the boy called Leroy said.

"She better," Buster said. "You know she better. If she pass by here again, we gonna jump her, you hear?"

"Sure, man," Leroy said. "The three of us can grab her easy."

"Then we can all three of us have some fun. Oh, *yeah*, man," the youngest boy said. He sounded as if he might be about fourteen.

Leroy said, "We oughta get Roland and J.T. too. For a whole pack of cigarettes she oughta treat all five of us."

"Aw, man, why tell Roland and J.T.?" the youngest voice whined. "They ain't in it. Them was *our* cigarettes."

"They was *my* cigarettes, you mean," Buster said with authority. "You guys better quit it before I decide to cut you out."

"Oh, man, don't do that. We with you, you know that."

"Sure, Buster, we your aces, man."

"All right, that's better." There was a minute of silence.

Then, "What we gonna do with the girl, Buster?" the youngest one wanted to know.

"When she come back we gonna jump the bitch, man. We gonna jump her and grab her. Then we gonna turn her every way but loose." He went on, spinning a crude fantasy that got wilder each time he retold it, until it became so secretive that their voices dropped to a low indistinct murmur punctuated by guffaws. Now and then Judy could distinguish the word "girl" or the other word they used for it; these words always produced the loudest guffaws of all. She shook off her fear with the thought that Lucy Mae was too smart to pass there again today. She had heard them at their dirty talk in the alley before and had always been successful in ignoring it; it had nothing to do with her, the wall protected her from their kind. All the ugliness was on their side of it, and this side was hers to fill with beauty.

She turned on her radio to shut them out completely and began to weave her tapestry to its music. More for practice than anything else, she started by picturing the maps of the places to which she intended to travel, then went on to the faces of her friends. Rose Griffin's sharp, Indian profile appeared on the wall. Her coloring was like an Indian's too and her hair was straight and black and glossy. Judy's hair, naturally none of these things, had been "done" four days ago so that tonight it would be "old" enough to have a gloss as natural-looking as Rose's. But Rose, despite her handsome looks, was silly; her voice broke constantly into high-pitched giggles and she became even sillier and more nervous around boys.

Judy was not sure that she knew how to act around boys either. The sisters kept boys and girls apart at the Catholic high school where her parents sent her to keep her away from low-class kids. But she felt that she knew a secret: tonight, in that dress, with her hair in a sophisticated upsweep, she would be transformed into a poised princess. Tonight all the college boys her mother described so eagerly would rush to dance with her, and then from somewhere *the boy* would appear. She did not know his name; she neither knew nor cared whether he went to college, but she imagined that he would be as dark as she was, and that there would be awe and diffidence in his manner as he bent to kiss her hand. . . .

A waltz swelled from the radio; the wall, turning blue in deepening twilight, came alive with whirling figures. Judy rose and began to go through the steps she had rehearsed for so many weeks. She swirled with a practiced smile on her face, holding an imaginary skirt at her side; turned, dipped, and flicked on her bedside lamp without missing a fraction of the beat. Faster and faster she danced with her imaginary partner, to an inner music that was better than the sounds of the radio. She was "coming out," and tonight the world would discover what it had been waiting for all these years.

"Aw, git it, baby." She ignored it as she would ignore the crowds that lined the streets to watch her pass on her way to the Ball.

"Aw, do your number." She waltzed on, safe and secure on her side of the wall.

"Can I come up there and do it with you?"

At this she stopped, paralyzed. Somehow they had come over the wall or around it and into her room.

"Man, I sure like the view from here," the youngest boy said. "How come we never tried this view before?"

She came to life, ran quickly to the lamp and turned it off, but not before Buster said, "Yeah, and the back view is fine, too."

"Aw, she turned off the light," a voice complained.

"Put it on again, baby, we don't mean no harm."

"Let us see you dance some more. I bet you can really do it."

"Yeah, I bet she can shimmy on down."

"You know it, man."

"Come on down here, baby," Buster's voice urged softly, dangerously. "I got a cigarette for you."

"Yeah, and he got something else for you, too."

Judy, flattened against her closet door, gradually lost her urge to scream. She realized that she was shivering in her underwear. Taking a deep breath, she opened the closet door and found her robe. She thought of going to the window and yelling down, "You don't have a thing I want. Do you understand?" But she had more important things to do.

Wrapping her hair in protective plastic, she ran a full steaming tub and dumped in half a bottle of her mother's favorite cologne. At first she scrubbed herself furiously, irritating her skin. But finally she stopped, knowing she would never be able to get cleaner than this again. She could not wash away the thing they considered dirty, the thing that made them pronounce "girl" in the same way as the other four-letter words they wrote on the wall in the alley; it was part of her, just as it was part of her mother and Rose Griffin and Lucy Mae. She relaxed then because it was true that the boys in the alley did not have a thing she wanted. She had what they wanted, and the knowledge replaced her shame with a strange, calm feeling of power.

After her bath she splashed on more cologne and spent forty minutes on her makeup, erasing and retracing her eyebrows six times until she was satisfied. She went to her mother's room then and found the dress, finished and freshly pressed, on its hanger.

When Mrs. Simmons came upstairs to help her daughter she found her sitting on the bench before the vanity mirror as if it were a throne. She looked young and arrogant and beautiful and perfect and cold.

"Why, you're dressed already," Mrs. Simmons said in surprise. While she stared, Judy rose with perfect, icy grace and glided to the center of the room. She stood there motionless as a mannequin.

"I want you to fix the hem, Mother," she directed. "It's still uneven in back."

Her mother went down obediently on her knees, muttering, "It looks all right to me." She put in a couple of pins. "That better?"

"Yes," Judy said with a brief glance at the mirror. "You'll have to sew it on me, Mother. I can't take it off now. I'd ruin my hair."

Mrs. Simmons went to fetch her sewing things, returned and surveyed her daughter. "You sure did a good job on yourself, I must say," she admitted grudgingly. "Can't find a thing to complain about. You'll look as good as anybody there."

"Of course, Mother," Judy said as Mrs. Simmons knelt and sewed. "I don't know what you were so worried about." Her secret feeling of confidence had returned, stronger than ever, but the evening ahead was no longer the vague girlish fantasy she had pictured on the wall; it had hard, clear outlines leading up to a definite goal. She would be the belle of the ball because she knew more than Rose Griffin and her silly friends; more than her mother, more, even, than Lucy Mae, because she knew better than to settle for a mere pack of cigarettes.

"There," her mother said, breaking the thread. She got up. "I never expected to get you ready this early. Ernest Lee won't be here for another hour."

"That silly Ernest Lee," Judy said, with a new contempt in her young voice. Until tonight she had been pleased by the thought of going to the dance with Ernest Lee; he was nice, she felt comfortable with him, and he might even be the awe-struck boy of her dream. He was a dark, serious neighborhood boy who could not afford to go to college; Mrs. Simmons had reluctantly selected him to take Judy to the dance because all the Gay Charmers' sons were spoken for. Now, with an undertone of excitement, Judy said, "I'm going to ditch him after the first dance, Mother. You'll see. I'm going to come home with one of the college boys."

"It's very nice, Ernest Lee," she told him an hour later when he handed her the white orchid, "but it's rather small. I'm going to wear it on my wrist, if you don't mind." And then, dazzling him with a smile of sweetest cruelty, she stepped back and waited while he fumbled with the door.

"You know, Edward, I'm not worried about her any more," Mrs. Simmons said to her husband after the children were gone. Her voice became harsh and grating. "Put down that paper and listen to me! Aren't you interested in your child?—That's better," she said as he complied meekly. "I was saying, I do believe she's learned what I been trying to teach her, after all."

Theodore Weesner
Stealing Cars

ALEX HOUSMAN WAS DRIVING A BUICK RIVIERA. The Buick, copper-tone, white sidewalls, was the model of the year, a '59, although the 1960 models were already out. The upholstery in the car was black, the windshield was tinted a thin color of motor oil. The Buick's heater was issuing a stale and odorous warmth, but Alex remained chilled. He had walked several blocks through snow and slush to the car, wearing neither hat nor gloves nor rubbers. The steering wheel was icy in his hands, and he felt icy within, throughout his veins and bones. Alex was sixteen; the Buick was his fourteenth car.

The storm was early to Michigan's Thumb. It was not yet November. The previous day had been predictably autumn, drizzling all day, leaves still hanging apple-colored overhead among the city's black wires, and lying soggy underfoot. But by evening a chilling breeze had begun moving through the city, blowing over the wide bypasses and outerdrives. In the morning the snow covering was overall. It was five or six inches deep, as wet as a blanket soaked in water, as gray and full in the sky as smoke from the city's automobile factories.

A cigarette Alex had not wanted so early in the morning was wedged in the teeth of the ashtray drawer. He could not remember having lighted it, and he thought to snuff it out, but made no move to do so. The dry smoke reached over the dashboard like a girl's hair in water. Taking the cigarette up, discovering either weakness or nervousness in his fingers, he drew his lungs full and replaced it in the teeth of the drawer. The smoke seemed to burn his eyes from within. He squinted as they watered, and shivered. Before him the windshield wipers slapped back and forth quietly, slapping the melting snow to streams trailing to the sides. The view was on again, off again.

He saw that he was heading out of town. He had crossed a line somewhere and now he was no longer going in the direction of Central High

School, he was going away. There was little traffic on his side of the street but on the other side crept a double line of cars and buses. Their headlights sparkled by, in the gray white of the storm. Glimpsing himself going in the wrong direction once again, on an edge of consciousness, he turned to the radio to search for music. Before long, still turning the dial, he was not listening to the stations. Soon he removed his hand. Driving. On the thought alone, the tediousness of driving raised its head.

He drove on. He pressed the accelerator and the heavy Buick moved out faster. He had switched license plates the first night he took the Buick, but he had been driving it ten or twelve days now, too long, he knew, to keep a car so easily identified. He knew he should trade the Buick for a Chevrolet, if only to save on gas money. He knew it every day, but he did not trade it. His father left him a dollar bill on their kitchen table each morning for his lunch and bus fare, and he suffered through giving up the dollar (for gas, never oil; regular, never ethyl) as he suffered through other things he had given up, other things he was leaving undone.

Alex had been driving to the country schools since September. He had discovered the first one by accident, merely driving one day when he should have been in his own; thereafter he searched them out intentionally. In easy fantasies, imagining he was the owner of the car, he drove around the corners and fronts of the strange schools in the movements of their lunch hours, to let himself be seen. Riding a copper-tone stallion. He returned to one school or another for several days running, picking out a girl and looking at her, and looking for her, and partially following her, returning to the same place the next day to watch for her to appear, almost never speaking or approaching. Then, frightened by the 4-H football types in threes and fours who always began to stare at him and say things to each other, he went on to another school, to Flushing and Linden and Grand Blanc and Atlas and Montrose. They were schools only an eighth or a tenth the size of his city high school—two or three hundred students versus three thousand—but there had been a wonder and excitement those fall days of discovering that the students were, incredibly, always fifteen and sixteen and seventeen, with the same recognizable bodies and backs and leg lengths and postures, except, when they turned, for their faces. Their faces were different: unknown and unknowing. He drove among them, and walked among them. He intentionally parked his Chevrolet Bel Air or his Buick Riviera under their eyes, left the car and reentered the car under their eyes, able to see himself in these moments as he imagined he was seen by them, as a figure from a movie, a stranger, some newcomer come to town, some new cock of the walk with a new car, with a plume of city hair.

Fifteen miles from the city he took the familiar ramp off the highway and continued right on the road to Shiawassee. Within a half mile he passed the side road down which Eugenia Rodgers lived, down which she had walked several times to meet him, for she was not allowed to have boys pick her up at her house.

His brother, Howard, also lived in this direction. Howard, who was three years younger, lived with their mother and her second husband some twenty-five miles from the city, where they operated a lakeside tavern. Alex did not know where they lived, but he knew where the tavern was. He was thinking of Howard, now, trying to call up images of him, trying to make the images stand still as he drove. What would Howard think if he saw him in the Buick? The thought of seeing Howard, of actually seeing him, made Alex shudder.

He leaned closer over the steering wheel, to concentrate on the on-again, off-again view presented by the wipers. In the weeks that he had been driving to Shiawassee he had thought of Howard a few times, but he had never considered going there, to Lake Nepessing. Nor did he plan on going there now. What he saw of himself he did not wish his brother to see. He had not seen Howard since a day late in the summer, three years before, when their mother, a stranger—they had not seen her in five or six years— came and took Howard away in her car, carrying his possessions, his clothes, in cardboard boxes. It was a miserable thing to remember, and shuddering again, Alex admitted to himself only that it had been a bad time, a bad week, and looked away from thinking about it. But the idea of seeing Howard became more pleasant, and he let it have its pleasant way, let it occupy him, and drove on, with no intention of going there.

Eugenia Rodgers was his age, sixteen, although he had told her he was nineteen. Nineteen seemed a proud age to his mind; sixteen possessed no such quality. He had met Eugenia, or picked her up, several weeks before, and now, even if it was no more than nine-thirty or ten and she would be in school, her town and her country school were a place to drive to, a place to believe he was headed for, rather than the lake beyond, rather than nowhere.

If he saw Eugenia he might apologize, after a fashion. He had picked her up at school two days before, during her lunch hour, and when they had driven into the country, to a lake, and the lunch hour was ending, he had refused to take her back. It had been autumn then, two days ago. They had gone, as they had several times before, to a lakeside park which was deserted in October. She wanted to go back, because if she missed again, the teacher was going to call her mother again, and her mother, who had remarried not long ago, was going to confine her. But he had refused to take her back, not when she begged, not when she let him feel her breasts, not when she became angry and started walking. He followed her with the car, and stopped before her on the shoulder of the road, watching her through the rearview mirror as she bent forward to begin running, pressing the accelerator as she came close. He convinced her twice more that he was stopping to pick her up, and left both times. The next time he stopped, she walked past the car and did not look at him, and he let her walk perhaps a quarter of a mile before he went after her again. When she finally got into the car, it was nearly two o'clock. She sat still and said nothing, and he looked at her now and then as he drove. In town, when he stopped at a corner, she left the car, slammed the door, and he had not seen her since. He felt like a fool, remembering, but he knew if he told her some story, that he had killed someone, had hit them with the car, or that he had killed his father, that she would listen, and would not believe him, but would, in her way, forgive.

He decided to go ahead and drive to Lake Nepessing. He did not care now; he felt he could talk to Howard somehow. What did it matter what he said, what they said, what they did not say? The idea of actually seeing Howard swept through him and from the tinted interior of the car, in the surrounding whiteness, he began to fantasize that there had been a catastrophe, that a war had come home, that he and Howard were two who were lost and all they needed in the world was to find each other, that with their ratlike cunning they would survive, they would effect a new life. Automobiles, schools, families, all would vanish. They would effect life itself.

Lake Nepessing was both a lake and a village, east on a winding road off the highway, north of Shiawassee. By the time he was on the road and undeniably headed for the village, his resolve had faded some, but not enough to make him turn back. The tavern was several miles past the village. He passed houses here and there along the winding road, then there were houses along both sides, and then a sign:

LAKE NEPESSING
SPEED LIMIT
25 MPH.

He drove slowly, beginning to feel nervous again.

Driving through the town, he noticed a woman leaving a car, keeping her head down as she stepped over to the sidewalk, and he wondered if she might be his mother. He wondered, given all the times he had walked on sidewalks in the city, if she had ever passed him? Had she known she was passing him? It did not matter if she did; he felt neither love nor hate for her. If he felt anything it was a distant curiosity. He did not want to talk to her; but he'd like to see her to look her over without being seen.

The tavern had not opened yet. The front windows were dark and there were no cars or tire marks in the parking lot in front. The neon sign LAKE-VIEW TAVERN was unlighted and hardly visible inside one of the windows, although some small neon beer signs along the windowsill were lighted, Blatz and Falstaff, red and yellow. He had all but stopped on the highway, and now he pulled over, into the parking lot. He sat in the car with the motor running and looked around. He felt as nervous as he had the first time he took a car. Then, as if climbing further into the thin branches of a tree, he opened the door, and left the motor running, stepped out into the snow and damp air. He heard a car coming on the highway behind him, and stood still, without looking, as it passed.

At the dark glass of the tavern he held his hands like blinders. He had never seen the inside of the tavern. Empty of people it looked disappointingly worn and threadbare. The lights over a shuffleboard were out, but behind the bar, among mirrors and bottles and glasses, a Miller's Highlife clock was lighted. It was twenty-three minutes after ten, the second hand revolving. For no reason, he tapped the window lightly with his fingers. However loud the tapping seemed, no one appeared, nothing happened. There was his reflection in the dark glass, in the gray air, and it occurred to him that the figure he saw was lost in some way he could not understand.

Against the rising of nervousness he walked around the end of the tavern, stepping through the unmarked slush, along a driveway which led down behind the building to a boat launching ramp. A T-shaped dock was in the water, and an old red gas pump stood on the bank. A rowboat was in the water, moving slightly, lifting a little toward shore and out again on a slack rope. On the dock he looked down into the water; it was more green here than black. Crouching to see better, he felt the snow fall on the back of his neck. The sky reflected its gray colors on the surface, and as he leaned forward his face and shoulders reflected darkly. The shreds of snow parachuted onto the water, shriveled gray and disappeared; his mind was ranging off as if in judgment of things the size of the universe, and of himself, but of nothing he could see in particular.

Turning his neck down, looking directly into his reflection, he found he could see through his face into the water. He worked his reflection like a flashlight to reveal the bottom. It was still autumn down there, brown and green, the sand blond, the moss hair wavering black from green stones, from the dock piles. Two nearly translucent fish, no deeper or longer than a finger, hovered unconcerned. A slight seizure came turning into his stomach and he leaned over all the more, bent his head between his knees to tighten his stomach against it. He glimpsed the sweep of his trouble and it was so wide and unknown, his face began trembling while his mind told him nothing.

An hour later he had driven back to Shiawassee. It was a town of five or six blocks of stores, with a movie theater and new parking meters, and with the streetlights lighted under the dark sky. The high school was on Main Street, set back from the street, with two dairy bars directly opposite. The two floors of school windows in the brick building were lighted, the same diamond color through the storm as car headlights. He saw a woman teacher's back close to a window on the second floor. He parked where he always parked to wait for Eugenia, where he could see the door of her school. He did not know what he was going to do and did not think much about it; it was not a new problem.

He sat in the car a long time, smoking and looking around. Then he yawned, yawned within the yawn, and deflated into himself. His eyes watered from exhaustion; they itched and he rubbed them. He had not known he was so tired. He considered lying over on his side in the front seat, to sleep, but did not. It was dangerous, inviting to strolling policemen. Still he slumped in the seat, and his head bobbed; he was waiting for Eugenia Rodgers to come out, and not waiting for her either, but merely waiting.

He heard no bells ring, but at last, as he was watching, the main door opened and two boys came out. Then a girl came out, alone, and he was not sure at first that it was her. He looked at the door again, which did not close all the way as one student after another kept it swinging open. Then he looked at the girl again and realized it was her. She walked with her face down against the snow, without a hat, her coat collar turned up and her shoulders high against her neck.

The coat: she was wearing the coat he had given her. It had been in the back seat of one car or another, a lady's camel's-hair coat with a small chain sewn inside the collar. He had forgotten the coat. It was too large for her, too long, and she walked with her hands drawn into the sleeves. He imagined her fuzzed and ratted sweater, her thickness of lipstick, the odors of her neck and hair, her large and firm breasts, and he felt aroused to see her. If he touched the horn for the slightest beep he knew she would look over at him, and she would turn away from her bearing across the street and walk to the car as she had before, without looking at him on the way. In the car she might pause before looking at him; she might ask for a cigarette and conceal herself with a search for matches, or she might ask for a light and conceal herself in a search for a cigarette, or she might close her eyes and lean over to kiss his ear, to use her tongue, or in their game of profanity she might say *you son of a bitch* and smile her shy and uncertain smile.

He did not touch the horn. He watched her walk along. She, like himself, had not worn boots. He knew she was on her way to one of the dairy bars, and he thought of taking her off somewhere to buy her some warm hamburgers. She usually bought cigarettes with the few coins she scraped or stole from her mother, and she loved hamburgers and French fries. But he watched her pass from view, like a thin song, and was relieved when it was over.

He drove through the students who were too concerned with the snow, or too sure of their world to look for cars, although they seemed to see the Buick's brushing fenders and headlights as he inched among them. Passing the dim windows of the dairy bar he glanced to see if she might see him, and he saw bodies and faces inside the glass, and the gold-flecked backside of one of the pinball machines. He imagined she had seen him; he had never driven away like this from anyone and it gave him a little strength, as if something were finally passing, finally ending.

For a moment, driving through Shiawassee, he saw a clarity in his life, or a determination. His troubles seemed for the moment to focus away. If they did not actually catch him driving a car, how could they prove it? With the cars recovered, would they care? It was a soothing idea; it seemed an easy road to follow. If he could begin, if he drove back to the city, and parked the car, and walked to school—It seemed that if he could begin, if he could stay calm, he could follow the road to its end, and there, where it stood waiting, he could secretly step into a new idea of himself.

He parked the Buick three blocks from the school, where he had parked the day before, and walked back. The snow was turning to rain by now and the leather of his shoes was quickly soaked black. He had thought to clear the car of evidence, to wipe away fingerprints and to empty the ashtray, but for no clear reason he simply parked it and let it stand. About ten minutes remained in the lunch hour, and as he walked back, the feeling of drawing nearer to the school moved through him with the air of a wind rising and falling, rising again.

Within the warmth of the heavy double door, he foolishly stomped his feet on the link-metal mat, splashing the water the mat lay in on his pants legs. He walked on into the first-floor corridor. In spite of all else there was a faint feeling of coming home after having been away. Here was the tile floor, the familiar hallways lined with dark green lockers, the whiskey-colored varnished molding, the globes hanging from the ceiling. Except for two girls walking away on the right, the corridor was empty. Far off, also to the right, music was playing, record music from the noon-hour dance in the girls' gym, which because he had never learned how to dance, he had avoided.

His locker was to the left, in the basement near his homeroom. He walked along. Going down the stairs to the basement, he met his homeroom teacher, Mr. Hewitt, coming up. Mr. Hewitt, besides teaching history, was the varsity baseball coach, and a quiet man, neither popular nor unpopular. He nodded lightly at Alex as they passed, then, behind him, Alex heard Mr. Hewitt say, "Alex, were you here this morning?"

Pausing Alex said, "No."

"Where were you?"

Rather than condemnation there was some kindness in the man's voice, and Alex, stopped on the steps, was affected and weakened by it. He found it hard to look up at Mr. Hewitt, who stood waiting. At last, glancing up, Alex said, "I'm back to school now."

Mr. Hewitt was amused. "You're back. Good, I'm glad to hear that. Where have you been?"

"Nowhere," Alex said. "Just messing around." He stood where he was, looking down again, knowing that Mr. Hewitt was standing there looking at him.

"You have a minute?" Mr. Hewitt said. "I'd like to talk with you."

Alex hunched his shoulders, to say yes, and walked along slightly to the rear of the teacher. They went past Alex's locker, and into the homeroom, and Alex found it hard to look up. It seemed if he did, something like whimpering would spread from his chest to his throat. He glanced up enough to see that a girl was sitting at a desk in the homeroom, reading, and looked away as Mr. Hewitt said to her, "Would you excuse us a minute, please?"

She did not quite understand, and Mr. Hewitt added after a pause, "We'd like to have a talk in private for a minute."

"Oh," she said. Alex heard her gather her things and heard Mr. Hewitt step over to close the door behind her.

Mr. Hewitt said, "Sit down."

Alex sat down, looking ahead to look away. He saw the bottom half of Mr. Hewitt move to a seat on a desktop. Mr. Hewitt said, "You've gotten yourself into some kind of dilemma, haven't you? Can you tell me what's happened?"

"Oh, I don't know," Alex said quickly.

"Why are you so upset?" Mr. Hewitt said.

Alex hunched his shoulders and lips again, as if not knowing, or not wanting to say.

"Something at home?"

"Nah," Alex said.

"I know you've missed a lot of school lately. What have you been doing? I'm not going to punish you or anything. Perhaps I can help."

"Ah, just a lot of bad things," Alex said. But his voice failed to work clearly—it rose at the end—and he continued to look ahead at nothing, angry with his voice, with himself.

"What kind of bad things? You mean skipping school?"

"No."

"What, exactly? Can you tell me? You feel free to tell me?"

Unable to speak and unable to look, Alex hunched his shoulders again— he didn't know. He felt his lower lip reaching out.

Someone opened the door and came walking in. Alex's view to the door was blocked and he did not look anyway, but Mr. Hewitt said, impatiently, "Please wait outside and close the door."

After a pause, almost in a whisper, Mr. Hewitt said, "Serious bad things?"

Alex nodded once. He did not look up. He knew Mr. Hewitt was studying him and, in his pause, that Mr. Hewitt believed him. For a moment neither of them spoke or moved. Then Mr. Hewitt said, "I'm afraid the class is about to start. But I want you to do me a favor—I want you to come back this afternoon after school—immediately after—will you do that?"

Alex moved his shoulders again and more or less nodded that he would.

He stood up as Mr. Hewitt stood up, but he still could not look at the man. He walked over toward the door without looking back, and heard Mr. Hewitt say behind him, "Don't get too worried now. It'll work itself out."

Alex said nothing; before him through the glass half of the door he saw faces on top of and beside each other, beginning to separate and back off before he touched the doorknob.

He stepped through them without looking at a face, saw bodies before him in the thickening corridor, and heard someone whisper, "*What's going on?*" The bell, ringing suddenly, startled him.

At his locker, facing the wall and holding his lock in his hand, he tried to tell himself the numbers. They floated close but he could not quite catch them. He fingered the lock's black face, and beside him, someone said, "Hey, what was that all about?"

Alex turned and looked at the boy beside his shoulder but could not think of his name, however familiar his face. "*What?*" he said to the boy.

The boy spoke again, but Alex's mind was hearing Mr. Hewitt again and he did not hear the boy. Alex turned his back on him, as if to conceal the working of his combination, and the boy's hand fell on his shoulder. "Hey," the boy said, and Alex, not looking back, suddenly, violently, whipped his shoulder to shake off the hand. The hand did not return. Nor did Alex look back. He continued staring down, hardly seeing the lock cupped in his hand.

In a moment he knew, decided in the knowing, that he was not going to the afternoon classes. What was he doing here? How could he have thought of coming to school? Sitting at a desk, sitting there, sitting there, sitting there. He closed his eyes for a moment, still facing the wall. But he could not see what he seemed to have been trying to see. At last he let the lock drop and turned to leave, making his way as calmly as he could through the confusion of corridor movement, aiming for the side door on the landing, fifty feet away, aiming for the gray and cold air outside.

Moving down the steps, walking away, he felt the school itself was watching his back, and he felt diminished being watched. He hurried along. Some relief came when he made it around a corner and out of sight of the buildings. His feet were so wet by now they were squishing water inside his shoes. He thought of going home, to undress and put on dry clothes, but he would have to wait until his father had left for work. He walked on. Water was dripping from his hair, down his neck and down his forehead, and from his sideburns. Clear water was gathering in the slush over the sidewalk, small pools in the nickel-colored foot marks. He walked along at a good pace, thinking he had never been so wet, but it was not until he was among the stores and buildings of downtown that it occurred to him that he had left the Buick behind. He had forgotten it completely. Not sure if it was funny or crazy, he tried again, without success, to laugh at himself.

In the men's room of the Fox Theater he used paper towels to wipe his hair and neck and face. Downstairs at the curtained aisle entrance he removed his coat and walked in. An orange-tinted advertisement for a dry cleaner was on the screen, but the lights were not yet completely dark. Perhaps fifteen people were scattered about the cavern, and he took a seat as removed from any of them as possible, on the right, the second seat in, opening his coat over the back of the third seat to dry. He never felt at ease until a theater was completely dark—the worst moment was when a movie ended and the lights came on, a moment he usually avoided by turning to watch the end as he walked up the hill of the aisle, slipping out and away before the lights came on. Now, his timing was lucky. Just as he slouched down into the cushioned seat, to conceal himself, the remaining overhead lights dimmed to darkness and *Previews of Coming Attractions* was fanning over the screen.

When the telephone rang, Alex was asleep on the couch in the living room. He was in his underwear, wrapped in an old Indian blanket he and his father kept on the couch, his clothes on the floor beside him where he had pulled them off. The only light in the room came from the opened door to the bathroom, off the living room at the end of a short hallway.

In the blur of his sleep—it had been short, but long enough to thicken his response—he made his way into the kitchen to the phone, and took up the receiver. As he answered, holding his forehead with his other hand, someone began half whispering in a hurry, and it was a moment before he realized it was Eugenia Rodgers. She was in a state of some kind, but he hardly had voice enough yet for talking and asked no questions. And even when he began to understand what had happened and why she had called, he did not want to appear frightened, and said little. More or less whispering, because she was whispering, he said, "Oh," and "They found the coat?" She carried on like a child herself, no longer bluffing, saying something about hating her stepfather for his promise not to tell if she told and about his telling just the same.

He stood, cold in his underwear, and closed his eyes for a moment. Then he opened them. The call seemed to have taken place in a dream from which he was now awakening. Off in the dream Eugenia Rodgers said she had told them "everything" and they had "called the police."

Stepping over to feel the wall for the light switch, he discovered that his hand was weak. The fluorescent lights came faltering on. He squinted. By the wall clock it was nine or ten minutes after ten. The day was refusing to die. He stood still a moment, not knowing what to do. He remembered the call again as if he had already forgotten. They found the coat. He was thinking she should have said they found her wearing the coat, and he was thinking he should have thanked her for calling—he had not—and he should have apologized for the other day. A yawn took him then, journeyed him a second or two to the tip of his head, made his eyes water with exhaustion. He exhaled to nearly collapsing, envisioned the blue-uniformed police, and felt far too tired to fight, or to run, or to think, felt no more than a thought away from anything.

In the bathroom he looked at himself in the mirror. Except that he had no need of shaving, there was a resemblance to his father when his father got up from sleeping after he'd been drinking. His hair, extra thick like his father's hair, was pressed high on the right, as were the veins on the side of his face. He felt another, stranger resemblance on the inside—felt gummed and swollen—and he was beginning to tremble. He tried to decide what to do. Should he run or should he stay? The idea of running, out in the rain, hitchhiking, taking another car, was like something from a movie. He had no energy to think about it. It only meant more trouble, more fear.

He would stay. His decision was easy. Whatever might happen, he would stay.

He sat on the toilet stool as a place to sit. With his elbows on his knees he rested his eye sockets and head on the heels of his hands. He had not forgotten the call, but still he kept remembering. His father. The thought of his father was different now. It made his heart wince somewhat. He knew at last what his father would feel. He would not feel anger, he would have no strong words. His father would feel as he felt now.

He drew bath water. He did not like baths and usually did his bathing at school in the showers. But he had not showered for several days, and besides, a bath was a way to get warm, to wake up. He drew the tub half-full, wadded his underclothes and laid them on the floor, and stepped into the water. He did not wash at first, but lay soaking. The telephone call kept returning to his thoughts, like something he could still not quite remember, or believe, or forget. Of all the places of disclosure—his teachers, the basketball team, Mr. Hewitt, students—only one made him shudder now, his father.

The police? Would they actually come here, rap on the door, take him away? Were they coming here now? He moved along more quickly on the idea, not to be caught in the tub, to be dressed. He wondered if the police would be impressed with his ingenuity of switching license plates, siphoning gas, impressed with his cooperative answers, impressed with him? How could such an intelligent young man, a fine young man, a basketball player, get into such a mess? No, he thought, they would not see it that way.

In his bedroom he put on clean underwear and socks, and a pair of clean khaki pants, and for its little flair of style, his only white shirt. He had grown some since his father gave him money to buy the shirt, together with a tie and a jacket. They were for his ninth-grade graduation dance, which he walked to, dateless, to spend the evening in the corner with some other boys who did not know how to dance, telling jokes, less angered or nervous in their presence, leaving the corner only once, when everyone circled around Miss Long, the music teacher, dancing with Mr. Fulton, the metal-shop teacher.

Before the mirror, he combed his hair. He looked better now; he was shiny-faced, combed, in a clean shirt. Something was over; he felt lean. And he began to feel hungry. He had drunk water and pop, but he could not remember having eaten all day. The feeling of hunger was pleasant, tenuous, and he tried to sustain it. He tried to believe that something was in fact over.

He fixed an elaborate meal: bacon and eggs, chopped onion and green pepper in the eggs, scrambled, rye bread toasted, cold milk. It was the only meal Alex knew how to cook for himself, and his dinner was usually a choice between this and a slab of rubbery cheese on dry bread, or peanut butter, stuffing the sandwich home on his way back down the stairs and down the driveway, clearing his throat somewhere along the way with a bottle of pop.

He ate until he remembered again. He had eaten a little more than half. As he remembered, his stomach filled and his appetite immediately disappeared. He sat at the table, holding his fork aloft, and a moment later he was hurrying to the bathroom. He stood several minutes over the toilet, bending as if to work a snake from his throat, resting his hand against the wall, and bending again. He placed his hand against the wall again finally, trying to even his breath. He believed it now. Sitting on the stool, his stomach cramping but with nothing there to be released, he shivered with goose bumps. He felt as able as a six-year-old; he was afraid.

By the clock in the kitchen it was ten minutes to twelve. His father was out of work by now. But his father seldom came home before twelve-thirty, or one, or sometime in the night after the bars closed at two-thirty. He had no thought of telling his father, but like a child alone in a house, he longed for his father to be there.

There were the dirty dishes. They had a pact of always washing their dishes and wiping the table and counter. It was only when things went bad for his father that the dishes began to stack—a mess which started at the start of heavy weekend drinking, so Alex failed as well and the sink soon filled with dishes and cloudy water and bits of egg and bread and cigarette butts floating. When the drinking ended, the kitchen was cleaned. It might be shining some afternoon when Alex came home from school, peace floating comfortably throughout the apartment. Or they might do the job together on a weekend morning, washing the dishes and scalding them with water from the tea kettle, cleaning the refrigerator, mopping the floor, beginning another string of fixing separate meals, washing a separate set of dishes, one leaving it clean for the other.

He left the mess. In the living room he looked down at Chevrolet Avenue from the window, thinking of the police, thinking it might be better if they came first, or at the same time, to counter his having to face his father.

He was in the kitchen again when he heard someone outside. It was still no more than twenty to one, and if it was his father, he was probably sober. He heard the several sounds, the car, the car door slamming, and in a moment, footsteps on the stairway, coming up. He stepped from the kitchen, and reentered as his father was coming through the door. His father looked pleased to see him, and spoke quietly, saying, "You're still up," as he was closing the door.

The sweep of cold air he had admitted passed over the room. Alex felt chilled anyway. His father placed his lunch bucket on the table and removed his coat, a blue denim finger-length workcoat. He was clearly sober, and in a calm mood. He rubbed his hands together. "Whatcha doing up so late? Schoolwork?"

Alex nodded.

"Why so glum, chum? Everything okay?"

"Sure."

His father was turning back his cuffs. The odor he carried of the factory was flowing now over the kitchen, an odor of oil, of machines. He turned to the sink to wash his hands. He wore a khaki shirt, from the army, and blue denim work pants. Alex thought to tell him now, to say, when he turned back, that something was wrong, that he had done something awful, that he was in trouble. But he did not. Always before when he wanted something, some dollars, or permission, or a baseball glove or a white shirt and tie, he approached his father when he was drinking, when he was flushed with love or generosity or something. It was different when he was sober.

Drying his hands, his father said, "You hungry? How about some bacon and eggs?"

"I already ate."

His father was at the refrigerator, removing the carton of eggs and the bacon. Alex began picking up his dirty dishes, but his father said, "Don't worry about those, I'll do them with mine."

"I guess I'll go to bed," Alex said.

"You tired?"

"Oh, a little."

For a moment then, as his father was working at the counter, neither of them spoke. Then Alex said, "I guess I'll go to bed then."

"Sure you won't have a bite to eat?" His father was looking at him now.

"No, I'm pretty tired," Alex said, looking away from looking at his father. He paused a moment, aware that his father was watching him, and then he walked from the kitchen, saying no more.

In his bedroom, not turning on his light, he sat on the edge of his bed to remove his socks, and when they were off, he still sat on the bed. At last, standing, he removed his shirt and pants. He knew his father knew something was wrong, and he knew this was the time to talk to him, but he still could not do it.

Then his father came to the door. Alex was turning his covers down, straightening the pillow of his unmade bed. His father half whispered from the doorway, "You going to bed now?"

"Yes."

"Well—okay. You have yourself a good sleep now, son."

"I will."

"Good night now."

"Good night."

Still his father paused. Then he said, "You want your door closed?"

"Okay."

"Good night now, son. Have a good sleep." His father closed the door softly, as if not to disturb something.

Pushing in between his old sheets, pulling up his covers, Alex lay on his side and kept his eyes open. In a moment he recognized the sound of the rain on his window, and then he could see more clearly the light which came around his shade from the lights in the street outside. His place in bed grew a little warmer and it was almost comfortable lying there, more comfortable than otherwise, he knew, with his father there, and sober, and a little worried about him. Nor could he help seeing the reversal of things. The misery was usually in those outer rooms, the old records playing, perhaps a sudden smashing of something, a dish, a cup, a fist against a wall or door, or a sudden laugh, or perhaps the throwing open of his bedroom door and the black silhouette of his father in the harsh light of the doorway —*son, hey son, old pal, wake up a minute*—perhaps nothing but the music and his father's silent presence through the night.

He was arrested the next day, but not until school had nearly ended. With no more than five minutes remaining in his last class, geometry, a girl from the principal's office entered the room with a white slip of paper.

It had been a day of questions and answers, of failures to answer. In homeroom that morning, Mr. Hewitt had leaned over his desk and whispered, "What happened to you yesterday? I looked for you."

"I guess I forgot," Alex had whispered back. "Everything's okay now."

Mr. Hewitt had looked at him as he straightened up, as if asking with his eyebrows if Alex was sure, and Alex had signaled with a small nod that he was.

During lunch hour he had walked past the parked Buick. It stood as he had left it, but looking somehow larger. He did not turn his eyes to it as he passed, but looked ahead, as if both he and the car were being watched. He circled the block so as not to pass it again, and this time he crossed the street and entered the lunchroom on the corner. It was filled with bodies and noise, cigarette smoke layering toward the ceiling, the juke box playing. Entering, not knowing just where to go or stand, he overheard someone say something about the noon-hour dance being about to start, and something grated within him, as always.

He recognized the girl entering the room as one who worked in the principal's office. When the teacher, Mrs. Scholls, read the note and looked in his direction, he was not surprised. But he may have been stunned in a way, for he could not quite recall afterward how the next minute or two passed. Mrs. Scholls came to his desk and said softly, "You're to report to the principal's office," and as if transferred by magic, a moment later he was in front of the wooden counter in the office where four or five girls and women were working at desks. He knew Mr. Spencer's office was to the left, but as a girl looked at him for his question, he said, his voice quite clear, "I'm supposed to see the principal." The girl directed him, but he hardly heard her words. In an outer office, a lady at a desk said from a distance, "Alex Housman?" and he nodded that he was.

He stopped at the doorway to the principal's office. He had never been here before. Mr. Spencer, from his desk, and two men, standing, in suits and unbuttoned topcoats, had their faces turned to the door. Alex had never met Mr. Spencer, but the man said, "Come in, Alex."

He took two or three steps into the office, and Mr. Spencer rose and came around his desk as if to shake hands, but stepped past him to close the door.

One of the men was walking over to him, reaching inside his topcoat to remove his wallet, which he flopped open. Alex glimpsed an intricate gold badge, some blue on it, then it was gone. Mr. Spencer was behind his desk again, standing, although Alex had not seen him return. The man introduced himself, Lieutenant Somebody, and the other man, Detective Somebody, but Alex did not listen carefully enough to register their names. He saw their faces looking at him. The lieutenant said, "I guess you know why we're here?"

"Yes," Alex said.

A moment later they were in the corridor, and the first students, the fast-walkers, were already in motion, although Alex had not heard the first bell ring. But classroom doors were open, or opening, classes were on their feet, and the day was ending.

They had to go to the basement for Alex to get his coat from his locker. Both detectives walked with him. He laid his books on the shelf and slipped his coat on, and locked up again. When they returned the way they had come, the corridor had thickened to a slow herding. Alex was not between the two men—both were on his right—but he noticed passing students glancing from him to them and back again, and he tried then to walk without looking into faces. Just before they reached the outside door, the men both slipped on porkpie rain hats. The man who had done the talking, the lieutenant, held the door for them, and when he came up he was on the other side so Alex was in the middle. He thought for the first time to run; it was one thing he could somehow do well.

Their car was parked in the no-parking space where the sidewalk met the street, half blocking the way over to the bus stops and lunchrooms. It was a black car, unmarked except for a small antenna coming from the roof. The mass of students was passing around the car as water passes around a dock pile. The lieutenant opened the rear door for Alex, and when he had stepped in and sat down, the door was slammed behind him. The lieutenant took the seat in front of him, and the other detective, a younger man, went around to the driver's side. The car was dirty, cigarette ashes all around, the floor ribbed metal without carpet; the motor was as noisy and loose as a truck's motor. They nosed through the flow of students in a J-turn, and headed downtown.

He spent several hours in the police station, from about three-thirty until eight or eight-thirty, getting stranded somehow in a shift change and in the dinner hour. A man finally came from the first office, folded handcuffs hanging from his belt, catching Alex smoking, and said, "That's all right— don't put it out. Come on in."

The man was conversational. He asked Alex how he was doing, how was school, and who was going to win the Pontiac game, and he asked many questions about full name and date of birth and address, and then if Alex had a girl friend, and what he wanted to be when he grew up. Alex cooperated. He said he sort of had a girl friend, but that he did not know what he wanted to be when he grew up. They talked about drafting and apprenticeships in factories and the General Motors Institute of Technology, and at last the man said, "What about the cars? Let's talk about them. When did you take the first one?"

"You mean the exact date?"

"Sure. Do you remember it?"

"Well, it was Friday. The first Friday in September. After school started."

"What was the car?"

"It was a Chevrolet, a Bel Air. Green, two-door."

"You got a good memory. Where did you find it? How long did you keep it? Where did you leave it?"

"I just kept in one night. I found it out at Lakeside Park, and I left it down on East Kearsley Street, about two in the morning."

"Who was with you?"

"Nobody."

"Come on. Who was with you?"

"Nobody."

"You took these cars alone?"

"Yes."

The man eyed him. Then he said, "Okay—keep your memory going. What was the next car. All the details."

Alex's memory remained clear. He could remember all but the numbers of the license plates he had switched. He talked for about an hour, told of smashing one car into a parked truck, and of trading the spare tire of another for three dollars in gas, up to and including the copper-tone Buick Riviera, telling where they could pick it up. When he finished, the man said, "Go on."

"That's it," Alex said.

"You sure?"

"Yes."

The man took up a sheet of paper. "What about the Olds Eighty-eight you took on September twenty-seventh? Why'd you leave that off the list?"

"I didn't take it," Alex said.

"Let's see your wallet."

Alex laid his wallet on the desk. The man picked it up and looked through it.

"This your phone number?" he said.

"Must be."

"Who's home?"

"Nobody."

"Your mother's not home? She work?"

"I just live with my father."

"Aah so. Where's he?"

"At work."

"Where?"

"Chevie."

"What shift does he work?"

"Second."

"You and your old man get along okay?"

"Sure."

The man was shaking his head, looking at him. "Why?" he said. "It makes no sense."

Alex said nothing; he knew no answer.

The man, rising, said, "What you doing in a mess like this? You nuts? Don't you know this is for real?"

Alex said nothing.

"Well, let's go," the man said. "I'm gonna have to put you in the detention home."

Alex was taken to another part of the police station. He was left sitting on a bench, not far from the main door and opposite the complaint desk, a moon-shaped counter with openings like those at a bank. He was waiting for the ID Clerk to come on duty. The blue-shirted policemen behind the counter paid little attention to him, much less than he paid to them. He listened to their radio and telephone conversations and orders and questions. He smoked. He stood up several times to relieve the numb pain growing on his tailbone from sitting, and he stepped over several times to press a swig of water from a cooler. The fact that he was waiting to be taken to the detention home floated over his thoughts as coolly as an impending basketball game, or an impending fight between others. He did not quite believe it.

At last a young man came hurrying in, wearing civilian clothes, popular, for it seemed all the policemen behind the counter called out something— *Hey, DJ, where the hell you been? DJ, how's duck hunting? Hey, old Murphy's hot after your ass.* And, among them: *You got a customer there.*

The young man was already past Alex but he looked back and said, "Be with you in a minute." He went on through a door and lights came on all along the upper half of a milk-colored glass wall. Alex saw the young man's shadow move across the room, then disappear. Ten minutes later he opened the door and said, "Okay, let's go."

Alex was photographed in an alcove marked with heights—look to the right, flash, chin up, flash—and his fingers were separated, rolled over an ink pad and then over a white card. The young man moved very fast. He wore a white shirt and tie, but with his sleeves rolled above his elbows, a cigarette behind one ear. He asked questions and clicked at a typewriter as Alex answered, spun the card out, and Alex was soon left sitting at another bench, within the ID room this time, to wait.

Two men passed through while he sat there, each accompanied by a uniformed policeman—one a tough, mean-looking man of about thirty who had been in a fight, little more than his eyebrow showing from one eye, and blood on his face, neck, and shirt, the other an egg-shaped old man dressed in a mismatched coat and tie and pants. Later Alex heard DJ on the phone—"Where the hell is Watt? I got a prisoner over here. No, no, juvenile."

Alex sat smoking, reaching out to throw matches and flick ashes into a metal wastebasket beside a desk. In time a uniformed policeman walked in, with a card in his hand. "Housman?" he said to Alex. Alex nodded. "Let's take a ride," he said. Alex rose. He put out his cigarette against the inside of the wastebasket.

Outside it was dark. They went down to the garage in one of the elevators, and out into the cold air. It was shivering cold to Alex, for all this time he had not removed his coat. Nor had he eaten, had barely eaten all day, but he was not hungry. He did not know the time. He felt it must have been past eight, perhaps close to nine. He and the policeman walked across a low-ceilinged garage, and, coming to a marked police cruiser, the policeman told him to get in front. They pulled out from under the building and across the lighted parking lot. Alex sat with his hands in his coat pockets, still shivering. The policeman said almost nothing. It had been raining, but the rain had stopped and there were only wet spots left, with traces of snow in the gutters.

They drove through the city, for a time in the direction of Alex's house, then turning east. They passed close to the factories along the river where his father worked, and must have been working at the time.

Some ten minutes later, in the country, going along a dark, paved road, the policeman suddenly put on his blinker—it flashed green on the dashboard—then braked and turned to enter a long driveway. The buildings were there, but they were poorly lighted and just visible in the sweep of headlights. Alex saw the brick to the right, with blacker spaces in the receding darkness where the windows must have been. He could not see how high the brick went, for there were small outdoor lights on the corners of the building, and blackness above. To the left, in a glimpse, the headlights flashed over part of a wire fence about eight feet high. The policeman said, "Let's go," and Alex realized the man had automatically disliked him.

The policeman came around from the driver's side, leaving the motor running, tall with his hat and his leather gear squeaking, and walking beside Alex to a door. Alex could see now that the building went on perhaps another hundred feet, that the other end was not lighted and disappeared in darkness. He glanced up and saw that the building was even higher than he had imagined, not two stories but three, perhaps four. From the darkness overhead, not very loud in the stillness, a Negro voice said, *"Hey, you new man—poleece catch yo ass?"* Laughter, barely audible, came from within.

The policeman said nothing. At the doorway he pressed a button and they stood waiting. A faint clicking came from inside the door, then it opened and a man was standing there. The policeman handed the card he had carried to the man. He said, "Here's a new one for you."

The man, who was short, said, "Give you any trouble?"

"No," said the policeman.

The policeman did not go in. The man nodded for Alex to enter, and Alex stepped inside. The man said something to the policeman and then closed the door. It caught cleanly and locked, a heavy door.

In the corridor the man told Alex to walk ahead. Alex walked ahead of him to where the corridor ended, where the door on the left was made of metal. With a key extracted from a ring on his belt, the man unlocked the door, reached in to switch on another light, and said, "Up you go."

Alex went up a circular metal stairway ahead of the man. Overhead somewhere he thought he heard something, voices, or the creaking of beds, within the sound of their footsteps on the metal. At the top, at a landing, there was another metal door, one with a hole about four inches wide in the center. The light switch here was on the outside. The man flipped the switch and looked in before he unlocked the door. Alex entered first. It was another corridor, not much wider than the door itself, lined with doors on one side some six or seven feet apart. Both walls were marked the full length with initials and messages and drawings dug and scratched into the white plaster. Two or three caged lights along the runway were lighted. The man closed the door behind him before he continued. Alex felt the sense now of confinement, of being cornered.

"Go on," the man said.

Each door along the way had a hole like that in the main door, with numbers stenciled over the holes, several of the numbers rubbed and scratched as if from within, all marked from without, but still readable.

"Right here," the man said.

It was number 11. Alex stood waiting while the man found another key to unlock the door. He pushed it open but did not go in himself. "In you go," he said.

Alex stepped into the room. For just a moment, from the light around his shadow, he saw more marked walls, a cot, a commode against the wall. The door was pulled shut at once behind him and there was only the circle of light from the hole in the door. Then the door was being locked, the key was working, and he turned to look back. There was nothing to see but the hole. A moment later he heard the door at the other end of the runway being opened. Immediately he was in full darkness, although he had not heard the click of the light switch. The sound of footsteps on the metal stairway followed, then, fainter, the opening, closing, and locking of the door at the bottom of the stairs.

He realized the room had a window.

Someone spoke then, calmly and soft. "Hey man, what you in for?"

Alex looked toward the door again, but did not answer.

Someone else said, "Hey, how you like the service in this hotel?" A high-pitched *hee-hee-hee* followed, and other laughter, but it settled quickly.

Alex stood waiting, listening. He thought he also heard the sound of steady breathing, someone asleep. There was also a light hissing sound of steam.

The lighter shape of the window was visible now, and he stepped over to it. The window was not barred, but it was covered on the outside with heavy mesh wire. The wire crossed at right angles in squares of about an inch, and was not quite as thick as a pencil.

There was little to see, except that it must have been the back of the building, away from the road. There were no lights. Nor did he see any stars visible in the dark sky. But then, far off, perhaps a mile away, he saw lights which seemed to come from a house.

He stood by the window. He was not very tired; it could not be much later than nine-thirty. He could see the shape of the cot now but he had no feeling to lie down. He stood quite a long time this way, thinking but barely following his thoughts. The excitement of being in jail, the notoriety, had already faded away. He thought he had been here about an hour, but was not sure. It may have been no more than fifteen minutes. He stood thinking, thinking naturally of himself, scanning his life as if to see what it was that had brought him here, and unable at the same time to see anything very clearly.

He wondered if there was any talk of him at the football game over in the city, any talk of his being here, of the detectives taking him from school. Probably not, for not many would know where he had been taken, and if they did, it did not much matter. He remembered the years he had sold popcorn at the stadium, for both football and baseball games. He had made one cent of each ten he collected, and on a good night, besides his admission, he made about two dollars. He worked at the stadium until he went to high school; he quit because he wanted to join the spectators sitting in the stands.

Right now his father was probably working at Plant 4, across the river from the lighted stadium. From there as well as from their apartment, the big plays and the touchdowns could be heard. He wondered if his father, hearing the crowd tonight, would think of him and think he was there. Or would his father know by now? He doubted it. He doubted the police would have notified him at the factory. His father would probably go home and find the apartment empty and think he was out late. Would he think he was at a party, a dance? It was something they never talked about.

Football games; he had always felt depressed during and after football games. He never liked to simply go back home, and he was afraid to go to the dances. He usually left in the general crowded movement and walked along into town, along with the lines of cars moving bumper to bumper, the policeman waving red flashlights. But in town the procession soon passed. The people who stopped there were always older people who parked and disappeared into the cocktail bars, and he continued walking along, looking in store windows, never in a mood at those times to go to a late movie, sometimes trying to pick up stray girls at bus stops, inviting them to milk shakes, or to walk, but with little luck. Usually, before long, he shot a few games of pool somewhere and walked home again. It was only that first night, and the nights after, when he had a car, that he did not go home early.

He shivered. The air around the window made it seem colder. The fear, and then the excitement, and then the calm he had felt since being locked up, were gone now, replaced by a small sickness of self-pity. The warmth of work and life in a factory seemed now all the richness one wanted to ask for under the sun. Life in school, with books and dreams and romance— it seemed the private, far-off world of the privileged, lying safe over there, sleeping well now after a night out.

He remembered the night at Lakeside Park, when he had stood looking as he stood now, and shivering, without being cold. He stood at the edge of the dark gymnasium floor that night, and all the time he was there he hardly moved a foot. The backboards had been raised, unseen in the overhead darkness, to make room for the dance, and colored lights, reds and greens, blues and violets, revolved overhead, over all, over his face where he stood, over the shadowed bodies of those dancing on the floor. Music was furnished by musicians from his school he had not known were musicians. He had taken two buses, the second to the end of the line, and walked another three quarters of a mile to get there; it was the first time he had ever gone to a school dance. And he thought he had been the last to have the back of his hand stamped at the door—where two girls had to check his name in a book to be sure he was from Central High School—but after a time the victorious football team came in and a brief uproar passed through the half-dark room. He still did not move. The uproar settled quickly, was absorbed quickly, as if by the darkness, and the music, and the dancers continued to dance, and he stood watching. Occasionally, passing, the brighter red or yellow light caught someone's upturned face, and when it caught his own, he stiffened and did not change his expression. He did not stay long. When he left, on his way to the door, sidestepping politely through the dancers, he had to pause once to let a couple not looking avoid bumping into him. He smiled lightly over this, as if over something cute, something youthful, but if they had bumped into him, and if he had had a knife, he would have ripped their throats with it. Out in the parking lot, he took his first car, a Chevrolet Bel Air with keys hanging in the ignition.

Jeremy Larner
Hector Rodriguez

I STARTED TAKING NARCOTICS IN THE BRONX, when I was eleven. I was curious, but I wasn't using them that much—I was just taking marijuana once in a while and snorting; I wasn't shooting it up, I was just skinning it then. Skinning is just where you hit anywhere in your body and shoot the dope in. That's with heroin. And snorting is where you snort it up your nose, just like if you're sniffing something. And burning marijuana, that's just like smoking a cigarette, the only thing you inhale it, you don't let it out, you just try to hold it in.

I was using it up there, and then when I moved down here, I was still using it, you know, but I didn't have no habit or nothing. Like when I started going to school, I would go to school high, and I learned how to read a little high. You know, like I wanted to learn something, the things I need in life, but the teachers wouldn't teach me. They used to ignore me, and pay attention to the other kids. Then when I didn't want to learn, they used to come and try to teach me how to learn. Like I couldn't see that; it used to burn me up. I used to go to school high and start nodding all over the classroom, get drowsy, and that's when I started staying out of school; I didn't go to school no more than three or four months in a year.

That's when I started mainlining, when I got to be fifteen; I started mainlining like a dog. Then when I was sixteen, about three or four months ago, I told my mother I was on narcotics. She started crying, but I told her don't cry, if I was another kid I would probably keep it to myself and die by myself. All I want you to do is give me your signature. That way I can go away to Riverside and help myself. The day that I was going away my mother came and gave me some money, my sister gave me some money, and my mother said, I can't see you go, and I said, well go home, 'cause I can't see myself go, 'cause I love you and I know I done one of the most stupidest mistakes in my life. My mother left crying and that hurt me, you know, but I had to take it like a man, because I knew that I stepped into something that was bigger than myself.

Then when I went to Riverside, it wasn't that bad kicking, because they give you medication to calm down your sickness, and that way you can kick in peace I was wrapped up in a blanket for five days with cold sweats, and when they came to bring my food I couldn't eat. Then after five days I started out with soup and milk, and I couldn't hold that in my system. After that when I started eating, I started going down to my social worker, having my team meetings.

I was on Team Two. Mr. W. was my social worker, Mr. Z. was my psychiatrist; then I had Mr. P. my psychologist, and I had a few other people there that I forgot their names. I used to go down and tell them my troubles and when they asked me how come I started using narcotics, I told them I was curious, because that was the truth; it wasn't because I had a problem or nothing, I was just curious, I played it stupid. I used to see my friends using it, I used to see them having fun, and I wanted to know what it was. When I got my hands on it I started to like it, so then it was too late to back out of it. So then I turned myself over to Riverside. They understood it, and at first they wanted to keep me six months, but I told them I wanted to come out, I wanted to start straight, see if I could get me a job, you know, to help out my parents. With a job I could occupy my time, kill time, stay away from everything. So they let me out, and every Thursday at six o'clock I got to check into the after-care clinic. I'm on three years' probation, and if I get caught with narcotics, I get taken in again, and this time they hit me with six months. And if I keep getting in trouble, they give me a year or send me upstate.

Marijuana smells like tea and olive seasoning mixed up together. Once you got it in you it makes you feel drowsy and it makes you forget about things you don't even want to know about. Or it just brings you out so you can have a gay time. If you want to jump around, you jump around; if you want to sit down and just be in a world of your own, you just sit down and look for your own kicks on it. Like if you see somebody and they come talk to you and something strikes you funny, you just crack up laughing. And you sit down, talk to a girl or boy, you know, like you got some company. You just stay sitting down in a corner and nobody can bother you, no trouble, no nothing. Since marijuana isn't habit-forming you can take it any time you feel like it. If you're in a good mood, you want to get gay, you haven't got nothing to do, you just go and buy yourself a couple of sticks, if you know anybody that sells it. You need to know the right person, 'cause you can go ask a cop for all I know, you need to know the right connection. If you get it, you just take it and there you are, in your own world.

I used to get it uptown, anywhere in Prospect Avenue, right in the streets. Like if you see a junkie and you know him, you just ask him where can I cop some pot? If he knows he'll take you, he'll cop for you. I paid 75 cents a stick, or a dollar for a bomb. A bomb is about as big as a Pall Mall and as fat as a Pall Mall. Like a regular cigarette The other one is skinnier. I used to smoke it anywhere, like I coulda smoked it in a hallway, smoke it in my house, and if I wanted to just start walking down the street smoking it without nobody seeing me. Just cuff it up in my hand without nobody seeing me and keep on smoking it, just like if I'm smoking a cigarette. Like I would light up a cigarette and light up a joint, start smoking the joint, and everytime I would see a cop or a person coming up I would hide it in my hand or in my pocket and just take out the cigarette, keep on walking. That way nobody would suspect.

I was eleven when I started with marijuana and heroin, too. I stole the heroin off of some guys. I seen them put it up on a roof. I didn't like them because they push me around too much. And I said I don't know what it is, but the only way I can get even with them is by taking it. And I got two of my friends, you know, they were brothers; one of them was twelve and the other was thirteen, like they would shoot up and all. So I took it; since I had seen them doing it, I knew what it was already, more or less. I went and took it and then I knew what it felt like and I liked it. Then from there on I kept on using it.

When you snort heroin, you know, it got a bad bitter taste, like a taste that would turn your stomach inside out. It got some way-out taste. I couldn't snort because I couldn't take that taste; so I started shooting up. Shooting up you don't get the taste; all you get is a fast rush and a boss feeling, you know, like then you got a higher kick than marijuana. You feel drowsy, sit in a corner nodding, nobody to bother you, you're in your own world, in other words. You ain't got no problems whatsoever, you think freely, you don't think about things you were thinking about before shooting up, like you're in your own world, nobody to bother you or nothing.

The first time I skinned, like I wouldn't hit the vein, just pick up the spike and shove it in. Skin-popping, it takes quite a while before you feel it— take a couple of minutes, but it still do the same effect. Skin-popping you don't get no tracks or nothing. Now mainlining you get tracks, and you're hitting directly in the vein. You get a faster habit and while you're main-lining you can feel the stuff faster. Tracks are marks, black marks, like a long black streak coming down your arm directly over your vein; that comes from hitting in the same place so much. Now when you skin-pop you hit all over your body; you can't keep up with tracks. You lose them; they just keep falling off.

I was fifteen when I started mainlining. I got a set of works: a spike, a whisky bottle cap with a bobby pin around it to make like a handle, an eyedropper, and a baby's pacifier. Now when you cook the stuff you just put it inside the bottle cap, draw it up with the eyedropper, tie the dropper to the spike and just shoot it in your veins. You need water to cook it up— a lot of guys carry a little bottle. You have a special spot to shoot up, that's where you have your water stashed. You measure out the heroin into the water, light a match, and cook it up in the cooker just like when you're heat-ing up a bowl of soup or something. They got a piece of cotton inside the cooker to help them draw it all up. They put the spike on the dropper, strap the arm up and wait till the veins come up and then just hit directly. You put the spike in slow, and the only way you know you got a hit is by watching the blood come up; then you just take off the strap and squeeze it in. Then you feel that rush all over your body and you got your high.

Once you squeeze it in, the drug circulates with your blood, it will come around your system, and all of a sudden your eyes will feel like they gonna close up on you. You feel drowsy, your mouth will dry up on you, your spit will turn into cotton balls, right?; then you just start nodding all over the place, take out the works, clean 'em and hide 'em. Then you got that boss feeling, man, like you're your own boss, there ain't nobody can tell you what to do in this world.

If you're weak-minded, if you get a habit, your body will like cramp up on you, your skin'll start shrinking up, you'll start getting sick and need a fix, you'll start sweating at the same time you'll feel cold, you'll be wrapped up in blankets. You'd do anything just to get a fix. For me to get my habit without mainlining it took me six months. I just kept on using it, and I kept on getting the money, right?, so I didn't have to worry about me getting sick. When I started to get sick and I needed the money for a fix, I would go tell my Mom, look I have to buy my girl a present, this and that, and my Mom would fall for it. She would give me the money, I would run down for a shot, take off, and my body would feel relieved, feel at ease. You know, I don't cramp up, then I feel boss. Then when I had money I got my works, and anybody want to use them have to give a taste of their junk, and somehow I kept up with my habit. Till I finally realized that I didn't want to use it no more, I wanted to straighten up, I wanted to go to work, help out my parents.

I have my own works, right? Now you're using junk yet you ain't got your own works. Well, you will come to use mine, 'cause you can't snort and you need a shoot-up. Now I'll tell you you have to give me a fix before using my works. You ain't got no choice, you have to give me a fix or go on without one. I had a bathroom in Henry Street and then I had a roof in Henry Street. Inside the bathroom they got the box upstairs, the clean water, fresh water comes down to wash out the bowl; well we just take a canful and bring it down. I had a special rule, you know: nobody could come up and get me till after nine o'clock in the morning, 'cause I was out all night. I had two sets of works—the one at home and the one I lend out to the people. Now sometimes I tell them, look, I've already shot up, I don't want to shoot up, just put a little bit inside of this bag—and I'll go shoot that home. Then we would shoot up in that bathroom or up on the roof. After that I would stash the works downstairs where nobody could see me, go home and during the night when I'm sick I have my own works home. I would lock myself in the bathroom where nobody see me and shoot up there, all by myself.

That bowl, you know, in the bathroom—I used to move it, and we had like a loose brick where I stash them; and the minute I move it back in place it look like it was built there and nobody could move it. Now before I hide them I tell my fellas, okay now go downstairs, and I start walking upstairs. They would think that I'm hiding upstairs and I would just watch them leave, and then I would just run down and hide them, go upstairs and come down through the next building. That way they wouldn't know where I had them.

The works that I had home, I used to clean up the spike and wrap it up in a piece of aluminum paper. Then I would wrap up the cooker in a piece of aluminum paper. The eye-dropper I would wrap up in a piece of bag paper, and put it all inside a box of Marlboro, you know, an empty pack of cigarettes, keep those home. Now the other works I used to wrap them up the same but wrap them up in a hanky and stash them. I kept this up till I was ready to go to Riverside, then I threw the works away, flushed them down the bowl piece by piece.

During a day I would take up two at a time; altogether it would come out to about sixteen fellas. Now you know if I was high, I wasn't gonna shoot up sixteen times, so I say okay, just start putting what you gonna give me inside this bag; then I just used to save it all up, and the next day I have my fix. I didn't have to worry about getting money or nothing.

The others couldn't get works. I had to steal my spike out of the hospital. Like when I went to the hospital for my penicillin shot when I had the Asiatic Flu, as the nurse walked out I seen where she threw the spike, inside a big jug full of alcohol. I just put my hand in and grabbed a whole bunch of spikes. I came out and I sold a whole lot of them to a whole lot of guys. And they lost them. But I still had two of them left, and I had my two sets of works, one home and one at the bathroom. And everybody after they lost theirs started coming to me. And I just kept collecting fixes.

I kept earning, I wouldn't sell nothing out. I figured if I sold something, I would spend the money, and later on like I be sick and nobody will come to give me a fix and I be stuck right there. So I used to keep taking in but I wouldn't give none out. A bag would be about a square inch—of that bag they would give me about a third. Now I would shoot up about four bags a day, right? The rest I would save and then I would have me about two more bags. I had it in my house stashed under the bureau. Or in the bathroom under the toilet bowl. I looked a long time before I found that place.

If one of them was nervous and he couldn't hit himself, if he would ask me I would hit him myself. I hit a lot of guys in my days. Now if a fella is capable to hit his own self, I would let him. I would let him judge his own self. Now I tell you I used to hit my own self. I wouldn't let no one hit me. I wouldn't take the chance. They might be nervous and run right through my vein, and who's gonna get messed up? Me.

In the morning, that's when everybody comes out sick, you know, to cop, and that's when I used to be ready with my works, just waiting for these people to come over my way. They used to come, boom! I would be collecting right there and then. They meet me in Henry Street. I wouldn't take nobody up to my house to shoot up, because I didn't want my parents to get a bad name. If I had a bad name why mess it up for my parents? I have to clear that up in my own ways. I would wait next to La Guardia Park, let 'em meet me there. When they come on I would say okay, go ahead, you know where to meet me. When they walk I would just run ahead, have the works and everything ready. I had a short-cut and I'd be there waiting for them.

About the junk itself, it is different depending on where and who you get it from. Now if one of these big operators, you know, the brain of the gang, if he would go and cop, and if he cops a piece that already been cut, he won't have to mess around with it unless he want to mess it up, you know, to make a little more out of it. Now if he go and cop a pure piece, that piece ought to be cut six and one, but he would come down and cut it two and one, make it nice and strong. Right there and then you got good junk, good heroin. Now if he were going to mess it up to get more junk than what he's supposed to get, he'll cut it up six and four, he'll loosen it up and make it weak, like guys won't cop off of him every day. By six and four I mean cutting it one spoon of pure heroin and six or four of sugar. They say it's supposed to be six and one, but if the dealer is wise, he wants everybody to keep coming to him, and he wants to give them a nice count so they can fall out, he will go and cut it two and one, or three and one, make it nice and strong.

Uptown they had this broad, you know, she was a woman already, she was married and she had three kids. She was a junkie and every time she would send somebody out to cop for her—'cause she wouldn't take the chance of going and buying for herself—they would beat her out of her money. And she started marking down the people who started doing that. And she lost her head. So she went and bag up a couple of bags full of rat poison, and when the guys came, you know, she told 'em, well I'm dealing now; and when they cop off her she say, well this guy didn't beat me or nothing, he didn't take my money, so she gave him a good bag. And she say, why this guy beat me, six times, so far he got 150 of my money. Boom! We'll give him a bag of rat poison and mess him up. Now if the guy taste it and know it's rat poison he can't do nothing about it, 'cause he beat her. If he shoots it up he's gonna die instantly.

I taste every bit of junk myself before I use it. I wouldn't take the chance —somebody could be sick, and they might want to get my money so they could get their real cure, and they might sell me a bag of Ajax or a bag of rat poison. And if I wouldn't taste it, if I would play stupid, I would just shoot it up, and like I would go out. Because rat poison cooks up. Now Ajax it cakes up on you, like it bubbles up, and I know if it's junk or not. I make a practice of tasting it, so I know what I'm getting and no one beats me for my money or tries to mess me up.

I had two overdoses in my life. One of them I had in Henry Street when I shot up, but it didn't hit me then, I didn't feel nothing till I walk downstairs. Boom! As soon as I hit the street I passed out. A guy took me up to his house, to his girl's house, and they woke me up. Then the second time I took too much, we were driving around inside a car and we were shooting up inside the car. I wind up in Jackson Park, unconscious, I done passed out, and the guys took me all the way back to Henry Street, took me up to a girl's house, gave me a salt shot, made me drink milk, forced milk down my system while I was out. Then they gave me some more salt shots and started slapping me out of it. Then when I opened one eye, they started walking me around. I was bleeding through my nose like a dog. After I woke up I thought I wasn't myself, because I was more than high. I still had that junk inside my system, and I was drowsy all over the street, I couldn't see where I was going.

It's very dangerous. If you go and shoot up someplace by yourself and you take an O.D. and you ain't got nobody to give you a salt shot, to help you out one-two-three, you'll die right there. You'll have white foam coming out of your mouth, you'll be bleeding. . . . This boy called Bobby, he died in a bathroom up here in Henry Street. He took an O.D. It was where Paul used to live. Paul came down and he was dead and Paul just stepped right over him. I know a lot of people died of overdoses.

I almost got yellow jaundice twice. I was here in Henry Street, and I was nodding. My friend came up and told me, hey, like your face is real yellow, man. Your whole body is yellow. Then when I went to the bathroom, my urinal came out like the color of tea. And the fellas told me, you know you could have yellow jaundice, and I told them no. And they looked at my eyes, made me stick out my tongue, and they said could you eat? And I told them no, and they said you got the reflex towards yellow jaundice, but we can't say for sure you got it. And like I didn't have it. I almost had it those two times, but I didn't get it. I didn't make it because I cut out in time.

I knew this Italian fellow who died of yellow jaundice in Bellevue. Like I knew George from Monroe Street. He had yellow jaundice, his eyes were all yellow; all you could see was a little black pit and the rest was all yellow. He went to the hospital and he came out all right, thank God. And a guy almost got his arm contaminated, they almost had to cut it off, because he blew air inside. He put air inside his veins and puffed them up. He was in the hospital for quite a while.

I've been walking around since I've been back, but I ain't seen none of the fellows who used to use my works. Except one, and he got popped the other day. He got picked up. I'm lucky I kicked.

Constance Crawford
The Boats

EVERYONE HAD TO COME TO Walt Pener's boathouse eventually since it was the only place on the lake which sold gasoline for the speedboats and repaired them when they leaked, sputtered, or would not go fast enough. The boathouse leaned back against the steep sandstone cliff, and docks were strung along the shore, flapping and creaking as the wind pushed the water under and between the metal barrels which floated them. The docks and the yard were usually in a state of workmanlike confusion, and on week ends the slips by the gasoline pumps were so crowded that there were always several people circling their boats slowly, offshore, waiting their turn. The men in loud shirts and boys with backs the color of their mahogany speedboats were always bustling in and out, discussing horsepower and varnishes and racing technique with the big husky Swedes Walt Pener hired as mechanics and dock boys. The few sailboat owners who came to have sails mended or rudders repaired were quiet and a little out of place.

Everybody seemed to know everybody else at the boathouse, and Joan Halderman liked to come here, especially lately, and watch, pretending that she, also, knew everybody and they knew her. Now she sat on a pile of boards, facing away from the blinding late-afternoon glare of the water. The sun was warm on her back, browning it still deeper, but the wind off the lake was rising, rustling the row of poplars, rushing in the pines on top of the cliff. Her shadow lay before her on the asphalt of the yard, and she watched the wind pick up long strands of her hair and wave them out from her head—like flames.

Wondering if her hair had grown to reach her waist yet, she bent her head back and her hair fell down, soft and thick and tickling. By twisting her arm behind her, Joan could feel that the longest hairs came all the way to her waist. But she jerked her head up quickly when she remembered that Ed might be watching and think she was foolish and a sissy. Ed was a friend of hers who worked with boats better than anyone, better, even, than Walt Pener himself. Ed had beautiful lumpy, strong arms and Joan wondered if he ever noticed how long and wavy her hair was and how well she could judge boats herself.

Then, with a shiver of anticipation, Joan saw that the thing she had been waiting for was going to begin, and she forgot about her hair. The gray work boat had reached the dock, towing a big speedboat that was listing badly. It belonged to Mr. DeYoung, Joan knew, who was a Yacht Club officer. This afternoon the boat had been found loose, banging against the rocks in a windy, deserted bay on the north shore. Now one man floated the boat onto the carriage, which was on a steep track leading down under the water. Ed started the mechanical winch, and the carriage was drawn up the track into the yard. The boat was glossy and dripping, and water spouted from the cracked bottom. Above the water line was a great splintered hole. Joan stood up to see better as Ed started to work, taking out the ruined plank. He was deft and strong.

"What happened this time, Ed?" she asked, and he glanced at her, squinting against the sun.

"You here again, kid? Look out now." He wrenched a piece of wood free and Joan could peer through the wound into the boat's very insides. "Found her banging on the rocks somewhere. Fifth time this *week* a boat's been turned loose. People better start buying locks. Yes, sir." His voice trailed off, and he was absorbed in his work.

"Yeah," said Joan, sitting down again. "They've all been nice boats, too, you notice?" She waited for an answer and then continued. "This has a hundred and seventy-five horse Fireball, doesn't it?"

"Yeah," he said. "Say, girls aren't supposed to know about engines." But he said it slowly, still working, as though he weren't even thinking about her.

"But *I* do," Joan said.

"H'm. How old are you?"

"Thirteen. Well, really nearly fourteen," she said, knowing he would believe her, for she looked much older than twelve and a half.

But he only said, "H'm."

Ed swooped the plane again and again along a plank, and the shavings curled up and dropped off as though his swinging movements had made them grow, by magic, out of the metal tool. His arms were strong and brown, with yellow hair on them. Joan imagined him wrapped in a red and gold cloth, stalking through a green jungle, cutting the creepers and twining things from his path with a long knife. "When I was little," she said, "about eight, my father and I sailed a boat around in the South Seas. That's where I learned it all. About boats." She was going to go on, but Ed straightened and looked up the road which led down from the top of the cliff.

A yellow Cadillac stopped in the yard, and a man in bright Hawaiian-print trunks and shirt got out and came over to Ed. The man took the cigar from between his teeth and puffed the air out of his red-veined cheeks with a hiss of exasperation as he saw the hole in the side of the boat. He grunted. "They'll jew me plenty again this time. Huh, Ed?"

"At least it didn't get to the motor, Mr. DeYoung," said Ed.

"Your boss'd say that's a damn shame." The man laughed, belching a cloud of smoke into the air. Joan sat on the pile of boards and listened only halfway to their voices. She studied Mr. DeYoung's feet in their leather sandals, and then his knobby, hairy knees. His shirt was open, hanging on each side of his round stomach. The smell of his cigar called up from somewhere, far back, the remembrance of her father, who had once scooped her up from the floor and set her on the table, which was wet from a glass someone had spilled. Everyone had laughed, and the smell of the cigars had hung all through the room. Joan hadn't thought of her father for a long time—maybe for the whole summer—and she wondered a little what he was doing, if perhaps he *could* be hunting big game or horse racing as she sometimes told the people who asked.

"Son of a bitch," muttered Mr. DeYoung, running his hand over the chrome strip on the hull. Joan began to listen, knowing he was thinking of the person who had turned his boat loose to drift. She watched with pleasure as he winced, noticing another deep scratch on the side. He groaned again. "The cops are going to get that guy, believe me."

"I guess people will have to begin buying locks," said Ed quietly, and Joan hid her smile behind her hand. She hoped Mr. DeYoung would scream and threaten the culprit with death, but he only muttered, "Son of a bitch," and "Who the devil . . . ?" a few times more, slapped Ed on the shoulder, and drove away. The tires of the Cadillac skidded on the gravel as he turned onto the main road at the top.

Joan watched Ed for a while longer. She hugged her knees and kept her feet up off the cold asphalt, listening to the roar of the wind. She dreamed of speed—flying, running, riding on a wild black horse, the biggest and wildest horse.

"Time to quit," said Ed, putting his tools in a box. "So long, kid."

The wind had begun to cut through the sun's warmth on Joan's back, and she was glad to get up. "So long, Ed." Though the boards were splintery, she skipped down the docks, because Ed was her friend and it had been an exciting afternoon. She decided to walk along the beach instead of taking the regular trail that ran through the pines and was smooth and civilized for the city people. The sand was cold, but, to show herself that she was tough, she ran where the water was ankle-deep. The golden spray shot up all around, and the drops, when they struck her, stung like hailstones. At the point, the wind always drove the foaming water onto the sand in miniature breakers which, if she watched long enough, would turn into real ones, salty and roaring. The rocks here, now turning bluer and colder as the sun sank, were jumbled down the beach and out into the water. Joan always thought it was as though a giant had sat once on top of the sandstone cliff and let gravel trickle idly through his fingers.

Since the sun was still up, Joan knew it must not even be six-thirty, and her mother and Steve would be having just their first highballs. It was too early to go home, for if she did, she would get there before dinner and they would think that she had nothing to keep her busy. In the next inlet, the public beach would be empty now. Joan decided to go around and sit on the diving board for a while and watch the seaweed which always twirled around the string of floats used to keep the dude swimmers in the shallow water.

Back in the bay, the water, sheltered by the point, became quiet suddenly, smeared with green reflections from the opposite shore. Joan lay on her stomach and dangled her arms over the sides of the diving board, feeling her hands grow heavy. She hung her head over the end, looking back at the beach, making herself believe that the sky and the sand had changed places and that the trees here were rooted by their slender tops. Then three boys came onto the sand, intruding into that strange world, destroying the illusion that it was the earth, and not she, that had turned upside down. Joan sat up quickly, and, hugging her knees, stared past the boys with cool, gray eyes to show her unconcern. They sounded like little children, giggling loudly. They, who could not possibly have understood, had interfered with her. The breeze lifted her hair softly, and she felt solitude around her like a cloak. But when the boys began skipping rocks over the water, she watched in spite of herself.

One of them they called Mort, and he had red hair which jerked in front of his eyes whenever he drew his long, freckled arm back to throw. Once the smallest boy took such a running windup that he splashed into the water, soaking his tennis shoes. They all laughed loudly, the other two patting the little one on his back. Joan no longer was protected by her isolation, but felt shut out of their gaiety. She let her legs down over the side of the diving board and swung them rapidly, gazing up at the pines bordering the beach, but the boys did not even glance at her. They had seen a frog squatting on a rock which jutted out of the water, some distance from shore. The frog stared arrogantly from bulging, half-closed eyes.

"O.K., ol' frog," the boys said, but even when the stones started splashing into the water around him, the frog sat motionless, disdainful. The boys became more earnest, gathering handfuls of rocks, taking careful aim, but always missing their target. They can't do it, Joan thought, they can't do it. She leaned back and contemplated the opposite shore. Out of the corners of her eyes she could see the boys were getting exasperated, and their throws became wilder and wilder. Two of them finally gave up, and only the red-haired boy kept on.

Joan got up slowly, dropped onto the sand, and chose her rock. A round one with enough roughness to give a good grip, she made sure. Scuffing her feet a little, she walked down the beach to get a better aim. She noticed with pride how quiet and steady her heart beat against her ribs. She was the heroine who, with only a whip and a chair, approaches the ferocious tiger. She took aim, and the boys turned to watch her. She missed the frog, but her stone struck the bigger rock just at the water line with a hard *splut* sound which Joan remembered clearly afterward. The frog leapt upward with a little squawk, flopped into the water belly first, and disappeared.

Placing her feet deliberately, looking straight ahead, Joan walked away up the beach, as a heroine should, curbing her urge to run and laugh, until she was on the trail, hidden in the pines. Then she ran as hard as she could, and as gracefully, beautifully. Horrid, stupid boys. But she hoped she would see them again and they would ask her who she was. Her legs obeyed her especially well tonight, gathering up, loosening out, taking the ground with great strides, great—powerful—strides. It was what they said about race horses.

In front of the Yacht Club dock the trail tipped downhill and threaded between the boulders. Joan disdained the people who took the easy way, and she could run straight over the pile of rocks without slackening speed. Little rock, big rock, one with moss; black one, cracked one, jump across— the words always chanted themselves through her head, and tonight they had to go faster than ever to keep up with her feet. Her hair flew and jerked and swished over her back. The rocks blurred by under her and she landed lightly on the pine needles on the other side, breathing hard with excitement.

Here the houses began, and Joan could see their lights blinking on, up the hill. The wild part of the trail was past, and so she walked slowly, as quiet as an Indian, through the darkening columns of the tree trunks. She was a scout, and if any of the white men, in their hillside forts, should look out, searching, they would glimpse a shadow, only for an instant, and would hear no sound.

Before climbing the hill to her own house, Joan stopped and looked past the docks, out over the open water, where the bats were darting to and fro in the half-light. She heard the rising rush of the wind far away in the trees on the opposite shore, and even here, on the sheltered side, the water was slapping against the creaking docks. She decided that later tonight she would walk clear around to Forster's, where the hills were low and the wind swept down across the bay.

Climbing the hill toward the houses, Joan realized how cold her feet were and how hungry she had become, but she did not hurry. In this neighborhood only the lake-front houses had great terraces and wide windows, and the farther Joan got from these, the smaller the houses were. Now there were dinner smells in the air, and people were sitting inside, in the flat yellow electric light of their dining rooms. Mrs. Ketcham, a blue bandanna around her head, greeted Joan from her kitchen window. Finally deciding to answer, Joan said, "Hello," and walked on. Jim Cannon, who had one of the fastest boats on the lake, was in his yard, hurriedly putting varnish on a water ski. He had never given Joan a ride in his boat, and she was glad he did not notice her now.

Then she saw the lights of her own house. She disliked their cabin, for that was what it was, a cabin, with blue trim and a steep little roof. There was only one real bedroom downstairs for her mother and Steve, and Joan had to use the slant-walled, half-finished room upstairs. Her windows were not wide casements opening out over the water but dormer windows looking at the steep side of the hill and at the main road just above, where, on week ends, the drunks squealed their tires going around the mountain curves.

When Joan opened the front door, her mother was stretched out on the bamboo chaise longue, and Joan could see that she was not in a good mood, even though the glass in her hand was nearly empty.

"*Well,* the wanderer returneth," her mother called to Steve, whom Joan could see through the open kitchen door. He was stirring something in a pan on the stove and had a dish towel tied around his waist. He turned and glanced at Joan. "Here, set the table, will you Joan? This damn gravy won't thicken."

Joan was annoyed; she *had* come back too soon. As she got the spoons out of the drawer in the kitchen, she noticed that Steve's mustache looked ragged and his blond hair fell over his sweaty forehead. When Steve had first come to live with them, and they had moved to the mountains, Joan had thought he was very handsome, with his smooth blond hair, jutting eyebrows, and shoulders like the men in magazines. But lately, since he went around in his shirt sleeves most of the time, his shoulders were narrower than Joan had thought. "Don't forget the milk," he said.

"Do we *always* have to . . ."

"*You* should have milk—yes, always."

Joan opened the icebox door and slammed it back against the sink. Steve was always treating her like a child. Still, she got the milk bottle out and brought it to the table in the living room, where they ate. She and Steve did have lots of fun, sometimes. Joan stood by the table and looked at her mother. "Are you sick again?" Joan asked.

"Exhausted," said her mother. "So sweet old Steve is fixing dinner. Have you ever thought, Joan, where you and I would be without Steve?"

"Cut it out, Marcia," said Steve quietly, carrying dishes to the table.

Joan had noticed that ever since her mother had left the rest home last winter she was always tired, although she got more beautiful all the time. Joan wondered if she would ever be so beautiful that a man would work for her the way Steve did for her mother. Even so, she didn't like having Steve with a towel around his waist. "Why don't we get a maid?" Joan asked, after a long silence. "The Bergen kids are always talking about their maid."

Her mother smiled, showing her even, white teeth. "Why, what a little snob you're getting to be!" Her smile faded. "Well, I'd like one, too, but where would we put her? And Steve thinks we should conserve my money." Steve turned and went into the kitchen. Joan's mother got up and came to the table. She had on the dress that Joan liked the best of all. It was bright blue and startling against her white skin and the dark, perfect waves of her hair. Joan had hated her own long, light, tangled hair until one day when Steve and her mother had been laughing and having fun together, and in a loud, jolly voice Steve had called Joan "the gray-eyed, golden-haired goddess, Athena." Joan wondered where he had got the name Athena, but she liked it and thought of changing her name when she grew up. Athena Halderman. Ever since then, studying her face in the mirror, she had seen new things, and she knew that she was beautiful, almost like her mother.

Steve brought in the dish of stew and they sat down. Joan poured herself a glass of milk, hoping Steve would notice how she scowled. When her mother started to eat, Joan noticed a bandage around the tip of her index finger. It looked strange beside the other long, scarlet fingernails.

"Another one broke?" said Joan regretfully.

"Don't remind me," said her mother, putting her hand out of sight. "I'm so mad I could scream. I did it on the damn garbage can." Joan knew her mother had been letting her fingernails grow ever since she had been sick. They made her long, blue-veined hands even more graceful, and sometimes when she let her hands droop over the arms of her chair, Joan thought the nails looked like the polished claws of a tiger or a lion. Joan wanted to tell her mother how sorry she was about the broken one, but they were talking of something else and she knew they would not listen to her.

Joan played with her food, eating only when she thought Steve would not see. Wishing they would pay attention to her, she puckered her forehead, trying to draw her eyebrows up in the middle as her mother did when she was disturbed. Sometimes Joan even put on special clothes or combed her hair differently to make them notice, but Steve had never called her gray-eyed Athena again.

Then Joan remembered how the frog had jumped off the rock this afternoon, frightened by her miraculous throw. Those stupid boys must have stared and gaped and wondered who she was as she walked coolly away, not giving them even so much as a glance. She wondered if Steve and her mother would realize how magnificent it had been if she told them about it. But they were talking about people Joan had never heard of, and Steve only looked at her once and said, "Joan, stop fooling around and eat."

All right, she would eat and they could go to hell. She would keep all her secrets—and she had plenty. Joan began stuffing the food into her mouth, gulping and chewing as noisily as she could. A piece of cold carrot fell off her spoon and slid down her bare leg. She would not even tell them the biggest, best secret of all. Just thinking about it made her heart beat faster with excitement. She knew other ways than talking to make people notice her, she thought.

Suddenly, in the middle of their incomprehensible talk, Joan's mother turned to her and said, "Maybe *Joan* said something. Has anyone been asking you about your father?"

"No," Joan said, "but those Bergen kids kept talking about how *their* father did this and *their* father did that. So I just told 'em something about *my* father, for a change." Joan remembered with pleasure that they had believed it all, even the part about Alaska. "Where is he anyway?" she asked, half afraid of a disappointing answer.

But her mother only said, "So that's it. I suppose Mrs. Bergen heard this conversation, too?"

Joan watched her mother's eyes, so dark that behind the reflections of light in them you could not even guess how deep they went. She enjoyed having her mother look at her so closely. "I don't know what I said," Joan answered, slowly, to keep her mother's eyes on her.

Her mother gave a breathy, mirthless little laugh. "And I suppose you forgot that my name is Mrs. Walch now, and not Mrs. Halderman."

"I don't know," said Joan again, suddenly not caring.

Her mother stood up, her mouth set in a smile, but Joan saw that where the dimples usually came, there were only dark lines instead. "Well, it makes no difference," her mother said. "I was a fool to think Lake Benton would be any different from any other place. They're *all* full of catty women."

"I don't see why getting into their stupid Yacht Club is anything to be desired," said Steve. "You wouldn't *like* them, even if they did ask you to play bridge. Now let's go somewhere and forget about it."

"All right," she said lightly. "Where shall it be? To the club for drinks and dancing? To the lovely house of some of our many friends for sparkling conversation? To a lively party, overlooking the lake?"

Steve stood up and smiled at her—a little sadly, Joan saw with bewilderment. "Why not the theater," he said, "joining the gay, after-dinner crowds?"

"Perfect!" said Joan's mother. "There's a new thing with John Wayne and Maureen O'Hara, isn't there? The critics *raved* about it." They both laughed together, quietly, leaning against the table.

Joan could not understand; they had a secret and she was left out. Then she remembered the secret *she* had from them, from everybody, and she began to laugh, too. It was hard at first but then came easier until the tears filled her eyes. But somehow, nothing was funny.

Then Joan's mother went into the bedroom to get her coat, and the laughter subsided. Joan was still vaguely troubled. "Want to come to the movie, Joan?" asked Steve. "You've been getting to bed early lately."

"No, I think I'll stay home," said Joan. "I have some things I want to do."

"O.K.," he said. "So long." And they went out.

Joan waited until she heard the car start outside and then ran up the stairs, two at a time, to her bedroom. She did not switch on the light but got the package of matches which she kept hidden under her mattress. She lit the candle which she had stood in a saucer on the old chiffonier. Joan loved the way the glow filled the long mirror, as though from under water. She took off her faded bathing suit, got the green one from the bottom drawer, and put it on. It hugged her tightly, and in the candle light it had a soft, half-sheen. She liked to run in this bathing suit; it seemed to stretch and relax with her, helping her. She shook her hair down, admiring it. Moving close to the mirror, she smoothed her eyebrows and looked for a long time into the gray eyes in the reflection. The candle was a tiny flame in each one. Finally she blew out the candle and went to the window. She knew the branches of the pine tree outside by heart, and could let herself down to the ground even on moonless, cloudy nights. She never went down the stairs, even when Steve and her mother were gone.

The air was cold now, and Joan shivered standing by the corner of the house, trying to decide where to go. Somehow, this time, it was different. The excitement of the afternoon had left her. The wind had risen, as she had thought it would, but it only made her colder; the moon was thin, already close to the jagged treetops on Wheeler Ridge. Then Joan remembered her resolve to go clear to Forster's on the big bay, and she started down the hill, trotting to keep warm. She tried leaping the ferns, and she noticed that her feet were now so tough that the pine needles only felt slippery and never pricked her as they used to. By the time she was on the trail by the shore, she felt much better, and began watching, as usual, for strange animal eyes and lurking danger. Thinking how surprised her mother and Steve would be if they knew, she almost laughed aloud, but then remembered how important it was for her to keep perfectly silent. The familiar excitement returned, tightening her muscles and making her ready, she felt, to perform miraculous feats of agility and daring if necessary.

But it was farther to the bay than she had thought. The woods became thicker, and the lights of the houses retreated far back in the trees. At one place, the trail crossed a wide stretch of sand where a stream, now dry, ran down from the hills in the spring, when the snow melted. The sand glimmered faintly around her. The wind carried the smell of the marshy plants which grew in the mud where the lake had receded through the rainless summer. Joan shivered; when she was nearly across the sand and into the trees again, a loud grating, rasping cry boomed from the shore where the row of docks floated on the black water. Joan gasped and stood rigid; the sound came again, like a groaning voice. And suddenly, from the trees, great, dark creatures rose into the sky with a rush of air all around, covering the sliver of moon. Joan cried out and ran, hardly realizing she had done so until she found herself standing among the tree trunks, her own scream echoing in her ears. Her heart filled her temples with pulse beats.

The lights of the Bergens' house showed a little distance up the hill, yellow and warm. While Joan looked at them, the sound came again. Then she knew it was only a fat bullfrog sitting somewhere in his cold, muddy world under the docks. And she must have frightened the cranes which always sat in the tops of the pine trees, like marble statues, until suddenly they would leap into the air with a rush of wings. Joan felt ridiculous standing, cold, in the middle of the trail, her knees shaking. Scared by a frog and some dumb cranes, like a city sissy, she thought with disgust. But she looked at the squares of yellow light from the Bergens' house, and longed to be inside with them. She knew that Mrs. Bergen sometimes read to the two girls and that they always had something good to eat in their hands when they came out to play. They were her friends. Joan started up the little path leading to the house.

But the Bergen girls had straight brown hair and tender feet. They bragged about their boat and the Yacht Club and their father. Joan remembered how they smirked at her sometimes, hating her. Often when she came to play, they wouldn't let her in the house and giggled at her from their bedroom window upstairs. Joan remembered, too, that, in some way, Mrs. Bergen had hurt her mother. Somehow she, like Joan, had been left out.

Joan smiled to herself in the dark, thinking how much the Bergens missed, even though they did have a fast boat. They never had adventures; they just sat and giggled. Those girls never knew how dark and thrilling it was at night, because they went inside and turned on all the lights. Joan forgot about going to Forster's, and she went back down the path quietly.

On the main trail, Joan stopped and listened, looking about her; there was nothing, no sound but the wind. She ran through the ferns down to the shore, out onto the Bergens' dock. It was littered with pieces of rope, a canoe paddle, a fishing pole, and several canvas chairs, one lying on its side. The Bergen girls never put away their things. Joan stood by the slip where the speedboat was tied—loosely tied, Joan saw, so that it banged against the dock when a gust of wind caught it. The canvas cover was thrown over the top of the boat and not fastened. She smoothed the cover and tied it down carefully, as if everything had belonged to her. Excitement flooded through her, more intensely than at any of the other times.

Joan unlooped the stern lines and then had to work over the knotted rope at the prow before it would loosen. Gripping the sides of the boat and bracing her feet against the cleats on the dock, Joan pushed with her full weight. The heavy boat started to slide out into the open water. When it was just free of the dock, she gave one last shove and the dark shape drifted out quietly, away from her. The momentum of her push spent itself, and the boat hung in a glassy strip of water for a moment, before the wind caught it. Then the stern swung crosswise to the wind, and the waves pushed against the mahogany sides. Joan watched until the boat disappeared in the darkness. Even though she held her hands over her mouth, she let out a high, thin little cry of exaltation.

5
Schools, Students, and Teachers

A GOOD PART OF WHAT public and private schools teach today was taught
not too long ago by the home and church; moral, social, political, and
economic instruction are now as much a part of school curricula as those in
reading, writing, and arithmetic. In shaping the lives of adolescents, schools
exert a powerful, if not the primary, influence. Teachers have in some
respects become surrogate parents. Often teachers can be freer, and at the
same time more objective, in their relations with students than parents can
be with their children. Students are also afforded a wider variety of talents
and personalities to learn from in their schools than is normally found in
their homes. Though some teachers may be unappealing, students often
find positive models they can admire, seek advice from, or emulate. Schools
also provide a place where adolescents can interact both in informal groups
or in more structured ones such as athletic teams, special-interest clubs, and
drama societies.

Within the school situation the expectations of students and teachers are
frequently different. Teachers traditionally emphasize the acquisition of
knowledge and academic success, while students often see social interaction
and having a good time as being more important. Cars, dates, clothes, music,
belonging to the right clique, and getting ahead in the world vie for the
attention of adolescents, and, as a result, academic issues become a
secondary interest for many. Still, most students are able to meet the
academic and extracurricular demands of their schools. Those who fail have
a low opinion of themselves—and are held in low esteem by others.

In large measure what has been said about high schools applies to colleges. The majority of students don't place a special value on intellectual accomplishments per se but rather are concerned with the prestige of becoming a college graduate. Friendships and future professional contacts are sought out and established. Students—and a growing number of teachers—often question the meaning and relevancy of what is taught. Implicitly and explicitly they often ask, "What really is the function of American education?"

Since World War II, writers of short fiction have reconsidered the relationship between students and teachers. No longer are they frequently shown as adversaries. Given the predictable limitations of the traditional classroom structure on interpersonal relations, students and teachers often develop a workable and occasionally a remarkable respect for one another in recent short stories. The stereotype of the idiosyncratic, disinterested, and frequently unreasonable schoolmaster of the nineteenth century has all but disappeared from the scene in contemporary short fiction. "The Heart of This or That Man," "Stealing Cars" (section 4), and "A Kind of Savage" are cases in which teachers and administrators go well beyond what is expected of them to help troubled students. The easy complacency of teachers in prewar fiction has been replaced with much doubt about the purpose of schools and the teachers' roles within them. Mr. Shapiro in "The Heart of This or That Man" wonders as he goes to meet his Friday class of problem students: "What am I doing here? I should be home reading, getting my Ph.D., getting laid, getting money." These would hardly seem the thoughts of a dedicated teacher, yet when one of his students, Jaime, is troubled, Mr. Shapiro goes out of his way to help him. His thoughts appear selfish; his actions are generous. Similarly, the Dean of Women who is suffering from the grinding irritations of her office in "A Kind of Savage" displays an uncommon patience in dealing with her faculty members and Courtney Pettit, an irrepressibly derelict coed. Both characters, however, have much in common, for Courtney's expulsion from college and the Dean's move off campus result from their mutual inability to cope with the insidious pressures of campus life. Because their problems are often similar, communication between students and teachers is more honest and personal in recent short fiction.

The majority of the stories about schools are set outside the classroom, for it is away from the regimen and structure of its confinement that students most often have their meaningful experiences. The classroom is only part of a larger academic backdrop against which the dramas of social and psychological development take place. Both "The Potato Baron and the Line" and "Sentimental Education" (section 1) examine the theme of young adults being in love, living together, and reaching a point in their relationships where they must reconsider how their lives have become intertwined and whether they should continue in the same direction they are going. Most stories of this type end with the couples breaking up or at least seriously contemplating it. The subtle stresses of academic life, personalities growing in different directions, and a desire (usually subconscious) to escape back to an earlier, more irresponsible state contribute to a bittersweet parting of ways. As relationships such as those in "The Potato Baron and the Line" and "Sentimental Education" are explored, much is revealed about dormitory life, parietals, and a host of other campus customs. "Phineas" (section 7) captures the out-of-class atmosphere of an exclusive New England prep school, especially the intensity of friendships and hatreds that develop when adolescents live together in close quarters. The joys and sorrows that occur in stories such as this have little to do with what goes on in the classroom.

The compelling task at hand for most adolescents in school, particularly in boarding school or college where there is no daily escape to the family, is how to become a member of some group that will give them a sense of worth and allow them to discover who they are. Numerous stories—"Mr. Princeton" and "A Kind of Savage" are good examples—consider the fate of students who, for one reason or another, don't fit into the social structures of academe. Naftoli Gold very quickly senses his alien status in "Mr. Princeton" after his interview for admission and overhearing the conversations of some students. His unpretentious Jewish upbringing is worlds apart from that of his worldly, prospective classmates. On the other hand, Courtney's free-spirited, bohemian ways in "A Kind of Savage" finally get her expelled from a staid private college for young ladies. Adjustment in school is difficult for most students and all but impossible for those who cannot or will not conform to fixed institutional and peer-group expectations. Every once in a while, colorful individualists by virtue of their charismatic personalities are able to operate outside the rules of conduct binding their peers, but this is rare and short-lived.

There are few stories that capture classroom atmosphere as well as "Tomorrow and Tomorrow and So Forth." Thumbnail sketches of the "jock," "brain," "dimwit," "siren," "snoozer," and other distinctive personalities are fixed in an archetypal snapshot of a public high-school class. In another type of classroom story, friction results when the information supplied by teachers is considered misinformation by students. Ozzie's refusal to believe that Jesus is not divine in "The Conversion of the Jews" (section 6) causes him openly to revolt and ultimately forces his teacher to recant, something all students fantasize about doing at one time or another. Few students, however, are as foolhardy or desperate as Ozzie and simply pretend they believe what appears to be incomprehensible or untrue.

Donald Gropman
The Heart of This
or That Man

MR. SHAPIRO FUMBLED WITH THE WINDOW POLE. Nine C would be here in a few minutes for its weekly session and he was not prepared. Open the window, remove his jacket, set out the jars of paint and the brushes he argued for each week.

"Now, Allan," Miss Katz would say, "I don't know if this request is covered by any rule. After all, I'm the art teacher and you teach English."

"Well, Miss Katz," he would say, "if you don't tell anyone, and I don't tell anyone, it will be our little secret. You know," and here he would smile, a little less broadly each week, "it's like giving an anonymous donation to the CJA or Red Feather. You and I help these kids, but we don't brag about it. Inside we know we are doing something good."

"Well, all right, Allan, what somebody doesn't know won't hurt him. Now remember to have them wash the brushes and wipe down the jars. Your boys are awfully messy. And by the way, do you really need so much paper?"

He still fumbled to fit the metal hook into the slot at the top of the window. He had read somewhere that an open window provides fresh air and inspiration. Through the high many-paned window he could see the street below him. The pale lemon light of a two o'clock winter afternoon drifted down from a silent and spent sky, but did not seem to fall on the brown heaps of snow and slush.

A policeman walked by, and Mr. Shapiro noticed that he could not see the small balloons of breath puff out over the policeman's shoulder. Was it warmer, what was it, March? Or April already? Snow on the streets in April? No matter. He liked to watch the breath balloons and fill them in. For policemen he inserted things like: *I am a policeman, sometimes I'm your friend; I like to find robbers 'cause I'm partners with them.* The policeman crossed the street. Mr. Shapiro looked over and saw Jaime sitting in a doorway. He was looking up at the empty sky and started up when the policeman burst into his sight. The policeman leaned over and Jaime waved his arms, shook his head, and pointed at Mr. Shapiro. No, Mr. Shapiro thought, he is pointing at the whole school. The policeman now shook his head and crossed back to the school side of the street with Jaime. The policeman disappeared at the side of the window and Jaime disappeared beneath it. Did the policeman invoke me, Mr. Shapiro thought, to make Jaime come to class and stop being truant?

The bell rang to start the last class as Mr. Shapiro was folding his suit jacket over the back of his chair. He had read somewhere that a teacher in shirtsleeves provokes less resistance in these students. The students started to drift into the room, singly or in twos. Mr. Shapiro had a moment of panic. What am I doing here? I should be home reading, getting my Ph.D., getting laid, getting money. What good can I do, help these poor under-privileged bastards become privileged so they can assimilate, have appliances and not live on welfare, and use toilet paper to wipe their asses instead of *El Diario de Nueva York*, so that in the final end they'll fill me with loathing like all the rest of the smug, consuming bastards. Shapiro's law of human nature, not too romantic I hope, says, a human being evinces more interesting manifestations while being consumed than while consuming. A contemporary aesthetic: What is the most beautiful thing in the world, the ultimate perfection? A young girl dying of consumption? No. A whole ethnic group being consumed.

Am I merely stupid, or expiating guilt? Anyway, why do these kids call me Mr. Shapiro? Everyone else calls me Allan, in the army they called me kike, my wife calls me *schmouk*, my professors call me dummy, although I never heard them.

Hey Al baby, what's shakin'? Man, this is a wise scene and you a real wig. Catch some pot Al, it's just a fifty pinney joint, but like it's all I carry. You not like those other teachers, they hard bastards, but you okay man, you go it everywhere, and the boy would use his index finger as a wand to touch his own temple, his chest, and his sex. The monologue elated Mr. Shapiro even though he could not recognize the student in the daydream.

On Friday afternoon the class with Nine C always went well. Four times a week Mr. Shapiro tried to teach them English. They wrote compositions and read *Silas Marner*. They had spelling quizzes and tried to parse sentences on the board. Whenever his wife, or anyone else not connected with the school, asked him about the class, Mr. Shapiro had one stock answer, "They just don't give a shit." But one thing did seem to interest them and that was the Friday session.

Mr. Shapiro had decided it would be a good idea to read them poems and let them paint what the poems meant to them. This would serve several functions: they will hear some poetry, they will express themselves in the paintings and, maybe, Mr. Shapiro hoped, I can get through to them. In September he had found a box of gold stars in his desk, the only trace left of the teacher before him. Each week he pasted a star on a painting, trying to give the star where he felt it would do the most good.

He tried to select poetry from the high school reader that would appeal to them. This afternoon he was going to read some Robert Frost. He felt it would make sense to them, offer them images they could instinctively grasp.

While he sat on his desk thinking, the students took paper and jars of paint. Two of them went into the hall to fill the water pitchers, for they had finally accepted the fact that the paints worked better if they were thinned. Most of the class was busy mixing paint when Jaime walked in. He didn't look at Mr. Shapiro. He went to his seat and sat down.

Mr. Shapiro leafed through the reader, but he watched Jaime. The boy was probably older than he looked, perhaps, fifteen or sixteen, but he was no bigger than a twelve-year-old. He always left the two top buttons of his shirt open and he wore no undershirt, so Mr. Shapiro could see the middle of his pale honey-colored chest, the skin pulled taut across the knobby clavicles.

Jaime didn't move. He sat staring at his desk, his thin fingers buried themselves in his matted black hair.

Mr. Shapiro walked up the aisle. "Don't you have any paints, Jaime?"

Jaime looked up at him. Mr. Shapiro saw a bleached face. The black eyes seemed gray, the hirsuteness on the upper lip seemed white. Mr. Shapiro's legs felt suddenly weak, he felt a large parching knot in his throat.

"What's wrong?" he asked, his voice much softer than he had intended.

"Nothing, Mr. Shapeiro. There's nothing is wrong."

"Come with me, I'll help you to get some paints and a piece of paper." He felt foolish mouthing these words, silly words about bottles of paint and empty paper, but he could think of nothing else.

Jaime was seated again, his paints before him on his desk. Mr. Shapiro waited until he was reading, smiled at him and began to read. As he read the first words of "Mending Wall" they too sounded silly to his ears. He felt embarrassed and knew that his face was turning red. The volume of his voice dropped from the pitch it started at, he mouthed the words as quickly as he could, droning them out like some primitive and unyielding chant. He looked up from the book while mouthing familiar phrases and saw the class looking at him strangely.

"Am I reading too quickly?" he asked, trying to control his fluster, restraining himself from hurling the high school reader through one of the many-paned windows and leaving the high school and the students forever. "Am I reading too quickly for you to follow me?" He despised himself for the touch of condescension in his voice, but he would have augmented it if a student hadn't answered.

"Yes, Mr. Shapeiro, much too fast." It was Jaime. He was still sitting with his elbows on his desk and his fingers buried in his matted black hair.

"Sounds like the IRT," another student said, and there was general laughter, even from Mr. Shapiro.

"I guess you're right, I was going a little fast. I'll begin again."

> *Something there is that doesn't love a wall,*
> *That sends the frozen-ground-swell under it,*
> *And spills the upper boulders in the sun;*
> *And makes gaps even two can pass abreast.*

Mr. Shapiro read the whole poem, slowly and with emotion. Now that the poem was fresh in his mind he recited most of it from memory. Before him at the rows of desks he could see the pale honey-colored faces, some with their dark eyes on his face, others staring at the book in his hands. Jaime had not changed his position. Mr. Shapiro could still see where the boy's fingers started to disappear into his black hair. He repeated the last line twice.

> *He says again, "Good Fences make good neighbors."*

The class stirred itself, Mr. Shapiro had an ephemeral sense of accomplishment. Maybe there was a contact, he thought, maybe I had their attention, that is the start of a dialogue. "Any questions?" he asked.

One boy asked why the wall was there anyway if it didn't do any good, and Mr. Shapiro started to answer. He started to explain the significance of New England stone walls, how they originated when the farmers had to pick the stones out of the soil in order to plant a crop, and how they have become a tradition in that part of the country. He started to explain further the irony of the dialogue between the two farmers, and felt he was losing the class again, so he cut it short, "Any other questions?"

"Yes, Mr. Shapeiro." It was Jaime again. "Can you read that part again where they carry rocks like wildmen?"

Mr. Shapiro picked up the book:

> *I see him there*
> *Bringing a stone grasped firmly by the top*
> *In each hand, like an old-stone savage armed.*
> *He moves in darkness, as it seems to me,*
> *Not of the woods only and the shade of trees.*

"What did you want to know about them, Jaime?"

"Nothing, Mr. Shapeiro, I just wanted to hear you read them again."

"All right. All right, class, we'll begin painting now. It wasn't a long poem and it didn't take up much time. Maybe there will be time enough for two paintings."

It was Mr. Shapiro's practice not to bother the students while they were painting, he felt his looking over their shoulders might inhibit or intimidate them. He took his jacket and went to the teacher's room for a cigarette. It was not the standard procedure, leaving a class alone, especially Nine C, but he had done it before on Fridays and there were never any complaints from the adjoining rooms.

The lounge for male teachers was next to that for female teachers. At the door he saw Miss Katz. He didn't want to talk to her. He didn't even want her to see him.

"Allan, you naughty, have you left your class unattended? And with poster paints yet! I hope you don't have any trouble," Miss Katz said, walking up to him. She had an empty cup in her hand. Mr. Shapiro knew that if it was wet she was leaving the lounge and if it was dry she was just arriving. But Miss Katz held the cup upside down and he couldn't tell. At first he didn't hear her words. He was convinced she was holding the cup that way just to keep him from knowing if it was wet or dry. "I hope you've never left them before, this could raise a problem for you."

"No," Mr. Shapiro said, "I haven't. I had to go to the bathroom." He had wanted to say *I had to take a wicked leak*, or *I suddenly, for no reason at all, felt like puking*, but he only said, and repeated, "I had to go to the bathroom." He hated himself again, for not saying what he wanted to say, for putting the bathroom excuse in some vague past tense, as if everyone didn't have to empty out at least once a day. He thought of the kids in the room, their honey-colored faces screwed up over their paintings, dreaming in their heads of orchards and fields, and he blurted out, "Do you know, Miss Katz, they are really more ginger-colored than honey-colored," and he leaped into the male lounge.

When he returned to the classroom it was just as he'd imagined. He saw rows of heads, almost every one of the heads covered with very black hair, bent over the desks. He felt pleased, he forgot all about Miss Katz and the probability that she was at that moment telling some other faculty member what he had said to her. When Mr. Shapiro thought about this in the lounge he tried to re-create Miss Katz's language. "You know, Louise, we were talking about his leaving his class unattended, and he was looking strange to begin with, staring at my teacup, and suddenly he shouted at me something about ginger and honey. Then he flew into the men's lounge and slammed the door. Don't you think he's disturbed?" He had ground his cigarette out on the floor of the lounge, and Miss Katz with it.

He stood at the window looking out. The sun was still shining, but it really wasn't shining, he thought, that is too active a description. The sunlight is drifting down, it is settling like a cloud of pale dust, it is falling because of gravity. He glanced at the students and saw Jaime. His head was bent over his desk, but both his hands were buried in his hair. Mr. Shapiro walked over to him. "What's wrong, Jaime, don't you feel like painting today?"

"Yes, Mr. Shapeiro, I'm all done."

Mr. Shapiro looked at the painting on Jaime's desk. There were two huge figures, manlike but inanimate, facing each other. Both figures had their arms raised above their heads and in their hands held stones. There were bright carmine streaks on their heads, faces and shoulders. Between them was a black wall that began in the absolute foreground of the painting and ran right through the depth and off the paper. Mr. Shapiro looked more closely and saw a third figure, a smaller one, crouched in a blob of gray on the wall. He felt the same weakness in his legs and the knot in his throat that he had when he looked into Jaime's face at the start of the class.

"What does it mean?" His voice was gruff, almost angry. Two or three of the other students looked up at him, then turned back to their paintings.

"Nothing."

"It can't mean nothing. Everything means something. It has to mean something." His voice was more insistent, hatred for himself ran through his body like a chill. "What does it mean?"

"Nothing," Jaime said, looking up at him with the gray eyes and white hirsuteness on his upper lip. "It don't mean nothing."

Mr. Shapiro straightened up, he looked at the painting again from his new and more distant perspective. The two large figures were both all green. He hadn't noticed that before. And the sky was watery yellow. The ground, where there was grass in the poem, was grape-purple. His eyes were drawn to the small blotted figure crouched on the wall. He leaned over again to have a closer look at it. "Who is that little figure supposed to be, the one on the top of the wall?"

Jaime looked up at him for a moment, then slid his fingers back into his hair and started to look at his painting again.

Mr. Shapiro looked at the clock over the door. There were only ten minutes left to the class. Ten minutes and the day was over, and the week. "All right, class, let's start cleaning up. While you clean the brushes and wipe off the jars I'll come around and pick the star-winner for today."

Most of the paintings tried to show the two farmers standing by the wall, and most of them had green grass and blue skies. But Mr. Shapiro could not think about any of them. He looked at them all, made a comment here, gave a word of encouragement there, but his imagination wasn't in it.

He walked up the aisle Jaime sat in. He paused a little longer at each painting as he got closer to Jaime. When he got to him he walked right by.

The brushes were all washed and standing in a jar, the bottles of paint were all cleaned on the outside, the empty water pitchers stood beside them. Mr. Shapiro looked at the clock. The bell would ring in two minutes. He had to announce a winner. "All right, class, the best painting today was done by Jaime Morales. Come up, Jaime, and I'll give you your gold star." The usual practice was to exhibit the best painting at the front of the room, and explain why it was the best. But today Mr. Shapiro didn't do this. He only announced the winner, and when Jaime didn't come forward he repeated, "Jaime, come up and I'll give you your star."

He looked at Jaime. The boy was still sitting as he had sat for all the time Mr. Shapiro saw him in class. He saw the top of his head, the thin fingers buried in the thick black hair. But now the fingers were clutching at Jaime's scalp. He was crying.

A few of the students around him looked at him, and then looked at Mr. Shapiro. Mr. Shapiro looked back at them vacantly. Jaime started to cry louder. Mr. Shapiro saw the bony clavicles in Jaime's pale honey-colored chest jerk in and out, he saw the boy's forehead and cheek muscles clench up to hold back the tears.

"What the hell is wrong?" he shouted, running up the aisle. "What's wrong now, what did I do?" The whole class was staring at them now, at Jaime and Mr. Shapiro. "What's wrong? Answer me!" he shouted. He didn't care that he was shouting, or that the whole class was watching him. Jaime looked up at him. Now his gray eyes were flecked with red. He stopped crying. "Nothing is wrong, ever."

The bell rang. Mr. Shapiro was still standing over Jaime. Some of the class got up, others waited for Mr. Shapiro to dismiss them. "Okay," he said, his voice cracking and weary, "you can all go now."

Mr. Shapiro was still leaning over Jaime. He was looking at the painting. He was still drawn to the small gray figure.

"What's wrong, Jaime, you can tell me now, everyone is gone."

"There's nothing wrong."

"Come on," Mr. Shapiro said, his confidence returning, "you can tell me."

"I have nothing to tell."

"Well, in that case, how about helping me carry the supplies back to the art room?"

Mr. Shapiro felt that he had suppressed whatever it was that made his legs weak and made him shout. Together, in two trips, they returned all the supplies. Now the week was over, but Mr. Shapiro knew something in it was unfinished. He wanted to know why Jaime had cried. He wanted to know because he wanted to help the boy. He wanted to understand him, to communicate with him and thereby comfort and help him. He could be honest with himself again, now that he had himself in control, and he could admit that he also wanted to know just for the sake of knowing.

"C'mon, Jaime, I go your way, I'll walk you home." They started out the door, "Wait a minute, you forgot your painting." Jaime went back to get it. Mr. Shapiro remembered the open windows and began to close them. The pale lemon light of an hour ago had turned to grayish-yellow. The sun seemed to be drawing into itself, absorbing its light back from the world.

He turned from the window and saw that Jaime was crying.

The slush had hardened on the sidewalk. Mr. Shapiro could see breath balloons when Jaime exhaled, but he could think of no words to fill them. "I'll buy you a Coke, or a hot chocolate," he said, and they went into a Nedick's. Jaime had his painting rolled up, and he put it on the floor beside him. They both ordered hot chocolates and Jaime put two teaspoons of sugar into his. They blew into their cups without talking. Jaime took a sip of his chocolate and smacked his lips. It was too hot.

"Do you want to know why I cried?"

"Yes, if you want to tell me."

"I want to tell you, Mr. Shapeiro, but it's not easy. It's hard."

"Start at the beginning, then, take it slow." Mr. Shapiro felt very comfortable sitting at the counter in Nedick's on a Friday afternoon with one of his students. Before Jaime started to talk, he already felt a sense of accomplishment.

"It's account of my painting."

Mr. Shapiro was mildly disappointed. "How could that painting make you cry? And anyway, you won the star this week. It was the best painting. You should be proud of it." Mr. Shapiro had not yet tasted his chocolate, but he felt warm inside. He said again, "You should be proud of it."

"I am, I am, I wanted to win a star, but now I don't have anything to do with it."

Mr. Shapiro was hardly listening. He felt expansive inside himself. The questions that had nagged at him earlier in the day seemed resolved. He knew why he was here, why he was teaching and not doing something else, why he was teaching in this particular school. He knew why he was teaching students like Jaime. He was helping them. He would never despise them for assimilating or becoming bourgeois. He was their friend, not their critic. He understood them. They needed him.

"What did you say, Jaime?"

"I don't have anything to do with it now, nothing at all."

"Why don't you keep it in your wallet as a memento, so you can look at it and feel good when you want to."

"What do you mean, Mr. Shapeiro, it can't fit in my wallet, it's too big."

"Oh, you're talking about the painting. I thought you meant my gold star."

"The painting, that's what I can't do anything with," Jaime said, his voice cracking and he started to cry again.

Mr. Shapiro was upset. "What is it, Jaime, you're not telling me everything. What is it? I have a right to know."

"I'm proud of my painting, Mr. Shapeiro, I'm glad I got the star today." Jaime huddled up on his stool, he crouched over his hot chocolate and held the cup in both his hands. "We live in a room with four other families," he said, and he looked at Mr. Shapiro. Mr. Shapiro didn't want to hear what Jaime was saying. He looked at the boy's eyes. They were black now, and shining. Tears rolled like pebbles down his smooth face. Mr. Shapiro blew into his chocolate. He drank some, it scalded and stuck in his throat. "Would you like a doughnut?" he sputtered.

"We live in a room with four other families. Every month we change places in the room. This month is our turn in the middle. I want to hang my painting but I have no wall." Jaime stopped. He was still looking at Mr. Shapiro. "I have no wall!" he shouted into Mr. Shapiro's face, and ran out of the Nedick's.

Mr. Shapiro sat at the counter. He looked down and saw Jaime's painting on the floor. He picked it up. A chill ran up his arm and down his back. He pushed his cup of chocolate aside and unrolled the painting. One end of the black stone wall drilled into Nedick's countertop, the wider end thrust at him.

When he first saw the painting in the classroom he knew what it was about, but he had tried to fool himself. Now his eyes fell on the green figures planted on the grape-purple grass. So, he thought, so I've come to this.

He glanced around Nedick's, but nothing seemed as real as the green men stiffly raging on the purple lawn beneath the streaked and watery sky.

He folded the painting and stuffed it into his coat pocket. He lit a cigarette and sipped some chocolate. Miss Katz's teacup, dry or wet, what was the difference? Why had he let it matter?

He felt sorry.

Mr. Shapiro slapped the edge of the countertop with his fingers. The countergirl asked what he wanted, but he did not look up. It has always been walls, he thought. Hearts of men sometimes pushed against walls. But the heart of this or that man, he thought, is the heart of this or that man ever strong enough to force the issue, to burst the walls and let the outside pour in?

He did not know. He was sorrier now, for his brains had failed him. *Kike* they called him, *schmouk, dummy*. They may be right. He nestled deeper into his shame. But it was more bitter than that. He knew now, with a fierce hatred for all mankind, that he did not have the heart to reject his own sorrow.

John Updike
Tomorrow and Tomorrow and So Forth

WHIRLING, TALKING, 11D BEGAN TO ENTER ROOM 109. From the quality of their excitement Mark Prosser guessed it would rain. He had been teaching high school for three years, yet his students still impressed him; they were such sensitive animals. They reacted so infallibly to merely barometric pressure.

In the doorway, Brute Young paused while little Barry Snyder giggled at his elbow. Barry's stagy laugh rose and fell, dipping down toward some vile secret that had to be tasted and retasted, then soaring artificially to proclaim that he, little Barry, shared such a secret with the school's fullback. Being Brute's stooge was precious to Barry. The fullback paid no attention to him; he twisted his neck to stare at something not yet coming through the door. He yielded heavily to the procession pressing him forward.

Right under Prosser's eyes, like a murder suddenly appearing in an annalistic frieze of kings and queens, someone stabbed a girl in the back with a pencil. She ignored the assault saucily. Another hand yanked out Geoffrey Langer's shirt-tail. Geoffrey, a bright student, was uncertain whether to laugh it off or defend himself with anger, and made a weak, half-turning gesture of compromise, wearing an expression of distant arrogance that Prosser instantly coordinated with feelings of fear he used to have. All along the line, in the glitter of key chains and the acute angles of turned-back shirt cuffs, an electricity was expressed which simple weather couldn't generate.

Mark wondered if today Gloria Angstrom wore that sweater, an ember-pink angora, with very brief sleeves. The virtual sleevelessness was the disturbing factor: the exposure of those two serene arms to the air, white as thighs against the delicate wool.

His guess was correct. A vivid pink patch flashed through the jiggle of arms and shoulders as the final knot of youngsters entered the room.

"Take your seats," Mr. Prosser said. "Come on. Let's go."

Most obeyed, but Peter Forrester, who had been at the center of the group around Gloria, still lingered in the doorway with her, finishing some story, apparently determined to make her laugh or gasp. When she did gasp, he tossed his head with satisfaction. His orange hair bobbed. Redheads are all alike, Mark thought, with their white eyelashes and pale puffy faces and thyroid eyes, their mouths always twisted with preposterous self-confidence. Bluffers, the whole bunch.

When Gloria, moving in a considered, stately way, had taken her seat, and Peter had swerved into his, Mr. Prosser said, "Peter Forrester."

"Yes?" Peter rose, scrabbling through his book for the right place.

"Kindly tell the class the exact meaning of the words 'Tomorrow, and tomorrow, and tomorrow/Creeps in this petty pace from day to day.'"

Peter glanced down at the high-school edition of *Macbeth* lying open on his desk. One of the duller girls tittered expectantly from the back of the room. Peter was popular with the girls; girls that age had minds like moths.

"Peter. With your book shut. We have all memorized this passage for today. Remember?" The girl in the back of the room squealed in delight. Gloria laid her own book face-open on her desk, where Peter could see it.

Peter shut his book with a bang and stared into Gloria's. "Why," he said at last, "I think it means pretty much what it says."

"Which is?"

"Why, that tomorrow is something we often think about. It creeps into our conversation all the time. We couldn't make any plans without thinking about tomorrow."

"I see. Then you would say that Macbeth is here referring to the, the date-book aspect of life?"

Geoffrey Langer laughed, no doubt to please Mr. Prosser. For a moment, he *was* pleased. Then he realized he had been playing for laughs at a student's expense.

His paraphrase had made Peter's reading of the lines seem more ridiculous than it was. He began to retract. "I admit—"

But Peter was going on; redheads never know when to quit. "Macbeth means that if we quit worrying about tomorrow, and just lived for today, we could appreciate all the wonderful things that are going on under our noses."

Mark considered this a moment before he spoke. He would not be sarcastic. "Uh, without denying that there is truth in what you say, Peter, do you think it likely that Macbeth, in his situation, would be expressing such" —he couldn't help himself—"such sunny sentiments?"

Geoffrey laughed again. Peter's neck reddened; he studied the floor. Gloria glared at Mr. Prosser, the anger in her face clearly meant for him to see.

Mark hurried to undo his mistake. "Don't misunderstand me, please," he told Peter. "I don't have all the answers myself. But it seems to me the whole speech, down to 'Signifying nothing,' is saying that life is—well, a *fraud*. Nothing wonderful about it."

"Did Shakespeare really think that?" Geoffrey Langer asked, a nervous quickness pitching his voice high.

Mark read into Geoffrey's question his own adolescent premonitions of the terrible truth. The attempt he must make was plain. He told Peter he could sit down and looked through the window toward the steadying sky. The clouds were gaining intensity. "There is," Mr. Prosser slowly began, "much darkness in Shakespeare's work, and no play is darker than *Macbeth*. The atmosphere is poisonous, oppressive. One critic has said that in this play, humanity suffocates." This was too fancy.

"In the middle of his career, Shakespeare wrote plays about men like Hamlet and Othello and Macbeth—men who aren't allowed by their society, or bad luck, or some minor flaw in themselves, to become the great men they might have been. Even Shakespeare's comedies of this period deal with a world gone sour. It is as if he had seen through the bright, bold surface of his earlier comedies and histories and had looked upon something terrible. It frightened him, just as some day it may frighten some of you." In his determination to find the right words, he had been staring at Gloria, without meaning to. Embarrassed, she nodded, and, realizing what had happened, he smiled at her.

He tried to make his remarks gentler, even diffident. "But then I think Shakespeare sensed a redeeming truth. His last plays are serene and symbolical, as if he had pierced through the ugly facts and reached a realm where the facts are again beautiful. In this way, Shakespeare's total work is a more complete image of life than that of any other writer, except perhaps for Dante, an Italian poet who wrote several centuries earlier." He had been taken far from the Macbeth soliloquy. Other teachers had been happy to tell him how the kids made a game of getting him talking. He looked toward Geoffrey. The boy was doodling on his tablet, indifferent. Mr. Prosser concluded, "The last play Shakespeare wrote is an extraordinary poem called 'The Tempest.' Some of you may want to read it for your next book reports—the ones due May 10th. It's a short play."

The class had been taking a holiday. Barry Snyder was snicking BBs off the blackboard and glancing over at Brute Young to see if he noticed. "Once more, Barry," Mr. Prosser said, "and out you go." Barry blushed, and grinned to cover the blush, his eyeballs sliding toward Brute. The dull girl in the rear of the room was putting on lipstick. "Put that away, Alice," Mr. Prosser commanded. She giggled and obeyed. Sejak, the Polish boy who worked nights, was asleep at his desk, his cheek white with pressure against the varnished wood, his mouth sagging sidewise. Mr. Prosser had an impulse to let him sleep. But the impulse might not be true kindness, but just the self-congratulatory, kindly pose in which he sometimes discovered himself. Besides, one breach of discipline encouraged others. He strode down the aisle and shook Sejak awake. Then he turned his attention to the mumble growing at the front of the room.

Peter Forrester was whispering to Gloria, trying to make her laugh. The girl's face, though, was cool and solemn, as if a thought had been provoked in her head. Perhaps at least *she* had been listening to what Mr. Prosser had been saying. With a bracing sense of chivalrous intercession, Mark said, "Peter, I gather from this noise that you have something to add to your theories."

Peter responded courteously. "No, sir. I honestly don't understand the speech. Please, sir, what *does* it mean?"

This candid admission and odd request stunned the class. Every white, round face, eager, for once, to learn, turned toward Mark. He said, "I don't know. I was hoping *you* would tell *me*."

In college, when a professor made such a remark, it was with grand effect. The professor's humility, the necessity for creative interplay between teacher and student were dramatically impressed upon the group. But to 11D, ignorance in an instructor was as wrong as a hole in a roof. It was as if he had held forty strings pulling forty faces taut toward him and then had slashed the strings. Heads waggled, eyes dropped, voices buzzed. Some of the discipline problems, like Peter Forrester, smirked signals to one another.

"Quiet!" Mr. Prosser shouted. "All of you. Poetry isn't arithmetic. There's no single right answer. I don't want to force my own impression on you, even if I *have* had much more experience with literature." He made this last clause very loud and distinct, and some of the weaker students seemed reassured. "I know none of *you* want that," he told them.

Whether or not they believed him, they subsided, somewhat. Mark judged he could safely reassume his human-among-humans attitude again. He perched on the edge of the desk and leaned forward beseechingly. "Now, honestly. Don't any of you have some personal feeling about the lines that you would like to share with the class and me?"

One hand, with a flowered handkerchief balled in it, unsteadily rose. "Go ahead, Teresa," Mr. Prosser said encouragingly. She was a timid, clumsy girl whose mother was a Jehovah's Witness.

"It makes me think of cloud shadows," Teresa said.

Geoffrey Langer laughed. "Don't be rude, Geoff," Mr. Prosser said sideways, softly, before throwing his voice forward: "Thank you, Teresa. I think that's an interesting and valid impression. Cloud movement has something in it of the slow, monotonous rhythm one feels in the line 'Tomorrow, and tomorrow, and tomorrow.' It's a very gray line, isn't it, class?" No one agreed or disagreed.

Beyond the windows actual clouds were bunching rapidly, and erratic sections of sunlight slid around the room. Gloria's arm, crooked gracefully above her head, turned gold. "Gloria?" Mr. Prosser asked.

She looked up from something on her desk with a face of sullen radiance. "I think what Teresa said was very good," she said, glaring in the direction of Geoffrey Langer. Geoffrey chuckled defiantly. "And I have a question. What does 'petty pace' mean?"

"It means the trivial day-to-day sort of life that, say a bookkeeper or a bank clerk leads. Or a schoolteacher," he added, smiling.

She did not smile back. Thought wrinkles irritated her perfect brow. "But Macbeth has been fighting wars, and killing kings, and being a king himself, and all," she pointed out.

"Yes, but it's just these acts Macbeth is condemning as 'nothing.' Can you see that?"

Gloria shook her head. "Another thing I worry about—isn't it silly for Macbeth to be talking to himself right in the middle of this war, with his wife just dead, and all?"

"I don't think so, Gloria. No matter how fast events happen, thought is faster."

His answer was weak; everyone knew it, even if Gloria hadn't mused, supposedly to herself, but in a voice the entire class could hear, "It seems so *stupid*."

Mark winced, pierced by the awful clarity with which his students saw him. Through their eyes, how queer he looked, with his long hands, and his horn-rimmed glasses, and his hair never slicked down, all wrapped up in "literature," where, when things get rough, the king mumbles a poem nobody understands. The delight Mr. Prosser took in such crazy junk made not only his good sense but his masculinity a matter of doubt. It was gentle of them not to laugh him out of the room. He looked down and rubbed his fingertips together, trying to erase the chalk dust. The class noise sifted into unnatural quiet. "It's getting late," he said finally. "Let's start the recitations of the memorized passage. Bernard Amilson, you begin."

Bernard had trouble enunciating, and his rendition began " 'T'mau 'n' t'mau 'r' t'mau.' " It was reassuring, the extent to which the class tried to repress its laughter. Mr. Prosser wrote "A" in his marking book opposite Bernard's name. He always gave Bernard A on recitations, despite the school nurse, who claimed there was nothing organically wrong with the boy's mouth.

It was the custom, cruel but traditional, to deliver recitations from the front of the room. Alice, when her turn came, was reduced to a helpless state by the first funny face Peter Forrester made at her. Mark let her hang up there a good minute while her face ripened to cherry redness, and at last forgave her. She may try it later. Many of the youngsters knew the passage gratifyingly well, though there was a tendency to leave out the line "To the last syllable of recorded time" and to turn "struts and frets" into "frets and struts" or simply "struts and struts." Even Sejak, who couldn't have looked at the passage before he came to class, got through it as far as "And then is heard no more."

Geoffrey Langer showed off, as he always did, by interrupting his own recitation with bright questions. " 'Tomorrow, and tomorrow, and tomorrow,' " he said, " 'creeps in'—shouldn't that be '*creep* in,' Mr. Prosser?"

"It is 'creeps.' The trio is in effect singular. Go on." Mr. Prosser was tired of coddling Langer. If you let them, these smart students will run away with the class. "Without the footnotes."

" '*Creepsss* in this petty pace from day to day, to the last syllable of recorded time, and all our yesterdays have lighted fools the way to dusty death. Out, out—' "

"No, no!" Mr. Prosser jumped out of his chair. "This is poetry. Don't mushmouth it! Pause a little after 'fools.' " Geoffrey looked genuinely startled this time, and Mark himself did not quite understand his annoyance and, mentally turning to see what was behind him, seemed to glimpse in the humid undergrowth the two stern eyes of the indignant look Gloria had thrown Geoffrey. He glimpsed himself in the absurd position of acting as Gloria's champion in her private war with this intelligent boy. He sighed apologetically. "Poetry is made up of lines," he began, turning to the class. Gloria was passing a note to Peter Forrester.

The rudeness of it! To pass notes during a scolding that she herself had caused! Mark caged in his hand the girl's frail wrist and ripped the note from her fingers. He read it to himself, letting the class see he was reading it, though he despised such methods of discipline. The note went:

> Pete—I think you're *wrong* about Mr. Prosser. I think he's
> wonderful and I get a lot out of his class. He's heavenly with
> poetry. I think I love him. I really do *love* him. So there.

Mr. Prosser folded the note once and slipped it into his side coat pocket. "See me after class, Gloria," he said. Then, to Geoffrey, "Let's try it again. Begin at the beginning."

While the boy was reciting the passage, the buzzer sounded the end of the period. It was the last class of the day. The room quickly emptied, except for Gloria. The noise of lockers slamming open and books being thrown against metal and shouts drifted in.

"Who has a car?"

"Lend me a cig, pig."

"We can't have practice in this slop."

Mark hadn't noticed exactly when the rain started, but it was coming down fast now. He moved around the room with the window pole, closing windows and pulling down shades. Spray bounced in on his hands. He began to talk to Gloria in a crisp voice that, like his device of shutting the windows, was intended to protect them both from embarrassment.

"About note passing." She sat motionless at her desk in the front of the room, her short, brushed-up hair like a cool torch. From the way she sat, her naked arms folded at her breasts and her shoulders hunched, he felt she was chilly. "It is not only rude to scribble when a teacher is talking, it is stupid to put one's words down on paper, where they look much more foolish than they might have sounded if spoken." He leaned the window pole in its corner and walked toward his desk.

"And about love. 'Love' is one of those words that illustrate what happens to an old, overworked language. These days, with movie stars and crooners and preachers and psychiatrists all pronouncing the word, it's come to mean nothing but a vague fondness for something. In this sense

I love the rain, this blackboard, these desks, you. It means nothing, you see, whereas once the word signified a quite explicit thing—a desire to share all you own and are with someone else. It is time we coined a new word to mean that, and when you think up the word *you* want to use, I suggest that you be economical with it. Treat it as something you can spend only once—if not for your own sake, for the good of the language." He walked over to his own desk and dropped two pencils on it, as if to say, "That's all."

"I'm sorry," Gloria said.

Rather surprised, Mr. Prosser said, "Don't be."

"But you don't understand."

"Of course I don't. I probably never did. At your age, I was like Geoffrey Langer."

"I bet you weren't." The girl was almost crying; he was sure of that.

"Come on, Gloria. Run along. Forget it." She slowly cradled her books between her bare arm and her sweater, and left the room with that melancholy shuffling teen-age gait, so that her body above her thighs seemed to float over the desks.

What was it, Mark asked himself, these kids were after? What did they want? Glide, he decided, the quality of glide. To slip along, always in rhythm, always cool, the little wheels humming under you, going nowhere special. If Heaven existed, that's the way it would be there. "He's heavenly with poetry." They loved the word. Heaven was in half their songs.

"Christ, he's humming." Strunk, the physical-ed teacher, had come into the room without Mark's noticing. Gloria had left the door ajar.

"Ah," Mark said, "a fallen angel, full of grit."

"What the hell makes you so happy?"

"I'm not happy, I'm just serene. I don't know why you don't appreciate me."

"Say." Strunk came up an aisle with a disagreeably effeminate waddle, pregnant with gossip. "Did you hear about Murchison?"

"No." Mark mimicked Strunk's whisper.

"He got the pants kidded off him today."

"Oh dear."

Strunk started to laugh, as he always did before beginning a story. "You know what a goddam lady's man he thinks he is?"

"You bet," Mark said, although Strunk said that about every male member of the faculty.

"You have Gloria Angstrom, don't you?"

"You bet."

"Well, this morning Murky intercepts a note she was writing, and the note says what a damn neat guy she thinks Murchison is and how she *loves* him!" Strunk waited for Mark to say something, and then, when he didn't, continued, "You could see he was tickled pink. But—get this—it turns out at lunch that the same damn thing happened to Fryeburg in history yesterday!" Strunk laughed and cracked his knuckles viciously. "The girl's too dumb to have thought it up herself. We all think it was Peter Forrester's idea."

"Probably was," Mark agreed. Strunk followed him out to his locker, describing Murchison's expression when Fryeburg (in all innocence, mind you) told what had happened to him.

Mark turned the combination of his locker, 18–24–3. "Would you excuse me, Dave?" he said. "My wife's in town waiting."

Strunk was too thick to catch Mark's anger. "I got to get over to the gym. Can't take the little darlings outside in the rain; their mommies'll write notes to teacher." He clattered down the hall and wheeled at the far end, shouting, "Now don't tell You-know-who!"

Mr. Prosser took his coat from the locker and shrugged it on. He placed his hat upon his head. He fitted his rubbers over his shoes, pinching his fingers painfully, and lifted his umbrella off the hook. He thought of opening it right there in the vacant hall, as a kind of joke, and decided not to. The girl had been almost crying; he was sure of that.

Marvin Schiller
Mr. Princeton

IT SNOWED THE WHOLE NIGHT BEFORE NAFTOLI GOLD took the train to Princeton University. In the morning, the sun dazzled everywhere. Walking up the Brooklyn street Nafty was acutely aware of the fresh snow. He had taken it as a marvelous sign: it symbolized the eradication of all that was uneven in his past, not up to par. The sidewalks, transformed to coconut frosting, all smooth and white, untrammeled, stretched purely before him, portended a day that was to be marked by accomplishments, by recognition, reward for his many talents.

He batted together his gloved hands, thrilled. Within one of the gloves was hidden a ten-dollar bill, folded as small as a three-cent stamp, that his father had given him to cover expenses. His father was still doubtful about the expedition and had given in only after the insistence of his brother, Nafty's uncle, the pediatrician.

On the corner, in front of the synagogue of which Naftoli's father and grandfather were lifetime members, the *shamus* was shoveling snow, clearing a path for sunrise worshippers. The shovel, scraping the hidden sidewalk, made a hollow sound in the clean air. Noticing Naftoli, the *shamus* stopped his work and looked up, astonished.

"Sholom," he greeted in disbelief. "*Sholom aleichem*, Naftila."

At seventeen, athletic, mature from tip to toe, Nafty did not relish being accosted in the diminutive. He answered hurriedly, "*Sholom, sholom* already."

"So don't tell me you're coming to services?" said the *shamus*. He leaned on his long-handled shovel. Behind him the synagogue with its great blue dome and its thin, stained-glass windows rose from the snow with Byzantine solidity.

"Such clothes!" and "My, my," continued the *shamus*, now scrutinizing the boy, in a motherly way picking at his clothes, for an inspection of tidiness. "What is—second *bar mitzvah*, something?"

Nafty brushed an invisible flake of snow from his coat lapel. "You like it?" He was pleased to have found approval.

The coat was a powder blue: $18.50 at Crawfords, Pitkin Avenue. An A.F. type, so called because it left one's bottom exposed to the Brownsville breeze. He was hatless, but his hair was cast carefully into a stiff and prominent pompadour, arrived at by employing half a jar of green "Surcurl" waveset and an aluminum wave-clip (secretly) the night before. And he smelled desperately of Aqua Velva—his father's—the advantage of rising before the old man. And he had used his father's electric razor on the fluff beneath his nose, unafraid of waking the man; after all, this morning he had the excuse.

Now, he rubbed his nose that twitched in the cold: two thousand years to shape that projection, that teapot's spout. (He accepted his fate with jocularity. He could always be a night-club comic, a Jimmy Durante, a Danny Kaye. Already the girls who thought his family was richer than most were telling him, "You got a terrific sense humor, Nafty.")

"Hey," he said to the *shamus*, suddenly inspired. "Will you say a little prayer for me today? What do you say? Something to bring me luck?"

The old man returned to his shoveling. "What's the matter? You can't say your own prayers? Yeshiva boy like you?"

Nafty blushed and knew a moment of shame—for it was true. He had been educated in a Yeshiva, had led himself, his family and friends to believe he was going to become a big rabbi.

"You don't understand," Nafty said. "I'm going to college today."

The old man screwed up his face doubtfully. "You?"

"For an interview. You know. Big. Big time."

The old man, nodding, was obviously impressed. He tucked the shovel's handle under his chin. With an air of divinity he asked, "N.Y.U.?"

"Naah. An out-of-town college. Princeton!"

"Princeton!? For *goyim*?"

Nafty knew a shock of anxiety. He tried to explain that it was different these days, 1947. "It's a new policy. They're liberal now, very liberal. You know, Finkel, because of the war. My uncle, the doctor, he knows the dean."

"That's very nice."

"My uncle says I got a good chance to get in. I got good grades, and I'm a swimmer." And as if he didn't think the man understood, Nafty started to make a swimmer's motions—his arms flaying the morning air rapidly, his head tucked neatly into his shoulders.

When the demonstration ended the old *shamus* bent once again to his shoveling. "I hope you get what you wish."

"But say a little prayer, a little *brucha* for me, huh? It'll make me feel more confident, no kidding."

Gently, the *shamus* lifed a shovel full of snow. He carried it to the hedge and dumped it. He paused to examine the narrow walk he had created as if he no longer was aware of Nafty. Then he spoke, full of wisdom. "Believe me. Nafty, believe me, if I knew a *brucha* I could say for Princeton I would say it for you. For City College, maybe; but for Princeton—this *brucha* you know better than me."

"Ah—"

The train ride to Princeton seemed without end. In his seat, huddled up in his blue coat, as he stared out at the snow-covered province of New Jersey, as he neared his destination, he grew unsettled. He was a sailor coming into port, a Daniel awaiting the first roar. He girded himself, because more than anything he could imagine, Nafty Gold wished to be admitted to Princeton. Not so much Princeton *per se*; it could be Cornell or Yale, even the University of Michigan at Ann Arbor—any institution with the ability of lending him an air of unique and desirable belonging. But Princeton especially. Princeton, what a tradition! A name that fell musically from the lips and produced a nod of respect from one's listeners. Princeton . . . Prince-ton, in time to the wheels over the rails: Woodrow Wilson, Princeton; Nafty Gold, Princeton. . . .

He tried to make the rattling wheels lullaby away his trepidation but he was unsuccessful. The closer the train bore him to his destination the more fearful he grew. In his heart of hearts he knew he was not the master of interviews. He would either talk too much or too little. Or else he would sit down and his fly would yawn open cavernously. He would take out a pen to sign a document and the pen would leak all over his fingers. The train hurtled on. He grew unsure of his shirt—were all the buttons there? His tie, his suit, his shoes? Was there a hole in his socks? Even his not-so-bad looks began to bother him: his nose—it had figured in so many touchy scenes that he dreamed about it. Once, his nostrils had been made of two overturned red flowerpots with weeds growing out of them, downward, drily, darkly. Another time he had walked into a cave at a mountainside only to discover he was hiking up his own nose. He stood now in a sweat and went rocking down the aisle. He asked the conductor how long the ride would be, and being told it would not be very long at all he considered journeying with the train to Philadelphia instead. But he pasted himself down in his seat—the wrong seat, but he was too confused to notice it—and he watched the telegraph poles being plucked like black feathers from the soft down of the snowy trackside.

An hour later the train halted, panting, its white breath columning upward against the ultramarine sky. The station was not one of those bright toy stations with a yellow roof but was run-down, its dark timbers even darker against the blinding field of snow surrounding it. The campiness of the station had a soothing effect on the explorer. But it passed, that moment of easement, as even a lozenge passes, dissolves. Nafty Gold became aware of his aloneness. What Gold had ever traveled this far afield? Even his uncle had been city bred, city schooled. Had his uncle been correct in pressing this interview on him?

The train left him, his last link with the past, and Nafty looked around—not at all sure that this was the promised land. Above the platform roof, on the other side of the station, he made out the tops of the university buildings, shining like the tops of saltcellars in the distance, all silver. How did he get there? Was there a bus? Looking around, he noticed for the first time, on the opposite platform, four young men waiting for a train to New York. They stood huddled together; one was wearing a long orange and black Princeton scarf; and from time to time their voices rose in the clear air. Nafty was awed to realize that these were Princeton men. He had never been so close. . . .

"Why don't we just whip down in my Dad's Buick?" Nafty Gold overheard.

One of the young men leaped down onto the snow-cushioned rail bed and stared down the empty, glinting trainscape. He pulled the fur collar of his stormcoat around his ears, and yelled back to the coevals, "The goddam train must've busted down!" He kneeled down in the snow, immersed his pink, melony hands into it and shaped a snowball. Standing, he eased it into the air so that it landed with a dead thud on the platform roof just over Nafty Gold's head, making the boy start, as out of reverie.

"Sorry, Dad," the Princeton man called out, and Nafty, still awed, blushed, speechless, and watched the man hop back onto the platform to rejoin his dark, shivering Sanhedrin. One young man, the fellow with the scarf, kept repeating, "Why don't we just whip down in my Dad's Buick?"

"I keep telling you my girl's expecting me at the station," said the boy who had been on the tracks.

"Send her a telegram, ass."

"How can I send her a telegram? Her whole family is turning out for this cocktail party at the Vanderbilt."

How envious Naftoli Gold was of them! How desirable to partake in that conversation! But how impossible! What madness! Buicks—cocktail parties —telegrams, even, were beyond his manner of life. What was he doing there?

"Hey, did you lose something?"

He was aware of a voice addressing him. Focusing on the boys again, he saw that a skinny fellow was now standing on the edge of the platform, just across from him.

"You lost, or what?"

He couldn't find his voice. He wanted to burrow a hole in the snow and, rabbitlike, disappear from the face of the earth. What could he do?

"Can you tell me the way to the Admissions Office?" he finally squeaked across the tracks.

"Sure thing." And the skinny fellow relayed a series of careful instructions that Nafty clicked into his mind with successive inane noddings of his head.

"Cut through the athletic field," said the Princeton man.

There was something in the clarity of the fellow's voice that made Nafty feel like a visitor to a foreign city. He was thankful for the instructions, yet at the same time, he wished to move away—as if it were becoming too immediately apparent that there was something too vitally different between himself and the boys on the other platform. Sheepishly, he thanked the fellow and trudged away.

"A tux," he heard a voice fading behind him. "She was wearing my goddam tuxedo when I walked into the bedroom. This forty-dollar negligee I bought her was on the chair, and she was in bed wearing my goddam tuxedo!"

Nafty's ears burned; his head burned. Was it possible that this life could be his? Was an interview all that stood in his way? He had begun to run and his shoes made mouths in the snow.

He came to the main street of the town and slowed down. He walked for several blocks amid housewives out on shopping skirmishes with their children. Young college men were carrying books, walking in the gutters where the snow was packed down firmer; older persons who might or might not be professors were getting in and out of station wagons. He felt strange to the small town, as a decent crusader must have felt strange in passing through those distant cities. But it was attractive to Naftoli. It was what he wanted, this small-college-town life. He prayed that the interview would go well. His uncle had said it was the most important step in the Princeton procedure.

He came to those grey fortresses of buildings from which knights and monks and courtesans might properly have emerged, on horseback, mule-back, or in some gay cabriolet rocking through the snow. Somewhere a carillon had begun to ring. Was it to announce the triumphant appearance of Naftoli Gold? He glanced at his Ingersoll watch and saw that he had to hurry to be on time for his interview. Gothic archways yawned open for him, effigies winked, windows glittering in the scintillating sun were giggling in feminine conversation concerning the search for the admissions office by young Knight Nafty, Sir Gold. An oak door, broad and high as an ocean-going raft caught his eye, it was his port; he was terrified, but he forced himself to turn its handle. Within, a grey-haired lady, a Grandma Moses so placed as to put the most nervous of would-be Princetonians at their ease, greeted Nafty, took his coat and told him he was just on time. He stammered and his knees quaked, yet such was his passion to be admitted that he forced a degree of quietness upon himself. He pointed out to the terrible *molochs* in his brain that he was actually *there*, at Princeton, that he had been, in all certainty, granted an interview, that certainly he must have a good chance—or else why had they sent for him?

"Mr. Gold?"

The door to the dean's office had opened, and some dark shadowy book-case had materialized in silhouette against the room's far windows. Nafty stood and watched the bookcase slowly evolve into flesh and blood, a man in a dark suit with a vest and a trickle of gold across it, a short man with dark red hair, a thick red mustache, a corpulent face as soft looking as a ripe cantaloupe, with eyebrows and eyes as pale as a cantaloupe's seeds, the kind of man who would never step out into the bright sun if he could avoid it, who spent his vacations in the deep shade of a mountain cottage.

He held an index card in his hand and he was smiling like a crescent moon. "How are you, Mr. Gold?"

He extended a pudgy hand and Nafty took it weakly, mumbling something inarticulate. He had begun to shake again.

The dean ushered the boy into his office, shut the door behind them, and introduced Nafty to a chair that was to be his womb for the next twenty minutes. They boy accepted it, alert as a traffic cop now as the adrenalin began to pump through his veins. The dean sat behind an impressive desk littered with papers, and he faced Nafty squarely. The boy did not flinch. On the wall behind the dean was a painting of a man in academic robes. Built up of blacks, browns, and deep reds it gave a solemn air to the room. Naftly glanced at the other walls. They were paneled in a design that suggested hidden cubbyholes, and framed here and there were further paintings of ruddy men, some with circular gold-framed eyeglasses refining their academic eyes. On the desk was a photograph of a woman, encased in a large leather frame. Two lesser frames, of silver, displayed devil-may-care poses of a boy and a girl. Through the two windows on either side of the wall behind the desk a portion of the campus was visible, a field covered democratically by snow.

"Did you get a chance to look around at all?" the dean asked.

Nafty had to shake his head a number of times before the words fell free. "No, sir, not too much."

"You'll want to walk around. The PSO conducts a tour some time around noon. Miss Rampaw will tell you about it at the desk out front."

Nafty nodded stupidly. What was the PSO? Was he supposed to know? "I guess I would have looked myself," he began hesitantly, "only my train just got here about ten minutes ago."

"I guess we routed you out of Brooklyn pretty early this morning."

Nafty nodded. The word "Brooklyn" hung with a foreign crisp tang in the air. It was not like the name of his home town at all. He was beginning to feel vaguely queer. The very luxury of the room—he had dreamed about having a room with paneling—seemed unreal to him. From out of doors he heard the muffled shouts of two young men at play. He saw them far away, but could not make out their game, dark specks against the blue snow, nothing more.

"How do you like getting up with the dawn on a morning like this?" the dean was saying.

"We're usually up pretty early anyway."

"I'm the kind of fellow who's tempted to hide under the covers till noon in this weather. . . ." He went forward to straighten the silver frames on his desk. "But these kids of mine begin to tear the room down about 6:30, regardless of the weather."

Nafty bowed his head, understanding, but embarrassed by the dean's friendliness. In his own circle, a man was always cagey on the first meeting. Maybe this interview is to find out how friendly I am, he thought. Maybe you're just supposed to be very friendly. And the idea of friendliness became immovably locked in his mind.

"Family life, though," the dean observed. "Side effect of being a father, don't you think?"

"My father is pretty strict about getting up early. Whenever he catches me lolling around after a quarter to seven he says, 'Good morning, Mr. Morgenthau, and how much is in the treasury this morning?' "

Dean MacIntosh chuckled.

"I've got five brothers," Nafty said, brimming over with openness, his eyes gleaming with friendship. "Three of my brothers are in service. The other two are in the business."

"The business?"

"My father's business. He has a wurst-casing factory in Long Island City. That's just outside New York. He wants me to study business so I can step in."

"Into wurst casing?"

"The stuff that holds the hot dogs together. We sell to everybody. Hygrade. Nathan's in Coney Island, all of them."

The dean was smiling, his teeth showing like a young girl's fine milk teeth. He looked cherubic, if you could imagine a cherub with a thick mustache.

"I guess it's not the average business," said Nafty.

"No, it isn't, but oddly enough it reminds me of a story I once heard. Let's see . . ." The dean tapped his forehead as if he could cause to tumble into place the fragments of that old story. He smiled. "I think you'll enjoy this. It was in England, oh, about 1913, '14—they weren't in the war at the time, that's it. They were still shipping food to Germany. Among other things, wurst. Millions of sausages. They entered the war, of course, but still some manufacturers continued to export the sausage. Then one day a German Zeppelin was shot down just outside of London, and I'll give you five guesses what its skin was composed of."

"Wurst casing?"

"Right."

"That's pretty clever."

"The manufacturers were old German families. In cahoots with the German government. They were sent to prison."

"I'll have to tell that to my father."

Again the cherubic smile; then an awkward silence. Nafty waited. It was like an examination in school. You waited to see the question written out on the blackboard and you prayed to God you knew the answers. The dean was riffing through some papers on his desk. Nafty's gaze wandered to the windows again. He was warm. He heard the shouts come, muffled, through the windows, and he could now see two boys, up to their calves in snow, ridiculously practicing lacrosse. His head swarmed with the mere fact that he was at Princeton.

"I see you've been pretty active as a journalist."

Nafty caught something different, something of a less expansive nature in the dean's voice. Was he just imagining it?

"You really enjoy writing quite a bit, don't you?" The dean looked up studiously from the report.

Yes, there *was* something different. The joking voice had become a serious voice, the falsetto was now a basso profundo.

"All forms of writing?"

"Ever since I was a kid I've been writing," Nafty blurted. He felt that he was about to get tangled up in the soft web of his own honesty and friendliness. Friendliness. He couldn't shift into another gear the way the dean did. He could hardly find the clutch. "Writing, I mean, for instance, it goes back a long time."

"I'd like to hear about it," the dean said quietly.

"It goes back to English class I had in elementary school, around the 4A. I wrote a Mother's Day poem. It was part of a class assignment, but it was a strange thing for me to be doing because my mother had passed away the year before. I wrote it because I didn't want anyone to know I didn't have a mother. It was all about my heart being gay on the merry day; and the teacher thought it was pretty good. I had a feeling for poetry, she said, and my mother was sure to love it. 'Thank you,' I said. 'I hope so.' During drawing class we prepared cards, and inserted poems inside them. I remember drawing three tulips on my card; or maybe we were all assigned tulips. Then we were supposed to present them to our mothers. . . ."

"That could make a touching little story. . . ."

"When I got home I didn't know what to do with the card. I think I must have cried a little. Then I hid it in my commode, under a stack of underwear. Every week I hid it under something else. I didn't want anyone to find it. It's funny, I always used to imagine my aunts snooping through my things. Not my father or brothers, but my aunts. I used to think they were trying to find out what I was like, because in those years I was very solemn. That's pretty stupid, isn't it?"

"No, it isn't stupid at all, Naftoli—"

Of course it was stupid! How did he get started on all of that?

"Naftoli—is that how you pronounce your name?"

He nodded, a quick little rabbinical nod.

"Naftoli, tell me a little more about yourself. What do you like to read?"

"Oh, I read quite a few things. I browse a lot. That's funny too. Some months I'll pick up a hundred books and not finish more than four or five of them. I become bored very quickly. Magazines. I read a good many of those. *Look, Life, Reader's Digest, Model Airplane News*, back copies of *American Mercury* we have around the house, my next brother's *New Yorker, Writer's Digest*. This is crazy. You know what I do sometimes? I'll pick up the classified section of a newspaper and start to read it. Right from the beginning. I mean, I don't even have enough money to buy a war bond but I'll read all the Merchandise for Sale columns. I'm not in business, but

I read the Buyers' Wants. I read the Situations Wanted, the Commercial Notices, the Personals. Did you ever read the Personals?"

". . . ."

"I read the personals every day. It fascinates me. 'John Jones, no longer responsible for the debts of his wife.' Or, 'S.S., please come home. The family and Myra forgive you.' Jeezus, did you ever wonder about those people? I mean, what's going on in their lives?"

A buzzer sounded on the dean's desk before he could reply. For Nafty, it was the breaking of a spell. He was left stranded with his unanswered question, like the man taking a high dive on a motion picture screen, when the projector breaks down and he's left glued in place while the machine whirs incredibly fast behind you. Nafty's heart was beating, and he tried not to listen when the dean spoke into the phone and said he would be out in a few minutes. Nafty tried not to hear that fatal whir.

To realize that just a small chunk of time had been set aside for him, and that it was coming to a close—it was a death! He was in agony. And the dean remained so unperturbed!

"It's a very difficult decision, isn't it?" MacIntosh said softly. "Deciding what college to attend."

If it were only a matter of decision!

"I remember my father pressing me to go to Amherst because it was *his* school."

I don't have that problem, Nafty thought, I'm lucky.

"What I mean to say, Naftoli, is that you ought to be pretty darn clear in your mind as to what a school can offer you. You've got a good record. Stand by it. Get in as many interviews as you can. If you select Princeton, base your selection on a particular reason. If you've got a question about curriculum, that's what I'm here for."

"I just—"

"Yes?"

"I don't think I could have a particular reason. I just feel that I want to get in. Be here. Princeton. It means something just as it is."

"Suppose we can't accept you, Naftoli? What then?"

Ugly, fantastic pictures flashed through Nafty's mind: he was a vulgar night-club comic; a pin boy in a sleazy bowling alley, a lifetime of lifting leaden pins; he was pushing dress wagons, lost in a maze that resembled streets in the garment district. He flushed, feeling a moment of anger against MacIntosh, feeling the man had tricked him, cheated him out of his secret yearnings. His voice tightened. "Do I have any chance at all of getting in?"

"I'll put it on the line, Naftoli. We're in an unhappy position at Princeton. We don't like it—I don't think anybody does. But it's going to be this way for a few years. Because of the war. GIs and so on. We've got more outstanding applications than we know what to do with. It shames me to tell you how many fellows we can accept out of every three hundred that apply."

"How many?" snapped Nafty. "Fifty?"

"Eight, Mr. Gold."

"Eight—?" Mr. Gold was hushed. And so sincerely had the dean spoken that Nafty's soul filled with remorse not only for himself but for the 291 others who would never see the light of a Princeton morning. What chance did he have, a nut like him from Brooklyn?

"In a few days I'm going to send you an application form. I don't want you to get overexcited when you see it. It doesn't mean acceptance."

Nafty nodded sadly.

"I want you to fill it out. Take your time with it. I know you can do a bang-up job on it. Tell us what you plan to do with yourself."

The earlier feeling of unreality overwhelmed the boy again. He hardly heard what the man was saying. At first he did not see the dean rise and extend his hand, and when Nafty rose he felt clumsy.

"I'm glad you got here for the interview, Naftoli."

The adventurer nodded weakly, and when he saw the dean open the door he welcomed it, his escape, his release from bondage.

"How is your uncle? I haven't seen him since the cruise we took to Bermuda before the war. How is his practice?"

"Fine, Mr. MacIntosh. He's fine."

"Good. Glad to hear it."

"He sends his regards to you." The words fell by rote.

"Give him my best," and "Good luck to you," and the door closed, he was in the outer office, the interview was ended, and he wanted to scream in anguish. It had come to nothing! No signing on the dotted line, nothing!

A secretary he had not seen before wavered into focus in front of him, holding a sheet of paper in one hand.

"If you'll just fill out this information sheet for us, Mr. Gold."

For a moment Mr. Gold looked at the paper in her hand, confused.

"It's just your name and address and so on."

Nafty shook his head.

"You could mail it in, if you'd rather. The dean—"

"I told him everything already!" he cried out, his voice rising uncontrollably. He stopped himself, for again MacIntosh was framed like a bookcase in the doorway. And Nafty felt annihilated. For the first time he noticed another young man in the room. The dean looked away from Nafty, and read from an index card held between his delicate fingers. "Larry?"—as if he were embarrassed that his greeting would be overheard by Mr. Gold. Sheepishly, Mr. Gold watched the applicant march into the dean's office. The dean did not turn to him again; and Nafty walked out without taking the paper from the secretary.

What was the sense? he kept asking himself as he walked through the snow of the campus. All bottled up with nervous energy, Nafty could not bring himself to go back to the train station. He walked past the university buildings, lost in its quadrangles. What the hell had been the sense of trying in the first place?

He came to the athletic field, a tundra of snow, barren except for a clump here and there of willowy, sickly trees, looking as brittle as rust. Low grey buildings seemed lonely and sad in the middle of the field. Then he heard shouting, and he saw them come out from behind the trees. "Hey, hey!" he heard, and, "Hey, hey, chuck it, boy. Chuck, chuck." Two young men, identically dressed in sweat pants and dark turtle-neck sweaters. A small ball was flying through the air between them. They stood a hundred feet apart now, practicing lacrosse, stamping on the snow to keep warm, swinging their bats fancily, yelling encouragement to one another.

Sullenly, Nafty approached them. He leaned against a winterbare elm, and from a distance, he watched.

Between flings, one of the boys turned to Nafty and cried out, "What do you say, kid? What do you say?"

The kid said nothing. Even the sports were foreign to him. This strange game, with a bat like a snowshoe. Where did one get the knowledge of lacrosse? Where was it taught? In what back yard was it played? As he walked away he tried to convince himself that at the beginning these boys had probably been as unknowing as himself. There was the reason for coming to Princeton. To learn lacrosse. This was the place it was taught. And with practice he could be as they were. Lacrosse. Train rides to New York. Parties at the Vanderbilt. In later life, pleasure cruises to Bermuda. But even as he thought it, he knew he would never fill out Dean MacIntosh's application form.

He had walked back to the main street of the town. As if in a reverie he stopped to peer into the window of a haberdashery store. He did not want to go home. He stared hard into the window.

Inside a salesman caught his attention, pointed to a striped bow tie that was featured in the display, as though to ask Nafty's opinion of it. Orange and black, the school colors of Princeton. The salesman smiled, and Nafty, hardly aware of what he was doing, walked into the overheated shop.

"Did you like that tie?" the salesman asked.

"How much is it?" said Nafty. He walked to the window to look at it. The store was very warm, and he unbuttoned his short topcoat.

"Two bucks this week, on sale." The salesman lifted the tie from the display and dangled it in front of Nafty. "Try it on," urged the salesman, leading him to a mirror. "Going into New York?"

Nafty nodded, wondering if the salesman had mistaken him for a student.

"That's a big game this weekend."

"I know," said Nafty, though he did not follow the games. Nafty unwound his own tie, a blue wool hand-me-down from his older brother. Carefully, he knotted the new tie.

"That looks fine," said the salesman.

"I'll wear it now," said Nafty, and he paid for it, and stuffed his old tie in his coat pocket.

He was ready to go home now. He would wear the tie on the train and on the streets of Brooklyn. He would wear it to the synagogue where he would meet the *shamus*, turning on the outside lights because it grew dark early at that time of the year. "How do you like this tie?" Nafty would ask. "This is what all the boys at Princeton wear." No, the *shamus* wouldn't understand. Maybe he would show it to some girls. During the summer he would go away to the mountains. He would work as a bus boy. Instead of wearing those dinky black ties he would wear this one. "It's my school tie," he would explain. "It's a requirement to wear it all year around." He would buy a lacrosse bat, and he would practice against the handball courts. That's all that was needed, he felt. He had to practice, just keep on practicing and he would learn all the things a Princeton man is supposed to learn.

At the station he bought a ticket back to New York, and as he stood waiting for the train where earlier that day the four boys had stood, he thought to himself that he would make himself different, that there would be a time when he would walk into a room and people would nudge each other, sensing that Nafty Gold was different. "Mr. Princton," they would think to themselves. "Here comes a Mr. Princton." He turned to stare down at the empty trainscape, thinking to himself, the goddam train must've busted down. The wind came up and blew full in his face, fluttered his necktie against his collar, and froze at the corners of his eyes the tears that had begun to form there.

Stephen Tracy
The Potato Baron
and the Line

*"My own melancholy is often remedied by
the house. . . . I am a mustachioed potato
baron, once more basking in the aura of
power."*

STRAIGHT ACROSS THE BAY FROM MONTEREY is Santa Cruz, the last hazy bit
of shoreline you can see across Monterey Bay on a clear day. Back when
sardines and anchovies made Monterey a booming fishing center, Santa
Cruz's southern exposure and long white beaches made it a resort, with
its own boardwalk and merry-go-round and roller coaster. My father grew
up in Santa Cruz just before it began its decline into a shabby retirement
town, with hotels and mansions transformed into condominiums and boarding houses. I grew up in turn in Monterey after the fish had disappeared
and the city's businessmen had taken over Steinbeck's Cannery Row, making
steakhouses, theatres, bookstores, and quaint wine-tasting rooms out of
what had been huge whitewashed warehouses permeated with the stench
of fish—a vague putrescence that used to give the fog an acrid, substantial
character. Now, at nineteen, I'm back in Santa Cruz, which is suffering a
renaissance as a university town. I have a room off campus in a peeling
gray mansion built around the turn of the century by a potato baron, who,
with his fortune, wife and children, silk vest, and gold pocket watch, left
the Midwestern plains for the Pacific Coast, where he built his home.

Originally standing beside the beach, the old house was subsequently
moved up the hill to its present site above the city, where it has assumed
a slightly hunched attitude, as if its sagging walls hoped to expand with
one last, deep breath, in spite of termite-riddled timbers and attic beams
that were left charred by some long-ago fire. Sometimes prospective buyers
appear and tour the premises, but I think they are just curious or looking
for entertainment. My own melancholy is often remedied by the house. I
take strolls through the ground-floor rooms when the sliding doors are open,
so that huge, high-ceilinged rooms are formed, and I can imagine it as it
was originally decorated—plush and crowded, the pastel ceilings trimmed
in gold, the walls dark mahogany, the windows draped with velvet, and

the blazing chandelier lights creating movement in the woodwork. I am a mustachioed potato baron, once more basking in the aura of power that young capitalism brings to those who believe. There is more opportunity here on this great West Coast than Wall Street can imagine, Horatio—more than can be inferred from some silken debutante's sparkling eyes. This country here will grow. Opening the stained-glass windows in the tower-like cupola, I can look out and see its expansive potential.

Now, however, the house is filled with students. It is owned by a Mrs. Thurgood, who is a sociology professor. She has rented the place to under-graduates while she attempts to sell it. The floors are eternally scuffed, and some of the rooms have been painted obscenely bright colors. Expensive stereos have replaced the delicate consonance of a harpsichord. As the youngest potato baron, I am upset by all this. Things are fading; the potato is not as popular as it once was. There are termites in the cupola, and, not far away, the brown pelican and the blue whale are being exterminated. We are all concerned. In this house, peopled with students of biology, ecology, and mathematics, concern is an important part of us—a glint of urgency in our otherwise dull eyes, an almost subversive inflection in our usually monotonous tone of conversation. I think we are growing out of it. Already, our concern lacks imagination; we sometimes spend a weekend registering Democrats.

Jessica is the woman who lives with me in my room, our room. Together, we share the finest room on the first floor, and at night we huddle in bed watching the fire writhe in the tiny fireplace cage, framed by handmade tile and a carved-woodwork mantel, which one visitor guessed would be worth a great deal by itself in any antique market. Our room was once the library, and the bookshelves still remain, rising the entire fourteen feet to the ceiling. Many of the prospective buyers who are being shown the house think it is a shame that students are allowed to live here, because it is such a fine old house. At times, I share their dismay and contempt, but usually I am busy studying. I am studying calculus and the fundamentals of chemistry, so that when the crops give out and I am no longer a baron I will be able to do something useful and relevant, something other than simply studying or playing the violin. I will take organic chemistry, then genetics, physics, and a great deal of biology. Eventually, I will be a doctor, my curly brown hair tousled in the wind as I make my way through the streets of an impoverished neighborhood of Chicago, New York, or Los Angeles. I will be a doctor for the poor, whom I can help with my knowl-edge and ply with my care. Jessica, after some thought, told me that this was, at least, a rational plan.

For this logical trend in my own thinking I thank calculus. At the same time, I can feel a new complexity cropping up in me because of my habit of having to shape everything before it can be used—taking usable equations off a curve that knows no stopping, no self-reflection, but simply continu-ance. There is, of course, a power in one's ability to stop the continuity for a moment in order to get a glimpse of the slope and the direction of the entire line. Too often, I feel events scurrying off on their own straight paths while I am left with an imaginary construct, an elaborate framework—this crooked house and a crooked smile. With mathematical training, however, I am beginning to see more and more the workings of a mathematical divinity. Whenever I complain of being a mindless, bodiless vector moving unsteadily away from a point of origin through squares of no coordinates across the Cartesian plane, Jessica accuses me of being theatrical and says that this is the way life is supposed to be arranged and that I should stop complaining. Jessica was married for a while. At the age of seventeen, she worked as a bookkeeper to support her husband and herself during their stay together, and she is still very good at work requiring order, straight-line thinking, and discipline. But me, I'm growing soft on Communism; I remember children's stories and the green emerald on my mother's hand.

For most purposes, Jessica and I are a self-contained unit and spend most of our time together, in the same room. But there are other students in the house. In fact, it was the others who found the house at the beginning of summer, and we moved in only after they had already painted the ceilings, sanded the floors, and varnished some of the old wood, and had forced Mrs. Thurgood to repair the plumbing. Tom and Jim, both blue-eyed, blond, and eager, apparently did most of the work, and they still feud about how the kitchen is to be repaneled or whether or not the house money can be used to repair the dishwasher. After an especially devastating argument, Tom will retreat to his lab up on campus, where he is doing undergraduate research on plant development, and Jim will spend a day or two programming computers, although his declared major is political science. If the disagreement is relatively minor, Jim, a member of the university chorus, will spend an hour or two singing at the top of his lungs. These two share a room on the second floor.

The second floor also houses Jane, a thin, sweet girl with a permanent closed-mouth smile and arms that are freckled like cream-of-mushroom soup. Also Susan, a short and jolly senior in biology, who occasionally bakes us a sheet of very rich chocolate-chip cookies. Both have graduation as their primary concern. Wade, another second-floor resident, seems to have dismissed the idea of graduating and has dropped out for the fall quarter, occupying himself with photography and the acquisition of a girlfriend who has no objections to modelling in the nude. At one time or another, all the girls in the house have endured his pleading stare, which is magnified by thick-rimmed glasses. Sharon and Mary-Ann complete the original house population, sharing the first floor with Jessica and me. Sharon, with large wrists and deep voice, is a sloppy but energetic cook, who keeps a steady flow of bread, cakes, and gritty, massive salads coming from the kitchen. Mary-Ann, a senior in chemistry, spends the largest portion of her time pining away for her fiancé, stationed in Germany, who is only a rare phone call in the house. In all, there are nine of us living in seventeen rooms. For the most part, we are compatible. The size of the house allows escape into the attic or an empty room, but the distances we keep affect us; we become strangely and suddenly gentle, touching each other at times with a genuine kindness, an almost exploratory compassion.

I have been shut up in my room for an entire cold gray afternoon studying for the mid-December finals, and I begin to feel that the separations imposed by the house have become a permanent part of me, breeding a cold, gray melancholy. The house is quiet and there is no evidence of anyone else as I make a pot of coffee, but then, coming out of the kitchen, I notice Mary-Ann stretched out on the front-room rug. With my coffee, I stand in the doorway a moment, watching the place where her legs meet. They are big legs, and smooth. Rather like bananas, I imagine.

"Tired?" I ask.

She nods and says her neck is tight. She has been studying for her comprehensives in chemistry. I sit down beside her on the floor and take her neck in my hands, beginning an adventure beyond the established relationship. We have laughed together over dinner with the others and have joined in wild food throwing, in juggling glasses, in circus fantasies. Once, she got milk for a cup of coffee I was drinking, but we have never touched each other. I never thought of her as something to touch. So there is a strangeness to it, and an excitement in feeling the blond hair on her neck become sweaty with the warmth of my hand as I squeeze there and press and then relax and again push the muscles together until they are no longer tense. I try to think of other things, of things my hands have touched— cracked granite while building a retaining wall, sand, cold rusted metal protruding from the winter beach, jellyfish, mosaic tabletops, the waxberries of a neighbor's hedge, the soft feathers of a parakeet's breast, steel-wound gut violin strings, bread dough. Mary-Ann's neck is softer now.

I leave her sleeping on the shag carpeting, and I think how comfortably we all live here, our individual dreams uninterrupted by the revolution, all of us well-fed and healthy, and the house preserving us within its aura. Jessica, with whose warmness I sleep (sometimes a leg extending its own private warmth across my own), is the best cook. She prepares blueberry cheesecake, pancakes, loaves of whole-wheat bread, and spaghetti with cream cheese and herb sauce. Her delicately flavored soups are served quietly and with formality, as if the whole sometimes vulgar collection of us were a group of tiny Orientals in this fading house. Jessica has had offers to live with others, because of her cooking and because she has hair the color of wheat and dark skin setting off blue eyes. She laughs at the proposals. There seems to be no question about us—perhaps because I am still the potato baron, perhaps because I can still pretend that this derivative and comfortable stopping of our lives will not change someday into something lifeless and joyless. Perhaps because I can pretend in bed that we are whales on the verge of extinction, floating just beneath the surface as we make love, singing the low whale songs.

In truth, it is beginning to seem as if the whole of my life is an exercise, a strenuous test of my imagination. Even in this house, in which time moves so slowly, limits manifest themselves again and again. The day comes to an end gradually as the talk in the kitchen dwindles and the people wander off into their rooms, leaving me, the only one up, studying calculus out of a thick book bound with integral tables. I have memorized most of them and can graph almost any algebraic function. I can find the first, second, and third derivatives, and soon, I see, noticing the heading of a future chapter, I will be able to do work with transcendental functions, which I imagine as extending off the graphed paper and through the windows, or up the old walls, along the beams, and up into the attic, worming their way across the silver planks there, where they sit for a moment on the cupola windowsills, and then finally leaping into the night sky and integrating themselves into the far-off glimmerings and the smoky odor of night—a continuous river of soaring equations pouring into velvet stratosphere.

In our room, Jessica takes the bedcovers in both hands and sleepily pulls them over her head. I am increasingly tempted to join her, to sleep and legitimately dream, instead of grappling with this calculus, but the math, I remind myself, is something useful, scientific, and physical. Nevertheless, I am affected by limits: the blankets, the bookcases, and the doors, always necessarily at some point of being opened or closed. Late at night, when I can feel that calculus can exist without my understanding, doors and their definite positions bother me. When I sleep, Gertrude Stein haunts me. She is leading a small encounter group and talking it into nonexistence. "We must be aware of our nonexistence," she says to me. "We must meet it head on."

The landlady, never a popular figure in fiction or in this house, is making a move that may put an end to the stagnation that I have begun to feel here. Mrs. Thurgood is generally soft-spoken and sometimes motherly; she likes to refer to us as her "affluent brood." At one time she was quite a political figure here, running for office on Socialist Party tickets during the Depression, and she still keeps up a radical front, in spite of what we see as her exploitation of students. She is now in her late fifties, and freshly divorced. There is a property dispute with her ex-husband, who has threatened to come in and make off with the velvet curtains and the luxurious carpeting in the living room. All this is the cause of the first instability to threaten our lives here, for Mrs. Thurgood, who apparently believes her husband capable of anything, has decided to take up the carpet herself.

Jessica, a veteran of and deserter from the ranks of the married, sees all this as proof of the mess people get into when they accept marriage as any kind of ratification of an essentially personal relationship. "The government should build highways and hospitals, and leave people alone," she says.

And so the house slips into December. The school quarter will end on the fifteenth; today is the fifth, and the landlady was here for rent. I have gone to the market, a few blocks from the house, to buy tangerines and groceries for the rest of the household, whom I find gathered around the stove in the kitchen when I return. She has done it—taken up the carpet and left the bare floor, carpet nails, and this subdued fury. Tom points out that, together, we probably pay five times more than Mrs. Thurgood's mortgage payments on the house and that the removal of the carpeting is not going to mean a reduction in our rent. Tom uses the words "one iota."

"Not one iota," Jim says, in echo, "and now we don't have a rug in the living room."

Sharon comes stamping in. She has just finished taking down and hiding all the velvet curtains—an act of retribution. Now it is decided that we will move out "en masse" in a combination rent strike and exodus, possibly taking the curtains as spoils.

"Before we vacate, perhaps we should attempt some sort of negotiation," I suggest. But no one is going to be persuaded at this point.

"Well, then, how about an obscene phone call or a bomb threat?"

I am hoping to become a part of the mood, but they ignore me, their backs up against the drainboards and counters, rancor in their eyes. It is going to be a revolution without humor. Damned if I'll support such a dull venture! I hide my tangerines against the coming unheaval and notice that the sugar is running low in the pantry but that there is plenty of salt. Three cartons of half-gallon cans of whole beets seem to be an omen of grim days ahead. I had hoped that things wouldn't converge until the quarter was over, and that I could play a more significant part in the revolution, but history is always out of people's control.

Here in the kitchen—in headquarters, now that the decision has been made—reliable sources regard the mood as tense. The initial surge of self-righteousness has been followed by a lot of activity involving calls home and to real-estate agents. We'll soon be homeless, and, standing in the kitchen after hiding my tangerines, I see that the tenants are suffering; almost everyone is either down with a cold or just getting over the flu. It is the rainy season here, and the roof is leaking badly; the ceiling of the second floor let loose an island of plaster this morning. Looking out the kitchen window, I feel the stillness of the house. It stands quiet as the rain begins again, and the clouds turn pink in the dusk. The whole house is beginning to float. I leave the kitchen and find Jessica.

"At least it feels like Christmas," she says, peeling one of my carefully hidden tangerines.

" 'What would Christmas be without presents?' said Jo," I say. "And what's Christmas vacation going to be like if we have to spend it looking for a place to live?"

We huddle together on the bed. Jessica squeezes a section of tangerine into her tight lips, spits out a seed, and sniffles. "I'm beginning to feel unstable again," she says. "I thought we had a place where we could stay awhile, but this place is crumbling. The paint's cracking, and tomorrow we do the whole thing with the newspaper and telephone calls, the 'Are you a student? I'm sorry, we don't rent to students' routine. God."

"I'll do the calling then. I'll just be firm and confident. 'Hello, I'm a potato baron. I need a winter place by the ocean. A big back yard, furnished and large enough for me and my concubine.' 'What?' 'Concubine—you know, a potato-picking machine. A large garage will do fine.' There must be some old people who will show proper respect for the aristocracy. What ever happened to the University that is Mankind, the vast Studentdom?"

Jessica, unimpressed, unrolls some of the toilet paper we keep in the room, wipes her nose, and goes upstairs. I light my pipe and look out the window, where the yellow sour-grass flowers are being beaten down by the rain. Damn her.

We're tired. The future is usurping things; our energy is no longer ours. At one time, when we first moved in together, just seeing Jessica getting up from bed and walking to the closet through the shadows—two white crescents of buttocks and the comfortable arch of her back moving away— filled me with warm excitement. Now I feel we are pushed together too often by having to sleep in the same bed, share the room, and make plans as a unit. The unique intimacy is becoming habit. But we don't talk about it. I have begun reading magazines, especially the advertisements—calculations in fine wool, spotless complexions, rich smiles, and long fingers. How would they look in this old room, those long women making their way to the closet from this brass bed? It is a vision filled with energy, and I am in need of energy. I have become a house-hunter, and it is lonely.

House-hunting is put aside during the next week, the week of finals, and each of us again attempts his own miraculous academic pupation, from which we hope to emerge with shining new wings and brighter colors. Wade, with no courses and nothing to worry about, wanders around the house exclaiming, "What the hell has happened to you people?"

After finals, we continue to tighten our schedules, reducing alternatives and inhibiting tangents. It is musical chairs; we are trying to find a new place before the music stops. Michael, my first-year roommate, tells us of a small apartment—shower, tiny kitchen, and bedroom—that Jessica and I can rent for forty-five dollars a month.

We call the place, and an old voice answers. I ask if there is an apartment for rent.

"Well, maybe," the voice replies. "Are you a student?"

"Yes, I'm a biology major." I say, exuding uprightness, cleanliness, dedication, and reverence.

At the other end, she clears her throat. "How many of you are there?"

"There's one of me, and I have one friend. A young lady."

"A friend? Are you married?"

"Not at the moment."

She pauses. "You'd better talk to my sister. It's her house. I don't have anything to do with it."

"Hello?" her sister says. "Actually, we're looking for a single working man. No couples. It's just too small. No, I don't think that we want to rent to a couple."

"There's a possibility I might be living alone. Do you suppose I could come over and look at it?"

"You're not a hippie, are you?"

"No, I'm a biology major."

I hang up and put on a clean shirt and clean pants. Jessica and I walk the few blocks to the house, go up the front steps, and knock on the screen door. A lady, in curlers and jowls, meets us without a greeting.

"It's strictly for one person, you know," the woman says. "You can go around back and talk to my husband, if you want."

The door closes. Behind the lace curtains of a side window, a shadowy mass watches us—the sister. The entrance to the apartment is at the back of the house, and the apartment itself, it turns out, is in the basement. Inside, the husband has just finished repainting the shower. He shows us his work, complaining about the condition in which the place was left by the former tenants. "I cleaned the oven, too," he says. "Those three people left everything a mess."

"Three?"

"Yah. Of course, they were all boys. For you two, I'll move in a double bed. Maybe you want a desk, too? I've got a couch you could look at."

Jessica and I nod. We have decided to take the place, in spite of the old lady. We all go back outside.

"That'll be eighty dollars a month for the two of you," the man says, rubbing his scruffy chin with the back of his hand. He looks up at the sky, the telephone wires. Finally, he has to look back at us. "That too much?"

We shrug vaguely.

"All right. Because you're young and she's so pretty, sir, I'll let you have it for seventy. How's that?"

Smiling, we agree to it and shake hands. The door of the main house creaks open behind us. The man's wife leans her head out, her pudgy fingers on the latch. She says one word, "Telephone," and a magnificent wave of dread sweeps over the moment. The man goes into the house.

"Jessica, I think our plans are about to be hacked asunder," I say.

After a few minutes, the wife extends her head. Her grimace might be construed as a grin.

"I'm awfully sorry," she says, "but that was a single working man. You know—just what we wanted." She retracts her head and the door swings shut. We stand in the driveway for a few minutes, staring at the door, and then shuffle out of the yard.

I think somewhere in some chemistry book I might be able to find a formula for a bomb that would lift the white boredom out of that sagging house and fill it with the grand heat of vengeance. At the same time, I wish that instead of being a potato baron I could be a Single Working Man.

With Christmas only a week away, the melancholy seems to be deepening, as more and more of our various house-hunting ventures are unsuccessful. Wade, in an effort to cheer us up and still convey the epidemic nature of the despair, has christened the mood "melancholera." The rest of us are not comforted, but we are organizing our defenses. We are planning an extravaganza for the old house—something to fray the thread of our future, stretching from here to the beginning of next month, when the rent is due.

"It has to be *extravagant*," says Jim. As a first step, he invites the entire university chorus. On the day of the party, a keg of beer arrives and is dutifully tapped and tested. Sheets of cookies are turned out by our domestic faction, Susan and Sharon. A few of these cookies survive the strenuous test instituted by the rest of us. Emissaries are visiting the neighbors, borrowing their tablecloths and extending invitations. By this time, most of us have recovered from finals, but serious plans for the future are not possible until after the party. Tonight, the night of the party, a household resolution has been passed banning all serious talk and any further visits from "prospective buyers."

The guests, most of them chorus members, start arriving late in the evening, knocking at the door, rattling the old stained glass. Their Christmas concert was a success, and they are still singing. The party develops very much as I once imagined college parties to be. I walk about, watching it all—the fast drinking, the small contests and intense laughter, red faces, hands holding and moving. A bearded fellow I've never seen before has his arm around Sharon's big middle, and she is smiling sweetly. Sure that no one will miss us, Jessica and I retreat to our rooms waiting for the arrival of our own friends. Perhaps we have never been part of the household, but I'm not sure now that any of us were. Perhaps it was just a house.

Jessica and I build a fire in the fireplace cage and watch it through the gold effervescence of our beer. Michael, my old roommate, makes his entrance and introduces his guest, Anne, a violinist. Her chin is almost double, but she is still invested with a kind of controlled beauty. Michael, who sometimes used to play duets with me, tells us she is a *real* musician, one who warms up with the Tchaikovsky Violin Concerto. She has a slight blond mustache.

"Hello," she says. "Michael has told me about you. I understand we are all violinists."

"To some extent or another," I reply. She seems poised, damnably poised, and is probably fascinatingly disciplined.

Wade evidently had a successful finals week, for now he comes into our room with a new girlfriend, Elizabeth. We all make our way up to the cupola with a half gallon of white wine and several mugs of beer. Anne, it turns out, is not drinking. I take large swallows of wine and watch the lights of Santa Cruz through an open cupola window. Occasional doors slam in nearby houses, and there is a kind of music to the motors of the cars on the streets below—high octave stoppings and diminuendos at red lights, and a slow grumbling crescendo of the same motors as they begin again. Tonight, Jessica seems such little company. Sitting across from her in the cupola, I see no communication or strength in her tight little smile. How can this be? There is no interest there, and watching her fills my stomach with dry dust. I take another mouthful of wine, no longer tasting it, and I begin to think what it would be like to live with someone who could force herself to practice the violin five or six hours a day. I have decided that we all have intense passions and that it is endurance that finally makes the difference.

Anne, submerged now in a polite boredom, slightly tightening her lips and folding her hands in her lap, projects an air of two parts refusal and one part transcendence. With a nonchalant deliberation, I am getting drunk. I watch the blue veins in my hands.

Anne whispers to Michael about an early appointment in the morning, and together they rise to go, Michael a little embarrassed and Anne thanking Jessica for the wonderful time. They apologize for leaving so early. I stand also, consciously steady, and walk with them downstairs, seeing them out. There are mumbled good nights, and the door shuts softly. The car is starting, and in a kind of spasm of dejection I pull the door open again and scramble out to them before they pull away.

Anne rolls down the window.

"What is it?" Michael asks.

Ignoring him, I mumble something and take Anne's face in my hands, kissing her lips gently but drunkenly.

"Must taste like wine and beer," I say. "Awful."

"Not too bad," she says smiling a little. Michael says good night, and the car pulls away. From the cupola, Wade and Jessica yell down. I don't know if they saw.

Michael comes back at six the next morning and wakes me up. We have an old appointment to go to Monterey for a violin lesson. The distant knocking at the glass front door comes as a shock; I feel a little like rattled glass myself. Rolling out of bed in a panic, unsteady and weak, I remember four of us on my bed, and me taking Elizabeth, Wade's friend, and holding her face tightly between my hands, I kissed her desperately. I couldn't feel my hands but I could feel her cheeks, and I had to connect my face with what I could feel of hers. Jessica was trying to dissuade me, saying that the only thing she wanted was me. Sometime after that, she made her way to the closet, slipped into my Army-surplus overcoat, and left the room, and sometime after that I was sick.

Now Jessica is sleeping on our bed, but I don't remember her returning. I pull on my pants, nearly losing my balance as I painfully hop about on the cold wood. I take my violin and let Michael in the door. He asks if I feel well enough for a lesson.

"Almost." I fix a cup of black instant coffee. The kitchen is filled with froth-crusted beer mugs and there is a pot of cold, stiff noodles. Michael is silent.

Later, in his Volkswagen, Michael turns his eyes from the road and glances at me nervously. "Could I ask you something?" he says.

I nod.

"What did you mean last night? I mean, you don't have to answer if you don't want to, but were you serious?"

I look at him for a moment. He has thick, Biblical hands, like Moses' hands in Michelangelo's marble.

"I'm sorry, Michael," I say. "I was drunk. I didn't have anything in mind. She seemed so disciplined, so sure."

He looks straight ahead.

"You both seemed older," I say, "and I felt that the only thing left to do was kiss her. Actually, I don't think I would even like her. She seems so set and confident, and I can't stay drunk all the time, can I?"

"I was just curious," Michael says. "But you're right—she is hard. And aggressive. You're lucky to have someone like Jessica."

"I guess it's just difficult to do anything all the time. Being with someone all the time. Or practicing every day, putting your life in order."

The Volkswagen is rattling, but it relaxes me. Calculus formulas begin to re-form in my head, like green sprouts recovering from a flood. The drunkenness is wearing off. I am exhausted.

I think maybe Jessica will find a place by herself for the next quarter, maybe a house in the woods in the Santa Cruz mountains that she can share with someone else. I think I will move back on campus, to the colorless, comfortable dorms. On this simple gray Saturday, I think that I will move into a dormitory room, where there will be less confusion, less to worry about, and more time to study the violin, calculus, and chemistry.

James Baker Hall
A Kind of Savage

FOR THE SECOND TIME IN THREE WEEKS the housemother from Brewster Hall, Elizabeth Dickinson, class of '29, was sitting in the Dean's office yacking on and on about this girl from Lexington, Kentucky, who was going to wreck the entire dorm if something wasn't done. Knowing Elizabeth (dear old Elizabeth), the Dean halved everything she said and discounted the tone completely—which left little that could be construed as a dean's business. Courtney Pettit this, Courtney Pettit that! For lack of any other way to entertain herself, Dean Bradford leaned forward in her chair in a private parody of interest and attention.

Elizabeth Dickinson was a frail, nervous woman who whipped lickety-split along the campus walks with her head buried on her chest; every few yards her face would pop up, smiling, only to disappear again abruptly. For a while the Dean had thought that the housemother had a tic rather than any real interest in the world, but Elizabeth Dickinson knew as much about what was going on at Talcott College, from the lowest freshman right up through the President, as anyone around. The Dean often thought now that if you could draw her hair back while she was trotting along with her head down, you would find her ears standing at alert like a dog's. It wasn't simply Elizabeth Dickinson, class of '29, that brought out that sort of meanness in the Dean; it was Elizabeth Dickinson as one of many. They were like the Chinese Communists, these old alumnae still attached to the college; what they lacked in equipment they made up for in dedication and tactics and sheer number—they just kept coming in human waves. A whole squad of them operated out of the very place where the Dean lived and ate, and one or two evenings of every week she fled straight from her office into New Haven; it was either that or end up being insulting. Or, worse still, dead.

"If you and the girls can't handle something like this, what can you handle, Elizabeth?" the Dean said. "I don't know this Pettit girl nearly as well as you do, of course, but she impressed me as a very quiet and accommodating little girl."

"That's the way she impressed me! That's the way she impresses everybody!"

What the housemother didn't understand, what very few of the little old ladies around Talcott College understood, was that the refinements and distinctions that meant so much to them were largely lost on the girls, who saw you as either for them or against them; either you were on the side of life, of freedom and adventure, or you were some version of death itself. If they ever got the idea that you were an old maid, you'd *had it* as an influence in their lives. Not too many years ago Dean Bradford would have tried to get Elizabeth Dickinson to see that, but now she knew better than to try. Considering the sort of women that Talcott was trying to cultivate, and the personnel they had to do it with (on paper, half the faculty was male, but it was hard to tell sometimes which half), the Dean was inclined to marvel at what success the college had.

Before the appointment was over, the Dean was feeling sorry for Elizabeth and a little guilty about being unable to take her problems more seriously. By way of making amends, she invited herself over for a drink late that afternoon. She thought it was clear that this would be a purely social call, but the housemother misconstrued the whole thing; when the Dean arrived, expecting to flop down in a chair with a drink, there in the living room were three of Elizabeth's girls—Courtney's ex-roommate, the dorm president, and the chairman of the dorm discipline committee—and the Dean found herself listening to the same garbage she'd heard that morning. Courtney Pettit this, Courtney Pettit that, all over again. Somebody was always having to get up and let her in after the doors were locked; she stayed up all night and slept all day and never seemed to study; penalizing her with extra duties simply meant risking further humiliation because it was hard enough getting her to do her own share in the first place. It all struck the Dean as enough to make you fall in love with Courtney Pettit, sight unseen.

The girls left, and as she was having her drink with Elizabeth, she said, "What's this I hear about you hanging out your laundry on Miss Finch's lawn?"

The housemother, taking her ritual walk about the campus on a recent Sunday morning, had discovered two undergarments—one male, one female—tied to the branch of a tree on the President's lawn.

"*What?*" Elizabeth exclaimed. "Where in the *world* did you hear *that?*"

"From Miss Finch herself. She said she happened to look out of the window, and there you were hanging things out to dry on her trees."

"I was taking them *down!* Lord have mercy, I—oh, you had me *scared to death!*" The housemother, blushing, shook her head in bewilderment at the Dean's imagination. "No wonder the girls love you."

"I thought they were scared of me."

"Oh, underneath it all they love you. Dearly! You're really so young at heart. They *identify* with you."

"Let me catch one doing that! I haven't got a heart, Elizabeth, just a gizzard."

On the way home she grew conscience-stricken for having abused the poor timid woman all over again. Unlike some of the little old ladies on the faculty, Elizabeth Dickinson had no say in the college, so she was relatively harmless; what's more, compared with most of the old maids that the Dean was obliged to deal with day in and day out, Elizabeth was open and lively. That was cutting it pretty thin, aligning Elizabeth Dickinson with the life force, but as the girls would tell you, you had to get your kicks where you found them, and in a woman's college you could end up sometimes cutting things pretty thin.

The Dean had nothing against the college or her job that being able to get away from it every night wouldn't have relieved—or so she was fond of telling herself. When she'd first come there, after the war (she and Miss Finch had been in the Marines together, a fact that still set everybody— students, faculty, alumnae—off in seventeen different directions at once), she'd promised herself, even told Miss Finch, that if she wasn't allowed to live in New Haven after a time, she would find herself another job. That was a good many years ago, and she'd never mentioned it again. For one thing, she found the way of life on campus much less sterile and parochial than she'd imagined. It was, in fact, very lively in a quiet way—the lake, the arboretum, the library, the talk—and she'd found it possible to live a deeply civilized life. Still, she would probably have moved to New Haven long ago but for the fact that more and more of the young faculty, especially the men, were trying to do that. The administration had not been forced to draw the line yet, but Miss Finch had gone out of her way on numerous occasions to let it be known that she didn't intend trying to run a residential college with a commuting faculty. If the Dean hadn't been a dean, she would have gone ahead anyhow, knowing that quite a few others were getting by with it, but being in the administration carried a special burden in the matter, as in so many others.

A lot of people were saying that Courtney Pettit would never fit in, that she was the most egregious mistake Talcott College had made in years, but when the Dean finally did agree to call Courtney in, it was more from curiosity than concern.

She was all prepared, when Courtney came in, for another of those full-dress debates in which the college was accused of being an oppressive reactionary matriarchy, but Courtney showed no interest in representing the forces of life and freedom. She was the first to point out that Talcott College was Talcott College, that she had known more or less what she was getting into when she came, and that she could always leave if she didn't like it. It was like interviewing a Girl Scout with bad grades, not a chick who was feared to have revolution in her blood.

"Gosh, Miss Bradford," Courtney said. "I try, I really do."

"What's so immensely difficult about obeying a few simple rules?"

"It's terrible, I know."

"You haven't been to English in three weeks. How long do you think you can keep your grades up without attending classes?"

"Probably not even one more day. I've been lucky on all those English papers."

"Why didn't you wait on tables the other morning when you were supposed to? Now don't give me that stuff about how ashamed you are. I want the reasons—one, two, three."

"I was in bed."

"My dear child, we were *all* in bed until we got *up*. Did it ever occur to you that if you came back to the dorm on time and went to bed at some decent hour, you wouldn't be so sleepy?"

"Yes, ma'am, I know it. I've tried to go to bed early, but I always end up just lying there wide awake for hours and hours. I reckon it's my metabolism."

"Your metabolism, huh?"

"Oh, don't make fun of me, Miss Bradford. It's the truth, it really is!"

"You're driving Miss Dickinson to distraction, I trust you realize that."

"Yes ma'am."

There was a long silence.

"Well? Is that a matter of indifference to you?"

"No ma'am. I'm sorry about Miss Dickinson. I realize she has a hard time."

The Dean looked up sharply. "What do you mean by that?"

"Nothing," Courtney said. "Heavensakes, I don't have anything against Miss Dickinson or any of the girls, I really don't."

"Either you're going to learn how to get along in the dorm, or you're going to end up before the Student Council. Do you understand what that means? It's up to you."

"Yes, ma'am, I know it," Courtney said. "I'm going to get a good night's sleep tonight and start working off all those penalties tomorrow."

She waited on tables three times a day all that week, and when Elizabeth Dickinson called, wanting to know what in the world the Dean had done, the Dean was tempted to suggest that Courtney Pettit, far from being disrespectful of authority, understood and appreciated it quite well, because she responded only to the real thing; but instead, a little ashamed of the frequency with which she used housemothers and virgin girls to take an attractive measure of herself, she told Elizabeth simply that she'd done her bit and the whole thing was now back in the laps of the powers at Brewster Hall, where it should have stayed all along.

At the dorm, though, few believed that Courtney Pettit really wanted to reform, and the first time she didn't show up for breakfast duty, they were laying for her. The word spread over the dining room like news of an international crisis, leaving silence in its wake. The girls turned their chairs away from the tables; the waitresses, wearing their aprons like placards, lined up against the wall in protest; everybody trained attention on the door, waiting for the delinquent Courtney. A few girls got their own breakfasts, boycotting the protest, but the rest just sat indignantly, refusing to take a bite until Courtney Pettit reported for duty. They waited five minutes. Ten. Fifteen. They couldn't sit around waiting all morning—most of them had an eight-o'clock class—so they hastily assembled an *ad hoc* committee to roust Courtney out of bed. The five girls boarded the elevator and waited in grim silence, like a bunch of Marines in a landing barge, until someone pushed the button. When the committee got back, somebody pointed out that it was no good getting Courtney up because they had no way to keep her from going back to bed again. Somebody else suggested that getting Courtney Pettit to fulfill her responsibilities was considerably more trouble than it was worth, and that the reasonable thing was for them to go on about their business as though she didn't exist. Somebody else pointed out that, yes, that was true, and it was probably exactly what Courtney was counting on; she was putting them on no matter which way they turned. A senior jumped up to say that she had taken as much guff off a freshman as she intended to take, that she personally had served that little bitch her meals a half dozen times and would be *damned* if she would let her get out of New England without paying her debts; there was nothing personal about it, it was a matter of social justice. With that the whole dining room exploded into factions, and the upshot was that most of the girls had to go without break- fast in order to make their classes.

It was midwinter before the Student Council got anywhere near as worked up as the girls from Brewster Hall. The first time they called Courtney in they contented themselves with reviewing the trouble she'd caused and issuing rather severe warnings about what would happen if she persisted in thinking she was a law unto herself. Courtney was contrite, and left quite obviously chastened. Some of the Council members were seeing her for the first time, and they agreed afterward, despite the loud protests of the repre- sentative from Brewster, that anybody who would be upset by that little girl was looking for somebody to be upset by. "Just wait," the Brewster girl kept saying, "just wait and you'll see," and the more she said it the more fun they made of her.

For several weeks Courtney behaved herself, but then all of a sudden everything was right back where it had started, and this time the Council decided to confine her to the campus on weekends for a month. For the first time since Courtney had taken up residence in Brewster Hall the girls listened without complaint, at least on the weekends, to the jazz she played all night in her room. In fact, some of the more vindictive made a ritual of going to her door at date time on Friday and Saturday and Sunday nights and yoo-hooing good-bye to her. Everybody, Courtney very much included, seemed more or less satisfied that she'd gotten what she deserved, until she was seen in New Haven late the last of those Saturday nights—while back at the dorm the housemother and the Student Council representative, among others, were listening to all that jazz. A quick investigation revealed the possibility that Courtney had been taking her privileges all along, but it couldn't be proved, and so the Council, influenced again by Courtney's disavowals and pleas and resolutions, only repeated the original punishment. This time there was no jazz at all; in fact, in a touchingly conspicuous effort to overcome suspicion, Courtney kept out in the open in the library virtually every night until it closed. But then, with even the more skeptical admitting it was unlikely that she would try to pull anything now, she was seen in New Haven again, eating breakfast one Sunday morning with a bearded fellow, and the Student Council called a special meeting to lower the boom. Before long they had her confined to her room night and day, seven days a week, except for classes—at least on paper they had her confined to her room—and the entire college was up in arms. The editor of the paper put the student government on the spot by pointing out what everybody was becoming more and more aware of—the Council had no power that couldn't be ignored by each and every student. One group within the Council wanted to salvage what prestige it could by trying to cultivate Courtney's impulse to reform, another wanted to pursue the hard line with ultimatums that even they weren't sure they could enforce. Finally, in frustration, the Council made an unprecedented request that the administration take Courtney Pettit off their hands.

"What choice have we got?" the President asked the Dean. "The girls have done all they can do."

"What about allowing the Council to recommend probation or expulsion? It would give them at least the semblance of some real power."

There was a long silence at Miss Finch's end of the phone.

"Subject to the approval of the faculty adviser or something like that," the Dean added.

Finally Miss Finch said, "No, that could end up getting us all in a lot of trouble. I don't think we ought to encourage them to think they've got anything to say about that at all. What is it about this girl anyway? You're fond of her, aren't you?"

"She's tremendously entertaining," the Dean said. "*More* than that, actually: she doesn't for a minute expect or even want the college to underwrite her behavior. It's extraordinary. I haven't seen a girl like that in all my years here. She can give a more intelligent and eloquent defense of the way things are around here than some of those Westchester girls on the Council. Their trouble is, they think they'd be immensely better off if they could get rid of Courtney Pettit, when the truth of the matter is that they'd have to invent her if she didn't exist."

"Does she want to be expelled? Is she just leading everybody on?"

"If she were a little older I'd be inclined to think maybe she was one of the world's great straight-faced comedians, but I really doubt it now. You know how kids that age are: there are probably three or four mutually exclusive Courtney Pettits crashing around inside that girl, and whenever one gets on top for any length of time, there's bound to be a palace revolution. She's like the wolfman—about once a month the Talcott gentility and respectability has a full-moon effect on her; it turns her into a kind of savage. It's an adolescent response to the same damn conflict that produces people like . . ." The Dean named several of the more publicly tortured and convoluted personalities around the college.

"Look," Miss Finch said, "you go ahead and handle it in whatever way you see fit. Just keep me posted. If we're going to let somebody wreck the college for the sake of being entertained, I don't want to miss any of it."

"I'm not going to let her go too far, don't worry about that."

When she put the phone down, the Dean began dictating a note requesting Courtney to make an appearance tomorrow at eleven, but then she grew impatient with all that formality and told her secretary to get the girl on the phone. And when Courtney came in the next morning, the Dean laid it on the line: She was going to have one more chance to respect the authority of the Council; after that she'd find herself confronted with the administration. By way of dramatizing that she meant every word she said, the Dean announced that there would be another meeting of the Council, and that she personally would be there, in the role of an observer.

"Well, how about it?" she asked.

"Gee whiz," Courtney said. "If I have to meet with those mixed-up girls many more times I'll go out of my mind."

After Courtney left, the Dean thought of calling Miss Finch to share that remark with her, but chickened out at the last minute. She tried to think of somebody she *could* call; there were plenty of people around who would appreciate what Courtney had said, but none that she could phone for just that. Finally she buzzed for her secretary.

The typing stopped, and the secretary appeared in the doorway, her glasses in her hand. "Did you want me?" Just the sight of her, another stolid well-meaning old lady for whom the college was life, suddenly moved the Dean.

"Guess what I told Miss Finch when she told me to have another talk with that Pettit girl."

The secretary confessed that she couldn't guess.

"I told her," the Dean said, "that if I had to meet with that mixed-up girl many more times I'd go out of my mind."

"You know," the secretary said solemnly, "just to talk to that girl, you'd never know she was that way. All these girls running around in sweat shirts and blue jeans, *they're* the ones who don't go to chapel."

The Council put off the meeting for a week in order to prepare for it; despite the Dean's disclaimers, they believed they were being called on to show cause why the case should be taken to the administration, and they weren't about to be made fools of again.

The meeting, when it came, was a solemn occasion. The Council president sat at one end of the great oval table and Courtney at the other, linked by girls around both sides, many with manila folders before them. One girl submitted the fact that, according to certain reliable sources at Yale, Courtney's bearded boyfriend in New Haven was a Communist. Another girl (the head of the campus chapter of Young Americans for Freedom, a girl who was fond of calling William F. Buckley Jr. "Bill" and of knowing exactly what he was up to whenever the fuzzy-headed liberals said he was up to no good) brought up the subject of what her father would think of Talcott College for condoning "a girl like that." Obviously no one at the table thought for a minute that Courtney had stayed out all night with a bearded Communist to eat ice cream at Ho Jo's, but all of them saw the need to stick to matters that were their business and to accusations that could be proved if necessary.

"Every girl on this campus takes the honor of the college with her wherever she goes," the first girl said. "She's desecrating us all! She's desecrating you, and you, and you"—she went around the room—"she's desecrating Dean Bradford, she's desecrating me!" She subsided into an emotional silence, her hand pressed to her chest.

"Courtney?" the Council president said.

"Gee," Courtney said, "I hadn't thought of it that way."

"Do you understand how we feel?"

"You mean 'desecrated'?"

"I mean, do you understand or don't you!"

"It's not a question of her understanding it," the first girl said. "Any degenerate can *understand* it. It's a question of whether she respects it!"

"Golly," Courtney said. "I can't respect desecration—that's sick. Desecration gives me the willies."

"That not what I mean!"

"How am I going to keep somebody like you from feeling desecrated?" Courtney wanted to know. "If you feel desecrated, that's your problem, huh? Not mine. When it comes to feeling desecrated, it's every man for himself."

That did it. Up until then the proceedings had been fairly orderly, partly for the Dean's sake and partly out of the girls' recognition of the fact that things could easily get ugly if they weren't careful, but that last insolence loosed the hounds in them: They accused Courtney of being a dirty, drunken little slut. What they had been advertising as moral indignation was suddenly revealed to be nothing but hatred posing as righteousness. The Dean, assuming that Courtney was unaffected, that she would sit it out calmly and shame them all, was embarrassed for the girls and for herself too. She was about to leave the room, as a way of registering her protest and bringing the girls back to their senses, when the whole business took an abrupt turn.

Suddenly everybody was staring at the girl sitting there at the end of the oversized table, the fingers of both hands hooked over the edge. Courtney wasn't looking at anyone; she was just staring straight ahead, her round, innocent eyes sorrowful and hurt. She was close to tears.

"I try," she said, shaking her head, "I really do. I try as hard as I can. I don't want to cause trouble, I really don't."

No one knew what to say.

Finally the Council president pointed out that people had to be judged finally by what they did, not by what they intended to do. No girl there in that room had been admitted to Talcott College just because she'd tried hard, and no one would be graduated, no matter how hard she tried, unless she met certain objective requirements. It was just the right tone, conciliatory without being soft, apologetic without compromising the hard justice of the Council's position. All the girls nodded with relief and pride.

Then someone wanted to know, well, where did they stand? At which point, again to everyone's surprise, Courtney got out a typewritten statement and read it. No one, not even the Dean, doubted for a minute that she meant what she was saying. She spoke of the fall colors around the lake, the red and yellow and orange of sumac and maple, and of the fallen leaves scattered across the lawns and paths and parking lots; she called to mind the sound of the chapel bells, and the view of the lakeside tennis courts from the path up the hill; she spoke of the great rambunctious Brueghel scenes at dusk on a bitter winter day, when the frozen lake was crowded with skaters and dogs and racing children with hockey sticks; she spoke of the common rooms where some barefoot girl in a robe was forever ironing, of the long bull sessions with girls wandering in for a while and then back out again, of the transformation every weekend of teen-agers into chic young women in heels; she spoke of snowplows clearing the campus roads late at night, of the look of the lighted dorms on the snowy hillsides around the quad, of the couples courting outside those dorms just before the doors were locked, of the concerts, the plays, the readings, the lectures; she spoke of girls sunbathing on the roofs in spring, of the redwing blackbirds singing in the field below the gym, of the boys coming in from Yale and Wesleyan and Princeton and Amherst and colleges all over New England.

In closing she read the Donne passage about how no man is an island unto himself but each a part of the main, and when she finished the room was absolutely silent again. The Dean found herself deeply moved.

The Council president looked slowly around the room. "I don't think anything more needs to be said."

"I don't think anything more *could be*," someone said.

For several weeks the Dean waited for something to happen, but nothing did. She wasn't particularly comfortable with the idea that Courtney was on her way to becoming a thoroughbred Talcott girl, but it had happened before and no doubt would again. In time even Elizabeth Dickinson went on record as giving the girl a chance to grow up and become civilized. The Dean was about ready to chalk up another one for good old Talcott College when she got a note from the Dean of one of the sister colleges saying that she ought to know that some girl at Talcott, claiming to have the name and address of the greatest lover in France, was trying to organize a summer pilgrimage composed of one girl from each of the sister colleges.

And the very next Saturday, Courtney stayed out all night without signing out, and didn't return until a little before nine the next morning. The girls were pouring out of the dorms on their way to church when a bright red sports car, driven by a bearded man and followed by four motor scooters, idled in, deposited Courtney unceremoniously in front of Brewster, and idled back out again, the string of scooters wagging behind the sports car like a tired tail. The doors of the dormitory were wide open, but Courtney, who was still drunk, stood on the stone wall around the beech tree demanding to be let in. "Open up!" she kept shouting, as though it were late at night and the place locked up tight. "Open up!" Then she jumped off the wall, climbed into the housemother's car, which was parked near the door, and started blowing the horn, stiff-arming it with both hands. Before long every girl in the dorm was downstairs and out on the sidewalk. They had to wrestle Courtney inside and onto the elevator. Poor Elizabeth Dickinson spent the rest of the day under sedatives.

The next morning the Dean scotched all formalities and dialed Courtney's number herself. The phone rang and rang, but no one answered. The Dean sat there, elbows on the desk, and waited. There was something exhilarating in the fact that Courtney hadn't become a Talcott girl after all, but it was the sort of feeling she knew she couldn't indulge. Finally Courtney picked up the phone.

"Courtney?"

"Yes, ma'am."

"Dean Bradford."

"Yes ma'am."

Silence.

"Your metabolism is rather sluggish today. I've been ringing for five minutes."

"Yes ma'am, you know, I heard something ringing, but I thought it was the alarm."

"It *is* the alarm, my dear." The Dean paused, but nothing came over the phone except Courtney's breathing.

"Can't you say anything but 'Yes ma'am'?"

"Yes ma'am. I mean, no ma'am." Courtney laughed. "Sometimes I reckon I just don't know what it is people want me to say."

"What does that mean?"

"Well, sometimes I just don't know what you-all want."

You-all, huh? The Dean stalled for as long as she dared, hunting for an oblique way to distinguish herself from Elizabeth Dickinson and the Talcott girls, but she knew that Courtney had her.

"What we-all want, my dear, is for you to abide by the rules. That's all, I can assure you."

There was a long silence, by which Courtney managed to insinuate—or so it seemed to the Dean—that she knew that was a lot of guff, and that the Dean knew it too.

"I'll give you an hour to get dressed and get over here, Courtney. If you're not here in an hour—don't come."

By the time the girl arrived, the Dean had spoken with her parents, with Miss Finch, and with the housemother. Campus life could no longer tolerate Courtney (even the girl's father wanted her expelled), but the Dean, despite her own qualms, finally persuaded everybody that Courtney should be allowed to finish out the few remaining weeks of the year by living, under dormitory rules, with an uncle in New Haven.

The poor uncle was an elderly lawyer who had seen her no more than a dozen times in his life—one day he and his wife were living the perfectly civilized life of a New England couple of means, and the next Courtney Pettit was in residence. The rules were hard enough for the Talcott people themselves to understand, so it was no wonder he found them utterly confusing. Almost every day either he or his wife phoned to check Courtney's interpretations with the Dean's office.

The weekday eleven o'clock check-in, did that mean the girls had to be in their rooms or merely on the premises? He was asking because Courtney had sat in a car out in front of the house the previous night from eleven until nearly one A.M. No, the Dean said, eleven o'clock meant in the house with the doors locked. So the next night Courtney brought her New Haven friends in with her, five of them with three guitars. Neither he nor his wife had anything against young people having a good time, the uncle told the Dean, but he felt obliged to see that Courtney kept her part of the bargain, and he was beginning to suspect that she was taking advantage of his lack of familiarity with the rules. He hoped he wasn't being merely old-fashioned, but to be quite frank neither he nor his wife found much to appreciate in the young people she was bringing into their house—they certainly weren't the sort one would expect a Talcott girl to be running around with. A few days later he called the Dean the first thing in the morning and said that if that girl wasn't out of his house by dinner time, he was going to call her father to come after her.

The Dean got Courtney out of class to the phone.

"Guess who."

"Dean Bradford?"

"Guess what."

"I've had it," Courtney said.

"You said it, honey."

"What's the matter now?"

"You're attending classes at Talcott College, and you're no longer a student here, that's what's the matter."

"Really?"

"Really."

"Gee."

A long silence. Did Courtney honestly not care? Hard as it was for her to face, the Dean was afraid that this girl was insisting on their differences, and she felt betrayed. She knew that when it was all over, when she was left with those who cared about nothing else, that she would want Courtney not to have cared at all, that she would be drawn to the idea that there was somebody out there in the world who appreciated everything that Talcott had to offer and was still able to toss it all away with ease. Now, though, there was something in the Dean that wanted to see a little chink in the girl's armor. "How's the pilgrimage to France shaping up?"

"How did you find out about that?"

"I just assumed that's what you'd be doing this summer."

Courtney laughed appreciatively. "It's falling through. I've got a Cliffy and a girl from Barnard, but the others aren't coming through. Everybody over at Vassar is shook about the school's reputation. I haven't heard a word from Smith—are there people still sort of moving around and breathing over there at Smith?"

"Some, sort of," the Dean said.

Another silence.

"Your bearded Communist boyfriend, don't you think that's going just a bit far? I mean aesthetically? You disappoint me at times, Courtney."

"He's not a Communist, Miss Bradford."

Okay, so he wasn't a Communist. She ought to have known—another point for Courtney Pettit.

"I suppose you were just too ashamed to admit it, though."

Courtney laughed again, and the Dean found herself responding to the girl's appreciation.

"I went out on a limb for you, I trust you realize that."

"Yes ma'am, I know you did."

A pause.

"Do you want to come over here and talk about it? There's nothing that can be done, but we can talk about it." The minute she'd said that, she was sorry.

"I will if you want me to," Courtney said.

A long silence this time.

The Dean was suddenly disgusted with her own naïveté and weakness. "Forget it," she said. "Just get the hell out of here, will you? I don't want to see you around here after today, do you understand?"

"Yes ma'am."

Late that afternoon Elizabeth Dickinson telephoned to find out what had happened, and as the Dean sat there at her desk listening to the house-mother go on about the whole affair, she saw three girls pull off their shoes and walk across the lawn outside her window, dragging their feet sensually through the grass. Suddenly they tossed their books to the ground and raced up the long steep terrace, laughing and screaming, slowing as they approached the top, pulling their long shadows, until they were barely moving. Then, like stunt planes peeling off, they angled along the ridge of the terrace for a few yards, picking up speed again, and then they dove to the ground, one behind the other, and let themselves go, rolling like logs back down the hill. Their laughter rang out in the clear spring air; along the campus walks girls stopped and smiled and hugged their books and watched. Down they came, faster and faster, their supple bodies spinning through the lush grass, their skirts and blouses and legs and arms and hair a blur of freewheeling light on the green hillside. Unconsciously, the Dean lowered the phone against her neck, pressing Elizabeth Dickinson's voice out of hearing for the moment, and held her breath—held it for the girls' safety, for the sheer beauty of the life that was in them.

Elizabeth Dickinson said, "You know, there are some people who just don't appreciate Talcott College, and they just don't belong here—it's as simple as that."

"Maybe you're right," the Dean said. Why was it she couldn't acknowledge the claims those girls out there had on her without getting involved with the likes of Courtney Pettit? Sometimes her life seemed to be nothing but a crude mockery of the distinctions her mind lived on. "But nothing's as simple as that," she said to Elizabeth.

One drink that evening before dinner and she knew that she couldn't face the little old ladies in the dining room, so she just sat there in front of her TV in a kind of stupor, eating blue cheese and crackers and drinking bourbon. After a while she dozed off, woke, and struggled into the bedroom. Several minutes later she found herself sitting on the side of the bed with her shoes and stockings off and her blouse unbuttoned, but she couldn't figure out whether she was supposed to be dressing or undressing.

The phone rang, piercing her stupor. It was Miss Forman, the head of Physical Education, calling from the next apartment house. She needed the Dean's help with a little problem. The matron over at the gym had just phoned to say that the new young man in English, Mr. Klein, had played squash with a friend during the dinner hour and hadn't returned the squash-courts key. Since Mr. Klein was just across the hall there from the Dean, Miss Forman wondered if she would mind inquiring about the key. Why, of course, the Dean said, she'd be glad to. As it turned out, Mr. Klein hadn't pocketed the key—how could he? he said; it was wired to an old Ping-Pong paddle—he had left it, not at the matron's window, but around the corner on her desk, where he'd assumed it was conspicuous enough. The Dean phoned the information to Miss Forman and, though it was still early, went to bed.

It wasn't until the next morning that it hit her just how odd the whole business about the key really was. In the first place, what the dickens were they locking the squash courts for? Bravado? In the second place, with all the duplicate keys around, surely there was no immediate need to recover the one Mr. Klein had used—they were just antsy at the idea of a man (a new young man at that!) running off with a key to something they'd locked up. And even if they'd needed that particular key that very night, and been reasonable in suspecting that someone had run off with it, paddle and all, why had the matron called Miss Forman instead of Mr. Klein himself? And why had Miss Forman, instead of contacting Mr. Klein directly, carried the matron's foolishness just that much farther? And worse still, the Dean thought, what about herself? What really shook her up wasn't that she'd gone along with the whole silly thing, but that she hadn't seen anything silly about it. It had seemed a perfectly natural little problem being solved in a perfectly natural way—if a man runs off with one of your keys, then naturally you've got to get it back immediately, and naturally you can't just ask him for it. One doesn't go around insulting people, even when they do behave suspiciously! The Dean tried to make allowances for herself—she'd been drinking, hadn't she?—but she'd destroyed that excuse too many times in dealing with the girls. The real trouble, of course, was that all of it *was* perfectly natural—natural to the little old ladies at Talcott College.

The next morning, before she had a chance to change her mind, the Dean took an apartment in New Haven and informed the housing office that she was moving out; that afternoon she left her office early and loaded the back seat of her car with her belongings. If she got fired, well then she would just have to get fired, for it seemed clearly a matter of life and death to get some distance between herself and the college.

As she was waiting at the gate for a break in the rush-hour traffic, a horn beeped, and there behind her in a sleek little red sports car with the top down were Courtney Pettit and her bearded boyfriend. The Dean's heart jumped. Her eyes met Courtney's in the rear-view mirror, and they both smiled politely, the smiles growing steadily richer until, in unison, they burst out laughing. The moment was shattered, though, when the horn beeped again, this time with unmistakable mockery, telling her to move out or move over. The Dean's smile vanished, but Courtney only laughed that much harder. What they would infer from her loaded car the Dean didn't know, but she felt revealed before them, as though they were seeing something that she did not want them, of all people, to see. If they tooted that horn again, she would scream! No, she would just sit there, by God, until they quieted down, and then she would—Suddenly they swung out behind her, and with Courtney's head flung back in laughter, proceeded to show her how it was done. The Dean had been thinking that she would get out and walk back there calmly and say that maybe *they* weren't intimidated by rush-hour drivers, but she was just a hung-up Talcott lady herself and there was no telling how soon she would find her way into that kind of traffic—and then they shot around her, bluffed their way recklessly in and roared off toward New Haven, trailing Courtney's laughter like tin cans behind a marriage car, leaving her there alone at the college gate.

6
Religions and Values

ADULTS FREQUENTLY FEEL THAT RELIGION plays a relatively minor role in the lives of contemporary adolescents. Such an opinion needs to be examined closely before being accepted as fact. It is true that the codes of conduct and beliefs of today's adolescents seem less formed by orthodox religious instruction than they were before World War II. The decline of religious instruction in schools and homes, together with the postwar attitude of scientism, have been blamed in large part for the flagging interest in religion. Today's secularized schools have been blamed, too, for turning the attention of youth to the more worldly issues plaguing society: war, racial inequality, political corruption, global starvation, environmental pollution, and a host of other problems. The de-emphasis on religion has been cited as a primary cause for juvenile delinquency, drug and alcohol abuse, premarital sexual experimentation, and emotional instability. With little doubt, what would appear to be an irreligious attitude on the part of today's adolescents has caused adults a great deal of consternation.

Before considering how religious contemporary adolescents may or may not be, it may be helpful to define the term "religion." Religion is a form of worship that contains two essential elements: a system of beliefs and a set of related practices that are held in common by an identifiable group. Usually these beliefs and practices are codified, and the observance of them, either public or private, is fairly uniform throughout a congregation. Much popular opinion about the supposed irreligiosity of adolescents is based on their lack of participation in formalized church affairs. It must be noted that few investigations have examined what adolescents' systems of beliefs consist of and how and from whom they are acquired. Elizabeth B. Hurlock has observed that almost all studies concerning the religious beliefs of adolescents have dealt with high-school and college students. Two large segments of adolescent society—primarily the high-school dropouts and those who do not attend college—have not been included in these studies. The current results about the religious attitudes of today's youth are at best incomplete and tentative.[1]

The studies that have been done clearly indicate that adolescents are not particularly irreligious, contrary to much popular opinion. Since adolescence is a time of searching for a set of values, most young people are in the process of questioning those of their childhood and exploring new ones. The very act of establishing a meaningful set of beliefs is often mistaken for an irreligious attitude by parents—particularly if the family religion is rejected in favor of another, or none at all. When adolescents fail to go to church, they are quite often implying much more about the appeal of the service than they are about their faith in religion as such. Studies show that adolescents attend church as often as their parents; and they spend a good deal of time in informal conversations talking about religions, the nature of God, and man's relationship to them.[2] Most students—particularly girls, who show more interest in religion than boys—profess a belief in God and claim they plan to give their children specific religious instruction. Many adolescents actively search for a religion or in some cases a less codified set of values they feel will serve them well in shaping their lives. Most question the easy acceptance of their parents' religion, though it is the exception when an adolescent switches to another.

The swelling enrollment in such college courses as the psychology of religion and comparative religion strongly suggests that religion is a serious concern of contemporary adolescents. The recent phenomenon of the Hari Krishna, Jesus, and Sun Moon movements points up the intensity of religious expression that is occasionally displayed by older adolescents. This is not the norm. Most high-school and college students are moderate in their beliefs and expressions of them. Because adolescence is more often than not a time of self-doubt, religion offers a sense of security, a system of values that gives direction, a belief in life, and a feeling of worth. Adolescents are inclined to believe in a religion if they see people around them sincerely involved in its practice.

In stories that consider the religious experiences of adolescents, the protagonists are nearly always between the ages of thirteen and fifteen— as four of the five stories in this section indicate. Typically these youngsters are precocious, intelligent, and sensitive (sometimes to a fault). They are involved in the difficult process of consciously formulating a meaningful philosophy that will give positive direction to their lives. At the same time,

1. Elizabeth B. Hurlock, *Adolescent Development*, 4th ed. (New York: McGraw-Hill, 1973), p. 226.
2. Ibid., pp. 226–227.

they are planning on careers as writers, teachers, artists, professionals, or members of religious groups—all requiring the perceptive, committed intelligence they possess in abundance.

As a vital part of their religious training, almost all sense the necessity of acquiring an advanced education leading toward a career, feeling that a great deal of meaning will derive from work that is an outward expression of their philosophy of life. When Billy says in "Like a Piece of Blues," "yes, education, I must get that," he consciously voices a basic need of those trying to shape their lives. The education he refers to comes not only from schools but also from home, church and friends—who are usually older and more experienced.

Of the several types of stories written about the religious experiences of adolescents, one that predominates deals with young people who are rigorously questioning the basic tenets of their religion. Protestant, Jewish, and Catholic youngsters alike reach a point in early adolescence when the most cherished and securely held beliefs of childhood are scrutinized. Turmoil results when they are unable to make the basic doctrines of their faith compatible with the logic of their own reasoning. "The Conversion of the Jews" illustrates such a situation. Ozzie Freedman's belief that Jesus Christ is divine runs counter to the teaching of Judaism and precipitates the tragicomic results between him and Rabbi Binder, who is preparing Ozzie for his bar mitzvah. Ozzie's child-simple logic seems irrefutable to him: if God could create heaven and earth in six days, surely the virgin birth of Christ as God-man would be no large task to perform. Further, Ozzie knows that the Catholics hold his belief in the divinity of Christ, so he does not feel he is being willfully perverse; it is that simple to his way of thinking, and he maintains his heretical belief to the end of the story.

In other stories adolescents begin to doubt their religion when they look at the less-than-perfect practitioners of it. The sanctimonious smugness of his father's congregation raises serious questions in Billy's mind about his religion in "Like a Piece of Blues." Also, his older friend, the Black Muslim Rashman, stimulates his thinking in such a peppery way that the comfortable salvation to be found in his church is lost to Billy forever. This story is typical of those in which the religion of the parents—one that is passed from generation to generation through custom and indoctrination—is frequently viewed by contemporary adolescents as empty and stagnant. In these stories adolescents move from rigorously formal to less formal religions or to none at all. Those who are in the process of defining a set of religious values have little difficulty identifying those who only give lip service to their religion. If too many of these people exist within a congregation, adolescents frequently abandon it together with the faith it represents.

Another type of story that has become popular in recent years deals with adolescents who find meaning in radical religions. The majority of these are westernized versions of Near, Middle, and Far Eastern creeds; and the one that has been most popular with writers is the Black Muslim. These alternate religions have special appeal for minority groups, the disenfranchised, those espousing radical politics, or people who do not feel at ease within the traditions of the more widely supported religions such as Judaism, Catholicism, or Protestantism. The vitality of newly formed religious groups with a special mission to perform or a new niche to fill attracts many adolescents. The appeal also reaches well beyond this age group, as can be seen in the gray-haired Rashman's participation in the Black Muslim movement.

The problem of adolescents controlling human impulses that are contrary to religious teachings is another theme of great interest to writers. "If They Knew Yvonne" explicitly explores the guilt, anxiety, and, at times, despair Harry feels as he tries to repress his troublesome sexual desires. His lapses into masturbation and premarital coitus generally create in him a sense of self-debasement. As he matures into early adulthood, he with great difficulty comes to terms with the dictates of his body and church. At the end of the story Harry concludes with a note of affirmation as he looks at the tanned bodies of his nephews crabbing from a wharf: he "hoped they would grow well, those strong little bodies, those kind hearts." In contrast, the closing lines of "The Outing" strongly suggest an estrangement from the church and a minister father because of Johnnie's budding homosexuality: "After a moment Johnnie moved and put his head on David's shoulder. David put his arms around him. But now where there had been peace there was only panic and where there had been safety, danger, like a flower, opened." When the sexual drives of adolescents are at odds with the teachings of their church, there is quite often a temporary estrangement from it. In a few cases it is abandoned permanently.

There are, of course, other themes of adolescent religious experience. The contradictions apparent among the basic teachings of different religions bewilder young worshipers, who readily question these differences. The opposing views of birth control held by Protestants and Catholics in "If They Knew Yvonne" and the antithetical philosophies of Jews and Catholics concerning Christ's divinity in "The Conversion of the Jews" are problems that many adolescents find very difficult to deal with. Such contradictions often cause them to reject formal religion altogether and to seek a set of values for human conduct elsewhere, frequently in advanced education, where what is taught seems to be more palpable and consistent.

Another recurring theme considers adolescents who are incapable of a religious experience, either emotionally or intellectually. In "Point of Conversion," even though Vera is befriended by Mrs. Clementson and Father Sheehan during her illegitimate pregnancy and attends church regularly, she is incapable of becoming a Catholic or, for that matter, of forming any religious affiliations at all. She, like the protagonists in similar stories, has little interest in forming a religious commitment—although she is quite willing to take advantage of the facilities and friends of a particular church. For some adolescents an exposure to a religion, no matter how intense the experience, fails to pique their curiosity or to raise even the most basic questions about its articles of faith; religion is only a church building where people congregate, where they go when troubled, where they are baptized, wed, or buried.

Yet another type of story considers adolescents who are raised in a deeply religious atmosphere and forcefully reject it and all it includes. The reasons vary. The more intellectually inclined find the philosophical basis of their religion incompatible with their world view. Some, like Johnnie in "The Outing," find that they cannot experience the emotional intensity of the other worshipers during a service; in fact, they are often embarrassed by demonstrative displays of religious fervor. And others find the "religion" of academe more agreeable to their way of thinking and a better guide to their lives than traditional religious beliefs.

James Baldwin
The Outing

EACH SUMMER THE CHURCH GAVE AN OUTING. It usually took place on the Fourth of July, that being the day when most of the church-members were free from work; it began quite early in the morning and lasted all day. The saints referred to it as the 'whosoever will' outing, by which they meant that, though it was given by the Mount of Olives Pentecostal Assembly for the benefit of its members, all men were free to join them, Gentile, Jew or Greek or sinner. The Jews and the Greeks, to say nothing of the Gentiles —on whom, for their livelihood, most of the saints depended—showed themselves, year after year, indifferent to the invitation; but sinners of the more expected hue were seldom lacking. This year they were to take a boat trip up the Hudson as far as Bear Mountain where they would spend the day and return as the moon rose over the wide river. Since on other outings they had merely taken a subway ride as far as Pelham Bay or Van Cortlandt Park, this year's outing was more than ever a special occasion and even the deacon's two oldest boys, Johnnie and Roy, and their friend, David Jackson, were reluctantly thrilled. These three tended to consider themselves sophisticates, no longer, like the old folks, at the mercy of the love or the wrath of God.

The entire church was going and for weeks in advance talked of nothing else. And for weeks in the future the outing would provide interesting conversation. They did not consider this frivolous. The outing, Father James declared from his pulpit a week before the event, was for the purpose of giving the children of God a day of relaxation; to breathe a purer air and to worship God joyfully beneath the roof of heaven; and there was nothing frivolous about *that*. And, rather to the alarm of the captain, they planned to hold church services aboard the ship. Last year Sister McCandless had held an impromptu service in the unbelieving subway car. She played the tambourine and sang and exhorted sinners and passed through the train distributing tracts. Not everyone had found this admirable, to some it seemed that Sister McCandless was being a little ostentatious. "I praise my Redeemer wherever I go," she retorted defiantly. "Holy Ghost don't leave *me* when I leave the church. I got a every day religion."

Sylvia's birthday was on the third, and David and Johnnie and Roy had been saving money for her birthday present. Between them they had five dollars but they could not decide what to give her. Roy's suggestion that they give her underthings was rudely shouted down: did he want Sylvia's mother to kill the girl? They were all frightened of the great, rawboned, outspoken Sister Daniels and for Sylvia's sake went to great pains to preserve what remained of her good humor. Finally, and at the suggestion of David's older sister, Lorraine, they bought a small, gold-plated pin cut in the shape of a butterfly. Roy thought that it was cheap and grumbled angrily at their combined bad taste ("Wait till it starts turning her clothes green!" he cried) but David did not think it was so bad; Johnnie thought it pretty enough and he was sure that Sylvia would like it anyway; ("When's *your* birthday?" he asked David). It was agreed that David should present it to her on the day of the outing in the presence of them all. ("Man, I'm the oldest cat here," David said, "you know that girl's crazy about me.") This was the summer in which they all abruptly began to grow older, their bodies becoming troublesome and awkward and even dangerous and their voices not to be trusted. David perpetually boasted of the increase of down on his chin and professed to have hair on his chest—"and somewhere else, too," he added shyly, whereat they all laughed. "You ain't the only one," Roy said. "No," Johnnie said, "I'm almost as old as you are." "Almost ain't got it," David said. "Now ain't this a hell of a conversation for church boys?" Roy wanted to know.

The morning of the outing they were all up early; their father sang in the kitchen and their mother, herself betraying an excitement nearly youthful, scrubbed and dressed the younger children and laid the plates for breakfast. In the bedroom which they shared Roy looked wistfully out of the window and turned to Johnnie.

"Got a good mind to stay at home," he said. "Probably have more fun." He made a furious gesture toward the kitchen. "Why doesn't *he* stay home?"

Johnnie, who was looking forward to the day with David and who had not the remotest desire to stay home for any reason and who knew, moreover, that Gabriel was not going to leave Roy alone in the city, not even if the heavens fell, said lightly, squirming into clean underwear: "Oh, he'll probably be busy with the old folks. We can stay out of his way."

Roy sighed and began to dress. "Be glad when I'm a man," he said.

Lorraine and David and Mrs. Jackson were already on the boat when they arrived. They were among the last; most of the church, Father James, Brother Elisha, Sister McCandless, Sister Daniels and Sylvia were seated near the rail of the boat in a little semi-circle, conversing in strident tones. Father James and Sister McCandless were remarking the increase of laxity among God's people and debating whether or not the church should run a series of revival meetings. Sylvia sat there, saying nothing, smiling painfully now and then at young Brother Elisha, who spoke loudly of the need for a revival and who continually attempted to include Sylvia in the conversation. Elsewhere on the boat similar conversations were going on. The saints of God were together and very conscious this morning of their being together and of their sainthood; and were determined that the less enlightened world should know who they were and remark upon it. To this end there were a great many cries of "Praise the Lord!" in greeting and the formal holy kiss. The children, bored with the familiar spectacle, had already drawn apart and amused themselves by loud cries and games that were no less exhibitionistic than that being played by their parents. Johnnie's nine year old sister, Lois, since she professed salvation, could not very well behave as the other children did; yet no degree of salvation could have equipped her to enter into the conversation of the grown-ups; and she was very violently disliked among the adolescents and could not join them either. She wandered about, therefore, unwillingly forlorn, contenting herself to some extent by a great display of virtue in her encounters with the unsaved children and smiling brightly at the grown-ups. She came to Brother Elisha's side. "Praise the Lord," he cried, stroking her head and continuing his conversation.

Lorraine and Mrs. Jackson met Johnnie's mother for the first time as she breathlessly came on board, dressed in the airy and unreal blue which Johnnie would forever associate with his furthest memories of her. Johnnie's baby brother, her youngest, happiest child, clung round her neck; she made him stand, staring in wonder at the strange, endless deck, while she was introduced. His mother, on all social occasions, seemed fearfully distracted, as though she awaited, at any moment, some crushing and irrevocable disaster. This disaster might be the sudden awareness of a run in her stocking or private knowledge that the trump of judgment was due, within five minutes, to sound: but, whatever it was, it lent her a certain agitated charm and people, struggling to guess what it might be that so claimed her inward attention, never failed, in the process, to be won over. She talked with Lorraine and Mrs. Jackson for a few moments, the child tugging at her skirts, Johnnie watching her with a smile; and at last, the child becoming always more restive, said that she must go—into what merciless arena one dared not imagine—but hoped, with a despairing smile which clearly indicated the improbability of such happiness, that she would be able to see them later. They watched her as she walked slowly to the other end of the boat, sometimes pausing in conversation, always (as though it were a duty) smiling a little and now and then considering Lois where she stood at Brother Elisha's knee.

"She's very friendly," Mrs. Jackson said. "She looks like you, Johnnie."

David laughed. "Now why you want to say a thing like that, Ma? That woman ain't never done nothing to you."

Johnnie grinned, embarrassed, and pretended to menace David with his fists.

"Don't you listen to that old, ugly boy," Lorraine said. "He just trying to make you feed bad. Your mother's real good-looking. Tell her I said so."

This embarrassed him even more, but he made a mock bow and said, "Thank you, Sister." And to David: "Maybe now you'll learn to keep your mouth shut."

"Who'll learn to keep whose mouth shut? What kind of talk is that?"

He turned and faced his father, who stood smiling on them as from a height.

"Mrs. Jackson, this is my father," said Roy quickly. "And this is Miss Jackson. You know David."

Lorraine and Mrs. Jackson looked up at the deacon with polite and identical smiles.

"How do you do?" Lorraine said. And from Mrs. Jackson: "I'm very pleased to meet you."

"Praise the Lord," their father said. He smiled. "Don't you let Johnnie talk fresh to you."

"Oh, no, we were just kidding around," David said. There was a short, ugly silence. The deacon said: "It looks like a good day for the outing, praise the Lord. You kids have a good time. Is this your first time with us, Mrs. Jackson?"

"Yes, said Mrs. Jackson. "David came home and told me about it and it's been so long since I've been in the country I just decided I'd take me a day off. And Lorraine's not been feeling too strong, I thought the fresh air would do her some good." She smiled a little painfully as she spoke. Lorraine looked amused.

"Yes, it will, nothing like God's fresh air to help the feeble." At this description of herself as feeble Lorraine looked ready to fall into the Hudson and coughed nastily into her handkerchief. David, impelled by his own perverse demon, looked at Johnnie quickly and murmured, "That's the truth, deacon." The deacon looked at him and smiled and turned to Mrs. Jackson. "We been hoping that your son might join our church someday. Roy brings him out to service every Sunday. Do you like the services, son?" This last was addressed in a hearty voice to David; who, recovering from his amazement at hearing Roy mentioned as his especial pal (for he was Johnnie's friend, it was to be with Johnnie that he came to church!) smiled and said, "Yes sir, I like them alright," and looked at Roy, who considered his father with an expression at once contemptuous, ironic and resigned and at Johnnie, whose face was a mask of rage. He looked sharply at the deacon again; but he, with his arm around Roy, was still talking.

"This boy came to the Lord just about a month ago," he said proudly. "The Lord saved him just like that. Believe me, Sister Jackson, ain't no better fortress for nobody, young or old, than the arms of Jesus. My son'll tell you so, ain't it, Roy?"

They considered Roy with a stiff, cordial curiosity. He muttered murderously, "Yes sir."

"Johnnie tells me you're a preacher," Mrs. Jackson said at last. "I'll come out and hear you sometime with David."

"Don't come out to hear me," he said. "You come out and listen to the Word of God. We're all just vessels in His hand. Do you know the Lord, sister?"

"I try to do His will," Mrs. Jackson said.

He smiled kindly. "We must all grow in grace." He looked at Lorraine. "I'll be expecting to see you too, young lady."

"Yes, we'll be out," Lorraine said. They shook hands. "It's very nice to have met you," she said.

"Goodbye." He looked at David. "Now you be good. I want to see you saved soon." He released Roy and started to walk away. "You kids enjoy yourselves. Johnnie, don't you get into no mischief, you hear me?"

He affected not to have heard; he put his hands in his pants' pockets and pulled out some change and pretended to count it. His hand was clammy and it shook. When his father repeated his admonition, part of the change spilled to the deck and he bent to pick it up. He wanted at once to shout to his father the most dreadful curses that he knew and he wanted to weep. He was aware that they were all intrigued by the tableau presented by his father and himself, that they were all vaguely cognizant of an unnamed and deadly tension. From his knees on the deck he called back (putting into his voice as much asperity, as much fury and hatred as he dared):

"Don't worry about me, Daddy. Roy'll see to it that I behave."

There was a silence after he said this; and he rose to his feet and saw that they were all watching him. David looked pitying and shocked. Roy's head was bowed and he looked apologetic. His father called:

"Excuse yourself, Johnnie, and come here."

"Excuse me," he said, and walked over to his father. He looked up into his father's face with an anger which surprised and even frightened him. But he did not drop his eyes, knowing that his father saw there (and he wanted him to see it) how much he hated him.

"What did you say?" his father asked.

"I said you don't have to worry about me. I don't think I'll get into any mischief." And his voice surprised him, it was more deliberately cold and angry than he had intended and there was a sardonic stress on the word "mischief." He knew that his father would then and there have knocked him down if they had not been in the presence of saints and strangers.

"You be careful how you speak to me. Don't you get grown too fast. We get home, I'll pull down those long pants and we'll see who's the man, you hear me?"

Yes we will, he thought and said nothing. He looked with a deliberate casualness about the deck. Then they felt the lurch of the boat as it began to move from the pier. There was an excited raising of voices and "I'll see you later," his father said and turned away.

He stood still, trying to compose himself to return to Mrs. Jackson and Lorraine. But as he turned with his hands in his pants' pockets he saw that David and Roy were coming toward him and he stopped and waited for them.

"It's a bitch," Roy said.

David looked at him, shocked. "That's no language for a saved boy." He put his arm around Johnnie's shoulder. "We're off to Bear Mountain," he cried, "*up* the glorious Hudson"—and he made a brutal gesture with his thumb.

"Now suppose Sylvia saw you do that," said Roy, "what would you say, huh?"

"We needn't worry about her," Johnnie said. "She'll be sitting with the old folks all day long."

"Oh, we'll figure out a way to take care of *them*," said David. He turned to Roy. 'Now you the saved one, why don't you talk to Sister Daniels and distract her attention while we talk to the girl? You the baby, anyhow, girl don't want to talk to you.'

"I ain't got enough salvation to talk to that hag," Roy said. "I got a Daddy-made salvation. I'm saved when I'm with Daddy." They laughed and Roy added, "And I ain't no baby, either, I got everything my Daddy got."

"And a lot your Daddy don't dream of," David said.

Oh, thought Johnnie, with a sudden, vicious, chilling anger, *he doesn't have to dream about it!*

"Now let's act like we Christians," David said. "If we was real smart now, we'd go over to where she's sitting with all those people and act like we wanted to hear about God. Get on the good side of her mother."

"And suppose *he* comes back?" asked Johnnie.

Gabriel was sitting at the other end of the boat, talking with his wife. "Maybe he'll stay there," David said; there was a note of apology in his voice.

They approached the saints.

"Praise the Lord," they said sedately.

"Well, praise Him," Father James said. "How are you young men today?" He grabbed Roy by the shoulder. "Are you coming along in the Lord?"

"Yes, sir," Roy muttered, "I'm trying." He smiled into Father James's face.

"It's a wonderful thing," Brother Elisha said, "to give up to the Lord in your youth." He looked up at Johnnie and David. "Why don't you boys surrender? Ain't nothing in the world for you, I'll tell you that. He says, 'Remember thy Creator in the days of thy youth when the evil days come not.'"

"Amen," said Sister Daniels. "We're living in the last days, children. Don't think because you're young you got plenty of time. God takes the young as well as the old. You got to hold yourself in readiness all the time lest when He comes He catch you unprepared. Yes sir. Now's the time."

"You boys going to come to service today, ain't you?" asked Sister Mc-

Candless. "We're going to have service on the ship, you know." She looked at Father James. "Reckon we'll start as soon as we get a little further up the river, won't we, Father?"

"Yes," Father James said, "we're going to praise God right in the middle of the majestic Hudson." He leaned back and released Roy as he spoke. "Want to see you children there. I want to hear you make a *noise* for the Lord."

"I ain't never seen none of these young men Shout," said Sister Daniels, regarding them with distrust. She looked at David and Johnnie. "Don't believe I've ever even heard you testify."

"We're not saved yet, sister," David told her gently.

"That's alright," Sister Daniels said. "You *could* get up and praise the Lord for your life, health and strength. Praise Him for what you got, He'll give you something more."

"That's the truth," said Brother Elisha. He smiled at Sylvia. "I'm a witness, bless the Lord."

"They going to make a noise yet," said Sister McCandless. "Lord's going to touch everyone of these young men one day and bring them on their knees to the altar. You mark my words, you'll see." And she smiled at them.

"You just stay around the house of God long enough," Father James said. "One of these days the Spirit'll jump on you. I won't never forget the day It jumped on me."

"That *is* the truth," Sister McCandless cried, "so glad it jumped on me one day, hallelujah!"

"Amen," Sister Daniels cried, "amen."

"Looks like we're having a little service right now," Brother Elisha said smiling. Father James laughed heartily and cried, "Well, praise Him anyhow."

"I believe next week the church is going to start a series of revival meetings," Brother Elisha said. "I want to see you boys at every one of them, you hear?" He laughed as he spoke and added as David seemed about to protest, "No, no, brother, don't want no excuses. You *be* there. Get you boys to the altar, then maybe you'll pay more attention in Sunday School."

At this they all laughed and Sylvia said in her mild voice, looking mockingly at Roy, "Maybe we'll even see Brother Roy Shout." Roy grinned.

"Like to see you do some Shouting too," her mother grumbled. "You got to get closer to the Lord." Sylvia smiled and bit her lip; she cast a glance at David.

"Now everybody ain't got the same kind of spirit," Brother Elisha said, coming to Sylvia's aid. "Can't *all* make as much noise as you make," he said, laughing gently, "we all ain't got your energy."

Sister Daniels smiled and frowned at this reference to her size and passion and said, "Don't care, brother, when the Lord moves inside you, you bound to do something. I've seen that girl Shout all night and come back the next night and Shout some more. I don't believe in no dead religion, no sir. The saints of God need a revival."

"Well, we'll work on Sister Sylvia," said Brother Elisha.

Directly before and behind them stretched nothing but the river, they had long ago lost sight of the point of their departure. They steamed beside the Palisades, which rose rough and gigantic from the dirty, broad and blue-green Hudson. Johnnie and David and Roy wandered downstairs to the bottom deck, standing by the rail and leaning over to watch the white, writhing spray which followed the boat. From the river there floated up to their faces a soft, cool breeze. They were quiet for a long time, standing together, watching the river and the mountains and hearing vaguely the hum of activity behind them on the boat. The sky was high and blue, with here and there a spittle-like, changing cloud; the sun was orange and beat with anger on their uncovered heads.

And David muttered finally, "Be funny if they were right."

"If who was right?" asked Roy.

"Elisha and them—"

"There's only one way to find out," said Johnnie.

"Yes," said Roy, "and I ain't homesick for heaven yet."

"You always got to be so smart," David said.

"Oh," said Roy, "you just sore because Sylvia's still up there with Brother Elisha."

"You think they going to be married?" Johnnie asked.

"Don't talk like a fool," David said.

"Well it's a cinch you ain't never going to get to talk to her till you get saved," Johnnie said. He had meant to say 'we.' He looked at David and smiled.

"Might be worth it," David said.

"*What* might be worth it?" Roy asked, grinning.

"Now be nice," David said. He flushed, the dark blood rising beneath the dark skin. "How you expect me to get saved if you going to talk that way? You supposed to be an example."

"Don't look at me, boy," Roy said.

"I want you to talk to Johnnie," Gabriel said to his wife.

"What about?"

"That boy's pride is running away with him. Ask him to tell you what he said to me this morning soon as he got in front of his friends. He's your son, alright."

"What did he say?"

He looked darkly across the river. "You ask him to tell you about it to-night. I wanted to knock him down."

She had watched the scene and knew this. She looked at her husband briefly, feeling a sudden, outraged anger, barely conscious; sighed and turned to look at her youngest child where he sat involved in a complicated and strenuous and apparently joyless game which utilized a red ball, jacks, blocks and a broken shovel.

"I'll talk to him," she said at last. "He'll be alright." She wondered what on earth she would say to him; and what he would say to her. She looked covertly about the boat, but he was nowhere to be seen.

"That proud demon's just eating him up," he said bitterly. He watched the river hurtle past. "Be the best thing in the world if the Lord would take his soul." He had meant to say "save" his soul.

Now it was noon and all over the boat there was the activity of lunch. Paper bags and huge baskets were opened. There was then revealed splendor: cold pork chops, cold chicken, bananas, apples, oranges, pears, and soda-pop, candy and cold lemonade. All over the boat the chosen of God relaxed; they sat in groups and talked and laughed; some of the more worldly gossiped and some of the more courageous young people dared to walk off together. Beneath them the strong, indifferent river raged within the channel and the screaming spray pursued them. In the engine room children watched the motion of the ship's gears as they rose and fell and chanted. The tremendous bolts of steel seemed almost human, imbued with a relentless force that was not human. There was something monstrous about this machine which bore such enormous weight and cargo.

Sister Daniels threw a paper bag over the side and wiped her mouth with her large handkerchief. "Sylvia, you be careful how you speak to these unsaved boys," she said.

"Yes, I am, Mama."

"Don't like the way that little Jackson boy looks at you. That child's got a demon. You be careful."

"Yes, Mama."

"You got plenty of time to be thinking about boys. Now's the time for you to be thinking about the Lord."

"Yes'm."

"You *mind* now," her mother said.

"Mama, I want to go home!" Lois cried. She crawled into her mother's arms, weeping.

"Why, what's the matter, honey?" She rocked her daughter gently. "Tell Mama what's the matter? Have you got a pain?"

"I want to go home, I want to go home." Lois sobbed.

"A very fine preacher, a man of God and a friend of mine will run the service for us," said Father James.

"Maybe you've heard about him—a Reverend Peters? A real man of God, amen."

"I thought," Gabriel said, smiling, "that perhaps I could bring the message some Sunday night. The Lord called me a long time ago. I used to have my own church down home."

"You don't want to run too fast, Deacon Grimes," Father James said. "You just take your time. You been coming along right well on Young Ministers' Nights." He paused and looked at Gabriel. "Yes, indeed."

"I just thought," Gabriel said humbly, "that I could be used to more advantage in the house of God."

Father James quoted the text which tells us how preferable it is to be a gate-keeper in the house of God than to dwell in the tent of the wicked; and started to add the dictum from Saint Paul about obedience to those above one in the Lord but decided (watching Gabriel's face) that it was not necessary yet.

"You just keep praying," he said kindly. "You get a little closer to God. He'll work wonders. You'll see." He bent closer to his deacon. "And try to get just a little closer to the *people*."

Roy wandered off with a gawky and dazzled girl named Elizabeth. Johnnie and David wandered restlessly up and down the boat alone. They mounted to the topmost deck and leaned over the railing in the deserted stern. Up here the air was sharp and clean. They faced the water, their arms around each other.

"Your old man was kind of rough this morning," David said carefully, watching the mountains pass.

"Yes," Johnnie said. He looked at David's face against the sky. He shivered suddenly in the sharp, cold air and buried his face in David's shoulder. David looked down at him and tightened his hold.

"Who do you love?" he whispered. "Who's your boy?"

"You," he muttered fiercely, "I love you."

"Roy!" Elizabeth giggled, "*Roy Grimes*. If you *ever* say a thing like that *again*."

Now the service was beginning. From all corners of the boat there was the movement of the Saints of God. They gathered together their various possessions and moved their chairs from top and bottom decks to the large main hall. It was early afternoon, not quite two o'clock. The sun was high and fell everywhere with a copper light. In the city the heat would have been insupportable; and here, as the saints filed into the huge, high room, once used as a ballroom, to judge from the faded and antique appointments, the air slowly began to be oppressive. The room was the color of black mahogany and coming in from the bright deck, one groped suddenly in darkness and took one's sense of direction from the elegant grand piano which stood in the front of the room on a little platform.

They sat in small rows with one wide aisle between them, forming, almost unconsciously, a hierarchy. Father James sat in the front next to Sister McCandless. Opposite them sat Gabriel and Deacon Jones and, immediately behind them, Sister Daniels and her daughter. Brother Elisha walked in swiftly, just as they were beginning to be settled. He strode to the piano and knelt down for a second before rising to take his place. There was a quiet stir, the saints adjusted themselves, waiting while Brother Elisha tentatively ran his fingers over the keys. Gabriel looked about impatiently for Roy and Johnnie, who, engaged no doubt in sinful conversation with David, were not yet in service. He looked back to where Mrs. Jackson sat with Lorraine, uncomfortable smiles on their faces, and glanced at his wife, who met his questioning regard quietly, the expression on her face not changing.

Brother Elisha struck the keys and the congregation joined in the song, *Nothing Shall Move Me from the Love of God*, with tambourine and heavy hands and stomping feet. The walls and the floor of the ancient hall trembled and the candelabra wavered in the high ceiling. Outside the river rushed past under the heavy shadow of the Palisades and the copper sun beat down. A few of the strangers who had come along on the outing appeared at the doors and stood watching with an uneasy amusement. The saints sang on, raising their strong voices in praises to Jehovah and seemed unaware of those unsaved who watched and who, some day, the power of the Lord might cause to tremble.

The song ended as Father James rose and faced the congregation, a broad smile on his face. They watched him expectantly, with love. He stood silent for a moment, smiling down upon them. Then he said, and his voice was loud and filled with triumph:

"Well, let us all say, Amen!"

And they cried out obediently, "Well, Amen!"

"Let us all say, praise Him!"

"Praise Him!"

"Let us all say, hallelujah!"

"Hallelujah!"

"Well, glory!" cried Father James. The Holy Ghost touched him and he cried again, "Well, bless Him! Bless His holy name!"

They laughed and shouted after him, their joy so great that they laughed as children and some of them cried as children do; in the fullness and assurance of salvation, in the knowledge that the Lord was in their midst and that each heart, swollen to anguish, yearned only to be filled with His glory. Then, in that moment, each of them might have mounted with wings like eagles far past the sordid persistence of the flesh, the depthless iniquity of the heart, the doom of hours and days and weeks; to be received by the Bridegroom where He waited on high in glory; where all tears were wiped away and death had no power; where the wicked ceased from troubling and the weary soul found rest.

"Saints, let's praise Him," Father James said. "Today, right in the middle of God's great river, under God's great roof, beloved, let us raise our voices in thanksgiving that God has seen fit to save us, amen!"

"Amen! Hallelujah!"

"—and to keep us saved, amen, to keep us, oh glory to God, from the snares of Satan, from the temptation and the lust and the evil of this world!"

"Talk about it!"

"*Preach!*"

"Ain't nothing strange, amen, about worshiping God *wherever* you might be, ain't that right? Church, when you get this mighty salvation you just can't keep it in, hallelujah! you got to talk about it—"

"Amen!"

"You got to live it, amen. When the Holy Ghost touches you, you *move*, bless God!"

"Well, it's so!"

"Want to hear some testimonies today, amen! I want to hear some *singing* today, bless God! Want to see some *Shouting*, bless God, hallelujah!"

"Talk about it!"

"And I don't want to see none of the saints hold back. If the Lord saved you, amen, He give you a witness *every*where you go. Yes! My soul is a witness, bless our God!"

"Glory!"

"If you ain't saved, amen, get up and praise Him anyhow. Give God the glory for sparing your sinful life, *praise* Him for the sunshine and the rain, praise Him for all the works of His hands. Saints, I want to hear some praises today, you hear me? I want you to make this old boat *rock*, hallelujah! I want to *feel* your salvation. Are you saved?"

"Amen!"

"Are you sanctified?"

"Glory?"

"Baptized in fire?"

"Yes So glad!"

"*Testify!*"

Now the hall was filled with a rushing wind on which forever rides the Lord, death or healing indifferently in His hands. Under this fury the saints bowed low, crying out "holy!" and tears fell. On the open deck sinners stood and watched, beyond them the fiery sun and the deep river, the black-brown-green, unchanging cliffs. That sun, which covered earth and water now, would one day refuse to shine, the river would cease its rushing and its numberless dead would rise; the cliffs would shiver, crack, fall and where they had been would then be nothing but the unleashed wrath of God.

"Who'll be the first to tell it?" Father James cried. "Stand up and talk about it!"

Brother Elisha screamed, "Have mercy, Jesus!" and rose from the piano stool, his powerful frame possessed. And the Holy Ghost touched him and he cried again, bending nearly double, while his feet beat ageless, dreadful signals on the floor, while his arms moved in the air like wings and his face, distorted, no longer his own face not the face of a young man, but timeless, anguished, grim with ecstasy, turned blindly toward heaven. *Yes, Lord, they cried, yes!*

"Dearly beloved . . ."

"Talk about it!"

"Tell it!"

"I want to thank and praise the Lord, amen . . ."

"Amen!"

". . . for being here, I want to thank Him for my life, health, and strength. . . ."

"Amen!"

"Well, glory!"

". . . I want to thank Him, hallelujah, for saving my soul one day. . . ."

"*Oh!*"

"Glory!"

". . . for causing the light, bless God, to shine in *my* heart one day when I was still a child, amen, I want to thank Him for bringing me to salvation in the days of my *youth*, hallelujah, when I have all my faculties, amen, before Satan had a chance to destroy my body in the world!"

"Talk about it!"

"He saved me, dear ones, from the world and the things of the world. Saved me, amen, from cardplaying . . ."

"Glory!"

". . . saved me from drinking, bless God, saved me from the streets, from the movies and all the filth that is in the world!"

"I *know* it's so!"

"He saved me, beloved, and sanctified me and filled me with the blessed Holy Ghost, *hallelujah!* Give me a new song, amen which I didn't know before and set my feet on the King's highway. Pray for me beloved, that I will stand in these last and evil days."

"Bless your name, Jesus!"

During his testimony Johnnie and Roy and David had stood quietly beside the door, not daring to enter while he spoke. The moment he sat down they moved quickly, together, to the front of the high hall and knelt down beside their seats to pray. The aspect of each of them underwent always, in this company a striking, even an exciting change; as though their youth, barely begun, were already put away; and the animal, so vividly restless and undiscovered, so tense with power, ready to spring had been already stalked and trapped and offered, a perpetual blood-sacrifice, on the altar of the Lord. Yet their bodies continued to change and grow, preparing them, mysteriously and with ferocious speed, for manhood. No matter how careful their movements, these movements suggested, with a distinctness dreadful for the redeemed to see, the pagan lusting beneath the blood-washed robes. In them was perpetually and perfectly poised the power of revelation against the power of nature; and the saints, considering them with a baleful kind of love, struggled to bring their souls to safety in order, as it were, to steal a march on the flesh while the flesh still slept. A kind of storm, infernal, blew over the congregation as they passed; someone cried, "Bless them, Lord!" and immediately, honey-colored Sister Russell, while they knelt in prayer, rose to her feet to testify.

From the moment that they closed their eyes and covered their faces they were isolated from the joy that moved everything beside them. Yet this same isolation served only to make the glory of the saints more real, the pulse of conviction, however faint, beat in and the glory of God then held an undertone of abject terror. Roy was the first to rise, sitting very straight in his seat and allowing his face to reveal nothing; just as Sister Russell ended her testimony and sat down, sobbing, her head thrown back and both hands raised to heaven. Immediately Sister Daniels raised her strong, harsh voice and hit her tambourine, singing. Brother Elisha turned on the piano stool and hit the keys. Johnnie and David rose from their knees and as they rose the congregation rose, clapping their hands singing. The three boys did not sing; they stood together, carefully ignoring one another, their feet steady on the slightly tilting floor but their bodies moving back and forth as the music grew more savage. And someone cried aloud, a timeless sound of wailing; fire splashed the open deck and filled the doors and bathed the sinners standing there; fire filled the great hall and splashed the faces of the saints and a wind, unearthly, moved above their heads. Their hands were arched before them, moving, and their eyes were raised to heaven. Sweat stained the deacon's collar and soaked the tight head-bands of the women. Was it true then? and had there indeed been born one day in Bethlehem a Saviour who was Christ the Lord? who had died for them—for *them!*—the spat-upon and beaten with rods, who had worn a crown of thorns and seen His blood run down like rain; and who had lain in the grave three days and vanquished death and hell and risen again in glory—*was it for them?*

Lord, I want to go, show me the way!

For unto us a child is born, unto us a son is given—and His name shall be called Wonderful, the mighty God, the everlasting Father, the Prince of Peace. Yes, and He was coming back one day, the King of glory; He would crack the face of heaven and descend to judge the nations and gather up His people and take them to their rest.

Take me by my hand and lead me on!

Somewhere in the back a woman cried out and began the Shout. They looked carefully about, still not looking at one another, and saw, as from a great distance and through intolerable heat, such heat as might have been faced by the Hebrew children when cast bound into the fiery furnace, that one of the saints was dancing under the arm of the Lord. She danced out into the aisle, beautiful with a beauty unbearable, graceful with grace that poured from heaven. Her face was lifted up, her eyes were closed and the feet which moved so surely now were not her own. One by one the power of God moved others and—as it had been written—the Holy Ghost descended from heaven with a Shout. Sylvia raised her hands, the tears poured down her face, and in a moment, she too moved out into the aisle, Shouting. Is it true then? the saints rejoiced, Roy beat the tambourine. David, grave and shaken, clapped his hands and his body moved insistently in the rhythm of the dancers. Johnnie stood beside him, hot and faint and repeating yet

again his struggle, summoning in panic all his forces, to save him from this
frenzy. And yet daily he recognized that he was black with sin, that the
secrets of his heart were a stench in God's nostrils. *Though your sins be as
scarlet they shall be white as snow. Come, let us reason together, saith the
Lord.*

Now there was a violent discord on the piano and Brother Elisha leapt
to his feet, dancing. Johnnie watched the spinning body and listened, in
terror and anguish, to the bestial sobs. Of the men it was only Elisha who
danced and the women moved toward him and he moved toward the
women. Johnnie felt blow over him an icy wind, all his muscles tightened,
as though they furiously resisted some imminent bloody act, as the body
of Isaac must have revolted when he saw his father's knife, and, sick and
nearly sobbing, he closed his eyes. It was Satan, surely, who stood so foully
at his shoulder; and what, but the blood of Jesus, should ever set him free?
He thought of the many times he had stood in the congregation of the
righteous—and yet he was not saved. He remained among the vast army
of the doomed, whose lives—as he had been told, as he now, with such
heart-sickness, began to discover for himself—were swamped with wretch-
edness and whose end was wrath and weeping. Then, for he felt himself
falling, he opened his eyes and watched the rejoicing of the saints. His eyes
found his father where he stood clapping his hands, glittering with sweat
and overwhelming. Then Lois began to shout. For the first time he looked
at Roy; their eyes met in brief, wry wonder and Roy imperceptibly shrugged.
He watched his mother standing over Lois, her own face obscurely troubled.
The light from the door was on her face, the entire room was filled with this
strange light. There was no sound now except the sound of Roy's tambourine
and the heavy rhythm of the saints; the sound of heavy feet and hands
and the sound of weeping. Perhaps centuries past the children of Israel led
by Miriam had made just such a noise as they came out of the wilderness.
For unto us is born this day a Saviour who is Christ the Lord.

Yet, in the copper sunlight Johnnie felt suddenly, not the presence of the
Lord, but the presence of David, which seemed to reach out to him, hand
reaching out to hand in the fury of flood time, to drag him to the bottom
of the water or to carry him safe to shore. From the corner of his eye he
watched his friend, who held him with such power; and felt, for that
moment, such a depth of love, such nameless and terrible joy and pain, that
he might have fallen, in the face of that company, weeping at David's feet.

Once at Bear Mountain they faced the very great problem of carrying
Sylvia sufficiently far from her mother's sight to present her with her birthday present. This problem, difficult enough, was made even more difficult
by the continual presence of Brother Elisha; who, inspired by the afternoon's service and by Sylvia's renewal of her faith, remained by her side
to bear witness to the goodness and power of the Lord. Sylvia listened with
her habitual rapt and painful smile. Her mother, on the one side and Brother

Elisha on the other, seemed almost to be taking turns in advising her on her conduct as a saint of God. They began to despair, as the sun moved visibly westward, of ever giving her the gold-plated butterfly which rested uncomfortably in David's waistcoat pocket.

Of course, as Johnnie once suggested, there was really no reason they could not go up to her, surrounded as she was, and give her the jewel and get it over with—the more particularly as David evinced a desire to explore the wonders of Bear Mountain until this mission should have been fulfilled. Sister Daniels could scarcely object to an innocuous memento from three young men, all of whom attended church devoutly and one of whom professed salvation. But this was far from satisfactory for David, who did not wish to hear Sylvia's "thank-you's" in the constricting presence of the saints. Therefore they waited, wandering about the sloping park, lingering near the lake and the skating rink and watching Sylvia.

"God, why don't they go off somewhere and sleep? or pray?" cried David finally. He glared at the nearby rise where Sylvia and her mother sat talking with Brother Elisha. The sun was in their faces and struck from Sylvia's hair as she restlessly moved her head, small blue-black sparks.

Johnnie swallowed his jealousy at seeing how Sylvia filled his comrade's mind; he said, half-angrily, "I still don't see why we don't just go over and give it to her."

Roy looked at him. "Boy, you sound like you ain't got good sense," he said.

Johnnie, frowning, fell into silence. He glanced sidewise at David's puckered face (his eyes were still on Sylvia) and abruptly turned and started walking off.

"Where you going, boy?" David called.

"I'll be back," he said. And he prayed that David would follow him.

But David was determined to catch Sylvia alone and remained where he was with Roy. "Well, make it snappy," he said; and sprawled, full length, on the grass.

As soon as he was alone his pace slackened; he leaned his forehead against the bark of a tree, shaking and burning as in the teeth of a fever. The bark of the tree was rough and cold and though it offered no other comfort he stood there quietly for a long time, seeing beyond him—but it brought no peace—the high clear sky where the sun in facing glory traveled; and the deep earth covered with vivid banners, grass, flower, thorn and vine, thrusting upward forever the brutal trees. At his back he heard the voices of the children and the saints. He knew that he must return, that he must be on hand should David at last outwit Sister Daniels and present her daughter with the golden butterfly. But he did not want to go back, now he realized that he had no interest in the birthday present, no interest whatever in Sylvia—that he had had no interest all along. He shifted his stance; he turned from the tree as he turned his mind from the abyss which suddenly yawned, that abyss, depthless and terrifying, which he had encountered already in dreams. And he slowly began to walk, away from the saints and the voices of the children, his hands in his pockets, struggling to ignore the question which now screamed and screamed in his mind's bright haunted house.

It happened quite simply. Eventually Sister Daniels felt the need to visit the ladies' room, which was a long ways off. Brother Elisha remained where he was while Roy and David, like two beasts crouching in the under-brush, watched him and waited their opportunity. Then he also rose and wandered off to get cold lemonade for Sylvia. She sat quietly alone on the green rise, her hands clasped around her knees, dreaming.

They walked over to her, in terror that Sister Daniels would suddenly reappear. Sylvia smiled as she saw them coming and waved to them merrily. Roy grinned and threw himself on his belly on the ground beside her. David remained standing, fumbling in his waistcoat pocket.

"We got something for you," Roy said.

David produced the butterfly. "Happy birthday, Sylvia," he said. He stretched out his hand, the butterfly glinted oddly in the sun, and he realized with surprise that his hand was shaking. She grinned widely, in amazement and delight, and took the pin from him.

"It's from Johnnie too," he said. "I—we—hope you like it—"

She held the small gold pin in her palm and stared down at it; her face was hidden. After a moment she murmured, "I'm so surprised." She looked up, her eyes shining, almost wet. "Oh, it's wonderful," she said. "I never expected anything. I don't know what to say. It's marvelous, it's wonderful." She pinned the butterfly carefully to her light blue dress. She coughed slightly. "Thank you," she said.

"Your mother won't mind, will she?" Roy asked. "I mean—" he stammered awkwardly under Sylvia's sudden gaze—"we didn't know, we didn't want to get you in any trouble—"

"No," David said. He had not moved; he stood watching Sylvia. Sylvia looked away from Roy and up at David, his eyes met hers and she smiled. He smiled back, suddenly robbed of speech. She looked away again over the path her mother had taken and frowned slightly. "No," she said, "no, she won't mind."

Then there was silence. David shifted uncomfortably from one foot to the other. Roy lay contentedly face down on the grass. The breeze from the river, which lay below them and out of sight, grew subtly more insistent for they had passed the heat of the day; and the sun, moving always west-ward, fired and polished the tips of trees. Sylvia sighed and shifted on the ground.

"Why isn't Johnnie here?" she suddenly asked.

"He went off somewhere," Roy said. "He said he'd be right back." He looked at Sylvia and smiled. She was looking at David.

"You must want to grow real tall," she said mockingly. "Why don't you sit down?"

David grinned and sat down cross-legged next to Sylvia. "Well, the ladies like 'em tall." He lay on his back and stared up at the sky. "It's a fine day," he said.

She said, "Yes," and looked down at him; he had closed his eyes and was bathing his face in the slowly waning sun. Abruptly, she asked him:

"Why don't you get saved? You around the church all the time and you not saved yet? Why don't you?"

He opened his eyes in amazement. Never before had Sylvia mentioned salvation to him, except as a kind of joke. One of the things he most liked about her was the fact that she never preached to him. Now he smiled uncertainly and stared at her.

"I'm not joking," she said sharply. "I'm perfectly serious. Roy's saved—at least he *says* so—" and she smiled darkly, in the fashion of the old folks, at Roy—"and anyway, you ought to be thinking about your soul."

"Well, I don't know," David said. "I *think* about it. It's—well, I don't know if I can—well, live it—"

"All you got to do is make up your mind. If you really want to be saved, He'll save you. Yes, and He'll keep you too." She did not sound at all hysterical or transfigured. She spoke very quietly and with great earnestness and frowned as she spoke. David, taken off guard, said nothing. He looked embarrassed and pained and surprised. "Well, I don't know," he finally repeated.

"Do you ever pray?" she asked. "I mean, *really* pray?"

David laughed, beginning to recover himself. "It's not fair," he said, "you oughtn't to catch me all unprepared like that. Now I don't know what to say." But as he looked at her earnest face he sobered. "Well, I try to be decent. I don't bother nobody." He picked up a grass blade and stared at it. "I don't know," he said at last. "I do my best."

"*Do* you?" she asked.

He laughed again, defeated. "Girl," he said, "you *are* a killer."

She laughed too. "You black-eyed demon," she said, "if I don't see you at revival services I'll never speak to you again." He looked up quickly, in some surprise, and she said, still smiling, "Don't look at me like that. I mean it."

"All right, sister," he said. Then: "If I come out can I walk you home?"

"I got my mother to walk me home—"

"Well let your mother walk home with Brother Elisha," he said, grinning, "Let the old folks stay together."

"Loose him, Satan!" she cried, laughing, "loose the boy!"

"The brother needs prayer," Roy said.

"Amen," said Sylvia. She looked down again at David. "I want to see you at church. Don't you forget it."

"All right," he said. "I'll be there."

The boat whistles blew at six o'clock, punctuating their holiday; blew, fretful and insistent, through the abruptly dispirited park and skaters left the skating rink; boats were rowed in furiously from the lake. Children were called from the swings and the seesaw and the merry-go-round and forced to leave behind the ball which had been lost in the forest and the torn kite which dangled from the top of a tree. ("Hush now," said their parents, "we'll get you another one—come along." "*Tomorrow?*"—"Come along, honey, it's time to go!") The old folks rose from the benches, from the grass, gathered together the empty lunch-basket, the half-read newspaper, the Bible which was carried everywhere; and they started down the hillside, an army in disorder. David walked with Sylvia and Sister Daniels and Brother Elisha, listening to their conversation (good Lord, thought Johnnie, don't they ever mention anything but sin?) and carrying Sylvia's lunch-basket. He seemed interested in what they were saying; every now and then he looked at Sylvia and grinned and she grinned back. Once, as Sylvia stumbled, he put his hand on her elbow to steady her and held her arm perhaps a moment too long. Brother Elisha, on the far side of Sister Daniels, noticed this and a frown passed over his face. He kept talking, staring now and then hard at Sylvia and trying, with a certain almost humorous helplessness, to discover what was in her mind. Sister Daniels talked of nothing but the service on the boat and of the forthcoming revival. She scarcely seemed to notice David's presence, though once she spoke to him, making some remark about the need, on his part, of much prayer. Gabriel carried the sleeping baby in his arms, striding beside his wife and Lois—who stumbled perpetually and held tightly to her mother's hand. Roy was somewhere in the back, joking with Elizabeth. At a turn in the road the boat and the dock appeared below them, a dead gray-white in the sun.

Johnnie walked down the slope alone, watching David and Sylvia ahead of him. When he had come back, both Roy and David had disappeared and Sylvia sat again in the company of her mother and Brother Elisha; and if he had not seen the gold butterfly on her dress he would have been aware of no change. She thanked him for his share in it and told him that Roy and David were at the skating rink.

But when at last he found them they were far in the middle of the lake in a rowboat. He was afraid of water; he could not row. He stood on the bank and watched them. After a long while they saw him and waved and started to bring the boat in so that he could join them. But the day was ruined for him; by the time they brought the boat in, the hour, for which they had hired it, was over; David went in search of his mother for more money but when he came back it was time to leave. Then he walked with Sylvia.

All during the trip home David seemed preoccupied. When he finally sought out Johnnie he found him sitting by himself on the top deck, shivering a little in the night air. He sat down beside him. After a moment Johnnie moved and put his head on David's shoulder. David put his arms around him. But now where there had been peace there was only panic and where there had been safety, danger, like a flower, opened.

George Davis
Like a Piece of Blues

IT WAS NOT UNTIL RASHMAN X, the little Black Muslim, began talking to us, my friend Teddy Crawford and me, that I began to notice. For him the teasing seemed all for fun, but I was 15, living through a very serious, vulnerable summer, so there was something deeper than fun in it for me.

Rashman was a small man, four inches shorter than I, and though I was skinny then, Rashman was skinnier. He was a neat, taut man with skin the color of pitch. His neatness and his dignity prevented his looking scrawny even with his knees and elbows coming to points as they did when he bent them beneath his starched, white barber's uniform. His hair was pepper-gray and always neat and parted, and I never saw him once when he needed a shave.

That Saturday morning when Teddy Crawford and I entered his barber-shop, the bums of Ninth Street followed us, bringing with them their usual odor of tobacco, filth, and wine to mix with the odor of talc and after-shave lotion inside. They took seats along the wall to wait for the teasing that always followed when Rashman and I got together.

Rashman's wit was as sharp as the razor he shaved himself with, and I was foolish enough to challenge him. He had a clever way of making small things seem significant; thus leaving them no longer small. For example, that Saturday while I was in the chair he brought to my attention that of all the women in my father's church's Woman's Society for Christian Service none were even as dark as Teddy Crawford and I, and we were only medium brown.

Yes, and I remember how Rashman had stopped me when I said "only medium brown," thus succeeding cleverly at making the bums think that I had said that we had fallen away from grace by only that much, that at least we were not black.

"I didn't say that," I challenged quickly, but Rashman was already laugh-

287

ing what I called then his little wicker-wire laugh way back in the roof of his mouth. He cut me off so I would not have a chance to explain myself. "Don't let folks brainwash you, son," he said.

Whenever we faced off like this and he scored first, he always spoke rapidly so I wouldn't be able to score back. "I guess the Christians taught you that black is the color of evil." He laughed deliciously. "Be careful, son. Be careful . . . Then of course brainwashing is seldom very painful, and if it's done subtly you never know it's happened. I knew a fellow once who went his entire life brainwashed. Died happy, though." He winked at the bums and bent over to pump my chair up a little higher. The bums smiled. A few of them cleared their throats, and there I was defenseless sitting in the middle of the shop with the silly barber's cloth tied around my neck.

"Wait. You're trying to make these gentlemen think that I . . ."

"No. I'm not criticizing you. No-o-o. I don't blame you one little bit. It's very hard to stand against the entire Christian civilization. It's no fun having to make up everything from scratch . . . better a servant in the house of the Lord than a king among the unholy, huh? Is that the way the Bible says it?" He laughed again. "I don't blame you one iota. Why . . . why enter the woods if you're not sure you can find your way out?"

The bums laughed partly at me and partly with me. "We all have to enter the woods sometime," I said.

"Oh sure, yes, yes, it's not bad to come in. Just don't come too deep. Come in, look around, then scat back." He spun my chair.

"You jump to conclusions too fast," I said, but this was not one of my good answers. It did not get a rise out of the bums as some of my cracks used to do.

"Yes I do. I do. I shouldn't blame you for . . ."

"Give me a chance to talk."

"Oh! Yes, all right."

I got down out of the chair talking, trying to hit on something that would swing the bums to my side, but Rashman had me too far down. He could afford to smile complacently while I argued. Someone else got in the chair and he began pumping the chair up again.

After much grumbling from Teddy Crawford, we left, but only after I declared that I would be back as soon as I got myself together. He sent me out onto the sidewalk with laughter and catcalls following me. I laughed myself. I liked Rashman, and I knew that he and the bums liked me. But the only bad thing was he had been defeating me too soundly and too often ever since back in May when too much seriousness began to creep into my mood.

Rashman's barber shop was the cleanest business on Ninth Street. However, my father warned me many times not to go there and listen to Rashman's bile; but Teddy Crawford and I, with our money in our pockets, would go down to Ninth Street on Saturday morning and wander around until I could talk Teddy into going to Rashman's shop instead of to one of the others.

I always had to promise him that afterwards I would go with him up to Maxine Green's apartment over the Tom Thumb Tailor Shop. Maxine's mother was never home on Saturday mornings, so I kept Maxine's three younger brothers outside while Teddy slipped the meat to her in the bedroom

"Okay," Teddy said on the first Saturday in July, only one week after he had promised never to go with me again. "I'll go if you promise not to waste all day arguing with that nut."

"Okay, to hell with Rashman," I said as we were coming down from Teddy's house toward the upper end of Ninth Street.

"Now you're talking, baby," Teddy said, walking wide-legged, filling his lungs with air, obviously thinking about Maxine Green.

"Hey, loka here," Rashman said as I pushed his front door open. "My little friends from the hill have come back." The heavy glass door sucked closed behind us. "I thought I scared you children away last time, making light of your Lord and Saviour Jesus Christ like I did." He spoke loud enough for everyone in the shop to hear. At least ten men had followed us in. Two of them had to stand because there were not enough seats. Teddy and I took our seats along the wall under the row of gleaming mirrors to wait our turns in the chairs. Rashman's assistant, a lean, quiet boy who came in from St. Louis each weekend to work at Rashman's Mosque #6 Barber Shop, always cut Teddy's hair. He liked to cut close, and that was the way Teddy's mother liked it.

Rashman did not say anything more to me until I got in the chair. This was a tactic of his. Then: "How are things up home?" he said as I sat down. "Did you tell the reverend what I said last week?"

"Yeah," I lied. "He said one of these days a bolt of lightning's going to hit your vilifying soul."

Shadezow, who had just sat down in the seat I had vacated, laughed and repronounced my word. Rashman laughed and shook out the large pin-striped cover cloth. He waved it in front of me like a magician.

Teddy got into the chair next to mine. The two men who had been play-ing checkers back near the shoeshine stand turned around to watch.

The bums seemed out of place with their tattered clothing and dirty bodies in the gleaming tile, glass, and porcelain shop. The bright July sun-light passing thru the large clean front windows highlighted their filth. It showed clearly the spittle in the mouth of one toothless one who was smiling as Rashman spun me around.

Rashman began by combing my hair briskly. It was kinky because with all the reading I was doing I didn't have time to care for it. He made it pop and made the dust fly to put me further at a disadvantage. By now all the bums were smiling, waiting for the argument between me and Rashman X, the only Negro in town who had courage enough to turn his back com-pletely on Christianity.

"What words of wisdom do you have for us today, my young man?" Rashman asked.

"None," I answered, and looked over at Teddy Crawford.

"Still believe in the saving grace of Jesus Christ?" he asked, biblically, knowing that I was going to say, "yes." "Doesn't it frighten you being in here where lightning might strike, then?"

"No."

"How about you, young man?" Rashman asked, spinning Teddy's chair so abruptly that the other barber had to jerk his clippers back.

Teddy smiled fawningly. His oily, peanut-smooth complexion reddened. His fat slick cheeks and round slick head seemed to fill up with blood. "No, sir."

Rashman let him go. Teddy was not the one he wanted. He wanted me. I was the outspoken one. Besides, I had secretly been considering following my father into the Christian ministry. I suspected that Rashman knew this, and this was why he taunted me more than Teddy.

We argued, but every time I was about to make a good point, Rashman would spin me away from my audience. I would be facing myself, self-consciously, in the mirror behind the chair, the image of the row of bums bouncing back and forth between the mirrors on the opposite walls. Then Rashman would pop my hair, and the bums would roar.

I stood up when he was done and let him brush the hair off my green and yellow polo shirt. Teddy was finished long before I was. He was in a hurry to get up to Maxine's.

"Christianity is dead. That's a fact, and it makes you a necrophiliac," Rashman sang.

The bums broke up over his word. They smacked their thighs and laughed: "Amen," "Yea," "Tell it like it is."

I waved Rashman away as I followed Teddy toward the door. I had to laugh, too, when Shaderow almost choked trying to repronounce, "necrophiliac." But my laughter was not deep. Too much of what Rashman said was too important.

II

The next Sunday was a bright, hot day. I got up early, let the sun into my room, dressed carelessly, and went outside thinking about Rashman. I wanted to skip church, but I knew that I would not be able to tell my father why. I walked around for a long time trying to decide what to do.

Our church was the largest Negro Methodist church in the district, and there were only three or four white churches larger—all of them city churches up in St. Louis. It was a natural stone building like the parsonage in which we lived. They both sat on a grassy plot a block and a half from the Negro college.

The neighborhood was not at all like you would picture a Negro ghetto. The houses and lawns were all well cared for. Most of the houses were brick or stone, and the few of them that were wood frame were in good repair. The vacant lots around the campus and the church were all well cared for The streets were all paved. Sidewalks ran on both sides all the way up from Ninth Street back past Carson Avenue and laterally on all sides from Bullock to Canterberry (except for the two blocks where the wall and the iron fence of the community cemetery precluded sidewalks).

Nearly everyone in the entire neighborhood was a member of my father's church.

Most of them were teachers at H. L. Single High School or over at the college. Ours was a world of secure jobs and easy living. The bigotry and injustice which menaced the lives of so many black people during these years was closed out of it. I walked down toward Mason Street thinking about that. When I got down almost to where Teddy Crawford lived, younger children started to come out of the houses dressed for Sunday School. I thought it best that I beat it back and get ready to teach my Sunday School class.

All during the hour I was hot with anxiety in the air-conditioned building. The lesson was about David the Shepherd. What, I wondered, did that have to do with anything.

Obviously, Rashman had a way of getting weekly bulletins from the church, for just as he said this was installation Sunday for the new officers of the Woman's Society for Christian Service. I watched them as they filed past me toward the front of the church.

"Ah! and you watch them," Rashman had said. "Everyone of them past the age thirty has to wear glasses because their eyes are weak. Mongrelization's done it. And you watch, every one of them will be fat from over-indulgence and lack of discipline."

On Sunday, as I watched the women, I hated their stuffy, sanctimonious smiles. All of them were light-skinned, plump, and slightly bent. All except two wore glasses. I wondered if this was just a coincidence that Rashman had noticed and decided to use against me, or whether, however silly scientifically it might seem, his statement about mongrelization had some truth to it. I thought for a moment, then I shook my head, no. I could picture him behind his chair, his image in the mirror showing his scissors poised above my unkempt hair, his face caught for one static moment between smiles, his own eyes aided by thin, rimless glasses. As I sat there in church, I thought that I could hear his brief, wickerwire laughter.

Old Mrs. Turner, my high school civics teacher, was standing two down from the end. She had been called forward as the new recording secretary. I focused my attention on her. She used to call me her little preacher. I shook with fear at the prospect that Rashman might find out and tell it in the crowded barber shop.

As I looked at Mrs. Turner, I filled up with anger because even now I was arguing with Rashman and losing. Mrs. Turner was too much for me to explain to someone like the bums. Rashman would get the better of me.

Mrs. Turner was a big butter-colored woman who wore heavy coke bottle-bottom glasses. She hated her job, and she hated the kids she had to teach. All she taught for was the money in it; that was plain from the way she acted. I knew how much Rashman would make of the contempt she had for the poorer kids from over in Chambers who came to school poorly dressed and often a little dirty. These kids were either timid and backward or too manish or womanish for their ages to suit Mrs. Turner. The one group she ignored as often as she could, and the others she expelled whenever she could get away with it. I knew how Rashman would tease me about the way Mrs. Turner complimented me for not being like them: "her little preacher." I shook my head again.

She did have the biggest tits on the faculty. I could score with the bums by mentioning that and by adding that I was sure they didn't grow because of heavy sexual activity. "She must play with them every night. And, boy, you ought to see them big yellow thighs when she sits up in the window sill at school," I would say to make the bums laugh, "I'd sure like to get some of that stuff." They would break up over that—little skinny me and big Mrs. Turner. Still I would lose the argument with Rashman because he knew me too well to be sidetracked.

But I was beginning to know Rashman, too. He was wrong. His science was screwed up. Shaderow and the others knew he was wrong, too. They were Christians. I had heard how groups of them would get juiced up on Saturday night and pile into Filbert's car and go over to Elder Nash's church and sing and cry about whatever they had lost—a mother or father or something.

But Rashman was right about them in a way. Christianity would never do more for them than make them feel a little better for a little while, like a piece of blues.

III

For a month I did not go back to see Rashman. I was not ready to face him. He was wrong; but I did not know how to convince him.

His house sat across a vacant lot from his shop. It was one of only three or four neat houses amid the squalor that was Ninth Street. The house seemed very small sitting by itself behind a very straight, wire fence. Unlike most of the houses around it, it was freshly painted and all the boards were in place. The house sat on piles and back under it the dirt was raked as level as concrete. Usually after eight o'clock in the evening the windows in his house would darken. I would see them as I passed taking Nancy Adkins home to Chambers. As far as I knew, the lean boy from St. Louis was the only non-relative who had ever entered Rashman's house. Shaderow and Filbert never had, even the insurance man left him alone. Often I wanted to stop by. Nancy would say that it was all right with her, but I was always a little too afraid. I knew that Rashman would be different without the bums to show off for—different and deeper. Often as I passed the house I would comment on how lonely it must get for Rashman in there because at heart he was a talker. The windows in the little old house would seem like half-closed, darkened eyes looking out on this dumping ground of Christian civilization.

I went for six weeks without seeing Rashman. When my mother made what seemed her final threat, I went to Mr. Granison's barber shop to get my hair cut. But the Sunday after father let the man from the State Fish and Game Board mealy-mouth the morning service, I decided to go down to see Rashman.

I was met at the door by his wife. She was a small black woman who looked ten or twelve years older than Rashman. "My husband is not home," she said, "but do come in." She did not wait to see if I was going to follow but simply turned and walked ahead of me down the hallway into the living room. The house had a stale odor inside, like the odor inside the houses of very old people. No sunlight came through the windows, which were heavily draped. The living room that we entered was small. The heavy, old-fashioned chair and sofa were covered with matching, faded, flowery slipcovers. The rug was of a hard weave. On the wall was a picture of Rashman receiving his diploma from a high school in St. Louis. This made me wonder how old Rashman really was. He had many gray hairs, but his skin was very smooth. He could be any age. I examined the picture for a date but found none. When I turned away from the wall, Mrs. X motioned for me to sit in the chair under the picture. She sat on the sofa across the room. "Rashman has gone to St. Louis now for a little while," she said. "He was very discontented here. . . . He told me a lot about you. Said you were the smartest youngster he had seen in a while."

"Not really," I said, and waved her comment away.

She looked at me and smiled. "He said when you get out of college you will be a great asset to the race. The masses of our people need so much. It always must be hoped that your generation will do much better than ours." She examined me again with that curious look of hers.

Two barefooted, bald-headed boys of about four or five ran to the living room door and peeped in. She laughed and called them forward. "Pharoah and Benda, this is Mr. Billy Aaron." She pushed them forward to meet me.

The bigger one took his fingers out of his mouth and gave me his wet hand to shake. I was glad for their presence because I felt that their mother was very sad about something, and I was not sure that I would know how to respond to it if she would decide to tell me what it was.

I took the smaller boy and tossed him toward the ceiling. The bigger one pushed into my arms for some of the same treatment. While I was engaged with them, their mother slipped out of the room and brought back a glass of iced tea. The two boys sat on my knees while I drank.

Then I heard their sister come downstairs. I knew that it was Shera because I remembered that she was a very slow walker. At home she was a much more imposing girl than at school. She wore no make-up, and her hair had been cut very short and had not been hot combed in a long time.

"How was church this morning?" she asked. She did not call me "Billy" as she did at school but "Mr. Aaron" as her mother called me when she asked, "Shera, you do know Mr. Aaron, do you not?"

"Yes, mother, Mr. Aaron is the best athlete in the tenth grade."

"Well," her mother said rather sage-like, "Rashman told me that."

"How was church?" Shera asked and smiled.

"Good," I said, and shrugged. She must have known about the man from the Fish and Game Board. I did not know if she were going to tell Rashman. I did not know if I really cared.

"We were Christians once, even Shera was," Mrs. X said. "We were Church of God in Christ." She waited for a moment. She seemed happy remembering. "You don't sing spirituals in your church, do you?"

"No. We sing anthems, chorals." Neither word sounded right, so I tried again. "You know, hymns."

"Yes," she said, "chorals are nice."

I knew she was saying this to make me feel good. She looked like the kind who had loved spirituals in that other life of hers.

I talked for a long time with Shera and Mrs. X about my plans to go to college and someday to be a writer. As I talked, I kept thinking: yes education, I must get that, I cannot allow this disenchantment in me to drive me to the same conclusions that Rashman's had driven him, for I was sure now that his wife had, with sadness, let him go away to do whatever his restlessness was forcing him to do. I was sure that when he left home, he did not know himself exactly what that was. In St. Louis, the Black Muslims had started to make stands against the police. I hoped very hard that this would not lead to violence.

In his absence I felt closer to Rashman than I ever had. I was afraid for him. I was afraid that he had gone away to do what he said, to make a stand against an entire civilization. I wished that he had not gone. I wanted to argue with him again. I wanted to convince him that what he felt he had to do was not necessary, but I was sure that if I had been given the chance to talk to him again, I would not have known what to say.

Andre Dubus
If They Knew Yvonne

I GREW UP IN LOUISIANA, and for twelve years I went to a boys' school taught by Christian Brothers, a Catholic religious order. In the eighth grade our teacher was Brother Thomas. I still have a picture he gave to each boy in the class at the end of that year: it's a picture of Thomas Aquinas, two angels, and a woman. In the left foreground Aquinas is seated, leaning back against one angel whose hands grip his shoulders; he looks very much like a tired boxer between rounds, and his upturned face looks imploringly at the angel. The second angel is kneeling at his feet and, with both hands, is tightening a sash around Aquinas's waist. In the left background of the picture, the woman is escaping up a flight of stone stairs; her face is turned backward for a final look before she bolts from the room. According to Brother Thomas, some of Aquinas's family were against his becoming a priest, so they sent a woman to his room. He drove her out, then angels descended, encircled his waist with a cord, and squeezed all concupiscence from his body so he would never be tempted again. On the back of the picture, under the title *Angelic Warfare*, is a prayer for purity.

Brother Thomas was the first teacher who named for us the sins included in the Sixth and Ninth Commandments which, in the Catholic recording of the Decalogue, forbid adultery and coveting your neighbor's wife. In an introductory way, he simply listed the various sins. Then he focused on what apparently was the most significant: he called it self-abuse and, quickly sweeping our faces, he saw that we understood. It was a mortal sin, he said, because first of all it wasted the precious seed which God had given us for marriage. Also, sexual pleasure was reserved for married people alone, to have children by performing the marriage act. Self-abuse was not even a natural act; it was unnatural, and if a boy did it he was no better than a monkey. It was a desecration of our bodies, which were temples of the Holy Ghost, a mortal sin that resulted in the loss of sanctifying grace and therefore could sent us to hell. He walked a few paces from his desk, his legs hidden by the long black robe, then he went back and stood behind the desk again and pulled down on his white collar: the front of it hung straight down from his throat like two white and faceless playing cards.

"Avoid being alone," he said. "When you go home from school, don't just sit around the house—go out and play ball, or cut the grass, or wash your dad's car. Do *anything*, but use up your energy. And pray to the Blessed Mother: take your rosary to bed at night and say it while you're going to sleep. If you fall asleep before you finish, the Blessed Mother won't mind—that's what she *wants* you to do."

Then he urged us to receive the Holy Eucharist often. He told us of the benefits gained through the Eucharist: sanctifying grace, which helped us fight temptation; release from the temporal punishment of purgatory; and therefore, until we committed another mortal or venial sin, a guarantee of immediate entrance into heaven. He hoped and prayed, he said, that he would die with the Holy Eucharist on his tongue.

He had been talking with the excited voice yet wandering eyes of a man repeating by rote what he truly believes. But now his eyes focused on something out the window, as though a new truth had actually appeared to him on the dusty school ground of that hot spring day. One hand rose to scratch his jaw.

"In a way," he said softly, "you'd actually be doing someone a favor if you killed him when he had just received the Eucharist."

I made it until midsummer, about two weeks short of my fourteenth birthday. I actually believed I would make it forever. Then one hot summer night when my parents were out playing bridge, Janet was on a date, and I was alone in the house, looking at *Holiday* magazine—girls in advertisements drinking rum or lighting cigarettes, girls in bulky sweaters at ski resorts, girls at beaches, girls on horseback—I went to the bathroom, telling myself I was only going to piss, lingering there, thinking it was pain I felt but then I knew it wasn't, that for the first wakeful time in my life it was about to happen, then it did, and I stood weak and trembling and shutting my eyes saw the faces of the Virgin Mary and Christ and Brother Thomas, then above them, descending to join them, the awful diaphanous bulk of God.

That was a Tuesday. I set the alarm clock and woke next morning at six-thirty, feeling that everyone on earth and in Heaven had watched my sin, and had been watching me as I slept. I dressed quickly and crept past Janet's bedroom: she slept naked, on her side, one sun-dark arm on top of the sheet; then past the closed door of my parents' room and out of the house. Riding my bicycle down the driveway, I thought of being struck by a car, so I rode on the sidewalk to church and I got there in time for confession before Mass. When I got home Janet was sitting on the front steps, drinking orange juice. I rode across the lawn and stopped in front of her and looked at her smooth brown legs.

"Where'd you go?"

"To Mass."

"Special day today?"

"I woke up," I said. "So I went."

A fly buzzed at my ear and I remembered Brother Thomas quoting some saint who had said if you couldn't stand an insect buzzing at your ear while you were trying to sleep, how could you stand the eternal punishment of hell?

"You set the alarm," she said. "I heard it."

Then Mother called us in to breakfast. She asked where I had been, then said, "Well, that's nice. Maybe you'll be a priest."

"Ha," Daddy said.

"Don't worry, Daddy," Janet said. "We don't hate Episcopalians anymore."

I got through two more days, until Friday, then Saturday afternoon I had to go to confession again. Through the veil over the latticed window Father Broussard told me to pray often to the Virgin Mary, to avoid those people and places and things that were occasions of sin, to go to confession and receive Communion at least once a week. The tone of his whispering voice was kind, and the confessional itself was constructed to offer some comfort, for it enclosed me with my secret, and its interior was dark as my soul was, and Christ crucified stared back at me, inches from my face. Father Broussard told me to say ten Our Fathers and ten Hail Marys for my penance. I said them kneeling in a pew at the rear, then I went outside and walked around the church to the cemetery. In hot sun I moved among old graves and took out my rosary and began to pray.

Sunday we went to eleven-o'clock Mass. Janet and I received Communion, but Mother had eaten toast and coffee, breaking her fast, so she didn't receive. Most Sundays she broke her fast because we went to late Mass, and in those days you had to fast from midnight until you received Communion; around ten in the morning she would feel faint and have to eat something. After Mass Janet started the car and lit a cigarette and waited for our line in the parking lot to move. I envied her nerve. She was only sixteen, but when she started smoking my parents couldn't stop her.

"I just can't keep the fast," Mother said. "I must need vitamins."

She was sitting in the front seat, opening and closing her black fan.

"Maybe you do," Janet said.

"Maybe so. If you have to smoke, I wish you'd do it at home."

Janet smiled and drove in first gear out of the parking lot. Her window was down and on the way home I watched her dark hair blowing in the breeze.

That was how my fourteenth summer passed: baseball in the mornings, and friends and movies and some days of peace, of hope—then back to the confessional where the smell of sweat hung in the air like spewed-out sin. Once I saw the student body president walking down the main street;

he recognized my face and told me hello, and I blushed not with timidity but shame, for he walked with a confident stride, he was strong and good while I was weak. A high-school girl down the street gave me a ride one day, less than an hour after I had done it; and I sat against the door at my side and could not look at her; I answered her in a low voice and said nothing on my own and I knew she thought I was shy, but that was better than the truth, for I believed if she knew what sat next to her she would recoil in disgust. When fall came I was glad, for I hoped the school days would break the pattern of my sins. But I was also afraid the Brothers could see the summer in my eyes; then it wasn't just summer, but fall and winter too, for the pattern wasn't broken and I could not stop.

In the confessional the hardest priest was an old Dutchman who scolded and talked about manliness and will power and once told me to stick my finger in the flame of a candle, then imagine the eternal fire of hell. I didn't do it. Father Broussard was firm, sometimes impatient, but easy compared to the Dutchman. The easiest was a young Italian, Father Grassi, who said very little: I doubt if he ever spoke to me for over thirty seconds, and he gave such light penances—three or four Hail Marys—that I began to think he couldn't understand English well enough to know what I told him.

Then it was fall again, I was fifteen, and Janet was a freshman at the college in town. She was dating Bob Mitchell, a Yankee from Michigan. He was an airman from the SAC base, so she had to argue with Mother for the first week or so. He was a high-school graduate, intelligent, and he planned to go to the University of Michigan when he got out. That's what she told Mother, who for some reason believed a man in uniform was less trustworthy than a local civilian. One weekend in October Mother and Daddy went to Baton Rouge to see L.S.U. play Ole Miss. It was a night game and they were going to spend Saturday night with friends in Baton Rouge. They left after lunch Saturday and as soon as they drove off, Janet called Bob and broke their date, then went to bed. She had the flu, she said, but she hadn't told them because Mother would have felt it was her duty to stay home.

"Would you bring me a beer?" she said. "I'll just lie in bed and drink beer and you won't have to bother with me at all."

I sat in the living room and listened to Bill Stern broadcast Notre Dame and S.M.U. I kept checking on Janet to see if she wanted another beer; she'd smile at me over her book—*The Idiot*—then shake her beer can and say yes. When the game was over I told her I was going to confession and she gave me some money for cigarettes. I didn't know how to tell her no, so I took the money but I didn't buy the cigarettes. I had enough to be ashamed of without people thinking I smoked too. When I got home I told her I had forgotten.

"Would you see if Daddy left any?"

I went into their room. On the wall above the double bed was a small crucifix with a silver Christ (Daddy called it a graven image, but he smiled when he said it); stuck behind the crucifix was a blade from a palm frond, dried brown and crisp since Palm Sunday. I opened the top drawer of Daddy's bureau and took out the carton of Luckies. Then something else red-and-white caught my eye: the corner of a small box under his rolled-up socks. For a moment I didn't take it out. I stood looking at that corner of cardboard, knowing immediately what it was and also knowing that I wasn't learning anything new, that I had known for some indefinite and secret time, maybe a few months or a year or even two years. I stood there in the history of my knowledge, then I put down the cigarette carton and took the box of condoms from the drawer. I had slid the cover off the box and was looking at the vertically arranged rolled condoms when I heard the bedsprings, but it was too late, her bare feet were already crossing the floor, and all I could do was raise my eyes to hers as she said, "Can't you find—" then stopped.

At first she blushed, but only for a second or two. She came into the room, gently took the box from me, put the cover on, and looked at it for a moment. Then she put it in the drawer, covered it with socks, got a pack of cigarettes and started back to her room.

"Why don't you bring me a beer," she said over her shoulder. "And we'll have a little talk."

When I brought the beer she was propped up in bed, and *The Idiot* was closed on the bedside table.

"Are you really surprised?" she said.

I shook my head.

"Does it bother you?"

"Yes."

"You're probably scrupulous. You confess enough for Eichmann, you know."

I blushed and looked away.

"Do you know that some people—theologians—believe a mortal sin is as rare as a capital crime? That most things we do aren't really that evil?"

"They must not be Catholics."

"Some of them are. Listen: Mother's only mistake is she thinks it's a sin, so she doesn't receive Communion. And I guess that's why she doesn't get a diaphragm—that would be too committed."

This sort of talk scared me, and I was relieved when she stopped. She told me not to worry about Mother and especially not to blame Daddy, not to think of him as a Protestant who had led Mother away from the Church. She said the Church was wrong. Several times she used the word *love*, and that night in bed I thought: love? love? For all I could think of was semen and I remembered long ago a condom lying in the dust of a country road; a line of black ants was crawling into it. I got out of bed, turned on a lamp, and read the *Angelic Warfare* prayer, which ends like this:

> O God, Who has vouchsafed to defend with the blessed cord of
> St. Thomas those who are engaged in the terrible conflict of
> chastity! grant to us Thy suppliants, by his help, happily to

overcome in this warfare the terrible enemy of our body and souls, that, being crowned with the lily of perpetual purity, we may deserve to receive from Thee, amongst the chaste bands of the angels, the palm of bliss . . .

Janet didn't do so well in the war. That January she and Bob Mitchell drove to Port Arthur, Texas, and got married by a justice of the peace. Then they went to Father Broussard for a Catholic marriage, but when he found out Janet was pregnant he refused. He said he didn't think this marriage would last, and he would not make it permanent in the eyes of God. My parents and I knew nothing of this until a couple of weeks later, when Bob was discharged from the air force. One night they told us, and two days later Janet was gone, up to Michigan; she wrote that although Bob wasn't a Catholic, he had agreed to try again, and this time a priest had married them. Seven months after the Texas wedding she had twin sons and Mother went up there on the bus and stayed two weeks and sent us post cards from Ann Arbor.

You get over your sister's troubles, even images of her getting pregnant in a parked car, just as after a while you stop worrying about whether or not your mother is living in sin. I had my own troubles and one summer afternoon when I was sixteen, alone in the house, having done it again after receiving Communion that very morning, I lay across my bed, crying and striking my head with my fist. It was a weekday, so the priests weren't hearing confessions until next morning before Mass. I could have gone to the rectory and confessed to a priest in his office, but I could not do that, I had to have the veiled window between our faces. Finally I got up and went to the phone in the hall. I dialed the rectory and when Father Broussard answered I told him I couldn't get to church but I had to confess and I wanted to do it right now, on the phone. I barely heard the suspicious turn in his voice when he told me to come to the rectory.

"I can't," I said.

"What about tomorrow? Could you come tomorrow before Mass, or during the day?"

"I can't, Father. I can't wait that long."

"Who is this?"

For a moment we were both quiet. Then I said, "That's all right."

It was an expression we boys used, and it usually meant none of your business. I had said it in a near whisper, not sure if I could speak another word without crying.

"All right," he said, "let me hear your confession."

I kneeled on the floor, my eyes closed, the telephone cord stretched tautly to its full length:

"Bless me, Father, for I have sinned; my last confession was yesterday—" now I was crying silent tears, those I hadn't spent on the bed; I could still talk but my voice was in shards—"my sins are: I committed self-abuse one time—" the word *time* trailing off, whispered into the phone and the empty hall which grew emptier still, for Father Broussard said nothing and I kneeled with eyes shut tight and the receiver hurting my hot ear until finally he said, "All right, but I can't give you absolution over the phone. Will you come to the rectory at about three?"

"Yes, Father."

"And ask for Father Broussard."

"Yes, Father, thank you, Father—" still holding the receiver after he hung up, my eyes shut on black and red shame; then I stood weakly and returned to the bed—I would not go to the rectory—and lay there feeling I was the only person alive on this humid summer day. I could not stop crying, and I began striking my head again. I spoke aloud to God, begging him to forgive me then kill me and spare me the further price of being a boy. Then something occurred to me: an image tossed up for my consideration, looked at, repudiated—all in an instant while my fist was poised. I saw myself sitting on the bed, trousers dropped to the floor, my sharp-edged hunting knife in my right hand, then with one quick determined slash cutting off that autonomous penis and casting it on the floor to shrivel and die. But before my fist struck again I threw that image away. No voices told me why. I had no warning vision of pain, of bleeding to death, of being an impotent freak. I simply knew: it is there between your legs and you do not cut it off.

2

Yvonne Miller finally put it to good use. We were both nineteen, both virgins; we started dating the summer after our freshman year at the college in town. She was slender, with black hair cut short in what they called an "Italian Boy." She was a Catholic, and had been taught by nuns for twelve years, but she wasn't bothered as much as I was. In the parked car we soaked our clothes with sweat, and sometimes I went home with spotted trousers which I rolled into a bundle and dropped in the basket for dry cleaning. I confessed this and petting too, and tried on our dates to keep dry, so that many nights I crawled aching and nauseated into my bed at home. I lay very still in my pain, feeling quasi-victorious: I thought Yvonne and I were committing mortal sins by merely touching each other, but at least for another night we had resisted the graver sin of orgasm. On other nights she took me with her hand or we rubbed against each other in a clothed pantomime of lovemaking until we came. This happened often enough so that for the first time in nearly seven years I stopped masturbating. And Saturday after Saturday I went proudly to confession and told of my sins with Yvonne. I confessed to Father Grassi, who still didn't talk much, but one Saturday afternoon he said, "How old are you, my friend?"

"Nineteen, Father."

"Yes. And the young girl?"

I told him she was nineteen. Now I was worried: I had avoided confessing to Father Broussard or the Dutchman because I was afraid one of them would ask about the frequency of our sins, then tell me either to be pure or break up with her and, if I did neither of these, I could not be absolved again. I had thought Father Grassi would not ask questions.

"Do you love her?"

"Yes, Father."

"At your age I think it is very hard to know if you really love someone. So I recommend that you and your girl think about getting married in two or three years' time and then, my friend, until you are ready for a short engagement and then marriage, I think each of you should go out with other people. Mostly with each other, of course, but with other people too. That may not help you to stay pure, but at least it will help you know if you love each other."

"Yes, Father."

"Because this other thing that's going on now, that's not love, you see. So you should test it in other ways."

I told him I understood and I would talk to my girl about it. I never did, though. Once in a while Yvonne confessed but I have no idea what she told the priest, for she did not see things the way I saw them. One night, when I tried to stop us short, she pulled my hand back to its proper place and held it there until she was ready for it to leave. Then she reached to the dashboard for a cigarette, tapped it, and paused as though remembering to offer me one.

"Don't you want me to do it for you?" she said.

"No, I'm all right."

She smoked for a while, her head on my shoulder.

"Do you really think it's a worse sin when it happens to you?" she said.

"Yes."

"Why?"

I told her what the Brothers had taught me.

"You believe that?" she said. "That God gave you this seed just to have babies with, and if you waste it He'll send you to hell?"

"I guess so."

"You have wet dreams, don't you?"

"That's different. There's no will involved."

"What about me? It just happened to me, and I didn't use up any eggs or anything, so where's my sin?"

"I don't know. Maybe sins are different for girls."

"Then it wouldn't be a sin for me to masturbate either. Right? I don't, but isn't that true?"

"I never thought of that."

"Well don't. You think too much already."

"Maybe you don't think enough."

"You're right: I don't."

"I'll tell you why it's a sin," I said. "Because it's reserved for married people."

"Climax?"

"Yes."

"But you're supposed to be married to touch each other too," she said. "So why draw the line at climax? I mean, why get all worked up and then stop and think that's good?"

"You're right. We shouldn't do any of it."

"Oh, I'm not sure it's as bad as all that."

"You're not? You don't think it's a sin, what we do?"

"Maybe a little, but it's not as bad as a lot of other things."

"It's a mortal sin."

"I don't think so. I believe it's a sin to talk about a girl, but I don't think what you do with her is so bad."

"All right: if that's what you think, why don't we just go all the way?"

She sat up to throw her cigarette out the window, then she nestled her face on my chest.

"Because I'm scared," she said.

"Of getting pregnant?"

"I don't think so. I'm just scared of not being a virgin, that's all."

Then she finished our argument, won it, soaked her small handkerchief in my casuistry. Next morning at breakfast I was tired.

"You're going to ruin your health," Mother said. "It was after one when you got home."

I flexed my biceps and said I was fine. But now Daddy was watching me from his end of the table.

"I don't care about your health," he said. "I just hope you know more than Janet did."

"*Honey,*" Mother said.

"She got it reversed. She started babies before she was married, then quit."

That was true. Her twin boys were four now, and there were no other children. Bob had finished his undergraduate work and was going to start work on a Ph.D. in political science. Early in the summer Mother had gone up there and stayed two weeks. When she got back and talked about her visit she looked nervous, as though she were telling a lie, and a couple of times I walked into the kitchen where Mother and Daddy were talking and they stopped until I had got what I wanted and left.

"I won't get pregnant," I said.

"Neither will Yvonne," Daddy said. "As long as you keep your pants on."

Then finally one night in early fall we drove away from her house where we had parked for some time, and I knew she would not stop me, because by leaving her house she was risking questions from her parents, and by accepting that she was accepting the other risk too. I drove out to a country road, over a vibrating wooden bridge, the bayou beneath us dark as earth on that moonless night, on through black trees until I found a dirt road into the woods, keeping my hand on her small breast as I turned and cut off the ignition and headlights. In a moment she was naked on the car seat, then I was out of my clothes, even the socks, and seeing her trusting face and shockingly white body I almost dressed and took her home but then she said, "Love me, Harry, love me—"

The Brothers hadn't prepared me for this. If my first time had been with a whore, their training probably would have worked, for that was the sort of lust they focused on. But they were no match for Yvonne, and next morning I woke happier than I had ever been. At school that day we drank coffee and held hands and whispered. That night on the way to her house I stopped at a service station and bought a package of condoms from a machine in the men's room. That was the only time I felt guilty. But I was at least perceptive enough to know why: condoms, like masturbation and whores, were something the Brothers knew about. I left that piss-smelling room, walked into the clear autumn night, and drove to Yvonne's, where they had never been.

For the rest of the fall and a few weeks of winter, we were hot and happy lovers. I marveled at my own joy, my lack of remorse. Once, after a few weeks, I asked her if she ever felt bad. It was late at night and we were sitting at a bar, eating oysters on the half shell. For a moment she didn't know what I meant, then she smiled.

"I feel wonderful," she said.

She dipped her last oyster in the sauce and leaned over the tray to eat it.

"Do we have enough money for more?" she said.

"Sure."

They were ninety cents a dozen. We watched the Negro open them, and I felt fine, eating oysters and drinking beer at one in the morning, having made love an hour ago to this pretty girl beside me. I looked at her hair and wondered if she ought to let it grow.

"Sometimes I worry, though," she said.

"Getting pregnant?"

"Nope, I never said you had to use those things. I worry about you."

"Why me?"

"Because you used to think about sins so much, and now you don't."

"That's because I love you."

She licked the red sauce from her fingers, then took my hand, squeezed it, and drank some beer.

"I'm afraid someday you'll start feeling bad again, then you'll hate me."

She was right to look for defeat in that direction, to expect me to move along clichéd routes. But, as it turned out, it wasn't guilt that finally soured us. After a couple of months I simply began noticing things.

I saw that she didn't really like football. She only enjoyed the games because they gave her a chance to dress up, and there was a band, and a crowd of students, and it was fun to keep a flask hidden while you poured bourbon into a paper cup. She cheered with the rest of us, but she wasn't cheering for the same thing. She cheered because we were there, and a young man had run very fast with a football. Once we stood up to watch an end chasing a long pass: when he dived for it, caught it, and skidded on the ground, she turned happily to me and brushed her candied apple against my sleeve. Watch out, I said. She spit on her handkerchief and rubbed the sticky wool. She loved sweets, always asked me to buy her Mounds or Hersheys at the movies, and once in a while she'd get a pimple which she tried to conceal with powder. I felt loose flesh at her waist when we danced, and walking beside her on the campus one afternoon I looked down and saw her belly pushing against her tight skirt; I lightly back-handed it and told her to suck her gut in. She stood at attention, saluted, then gave me the finger. I'm about to start my period, she said. Except for the soft flesh at her waist she was rather thin, and when she lay on her back her naked breasts spread and flattened, as though they were melting.

Around the end of November her parents spent a weekend with relatives in Houston, leaving Yvonne to take care of her sister and brother, who were fourteen and eleven. They left Saturday morning, and that night Yvonne cooked for me. She was dressed up, black cocktail dress, even heels, and she was disappointed when she saw I hadn't worn a coat. But she didn't say anything. She had already fed her brother and sister, and they were in the den at the back of the house, watching television. Yvonne had a good fire in the living room fireplace, and on the coffee table she had bourbon, a pitcher of water, a bucket of ice, and a sugar bowl.

"Like they do in Faulkner," she said, and we sat on the couch and drank a couple of toddies before dinner. Then she left me for a while and I looked into the fire, hungry and horny, and wondered what time the brother and sister would go to bed and if Yvonne would do it while they were sleeping. She came back to the living room, smiled, blushed, and said, "If you're brave enough, I am. Want to try it?"

We ate by candlelight: oyster cocktails, then a roast with rice and thick dark gravy, garlic-tinged. We had lemon icebox pie and went back to the fireplace with second cups of coffee.

"I love to cook," she said from the record player. She put on about five long-playing albums, and I saw that we were supposed to sit at the fire and talk for the rest of the evening. The first album was Jackie Gleason, *Music, Martinis, and Memories*, and she sat beside me, took my hand, and sipped her coffee. She rested her head on the back of the couch, but I didn't like to handle a coffee cup leaning back that way, so I withdrew my hand from hers and hunched forward over the coffee table.

"I think I started cooking when I was seven," she said to my back. "No, let's see, I was eight—" I looked down at her crossed legs, the black dress just covering her knees, then looked at the fire. "When we lived in Baton Rouge. I had a children's cookbook and I made something called 'Chili Concoction.' Everybody was nice about it, and Daddy ate two helpings for supper and told me to save the rest for breakfast and he'd eat it with eggs. He did, too. Then I made something called a strawberry minute pie, and I think it was pretty good. I'll make it for you sometime."

"Okay."

I was still hunched over drinking coffee, so I wasn't looking at her. I finished the coffee and she asked if I wanted more, and that irritated me, so I didn't know whether to say yes or no. I said I guess so. Then watching her leave with my cup, I disliked myself and her too. For if I wasn't worthy of the evening, then wasn't she stupid and annoyingly vulnerable to give it to me? The next album was Sinatra; I finished my coffee, then leaned back so our shoulders touched, our hands together in her lap, and we listened. Once she took a drag from my cigarette and I said, Keep it, and lit another. The third album was Brubeck. She put some more ice in the bucket, I made toddies, and she asked if I understood *The Bear.* I shrugged and said probably not. She had finished it the day before, and she started talking about it.

"Hey," I said. "When are they going to sleep?"

She was surprised, and again I disliked myself and her too. Then she was hurt, and she looked at her lap and said she didn't know, but she couldn't make love anyway, not here in the house, even if they were sleeping.

"We can leave for a while," I said. "We won't go far."

She kept looking at her lap, at our clasped hands.

"They'll be all right," I said.

Then she looked into my eyes and I looked away and she said, "Okay, I'll tell them."

When she came back with a coat over her arm I was waiting at the door, my jacket zipped, the car key in my hand.

We broke up in January, about a week after New Year's. I don't recall whether we fought, or kissed goodbye, or sat in a car staring mutely out the windows. But I do remember when the end started; or, rather, when Yvonne decided to recognize it.

On New Year's Eve a friend of ours gave a party. His parents were out of town, so everyone got drunk. It was an opportunity you felt obliged not to pass up. Two or three girls got sick and had to have their faces washed and be walked outside in the cold air. When Yvonne got drunk it was a pleasant drunk, and I took her upstairs. I think no one noticed: it was just past midnight, and people were hard to account for. We lay on the bed in the master bedroom, Yvonne with her skirt pulled up, her pants off, while I performed in shirt, sweater, and socks. She was quiet as we stood in the dark room, taking our pants off, and she didn't answer my whispered Happy New Year as we began to make love, for the first time, on a bed. Then, moving beneath me, she said in a voice so incongruous with her body that I almost softened but quickly got it back, shutting my ears to what I had heard: This is all we ever do, Harry—this is all we ever do.

The other thing I remember about that night is a time around three in the morning. A girl was cooking hamburgers, I was standing in the kitchen doorway talking to some boys, and Yvonne was sitting alone at the kitchen table. There were other people talking in the kitchen, but she wasn't listening; she moved only to tap ashes and draw on her cigarette, then exhaled into the space that held her gaze. She looked older than twenty, quite lonely and sad, and I pitied her. But there was something else: I knew she would never make love to me again. Maybe that is why, as a last form of possession, I told. It could not have been more than an hour later, I was drunker, and in the bathroom I one-upped three friends who were bragging about feeling tits of drunken girls. I told them I had taken Yvonne upstairs and screwed her. To add history to it, I even told them what she had said.

3

Waiting in line for my first confession in five months, I felt some guilt but I wasn't at all afraid. I only had to confess sexual intercourse, and there was nothing shameful about that, nothing unnatural. It was a man's sin. Father Broussard warned me never to see this girl again (that's what he called her: this girl), for a man is weak and he needs much grace to turn away from a girl who will give him her body. He said I must understand it was a serious sin because sexual intercourse was given by God to married couples for the procreation of children and we had stolen it and used it wrongfully, for physical pleasure, which was its secondary purpose. I knew that in some way I had sinned, but Father Broussard's definition of that sin fell short and did not sound at all like what I had done with Yvonne. So when I left the confessional I still felt unforgiven.

The campus was not a very large one, but it was large enough so you could avoid seeing someone. I stopped going to the student center for coffee, and we had no classes together; we only saw each other once in a while, usually from a distance, walking between buildings. We exchanged waves and the sort of smile you cut into your face at times like that. The town was small too, so occasionally I saw her driving around, looking for a parking place or something. Then after a while I wanted to see her, and I started going to the student center again, but she didn't drink coffee there anymore. In a week or so I realized that I didn't really want to see her: I wanted her to be happy, and if I saw her there was nothing I could say to help that.

Soon I was back to the old private vice, though now it didn't seem vice but an indulgence, not as serious as smoking or even drinking, closer to eating an ice-cream sundae before bed every night. That was how I felt about it, like I had eaten two scoops of ice cream with thick hot fudge on it, and after a couple of bites it wasn't good anymore but I finished it anyway, thinking of calories. It was a boring little performance and it didn't seem worth thinking about, one way or the other. But I told it in the confessional, so I could still receive the Eucharist. Then one day in spring I told the number of my sins as though I were telling the date of my birth, my height, and weight, and Father Broussard said quickly and sternly, "Are you sorry for these sins?"

"Yes, Father," I said, but then I knew it was a lie. He was asking me if I had a firm resolve to avoid this sin in the future when I said, "No, Father."

"No what? You can't avoid it?"

"I mean no, Father, I'm not really sorry. I don't even think it's a sin."

"Oh, I see. You don't have the discipline to stop, so you've decided it's not a sin. Just like that, you've countermanded God's law. Do you want absolution?"

"Yes, Father. I want to receive Communion."

"You can't. You're living in mortal sin, and I cannot absolve you while you keep this attitude. I want you to think very seriously—"

But I wasn't listening. I was looking at the crucifix and waiting for his voice to stop so I could leave politely and try to figure out what to do next. Then he stopped talking, and I said, "Yes, Father."

"*What?*" he said. "*What?*"

I went quickly through the curtains, out of the confessional, out of the church.

On Sundays I went to Mass but did not receive the Eucharist. I thought I could but I was afraid that as soon as the Host touched my tongue I would suddenly realize I had been wrong, and then I'd be receiving Christ with mortal sin on my soul. Mother didn't receive either. I prayed for her and hoped she'd soon have peace, even if it meant early menopause. By now I agreed with Janet, and I wished she'd write Mother a letter and convince her that she wasn't evil. I thought Mother was probably praying for Janet, who had gone five years without bearing a child.

It was June, school was out, and I did not see Yvonne at all. I was working with a surveying crew, running a hundred-foot chain through my fingers, cutting trails with a machete, eating big lunches from paper bags, and waiting for something to happen. There were two alternatives, and I wasn't phony enough for the first or brave enough for the second: I could start confessing again, the way I used to, or I could ignore the confessional and simply receive Communion. But nothing happened and each Sunday I stayed with Mother in the pew while the others went up to the altar rail.

Then Janet came home. She wrote that Bob had left her, had moved in with his girl friend—a graduate student—and she and the boys were coming home on the bus. That was the news waiting for me when I got home from work, Mother handing me the letter as I came through the front door, both of them watching me as I read it. Then Daddy cursed, Mother started crying again, and I took a beer out to the front porch. After a while Daddy came out too and we sat without talking and drank beer until Mother called us to supper. Daddy said, "That son of a bitch," and we went inside.

By the time Janet and the boys rode the bus home from Ann Arbor, Mother was worried about something else: the Church, because now Janet was twenty-three years old and getting a divorce and if she ever married again she was out of the Church. Unless Bob died, and Daddy said he didn't care what the Church thought about divorce, but it seemed a good enough reason for him to go up to Ann Arbor, Michigan, and shoot Bob Mitchell between the eyes. So while Janet and Paul and Lee were riding south on the Greyhound, Mother was going to daily Mass and praying for some answer to Janet's future.

But Janet had already taken care of that too. When she got off the bus I knew she'd be getting married again someday; she had gained about ten pounds, probably from all the cheap food while Bob went to school, but she had always been on the lean side anyway and now she looked better than I remembered. Her hair was long, about halfway down her back. The boys were five years old now, and I was glad she hadn't had any more, because they seemed to be good little boys and not enough to scare off a man. We took them home—it was a Friday night—and Daddy gave Janet a tall drink of bourbon and everybody talked as though nothing had happened. Then we ate some shrimp *étouffée* and after supper, when the boys were in bed and the rest of us were in the living room, Janet said by God it was the best meal she had had in five years, and next time she was going to marry a man who liked Louisiana cooking. When she saw the quick look in Mother's eyes, she said, "We didn't get married in the Church, Mama. I just told you we did so you wouldn't worry."

"You *didn't?*"

"Bob was so mad at Father Broussard he wouldn't try again. He's not a Catholic, you know."

"There's more wrong with him than that," Daddy said.

"So I can still get married in the Church," Janet said. "To somebody else."

"But Janet—"

"Wait," Daddy said. "Wait. You've been praying for days so Janet could stop living with that son of a bitch and still save her soul. Now you got it—right?"

"But—"

"Right?"

"Well," Mother said, "I guess so."

They went to bed about an hour past their usual time, but Janet and I stayed up drinking gin and tonic in the kitchen, with the door closed so we wouldn't keep anybody awake. At first she just talked about how glad she was to be home, even if the first sign of it was the Negroes going to the back of the bus. She loved this hot old sticky night, she said, and the June bugs thumping against the screen and she had forgot how cigarettes get soft down here in the humid air. Finally she talked about Bob; she didn't think he had ever loved her, he had started playing around their first year up there, and it had gone on for five years more or less; near the end she had even done it too, had a boyfriend, but it didn't help her survive at all, it only made things worse, and now at least she felt clean and tough and she thought that was the first step toward hope.

The stupid thing was she still loved the philandering son of a bitch. That was the only time she cried, when she said that, but she didn't even cry long enough for me to get up and go to her side of the table and hold her or something: when I was half out of my chair she was already waving me back in it, shaking her head and wiping her eyes, and the tears that had filled them for a moment were gone. Then she cheered up and asked if I'd drive her around tomorrow, down the main street and everything, and I said sure and asked her if she was still a Catholic.

"Don't tell Mother this," she said. "She's confused enough already. I went to Communion every Sunday, except when I was having that stupid affair, and I only felt sinful then because he loved me and I was using him. But before that and after that, I received."

"You can't," I said. "Not while you're married out of the Church."

"Maybe I'm wrong, but I don't think the Church is so smart about sex. Bob wouldn't get the marriage blessed, so a priest would have told me to leave him. I loved him, though, and for a long time I thought he loved me, needed me—so I stayed with him and tried to keep peace and bring up my sons. And the Eucharist is the sacrament of love and I needed it very badly those five years and nobody can keep me away."

I got up and took our glasses and made drinks. When I turned from the sink she was watching me.

"Do you still go to confession so much?" she said.

I sat down, avoiding her eyes, then I thought what the hell, if you can't tell Janet you can't tell anybody. So looking at the screen door and the bugs thumping from the dark outside I told her how it was in high school and about Yvonne, though I didn't tell her name, and my aborted confession to Father Broussard. She was kind to me, busying herself with cigarettes and her drink while I talked. Then she said, "You're right, Harry. You're absolutely right."

"You really think so?"

"I know this much: too many of those celibates teach sex the way it is for them. They made it introverted, so you come out of their schools believing sex is something between you and yourself, or between you and God. Instead of between you and other people. Like my affair. It wasn't wrong because I was married. Hell, Bob didn't care, in fact he was glad because it gave him more freedom. It was wrong because I hurt the guy." A Yankee word on her tongue, *guy*, and she even said it with that accent from up there among snow and lakes. "If Bob had stayed home and taken a *Playboy* to the bathroom once in a while I might still have a husband. So if that's a sin, I don't understand sin."

"Well," I said. Then looking at her, I grinned and it kept spreading and turned into a laugh. "You're something, all right," I said. "Old Janet, you're something."

But I still wasn't the renegade Janet was, I wanted absolution from a priest, and next morning while Mother and Daddy were happily teasing us about our hangovers, I decided to get it done. That afternoon I called Father Grassi, then told Janet where I was going, and that I would drive her around town when I got back. Father Grassi answered the door at the rectory; he was wearing a white shirt with his black trousers, a small man with a ruddy face and dark whiskers. I asked if I could speak to him in his office.

"I think so," he said. "Do you come from the Pope?"

"No, Father. I just want to confess."

"So it's you who will be the saint today, not me. Yes, come in."

He led me to his office, put his stole around his neck, and sat in the swivel chair behind his desk; I knelt beside him on the carpet, and he shielded his face with his hand, as though we were in the confessional and he could not see me. I whispered "Bless me, Father, for I have sinned," my hands clasped at my waist, my head bowed. "My last confession was six weeks ago, but I was refused absolution. By Father Broussard."

"Is that so? You don't look like a very bad young man to me. Are you some kind of criminal?"

"I confessed masturbation, Father."

"Yes? Then what?"

"I told him I didn't think it was a sin."

"I see. Well, poor Father Broussard: I'd be confused too, if you confessed something as a sin and then said you didn't think it was a sin. You should take better care of your priests, my friend."

I opened my eyes: his hand was still in place on his cheek, and he was looking straight ahead, over his desk at the bookshelf against the wall.

"I guess so," I said. "And now I'm bothering you."

"Oh no: you're no trouble. The only disappointment is you weren't sent by the Pope. But since that's the way it is, then we may just as well talk about sins. We had in the seminary a book of moral theology and in that book, my friend, it was written that masturbation was worse than rape, because at least rape was the carrying out of a natural instinct. What about that?"

"Do you believe that, Father?"

"Do you?"

"No, Father."

"Neither do I. I burned the book when I left the seminary, but not only for that reason. The book also said, among other things, let the buyer beware. So you tell me about sin and we will educate each other."

"I went to the Brothers' school."

"Ah, yes. Nice fellows, those Brothers."

"Yes, Father. But I think they concentrated too much on the body. One's own body, I mean. And back then I believed it all, and one day I even wanted to mutilate myself. Then last fall I had a girl."

"What does that mean, you had a girl? You mean you were lovers?"

"Yes, Father. But I shouldn't have had a girl, because I believed my semen was the most important part of sex, so the first time I made love with her I was waiting for it, like my soul was listening for it—you see? Because I wouldn't know how I felt about her until I knew how I felt about ejaculating with her."

"And how did you feel? Did you want to mutilate yourself with a can opener, or maybe something worse?"

"I was happy, Father."

"Yes."

"So after that we were lovers. Or she was, but I wasn't. I was just happy because I could ejaculate without hating myself, so I was still masturbating, you see, but with her—Does that make sense?"

"Oh yes, my friend. I've known that since I left the seminary. Always there is too much talk of self-abuse. You see, even the term is a bad one. Have you finished your confession?"

"I want to confess about the girl again, because when I confessed it before it wasn't right. I slept with her without loving her and the last time I slept with her I told some boys about it."

"Yes. Anything else?"

"No, Father."

"Good. There is a line in Saint John that I like very much. It is Christ praying to the Father and He says: 'I do not pray that You take them out of the world, but that You keep them from evil.' Do you understand that?"

"I think so, Father."

"Then for your penance, say *alleluia* three times."

Next afternoon Janet and I took her boys crabbing. We had an ice chest of beer and we set it under the small pavilion at the center of the wharf, then I put out six crab lines, tying them to the guard rail. I remembered the summer before she got married Janet and I had gone crabbing, then cooked them for the family: we had a large pot of water on the stove and when the water was boiling I held the gunny sack of live crabs over it and they came falling out, splashing into the water; they worked their claws, moved sluggishly, then died. And Janet had said: *I keep waiting for them to scream.*

It was a hot day, up in the nineties. Someone was water-skiing on the lake, which was salt water and connected by canal to the Gulf, but we had the wharf to ourselves, and we drank beer in the shade while Paul and Lee did the crabbing. They lost the first couple, so I left the pavilion and squatted at the next line. The boys flanked me, lying on their bellies and looking down where the line went into the dark water; they had their shirts off, and their hot tan shoulders and arms brushed my legs. I gently pulled the line up until we saw a crab just below the surface, swimming and nibbling at the chunk of ham.

"Okay, Lee. Put the net down in the water, then bring it up under him so you don't knock him away."

He lowered the pole and scooped the net slowly under the crab.

"I got him!"

"That's it. You just have to go slow, that's all."

He stood and lifted the net and laid it on the wharf.

"Look how big," Paul said.

"He's a good one," I said. "Put him in the sack."

But they crouched over the net, watching the crab push his claws through.

"Poor little crab," Lee said. "You're going to die."

"Does it hurt 'em, Harry?" Paul said.

"I don't know."

"It'd hurt me," he said.

"I guess it does, for a second or two."

"How long's a second?" Lee said.

I pinched his arm.

"About like that."

"That's not too long," he said.

"No. Put him in the sack now, and catch some more."

I went back to my beer on the bench. Paul was still crouching over the crab, poking a finger at its back. Then Lee held open the gunny sack and Paul turned the net over and shook it and the crab fell in.

"Goodbye, big crab," he said.

"Goodbye, poor crab," Lee said.

They went to another line. For a couple of hours, talking to Janet, I watched them and listened to their bare feet on the wharf and their voices as they told each crab goodbye. Sometimes one of them would stop and look across the water and pull at his pecker, and I remembered that day hot as this one when I was sixteen and I wanted to cut mine off. I reached deep under the ice and got a cold beer for Janet and I thought of Yvonne sitting at that kitchen table at three in the morning, tired, her lipstick worn off, her eyes fixed on a space between the people in the room. Then I looked at the boys lying on their bellies and reaching down for another crab, and I hoped they would grow well, those strong little bodies, those kind hearts.

Starkey Flythe
Point of Conversion

MRS. CLEMENTSON HAD PREGNANT GIRLS BEFORE. Father Sheehan sent them mainly, but they'd come from the welfare agency too. Even from the WACs. The girls came, swelled for their months, weeping copiously about the men who'd done them wrong, laid their egg, then painted their faces to go out and do it all over again. But they left. That was the point. They left. Verna hadn't. After Verna's baby was born, and Mrs. Clementson, or Clemmie as everybody called her—the social tongue never saw fit to title her—stood masked in the delivery room and saw a bungling nurse carry the baby out the wrong door for adoption so that Verna, alert, insistent on natural childbirth, the exercises, the breathing, saw the baby, saw *her* baby and Godknowswhoelse's baby, saw it was a *boy* baby, saw that she would never see him again, and in sobs stayed with Mrs. Clementson.

Clemmie was glad at first. In this garden that she as an ex-public health nurse ran, where girls blew up and never grew up, Verna seemed to learn. Was hurt. Would do better. Clemmie was retired now. Sixty-five, on a pension, living in her grandmother's house, dead now, the grandmother and the house, a victorian draft with a roof like a salt shaker. But rooms. Rooms gone to bed. So that was how Father Sheehan got her into this. And they paid her for it, too. They, the church, the county, the state, the government. "Did you know that?" she said to Mary Murphy, her oldest friend, her roommate, her sounding box. "Did you know that the government—you and I—pay for the girl to have her baby? Then give her six weeks of post natal care? The WACs. Did you know that?" Mrs. Murphy, oldest and dearest, yawned. She had become a crank. Was not retired. Completely taken up with her job at the Veteran's Hospital. Smoked. Wore her hair in a tumble.

When time finally shrank Verna, Clemmie got her a job at a friend's office. Typing out statements. The Madonna Shop. Bills. Orders. The shop sold greeting cards, penny pictures of vapid Jesuses made in Italy to women who stuck them in books and forgot about them. Verna was not a Catholic. And that was the wonder. After all, it was to Father Sheehan she talked in the months of agony when she wondered why the boy she loved wouldn't marry her and be happy with the child she was going to give him. "You wouldn't want to marry him if he doesn't love you now, would you?" Father asked the girl in the back room while Clemmie washed supper dishes, and wondered why he didn't close the door, though knowing that he could never forget—and how could *she*—that she was a convert, hence some different sort of clay, clay that had to have it explained by open doors and commonplace chats over commonplace cups of coffee, that there were no secrets in the Church, no mysteries that she herself couldn't partake of. "I could tell you what they're like. *Men*. Use you like Kleenex, then toss you in the garbage." Her own experience was brief. Husband who drank. Divorce that didn't leak.

Verna went on weeping. But she wouldn't be Baptized. Wouldn't. Went to mass with Clemmie, Sunday, twice a week, sometimes more. Sat there in the pew. Knelt. Recited. But wouldn't come in. "Why in heaven's name?" asked Mary Murphy. "She only talks to Father Sheehan. Thinks he's wonderful, goes with you fifty times a week to mass. Why?" she yawned. Verna said sometimes "I know everybody thinks I'll get over this. But I won't. You don't know. I'll never, never get over it." Clemmie looked in a blue horse notebook she kept and read the names of fourteen girls she'd kept who had had illegitimate babies. "And you won't get over it," she thought. So Verna kept on with the greetings cards and penny pictures and helped out at the house which didn't make Clemmie mad since she'd taken in two old ladies who couldn't stand a rest home, and whose two nieces said, "Will you take them? Clemmie?" and Clemmie, seeing the nieces' chops water in anticipation of the estate, smiled and said, "Yes. Two hundred apiece." Anyone else she would have done free. She liked to take care of people, wait on them. "You should've been a waitress," Mary Murphy said. "I was," Clemmie came back. "A waitress with bed pans and enemas and specimens. A white winged waitress." "Talk yourself into paradise if you can," cranked Mrs. Murphy.

Verna was young. Never answered back. Ran errands. To the grocery. To the parish hall. To wherever in the world Clemmie wanted her to go. Lickety-split. Clemmie was deep into the Catholic family parish life. Nuns from Sacred Heart School came to supper. She had, almost, a brogue, from Father Sheehan, from Mrs. Murphy, from the brothers, the sisters, the fathers. An occasional monsignor. People even said—people who knew her when she was Scotch, when she was Presbyterian, when her father played the pipe organ at the First Presbyterian Church and her mother taught Sunday school, people who knew her before the conversion—the conversion of St. Clemmie, Mrs. Murphy called it, and after half a bottle of sherry had drawn it on the table cloth; Clemmie struck by light, Clemmie on her knees, stigmata spiking her hands, her tennis shoed feet, Father Sheehan holding the reins of her bike—people said, at parties, or any other place where Clemmie, on her bike, in her Nash Metropolitan, went, said, "Now, look at her. If she isn't the epitome of Irish Catholic potato famine, the *epitome.*" And Clemmie didn't mind because her potato-famine Irish friends were jolly and common-to-the-core and who, she herself included, wasn't? And unimportant—"Broken pieces of pottery and you wrote the name of some crook politico on it and if he got enough—out, and I could think of a few, the mayor included, I'd like to break pottery on"—being ostracized from the *non*-Irish didn't mean anything but being taken in by the Irish. Besides it was 1970 and nobody was anybody but out of the pot. "Everybody else her age has a pot. Except her. She's always pedaling off her pot on her bike. Other ladies peddle insurance but fair Clemmie pedals pot." (Mrs. Murphy on the subject.) And Verna didn't feel so alone if someone else was ostracized. Verna. A mother without a mother's child. But wouldn't she come in? If the haves threw you out, shouldn't you go in with the have nots? Anyway, not all of them were so have not. The O'Shaughnessys owned a liquor store—a chain of them and if the haves didn't think that made mon, and fun . . . Mrs. O'What's-her-name shot Mr. O'What's-his-name's lover—and him with eight children . . . as the lover descended the bus at the corner of Amiens and Roule Street in full view of Tabby O'Something else who clerked in Mr. O's booze store number 6, but who refused to testify at the trial saying he was under the counter when it happened though as everybody who's ever had so much a sip of Italian Swiss Colony knows, store number 6 is a glass box with no counter to speak of and that inside you can see everything that takes place in this world including the mating of an insect which Tabby had also noticed, Mr. O' and his lady love having rented a room in the building opposite number 6. And every Christmas, Easter and All Saints' Day, having been acquitted, Mr. O' sent his lawyer, and Tabby, a case of Dewar's scotch and if that wasn't mon and fun, what was?

Why Verna wouldn't come in, in to that cozy, chatty, warm-your-bones-by-the-fire-with-a-little-whisky Irish life, God only knew. But she wouldn't.

She was from a little town in east Tennessee, a teeny eenie iny town of 150 with a high school that graduated two. (Verna was voted most likely, the other girl most beautiful.) Well, naturally, she was suspicious, but not old enough to have any prejudices, especially old prejudices. Ate her breakfast eggs any kind of way.

Thursday, Clemmie pedaled to the Madonna Shop. Verna was out to lunch and her boss, Clemmie's old friend, said, "I'm going. Closing up shop and going. Pilgrimage. The holy land or Rome. Can't decide. Or maybe even Dublin." This with a wink and a slap on the rear, a conscious Irish manner which all of a sudden Clemmie found not quite so cutie pie as she had pictured it to Verna who was on the outside looking in.

Verna was out of a job. It was all right when she was working and bringing in something for her room and board and going out on errands and helping around the house that really needed help. Now she wasn't part of the hive—the economic part—she'd never picked up with the social part. "Maybe I use her," thought Clemmie. "Maybe she uses me. The uses of uses. Anyway, she ought to have something, something to do."

Verna's unemployed status made her sulk, made her consider any employment—going to the grocery store, the parish—a drudge. Clemmie sent her to the green grocer and Verna banged the cabbage and squash down on the kitchen table with the change. "Here, here, this won't do," Clemmie school-teachered. And Verna female-logiced right back. "Won't do? Well, count the change. It's all there. Look at the ticket if you think I took any of your money," and stormed out of the room.

Thursday a week, Clemmie heard the front door slam. Tears—she heard tears—Verna going through the living room, the parlor, the dining room, then into her own room. Another slam. More tears. Clemmie went to the front door. "Now why wouldn't she go straight down the hall to her room instead of zigzagging through every chamber in this heavenly mansion?" Following Verna's steps—her tears, she thought, but actually it was raining—she found a letter moireed with the water from Verna's eyes or the sky's—she picked it up and read—none of her business but after all she had examined penises in the public health service and if that wasn't business what was:

> My dearest darling V. My thoughts—and my prayers have been with you this last month. I praid your baby—(your baby! bracketed Clemmie) was safely delivered. You would have been a wonderful and devoted mother. (You.) Since leaving you and the Army, I have tried to build a new life for myself. Dad is happy with the progress I am making in college and thinks I can easily assume a position in his business when I graduate. But I am not kidding myself. I know it will be hard work. The whole thing has been very painful for me. (Painful. Oh I wish men could lay eggs.) But I believe everything has worked out for the better. Dad has given me a new car and this afternoon, I have been out driving around with a friend. We stopped by a hillside and just walked around for hours, doing nothing, just staring off into space. Perhaps you and I can go for a ride some day. Seattle is a long way for you to come, though, but who knows?
>
> May the Lord help you as he has helped me. I know you will soon forget me and if sometime in the far distant future our paths should cross, you would say, Who was that, I don't remember. But I will never forget.
>
> Yours very truly,
> R. B. H., Jr.

When Mary Murphy came home from work, Clemmie said, "Verna is in her room crying." "Well, I'll be in mine crying if I don't get these shoes off." "Well, what's wrong with you?" "Cement."

At supper, her feet reposing in red bunny slippers, Mrs. Murphy read the letter. Verna would not come out of her room. The old ladies—two hundred dollars—ate in theirs. "Why should she cry over that?" "I can't guess," Clemmie said. Sarcasm.

"Well, I'll tell you one thing. Every country has its type. In La Belle it's the aging French bébé, England's got the moustache, and we have the Dear John." "Her name's Verna." "Don't smart it. Just pour the sherry," Mary said. "All right."

Verna wept for R. B. H., Jr., her job, her baby. "Well, can you get her another job?" Clemmie asked. "Yes, if we don't get flooded out the front door."

The next day, Mary Murphy paddled down the hall to the source of Verna's tears and told the girl she had a job for her—temporary replacement in a doctor's office. Verna stopped weeping long enough to go to work. A week went by and she liked it. Breezed in and out. Clemmie mopped up the hall.

Before, Verna had walked to work. Or ridden Clemmie's bike. The Madonna Shop was only four blocks away. Now she had to drive. Clemmie lent her the Nash. Mary: "Is she careful?" Clemmie: "Is she timely? I've got to go to mass five minutes before she gets back."

A month she was on time. Then she wasn't. Clemmie, in hat and coat, temporally and spiritually prepared for the mass, was in flame. "Where have you been? Where! You know I'm late to mass already when you get here. Now it's too late, and here I am lending you *my* car." "*That* car!" Verna said. "Well, you can walk tomorrow, then." Clemmie took off her hat and coat, her armor of light. Verna went to her room. Clemmie put on her apron and started peeling potatoes. "Verna!" She called, "You get in here and peel these!" Verna came out and peeled them, her large clumsy fingers leaving in the eyes and gouging out most everything else.

Next day she walked to work, came home with two friends, two pregnant friends. "This is Louanne and Becky. They were in the WACs with me. Now the same thing's happened to them." She giggled. They went to Verna's room. Shut the door. Giggles. Clouds of smoke.

When Mary got there, they came out and were introduced. They were leaving anyway. They giggled. Rested their arms on their stomachs. "What's so funny? You think a pin'll make that go down? Do you?" They giggled harder, went out the front door, up the street, laughing to cry.

At 8:15, Mrs. Tonley, the regular nurse in the office where Verna worked, called. Mary knew her. They were chummy. "I've asked her," Mrs. Tonley said. "She won't give me an answer. August is my vacation, I can't leave the doctor with nobody. I want to know if Verna's going to stay. Or what."

"We thought she loved the job." "I think she does. I just want to know. About August."

In the doctor's office next day Mrs. Tonley said to Verna, "What I want to know is are you going to be here August? Or aren't you? All of it." "See, I really do like it here. You and Dr. Blake are real good to me. I put in for this government job at the Fort. Teaching. That's what I did in the WACs. I don't know if I'll get it. Then you know I get the G.I. Bill. But I'm saving that." "That's fine. Are you going to be here August? Else I've got to get somebody who will." "Well, see, teaching—like I was doing in the Army— it's all I really know how to do. I know what to teach them." "I bet you do," said Mrs. Tonley, and the doctor rang. Some patient couldn't get back into his clothes. Geriatrics.

Next day, Mrs. Tonley said, "Which, Verna? *Now*. Decide." "Oh, Mrs. Tonley . . . If they accept my application at the Fort, I'd have to go right out. They have a lot of girls in line for the job. . ." "Which, Verna. Now!" "If they don't take me out there, I won't have a job." "Verna. I want somebody here for August." "I don't know."

Mrs. Tonley called Mary that night. "Tell her not to come in tomorrow. I got somebody else. I never saw anything like that girl. Wouldn't *say*." "Don't blame me. She's none of mine. It's Clemmie brings home the strays around here." "How is Clemmie, anyway?" "She's all right. This'll give her something to do. Finding Verna a job." "Something *else*."

When informed, Verna cried. Clemmie said, "Dear God," rising to the occasion by breaking out in hives. She couldn't lie on her bed. Couldn't wear clothes. Wouldn't give in. "I've got something better to do." In a hospital gown—all she could wear—hives and all, her hands pinching the flaps together over her naked behind, Clemmie went out to the hospital. "Don't you have some course out here in Practical Nursing?" "Yes ma'am. But you're too old." "Well now, sonny, how old do you have to be?" "Eighteen and a high school graduate. September 5th." "Well, she's that." On the spot, hives stinging like so many wasps. Clemmie enrolled Verna, at least as far as she could, she not having Verna's thumb prints, birth certificate, high school diploma and a spare notary public.

Verna said No, she wouldn't go, wouldn't use her G.I. Bill, wouldn't. Said Clemmie could go herself if she wanted to go so bad. But, September 5th, she got her history together, got it notarized publicly, and went. Two weeks later, a boy brought her home. She was wearing a starched uniform, pink and white stripes. Smiling. "You look fairly pretty," Mary Murphy said.

The boy turned out to be a male nurse. Clemmie disapproved. "He hasn't got bat brains. And he's three years younger than she is." "Oh, what do *you* know about love?" snided Mary. Clemmie had given Verna back the car. Verna was later and later. Clemmie gave up mass. Sundays Verna worked part time in a nursing home. With him. "She could do *that* around here," Mary said. "I'm worried," Clemmie said. "What you need is some more pg girls. To distract you. . . . What's the moon doing tonight?" "Gibbous waning." "Nothing there."

One afternoon, Clemmie and Verna were out shopping. They rode by the First Baptist Church, biggest church in town. "That's where I'm going to be married." "It's a lovely church," Clemmie said vaguely, wistfully. Vague because she couldn't think what Verna meant, or if she meant anything; wistful, because her own church took up two hundred dollars every other Sunday while this Goliath raked in a national debt.

He came to supper that night. During dessert—floating island—Verna said to him, him who never identified himself on the phone, said Is Verna there? nothing else, ran through amber lights—Him, seventeen and a male nurse—"Tell her." As easily as asking for more dessert—which he did—he told them.

Clemmie gritted her teeth: "I'm not going to break out in hives. *Not.*" After he left, she went to Verna's room. "Is that what you want? Really want?" "We love each other," Verna said. "You've been through one junk-bunk already. This probably won't be any better, will it?" "This is going to make everything in my life all right. Everything I went through. We're going to have our own apartment, our own job, our own friends, our own baby, our own *car.*"

Clemmie went with her to the First Baptist where the preacher said it was fifty dollars for non-members to be married in his church which squelched that. And to the Key wholesalers where they bought dishes and stainless steel, and sheets. . . . And what else does a man need to live by? Clemmie tried to remember.

Verna found another Baptist church—it was called either the Third Baptist Church or the Fourth Baptist Church. Mrs. Murphy didn't bother to say, "What about Father Sheehan?" Verna and her boy wondered whether to wait till their year course was up. Clemmie said, "Yes. Do. You'd better." They decided not to.

"What is it?" Clemmie demanded of Mary Murphy. "What don't we do right? I tried. I did for her . . . she can't deny that. Her parents wouldn't let her in the house. I let her. Maybe it's the generation gap." "Generation gap? I should hope so. One of those 'youths' tries to get familiar with me, I'll break its . . ." "No, I meant, maybe *we* can't talk to *them.*" "It's them can't talk to us. Mouths all stuffed up with bubble gum." "Oh, Mary. Sometimes you're a comfort," Clemmie changed gear to a snicker, "and sometimes you're not." "Has she told him?" Mary asked. "What?" "About the baby, the po' lil' unwanted baby. 'It was just a *little* baby, your honor.'" "Oh, dear God, Mary. It's not so funny. No. She hasn't told him." "Well, don't you think she oughter?" "She says he won't marry her if he knows." "Won't he find out? On the wedding night?" "She's going to a gynecologist." "A gynecologist!" "Yes, she says he can make her like she was before. . . . Like a virgin." "You get the name of that doctor, I'll have one of those."

When the male nurse kissed Verna good night in the hall, Clemmie, sitting up late with the Annals of Good St. Anne de Beaupré, saw them, thought, "What a pretty thing. Their kiss. Teeth hidden. Muted lips. Breathless wonder." He left her, lips first; last, the hands. As he left, Verna said, curiously, Clemmie thought, "Immersion?" "Total immersion," he said. Clemmie imagined, "Love. Totally immersed in love."

It was baptism they were speaking of, though. The following morning Rev. Reold called. "We are happy to have a new soul." "Who wouldn't be, brother?" thought Clemmie, fundamentalist emerging. "Happy with a new soul for our body, the church. Please tell the applicant to bring a large towel and a change of dry underwear." "She wouldn't bring wet, now would she," and Clemmie, the receiver safely down, Mary's personality drenching her.

Clemmie got it all together and at six she and Mary stood behind the altar in the Fourth Baptist Church and watched Verna in a white robe walk down into the water. Then in the robing room they dried her and saw her without makeup, naked, saw how plain she was, how young, how forlorn.

The next day they were married. Clemmie and Mary stood on the steps of the church, the prefabricated church, stark and new. ("Thank God for all our *papier maché*," confided Mary, hatted and respectable for the occasion) as Verna and her male nurse dashed for the Nash in a thin shower of rice given up by the two pregnant friends and Clemmie and Mary as far as their bursitised arms allowed. Clemmie thought of them driving—that was her wedding present, the car—driving, driving God knows where, God knows to what motel, driving, the insects, drawn by the lights, splattering against the windshield, and she felt a terrible sense of failure, terrible.

Philip Roth
The Conversion
of the Jews

"YOU'RE A REAL ONE FOR OPENING YOUR MOUTH in the first place," Itzie said. "What do you open your mouth all the time for?"

"I didn't bring it up, Itz, I didn't," Ozzie said.

"What do you care about Jesus Christ for anyway?"

"I didn't bring up Jesus Christ. He did. I didn't even know what he was talking about. Jesus is historical, he kept saying. Jesus is historical." Ozzie mimicked the monumental voice of Rabbi Binder.

"Jesus was a person that lived like you and me," Ozzie continued. "That's what Binder said—"

"Yeah? . . . So what! What do I give two cents whether he lived or not. And what do you gotta open your mouth!" Itzie Lieberman favored closed-mouthedness, especially when it came to Ozzie Freedman's questions. Mrs. Freedman had to see Rabbi Binder twice before about Ozzie's questions and this Wednesday at four-thirty would be the third time. Itzie preferred to keep *his* mother in the kitchen; he settled for behind-the-back subtleties such as gestures, faces, snarls and other less delicate barnyard noises.

"He was a real person, Jesus, but he wasn't like God, and we don't believe he is God." Slowly, Ozzie was explaining Rabbi Binder's position to Itzie, who had been absent from Hebrew School the previous afternoon.

"The Catholics," Itzie said helpfully, "they believe in Jesus Christ, that he's God." Itzie Lieberman used "the Catholics" in its broadest sense—to include the Protestants.

Ozzie received Itzie's remark with a tiny head bob, as though it were a footnote, and went on. "His mother was Mary, and his father probably was Joseph," Ozzie said. "But the New Testament says his real father was God."

"His *real* father?"

"Yeah," Ozzie said, "that's the big thing, his father's supposed to be God."

"Bull."

"That's what Rabbi Binder says, that it's impossible—"

"Sure it's impossible. That stuff's all bull. To have a baby you gotta get laid," Itzie theologized. "Mary hadda get laid."

"That's what Binder says: 'The only way a woman can have a baby is to have intercourse with a man.'"

"He said *that*, Ozz?" For a moment it appeared that Itzie had put the theological question aside. "He said that, intercourse?" A little curled smile shaped itself in the lower half of Itzie's face like a pink mustache. "What you guys do, Ozz, you laugh or something?"

"I raised my hand."

"Yeah? Whatja say?"

"That's when I asked the question."

Itzie's face lit up. "Whatja ask about—intercourse?"

"No, I asked the question about God, how if He could create the heaven and earth in six days, and make all the animals and the fish and the light in six days—the light especially, that's what always gets me, that He could make the light. Making fish and animals, that's pretty good—"

"That's damn good." Itzie's appreciation was honest but unimaginative: it was as though God had just pitched a one-hitter.

"But making light . . . I mean when you think about it, it's really something," Ozzie said. "Anyway, I asked Binder if He could make all that in six days, and He could *pick* the six days He wanted right out of nowhere, why couldn't He let a woman have a baby without having intercourse."

"You said intercourse, Ozz, to Binder?"

"Yeah."

"Right in class?"

"Yeah."

Itzie smacked the side of his head.

"I mean, no kidding around," Ozzie said, "that'd really be nothing. After all that other stuff, that'd practically be nothing."

Itzie considered a moment. "What'd Binder say?"

"He started all over again explaining how Jesus was historical and how he lived like you and me but he wasn't God. So I said I under*stood* that. What I wanted to know was different."

What Ozzie wanted to know was always different. The first time he had wanted to know how Rabbi Binder could call the Jews "The Chosen People" if the Declaration of Independence claimed all men to be created equal. Rabbi Binder tried to distinguish for him between political equality and spiritual legitimacy, but what Ozzie wanted to know, he insisted vehemently, was different. That was the first time his mother had to come.

Then there was the plane crash. Fifty-eight people had been killed in a plane crash at La Guardia. In studying a casualty list in the newspaper his mother had discovered among the list of those dead eight Jewish names (his grandmother had nine but she counted Miller as a Jewish name); because of the eight she said the plane crash was "a tragedy." During free-discussion time on Wednesday Ozzie had brought to Rabbi Binder's attention this matter of "some of his relations" always picking out the Jewish names. Rabbi Binder had begun to explain cultural unity and some other things when Ozzie stood up at his seat and said that what he wanted to know was different. Rabbi Binder insisted that he sit down and it was then that Ozzie shouted that he wished all fifty-eight were Jews. That was the second time his mother came.

"And he kept explaining about Jesus being historical, and so I kept asking him. No kidding, Itz, he was trying to make me look stupid."

"So what he finally do?"

"Finally he starts screaming that I was deliberately simple-minded and a wise guy, and that my mother had to come, and this was the last time. And that I'd never get bar-mitzvahed if he could help it. Then, Itz, then he starts talking in that voice like a statue, real slow and deep, and he says that I better think over what I said about the Lord. He told me to go to his office and think it over." Ozzie leaned his body towards Itzie. "Itz, I thought it over for a solid hour, and now I'm convinced God could do it."

Ozzie had planned to confess his latest transgression to his mother as soon as she came home from work. But it was a Friday night in November and already dark, and when Mrs. Freedman came through the door she tossed off her coat, kissed Ozzie quickly on the face, and went to the kitchen table to light the three yellow candles, two for the Sabbath and one for Ozzie's father.

When his mother lit the candles she would move her two arms slowly towards her, dragging them through the air, as though persuading people whose minds were half made up. And her eyes would get glassy with tears. Even when his father was alive Ozzie remembered that her eyes had gotten glassy, so it didn't have anything to do with his dying. It had something to do with lighting the candles.

As she touched the flaming match to the unlit wick of a Sabbath candle, the phone rang, and Ozzie, standing only a foot from it, plucked it off the receiver and held it muffled to his chest. When his mother lit candles Ozzie felt there should be no noise; even breathing, if you could manage it, should be softened. Ozzie pressed the phone to his breast and watched his mother dragging whatever she was dragging, and he felt his own eyes get glassy. His mother was a round, tired, gray-haired penguin of a woman whose gray skin had begun to feel the tug of gravity and the weight of her own history. Even when she was dressed up she didn't look like a chosen person. But when she lit candles she looked like something better; like a woman who knew momentarily that God could do anything.

After a few mysterious minutes she was finished. Ozzie hung up the phone and walked to the kitchen table where she was beginning to lay the two places for the four-course Sabbath meal. He told her that she would have to see Rabbi Binder next Wednesday at four-thirty, and then he told her why. For the first time in their life together she hit Ozzie across the face with her hand.

All through the chopped liver and chicken soup part of the dinner Ozzie cried; he didn't have any appetite for the rest.

On Wednesday, in the largest of the three basement classrooms of the synagogue, Rabbi Marvin Binder, a tall, handsome, broad-shouldered man of thirty with thick strong-fibered black hair, removed his watch from his pocket and saw that it was four o'clock. At the rear of the room Yakov Blotnik, the seventy-one-year-old custodian, slowly polished the large window, mumbling to himself, unaware that it was four o'clock or six o'clock, Monday or Wednesday. To most of the students Yakov Blotnik's mumbling, along with his brown curly beard, scythe nose, and two heel-trailing black cats, made of him an object of wonder, a foreigner, a relic, towards whom they were alternately fearful and disrespectful. To Ozzie the mumbling had always seemed a monotonous, curious prayer; what made it curious was that old Blotnik had been mumbling so steadily for so many years, Ozzie suspected he had memorized the prayers and forgotten all about God.

"It is now free-discussion time," Rabbi Binder said. "Feel free to talk about any Jewish matter at all—religion, family, politics, sports—"

There was silence. It was a gusty, clouded November afternoon and it did not seem as though there ever was or could be a thing called baseball. So nobody this week said a word about that hero from the past, Hank Greenberg—which limited free discussion considerably.

And the soul-battering Ozzie Freedman had just received from Rabbi Binder had imposed its limitation. When it was Ozzie's turn to read aloud from the Hebrew book the rabbi had asked him petulantly why he didn't read more rapidly. He was showing no progress. Ozzie said he could read faster but that if he did he was sure not to understand what he was reading. Nevertheless, at the rabbi's repeated suggestion Ozzie tried, and showed a great talent, but in the midst of a long passage he stopped short and said he didn't understand a word he was reading, and started in again at a drag-footed pace. Then came the soul-battering.

Consequently when free-discussion time rolled around none of the students felt too free. The rabbi's invitation was answered only by the mumbling of feeble old Blotnik.

"Isn't there anything at all you would like to discuss?" Rabbi Binder asked again, looking at his watch. "No questions or comments?"

There was a small grumble from the third row. The rabbi requested that Ozzie rise and give the rest of the class the advantage of his thought.

Ozzie rose. "I forget it now," he said, and sat down in his place.

Rabbi Binder advanced a seat towards Ozzie and poised himself on the edge of the desk. It was Itzie's desk and the rabbi's frame only a dagger's-length away from his face snapped him to sitting attention.

"Stand up again, Oscar," Rabbi Binder said calmly, "and try to assemble your thoughts."

Ozzie stood up. All his classmates turned in their seats and watched as he gave an unconvincing scratch to his forehead.

"I can't assemble any," he announced, and plunked himself down.

"Stand up!" Rabbi Binder advanced from Itzie's desk to the one directly in front of Ozzie; when the rabbinical back was turned Itzie gave it five-fingers off the tip of his nose, causing a small titter in the room. Rabbi Binder was too absorbed in squelching Ozzie's nonsense once and for all to bother with titters. "Stand up, Oscar. What's your question about?"

Ozzie pulled a word out of the air. It was the handiest word. "Religion."

"Oh, now you remember?"

"Yes."

"What is it?"

Trapped, Ozzie blurted the first thing that came to him. "Why can't He make anything He wants to make!"

As Rabbi Binder prepared an answer, a final answer, Itzie, ten feet behind him, raised one finger on his left hand, gestured it meaningfully towards the rabbi's back, and brought the house down.

Binder twisted quickly to see what had happened and in the midst of the commotion Ozzie shouted into the rabbi's back what he couldn't have shouted to his face. It was a loud, toneless sound that had the timbre of something stored inside for about six days.

"You don't know! You don't know anything about God!"

The rabbi spun back towards Ozzie. "What?"

"You don't know—you don't—"

"Apologize, Oscar, apologize!" It was a threat.

"You don't—"

Rabbi Binder's hand flicked out at Ozzie's cheek. Perhaps it had only been meant to clamp the boy's mouth shut, but Ozzie ducked and the palm caught him squarely on the nose.

The blood came in a short, red spurt on to Ozzie's shirt front.

The next moment was all confusion. Ozzie screamed, "You bastard, you bastard!" and broke for the classroom door. Rabbi Binder lurched a step backwards, as though his own blood had started flowing violently in the opposite direction, then gave a clumsy lurch forward and bolted out the door after Ozzie. The class followed after the rabbi's huge blue-suited back, and before old Blotnik could turn from his window, the room was empty and everyone was headed full speed up the three flights leading to the roof.

If one should compare the light of day to the life of man: sunrise to birth; sunset—the dropping down over the edge—to death; then as Ozzie Freedman wiggled through the trapdoor of the synagogue roof, his feet kicking backwards bronco-style at Rabbi Binder's outstretched arms—at that moment the day was fifty years old. As a rule, fifty or fifty-five reflects accurately the age of late afternoons in November, for it is in that month, during those hours, that one's awareness of light seems no longer a matter of seeing, but of hearing: light begins clicking away. In fact, as Ozzie locked shut the trapdoor in the rabbi's face, the sharp click of the bolt into the lock might momentarily have been mistaken for the sound of the heavier gray that had just throbbed through the sky.

With all his weight Ozzie kneeled on the locked door; any instant he was certain that Rabbi Binder's shoulder would fling it open, splintering the wood into shrapnel and catapulting his body into the sky. But the door did not move and below him he heard only the rumble of feet, first loud then dim, like thunder rolling away.

A question shot through his brain. "Can this be *me?*" For a thirteen-year-old who had just labeled his religious leader a bastard, twice, it was not an improper question. Louder and louder the question came to him—"Is it me? Is it me?"—until he discovered himself no longer kneeling, but racing crazily towards the edge of the roof, his eyes crying, his throat screaming, and his arms flying everywhichway as though not his own.

"Is it me? Is it me ME ME ME ME! It has to be me—but is it!"

It is the question a thief must ask himself the night he jimmies open his first window, and it is said to be the question with which bridegrooms quiz themselves before the altar.

In the few wild seconds it took Ozzie's body to propel him to the edge of the roof, his self-examination began to grow fuzzy. Gazing down at the street, he became confused as to the problem beneath the question: was it, is-it-me-who-called-Binder-a-bastard? or, is-it-me-prancing-around-on-the-roof? However, the scene below settled all, for there is an instant in any action when whether it is you or somebody else is academic. The thief crams the money in his pockets and scoots out the window. The bridegroom signs the hotel register for two. And the boy on the roof finds a streetful of people gaping at him, necks stretched backwards, faces up, as though he were the ceiling of the Hayden Planetarium. Suddenly you know it's you.

"Oscar! Oscar Freedman!" A voice rose from the center of the crowd, a voice that, could it have been seen, would have looked like the writing on scroll. "Oscar Freedman, get down from there. Immediately!" Rabbi Binder was pointing one arm stiffly up at him; and at the end of that arm, one finger aimed menacingly. It was the attitude of a dictator, but one—the eyes confessed all—whose personal valet had spit neatly in his face.

Ozzie didn't answer. Only for a blink's length did he look towards Rabbi Binder. Instead his eyes began to fit together the world beneath him, to sort out people from places, friends from enemies, participants from spectators. In little jagged starlike clusters his friends stood around Rabbi Binder, who was still pointing. The topmost point on a star compounded not of angels but of five adolescent boys was Itzie. What a world it was, with those stars below, Rabbi Binder below . . . Ozzie, who a moment earlier hadn't been able to control his own body, started to feel the meaning of the word control: he felt Peace and he felt Power.

"Oscar Freedman, I'll give you three to come down."

Few dictators give their subjects three to do anything; but, as always, Rabbi Binder only looked dictatorial.

"Are you ready, Oscar?"

Ozzie nodded his head yes, although he had no intention in the world—the lower one or the celestial one he'd just entered—of coming down even if Rabbi Binder should give him a million.

"All right then," said Rabbi Binder. He ran a hand through his black Samson hair as though it were the gesture prescribed for uttering the first digit. Then, with his other hand cutting a circle out of the small piece of sky around him, he spoke. "One!"

There was no thunder. On the contrary, at that moment, as though "one" was the cue for which he had been waiting, the world's least thunderous person appeared on the synagogue steps. He did not so much come out the synagogue door as lean out, onto the darkening air. He clutched at the doorknob with one hand and looked up at the roof.

"Oy!"

Yakov Blotnik's old mind hobbled slowly, as if on crutches, and though he couldn't decide precisely what the boy was doing on the roof, he knew it wasn't good—that is, it wasn't-good-for-the-Jews. For Yakov Blotnik life had fractionated itself simply: things were either good-for-the-Jews or no-good-for-the-Jews.

He smacked his free hand to his in-sucked cheek, gently. "Oy, Gut!" And then quickly as he was able, he jacked down his head and surveyed the street. There was Rabbi Binder (like a man at an auction with only three dollars in his pocket, he had just delivered a shaky "Two!"); there were the students, and that was all. So far it-wasn't-so-bad-for-the-Jews. But the boy had to come down immediately, before anybody saw. The problem: how to get the boy off the roof?

Anybody who has ever had a cat on the roof knows how to get him down. You call the fire department. Or first you call the operator and you ask her for the fire department. And the next thing there is great jamming of brakes and clanging of bells and shouting of instructions. And then the cat is off the roof. You do the same thing to get a boy off the roof.

That is, you do the same thing if you are Yakov Blotnik and you once had a cat on the roof.

When the engines, all four of them, arrived, Rabbi Binder had four times given Ozzie the count of three. The big hook-and-ladder swung around the corner and one of the firemen leaped from it, plunging headlong towards the yellow fire hydrant in front of the synagogue. With a huge wrench he began to unscrew the top nozzle. Rabbi Binder raced over to him and pulled at his shoulder.

"There's no fire . . ."

The fireman mumbled back over his shoulder and, heatedly, continued working at the nozzle.

"But there's no fire, there's no fire . . ." Binder shouted. When the fireman mumbled again, the rabbi grasped his face with both his hands and pointed it up at the roof.

To Ozzie it looked as though Rabbi Binder was trying to tug the fireman's head out of his body, like a cork from a bottle. He had to giggle at the picture they made: it was a family portrait—rabbi in black skullcap, fireman in red fire hat, and the little yellow hydrant squatting beside like a kid brother, bareheaded. From the edge of the roof Ozzie waved at the portrait, a one-handed, flapping, mocking wave; in doing it his right foot slipped from under him. Rabbi Binder covered his eyes with his hands.

Firemen work fast. Before Ozzie had even regained his balance, a big, round yellowed net was being held on the synagogue lawn. The firemen who held it looked up at Ozzie with stern, feelingless faces.

One of the firemen turned his head towards Rabbi Binder. "What, is the kid nuts or something?"

Rabbi Binder unpeeled his hands from his eyes, slowly, painfully, as if they were tape. Then he checked: nothing on the sidewalk, no dents in the net.

"Is he gonna jump, or what?" the fireman shouted.

In a voice not at all like a statue, Rabbi Binder finally answered. "Yes, yes, I think so . . . He's been threatening to . . ."

Threatening to? Why, the reason he was on the roof, Ozzie remembered, was to get away; he hadn't even thought about jumping. He had just run to get away, and the truth was that he hadn't really headed for the roof as much as he'd been chased there.

"What's his name, the kid?"

"Freedman," Rabbi Binder answered. "Oscar Freedman."

The fireman looked up a Ozzie. "What is it with you, Oscar? You gonna jump, or what?"

Ozzie did not answer. Frankly, the question had just arisen.

"Look, Oscar, if you're gonna jump, jump—and if you're not gonna jump, don't jump. But don't waste our time, willya?"

Ozzie looked at the fireman and then at Rabbi Binder. He wanted to see Rabbi Binder cover his eyes one more time.

"I'm going to jump."

And then he scampered around the edge of the roof to the corner, where there was no net below, and he flapped his arms at his sides, swishing the air and smacking his palms to his trousers on the downbeat. He began screaming like some kind of engine, "Wheeeee . . . wheeeeee," and leaning way out over the edge with the upper half of his body. The firemen whipped around to cover the ground with the net. Rabbi Binder mumbled a few words to Somebody and covered his eyes. Everything happened quickly, jerkily, as in a silent movie. The crowd, which had arrived with the fire engines, gave out a long, Fourth-of-July fireworks oooh-aahhh. In the excitement no one had paid the crowd much heed, except, of course, Yakov Blotnik, who swung from the doorknob counting heads. "Fier und tsvansik . . . finf und tsvantsik . . . Oy, Gut!" It wasn't like this with the cat.

Rabbi Binder peeked through his fingers, checked the sidewalk and net. Empty. But there was Ozzie racing to the other corner. The firemen raced with him but were unable to keep up. Whenever Ozzie wanted to he might jump and splatter himself upon the sidewalk, and by the time the firemen scooted to the spot all they could do with their net would be to cover the mess.

"Wheeeee . . . wheeeee . . ."

"Hey, Oscar," the winded fireman yelled, "What the hell is this, a game or something?"

"Wheeeee . . . wheeeee . . ."

"Hey, Oscar—"

But he was off now to the other corner, flapping his wings fiercely. Rabbi Binder couldn't take it any longer—the fire engines from nowhere, the screaming suicidal boy, the net. He fell to his knees, exhausted, and with his hands curled together in front of his chest like a little dome, he pleaded, "Oscar, stop it, Oscar. Don't jump, Oscar. Please come down . . . Please don't jump."

And further back in the crowd a single voice, a single young voice, shouted a lone word to the boy on the roof.

"Jump!"

It was Itzie. Ozzie momentarily stopped flapping.

"Go ahead, Ozz—jump!" Itzie broke off his point of the star and courageously, with the inspiration not of a wise-guy but of a disciple, stood alone. "Jump, Ozz, jump!"

Still on his knees, his hands still curled, Rabbi Binder twisted his body back. He looked at Itzie, then, agonizingly, back to Ozzie.

"OSCAR, DON'T JUMP! PLEASE, DON'T JUMP . . . please please . . ."

"Jump!" This time it wasn't Itzie but another point of the star. By the time Mrs. Freedman arrived to keep her four-thirty appointment with Rabbi Binder, the whole little upside down heaven was shouting and pleading for Ozzie to jump, and Rabbi Binder no longer was pleading with him not to jump, but was crying into the dome of his hands.

Understandably Mrs. Freedman couldn't figure out what her son was doing on the roof. So she asked.

"Ozzie, my Ozzie, what are you doing? My Ozzie, what is it?"

Ozzie stopped wheeeeeing and slowed his arms down to a cruising flap, the kind birds use in soft winds, but he did not answer. He stood against the low, clouded, darkening sky—light clicked down swiftly now, as on a small gear—flapping softly and gazing down at the small bundle of a woman who was his mother.

"What are you doing, Ozzie?" She turned towards the kneeling Rabbi Binder and rushed so close that only a paper-thickness of dusk lay between her stomach and his shoulders.

"What is my baby doing?"

Rabbi Binder gaped up at her but he too was mute. All that moved was the dome of his hands; it shook back and forth like a weak pulse.

"Rabbi, get him down! He'll kill himself. Get him down, my only baby . . ."

"I can't" Rabbi Binder said, "I can't . . ." and he turned his handsome head towards the crowd of boys behind him. "It's them. Listen to them."

And for the first time Mrs. Freedman saw the crowd of boys, and she heard what they were yelling.

"He's doing it for them. He won't listen to me. It's them." Rabbi Binder spoke like one in a trance.

"For them?"

"Yes."

"Why for them?"

"They want him to . . ."

Mrs. Freedman raised her two arms upward as though she were conducting the sky. "For them he's doing it!" And then in a gesture older than pyramids, older than prophets and floods, her arms came slapping down to her sides. "A martyr I have. Look!" She tilted her head to the roof. Ozzie was still flapping softly. "My martyr."

"Oscar, come down, *please*," Rabbi Binder groaned.

In a startlingly even voice Mrs. Freedman called to the boy on the roof. "Ozzie, come down, Ozzie. Don't be a martyr, my baby."

As though it were a litany, Rabbi Binder repeated her words. "Don't be a martyr, my baby. Don't be a martyr."

"Gawhead, Ozz—*be* a Martin!" It was Itzie. "Be a Martin, be a Martin," and all the voices joined in singing for Martindom, whatever *it* was. "Be a Martin, be a Martin . . ."

Somehow when you're on a roof the darker it gets the less you can hear. All Ozzie knew was that two groups wanted two new things: his friends were spirited and musical about what they wanted; his mother and the rabbi were even-toned, chanting, about what they didn't want. The rabbi's voice was without tears now and so was his mother's.

The big net stared up at Ozzie like a sightless eye. The big, clouded sky pushed down. From beneath it looked like a gray corrugated board. Suddenly, looking up into that unsympathetic sky, Ozzie realized all the strangeness of what these people, his friends, were asking: they wanted him to jump, to kill himself; they were singing about it now—it made them that happy. And there was an even greater strangeness: Rabbi Binder was on his knees, trembling. If there was a question to be asked now it was not "Is it me?" but rather "Is it us? . . . Is it us?"

Being on the roof, it turned out, was a serious thing. If he jumped would the singing become dancing? Would it? What would jumping stop? Yearningly, Ozzie wished he could rip open the sky, plunge his hands through, and pull out the sun; and on the sun, like a coin, would be stamped JUMP or DON'T JUMP.

Ozzie's knees rocked and sagged a little under him as though they were setting him for a dive. His arms tightened, stiffened, froze, from shoulders to fingernails. He felt as if each part of his body were going to vote as to whether he should kill himself or not—and each part as though it were independent of *him*.

The light took an unexpected click down and the new darkness, like a gag, hushed the friends singing for this and the mother and rabbi chanting for that.

Ozzie stopped counting votes, and in a curiously high voice, like one who wasn't prepared for speech, he spoke.

"Mamma?"

"Yes, Oscar."

"Mamma, get down on your knees, like Rabbi Binder."

"Oscar—"

"Get down on your knees," he said, "or I'll jump."

Ozzie heard a whimper, then a quick rustling, and when he looked down where his mother had stood he saw the top of a head and beneath that a circle of dress. She was kneeling beside Rabbi Binder.

He spoke again. "Everybody kneel." There was the sound of everybody kneeling.

Ozzie looked around. With one hand he pointed toward the synagogue entrance. "Make *him* kneel."

There was a noise, not of kneeling, but of body-and-cloth stretching. Ozzie could hear Rabbi Binder saying in a gruff whisper, ". . . or he'll *kill* himself," and when next he looked there was Yakov Blotnik off the doorknob and for the first time in his life upon his knees in the Gentile posture of prayer.

As for the firemen—it is not as difficult as one might imagine to hold a net taut while you are kneeling.

Ozzie looked around again; and then he called to Rabbi Binder.

"Rabbi?"

"Yes, Oscar."

"Rabbi Binder, do you believe in God?"

"Yes."

"Do you believe God can do Anything?" Ozzie leaned his head out into the darkness. "Anything?"

"Oscar, I think—"

"Tell me you believe God can do Anything."

There was a second's hesitation. Then: "God can do Anything."

"Tell me you believe God can make a child without intercourse."

"He can."

"Tell me!"

"God," Rabbi Binder admitted, "can make a child without intercourse."

"Mamma, you tell me."

"God can make a child without intercourse," his mother said.

"Make *him* tell me." There was no doubt who *him* was.

In a few moments Ozzie heard an old comical voice say something to the increasing darkness about God.

Next, Ozzie made everybody say it. And then he made them all say they believed in Jesus Christ—first one at a time, then all together.

When the catechizing was through it was the beginning of evening. From the street it sounded as if the boy on the roof might have sighed.

"Ozzie?" A woman's voice dared to speak. "You'll come down now?"

There was no answer, but the woman waited, and when a voice finally did speak it was thin and crying, and exhausted as that of an old man who had just finished pulling the bells.

"Mamma, don't you see—you shouldn't hit me. He shouldn't hit me. You shouldn't hit me about God, Mamma. You should never hit anybody about God—"

"Ozzie, please come down now."

"Promise me, promise me you'll never hit anybody about God."

He had asked only his mother, but for some reason everyone kneeling in the street promised he would never hit anybody about God.

Once again there was silence.

"I can come down now, Mamma," the boy on the roof finally said. He turned his head both ways as though checking the traffic lights. "Now I can come down . . ."

And he did, right into the center of the yellow net that glowed in the evening's edge like an overgrown halo.

7
Initiation and Identity

LIFE IS A SERIES OF TRANSITIONS from one stage of human development to another. Birth, puberty, becoming an adult, marriage, and death are traditionally accompanied by rites of passage that are similar in nature across cultures. Arnold Van Gennep's *The Rites of Passage* describes the archetypal pattern of initiation—most explicitly practiced today in preliterate cultures. In order for adolescents to become full-fledged adults, they must experience three stages in their transition. In the first, "separation," a symbolic death must occur that forces the initiates to leave behind them all their former habits, acquaintances, and associations; it is, quite simply, the death of childhood. The "transition," the second stage, requires that the initiates be severely tested physically, spiritually, and emotionally while at the same time being instructed in the customs of their society. For the initiation to be effective it must be performed by the older members of the community, who have the maturity and knowledge necessary for trans-forming children into adults. The length of the transition varies from culture to culture. It can be as short as a few days or as long as the better part of a year, depending primarily on the economic status of the society; those societies that are more affluent can afford the luxury of a longer and more elaborate ceremony. The last stage, "incorporation," is reserved for initiates who have successfully completed the first two stages and is marked by a public ceremony welcoming them into the ranks of adults. In preliterate societies these stages are more clearly expressed and ritualized than in highly technological societies, and it should be noted that though all the stages are necessary for a valid initiation, no two cultures emphasize them in the same way.[1]

In more technologically advanced societies, adulthood is not conferred on adolescents in a single ceremony. Nevertheless, rites still exist that at one time had that purpose. Two that are practiced today and should be mentioned are confirmation and the bar mitzvah, which signal a coming of age in certain religious communities, yet do not confer an adult status that carries over into secular life. Social scientists have observed that there is little formal guidance today for adolescents in learning the ways of adults, nor are there any rites for recognizing the physiological, psychological, or sociological changes that indicate the end of adolescence and the beginning of adulthood. Today's adolescents are faced with the dilemma of not knowing when they have reached maturity. Usually a cumulative series of incidents over a period of time subtly constitutes an informal rite of passage. Killing an animal, taking a long journey, first coitus, a dangerous act performed are but a few of the tests an adolescent may experience; yet, quite often there is a single experience that is more keenly felt than the others, one that precipitates an awareness of one's adult status. The absence of a formal rite of passage ceremony necessitates a longer and more uncertain transition, with much unguided groping, as adolescents try not only to establish their new adulthood but also their identity.

The primary question to be answered by adolescents is "Who am I?" and the journey to adulthood is basically a quest for an answer. Identity can be established in a number of ways. Well-adjusted older adolescents and young adults form a conception of themselves that is in keeping with a realistic assessment of their physical, emotional, social, and intellectual development, as well as life experiences. They are able to define themselves honestly in light of their strengths and weaknesses. For the most part they are emotionally and economically free from the constraints of their parents and independent in their actions. They are preparing for some occupation or profession and are or will soon be able to answer the question that is asked most often when people are first getting acquainted: "What do you do for a living?" Of course, identity goes well beyond the type of job people hold, but in American society today probably no other factor is as important in initially defining people. Also, by early adulthood, well-adjusted adolescents have developed a personality that sets them apart from other individuals. They feel unique.

"The Law" combines two types of initiation story. One type concerns adolescents imposing on themselves a difficult task, and the other considers their being required by adult society to participate in a formal ceremony. Danny, a very bad stutterer, insists that he give a speech during his bar mitzvah, even though he doesn't have to. Danny's decision is brave indeed considering how poorly he speaks: "He had a habit of closing his eyes as

1. Arnold Van Gennep, *The Rites of Passage.* Translated by Monika B. Vizedom and Gabrielle L. Caffee (Chicago: The University of Chicago Press, 1960), pp. vii, 10–11.

though he'd been told to visualize the word beforehand. It was agonizing to watch: the shut eyes, the deep breath, the pulsing beat in his neck, the chin jerking spasmodically, and spit gathering in the corners of his mouth." Danny believes that if he prays hard enough, his speech impediment will disappear. Sadly, it does not. During the ceremony he looks down on the crowd in the synagogue and makes up his mind "to assume the burden of what the reiteration of the Law of his Fathers had demanded from the first." Danny comes of age when he realizes that his speech defect is permanent and must be lived with. The bar mitzvah signals his formal initiation as an adult within his religious community, but it is confronting the chore of public speech-making that teaches Danny his most important lesson.

"Phineas," like "The Law," also deals with adolescents overcoming their fear to perform some demanding, self-imposed task. The stories differ because in the first the ritualized setting of the initiation is determined by established tradition and under the sponsorship of adults, whereas in the second the initiation (which consists of jumping from a tall tree into a river) is newly created and directed by a group of adolescents. The leap in "Phineas," which is required in order to become a member of the Super Suicide Society of the Summer Session at Devon preparatory school, ultimately cripples Finny. He is jounced from a limb by Gene, his friend, and plummets to the ground. In both "The Law" and "Phineas" the results of the initiatory experiences are similar. Although Danny's stutter remains and Finny's leg is permanently crippled, both begin to accept these disabilities as undeniable conditions of their lives. In stories where the initiation is sponsored by adolescents and some daredevil act is required, the initiates often overestimate their abilities and tragedy results. When adults are sponsors, this hardly ever happens.

The most written-about adolescent rite of passage concerns first sexual intercourse. "Barred" (section 1) represents a type of story, now out of vogue, in which adolescents lose their virginity to prostitutes. A predominant fictional pattern describes the mood of exhilarated anticipation on the part of these adolescents quickly giving way to despondency and guilt because of the loveless nature of their experiences. Stories of this nature are presented from the male point of view, and the emotions of prostitutes are seldom if at all considered. On the other hand, "Sentimental Education" (section 1) exemplifies an important trend in short fiction of the past twenty years or so in which the sexual initiation of both males and females is considered. In these stories, sexual and emotional relationships are each explored in detail and put in perspective one with the other. The emphasis in stories of this type is less on the sexual experience and more on the total involvement of two people falling in love for the first time; the sensationalism found in many stories of sexual initiation is absent.

A good number of stories in this anthology are about rites of passage, for they mark singular instances or short periods of time when adolescents pass from one stage of human experience to another. Being formally introduced to society at a debutante ball has traditionally been a custom of affluent socioeconomic groups. On the night Judy is presented to society in "Debut" (section 4), she begins to practice her mother's cynical philosophy of manipulating people. As she is incorporated into the world of adults, she brings with her a code of conduct that she intuits will help her not only to survive but also to prosper. Both "Louisa, Please Come Home" (section 3) and "The Sorcerer's Eye" explore the difficult passage adolescents must take as they leave their parents for good and begin to establish a life of their own in preparation for becoming parents themselves. Although the experience in each case is painful because the security of childhood is lost, the protagonists are compensated for this by their newly acquired adulthood. In "Homecoming" (section 3), the realities of death and the ambiguous way it affects those who must contend with it allow Susan to view life in a more mature fashion—and certainly more realistically than her mother. Her ability to evaluate human motivations is greatly increased.

In many stories in which adolescents are trying to establish their identities, they must first declare their independence. A few do it suddenly by running away, as in "The Sorcerer's Eye" and "Louisa, Please Come Home." Yet, their escape is never final, for after a while there is the inevitable return home because of necessity, curiosity, or a desire to recapture some essential element of childhood. It is actually this return that helps the runaways realize their self-sufficiency. And once their independence has been established, they are better able to define themselves and their destiny.

In "The Somebody" Chato impulsively declares his independence one morning to his father: "I'm checking out of this dump! You'll never see me again!" He then spends the day emblazoning his name on the walls of the ghetto in which he lives. With Chato's gang broken up and the territory it used to control in the hands of another gang, his identity and purpose are all but destroyed. Nevertheless he has decided to "be famous all over town," and to accomplish his purpose he sets about writing on any available wall "CHATO DE SHAMROCK with rays shooting out like from the Holy Cross." By contrast it is a serene, summer mood that pervades "The Grey Bird," one in which fifteen-year-old Natalie mystically merges with nature and becomes "Lois the silver girl," an imaginary ideal who will help her define her identity. As she swims away into the "grey-green distance," she leaves her childhood behind her.

In many stories of adolescence a particular incident, sometimes seemingly insignificant, precipitates an awareness of identity. The few hours Naftoli Gold spends on campus in "Mr. Princeton" (section 5) give him a disturbing insight into who he is and who his prospective classmates are. It becomes "too immediately apparent that there was something too vitally different between himself and the boys on the other platform" at the university train station. Naftoli is Jewish and they are not. He comes from relatively modest means and they do not. He does not fit. And he senses that his admissions interview has gone poorly and that he will not be admitted to the university. "The Four Sides of a Triangle" (section 3) culminates in an epiphany for Sam when he finally grasps the nature of love and the heartache of the betrayed lover. He thinks as he listens to the man his uncle has cuckolded, "I was suddenly shaken out of my self-centered adolescence. Suddenly, I knew he was speaking to me, and for everyone. All of my life was loss." Sam becomes an adult as he learns a basic, unsettling truth about life, even though he is only sixteen years old. And in "The Death of Horatio Alger" (section 4) it is during a fist fight that Mickey, a black, realizes that "Negroes and Italians beat and shaped me, and my allegiance is there. But the triumph of romanticism was parquet floors, yellow dresses, gardens, and sandy hair. I must have felt the loss and could not rise against a cardboard world of dark hair and linoleum. Reality was something I was convinced I could not have." His desire for the privileges of whites is as futile as the fight he is involved in, though he goes down desperately swinging his fists.

Sudden, often painful, revelations of one's identity are the central concern in numerous stories of adolescence. Most often such stories are about older adolescents who are on the threshold of becoming adults but who have yet to discover some essential truth about themselves, one that will put into perspective many of the events and experiences of their lives. More often than not what they learn about themselves has to do with a weakness or limitation they have not taken properly into account. Almost all stories of adolescence have something to do with young people answering the question "Who am I?"

Hugh Nissenson
The Law

ON AND OFF, THAT WHOLE SUMMER, I wondered what my uncle Willi was going to do about his son. The boy, Danny, was going to be thirteen on the twelfth of July, and as early as February, I remembered, Willi was talking about having his Bar Mitzvah at their Temple in Queens; the whole works—a service in the morning and a party for the family and their friends in the afternoon at their home.

"Nothing ostentatious, you understand," he told me. "Drinks and hors d'oeuvres. You know: franks, little pigs in a blanket, or lox on pieces of toast."

I said that I thought that the party was a nice idea but, though it was really none of my business, maybe that was enough.

"I mean why the whole service? You don't want to make him go through all of that speechmaking."

"Ah, but he insists," said Willi.

"Does he?"

"So help me. He says he wouldn't think of having one without the other, and his doctor says it's all right. The doctor says if he really wants to speak, then by all means. Treat him normal."

"What doctor?"

"Rhinehart. Didn't I tell you? Rhinehart's been treating him since the Fall."

"Who's Rhinehart?"

"I thought you knew. Didn't Helene tell you? Speech therapy. One of the big speech men in New York. He's connected with the Medical Center. Just since September, and he's done wonders."

"I didn't know. I'm glad to hear it."

"Will you come to the service?" he asked.

"When will it be?"

"The weekend after the Fourth. That Saturday, in the morning. The Fourth is on a Monday. That Saturday, the ninth," he said.

"Sure."

"Ten o'clock in the morning. Don't you forget now. Mark it down." he said.

I never thought he'd go through with it. For as long as I could remember, his son had a terrible stammer. Just to say "hello" was an effort. He had a habit of closing his eyes as though he'd been told to visualize the word beforehand. It was agonizing to watch: the shut eyes, the deep breath, the pulse beating in his neck, the chin jerking spasmodically, and the spit gathering in the corners of his mouth.

"H-h-h-hello, Joe," he'd greet me. "How-how-how are ya?"

Relaxed, silent, he seemed another kid, somehow altogether different-looking, resembling his mother, with a placid oval face, and large dark eyes, beautiful eyes, with long curly lashes, and delicate hands with bitten nails that were always in his mouth. To avoid speaking as much as possible, he had developed the facility of listening attentively, fixing those eyes on you, with a faint smile on his lips, nodding or shaking his head as the occasion demanded, so that he gave the impression of following whatever you said with a kind of ravenous intensity that made you self-conscious of being able to speak normally yourself. An intelligent defense. That he was really brilliant, there wasn't any doubt.

"An 'A' average in school," Willi told me, throwing his arm about the boy's shoulders. "He loves history," he added, as a kind of concession to me. A pause, as though I was supposed to test the boy's knowledge. Helene, his mother, glanced at me with alarm. I remained silent, smiling with a nod, and it seemed to me that the boy himself gave me a look of gratitude that went unnoticed by his father. At the time, I was teaching American history to the tenth grade in a private school on the Upper East Side. It was easy to imagine Danny's suffering in class, called upon by his teacher to recite, straining to express himself, while the other kids laughed behind their hands, or mimicked him, spraying the air with spit.

Anyhow, that was in February, as I've said. Came the summer and I didn't see much of them at first. I spent most of my time in the Forty-second Street Library doing research for my Ph.D. thesis on the Alien and Sedition Act. A couple of times in May Willi called me on the phone to invite me out to dinner, but I was too busy. He was really the only family I had left, but with one thing and another, we were never really close. My mother's younger brother, a man in his middle forties, short and powerfully built, running now to fat, with red cheeks and a fringe of dark hair about the crown of his head that resembled a monk's tonsure, he always reminded me of the picture of the jolly monk on the labels of imported German beer. He had been born in Germany, as a matter of fact. My mother had written and tried to persuade him to leave the country in 1935, but he intended to study law at Heidelberg, so the Nazis caught him and deported him to Bergen Belsen where he managed to survive the war, coming to this country in 1947, just before my mother's death. He had written a book about his experiences—*Mein Erlebnis*—that was never actually published, but everyone who knew him felt they had read it anyhow, from the way he constantly spoke of what had happened to him. When he spoke about the concentration camps, he sounded as if he was quoting by heart from a manuscript. He generally loved to talk, and if it was a blow to his pride that his son had so much trouble in getting a word out straight, he never let on, as far as I could see.

"Stammering? What's a stammer?" I once heard him tell the boy. "It's a sign of greatness. . . . Yes, I mean it. Demosthenes stammered, and Moses. *Moshe Ribenue*. Mose our Teacher himself."

"M-M-Moses?"

"The luckiest thing that ever happened, believe you me."

"H-h-how l-lucky?"

"How many Commandments are there?"

His son held up his ten fingers.

"Ten! There you are!" said his father. "Believe me, if he didn't have a stammer he would have given us a hundred. . . . Luck, eh? Luck or not?"

The boy laughed. His father had a way with words, there was no doubt of it, making a good living as a paper-box salesman for a company at New Hyde Park on the Island. I imagine he cleared over twenty thousand a year. He lived nicely enough, in one of those red-brick, two-story, semi-detached houses on Eighty-first Avenue in Queens, with a little rose garden in the back and a pine-paneled bar and rumpus room in the cellar where he intended to have the party after the Bar Mitzvah. I finally went out for dinner the second week in May. We had a drink downstairs.

"You can't help it," he said. "I figure about thirty, thirty-five people. What can I do? Helene's family, friends from the office, the kid's friends from school, the rabbi and his wife. Thirty-five, maybe more. . . . Helene says with that many we'll have to serve lunch. I thought maybe a cold buffet. We'll eat down here. I'm having it air-conditioned."

"It's a nice idea."

"It'll be a nice party, you wait and see. How about another Scotch?"

"Just a drop."

"Chivas Regal. Twenty years old. Like velvet water."

"Just a splash of water," I told him. "Where's Danny?"

"What's the time?"

"Just six."

"Be home any minute. He's at Hebrew school."

"How's he doing?"

"Wonderful. That rabbi does wonders. The boy can already read. Of course, it's all modern. To help him he has a recording of the Haftorah he has to say, put out by some company in New Jersey."

"Sounds like a wonderful idea."

"He's reciting from Numbers."

"I don't know too much about it."

"It's some of the Laws, and how they should organize themselves in the march through the desert."

"And Danny likes it?" I asked.

"You should hear him. The rabbi, the doctor, Rhinehart—I told you: everybody helps. Ask him yourself."

He came home about six-thirty, with his notebook under his arm. He had grown a little since I saw him last, become a little leaner, with bigger hands and feet, bony wrists. There was a slight down on his cheeks and upper lip, but so far as I could tell his speech was about the same. He went through the convulsions just to say hello—the suspended breath and shut eyes, the blue veins swelling on the sides of his neck. When we sat down at the dinner table, he remained standing by his place, with a loaf of bread covered by a linen napkin set before him, and a black silk skull-cap on the back of his head.

"*B-b-b-b-aruch atar a-adonoi,*" he mumbled—the Hebrew blessing of the bread—and when he finished, he looked pale and wiped the spit from his lips with the back of his hand.

"How was that?" Willi asked me.

"Nice."

"Practice. Practice makes perfect."

His son lowered his quivering eyelids. Helene served the roast chicken and wild rice, with little brown potatoes.

"You never learned the language?" Willi spoke to me again.

"I was never Bar Mitzvahed; no."

"Neither was I."

"Really?"

"In Germany, when I was growing up, it was—unfashionable to be given a Jewish education." He tore at a chicken wing with his teeth. "Once in a while in the camp I would run into somebody who could speak Hebrew. It's really an ugly language. It's just that . . . I don't know. It was nice to hear it spoken. It was *verboten*, of course, but still . . . how can I explain? It was something out of our past, the really distant past. It somehow seemed to me to be the only part of our consciousness that was left—uncontaminated. Not like Yiddish. . . . I always hated Yiddish. I used to pride myself on my command of German, the way I wrote particularly, a really educated style, but I learned to hate it. Sometimes for weeks I couldn't bring myself to say a word. The language of the S.S. . . . ."

"T-t-t-tell about H-H-Heinz," interrupted his son.

"Eat your chicken," his mother said. The tone of her voice made me look at her with surprise: black hair with a faint reddish tinge, and long curling eyelashes that shadowed her prominent cheekbones. Lucky enough to have been spared the later horrors, she too was a refugee, coming from Germany in 1936. I suddenly sensed that she disapproved and was even a little frightened of Willi's imposition of the whole thing on the boy's consciousness. In front of me, though, "eat your chicken" was all that she said. We finished the rest of the meal in silence—lemon meringue pie and coffee —and Willi, the boy, and myself went into the living room and sat down on the sofa.

"Cigar?" Willi asked.

"No thanks."

He belched and lit up, and began to pick his front teeth with the folded cellophane. "How about a little brandy?"

"That'd be nice."

"Napoleon: the best," he said, pouring some into two snifters that the boy had brought in from the kitchen. "Wonderful. . . . Too good. I'm getting too fat, I know. Soft," he said, patting his paunch. "The doctor tells me I ought to lose at least twenty pounds. An irony, eh? Did you know that when I got out of Belsen I weighed ninety pounds? Ninety, mind you, and now, like all the other Americans, I'm to die of overweight."

His eyes gleamed as though he derived some sort of satisfaction out of the thought.

"A living skeleton," he went on. "You must have seen photos after the liberation of a place like that. I don't have to tell you. . . ."

But he did, as I knew he would; he went on and on, while his son listened, his legs tucked under him, biting on one fingernail after the other.

"You can't know—thank God—not you, or Danny here, or Helene. . . . No one who was not there can even guess what it was like to be so hungry, to be literally starving to death on two slices of bread a day, and a pint of watery soup with a snip of turnip in it, if you're lucky. Twice a week a spoonful of rancid butter, and an ounce of sausage or cheese. . . . And the worst of it knowing that it's endless, knowing that no matter how hungry you are today there's absolutely no possibility of getting anything more to eat tomorrow but that the anguish will simply grow and grow and grow. . . . Words. . . ." He shrugged. "You aren't really listening and I can't blame you. What good are words to describe such things?"

He sucked on his cigar and screwed up his eyes to watch the smoke, as thick and white as milk, gather in the cone of light above the lamp on the coffee table. "There were two obsessions that everyone had. Ask anyone who was in such a place. Have you ever read any books about them? . . . Food first: dreaming about food, sitting down to a meal like we just had, and eating till you burst, and second: just staying alive so that you would be able to describe what was happening to you. Everyone wanted to write a book. Seriously. Just to tell the world, as though to convince ourselves as well that such things were really happening, that we were actually living through them. I wrote *Mein Erlebnis* in six weeks. . . ."

He waved the smoke away, and again his narrowed eyes had that peculiar gleam. The boy sat perfectly motionless, with his lips slightly parted in expectation of his father to continue, and for the first time I began to understand the nature of Willi's compulsion to talk so much about what he

had endured. Triumph. There was a flash of triumph in his eyes as he regarded his son. It was as if I were listening to a mountain climber—what's
his name, the one who climbed Everest—or the first man who will land on
the moon and live to tell about it. He talked and talked, partly, I am sure,
because it was essentially a personal victory that he was describing—and
gloating over, in spite of himself. It was a display of prowess before his son;
the supreme success, perhaps even the high point of his life, that he among
all those millions managed to live through it all.

From the kitchen came the swish of water and the hum of the automatic
dishwasher. Helene came into the living room with a bowl of fruit.

"An apple, Joe?"

"No thanks."

Willi peeled a banana, and to be polite perhaps, or maybe because of his
wife's feelings about talking as he did in front of the boy, he began to ask
me about my work.

"The Alien and Sedition Act, eh?" he said. "Yes. . . . Yes, interesting and
significant. . . . When was it again?"

"S-s-seventeen n-ninety-eight," said Danny.

Willi questioned me with a raised eyebrow. "That's right," I told him.

He grinned. "I told you he loves his history."

"He's right a hundred percent."

"Who was it?" Willi went on. "President Adams, wasn't it? Against the
Bill of Rights—the first suspension of habeas corpus."

"And M-M-Marshall," began the boy.

His father laughed with his mouth full of banana. "You can see for yourself he knows much more about it than me." The boy smiled, flushed to his
temples with pride. "Still, I remember: No freedom of speech, hundreds of
editors thrown into jail for criticizing the government, the prisons packed
with dissenters." From his voice, he sounded as though he momentarily
somehow enjoyed it.

"About twenty-five, all told," I said.

"You don't say. Just twenty-five?"

"That's it."

He grinned again. "How about that! America, you see?" he said to his
wife. "Imagine. A whole stink over that."

"There was more to it than that," I told him.

"Of course, but still—a crisis! Genuine indignation over the fate of just
twenty-five men. . . ."

"Yes, partly," I told him, suddenly weary, bleary-eyed from the dinner
and the drinks.

"And the Jews?" he asked me.

"I don't understand."

"There was no particular repression of the Jews, as such?"

"I never thought about it, to tell you the truth."

He laughed. "Seriously," I went on. "The law was directed against foreigners, mostly—the British and the French. French spies, for example. There was a lot of spying going on, and the law forced a lot of foreigners to leave the country."

"But nothing was specifically directed against the Jews."

"No. Why should there have been?"

Another laugh. "What's so funny?" I asked him.

"Don't you know the joke?"

"Which one?"

"You must have heard it. . . . The S.S. man in Berlin who grabs a Jew by the collar and kicks him in the shins. 'Tell me, Jew, who's responsible for all of Germany's troubles?' The Jew trembles. His teeth absolutely chatter; his knees knock together. 'The Jews, of course,' he answers. 'Good,' says the S.S. man. 'The Jews and the bareback riders in the circus,' the little Jew goes on. 'Why the bareback riders in the circus?' the S.S. man asks. 'Aha,' comes the answer. 'Exactly! So *nu?* Why the Jews?' "

The boy laughed, slapping his thigh, guffawing until the tears came into his eyes, as if he were delighted to find a release in a sound that he could express without impediment.

"Yes, yes," Willi continued, taking a last bite of the banana and throwing the peel into an ashtray. "He laughs, and it's true, the absurdity, and yet there's something more. There's a reason. . . . Why the Jews? There's the psychology of a Heinz to contend with, and not an isolated pathological case either, but common. More common than you'd care to know."

The boy shifted his position, leaning toward his father with one hand on the arm of the sofa, and both feet on the floor.

"Have a piece of fruit," Helene told me.

"No thanks. Who's Heinz?" I asked.

"*Herr Hauptsturmfuehrer Berger,*" said Will. "You know the type. Tall and blond, beautiful, really, the very image of manly perfection that you can see for yourself, today, just by going to the movies. . . . A movie star, so help me; six foot two at least, with straight blond hair, white flashing teeth, a positively captivating smile—dimples at the corners of his mouth—beautiful blue eyes. . . . The uniform? Perfection. Designed for him; tailor-made for that slim, hard body, broad shoulders. . . ." He spread his stubby hands in the air, reminding me more than ever of that monk making an invocation. "Black, all black and belted with what do you call them? Riding pants. Jodhpurs, and gleaming black boots. . . ."

"But I still don't understand," I said. "Who is he?"

"*Was,*" corrected Willi. "He was a guard in the camp. After the war the British caught him and he was tried and hanged. . . . *Was.* . . . Unfortunate. I mean it, too. Seriously. No one had the good sense to study him instead: how he used to stand, for example—very significant—with the thumb of one hand, his left hand, I remember, stuck in his belt, and the other grasping a braided riding whip that he would tap against those boots. The boots, the belt, the buckle, the buttons, all flashing in the sun—enough to blind you, believe me. White teeth, that dimpled smile. . . . He was convicted of murder. One day he killed a child, a little girl of seven. . . . In the camp, some of the barracks had three tiers of wooden beds along the wall, bare planks to sleep on, *boxen* in the jargon. We slept together packed like sardines. Often someone would die in the night, but it was impossible to move. We would sleep with the dead, but no matter. . . . Where was I?"

"The child," I said.

"Ah, yes. One of the *boxen* in the women's barracks was coming apart; one leg was coming off. Three tiers, mind you; hundreds of pounds of timber. . . . For some reason the child was on the floor, directly beneath it, on her hands and knees. Perhaps he—Heinz—had ordered it so. I don't know. I don't think so. She must just have been looking for something. A crust of bread, a crumb, perhaps, and in walks the *Hauptsturmfuehrer* smiling all the while as though to charm the ladies, immediately sizing up the situation; perfect. The child beneath the rickety bed, the girl's mother, Frau Schwarz, in one corner, binding up her swollen legs with a few rags.

"'*Grädige Frau* . . .' he greets her—the mother, who stands up nervously twisting a rag about her wrist.

"'Hilda!' she screams. . . . Not even a Jewish name, mind you; a good German name. . . . 'Hilda!' The child begins to rise, but it's too late. With a flick of his boot, a movement of that polished toe, our Heinz has already acted, kicking out the loose timber, bringing down the whole thing on the child's back. . . . A broken back.

"'Mama!' she cries. 'I can't move! My legs!' For a day and a half like that until she goes into convulsions and dies in her mother's arms. The woman comes to me and reproaches herself because she hasn't got the courage to commit suicide.

"'After all,' she says, 'I have the means. . . .' She's referring to the rags that she has woven into a noose. 'Just the courage is lacking. Mr. Levy, what's the matter with me?' She goes mad, and before she dies she wanders about the camp asking everyone to strangle her. . . . She even comes to Heinz. It was just outside the latrines. I witnessed this myself. Apparently he doesn't even remember who she is. He shoos her away, those beautiful blue eyes clouded for just an instant in complete bewilderment.

"'*Verrückt*,' he tells me. 'Insane.' With a shrug. I'm busy on my hands and knees scrubbing the concrete floor with a brush and a pail of lye and water, not daring to look up, blinded by those boots.

"'Here, here, Levy. No; to the left. Put some elbow grease into it.'

"A fanatic for order and cleanliness, you understand. He used to speak with me a great deal. I couldn't imagine why. Perhaps because we were both about the same age. He would constantly ask me questions about the Jews—technical questions, so to speak, about our beliefs, about the Torah, for example, all the Laws. He seemed sincerely interested and, as far as I could tell, he was genuinely disappointed when he realized that I knew next to nothing and had been educated like himself as a good, middle-class German—*Gymnasium*, and two semesters at Heidelberg. One day he was absolutely flabbergasted to find out that for the life of me I couldn't even recite the Ten Commandments. I couldn't get more than five, and not in order, either. 'Tsk! Tsk! Levy.' He shook that beautiful head and began reciting them all.

"'I am the Lord thy God who brought thee forth out of the land of Egypt, out of the house of bondage. . . . Thou shalt have no other gods before me.' Etc., etc. All of them, the whole business. . . . Imagine the scene. It was a Sunday, I remember, rest day, the one day off from man-killing labor the whole week. I had gone outside the barracks to get a little sun. Imagine it, I tell you. A vast desert, our own Sinai surrounding us, rolling sand dunes, green wooden shacks set in rows. In the distance, the silver birch trees of the women's camp like a mirage. The wire mesh gate of the main entrance to my right that always reminded me of the entrance to a zoo. Here and there, scattered on the ground, all heaped together, the mounds of bodies, the living dead and the dead—stiff, open eyes, gaping mouths, all heaped together, indistinguishable. It was early spring, and warm, with a weak sun, gray clouds, cumuli, with a flat base and rounded outlines, piled up like mountains in the western sky. . . . I remember that distinctly—cumuli. . . . It was a matter of life and death, learning to tell one type of cloud from another—the promise of a little rain. There was never enough water. Just two concrete basins to supply the entire camp. We were slowly dying of thirst in addition to everything else. I remember thinking that if the rain does come I shall try and remain outside the barracks as long as I can after roll call, with my mouth open. Crazy thoughts. What was it? Chickens, young *Truthahnen*—turkeys drown that way in the rain, too stupid to close their mouths. . . . Insane, disconnected thoughts while, according to regulation, I stood rigidly at attention, with my chin in, and chest out, my thumbs along the crease in my striped prison pants, as Heinz drones on and on.

"'Honor thy father and thy mother. . . . Thou shalt not murder. . . .' On and on to the end, and then, with what I can only describe as a shy expression on his face, the explanation:

"'We live in Saxony,' he tells me. 'Absolutely charming, Levy. Do you know East Prussia? Ah, the orchard and the flower beds—roses, red and white roses, growing in front of the church. My father's church. A pastor, Levy, and his father before him and before that. Three generations of pastors. When I was young, I thought I would go into the Church myself. I have the religious temperament.'

"'Yes, sir. *Jawohl, Herr Hauptsturmfuehrer.*'

"'Does that astonish you?'

"'Not at all, *Mein Herr.*'

"'It does, of course. . . . Sundays. . . . Ah, a day like today. The church bells echoing in the valley and the peasants in their black suits and creaking shoes shuffling between those rose beds to listen to Papa thunder at them from the pulpit, slamming down his fist. "Love, my friends! It is written that we are to love our neighbors as ourselves." The fist again. "Love!" he shouts, and I would begin to tremble, literally begin to shake. . . . Why,

Levy? I often asked myself. You ought to know. Jews are great psychologists. Freud. . . .'

"'I don't know, *Herr Hauptsturmfuehrer*.'

"'A pity. . . . He would preach love and all I could see from that front pew was that great fist—the blond hair on the backs of the fingers, the knuckles clenched, white. . . . That huge fist protruding from the black cuff like the hand of God from a thunder cloud. . . .' That was his image, I swear it. So help me, a literary mind. '*Die grosse Faust ist aus der schwarzen Manschette heraus gestreckt wie Gottes-hand aus einer Sturmwolke.* Yet, to be honest,' Heinz went on, 'he never struck me. Not once in my whole life, and I was never what you could call a good child, Levy. Secret vices, a rebellious spirit that had to be broken. . . . And obedience was doubly difficult for the likes of me, but, as I've said, whenever I misbehaved, he never once laid a hand on me. . . . Love. . . . He spoke about love and was silent. Talk about psychology! That silence for days on end; all he had to do was say nothing and I would lie in my bed at night, trembling. Can you explain that, Levy? I would lie awake praying that he would beat me instead, smash me with that fist, flay my back with his belt rather than that love, that silent displeasure. He had thin, pale lips, with a network of wrinkles at the corner of his mouth. . . . No dimples. I get my dimples from my mother. . . . To please him, I would learn whole passages of the Bible by heart; your Bible, Levy.'

"He tapped his whip against the top of his boots.

"'Tell me, Levy. . . .'

"'Yes, sir?'

"I know the Jews; a gentle people. Tell me honestly. Did your father ever beat you?'

"'No, sir.'

"'Not once?'

"'Never, sir.'

"'A gentle people, as I've said, but lax in your education, wouldn't you say?'

"'Yes, sir.'

"'Well, then we must remedy that. . . .'"

For the first time, the flow of words faltered. Willi paused to relight his cigar, and then, as though it had left a bad taste in his mouth, snubbed it out in the ashtray and picked a fleck of tobacco from the tip of his tongue. "Like some dog," he finally went on. "As if he were training some animal. . . . That whip across the back, the bridge of the nose, the eyes. . . . All afternoon I stood at attention while those clouds gathered and it began to rain, until I could repeat it all word for word. 'I am the Lord thy God who brought thee forth out of the land of Egypt.' He hit me in the adam's apple. I could hardly speak. The rain came down my face. . . ."

Another silence. The automatic dishwasher had long since stopped. Helene bit into an apple and looked at her watch. Before she had a chance to speak, the boy shook his head.

"Never mind," she told him. "It's late. Past ten. Time for bed."

"Ten?" I repeated, standing up. "I've got to go myself."

"Say good night to Joe," said Helene to her son.

"You w-w-w-wanna hear my r-r-record?" He asked me. "It'll only t-t-take a minute."

"O.K.; for a minute."

His room was at the head of the stairs. I followed him up and he shut the door.

"Y-you never heard about H-H-Heinz before?"

"Never."

"I have; o-often. It used to give me b-bad dreams."

On top of his desk was a phonograph record. He put it on the portable phonograph that stood in one corner of the room. For a time, sitting on the bed while the boy put on his pajamas, I listened to the deep voice chanting in the unintelligible tongue.

"D-don't you understand?"

"Not much," I said.

"How—how come you were never B-B-Bar Mitzvahed?"

"I wasn't as lucky as you. My father was dead, and my mother didn't care one way or the other."

"M-Mama doesn't care either," he said, tying his bathrobe around his waist. He rejected the record and stood by the window that faced the rose garden, biting his thumbnail.

"D-d-do you believe in G-G-God?"

"I don't know."

"I do—do."

"You're lucky there too."

"D-don't you ever pray?"

"No."

"I d-d-do; often."

I imagined that, rather like his laughter, that too must have been a wonderful relief; praying in silence, grateful and convinced that he was able to communicate something without a stammer.

"D-d-do you know what I p-pray for?" he asked me.

"What?"

"A-actually it's a s-s-secret."

"You can tell me if you like."

"S-sometimes, y-you know, when I think of all th-those people at the Temple—at the B-B-Bar Mitzvah, I mean—I get into a sweat."

"It'll be all right."

"There'll be h-hundreds of people there, M-Mama's whole family, G-G-Goldman's parents and all his family, and all their f-f-friends."

"Who's Goldman?"

"He's a f-f-fink. Sammy Goldman. We're being B-B-Bar Mitzvahed together. He's rich. His father owns a chain of delicatessens. He's t-told everybody about me. He didn't want to g-go with me. He has p-pimples from p-p-playing with himself."

"It's late," I told him. "I really ought to go."

"It's another m-m-month or so. More. Time enough. Anything can h-h-happen in time, don't you think?"

"It depends."

"If you b-b-believe enough?"

"Maybe so."

"The st-st-stammer, you know, is all psychological. Doctor Rhinehart says so. It c-came all of a sudden. W-when I started school."

"I didn't know."

"Oh yes. And if it c-c-came that way, it can g-g-go too; suddenly, I mean. That's l-l-logical, don't you think?"

"Anything is possible," I told him.

He smiled abruptly, and opened his mouth again, giving me the impression that he wanted to say something more. But for some reason, maybe because he was tired, he got stuck; his chin jerked spasmodically as he tried to force the word from his mouth, and then he shrugged and gave up, holding out a moist palm to say good night and good-by.

"Good luck," I told him.

About a week later his father gave me a ring. He had a customer in the garment district, on Seventh Avenue and Thirty-seventh Street, and he thought that if as usual I was working at the Forty-second Street Library, we could meet for a bite of lunch. I said fine. It was a hot day. His cheeks were purplish from the heat and he breathed heavily. We had a sandwich and a soda at Schrafft's and then he walked me back to the library where we sat for a while on the granite steps under the trees around the flagpole at the north entrance on the avenue. The place was jammed with shopgirls and clerks taking in a few minutes of the sun before they had to go back to work. We sat and watched the flow of crowds going into the stores; the cars and the buses and the cabs, the cop at the intersection, wearing dark glasses and a short-sleeved summer uniform, waving the traffic on.

"How's the work?" Willi asked me.

"Coming along. How's the family?"

"Fine. They send their best."

"Send my love."

"I will." He smoked a cigar and coughed. The air was thick with fumes. "You know, Danny doesn't say much, but he can't fool me."

"About what?"

"He's worried about the Bar Mitzvah. Speaking in front of all those people. I told him to take it slow and everything would be all right. What do you think?"

"You know best."

"Helene thinks I'm doing the wrong thing."

"It's hard for me to say."

"You heard me that night. . . . Sometimes I go on and on. She says I shouldn't fill his head with that sort of thing, but I say that he has a right to know."

"You may be right."

"He doesn't understand everything, of course. . . . That story about Heinz, for example. . . . But he will in time. . . . It was a revelation to me. You know, sometimes, in the camp, before I met Heinz, I used to wonder why it was all happening. Why the Jews, I mean. . . .

"Oh, there are other factors, of course. . . . But don't you see? The Commandments. All the Laws. . . ." He flicked away his cigar ash. "The Law, more than anything. . . . He taught me that, that day in the rain. They were murdering, humiliating us because whether it was true or not we had come to—how shall I say it?—embody, I suppose . . . In some strange way, we had come to embody that very Law that bound them too—through Christianity, I mean—and in destroying us . . . Heinz, for example, hating his father, the pastor, who preached love—love thy neighbor, from Leviticus, you know. . . . Of course, there's the fist: love and hate all mixed together. I really don't understand that part myself, but I do know that what all of them hated, somehow, was the yoke that we had given them so long ago. The Law that makes all the difference, that makes a man different from a beast, the civilized . . ." He coughed. "Can't you see what I mean?"

"I'm not sure. I think so."

"It's hard for me to keep it all straight myself. . . . I just feel that the least we can do is pass it on, the way we always have, from father to son. The Bar Mitzvah. . . . Of course, now with Danny, he doesn't really complain, but he suffers, I know. I'm not sure just what to do."

"What can I tell you?"

"Nothing, I know. I just wanted you to understand. . . . You know the irony is that he hates me."

"Don't be absurd."

"It's true—at least partly. Oh, he loves me too, but Rhinehart says that stammering is very often—it's very complicated—a kind of expression of hostility, resentment, to those whom you're supposed to love. . . . It all started you know when he began school. He was very bright. I've always demanded too damn much of him."

"It'll be O.K."

"Oh, I know it, eventually. It's only that in the meantime . . . I told him yesterday that if he wanted to call the whole service off, I'd be glad to do it in a minute."

"What'd he say?"

"Nothing doing. What he's been saying all along. Definitely not. . . . As a matter of fact, he smiled."

"Did he?" I said. "What are you going to do?"

"Go ahead, I guess. But I made it as clear as I could that any time he wants to drop the speech and just have the party at home, it was more than O.K. by me."

"Well," I told him. "I've got to get back to the books."

"I know. I didn't mean to keep you."

"Thanks for lunch."

"My pleasure. . . . Joe, you're the only blood relative I've got left. People talk. I just wanted you to understand."

I nodded, and left him standing there, smoking and coughing, in the dazzling pattern of light and shadow cast by the sunlight streaming through the dusty leaves of the trees.

The weeks went by. Once or twice he called again to have me out to dinner, and I asked him whether or not the service was still on. "Sure," he'd answer. "He's studying away." I was too busy getting my notes into shape to go out and see them. My work was going fairly well. I decided to attack the whole problem from the point of view of Chief Justice Marshall—the origin of judicial review—but with all of it, I got a good chunk of the reading done by the beginning of July, so that over the Fourth I was able to get away and spend the weekend visiting a classmate of mine at Columbia and his wife who had taken a cottage for the summer at Cape Cod. I got back Tuesday night. The service was scheduled for the following Saturday, so I called Willi to make absolutely sure once and for all that Danny was going to speak in the Temple.

"You bet," he told me. "You know, I think I've got a budding rabbi on my hands."

"How do you mean?"

"Religious? My God, you ought to see him. He gets up at six in the morning to pray."

The service was to be held at Temple Shalom on Seventy-eighth Avenue. I hadn't bought a present yet and I was stumped. For the life of me I couldn't think of anything original. In the end, I went to the bank and bought him a series-E savings bond for $25.00. Somehow it didn't seem enough, so in addition I bought him fourteen silver dollars—one extra for good luck—and had them packed in a velvet box with a clasp. I thought the kid might get a kick out of it.

Saturday at last: hot and muggy, a promise of rain, with a peculiar diffused light shining from behind the low gray clouds. It was too hot to sleep much the night before. I was up at six-thirty and out of the house by a quarter to eight. At first I thought that maybe I'd go out to the house and we'd all go to the Temple together. I don't know why; I decided against it. I loafed around instead, wasting time, and by the time I took the subway and arrived in Queens it was a quarter to ten. The crowds were already arriving at the Temple, Goldman's relatives, most of them people I didn't know, all dressed up in dark summer suits and light dresses, flowered prints and silks. It was so muggy that the powder flaked on the women's cheeks. I finally recognized Helene's brother and sister-in-law in the crush— a chiropodist who lived in Brooklyn. We chatted for a minute before they went inside.

"Willi here?" I asked.

"Not yet. I didn't see any of them," he said. "Maybe we ought to call up and find out if they're really coming. Between you and me, I never thought the kid would go through with it."

I waited alone just outside the big oaken doors. The air was stifling, and the sun had shifted and faded from behind the clouds darkening the streets. It began to rain. I went into the vestibule, and about three minutes of ten the family arrived.

"A rabbi, I told you," said Willi, folding his dripping umbrella. "He didn't want to take a cab on *Shabbos*. We had to walk here in the rain."

Helene took off her wilted straw hat. "Ruined," she said. The boy said nothing. With a white-silk prayer shawl over his arm, he was dressed in a dark-blue suit that emphasized the pallor of his face. All the color had gone from his cheeks; his lips were drawn and white.

"Congratulations," I told him.

He nodded. "We're late," said his father. "We ought to get seated." He took his wife by the elbow and they went inside. The boy hung back and pulled at my sleeve.

"D-d-d-do you think they'll l-laugh?" he asked.

"Of course not."

He shook his head and shrugged.

"I p-p-p-prayed and p-p-prayed."

We all sat in the front pew, to the left of the Ark. There were baskets of red roses set on the marble steps. The bronze doors of the Ark were open and the rabbi, young and handsome, wearing horn-rimmed glasses and prematurely gray at the temples, conducted the morning service. He was sweating and, while the cantor sang, he surreptitiously plucked a handkerchief from the sleeve of his robe and dabbed at his upper lip. The service went on, mostly in Hebrew, chanting and responsive reading, the drone of voices and the tinkle of silver bells as Willi and Mr. Goldman were called upon to elevate the Torah over the heads of the congregation and lay it open on the mahogany podium set on the edge of the steps. The rain beat against the stained glass windows. Danny sat to my right, picking at the cuticle of his thumb. When it came time for the recitation of the Haftorah, the Goldman kid went first. He would do well and he knew it—chanting the Hebrew in a high singsong voice that was just beginning to crack; rather good-looking, and tall for his age, with reddish blond hair, full lips, and pimpled cheeks. His father, seated on the stage to the rabbi's left and next to Willi, beamed at the audience. Then it was Danny's turn. The crowd shifted perceptively in their seats, and as he stood up two women in the row behind us nervously began to fan themselves with their prayer books. Evidently he was right: the Goldman boy had told everyone about his stammer. You could sense it. You could hear everyone in the place take a deep breath as he mounted the three steps with the fringed end of his prayer shawl dragging along the floor. He stood behind the opened Torah, and with a bitten forefinger found his place. The rustle of silks; the audience had shifted again, with a faint murmur. The wooden pews creaked and the noise must have startled him, because he suddenly glanced up. For a moment he was up to his old tricks, trying to stare them down, but it was no use. No one said anything. All at once he was just listening to the sound of their labored breathing. They pitied him and he knew it, and they hated him, in spite of themselves, for the embarrassment that he was causing them, and he was aware of that too. The rabbi wiped the sweat from his upper lip. With his left hand rubbing the side of his nose, Willi sat looking at his feet. Then, for a moment more, wide-eyed, and with trembling lips, the boy continued to stare down at the crowd until he caught my eye. He blinked and shrugged his shoulders again, and hunched forward, as though before he began to stammer the blessing he had made up his mind to assume the burden of what the reiteration of the Law of his Fathers had demanded from the first.

John Knowles
Phineas

IT WAS THE KIND OF PLACE I had expected all right, an old-rooted Massachusetts town. All of the homes along Main Street, from solid white mansions to neat saltboxes, were settled behind their fences and hedges as though invulnerable to change.

I approached a particular house. The yard was large but the house had been built close to the street. A hedge as high as my shoulder separated it from the sidewalk. I kept calm until I reached the break in the hedge and saw the marker. It was the name, in small, clear letters. I stood beneath an ancient, impregnable elm and got myself ready to knock at Finny's door.

Three months before, I had gone unsuspectingly to another door and first encountered him. The summer session of the Devon School convened that year in June, and when I opened the door of the room assigned me, there was Finny, standing in the middle of the floor and pulling handfuls of clothes carelessly out of a suitcase.

I had seen him at a distance around the school the previous winter and gotten the impression that he was bigger than I was. But when he straightened up, our eyes met dead level. For a second I thought he was going to say, "I'll bet my old man can lick your old man." Then his mouth broke into a grin, and he said, "Where did you get that dizzy shirt?"

It was like one of the shifts which made him so good at sports: exactly what the opponent didn't expect. I had been prepared to introduce myself, or to waive that and exclaim, "Well, I guess we're roommates!" or to begin negotiating an immediate, hostile division of the available floor space. Instead, he cut through everything and began criticizing my clothes—*my* clothes—while he stood there in hacked-off khaki pants and an undershirt. As a matter of fact, I was wearing a lime-green, short-sleeved sports shirt with the bottom squared and worn outside the pants, much admired in the South. "At home," I said. "Where did you think?"

"I don't know, but I can see that home is *way* down yonder." He had an unusual voice, as though he had some baritone instrument in his chest which would amaze you if he didn't keep it under control. You could clearly hear the music in it when he spoke: it was only when he tried to sing, which he often did, that music fled and his voice wailed off key ("Like an Arabian lament," the director of the Glee Club once commented).

Finny made me understand that we should be close friends at once. That first day, standing in our comfortless room amid his clothes, he began to talk and I began to listen. He wanted to establish a firm understanding on all subjects, so he covered the field, beginning with God and moving undeviatingly through to sex. "I'm not too bright about all this," he began, "and I don't understand much about theories, but the way it's always seemed to me . ." and then he outlined his beliefs. I didn't like them much; they had an eccentric, first-hand originality which cut straight across everything I had been told to believe. God, he felt, was Someone you had to discover for yourself. Nothing important had ever been written or said about Him. Sermons were usually hot air; formal prayers were drill.

Sex was vital, and that was why it was surrounded by even more fantasy than God. He had experienced it three times, and gave detailed, completely matter-of-fact and unboastful accounts of all three, omitting only the girls' names out of gallantry.

"How many times have you slept with a girl?" he asked, fixing his interested eyes on mine.

I was supposed to take up my story at this point. But my ideas would have been as dull as a catechism after his; it seemed as though I had never had an original thought in my life. Besides, this wasn't the way we talked with strangers in the South.

I hadn't asked for all these confidences, and I wasn't going to give mine in return. "I'll tell you about it someday," I answered in what I thought was a cool, rebuffing one.

"All right," exclaimed Finny with cheerful unconcern. "Will I be interested?"

"You'll be as interested as I was in yours." I liked the screened irony of this reply, lie though it was.

"Good!" He flung his empty suitcase into a corner, where it landed at an angle against the wall and stayed that way for the rest of the summer.

I wasn't going to be opened up like that suitcase, to have him yank out all my thoughts and feelings and scatter them around underfoot. So he went on talking and I kept on restively listening through the first weeks of summer.

Finny declared himself especially pleased with this weather, but I found later that all weathers delighted Phineas.

For that was his real name, and it is important for two reasons: first, it was just the kind of special old New England name he would have, and second, no one ever thought to kid him about it. At the Devon School kidding people, or "cutting them down," as it was called, gave place only to athletics as a field of concentration. No one could be allowed to grow above the prevailing level; anyone who threatened to must be instantly and collectively cut down. But Phineas at Devon was like the elms I came to find in his home town, so rooted and realized and proportional that the idea of felling them was unthinkable. Not that he wasn't kidded: his amazing way of dressing, his enjoyment of singing and his inability ever to be on key, the score of fourteen he got on a Latin examination, his habit of emptying his pockets on the floor at night, the icebox he bought which wouldn't hold ice or water, his failure to realize that he was naked when he went calling around the dormitory after a shower, all of these habits were kidded endlessly. But not cut down; they were too exceptional for that. We searched for ways to get at him for a while and then realized that it was impossible, because he never forced himself up.

All of us were at Devon for the summer session, the first in the history of the school. It was because of the war, to hurry us toward graduation before we became eighteen and draftable. We sixteen-year-olds were brought back for the summer and our pace stepped up noticeably. It's odd that such a peaceful summer should have resulted from war.

We became a muted New England adaptation of gilded youth that summer, we boys of sixteen. The masters were more benevolent toward us than at any other time. I think we relieved them of some of their pressure; we reminded them of what peace was like, of lives not bound up with destruction.

Phineas was the essence of this careless peace. Not that he was unconcerned about the war. On the third morning of the session he decided to wear his pink shirt, to memorialize the bombing of the Ploesti oil fields. It was a finely woven broadcloth, carefully cut, and very pink. No one else in the school could have worn it without some risk of having it torn from his back. But Finny put it on with the air of a monarch assuming the regalia. As he was buttoning the collar he at last acknowledged my absorbed stare, letting his eyes slide slowly from the mirror around to me.

"I figured it was a good day to put it on," he said stoutly, "on account of the oil fields." I just kept staring at him in mystification. "Well, you've got to do *something* to celebrate," he added rebukingly. "You can't just let something like that go by."

"Talk about *my* dizzy shirt!" I broke out indignantly at last.

"Yeah, but yours really is just a dizzy shirt. This is an emblem."

"Is that right!"

"Yeah, that *is* right,"

It was right. I watched him break it out during the next weeks for certain specific triumphs—his grade of C on a history quiz, the Battle of Midway, the retirement of Mrs. Carrian, our school dietitian, or "Lucrezia," as we called her. During the regular school terms, Phineas told me, he wore the shirt principally to celebrate the victories of the soccer, hockey, and lacrosse squads. He had elected to play, and therefore inevitably to star, on these three teams the previous year. He excelled at any sport because he had never yet realized that a player had to work for years to master completely one co-ordinated athletic movement, such as swinging a golf club. He thought an athlete naturally was good at everything at once. And he was right, for himself.

But why had he picked these teams, which drew smaller crowds and commanded less prestige than some of the others? It looked a little phony to me, deliberately turning his back on fame so that people would admire him even more. That might be it. So I asked him.

"Football!" he exclaimed in a tone of thrilling scorn. "Who would ever want to play football!" We were walking across the playing fields toward the gym after an hour of compulsory calisthenics. "It's just like those damn pushups and knee bends today. 'All together now, one-two-three,' that's football. Do you know they draw a map of every player's move, like it was geometry or something?"

Privately I thought that gave football a praiseworthy orderliness. I was going to say so, but Finney had encountered one of his principles, and wanted to enlarge on it.

"In a sport you've got to be loose," he went on. "You have to invent something new all the time. It's no fun if you don't."

This, as it turned out, was his personal athletic code. To be free, to invent, to create without any imposed plan. There was the essence of happiness. Or at least, as we walked back to the gym that late afternoon, so he gave me to believe.

He applied the same individualism, or anarchy, to his studies. We were sitting in our room memorizing the Presidents of the United States one night. "Washington-Adams-Jefferson-Madison-Monroe-Adams-Jackson," said Finny. "I've got those guys cold. Then who was there?"

"Van Buren-Harrison-Tyler-Polk-Taylor-Fillmore."

"What!" Finny cried. "Who ever heard of *them!*"

"Well, they were Presidents of the United States once."

He smiled as though at a wry, touching dream. "I guess *somebody* has to make up lists for schoolboys."

I turned back to the Cleveland-Harrison-Cleveland-McKinley-Roosevelt-Taft period with a divided mind. With Phineas sitting next to me day after day like some guiltless doubting Thomas, I began to wonder not whether history was real, but whether it was important.

I didn't do well in that course; that is, I got a B. At the end of the summer Mr. Patch-Withers told me that I didn't receive an A because of a "veiled flippance" in some of my work. But by that time nothing like grades mattered any more.

I knew Finny was interfering with my studies, and then I began to suspect why. I was smarter than he was. He couldn't stand that. I wasn't deceived by that amazed, happy grin of his when he learned I'd scored the highest grade in Latin, or his candid questions about how I balanced trigonometry equations in three steps while he took twelve. He was trying to take me in; he hated the fact that I could beat him at this. He might be the best natural athlete in the school, the most popular boy, but I was winning where it counted. Of all that there was to know about Phineas, I grasped this hidden enmity best.

And then I realized, with relief, that we were equals. He wasn't so unlike me, so peacefully himself, unconscious of conflict and rivalry, after all. He was as vulnerable and treacherous as everyone else. I began to feel more comfortable with him; I almost even liked him.

Summer moved on in its measureless peace. Finny put up with the compulsory calisthenics in the afternoons, but it was in the hour or two of daylight after supper that he set out to enjoy himself. One evening when five of us were sitting around the Common Room, all bored except Phineas, the idea came to him. His face lit up in inspiration. "I know, let's go jump in the river!" The rest of us looked up warily. "You know," he said, already full of enthusiasm, "out of that tree the seniors use to practice abandoning a troopship." He looked at us in the amused, cajoling way he had, as though we were a good but reluctant team and he was the coach. "Come on, don't just sit there waiting for the end of the world."

So we went out across the empty campus. There was a heightened, theatrical glow around us, as though we were crossing an empty stage with light flooding out from the wings. It gave what we were about to do the aura of a drama.

The tree grew alone and leaned out slightly over the river's edge. We looked up at its extraordinary height, and none of us believed that we would jump from it. None but Phineas. He stripped to his underpants and began scrambling up the wooden rungs nailed on the side of the tree. At last he stepped onto a branch which reached out a little farther over the water. "Is this the one they jump from?" he called down. None of us knew. "If I do it, will everybody do it?" We didn't say anything very clearly. "Well," he cried out, "here's my contribution to the war effort!" and he sprang out, fell through the tips of some lower branches, and smashed into the water.

"Great!" he cried, bobbing instantly to the surface again. "That's the most fun I've had this whole week. Who's next?"

I was. I hated the very existence of that tree. The idea of jumping from it revolted every instinct for self-preservation I had. But I would not lose in this to Phineas. I took off my clothes and began to climb. The branch he had jumped from was more slender than it looked from the ground, and much higher. It was impossible to walk out on it far enough to be well over the river. I would have to spring far out or risk falling into the shallows next to the bank. "Come on," drawled Finny from below, "don't admire the view. When they torpedo the troopship you can't stand around admiring the waves. Jump!"

It took one hatred to overcome another. I hated him at that moment, always trying to show me up, to get revenge for my procession of A's and his of D's. Damn him. I jumped.

The tips of branches snapped past me and then I crashed into the water. An instant later I was on the surface getting congratulations.

"I think that was better than Finny's," said Bobby Zane, who was bidding for an ally in the dispute he foresaw.

"Oh yeah?" Finny grimaced in pretended fury. "Let's see you pass the course before you start handing out grades. The tree's all yours."

Bobby's mouth closed as though forever. He didn't argue or refuse. He became inanimate. But the other two, Chet Douglass and Leper Lepellier, were vocal enough, complaining about school regulations, the danger of stomach cramps, chronic infirmities they had never mentioned before.

"It's you, pal," Finny said to me at last, "just you and me." He and I started back across the campus, preceding the others like two seigneurs.

But this made me feel no closer to Phineas. Neither did the document he drew up, the Charter of the Super Suicide Society of the Summer Session, inscribing his name and mine as charter members. He listed Chet, Bobby, and Leper as "trainees," and posted the paper in the Common Room. A few added their names to the trainee list and came with us in the evenings. The thing was respected: Finny's direct and aspiring pleasure in this game carried the whole dormitory with him.

August arrived with a deepening of all the summertime splendors of New Hampshire. There was a latent freshness in the air, as though spring were returning in the middle of the summer.

But examinations were at hand. I wasn't as ready for them as I should have been. The Suicide Society now met almost every evening, and all members were required to attend and jump. I never got inured to it. But when Phineas did it backwards one evening, so did I, with the sensation that I was throwing my life away. He promoted both of us on the spot to Senior Overseer Charter Members.

I would not let myself be shaken off, even though I began to see that it didn't really matter whether he showed me up at the tree or not. Because it was what you had in your heart that counted. And I had detected that Finny's was a den of lonely, selfish ambition. He was no better than I was, no matter who won all the contests.

A French examination was announced for one Friday late in August. Finny and I studied for it in the library Thursday afternoon; I went over vocabulary lists, and he wrote messages and passed them with great serious-ness to me, as *aides-mémoire*. Of course I didn't get any work done. After supper I went to our room to try again. Phineas came in.

"Arise," he began airily, "Senior Overseer Charter Member! Elwin 'Leper' Lepellier has announced his intention to make the leap this very night, to qualify, to save his face at last."

I didn't believe it. Leper Lepellier would go down paralyzed with panic on any sinking troopship before making such a jump. Finny had put him up to it, to finish me for good on the exam. I turned around with elaborate resignation. "If he jumps out of that tree I'm Mahatma Gandhi."

"All right," Finny agreed. He had a way of turning clichés inside out like that. "Come on. We've got to be there. Maybe he *will* do it this time."

"Jee-sus!" I slammed the French book shut.

"What's the matter?"

What a performance! His face was completely questioning and candid. "Studying!" I snarled. "You know, books. Examinations."

"Yeah . . ." He waited for me to go on, as though he didn't see what I was getting at yet.

"Oh, of course, *you* wouldn't know what I'm talking about. Not you." I stood up and slammed the chair against the desk. "Okay, we go. We watch little lily-liver Lepellier not jump from the tree, and I ruin my grade."

He looked at me with an interested expression. "You want to study?"

I sighed heavily. "Never mind, forget it. I know. I joined the club. I'm going."

"Don't go!" He shrugged. "What the hell, it's only a game."

I stopped halfway to the door. "What d'you mean?" I muttered. What he meant was clear enough, but I was groping for what lay behind his words. I might have asked, "Who are you, then?" instead. I was facing a total stranger.

"I didn't know you needed to study," he said simply. "I didn't think you ever did. I thought it just came to you."

It seemed that he had made some kind of parallel between my studies and his sports. He probably thought anything you were good at came without effort. He didn't know yet that he was unique.

I couldn't quite achieve a normal speaking voice. "If I need to study, then so do you."

"Me?" He smiled faintly. "Listen, I could study forever and I'd never break C. But it's different for you, you're good. You really are. If I had a brain like that, I'd—I'd have my head cut open so people could look at it."

He put his hands on the back of a chair and leaned toward me. "I know. We kid around a lot, but you have to be serious sometime, about something. If you're really good at something, I mean if there's nobody, or hardly anybody, who's as good as you are, then you've got to be serious about that. Don't mess around." He frowned. "Why didn't you say you had to study before?"

"Wait a minute," I said.

"It's okay. I'll oversee old Leper. I know he's not going to do it." He was at the door.

"Wait a minute," I said more sharply. "I'm coming."

"No you aren't, pal, you're going to study."

"Never mind my studying."

"You think you've done enough already?"

"Yes." I let this drop curtly, to bar him from telling me what to do about my work. He let it go at that, and went out the door ahead of me, whistling off key.

We followed our gigantic shadows across the campus, and Phineas began talking in wild French, to give me a little extra practice. I said nothing, my mind exploring the new dimensions of isolation around me. Any fear I ever had of the tree was nothing beside this. It wasn't my neck but my understanding that was menaced. He had never been jealous of me. Now I knew that there never had been and never could have been any rivalry between us. I was not of the same quality as he.

I couldn't stand this. We reached the others loitering around the base of the tree and Phineas began exuberantly to throw off his clothes, delighted by the challenge, the competitive tension of all of us. "Let's go, you and me," he called. A new idea struck him. "We'll go together, a double jump! Neat, eh?"

None of this mattered now: I would have listlessly agreed to anything. He started up the wooden rungs and I began climbing behind, up to the limb high over the bank. Phineas ventured a little way along it, holding a thin, nearby branch for support. "Come out a little way," he said, "and then we'll jump side by side." The countryside was striking from here, a deep-green sweep of playing fields and bordering shrubbery, with the school stadium white and miniature-looking across the river. From behind us the last long rays of light cut across the campus.

Holding firmly to the trunk, I took a step toward him, and then my knees bent and I jounced the limb. Finny, his balance gone, swung his head around to look at me for an instant with extreme interest, and then he tumbled sideways, broke through the little branches below and hit the bank with a sickening, unnatural thud. It was the first clumsy physical action I had ever seen him make. With unthinking sureness I moved out on the limb and jumped into the river, every trace of my fear of this forgotten.

None of us was allowed near the infirmary during the next days, but I heard all the rumors that came out of it. Eventually a fact emerged: one of his legs had been "shattered." I learned no more, although the subject was discussed endlessly. Everyone talked about Phineas to me. I suppose this was natural. I had been right beside him when it happened: I was his roommate.

I couldn't go on hearing about it much longer. If anyone had been suspicious of me, I might have developed some strength to defend myself. But no one suspected. Phineas must still be too sick, or too noble, to tell them.

I spent as much time as I could alone in our room, trying to empty my mind of every thought, to forget where I was, even who I was. One evening when I was dressing for dinner an idea occurred to me, the first with any energy behind it since Finny fell from the tree. I decided to put on his clothes. We wore the same size, and although he always criticized my clothes, he used to wear them frequently, quickly forgetting what belonged to him and what to me. I never forgot, and that evening I put on his cordovan shoes and his pants, and I looked for and finally found his pink shirt neatly folded, in a drawer. Its high stiff collar against my neck, the rich material against my skin excited a sense of strangeness and distinction; I felt like some nobleman, some Spanish grandee.

But when I looked in the mirror it was no remote aristocrat I had become. I was Phineas, Phineas to the life. I even had his humorous expression on my face, his sharp awareness. I had no idea why this gave me such intense relief, but it seemed, as I stood there in Finny's shirt, that I would never stumble over the twists and pitfalls of my own character again.

I didn't go down to dinner. The sense of transformation stayed with me throughout the evening, and even when I undressed and went to bed. That night I slept easily, and it was only on waking up that this illusion was gone, and I was confronted with myself, and what I had done to Finny.

Sooner or later it had to happen, and that morning it did. "Finny's better!" Dr. Stanpole called to me on the chapel steps. He steered me amiably into the lane leading toward the infirmary. "He could stand a visitor or two now, after these very nasty few days."

"You—you don't think I'll upset him or anything?"

"You? No, why? It'll do him good."

"I suppose he's still pretty sick."

"It was a messy break, but we'll have him walking again."

"*Walking* again!"

"Yes." The doctor didn't look at me, and barely changed his tone of voice. "Sports are finished for him after an accident like that, of course."

"But he must be able to," I burst out, "if his leg's still there, if you aren't going to amputate it—you aren't, are you?—then it must come back the way it was, why shouldn't it? Of course it will."

Dr. Stanpole hesitated, and I think glanced at me for a moment. "Sports are finished. As a friend you ought to help him face that and accept it."

I grabbed my head and the doctor, trying to be kind, put his hand on my shoulder. At his touch I lost all hope of controlling myself. I burst out crying into my hands; I cried for Phineas and for myself and for this doctor who believed in facing things. Most of all I cried because of kindness, which I had not expected.

"Now, that's no good. You've got to be cheerful and hopeful. He needs that from you. He wanted especially to see you. You were the one person he asked for."

That stopped my tears. Of course I was the first person he wanted to see. Phineas would say nothing behind my back; he would accuse me, face to face.

We were walking up the steps of the infirmary. Everything was very swift, and next I was in a corridor, being nudged by Dr. Stanpole toward a door. 'He's in there. I'll be with you in a minute."

I pushed back the door, which was slightly ajar, and stood transfixed on the threshold. Phineas lay among pillows and sheets, his left leg, enormous in its white bindings, suspended a little above the bed. A tube led from a glass bottle into his right arm. Some channel began to close inside me and I knew I was about to black out.

"Come on in," he said. "You look worse than I do." The fact that he could make a light remark pulled me back a little, and I went to a chair beside his bed. He seemed to have diminished physically in the few days which had passed, and to have lost his tan. His eyes studied me as though I were the patient. They no longer had their sharp good humor, but had become clouded and visionary. After a while I realized he had been given a drug. "What are *you* looking so sick about?" he went on.

"Finny, I—" there was no controlling what I said; the words were instinctive, like the reactions of someone cornered. "What happened at the tree? That damn tree, I'm going to cut down that tree. Who cares who can jump out of it? How did you fall, how could you fall off like that?"

"I just fell." His eyes looked vaguely into my face. "Something jiggled and I fell over. I remember I turned around and looked at you; it was like I had all the time in the world. I thought I could reach out and get hold of you."

I flinched violently away from him. "To drag me down too!"

He kept looking vaguely over my face. "To get hold of you, so I wouldn't fall."

"Yes, naturally." I was fighting for air in this close room. "I tried, you remember? I reached out but you were gone, down through those little branches."

"I remember looking at your face for a second. Funny expression you had. Very shocked, like you have right now."

"Right now? Well, of course, I *am* shocked. It's terrible."

"But I don't see why you should look so *personally* shocked. You look like it happened to you or something."

"It's almost like it did! I was right there, right on the limb beside you!"

"Yes, I know. I remember it all."

There was a hard block of silence, and then I said quietly, as though my words might detonate the room, "Do you remember what made you fall?"

His eyes continued their roaming across my face. "I don't know. I must have just lost my balance. It must have been that. I did have this feeling that when you were standing there beside me, y—I don't know. I must have been delirious. So I just have to forget it. I just fell, that's all." He turned away to grope for something among the pillows. "I'm sorry about that feeling I had."

I couldn't say anything to this sincere, drugged apology for having suspected the truth. He was never going to accuse me. It was only a feeling he had, and at this moment he must have been formulating a new commandment in his personal decalogue: Never accuse a friend of a crime if you only have a feeling he did it.

It was his best victory. If I had been the one in the hospital bed I would have brought Devon down around his ears with my accusations; I would have hounded him out of the school. And I had thought we were competitors! It was so ludicrous I wanted to cry.

And if Phineas had been sitting here in this pool of guilt, how would he have felt, what would he have done?

He would have told the truth.

I got up so suddenly that the chair overturned. I stared at him in amazement, and he stared back, his mouth gradually breaking into a grin. "Well," he said in his friendly, knowing voice, "what are you going to do, hypnotize me?"

"Finny, I've got something to tell you. You're going to hate it, but there's something I've got to tell you."

But I didn't tell him. Dr. Stanpole came in before I was able to, and then a nurse came in, and I was sent away. I walked down the corridor of elms descending from the infirmary to the dormitories, and at every tree I seemed to leave something I had envied Finny—his popularity, his skill at sports, his background, his ease. It was none of these I had wanted from him. It was the honesty of his every move and his every thought.

But the story wasn't yet complete. I had to wait for a while before ending it, because the day after I saw Finny, the doctor decided that he was not yet well enough for visitors, even old pals like me, after all. The summer session closed. Phineas was taken by ambulance to his home outside Boston, and I went south for a month's vacation. At the end of September I came back to Boston, en route to Devon for the fall term. I found the town where he lived, and I waited a little longer under that tree in front of Finny's house, struggling, maybe for the last time, with the risky emotions I had had for years. Tomorrow, back at Devon, I would be someone else. A week later I was going to turn seventeen and begin the last acceleration which would pitch me into some corner of the war.

The sun was going down much earlier those days, and it began to get chilly. I rehearsed what I was going to say once more, and then turned in through the hedge and knocked at Finny's door.

Danny Santiago
The Somebody

THIS IS CHATO TALKING, CHATO DE SHAMROCK, from the Eastside in old L.A., and I want you to know this is a big day in my life because today I quit school and went to work as a writer. I write on fences or buildings or anything that comes along. I write my name, not the one I got from my father. I want no part of him. I write Chato, which means Catface, because I have a flat nose like a cat. It's a Mexican word because that's what I am, a Mexican, and I'm not ashamed of it. I like that language too, man. It's way better than English to say what you feel. But German is the best. It's got a real rugged sound, and I'm going to learn to talk it someday.

After Chato I write "de Shamrock." That's the street where I live, and it's the name of the gang I belong to, but the others are all gone now. Their families had to move away, except Gorilla is in jail and Blackie joined the navy because he liked swimming. But I still have our old arsenal. It's buried under the chickens, and I dig it up when I get bored. There's tire irons and chains and pick handles with spikes and two zip guns we made and they shoot real bullets but not very straight. In the good old days nobody cared to tangle with us. But now I'm the only one left.

Well, today started off like any other day. The toilet roars like a hot rod taking off. My father coughs and spits about nineteen times and hollers it's six-thirty. So I holler back I'm quitting school. Things hit me like that—sudden.

"Don't you want to be a lawyer no more," he says in Spanish, "and defend the Mexican people?"

My father thinks he is very funny, and next time I make any plans, he's sure not going to hear about it.

"Don't you want to be a doctor," he says, "and cut off my leg for nothing someday?"

367

"*Due beast ine dumb cop,*" I tell him in German, but not very loud.

"How will you support me," he says, "when I retire? Or will you marry a rich old woman that owns a pool hall?"

"I'm checking out of this dump! You'll never see me again!"

I hollered it at him, but already he was in the kitchen making a big noise in his coffee. I could be dead and he wouldn't take me serious. So I laid there and waited for him to go off to work. When I woke up again, it was way past eleven. I can sleep forever these days. So I got out of bed and put on clean jeans and my windbreaker and combed myself very neat because already I had a feeling this was going to be a big day for me.

I had to wait for breakfast because the baby was sick and throwing up milk on everything. There is always a baby vomiting in my house. When they're born, everybody comes over and says: "*Qué* cute!" but nobody passes any comments on the dirty way babies act or the dirty way they were made either. Sometimes my mother asks me to hold one for her but it always cries, maybe because I squeeze it a little hard when nobody's looking.

When my mother finally served me, I had to hold my breath, she smelled so bad of babies. I don't care to look at her anymore. Her legs got those dark-blue rivers running all over them. I kept waiting for her to bawl me out about school, but I guess she forgot, or something. So I cut out.

Every time I go out my front door I have to cry for what they've done to old Shamrock Street. It used to be so fine, with solid homes on both sides. Maybe they needed a little paint here and there but they were cozy. Then the S.P. railroad bought up all the land except my father's place because he was stubborn. They came in with their wrecking bars and their bulldozers. You could hear those houses scream when they ripped them down. So now Shamrock Street is just front walks that lead to a hole in the ground, and piles of busted cement. And Pelón's house and Blackie's are just stacks of old boards waiting to get hauled away. I hope that never happens to your street, man.

My first stop was the front gate and there was that sign again, that big S wrapped around a cross like a snake with rays coming out, which is the mark of the Sierra Street gang, as everybody knows. I rubbed it off, but tonight they'll put it back again. In the old days they wouldn't dare to come on our street, but without your gang you're nobody. And one of these fine days they're going to catch up with me in person and that will be the end of Chato de Shamrock.

So I cruised on down to Main Street like a ghost in a graveyard. Just to prove I'm alive, I wrote my name on the fence at the corner. A lot of names you see in public places are written very sloppy. Not me. I take my time. Like my fifth-grade teacher used to say, if other people are going to see your work, you owe it to yourself to do it right. Mrs. Cully was her name and she was real nice, for an Anglo. My other teachers were all cops but Mrs. Cully drove me home one time when some guys were after me. I think she wanted to adopt me but she never said anything about it. I owe a lot to that lady, and especially my writing. You should see it, man—it's real smooth and mellow, and curvy like a blond in a bikini. Everybody says so. Except one time they had me in Juvenile by mistake and some doctor looked at it. He said it proved I had something wrong with me, some long word. That doctor was crazy, because I made him show me his writing and it was real ugly like a barb-wire fence with little chickens stuck on the points. You couldn't even read it.

Anyway, I signed myself very clean and neat on that corner. And then I thought, Why not look for a job someplace? But I was more in the mood to write my name, so I went into the dime store and helped myself to two boxes of crayons and some chalk and cruised on down Main, writing all the way. I wondered should I write more than my name. Should I write, "Chato is a fine guy," or, "Chato, is wanted by the police"? Things like that. News. But I decided against it. Better to keep them guessing. Then I crossed over to Forney Playground. It used to be our territory, but now the Sierra have taken over there like everyplace else. Just to show them, I wrote on the tennis court and the swimming pool and the gym. I left a fine little trail of Chato de Shamrock in eight colors. Some places I used chalk, which works better on brick or plaster. But crayons are the thing for cement or anything smooth, like in the girls' rest room. On that wall I also drew a little picture the girls would be interested in and put down a phone number beside it. I bet a lot of them are going to call that number, but it isn't mine because we don't have a phone in the first place, and in the second place I'm probably never going home again.

I'm telling you, I was pretty famous at the Forney by the time I cut out, and from there I continued my travels till something hit me. You know how you put your name on something and that proves it belongs to you? Things like school books or gym shoes? So I thought, How about that, now? And I put my name on the Triple A Market and on Morrie's Liquor Store and on the Zócalo, which is a beer joint. And then I cruised on up Broadway, getting rich. I took over a barber shop and a furniture store and the Plymouth agency. And the firehouse for laughs, and the phone company so I could call all my girl friends and keep my dimes. And then there I was at Webster and Garcia's Funeral Home with the big white columns. At first I thought that might be bad luck, but then I said, Oh, well, we all got to die sometime. So I signed myself, and now I can eat good and live in style and have a big time all my life, and then kiss you all goodbye and give myself the best damn funeral in L.A. for free.

And speaking of funerals, along came the Sierra right then, eight or ten of them down the street with that stupid walk which is their trademark. I ducked into the garage and hid behind the hearse. Not that I'm a coward. Getting stomped doesn't bother me, or even shot. What I hate is those blades, man. They're like a piece of ice cutting into your belly. But the Sierra didn't see me and went on by. I couldn't hear what they were saying but I knew they had me on their mind. So I cut on over to the Boys' Club, where they don't let anybody get you, no matter who you are. To pass the time I shot some baskets and played a little pool and watched the television, but the story was boring, so it came to me, Why not write my name on the screen? Which I did with a squeaky pen. Those cowboys sure looked fine with Chato de Shamrock written all over them. Everybody got a kick out of it. But of course up comes Mr. Calderon and makes me wipe it off. They're always spying on you up there. And he takes me into his office and closes the door.

"Well," he says, "and how is the last of the dinosaurs?"

Meaning that the Shamrocks are as dead as giant lizards.

Then he goes into that voice with the church music in it and I look out of the window.

"I know it's hard to lose your gang, Chato," he says, "but this is your chance to make new friends and straighten yourself out. Why don't you start coming to Boys' Club more?"

"It's boring here," I tell him.

"What about school?"

"I can't go," I said. "They'll get me."

"The Sierra's forgotten you're alive," he tells me.

"Then how come they put their mark on my house every night?"

"Do they?"

He stares at me very hard. I hate those eyes of his. He thinks he knows everything. And what is he? Just a Mexican like everybody else.

"Maybe you put that mark there yourself," he says. "To make yourself big. Just like you wrote on the television."

"That was my name! I like to write my name!"

"So do dogs," he says. "On every lamppost they come to."

"You're a dog yourself," I told him, but I don't think he heard me. He just went on talking. Brother, how they love to talk up there! But I didn't bother to listen, and when he ran out of gas I left. From now on I'm scratching that Boys' Club off my list.

Out on the street it was getting dark, but I could still follow my trail back toward Broadway. It felt good seeing Chato written everyplace, but at the Zócalo I stopped dead. Around my name there was a big red heart done in lipstick with some initials I didn't recognize. To tell the truth, I didn't know how to feel. In one way I was mad that anyone would fool with my name, especially if it was some guy doing it for laughs. But what guy carries lipstick? And if it was a girl, that could be kind of interesting.

A girl is what it turned out to be. I caught up with her at the telephone company. There she is, standing in the shadows, drawing her heart around my name. And she has a very pretty shape on her, too. I sneak up behind her very quiet, thinking all kinds of crazy things and my blood shooting around so fast it shakes me all over. And then she turns around and it's only Crusader Rabbit. That's what we called her from the television show they had then, on account of her teeth in front.

When she sees me, she takes off down the alley, but in twenty feet I catch her. I grab for the lipstick, but she whips it behind her. I reach around and try to pull her fingers open, but her hand is sweaty and so is mine. And there we are, stuck together all the way down. I can feel everything she's got and her breath is on my cheek. She twists up against me, kind of giggling. To tell the truth, I don't like to wrestle with girls. They don't fight fair. And then we lost balance and fell against some garbage cans, so I woke up. After that I got the lipstick away from her very easy.

"What right you got to my name?" I tell her. "I never gave you permission."

"You sign yourself real fine," she says.

I knew that already.

"Let's go writing together," she says.

"The Sierra's after me."

"I don't care," she says. "Come on, Chato—you and me can have a lot of fun."

She came up close and giggled that way. She put her hand on my hand that had the lipstick in it. And you know what? I'm ashamed to say I almost told her yes. It would be a change to go writing with a girl. We could talk there in the dark. We could decide on the best places. And her handwriting wasn't too bad either. But then I remembered I had my reputation to think of. Somebody would be sure to see us, and they'd be laughing at me all over the Eastside. So I pulled my hand away and told her off.

"Run along, Crusader," I told her. "I don't want no partners, and especially not you."

"Who are you calling Crusader?" she screamed. "You ugly, squash-nose punk."

She called me everything. And spit at my face but missed. I didn't argue. I just cut out. And when I got to the first sewer I threw away her lipstick. Then I drifted over to the banks at Broadway and Bailey, which is a good spot for writing because a lot of people pass by there.

Well, I hate to brag, but that was the best work I've ever done in all my life. Under the street lamp my name shone like solid gold. I stood to one side and checked the people as they walked past and inspected it. With some you can't tell just how they feel, but with others it rings out like a cash register. There was one man. He got out of his Cadillac to buy a paper and when he saw my name he smiled. He was the age to be my father. I bet he'd give me a job if I asked him. I bet he'd take me to his home and to his office in the morning. Pretty soon I'd be sitting at my own desk and signing my name on letters and checks and things. But I would never buy a Cadillac, man. They burn too much gas.

Later a girl came by. She was around eighteen, I think, with green eyes. Her face was so pretty I didn't dare to look at her shape. Do you want me to go crazy? That girl stopped and really studied my name like she fell in love with it. She wanted to know me, I could tell. She wanted to take my hand and we'd go off together just holding hands and nothing dirty. We'd go to Beverly Hills and nobody would look at us the wrong way. I almost said "Hi" to that girl, and, "How do you like my writing?" But not quite.

So here I am, standing on this corner with my chalk all gone and only one crayon left and it's ugly brown. My fingers are too cold besides. But I don't care because I just had a vision, man. Did they ever turn on the lights for you so you could see the whole world and everything in it? That's how it came to me right now. I don't need to be a movie star or boxing champ to make my name in the world. All I need is plenty of chalk and crayons. And that's easy. L.A. is a big city, man, but give me a couple of months and I'll be famous all over town. Of course they'll try to stop me—the Sierra, the police and everybody. But I'll be like a ghost, man. I'll be real mysterious, and all they'll know is just my name, signed like I always sign it, CHATO DE SHAMROCK with rays shooting out like from the Holy Cross.

Howard Nemerov
The Sorcerer's Eye

AROUND THE CASTLE WHERE I LIVED with my parents was a moat, half over-grown with weeds, where wild birds waded and swam. A corridor, which I liked to think was secret, led to a door at the water's edge, and there I used to go, against my father's absolute command, to meet the girl from outside. We spoke across the water.

"What is that you wear on the string around your neck?" she asked me once. I drew it from my shirt, a golden spoon it was, and showed it to her.

"Why a golden spoon?" she asked.

"Oh," I said, "it is something that happened long ago, a kind of family joke, though not a very good one. You wouldn't be interested."

"You're a sad boy, aren't you?" said she. "Do they really joke, in your family? Tell me."

"When I was little," I said, "my father once told me, he seemed angry about it, that I had been born with a golden spoon in my mouth. That puzzled me, since I didn't know it was a proverb, and I tried to think what it was like to be born, and why one would have a golden spoon in one's mouth at that time, and finally, seeing that my father really meant something, which it made him angry to mean, I started to cry. My mother then, to turn it into a joke, took a real golden spoon from the dinner table, tapped me on the shoulder with it, and said I was her knight of the golden spoon. So I have kept the spoon."

The girl smiled. She was dressed in black rags, and so beautiful.

"You love your mother, don't you?" she said.

"She is sick," I replied. "She lies on a sofa all day, and has little heart-shaped white pastilles, for her heart ailment. She reads novels, and sometimes I read them to her, though Father does not like me to be reading novels."

"There's a great lot your father doesn't like."

"He doesn't like at all for me to meet you and talk to you."

"I know," said she. "We're both lonely."

"I am so lonely," said I. "For I read in books about how people live, out in the world, and meet others, and make friends, and love another. I love you, I think."

"I love you," she said, "but it would be better not to talk of that."

"Because of your father?" I asked.

"Because of him, yes."

"I know about your father," I said, "for my father told me the tale on my eighteenth birthday, only a while ago. I have even seen your father, through the telescope in the tower room. He sits in the woods, a mile away. He sits on a throne of sorts, I think, and stares at our castle all the time. He is a sorcerer, isn't he, a kind of wizard?"

"He is," said she.

"And my father is frightened of him," I went on, "for he built this castle of ours by magic, before I was born, and my father fears that if he is offended he may tear it down, also by magic."

"That's true, he could," she said. "Your father must have been in terrible trouble, to need my father's help."

"My father used to live in the world," I said. "He was a captain in one of the great regiments, and he had epaulets of silver, high boots, silver spurs. But he lived too well, and gambled, and was in debt. One night, when he was drunk and losing everything, he bet against a brother officer and on his side the wager was that this man, if he won, might spend a night with my mother."

"That was a bad thing to do," said the girl.

"It was," I said, "for he lost. Everyone knew then that it was not only a bad bet but an impossible one, and they left him alone until sunrise, with a pistol on the table. My father was to shoot himself because of his dishonor; that was the understanding, in the regiment. But instead he went out and walked in the streets of the city until, near dawn, he met your father, who brought him into the deep forest, far away, and raised him up this fine castle which you see—all by a look of the eye he did this, and by a gesture of the hand."

"My father has a great and terrible power," the girl said. "There was a condition."

"The condition was simply this," I replied, "that we live here, that we never go outside."

"You are safe, at any rate."

"Yes," I said, "we are safe enough. But my father is unhappy, and that makes us all unhappy. He is unhappy because, I think, he believes still that he might somehow have got out of his desperate position and gone on to a grand career, and because my mother is ill and not much of a companion to him, and because she despises him, having never forgiven the wager. Finally," I said with some hesitation, "because he suspects, and fears, that after all his fellow officer might have taken advantage of his winning, on that night, so I would be not my father's child but his. About this, he has never asked my mother, as fearing her reply, as not wanting the burden of the knowledge, I don't know."

We were silent. The waters of the moat glittered between us. Behind me the castle stood towering in courses of great blocks of stone, behind her the trees flickered their green leaves in the light wind and the sunshine.

"I never knew my mother," said the girl at last.

"I'm sorry for that," said I.

"Nor have I been in the world," she said. "I am as much a prisoner as you are, and perhaps my father is as much a prisoner as yours. The keeper is always bound to his charge, so neither can be free."

"I should like to go into the world," I said, "but only if you would go with me."

"My father has two eyes," she said, musingly, and as if not replying at all, "of which the right one, of flesh and blood, is the eye of action, and the left one a glass orb, is the eye of thought. With the one, he does; with the other, he knows."

"That is a strange division," I said, "and yet, after all, quite appropriate in its way."

"I have been thinking," she said, "that as my father's eyes are fixed upon the castle, so that you and I are beneath his notice, we might go together, one time, and come up behind him, and you with your golden spoon could quickly remove an eye—"

"But that would be terrible," said I, "in itself and in its consequences."

"Terrible, how?" asked the girl. "I do not love my father."

"Nor I mine," I replied, "though I should be sorry to lose my mother. But the castle would fall."

"Not if you removed the glass eye," she said. "It would not hurt him to lose it, since it is glass, since it is the eye of knowledge he would never know he had lost it, so that it follows, surely, that he must keep the eye of action turned, as always, upon the castle, to keep it as it is, in being."

"That's true," I said, beginning to be fascinated with the idea. "But dangerous."

"You are afraid?" she asked, smiling again.

"I have never been afraid," I said, somewhat sternly, but yet not pridefully, for the fact was that my existence until this time had magically excluded the awareness of fear.

"When it is done," she said, "we shall go out into the world, away from castle and forest, and I promise to love you for as long as you will love me."

"I will do it for that promise," I said. "I will do it for you."

"Tonight," she said, "meet me here again, and I will lead you where he sits."

So we parted, agreeing to meet in the hour before dawn.

2

"You've been seeing that girl again," said my father during the course of the evening.

"No, sir," I said, looking him steadily in the eye. I thought that he had not seen me down there by the moat, but said this simply from a sad propensity, almost a wish, to know the worst, at all times, about everything.

"I hope you are not lying to me," he said, frowning. "You know how I regard a lie."

He had come to a stop facing me, but now he resumed his usual occupation of pacing the long hall, with his hands locked behind him. Whenever he turned toward me, however, he thought of something else to say.

"It's for your good, as well as mine, that I warn you" was one of these remarks. And another was "Don't imagine I shan't know what you do." And another: "I don't like to have to keep an eye perpetually on what my own son is up to; but I will, I will if it is necessary, make no mistake about that."

My silence during all this was meant to be respectful, though it was also shamefaced because of the lie; it seemed merely to provoke him further, so that at last he came to a definite halt in front of me, but spoke rather to the ceiling, or the walls, than to me.

"What difference does it make? What can I keep? What have I to defend? A merciless bargain. Are you my son? Are you?"

"I don't know," I said, though he still seemed to be talking at random rather than to me. "I cannot know if you don't, sir."

"Ah, I know you'll do as you please," he said roughly, and then, "If you see that child once more—once more—let me tell you, lad—"

"Yes, Father," said I meekly but by no means humbly.

"I will . . . I will . . . ah, what will I?" he rather groaned than said, and stalked away leaving me there. I felt sad for him in his merciless bargain, but undisturbed in my resolve. The bargain had not been mine, and perhaps what I was about to do had, in some way, been included in the pact to begin with, before I was born. He was an elegant, lean man, my father, still young-looking, and I had always thought him strong. But I now saw that his strength was of the sort which is purely for display and is always defeated in action; that is why it could continue to look like strength, because there was really for him, poor man, no world in which he might expend it.

My mother, though, was the image of a continuously victorious weakness. Fragile and lovely, with her romances and her little medicated confections for the heart, she lay there year after year, not so much indomitable—that was the quality she had lived on, and used up—as simply undefeated. I told her nothing, that night; but she felt a foreboding.

"Something . . . something . . . will happen, soon."

"Oh, Mother," I said quite boldly, "all will be well, you will live in your castle still. Whatever happens, trust your knight of the golden spoon, who will never let anything bad happen to you." For I believed at this time that

I was going to be their savior as well as my own. I should free myself, and go into the world, and love another, while they would possess their fine castle unconditionally, when I had removed the glass eye of knowledge from the sorcerer's head, so that it might never revoke the action of the other eye which kept the castle standing. So all would be well, with them and with me.

I reassured my mother, and then for a while read to her, as I sometimes did, from the novel she happened to be reading at the time. Because she read these novels far more when I was not there than had them read when I was, my impression of the life in them was flickering and discontinuous: someone would be happy at one reading, on the point of suicide at the next, married at the next, then dead, and so on; also, different people would have entered while I was away, and the people I knew from previous readings would have disappeared; I never knew, even, when one novel left off and a quite different one replaced it.

In the chapter I read that night a man abandoned his wife and child, on account of something he had done which doubtless had been described in an earlier part, but which I knew nothing of. As he left the house at night, he stood at the end of the street to look back once at the little light above the door emblem of a happiness lost and a security decayed, so that the author, a woman, was moved to exclaim to us readers, "The gleam of that lantern would illuminate his mind for many years," and, an instant later, "how far that little lantern threw its beams!" expressions which, sentimental as they may have been in that place, I have been unable to forget. At the time, however, I affected to regard them slightly, and may even have read these phrases with a tone of mockery, for my mother said to me, as I bent to kiss her good night and, as I thought, goodbye, that when one day I had gone into the world and married and knew what it was to be a father, I should perceive the bitter truth at the heart of those words which I now found merely sugary.

3

Before dawn, by the black waters of the moat, without a moon to silver them, I stood shivering. At her low, long call I dived as deep and far as I could, felt for an instant the weeds cling and grasp about me, and came up at her feet. We set off roundabout through the forest, she holding my hand and leading the way with a great certainty, though nothing could be seen.

"You remember what you have to do?" she whispered once. I whispered that I did, though really what went through my head was scarcely a thought, so much as the mere image of my bending over that high and crooked shoulder from behind and suddenly, violently, digging with my golden spoon.

We reached the glade in the forest at first light, when a few birds were beginning to cry out. The girl, my girl, was pale, pale as stone in this gray light, and, though I was not afraid, something of what fear was began to make itself known to me through her hand, sweating but coldly sweating, which clutched mine always more tightly as we crept into the clearing behind the old man's high throne, above which reared back his great shoulders cloaked in black and his massive, steady head, which never moved.

"Now!" she whispered, letting go my hand and pushing me out toward the figure in the glade. I took the spoon, tearing the cord which tied it to my neck, ran forward, and leaped up, grasping that head by its white hair so that it fell back while with my other hand I did with the spoon what I had come to do.

Oh, I saw his face at that instant, and it was terrible, and I knew now how to be afraid. The air was split by his one cry of anguish, which endured while I dropped to the ground and began to run. The girl caught me by the hand again; in my other hand I held the spoon, and in the spoon was held the eye, and his mighty voice screamed behind us as we ran, "I know you! I know you!"

"Not that way," that girl began to bicker at me, "not that way, that leads back to the castle."

"I know," said I. "I took the wrong eye."

"I know you!" screamed the voice behind us. "I know what you have done."

As we ran through the forest the sun rose before us, and its red and gold light flickered through the leaves in a rhythm like that beaten by my brain: I know you, I know you. The eye stuck to the spoon, the spoon was clenched in my hand. Now I was the leader, and I was afraid, while the girl tagged on behind me, and the great voice of agony wakened the forest and the whole world.

"I can't run any more," she began to cry out after a time, and when despite my terrible impatience and fear I turned to attend to her weakness I saw no beautiful young girl, whose white flesh peeped at the shoulder through her rags, and whom I loved, but a thickened, sallow, blotched creature dressed in a somewhat elegant gown which was, however, badly ripped and stained.

"I can't go on any more," she cried chokingly, and sagged to the ground. As I took up my flight again I heard her for a time begging me not to leave her, but I could not stop.

The castle, when I reached it, was a silent ruin. The moat had dried up, and in the dry ravine where it had been was a tangle of bushes and vines and tall grass. Great trees had fallen, it seemed centuries ago, against what was left of the castle walls, brought low now and with the contours of the great stones softened by moss and lichen. One of these trees I was able to use as a bridge, and in a moment stood atop a heap of marble slabs mingled with granite blocks. Before me, in a kind of pit formed by the inward collapse of battlements, my mother sat on a stone, with my father standing beside her. He held her by the hand. I saw that they were old, quite old, and wrinkled, with dry, papery faces. And I was frightened anew, even before my father cried out to me, in a shrill voice, "What have you done?

Monster, what have you done?" And my mother said, in a dull voice as though she cared for nothing in the world, "What is that in your hand?"

I looked at my hand, at the spoon, at the eye which quivered there like a jelly. In that instant I knew all the fear my childhood had been denied, all the fear, I think, of children all over the world when in their sinfulness and shame they stand before the mighty parents whom they are bidden to destroy. And as though by this means I might rid myself of the evidence of my guilt I raised the spoon to my mouth and swallowed down the eye.

"What's done is done," I said to them sternly. "Come, we shall leave here at once."

And that is what we did, with nothing in our hands except my golden spoon. My parents opposed me no more, and we walked out into the forest, in the heat of the day, where I could still hear as it were the leaves of the trees shaking in slight sound: "I know you!" And this great forest, which from the castle had once seemed of illimitable extent in every direction, proved to go on for a few miles only. By midafternoon we had come out on a highway, with rails sunk in it, and on the rails was what I later understood to be a tram car. Of course, as we had no money, it was necessary to walk. And when, some time later, we came into the city, it was hard at first to find food and lodging. But I was now the owner—despite himself—of the eye of power and action, and it is enough to say that I soon found work, which enabled me to provide for my parents while they lived.

It was not long. My mother was very shortly afterward taken by a fatal attack, and then my father, stealing money from me in order to do so, bought a pistol and with it one night blew out his brains, just as though he were a gallant young captain still, and nineteen years had never passed.

Since then, I have gone about my business in the world, preferring travel to residence, being, as you might say, an *entrepreneur*. I have done quite well with my life, following my many concernments from one town to another, living always in hotels, a long succession of them so that they seem to become one in my memory, with their marbles and potted palms and ancient elevators of open grillework in which the passengers arise and descend like angels in trousers and spats or in tea gowns and pumps. All those towns seem a single town in the flickering rhythm of my brain, Nineveh, perhaps, that great city which the Lord spared, as I read once, although there were therein so many persons that could not discern between their right hand and their left hand.

I have never married. And I have kept my golden spoon, for a watch charm. I used to eat my breakfast egg with it, but gave that up many years back as being bravado. And somewhere, in a small clearing in my busy brain, the black-robed magician sits still in his high chair and cries out in an anguish undiminished by time or by his impotence that he knows me, he knows me.

Hannah Green
The Grey Bird

ABOUT THREE IN THE MORNING Natalie Mitchell, a girl of fifteen, stood at a lighted window upstairs in an old frame house. She stood with her head hung forward. Her hair parted mussily at the nape of her neck and was moist close to the skin. Her eyes, large and green in her long beige-pale face, circled about furtively, sleepily, and stared for a moment vacant and wide out into the darkness where a maple branch reached with its broad leaf hands close to the window and scarcely quivered in the thick, humid night. Natalie let her shoulders slouch lower so that her wet pajama collar pulled tight against her neck and a chill went through her like a crazy shiver because it was so hot.

Turning from her window she stared for several moments at her desk which in the pale green room of old cream-colored bedroom furniture stood tall, heavy, and dark with its ornately carved baroque top only two inches below the ceiling and its bookshelves closed behind glass doors.

She looked at her clock. In half an hour they would all be up. In two hours they would be already on the road. Natalie rubbed her feet along the cool floor of the hall to her sister's room, opened the door, and whispered loudly into the darkness, "Hey, El, are you awake yet?"

"Huh?" Ellen swished her sheets and made a long, comfortable groan. "Huh? Yeah, I can't sleep at all."

"Neither can I. Shall I come in and we'll talk quietly?" Natalie kicked into a slipper and flopped down on Ellen's legs.

Ellen squirmed. "Ow, dammit, get off."

"It's almost three-thirty anyhow," whispered Natalie, standing up and taking a new position at the bottom of the bed.

"Just think, Nat, this afternoon we'll be swimming in West Bay."

"Yeah, just think," replied Natalie with tones of mystery and anticipation forced into her voice. "Quick plunge. One toe in and out." She said "out" way too loudly and they began to laugh.

"Shh,' and they laughed some more. They heard the low voices of their mother and father in the next room. "Shh, they're awake." Natalie's lips hung open and moved slightly as she breathed. She imagined the dark room with the low, relaxed voices side by side in the bed. In front of her father's voice a red point of cigarette light moved, grew brighter under his eyes, moved to the side, grew bright again, and flew finally into the darkness of an ash tray.

In their mother and father's bathroom the toilet flushed. Ellen turned on her light. "They're up," she announced, jerking up her chin.

They heard Kroupa's nails scratch the door of their mother and father's room and Natalie bounded to let him out.

"Oh, morning, morning, Kroupsie." His front end was buried in her embrace; the back part wagged wildly and then squirmed to freedom. Natalie followed him to Ellen's bed. "Up, Kroupa, up!" she commanded, and clapped her hands.

Ellen was then squealing under the sheet and Kroupa danced all over the wriggling body trying to find its head.

"Give her a real cold nose," cheered Natalie.

From under the pillow came, "Kroupa Mitchell, down! Ouch. Cut it out, Kroups." His black tail with the white tip went round and round in circles.

Their mother appeared in the doorway in her thin nightgown. Her hair stood out in strands around the creased flesh of her face.

"Children, pipe down, it's the middle of the night and you'll wake the Egberts," she whispered hoarsely, and half excited too. Her eyes had the wide startled look they always had in the early morning.

"Oh, Kroups, no breakfast for you," said Ellen, hugging him when their mother was gone. "We're going to West Bay and you better not throw up."

"Kroups won't." Natalie put her cheek down on his furry head. "Oh, pew, Kroupa's halitosis is worse than it ever was. Whew!" She pinched her nose. "Brother, what'll we do?"

Ellen laughed. Her mouth got a helpless look and her lids went half down over her blue eyes.

Natalie went to her father's door. "Daddy, what'll we do? Kroupa has the worst halitosis ever."

"I suggest a thorough purge." Natalie's father stood by his bureau brushing his hair. His legs were white and very skinny. Natalie looked at the red mark on the bridge of his nose which looked as though it hurt in the morning when his eyes without glasses were narrow and puffy.

She turned and dashed back to Ellen's room. "Hey, El, Daddy suggests a thorough purge." Ellen laughed some more.

After breakfast Natalie shut the door of her room and sat down at her desk. She rubbed her forehead against the worn brown velvet writing top, spread out her arms, and curled the fingers of her large-boned hands over the edge. The desk had been in her room since the fifth grade when her Great-Aunt Martha died. When it came she loved it at once because of its cubbyholes and compartments and the two thin drawers with partitions of various sizes which she could lock and unlock with a slim brass key. She studied at her desk and it gave her a sense of duty. She imagined that she had to study at her desk the way she did. In the sixth grade she studied geography, for instance, drawing out the time so that as she learned the temperature and products and climate of Indochina she felt herself wandering through rice paddies with her feet bare in the thick warm mud. It was pleasant to be neatly enclosed by the walls of her room, to be seated for hours in front of the huge desk into whose compartments, cubbyholes, and shelves everything she thought or did fitted neatly. Her mother and father said proudly that she belonged to an intellectual family, and occasionally she sat downstairs talking with her father about geography, her favorite subject.

Every summer Natalie went to her room before leaving for West Bay in order to say goodbye to her desk in such a way as to carry it with her in her mind for the summer. As she sat with her head against the worn velvet surface Ellen came into her room.

"Come on, Nat, it's time to go."

"O.K." Natalie didn't lift her head. She squeezed her eyes so tightly shut they throbbed in the darkness. She felt Ellen's eyes in the middle of her back. She wanted to leap up screaming with rage.

"What's wrong?" asked Ellen.

"Nothing. I'm coming."

Ellen went down the steps. Natalie stood up and looked vacantly at the glass doors of the bookshelves. She passed her fingers nervously and rapidly across the lines of the compartments and rubbed her finger on the small drawer. She opened it with the key and drew out a long yellow pad of paper with green lines and a red line for the margin. The pad was fat and its pages were rumpled from the perspiration of her hands. She had written through it that winter nearly to the back and had never torn away a page. Sitting at her desk at night unable to concentrate on her homework she wrote about a girl named Lois, a girl who was lovely with silver hair and silver skin and eyes deep like violets because she was seen only in the moonlight and only after a long time of climbing and climbing up the cold stone steps of a tower or struggling through the long sandy road of a forest to a field which was wavy with grass and filled with moonlight where Lois danced and danced in the moonlight. And she read over all that she had written in a sad thin voice that whispered and swelled and whined like the wind.

Natalie looked down at the pad, folded it over, put it in an old writing-paper box together with some blank papers and special pictures, and walked with it downstairs to the car.

Before backing out of the garage the father announced that the mileage was exactly 4,735.8 and the time precisely four-thirty-five Eastern Standard

Time. Ellen asked to be allowed to keep the record of gas and mileage that year.

The car stopped to turn onto Lontana and the street lamp at the corner was just beginning to fade into the greying light. "Good-bye, house," they called. The car moved smoothly down the street, and at the backs of lawns houses stood with their windows still asleep in the cool, dark morning. The village square was empty and dark except for the harsh white light in the drugstore window. The mother asked, "Are you sure we have everything? Did we shut all the windows?" The father pressed down on the brake and they turned out into the highway. "Good-bye, Mercator," they all called.

Ellen asked to know her Papa's arrival prediction, and he predicted in his deep matter-of-fact voice that barring heavy traffic, unforeseen detours, or difficult weather, they would pull up in front of the cottage at approximately three-thirty-eight.

They drove fast. The car began to fill with whirring noise and the head-lights faded greyer on the road. They passed trucks parked by the roadside. They didn't even slow down to go through Stockton. In one house the lights were on and the mother asked why those people were up so early, did they suppose. Ellen asked for a piece of chewing gum. The mother said, "Wait until seven at least." Ellen said, "But, Mama." They slowed down to go through Hamilton. The streets were empty. They stopped for a red light and nothing passed as they waited. Toward the edge of town a car passed them going very fast. Ellen said, "Let's guess where he's going."

Natalie settled comfortably into the seat. She liked the arrangement of the family, each with his own place, each facing forward, everyone excited and glad. Natalie sat behind her father, Ellen behind her mother, who sat with the map in her lap and the lunch basket and thermos at her feet. Natalie and Ellen kept their writing-paper boxes, diaries, and purses each on her own side of the seat. Kroupa nestled between them with his chin pressed down on Ellen's lap and his tail curved along the side of Natalie's leg.

"Why do I always get the bad end of Kroupa?" asked Natalie. Ellen let out a monstrous burst of laughter, gulped it up, and looked significantly at Natalie in the pleasant darkness of the car.

"Enter Galilee County, leave Cairo," called the father.

"I think this year I'll make a list of all the counties we go through," Ellen said loudly enough for her parents to hear.

"I'll write down the names of all the unincorporated towns," Natalie said very loudly.

The car sped on. When it slowed down for a town, the chatting of the mother and father emerged and then disappeared again into the whir when they were back on the open highway. Natalie looked out at the peaceful morning fields sliding by with jerking swoops between telephone poles.

"Enter Darke County, leave Galilee," announced Ellen. "Pretty soon we come to North Star, remember, Nat?"

"Sure. Just this side of North Star is the big fairground with the grey wooden wall and the grey buildings inside." Natalie imagined the grey wall and the tall dark tree trunks and the sweet green grass that grew inside the wall in the empty mornings when they sped by every year, never slowing down to look carefully.

"Two guesses," snapped Ellen. "Where's the ugly old courthouse right in the middle of the main street?"

"Greenville," sang out Natalie.

The hills began to flatten out and the dark grey clouds turned to thick pink lumps in the east.

"Red sky in the morning gives sailors warning," declaimed the mother cheerfully from the front seat.

When the sun rose it sped along with the car, a smooth red circle just over the fields and square wood plots. Natalie wanted to watch the sun and to feel its warm orange light on her face. She twisted forward and low to look through Ellen's window. Ellen leaned forward.

"Lean back, will you, Ellen?"

"Why should I? You've got your side."

"I want to see."

"Tough."

Natalie looked at Ellen's curved shoulder and the leg under her skirt and the soft skin below her chin. She turned, rolled down her window, and pressed her face into the thick fast air that blew by.

"Roll up your window, Natalie, you make me nervous," said the father. Natalie stared at the back of his head, rolled up the window, and pushed herself violently back into the seat.

As they drove into the outskirts of Eaton, Ohio, the sun was already high in the sky, but it was not quite seven-thirty and the town was still quiet. Ellen began to make jokes about Eaton houses, Eaton trees, and Eaton sidewalks. She forced herself to nearly die laughing when Kroupa put his paws on the window ledge, wagged, and then barked at an Eaton dog. She begged to stop at an Eaton gas station.

In the white tile ladies' room Natalie looked at herself in the mirror, patted her hair against her head, brushed at the shoulder of her rumpled green cotton, stuck out her tongue, and left the room pinching her oily-beige cheeks. The father stood tall and thin with his shoulders slightly hunched, chatting with the gas attendant by the front fender of the car. Every year the mother repeated how well he knew how to talk to people. Natalie walked over to where Kroupa tugged Ellen along on his leash on the thin margin of grass between the sidewalk and the street.

Natalie said, "Let me walk him now." Kroupa tugged after a scent and Natalie jerked at the leash, trying to lift his head. They left when the father determined that Kroupa's airing had been sufficient.

It began to get very hot in the car. Ellen twisted restlessly on the seat and began to write something on her pad. The pencil scratched steadily and smoothly under the noise of the speeding car. In the front seat the mother poured a drink. For a moment the car smelled fresh and pungent from gin. The car slowed slightly and Natalie heard water softly plopping into the paper cup. The father drank it in a single gulp. Kroupa tried to climb over Natalie. He panted from the heat. His tongue hung out and he slobbered as he panted. Natalie pushed him back impatiently and forced him down to the floor.

Ellen rooted to play the animal game. But first thing she accused Natalie of counting too many cows in one herd. The father said that to count the legs and divide by four was the only foolproof system. Natalie didn't want to play anyhow.

When they crossed the Michigan border they all burst into an uproarious rendition of "Oh, we don't give a damn for the whole state of Michigan." Natalie sang loud until it strained her voice. Her throat hurt and her face got red with the effort. Her shoulders twisted back and forth. "We're from O-hi-o, We're from O-hi-o."

Ellen stopped singing. Natalie continued furiously loud. She stopped suddenly and faced Ellen. Ellen stared at her.

"Why did you stop?" asked Natalie.

"How can I sing when you're so off tune?"

"Oh, you're just stupid!" Natalie looked down at her lap. She crossed her legs and smoothed the top of Kroupa's head with her shoes.

It got hotter. Kroupa was told to stay down. Natalie rubbed her hand across her writing box, then lifted out her pad and looked at what she had written. She began to read the words in a strange lovely whine silently inside her head. Suddenly Ellen's head brushed against her shoulder. Ellen read aloud in a taunting voice, "I had been climbing, climbing for hours up the narrow, bumpy, slippery steps that clung to the wall of the circular tower."

Natalie hugged the pad to her chest. "Get away, will you?"

Ellen trilled in a nasal singsong repetition, "I had been climbing, climbing, climbing for hours." Ellen reached at Natalie's chest and pulled at the pad.

"Leave me alone!" shrieked Natalie. "Leave me alone!"

"Natalie, be quiet," said the mother turning around.

Ellen sing-songed, "I had been climbing, climbing for hours," and contorted her body in climbing gestures.

"Mama, make her shut up."

"Ellen, for God's sake, what are you doing?"

"I'm going up in the tower, Mama, just like Natalie."

"Stop that this minute, Ellen Mitchell," commanded the mother.

Ellen continued; she stepped her feet up and down on the car floor, tipped back her head, and twisted her body. Natalie stared at her with the yellow pad hugged against her chest.

"You heard me, Ellen."

"I'll stop at the *end* of this minute."

The mother turned toward Natalie with a loud and irritated sigh. Natalie felt her mother's eyes on her face. She wanted to say something but she felt outside of herself and almost watched herself tilt her chin to the side and let her eyes become vacant and strange.

"You will be able to take interesting walks this summer, Natalie dear."

"Yes." Slowly Natalie's shoulders hunched up in the posture her father adopted when he wanted to keep her mother from looking into his eyes. She sat stiff and kept her writing pad tightly protected.

When Ellen subsided her mother turned around. Without looking at Ellen, Natalie piled her coat, her purse, and a box of Kleenex on the seat between them and hunched around to look out the window. Ellen began to sing to the tune of "Birmingham Jail" softly so that no one but Natalie could hear, "I had been climbing, climbing for hours."

Natalie pulled her hands up over her ears. She watched the reflection of her family seated in the car speeding dimly along just below the road. She pressed her face against the window and wanted something to concentrate on. She felt her mother turn and glance at her and she wanted to twist her back and be away, far away, in some private and beautiful place. But she couldn't think of anything. In the winter every day after school she went for a walk, and every day she stopped in the middle of the lawn with the tough, cold winter grass under her feet, turned, and looked up at the house. Every day she turned that way to see if her mother or sister were watching, and every day the tall thin windows of the house were shiny black and reflected back the outside to her; they reflected sky and naked tree branches. She moved from the yard and walked along the cinder mound by the railroad tracks with her shoulders slouched and her head hung forward and her eyes roving vacantly about the ground and the grey street pavement. She crossed the tracks and walked slowly up the hill road beyond the edge of the village. She walked between fields on the narrow black road, and when she reached the brow of the hill there was a thick wood of young pencil-thin trees on one side of the road and an old apple orchard on the other. She broke then into a wild run. She ran with her throat tipped back and her arms spread out like the wings of a bird. She ran until she reached the lamppost at the intersection and then turned back toward home. She never looked at much or thought of anything in particular as she walked. She was often startled to find herself crossing the railroad tracks toward home and could not even remember running to the intersection at the top of the hill. But at the dinner table every night she answered questions about her walk: Did she find any Osage oranges to roll down the hill, did she see red and black caterpillars basking in the sun on the road, did the village from up there look as though most of the leaves were out again.

In the afternoon, south of Cadillac, the land suddenly changed. For miles, from long hill to long hill, the white line of road stretched through green cedar forest. The mother announced from the front seat, as she did every year, that this was the most beautiful road in the country, this stretch of one-eleven. Between patches of dark cedar forest were fields with dry green

grasses and sand places where the wind swept the grass bare and only the
junipers and bracken began to creep again up toward the hilltops. There
were no houses except for an occasional dark, unpainted shack.

The talk in the car grew excited. I wonder if Ed has cut the grass yet.
Ellie and George must be out fishing now. I bet Mr. Lee is already sun-
burned. Do you think the Morrisons are out sailing this afternoon? Do
you s'pose Ed fixed the courts yet? I wonder how the cherries are this year.
We'll be able to have a fire tonight.

They stopped for gasoline in Cadillac. The father asked the man how
the weather had been, how was the cherry crop on the peninsula this year.
The man wanted to know how far had they come, the car was sure covered
with dust, and what kind of dog was that.

When they turned off onto the short cut they officially began to play "I-
see-West-Bay-first." They sat on the edge of their seats. The road wound
down hills, around lakes, and up through fields. Just before the brow of hills
they lifted their heads way up to the roof. The father didn't like it but no
one cared. Finally Ellen burst into a jumbled scream, "I-see-West-Bay-first!"

It was clean and cool and wide before them, with long arms of land
cupping it and stretching northward. The bay was a deep grey-blue and
there was a thick sheet of cloud in the west. Natalie let the cool bay fill her
head so that her thoughts became like fish swimming deep in the dark
night of her mind. They were all beautiful, and Lois the silver girl swam
under the water a long time in graceful darts as a minnow swims, climbed
out on the beach, and stood letting the wind blow the water off her in
lovely pure drops.

When the road reached the bay it wound along the shore. Natalie sat
languidly in the seat with her neck drooped toward the window, watching
for glimpses of the bay through the birches and pines and low beach bushes.
Just by the Harbor Grocery the climate changed. The air became cool and
clear and exciting. They rolled down the windows and the car turned onto
the brown gravel road which bent around the harbor through a deep pine
wood. Kroupa began to wag his tail.

"Daddy, how does Kroupa know, how can he know?" asked Ellen.

The mother said, "I hope they remembered to deliver our order today."

When they pulled up behind the cottage and first got out of the car they
felt dazed. Natalie felt very tall, with flimsy knees. She could smell the
musty-leaf floor of the forest mixed with the smell of the fire at the Hay-
docks'. The cottage looked small and shabby with the sand-earth splattered
up against the white kitchen wall. The ground was dotted with raindrop
marks and there were cobwebs and sand at the bottom of the woodpile.
The afternoon light came grey-green through the leaves.

Ellen ran excitedly into the house and Natalie followed. Ellen banged
up the stairs and shook the cottage. Natalie scuffed into the living room
across the dark grass rugs. The cottage smelled musty. The rooms were dark
and the wood walls seemed damp. Natalie stood in front of the fireplace with
her hands hanging heavily at her side.

From upstairs Éllen yelled, "Come on up, Nat, let's fix our beds first thing."

The mother answered from the kitchen where she had the water running, "Let's get the car unpacked first."

Natalie went to the closet and took out the toy sailboat which stood on the floor beside the porch pillows. She put it on the mantel at its place in the center and traced her finger idly across the thin, dusty sail.

From the back the father called, "Come see Kroupa digging his usual hole."

"Come on, Natalie," said her mother, appearing at the edge of the living room with a suitcase in her hand.

"How can you expect me to do more than one thing at a time?" Natalie whined. The mother went on upstairs.

In the back the father leaned against the tree with his arm hanging onto the clothesline. His white shirt was soft and mussed and his face was pale. "Kroupa's off chasing squirrels," he said, not looking directly at Natalie. He had already unloaded half the trunk, and a row of suitcases, newspaper bundles, tennis rackets, and tennis shoes stood beside the car. Natalie picked up her own black suitcase and her tennis racket and walked back into the cottage.

On the way back down the stairs she stopped at the landing and stroked the brown hunting jacket she had used the summer before for walking and sailing. She took it from its hook and put it on, then felt deep into its pocket and rubbed in her fingers the smooth surface of the stone she had kept there all winter. As she wandered out onto the front porch she rubbed the stone along in the sand at the bottom of the pocket, and it made a grinding, pleasant sound. She looked across at the top of the forest. The forest bent back, rustled, then stood for a moment straight and quiet.

Natalie heard her mother bounce friskily into the living room and could feel her just inside the door with the clown smile she put on her face to try and make them all have fun. Natalie didn't look around. Her mother went away and she could hear her father's slow steps going up the stairs.

She opened the screen door, jumped the last steps, and began to run. She ran in long loping steps over roots and through tall grass patches and onto the sandy-rutted road that went through the field. She ran furiously, twisting her back, twisting out the eyes she could feel watching her. She turned from the field and ran deep into the forest road before she stopped and bent over, breathing heavily, with her hand pressed against her stomach. The road was still wet from the rain, with only the tracks of Ed's truck marked neatly in the sand. She printed her feet neatly in the sand and walked on quietly in the forest world with her hands in the soft canvas pockets. Nothing moved in the wood but the occasional fragile shake of a leaf or the cracking of a stick. The beech trees grew tall and slim with their gray silver trunks, and above, the forest waved softly like the bay.

Toward the beach the forest changed to pine and the wind reached in and blew back the ferns and the low leaved trees. Natalie ran down the

last hill and out onto the beach through the juniper and beach myrtle. The
bay was wide and grey and thickly moving. She smelled the clean smell of
stones and fish and rain and lake. She took off her shoes and dug her feet
into the wet stones. She waded in and took a drink from her hands of the
sweet bay water, then scuffed along the shore, kicking gently through the
water toward the point where she would see the open lake beyond the bay.
The wind caught sweetly at her throat, swirled around her, and blew up her
hair in soft gusts. She tipped up her throat to feel the wind and ran along
the water's edge into the wind. With her mouth opened she ran in long
graceful-feeling leaps, spanked her feet against the wet sand, and stretched
out her arms until they quivered like the wings of a wild grey bird. She ran
farther and her feet began to feel heavy as she dug them with each step
out of soft sand. She pulled off her jacket and threw it on a bush back from
the water. Then she ran with her naked arms stretched out until she could
see the open lake smooth and wide to the north. The sky blew grey with
sea-soft clouds close over the water and the wind blew softly around her.
She held herself to keep from breathing hard and ran again. It was hard to
run. She lunged forward and threw herself down against the stones by the
water's edge. She took cool pebbles into her mouth and rubbed her face
in the wet stones. She shoved toward the water, put in her face so her
hair moved with the motion of the waves. The wind swooped down and
blew against her in a sudden gust. As she stood up and started to run her
foot kicked against a piece of wood. She stopped to pick it up. It was a
piece of driftwood shaped like a bird, a grey bird with its wings stretched
out. Natalie held it by its throat and walked along, looking at the open water
to the north. She tried to run, and she ran into the water with her dress on.
She swam under the surface and rubbed against the sand and felt the water
silken and sweet and cold around her. She dove again toward the bottom
and stayed quiet to listen to the stones shifting with the sand in the motion
of the bay. She drank some water and dove again under and swam into the
grey-green distance, swam in darts as a silver fish or as Lois the silver girl
swam. The grey bird lay on the shiny sand by the water's edge and shifted
slightly with the waves when they touched it.

Bibliography: Novels of Adolescence

1976

Christman, Elizabeth. *A Nice Italian Girl*. New York: Dodd, Mead.

Guest, Judith. *Ordinary People*. New York: Viking Press.

Mojtabai, A[nn] G[race]. *The 400 Eels of Sigmund Freud*. New York: Simon and Schuster.

Price, Richard. *Bloodbrothers*. Boston: Houghton Mifflin.

1975

Albert, Mimi. *The Second Story Man*. New York: George Braziller.

Bernays, Anne. *Growing Up Rich*. Boston: Little, Brown.

Brown, Claude. *The Children of Ham*. Briarcliff Manor, New York: Stein & Day.

Friedman, Sanford. *Still Life*. New York: Saturday Review Press.

Hobson, Laura Z. *Consenting Adult*. Garden City, New York: Doubleday.

Jacobs, Harvey. *Summer on a Mountain of Spices*. New York: Harper & Row.

Potok, Chaim. *In the Beginning*. New York: Knopf.

Rhodes, David. *Rock Island Line*. New York: Harper & Row.

Rhodes, Evan H. *The Prince of Central Park*. New York: Coward, McCann.

Stein, Sol. *The Childkeeper*. New York: Harcourt Brace Jovanovich.

Wersba, Barbara. *The Country of the Heart*. New York: Atheneum.

1974

Baldwin, James. *If Beale Street Could Talk*. New York: Dial Press.

Deal, Babs H. *The Reason for Roses*. Garden City, New York: Doubleday.

Fields, Jeff. *A Cry of Angels*. New York: Atheneum.

Howard, Maureen. *Before My Time*. Boston: Little, Brown.

Lurie, Alison. *The War Between the Tates*. New York: Random House.

McCall, Dan. *Jack the Bear*. Garden City, New York: Doubleday.

Madden, David. *Bijou*. New York: Crown.

Murray, Albert. *Train Whistle Guitar*. New York: McGraw-Hill.
Price, Richard. *The Wanderers*. Boston: Houghton Mifflin.

1973

Baker, Elliott. *Unrequited Loves*. New York: G. P. Putnam's.
Bowers, John. *No More Reunions*. New York: E. P. Dutton.
Chappell, Fred. *The Gaudy Place*. New York: Harcourt, Brace.
Churchill, Winston J. *Running in Place*. New York: George Braziller.
Early, Robert. *The Jealous Ear*. Boston: Houghton Mifflin.
Fraser, Sylvia. *Pandora*. Boston: Little, Brown.
Harris, Marilyn. *Hatter Fox*. New York: Random House.
Hotchner, A. E. *King of the Hill*. New York: Harper & Row.
Hough, John. *A Two-Car Funeral*. Boston: Little, Brown.
Logan, Jane. *The Very Nearest Room*. New York: Scribner's.
Newlove, Donald. *Leo & Theodore*. New York: Saturday Review Press.
Ogburn, Charlton. *Winespring Mountain*. New York: William Morrow.
Powers, John R. *The Last Catholic in America*. New York: Saturday Review Press.
Reeve, F. D. *White Colors*. New York: Farrar, Straus.
Taylor, Donald. *After the First Death*. New York: George Braziller.
Thomas, Audrey. *Songs My Mother Taught Me*. Indianapolis and New York: Bobbs-Merrill.

1972

Cain, George. *Blueschild Baby*. New York: McGraw-Hill.
Chute, B. J. *The Story of a Small Life*. New York: E. P. Dutton.
Covert, Paul. *Cages*. New York: Liveright.
DeLillo, Don. *End Zone*. Boston: Houghton Mifflin.
Ellis, Mel. *This Mysterious River*. New York: Holt, Rinehart and Winston.
Fair, Ronald L. *We Can't Breathe*. New York: Harper & Row.
Green, Hannah. *The Dead of the House*. Garden City, New York: Doubleday.
Greenan, Russell H. *The Queen of America*. New York: Random House.
Hannah, Barry. *Geronimo Rex*. New York: Viking Press.
Higgins, Colin. *Harold and Maude*. Philadelphia: J. B. Lippincott.
Hill, Weldon. *Jefferson McGraw*. New York: William Morrow.
Norman, Gurney. *Divine Right's Trip*. New York: Dial Press.
Oates, Joyce Carol. *Wonderland*. New York: Vanguard Press.
Peck, Robert Newton. *A Day No Pigs Would Die*. New York: Knopf.
Potok, Chaim. *My Name Is Asher Lev*. New York: Knopf.
Schiff, Ken. *Passing Go*. New York: Dodd, Mead.
Stallworth, Anne Nall. *This Time Next Year*. New York: Vanguard Press.
Stein, Sol. *The Magician*. New York: Delacorte Press.
Weesner, Theodore. *The Car Thief*. New York: Random House.
Yglesias, Rafael. *Hide Fox, and All After*. Garden City, New York: Doubleday.

1971

Athas, Daphne. *Entering Ephesus.* New York: Viking Press.

Atwell, Lester. *Life with Its Sorrow, Life with Its Tear.* New York: Simon & Schuster.

Beckham, Barry. *My Main Mother.* New York: Walker.

Blatty, William Peter. *The Exorcist.* New York: Harper & Row.

Brown, Kenneth H. *The Narrows.* New York: Dial Press.

Dizenzo, Patricia. *An American Girl.* New York: Holt, Rinehart and Winston.

Douglas, Michael. *Dealing; or, the Berkeley-to-Boston Forty-Brick Lost-Bag Blues.* New York: Knopf.

Dunn, Katherine. *Truck.* New York: Harper & Row.

Griffith, Patricia Browning. *The Future Is Not What It Used to Be.* New York: Simon & Schuster.

Hale, Nancy. *Secrets.* New York: Coward, McCann.

Hayes, Joseph. *Like Any Other Fugitive.* New York: Dial Press.

Herlihy, James Leo. *The Season of the Witch.* New York: Simon & Schuster.

Kennedy, Raymond. *Good Night, Jupiter.* New York: Atheneum.

Knowles, John. *The Paragon.* New York: Random House.

McCarthy, Mary. *Birds of America.* New York: Harcourt, Brace.

Morris, Wright. *Fire Sermon.* New York: Harper & Row.

Osborn, John Jay. *The Paper Chase.* Boston: Houghton Mifflin.

Raucher, Herman. *Summer of '42.* New York: G. P. Putnam's.

Read, Piers Paul. *The Professor's Daughter.* Philadelphia: J. B. Lippincott.

Reeve, F[ranklin] D. *The Brother.* New York: Farrar, Straus.

Renvoizé, Jean. *A Wild Thing.* Boston: Little, Brown.

Rubin, Michael. *In a Cold Country.* New York: McGraw-Hill.

Thompson, Earl. *A Garden of Sand.* New York: G. P. Putnam's.

Turner, Steven. *A Measure of Dust.* New York: Simon & Schuster.

Wersba, Barbara. *Run Softly, Go Fast.* New York: Atheneum.

1970

Arnow, Harriette Simpson. *The Weedkiller's Daughter.* New York: Knopf.

Dizenzo, Patricia. *Phoebe.* New York: McGraw-Hill.

Gagarin, Nicholas. *Windsong.* New York: William Morrow.

Goddard, J. R. *The Night Crew.* Boston: Little, Brown.

Horgan, Paul. *Whitewater.* New York: Farrar, Straus.

Horwitz, Julius. *The Diary of A. N.: The Story of the House on West 104th Street.* New York: Coward, McCann.

McMahon, T. *Principles of American Nuclear History.* Boston: Little, Brown.

Markfield, Wallace. *Teitelbaum's Window.* New York: Knopf.

Meriwether, Louise. *Daddy Was a Number Runner.* Englewood Cliffs, New Jersey: Prentice-Hall.

Michael, David J. *A Blow to the Head.* Boston: Houghton Mifflin.

Mitchell, Don. *Thumb Tripping.* Boston: Little, Brown.

Owens, Guy. *Journey for Joedel.* New York: Crown.

Piercy, Marge. *Dance the Eagle to Sleep*. Garden City, New York: Doubleday.

Robertson, Don. *The Greatest Thing That Almost Happened*. New York: G. P. Putnam's.

Segal, Erich. *Love Story*. New York: Harper & Row.

Swarthout, Glendon. *Bless the Beasts and Children*. Garden City, New York: Doubleday.

Young, Al. *Snakes*. New York: Holt, Rinehart and Winston.

1969

Barrett, B. L. *Love in Atlantis*. Boston: Houghton Mifflin.

Cleary, Jon. *Remember Jack Hoxie*. New York: William Morrow.

Elliott, David W. *Listen to the Silence*. New York: Holt, Rinehart and Winston.

Graves, Wallace. *Trixie*. New York: Knopf.

Hunter, Evan. *Sons*. Garden City, New York: Doubleday.

Irving, John. *Setting Free the Bears*. New York: Random House.

Leggett, John. *Who Took the Gold Away?* New York: Random House.

McAffee, Thomas. *Rover Youngblood: An American Fable*. New York: R. W. Baron.

Neufeld, John. *Lisa, Bright and Dark*. New York: S. G. Phillips.

Rader, Paul. *Professor Wilmess Must Die*. New York: Dial Press.

Robinson, Rose. *Eagle in the Air*. New York: Crown.

Shipley, C. L. *The Jade Piccolo*. New York: Atheneum.

Von Hoffman, Nicholas. *Two, Three, Many More*. New York: Quadrangle.

1968

Baker, Elliott. *The Penny Wars*. New York: G. P. Putnam's.

Baumbach, Jonathan. *What Comes Next*. New York: Harper & Row.

Bradford, Richard. *Red Sky at Morning*. New York: J. B. Lippincott.

Burland, Brian. *A Fall from Aloft*. New York: Random House.

Capote, Truman. *The Thanksgiving Visitor*. New York: Random House.

Daniels, Guy. *Progress, U.S.A.* New York: Macmillan.

Davis, L. J. *Whence All But He Had Fled*. New York: Viking Press.

Disney, Doris Miles. *Voice from the Grave*. Garden City, New York: Doubleday.

Horgan, Paul. *Everything to Live For*. New York: Farrar, Straus.

Hunter, Evan. *Last Summer*. Garden City, New York: Doubleday.

Kerouac, Jack. *Vanity of Duluoz: An Adventurous Education*. New York: Coward, McCann.

Kirkwood, James. *Good Times/Bad Times*. New York: Simon & Schuster.

Kline, Nancy E. *The Faithful*. New York: William Morrow.

Larner, Jeremy. *The Answer*. New York: Macmillan.

MacDonald, Ross. *The Instant Enemy*. New York: Knopf.

Mathews, F. X. *The Concrete Judasbird*. Boston: Houghton Mifflin.

Oates, Joyce Carol. *Expensive People*. New York: Vanguard Press.

Rogers, Thomas. *The Pursuit of Happiness*. New York: New American Library.

Rothberg, Abraham. *The Song of David Freed*. New York: G. P. Putnam's.

Sukenick, Ronald. *Up*. New York: Dial Press.

Van Dyke, Henry. *Blood of Strawberries*. New York: Farrar, Straus.

Zindel, Paul. *The Pigman*. New York: Harper & Row.

1967

Aaron, Chester. *About Us*. New York: McGraw-Hill.

Deal, Borden. *The Least One*. Garden City, New York: Doubleday.

Duhrssen, Alfred. *Memoir of an Aged Child*. New York: Holt, Rinehart and Winston.

Fox, William Price. *Moonshine Light, Moonshine Bright*. Philadelphia: J. B. Lippincott.

Gold, Herbert. *Fathers*. New York: Random House.

Green, Gerald. *To Brooklyn with Love*. New York: Trident.

Huntsberry, William E. *The Big Wheels*. New York: Lothrop.

Lipsyte, Robert. *The Contender*. New York: Harper & Row.

Marshall, Catherine. *Christy*. New York: McGraw-Hill.

Matthews, Jack. *Hanger Stout, Awake!* New York: Harcourt, Brace.

Morris, Wright. *In Orbit*. New York: New American Library.

Murphy, Robert. *A Certain Island*. New York: M. Evans.

Oates, Joyce Carol. *A Garden of Earthly Delights*. New York: Vanguard Press.

Perrin, Ursula. *Ghosts*. New York: Knopf.

Potok, Chaim. *The Chosen*. New York: Simon & Schuster.

Reed, Kit. *The Better Part*. New York: Farrar, Straus.

Rollins, Bryant. *Danger Song*. Garden City, New York: Doubleday.

Rosenberg, Jessie. *Sudina*. New York: E. P. Dutton.

Ross, Sam. *Hang-Up*. New York: Coward, McCann.

Salas, Floyd. *Tattoo the Wicked Cross*. New York: Grove Press.

Salter, James. *A Sport and a Pastime*. Garden City, New York: Doubleday.

Walton, Stephen. *No Transfer*. New York: Vanguard Press.

Welles, Patricia. *Babyhip*. New York: E. P. Dutton.

Wilkinson, Sylvia. *A Killing Frost*. Boston: Houghton Mifflin.

Williams, Vinnie. *Greenbones*. New York: Viking Press.

Yafa, Stephen H. *Paxton Quigley's Had the Course*. Philadelphia: J. B. Lippincott.

1966

Boynton, Peter. *Games in the Darkening Air*. New York: Harcourt, Brace.

Brautigan, Richard. *The Abortion: An Historical Romance*. New York: Simon & Schuster.

Farina, Richard. *Been Down So Long It Looks Like Up To Me*. New York: Random House.

Hersey, John. *Too Far to Walk*. New York: Knopf.

Hill, Weldon. *Rafe*. New York: David McKay.

Hoff, Marilyn. *Dink's Blues*. New York: Harcourt, Brace.

Nichols, John. *The Wizard of Loneliness*. New York: G. P. Putnam's.

Price, Reynolds. *A Generous Man*. New York: Atheneum.

Richert, William. *Aren't You Even Gonna Kiss Me Good-By?* New York: David McKay.

Richter, Conrad. *A Country of Strangers*. New York: Knopf.

Robertson, Don. *The Sum and Total of Now*. New York: G. P. Putnam's.

Schiller, Marvin. *Country of the Young*. New York: Crown.

Wilkinson, Sylvia. *Moss on the North Side*. Boston: Houghton Mifflin.

Wilner, Herbert. *All the Little Heroes*. Indianapolis and New York: Bobbs-Merrill.

1965

Bonham, Frank. *Durango Street*. New York: E. P. Dutton.

Brown, Claude. *Manchild in the Promised Land*. New York: Macmillan.

Clarke, Tom E. *The Big Road*. New York: Lothrop.

Dornfeld, Iris. *Boy Gravely*. New York: Knopf.

Drexler, Rosalyn. *I Am the Beautiful Stranger*. New York: Grossman.

Friedman, Sanford. *Totempole*. New York: E. P. Dutton.

Glyn, Caroline. *Love and Joy in Mabillon*. New York: Coward, McCann.

Kaufman, Bel. *Up the Down Staircase*. Englewood Cliffs, New Jersey: Prentice-Hall.

Nichols, John. *The Sterile Cuckoo*. New York: David McKay.

Rubin, Theodore Isaac. *Platzo: and The Mexican Pony Rider*. New York: Simon & Schuster.

Sprague, Gretchen. *A Question of Harmony*. New York: Dodd, Mead.

Wagoner, David. *The Escape Artist*. New York: Farrar, Straus.

Westheimer, David. *My Sweet Charlie*. Garden City, New York: Doubleday.

Weston, John. *Jolly*. New York: David McKay.

Winter, Alice. *The Velvet Bubble*. New York: William Morrow.

Wolff, Ruth. *A Crack in the Sidewalk*. Briarcliff Manor, New York: Stein & Day.

1964

Brace, Gerald Warner. *The Wind's Will*. New York: W. W. Norton.

Burwell, Basil. *A Fool in the Forest*. New York: Macmillan.

Crawford, Joanna. *Birch Interval*. Boston: Houghton Mifflin.

Friedman, Bruce Jay. *A Mother's Kisses*. New York: Simon & Schuster.

[Greenberg, Joanne] Green, Hannah. *I Never Promised You a Rose Garden*. New York: Holt, Rinehart and Winston.

Grumbach, Doris. *The Short Throat, the Tender Mouth*. Garden City, New York: Doubleday.

Horgan, Paul. *Things as They Are*. New York: Farrar, Straus.

Larner, Jeremy. *Drive, He Said*. New York: Dial Press.

Murphy, Robert. *The Pond*. New York: E. P. Dutton.

Oates, Joyce Carol. *With Shuddering Fall*. New York: Vanguard Press.

Plagemann, Bentz. *Father to the Man*. New York: William Morrow.

Richter, Conrad. *The Grandfathers*. New York: Knopf.

Wallart, Edward Lewis. *The Children at the Gate*. New York: Harcourt, Brace.

White, Robin. *All in Favor Say No*. New York: Farrar, Straus.

1963

Bennett, Jack. *Jamie*. Boston: Little, Brown.

Blechman, Burt. *The War of Camp Omongo*. New York: Random House.

Borland, Hal. *When the Legends Die*. Philadelphia: J. B. Lippincott.

Deal, Babs. *The Grail*. New York: David McKay.

Faasen, Neal. *The Toyfair*. New York: Simon & Schuster.

Hall, James Baker. *Yates Paul, His Grand Flights, His Tootings*. Cleveland, Ohio: World.

Owens, William A. *Look to the River*. New York: Atheneum.

Parks, Gordon. *The Learning Tree*. New York: Harper & Row.

Smith, Betty. *Joy in the Morning*. New York: Harper & Row.

Updike, John. *The Centaur*. New York: Knopf.

Wier, Esther. *The Loner*. New York: David McKay.

1962

Abbey, Edward. *Fire on the Mountain*. New York: Dial Press.

Bradbury, Ray. *Something Wicked This Way Comes*. New York: Simon & Schuster.

Daniels, Sally. *The Inconstant Season*. New York: Atheneum.

Dornfeld, Iris. *Jeeney Ray*. New York: Viking Press.

Eclov, Shirley. *My Father's House*. New York: Harper & Row.

Faulkner, William. *The Reivers*. New York: Random House.

Gover, Robert. *One Hundred Dollar Misunderstanding*. New York: Grove Press.

Hill, Patti. *One Thing I Know*. Boston: Houghton Mifflin.

Sandburg, Helga. *The Owl's Roost*. New York: Dial Press.

Sanguinetti, Elise. *The Last of the Whitfields*. New York: McGraw-Hill.

Sullivan, Scott. *The Shortest Gladdest Years*. New York: Simon & Schuster.

1961

Fast, Howard M. *April Morning*. New York: Crown.

Grau, Shirley Ann. *The House on Coliseum Street*. New York: Knopf.

Hamner, Earl, Jr., *Spencer's Mountain*. New York: Dial Press.

Johnson, Nora. *A Step Beyond Innocence*. Boston: Atlantic Monthly Press.

Lee, Marjorie. *The Eye of Summer*. New York: Simon & Schuster.

Lloyd, Norris. *A Dream of Mansions*. New York: Random House.

Perutz, Kathrin. *The Garden.* New York: Atheneum.

Roth, Arthur J. *The Shame of Our Wounds.* New York: Thomas Y. Crowell.

Rubin, Louis Decimus. *The Golden Weather.* New York: Atheneum.

Salinger, J. D. *Franny and Zooey.* Boston: Little, Brown.

Strom, Leslie Winter. *A Weed in the Garden.* New York: Random House.

Taylor, Robert Louis. *A Journey to Matecumbe.* New York: McGraw-Hill.

Williams, Thomas. *The Night of Trees.* New York: Macmillan.

1960

Abelson, Ann. *The Little Conquerors.* New York: Random House.

Albee, George Sumner. *By the Sea, by the Sea.* New York: Simon & Schuster.

Babcock, Havilah. *The Education of Pretty Boy.* New York: Holt, Rinehart and Winston.

Bennett, Eve. *April Wedding.* New York: Julian Messner.

Bourjaily, Vance. *Confessions of a Spent Youth.* New York: Dial Press.

Brace, Gerald Warner. *Winter Solstice.* New York: W. W. Norton.

DiDonato, Pietro. *Three Circles of Light.* New York: Julian Messner.

Dougherty, Richard. *A Summer World.* Garden City, New York: Doubleday.

Froscher, Wingate. *The Comforts of the Damned.* New York: Appleton-Century-Crofts.

Gold, Herbert. *Therefore Be Bold.* New York: Dial Press.

Herlihy, James Leo. *All Fall Down.* New York: E. P. Dutton.

Hill, Margaret. *Really, Miss Hillsbro!* Boston: Little, Brown.

Kapelner, Alan. *All the Naked Heroes.* New York: George Braziller.

Kirkwood, Jim. *There Must Be a Pony!* Boston: Little, Brown.

Knowles, John. *A Separate Peace.* New York: Macmillan.

Leahy, Jack Thomas. *Shadow on the Waters.* New York: Knopf.

Lee, Harper. *To Kill a Mockingbird.* Philadelphia: J. B. Lippincott.

Leslie, Warren. *Love or Whatever It Is.* New York: McGraw-Hill.

MacDonald, John D. *The End of the Night.* New York: Simon & Schuster.

McFarland, Philip. *A House Full of Women.* New York: Simon & Schuster.

Martin, Peter. *The Building.* Boston: Little, Brown.

Mayhall, Jane. *Cousin to Human.* New York: Harcourt, Brace.

Moore, Ruth. *Walk Down Main Street.* New York: William Morrow.

O'Connor, Flannery. *The Violent Bear It Away.* New York: Farrar, Straus.

Richter, Conrad. *The Waters of Kronos.* New York: Knopf.

Roberts, Dorothy James. *With Night We Banish Sorrow.* Boston: Little, Brown.

Solomon, Barbara Probst. *The Beat of Life.* Philadelphia: J. B. Lippincott.

Street, James Howell, and Tracy, Don. *Pride of Possession.* Philadelphia: J. B. Lippincott.

Swarthout, Glendon. *Where the Boys Are.* New York: Random House.

Walker, Mildred. *The Body of a Young Man.* New York: Harcourt, Brace.

Wood, William. *The Fit.* New York: Macmillan.

Zietlow, E[dward] R[obert]. *These Same Hills.* New York: Knopf.

1959

Angoff, Charles. *Between Day and Dark*. New York: Thomas Yoseloff.

Baker, Laura Nelson. *The Special Year*. New York: Knopf.

Ballard, James. *The Long Way Through*. Boston: Houghton, Mifflin.

Beaumont, Charles. *The Introducer*. New York: G. P. Putnam's.

Begner, Edith P. *Just off Fifth*. New York: Rinehart.

Bell, Robert E. *The Butterfly Tree*. Philadelphia: J. B. Lippincott.

Deal, Borden. *The Insolent Breed*. New York: Scribner's.

DeMott, Benjamin. *The Body's Cage*. Boston: Little, Brown.

Duffus, R[obert] L[uther]. *The Waterbury Record*. New York: W. W. Norton.

Ehle, John. *Kingstree Island*. New York: William Morrow.

Erno, Richard B. *The Hunt*. New York: Crown.

Farris, John. *Harrison High*. New York: Rinehart.

Garrett, Zena. *The House in the Mulberry Tree*. New York: Random House.

Gold, Herbert. *The Optimist*. Boston: Little, Brown.

Goodman, Aubrey. *The Golden Youth of Lee Prince*. New York: Simon & Schuster.

Gutwillig, Robert. *The Fugitives*. Boston: Little, Brown.

Hubler, Richard G. *True Love, True Love*. New York: Duell, Sloan & Pearce.

Hunter, Evan. *A Matter of Conviction*. New York: Simon & Schuster.

Jennison, Peter S. *The Mimosa Smokers*. New York: Thomas Y. Crowell.

Johnson, Curtis. *Hobbledehoy's Hero*. Chicago: Pennington Press.

Jones, Dorothy Holder. *The Wonderful World Outside*. New York: Dodd, Mead.

Kelley, William. *Gemini*. Garden City, New York: Doubleday.

Kerouac, Jack. *Doctor Sax*. New York: Grove Press.

————. *Maggie Cassidy*. New York: Avon.

Kirsch, Robert R. *In the Wrong Rain*. Boston: Little, Brown.

Kohner, Frederick. *Cher Papa*. New York: G. P. Putnam's.

Linkletter, Monte. *Cricket Smith*. New York: Harper & Row.

McGivern, William Peter. *Savage Streets*. New York: Dodd, Mead.

Manfred, Frederick. *Conquering Horse*. New York: McDowell, Obolensky.

Marshall, Lenore. *The Hill Is Level*. New York: Random House.

Marshall, Paule. *Brown Girl, Brownstones*. New York: Random House.

Miller, Warren. *The Cool World*. Boston: Little, Brown.

Mitchner, Stuart. *Let Me Be Awake*. New York: Thomas Y. Crowell.

O'Donnell, Eugene. *Berdoo*. New York: Rinehart.

Offit, Sidney. *He Had It Made*. New York: Crown.

Petrakis, Harry Mark. *Lion at My Heart*. Boston: Little, Brown.

Purdy, James. *Malcolm*. New York: Farrar, Straus.

Shulman, Max. *I Was a Teen-Age Dwarf*. New York: Bernard Geis.

Soman, Florence Jane. *A Break in the Weather*. New York: G. P. Putnam's.

Sterling, Dorothy. *Mary Jane*. Garden City, New York: Doubleday.

Stern, Daniel. *Miss America*. New York: Random House.

Suckow, Ruth. *The John Wood Case*. New York: Viking Press.

Sumner, Cid Ricketts. *Tammy Tell Me True*. Indianapolis and New York: Bobbs-Merrill.

Tamkus, Daniel. *The Much-Honored Man*. Garden City, New York: Doubleday.

Tembler, Paul. *The Spring Dance*. New York: Viking Press.

Tigue, Ethel Erkkilla. *Betrayal*. New York: Dodd, Mead.

Villarreal, José Antonio. *Pocho*. Garden City, New York: Doubleday.

1958

Boles, Paul Darcy. *Parton's Island*. New York: Macmillan.

Calitri, Charles. *Strike Heaven in the Face*. New York: Crown.

Carlile, Clancy. *As I Was Young and Easy*. New York: Knopf.

Chamberlain, Anne. *The Darkest Bough*. Indianapolis and New York: Bobbs-Merrill.

Daly, Edwin. *A Legacy of Love*. New York: Scribner's.

Davis, Christopher. *Lost Summer*. New York: Harcourt, Brace.

Davis, Wesley Ford. *The Time of the Panther*. New York: Harper & Row.

Dempsey, David K. *All That Was Mortal*. New York: E. P. Dutton.

Elliott, George P. *Parktilden Village*. Boston: Beacon Press.

Ellison, James Whitfield. *The Freest Man on Earth*. Garden City, New York: Doubleday.

Faralla, Dana. *The Madstone*. Philadelphia: J. B. Lippincott.

Feibleman, Peter S. *A Place Without Twilight*. Cleveland, Ohio: World.

Flagg, Kenneth. *Andrew*. New York: G. P. Putnam's.

Frede, Richard. *Entry E*. New York: Random House.

Gutterson, Herbert. *The Last Autumn*. New York: William Morrow.

Gutwillig, Robert. *After Long Silence*. Boston: Little, Brown.

Hitchens, Dolores. *Fool's Gold*. Garden City, New York: Doubleday.

Humphrey, William. *Home from the Hill*. New York: Knopf.

Johnson, Nora. *The World of Henry Orient*. Boston: Little, Brown.

Karmel, Alex. *Mary Ann*. New York: Viking Press.

Kozol, Jonathan. *The Fume of Poppies*. Boston: Houghton Mifflin.

Loveland, Constance. *Veronica*. New York: Vanguard Press.

[Miller, Warren] Amanda Vail. *The Bright Young Things*. Boston: Little, Brown.

Nabokov, Vladimir. *Lolita*. New York: G. P. Putnam's.

Robinson, Alice M. *The Unbelonging*. New York: Macmillan.

Salamanca, J. R. *The Lost Country*. New York: Simon & Schuster.

Sandburg, Helga. *The Wheel of Earth*. New York: McDowell, Obolensky.

Smith, Betty. *Maggie-Now*. New York: Harper & Row.

Wagoner, David. *Rock*. New York: Viking Press.

Weidman, Jerome. *The Enemy Camp*. New York: Random House.

Wilson, Sloan. *A Summer Place*. New York: Simon & Schuster.

Wright, Richard. *The Long Dream*. Garden City, New York: Doubleday.

1957

Abaunza, Virginia. *Sundays from Two to Six.* Indianapolis and New York: Bobbs-Merrill.

Bradbury, Ray. *Dandelion Wine.* Garden City, New York: Doubleday.

Byron, Gilbert. *The Lord's Oysters.* Boston: Little, Brown.

Carson, Josephine. *Drives My Green Age.* New York: Harper & Row.

Daly, Edwin. *Some Must Watch.* New York: Scribner's.

Faulkner, William. *The Town.* New York: Random House.

Ham, Roswell G., Jr. *Fish Flying Through the Air.* New York: G. P. Putnam's.

Harris, Mark. *Something About a Soldier.* New York: Macmillan.

Head, Ann. *Fair with Rain.* New York: McGraw-Hill.

Kerouac, Jack. *On the Road.* New York: Viking Press.

Kohner, Frederick. *Gidget.* New York: G. P. Putnam's.

[Miller, Warren] Amanda Vail. *Love Me Little.* New York: McGraw-Hill.

Nemerov, Howard. *The Homecoming Game.* New York: Simon & Schuster.

Nusser, J[ames] L. *Scorpion Field.* New York: Appleton-Century-Crofts.

Purdy, James. *"63: Dream Palace" in Color of Darkness.* New York: New Directions.

Roark, Garland. *The Cruel Cocks.* Garden City, New York: Doubleday.

Simmons, Herbert. *Corner Boy.* Boston: Houghton Mifflin.

Sourian, Peter. *Miri.* New York: Pantheon Books.

Thompson, Charles. *Halfway Down the Stairs.* New York: Harper.

Wetzel, Donald. *The Rain and the Fire and the Will of God.* New York: Random House.

Winsor, Kathleen. *America, with Love.* New York: G. P. Putnam's.

Yaffe, James. *Nothing but the Night.* Boston: Little, Brown.

1956

Algren, Nelson. *A Walk on the Wild Side.* New York: Farrar, Straus.

Athas, Daphne. *The Fourth World.* New York: G. P. Putnam's.

Beheler, Laura. *The Paper Dolls.* Boston: Houghton Mifflin.

Boylen, Margaret. *The Marble Orchard.* New York: Random House.

DuBois, William. *A Season to Beware.* New York: G. P. Putnam's.

Eddy, Roger W. *The Bulls and the Bees.* New York: Thomas Y. Crowell.

Fenwick, Elizabeth. *Days of Plenty.* New York: Harcourt, Brace.

Gipson, Fred. *Old Yeller.* New York: Harper & Row.

Hunter, Evan. *Second Ending.* New York: Simon & Schuster.

Karney, Jack. *Work of Darkness.* New York: G. P. Putnam's.

Levin, Meyer. *Compulsion.* New York: Simon & Schuster.

Levy, Melvin P. *Lafayette Carter.* Philadelphia: J. B. Lippincott.

Metalious, Grace. *Peyton Place.* New York: Julian Messner.

Moore, Pamela. *Chocolates for Breakfast.* New York: Rinehart.

Rehder, Jessie C. *Remembrance Way.* New York: G. P. Putnam's.

Rooney, Frank. *The Heel of Spring.* New York: Vanguard Press.

Saroyan, William. *Mama, I Love You*. Boston: Little, Brown.

Shaw, Irwin. *Lucy Crown*. New York: Random House.

Shulman, Irving. *Children of the Dark*. New York: Henry Holt.

————. *Good Deeds Must Be Punished*. New York: Henry Holt.

Steuer, Arthur. *The Terrible Swift Sword*. New York: Coward, McCann.

Street, James. *Captain Little Ax*. Philadelphia: J. B. Lippincott.

1955

Angoff, Charles. *The Sun at Noon*. New York: Beechhurst Press.

Chamberlain, Anne. *The Tall Dark Man*. Indianapolis and New York: Bobbs-Merrill.

Ellison, James Whitfield. *I'm Owen Harrison Harding*. Garden City, New York: Doubleday.

Ellson, Hal. *Rock*. New York: Ballantine Books.

Erno, Richard B. *My Old Man*. New York: Crown.

Grace, Carol. *The Secret in the Daisy*. New York: Random House.

Halevy, Julian. *The Young Lovers*. New York: Simon & Schuster.

Oakey, Virginia. *Thirteenth Summer*. New York: A. A. Wyn.

Phillips, Thomas Hal. *The Loved and the Unloved*. New York: Harper's.

Plagemann, Bentz. *This Is Goggle*. New York: McGraw-Hill.

Porter, Monica E. *Mercy of the Court*. New York: W. W. Norton.

[Seid, Ruth] Jo Sinclair. *The Changelings*. New York: McGraw-Hill.

Swados, Harvey. *Out Went the Candle*. New York: Viking Press.

[Tanner, Edward Everett] Patrick Dennis. *Auntie Mame*. New York: Vanguard Press.

Weeks, Joseph. *All Our Yesterdays*. New York: Rinehart.

Wouk, Herman. *Marjorie Morningstar*. Garden City, New York: Doubleday.

1954

Davis, Clyde Brion. *The Newcomer*. Philadelphia: J. B. Lippincott.

Dubin, Harry Ennis. *Hail, Alma Pater*. New York: Hermitage House.

Faralla, Dana. *Black Renegade*. Philadelphia: J. B. Lippincott.

Fisher, Steve. *Giveaway*. New York: Random House.

Hunter, Evan. *Blackboard Jungle*. New York: Simon & Schuster.

Lumbard, C[harles] G[ilbert]. *Senior Spring*. New York: Simon & Schuster.

Miller, Nolan. *Why I Am So Beat*. New York: G. P. Putnam's.

Scott, Glenn. *A Sound of Voices Dying*. New York: E. P. Dutton.

Stolz, Mary. *Pray Love, Remember*. New York: Harper & Row.

Street, James. *Good-bye, My Lady*. Philadelphia: J. B. Lippincott.

Tunis, John. *Go, Team, Go!* New York: William Morrow.

West, Jessamyn. *Cress Delahanty*. New York: Harcourt, Brace.

1953

Angoff, Charles. *In the Morning Light*. New York: Beechhurst Press.

Baldwin, James. *Go Tell It on the Mountain*. New York: Knopf.

Bellow, Saul. *The Adventures of Augie March*. New York: Viking Press.

Bro, Margueritte Harmon. *Stub: A College Romance.* Garden City, New York: Doubleday.

Burress John. *Apple on a Pear Tree.* New York: Vanguard Press.

Burt, Nathaniel. *Scotland's Burning.* Boston: Little, Brown.

Clayton, John Bell. *Wait, Son, October Is Near.* New York: Macmillan.

Davis, Reuben. *Shim.* Indianapolis and New York: Bobbs-Merrill.

Edmonds, Walter D. *The Boyds of Black River.* New York: Dodd, Mead.

Ellson, Hal. *Summer Street.* New York: Ballantine Books.

Halper, Albert. *The Golden Watch.* New York: Henry Holt.

Kennedy, Mark. *The Pecking Order.* New York: Appleton-Century-Crofts.

Keogh, Theodora. *The Tatooed Heart.* New York: Farrar, Straus.

[Marquand,] John Phillips [Jr.]. *The Second Happiest Day.* New York: Harper & Row.

Moody, Ralph. *The Fields of Home.* New York: W. W. Norton.

Shulman Irving. *The Square Trap.* Boston: Little, Brown.

Stolz, Mary. *Ready or Not.* New York: Harper & Row.

Wallop, Douglass. *Night Light.* New York: W. W. Norton.

Weldon, John Lee. *The Naked Heart.* New York: Farrar, Straus.

1952

Burt, Katharine Newlin. *Escape from Paradise.* New York: Scribner's.

Calitri, Charles. *Rickey.* New York: Scribner's.

Clayton, John Bell. *Six Angels at My Back.* New York: Macmillan.

Davis, H[arold] L[enoir]. *Winds of Morning.* New York: William Morrow.

Davis, Kenneth S. *Morning in Kansas.* Garden City, New York: Doubleday.

DeJong, David Cornel. *Two Sofas in the Parlor.* Garden City, New York: Doubleday.

Doan, Daniel. *The Crystal Years.* New York: Abelard Press.

Ellison, Ralph. *Invisible Man.* New York: Random House.

Ellson, Hal. *The Golden Spike.* New York: Ballantine Books.

Emery, Anne. *Sorority Girl.* Philadelphia: Westminster Press.

Gorham, Charles. *Trial by Darkness.* New York: Dial Press.

Harris, Sara. *The Wayward Ones.* New York: Crown.

Macauley Robie. *The Disguises of Love.* New York: Random House.

Mandel, George. *Flee the Angry Strangers.* Indianapolis and New York: Bobbs-Merrill.

[Mayer, Jane, and Spiegel, Clara] Clare Jaynes. *Early Frost.* New York: Random House.

Michaelson, John Nairne. *Morning, Winter, and Night.* New York: Sloane.

Smith, Madeline Babcock. *The Lemon Jelly Cake.* Boston: Little, Brown.

Stafford, Jean. *The Catherine Wheel.* New York: Harcourt, Brace.

Steinbeck, John. *East of Eden.* New York: Viking Press.

Thacher, Russell. *The Tender Age.* New York: Macmillan.

1951

Abel, Hilde. *The Guests of Summer.* Indianapolis and New York: Bobbs-Merrill.

Agee, James. *The Morning Watch*. Boston: Houghton Mifflin.
Capote, Truman. *The Grass Harp*. New York: Random House.
Jackson, Shirley. *Hangsaman*. New York: Farrar, Straus.
L'Engle, Madeleine. *Camilla Dickinson*. New York: Simon & Schuster.
Lincoln, Victoria. *Out from Eden*. New York: Rinehart.
Moody, Ralph. *Man of the Family*. New York: W. W. Norton.
Moore, Ruth. *Candlemas Bay*. New York: William Morrow.
Phillips, Thomas Hal. *The Golden Lie*. New York: Rinehart.
Salinger, J[erome] D[avid]. *The Catcher in the Rye*. Boston: Little, Brown.
Shulman, Max. *The Many Loves of Dobie Gillis*. Garden City, New York: Doubleday.
Styron, William. *Lie Down in Darkness*. Indianapolis and New York: Bobbs-Merrill.
West, Jessamyn. *The Witch Diggers*. New York: Harcourt, Brace.

1950

[Adams, Alger] Philip B. Kaye. *Taffy*. New York: Crown.
Armstrong, Charlotte. *Mischief*. New York: Coward, McCann.
Barton, Betsey. *Shadow of the Bridge*. New York: Duell, Sloan & Pearce.
Demby, William. *Beetlecreek*. New York: Rinehart.
Ellson, Hal. *Tomboy*. New York: Scribner's.
Faulkner, John. *Chooky*. New York: W. W. Norton.
Gipson, Fred. *The Home Place*. New York: Harper & Row.
Goodin, Peggy. *Take Care of My Little Girl*. New York: E. P. Dutton.
Harnden, Ruth. *I, a Stranger*. New York: Whittlesey House.
Jackson, Charles. *The Sunnier Side*. New York: Farrar, Straus.
Keogh, Theodore. *Meg*. New York: Creative Age Press.
Lamson, Peggy. *The Charmed Circle*. Philadelphia: J. B. Lippincott.
[Masters, Kelly R.] Zachary Ball. *Piney*. Boston: Little, Brown.
Moody, Ralph. *Little Britches*. New York: W. W. Norton.
Pease, Howard, *The Dark Adventure*. Garden City, New York: Doubleday.
Ritner, Ann. *The Green Bough*. Philadelphia: J. B. Lippincott.
Stewart, John Craig. *Through the First Gate*. New York: Dodd, Mead.
Stillwell, Hart. *Campus Town*. Garden City, New York: Doubleday.
Stuart, Jesse. *Hie to the Hunters*. New York: Whittlesey House.
Taylor, Peter. *A Woman of Means*. New York: Harcourt Brace Jovanovich.
Westheimer, David. *The Magic Fallacy*. New York: Macmillan.
Willingham, Calder. *Geraldine Bradshaw*. New York: Vanguard Press.
Witherspoon, Mary-Elizabeth. *Somebody Speak for Katy*. New York: Dodd, Mead.
Wong, Jade Snow. *Fifth Chinese Daughter*. New York: Harper & Row.

1949

Barber, Elsie Oakes. *The Trembling Years*. New York: Macmillan.
Baumer, Marie. *The Seeker and the Sought*. New York: Scribner's.
Bro, Margueritte Harmon. *Sarah*. Garden City, New York: Doubleday.

Caldwell, Erskine. *Place Called Estherville*. New York: Duell, Sloan & Pearce.
Edwards, E[dward] J. *The Chosen*. New York: Longmans, Green.
Ellson, Hal. *Duke*. New York: Scribner's.
Gipson, Fred. *Hound-Dog Man*. New York: Harper & Row.
Grant, Dorothy Fremont. *Devil's Food*. New York: Longmans, Green.
Lampell, Millard. *The Hero*. New York: Julian Messner.
Lincoln, Victoria. *Celia Amberley*. New York: Rinehart.
McCarthy, Catherine Ridgeway. *Definition of Love*. Boston: Houghton Mifflin.
Marquand, John P. *Point of No Return*. Boston: Little, Brown.
Mende, Robert. *Spit and the Stars*. New York: Rinehart.
Morrison, Ray. *Angels Camp*. New York: W. W. Norton.
Norman, Charles. *The Well of the Past*. Garden City, New York: Doubleday.
[Proffit, Josephine] Sylvia Dee. *And Never Been Kissed*. New York: Macmillan.
Tunis, John. *Son of the Valley*. New York: William Morrow.
Vidal, Gore. *The Season of Comfort*. New York: E. P. Dutton.
Winslow, Anne Goodwin. *The Springs*. New York: Knopf.
Yoseloff, Martin. *The Girl in the Spike-Heeled Shoes*. New York: E. P. Dutton.

1948
Ader, Paul. *The Leaf Against the Sky*. New York: Crown.
Bromfield, Louis. *The Wild Country*. New York: Harper & Row.
Capote, Truman. *Other Voices, Other Rooms*. New York: Random House.
Faulkner, William. *Intruder in the Dust*. New York: Random House.
Gorham, Charles. *The Future Mr. Dolan*. New York: Dial Press.
Millar, Margaret. *It's All in the Family*. New York: Random House.
Moore, Ruth. *The Fire Balloon*. New York: William Morrow.
Morley, Blythe. *The Intemperate Season*. New York: Farrar, Straus.
Nathan, Robert. *Long After Summer*. New York: Knopf.
Plageman, Bentz. *Into the Labyrinth*. New York: Farrar, Straus.
Raphaelson, Dorshka. *Morning Song*. New York: Random House.
Rendina, Laura Cooper. *Roommates*. Boston: Little, Brown.
Shaw, Irwin. *The Young Lions*. New York: Random House.
Summers, Hollis. *City Limit*. Boston: Houghton Mifflin.
Sumner, Cid Rickett, *Tammy Out of Time*. Indianapolis and New York: Bobbs-Merrill.
Vidal, Gore. *The City and the Pillar*. New York: E. P. Dutton.
Wouk, Herman. *The City Boy*. New York: Simon & Schuster.
Yoseloff, Martin. *The Family Members*. New York: E. P. Dutton.

1947
Athas, Daphne. *The Weather of the Heart*. New York: Appleton-Century-Crofts.

Eddy, Roger W. *The Rimless Wheel*. New York: Macmillan.

Faralla, Dana. *The Magnificent Barb*. Philadelphia: J. B. Lippincott.

Foff, Arthur. *Glorious in Another Day*. Philadelphia: J. B. Lippincott.

Henning, William E. *The Heller*. New York: Scribner's.

Lewiton, Mina. *The Divided Heart*. New York: David McKay.

[McLean, Kathryn] Kathryn Forbes. *Transfer Point*. New York: Harcourt, Brace.

Motley, Willard. *Knock on Any Door*. New York: Appleton-Century-Crofts.

Ricks, Peirson. *The Hunter's Horn*. New York: Scribner's

Scott, Virgil. *The Dead Tree Gives No Shelter*. New York: William Morrow.

Shulman, Irving. *The Amboy Dukes*. Garden City, New York: Doubleday.

Sklar, George. *The Two Worlds of Johnny Truro*. Boston: Little, Brown.

Stafford, Jean. *The Mountain Lion*. New York: Harcourt, Brace.

Whitney, Phillis A. *Willow Hill*. New York: Reynal & Hitchcock.

Willingham, Calder. *End as a Man*. New York: Vanguard Press.

Young, I[sador] S. *Jadie Greenway*. New York: Crown.

1946

Goodin, Peggy. *Clementine*. New York: E. P. Dutton.

Johnson, Josephine W. *Wildwood*. New York: Harper & Row.

McCullers, Carson. *The Member of the Wedding*. Boston: Houghton Mifflin.

Marquand, John P. *B. F.'s Daughter*. Boston: Little, Brown.

Pratt, Theodore. *Valley Boy*. New York: Duell, Sloan & Pearce.

Rosenfeld, Isaac. *Passage from Home*. New York: Dial Press.

Scott, Jessie. *Charity Ball*. New York: Macmillan.

[Sture-Vasa, Mary] Mary O'Hara. *The Green Grass of Wyoming*. Philadelphia: J. B. Lippincott.

Treynor, Blair. *She Ate Her Cake*. New York: William Morrow.

1945

Clark, Walter Van Tillburg. *The City of Trembling Leaves*. New York: Random House.

Karig, Walter. *Lower than Angels*. New York: Farrar & Rinehart.

Kehoe, William. *A Sweep of Dusk*. New York: E. P. Dutton.

L'Engle, Madeleine. *The Small Rain*. New York: Vanguard Press.

Maxwell, William. *The Folded Leaf*. New York: Harper & Row.

Means, Florence. *The Moved Outers*. Boston: Houghton Mifflin.

Roberts, Dorothy James. *A Durable Fire*. New York: Macmillan.

Rosaire, Forrest. *East of Midnight*. New York: Knopf.

Seley, Stephen. *The Cradle Will Fall*. New York: Harcourt, Brace.

Wadelton, Tommy. *Silver Buckles on His Knee*. New York: Coward, McCann.

Wickenden, Dan. *The Wayfarers*. New York: William Morrow.

Bibliography:
Textbooks on Adolescence

Abell, Walter H. *The Collective Dream in Art: A Psycho-historical Theory of Culture Based on Relations Between the Arts, Psychology, and Social Sciences.* Cambridge, Massachusetts: Harvard University Press, 1957.

Adams, James F. *Understanding Adolescence: Current Developments in Adolescent Psychology.* 3rd ed. Boston: Allyn & Bacon 1976.

Adelman, Clifford. *Generations: A Collage on Youthcult.* New York: Praeger, 1972.

Aichorn, August. *Wayward Youth.* New York: Viking Press, 1965.

Aldridge, John W. *In Search of Heresy: American Literature in an Age of Conformity.* New York: McGraw-Hill, 1956.

Alexander, Theron. *Children and Adolescents: A Biological Approach to Psychological Development.* Chicago: Aldine, 1969.

Allport, Gordon W. *Becoming.* New Haven: Yale University Press, 1955.

————. *The Use of Personal Documents in Psychological Science.* New York: Social Science Research Council, 1942.

Altbach, Philip G., and Laufer, Robert S., eds. *The New Pilgrims: Youth Protest in Transition.* New York: David McKay, 1972.

Arms, Myron, and Denman, David. *Touching the World.* New York: Scribner's, 1975.

Ausubel, David P. *Theory and Problems of Adolescent Development.* New York: Grune & Stratton, 1954.

Babin, Pierce. *Faith and the Adolescent.* New York: Seabury Press, 1967.

Balser, Benjamin H., ed. *Psychotherapy of the Adolescent: At Different Levels of Psychiatric Practice with Special Emphasis on the Role of the School.* New York: International Universities Press, 1969.

Bandura, Albert, and Walters, Richard H. *Adolescent Aggression: A Study of the Influence of Child-Training Practices and Family Inter-Relationships.* New York: Ronald Press, 1959.

Barron, Milton L. *The Juvenile in Delinquent Society.* New York: Knopf, 1954.

Bergler, Edmund. *The Writer and Psychoanalysis.* New York: Brunner, 1954.

Bernard, Harold W. *Adolescent Development in American Culture.* Yonkers, New York: World, 1957.

Bettleheim, Bruno. *Symbolic Wounds: Puberty Rites and the Envious Male.* New York: Macmillan, 1962.

Bloch, Herbert A., and Flynn, Frank T. *Delinquency: The Juvenile Offender in America Today.* New York: Random House, 1956.

———, and Niederhoffer, Arthur. *The Gang.* Westport, Connecticut: Greenwood Press, 1976.

Blos, Peter. *The Adolescent Personality: A Study of Individual Behavior.* New York: Appleton-Century-Crofts, 1941.

———. *On Adolescence: A Psychoanalytic Interpretation.* New York: Free Press, 1962.

———. *The Young Adolescent: Clinical Studies.* New York: Free Press, 1970.

Bressler, L., and Bressler, M. *Youth in American Life.* New York: Houghton Mifflin, 1972.

Buxton, Claude E. *Adolescents in School.* New Haven, Connecticut: Yale University Press, 1973.

Cantwell, Zita, and Svajian, Pergrouhi, eds. *Adolescence: Studies in Development.* Itasca, Illinois: F. E. Peacock, 1974.

Caplan, Gerald, and Lebovici, Serge, eds. *Adolescence: Perspectives.* New York: Basic Books, 1969.

Carlsen, G. Robert. *Books and the Teen-Age Reader.* New York: Harper & Row, 1971.

Cohen, Albert K. *Delinquent Boys: The Culture of the Gang.* Glencoe, Illinois: Free Press, 1955.

Cole, Luella, and Hall, Irma N. *Psychology of Adolescence.* 7th ed. New York: Holt, Rinehart and Winston, 1970.

Coleman, James S. *Adolescent Society.* New York: Free Press, 1971.

———, et al. *Youth: Transition to Adulthood—Report on Youth of the President's Advisory Committee.* Chicago: University of Chicago Press, 1974.

Coles, Robert, et al. *Twelve to Sixteen: Early Adolescence.* New York: W. W. Norton, 1973.

Conger, John J. *Adolescence and Youth: Psychological Development in a Changing World.* New York: Harper & Row, 1973.

———. *Contemporary Issues in Adolescent Development.* New York: Harper & Row, 1975.

Crow, Lester D., and Crow, A. *Adolescent Development and Adjustment.* 2nd ed. New York: McGraw-Hill, 1965.

Drane, James F. *A New American Reformation: A Study of Youth Culture and Religion.* Totowa, New Jersey: Littlefield, Adams, 1974.

Dreyfus, Edward A. *Adolescence: Theory and Experience.* Indianapolis and New York: Bobbs-Merrill, 1976.

Edelston, H. *Problems of Adolescence*. New York: Philosophical Library, 1957.

Eliade, Mircea. *Rites and Symbols of Initiation: The Mysteries of Birth and Rebirth*. New York: Harper & Row, 1965.

Erikson, Erik. *Childhood and Society*. New York: W. W. Norton, 1950.

———. *Identity: Youth and Crisis*. New York: W. W. Norton, 1968.

———. *Youth: Change and Challenge*. New York: Basic Books, 1963.

Esman, Aaron H., ed. *The Psychology of Adolescence: Essential Readings*. New York: International Universities Press, 1975.

Flacks, Richard. *Youth and Social Change*. New York: Random House, 1971.

Fleming, Charlotte M. *Adolescence: Its Social Psychology*. New York: International Universities Press, 1969.

Frank, Lawrence K., et al. *Personality Development in Adolescent Girls*. Millwood, New York: Krause Reprint, 1951.

Freud, Anna. "Adolescence," in Eissler, Ruth S., et al., eds. *The Psychoanalytic Study of the Child*. New York: International Universities Press, 1958.

———. *The Ego and the Mechanisms of Defense*. New York: International Universities Press, 1946.

Friedenberg, Edgar Z. *Coming of Age in America: Growth and Acquiescence*. New York: Random House, 1965.

———. *Vanishing Adolescent*. Boston: Beacon Press, 1959.

Fuchs, Estelle, ed. *Youth in a Changing World: Cross-Cultural Perspectives on Adolescence*. Chicago: Aldine, 1976.

Gallagher, J. Roswell, and Harris, Herbert I. *Emotional Problems of Adolescents*. New York: Oxford University Press. 1958.

Gallatin, Judith E. *Adolescence and Individuality: A Conceptual Approach to Adolescent Psychology*. New York: Harper & Row, 1975.

Gennep, Arnold Van. *The Rites of Passage*. Chicago: University of Chicago Press, 1960.

Gillespie, James M., and Allport, Gordon W. *Youth's Outlook on the Future*. Garden City, New York: Doubleday, 1955.

Glueck, Sheldon, and Glueck, Eleanor. *Unravelling Juvenile Delinquency*. Cambridge, Massachusetts: Harvard University Press, 1950.

Goodman, Paul. *Growing Up Absurd*. New York: Random House, 1960.

Gordon, C. W. *The Social System of the High School: A Study in the Sociology of Adolescence*. Glencoe, Illinois: Free Press, 1957.

Gottlieb, David, et al. *Emergence of Youth Societies*. New York: Free Press, 1969.

Guardo, Carol J. *The Adolescent as Individual: Issues and Insights*. New York: Harper & Row, 1975.

Gutsch, Kenneth, and Peters, Herman J. *Counseling with Youth: In Search for Identity*. Indianapolis and New York: Bobbs-Merrill, 1973.

Haim, Andre. *Adolescent Suicide*. New York: International Universities Press, 1975.

Hall, Stanley G. *Adolescence* (reprint of 1905 edition). New York: Arno Press, 1970.

Hansen, James C., and Maynard, Peter E. *Youth: Self-Concept and Behavior.* Indianapolis and New York: Bobbs-Merrill, 1973.

Hartmann, Heinz. *The Ego and the Problem of Adaptation.* New York: International Universities Press, 1958.

Havighurst, Robert James. *Human Development and Education.* New York: David McKay, 1967.

————, et al. *A Survey of the Education of Gifted Children.* Chicago: University Press, 1955.

Holmes, Donald J. *Adolescent in Psychotherapy.* Boston: Little, Brown, 1964.

Hudgens, Richard W. *Psychiatric Disorders in Adolescents.* Baltimore: Williams & Wilkens, 1974.

Hurlock, Elizabeth B. *Adolescent Development.* 4th ed. New York: McGraw-Hill, 1973.

Jersild, Arthur T. *In Search of Self.* New York: Teachers College, 1952.

————. *Psychology of Adolescence.* 2nd ed. New York: Macmillan, 1963.

Keniston, Kenneth. *Young Radicals: Notes on Committed Youth.* New York: Harcourt, Brace, 1968.

Kiell, Norman. *The Adolescent Through Fiction: A Psychological Approach.* New York: International Universities Press, 1965.

————. *The Universal Experience of Adolescence.* New York: International Universities Press, 1964.

Konopka, Gisela. *Adolescent Girl in Conflict.* Englewood Cliffs, New Jersey: Prentice-Hall, 1966.

Lehner, George F. J., and Kube, Ella. *The Dynamics of Personal Adjustment.* Englewood Cliffs, New Jersey: Prentice-Hall, 1955.

MacLennan, Beryce W., and Felsenfeld, Naomi. *Group Counseling and Psychotherapy with Adolescents.* New York: Columbia University Press, 1970.

Manaster, Guy J. *Adolescent Development and the Life Tasks.* Boston: Allyn & Bacon, 1977.

Matterson, James F., Jr. *Psychiatric Dilemma of Adolescence.* Boston: Little, Brown, 1967.

Matteson, David R. *Adolescence Today: Sex Roles and the Search for Identity.* Homewood, Illinois: Dorsey Press, 1975.

Mays, John B. *Young Pretenders: Teenage Culture in Contemporary Society.* 2nd ed. New York: Schocken Books, 1968.

Muuss, Rolf E. *Theories of Adolescence.* New York: Random House, 1962.

O'Doherty, E. F. *The Religious Formation of the Adolescent.* New York: Alba House, 1973.

Pearson, Gerald H. J. *Adolescence and the Conflict of Generations.* New York: W. W. Norton, 1958.

————. *Psychoanalysis and the Education of the Child.* New York: W. W. Norton, 1954.

Peel, E. A. *The Nature of Adolescent Judgment*. New York: Halsted Press, 1972.

Powell, Marvin. *Youth: Critical Issues*. Indianapolis and New York: Bobbs-Merrill, 1972.

Reich, Charles A. *The Greening of America: How the Youth Revolution Is Trying to Make America Livable*. New York: Random House, 1970.

Rice, F. Philip. *Adolescent: Development, Relationships, and Culture*. Boston: Allyn & Bacon, 1975.

Rinzler, Alan, ed. *Manifesto Addressed to the President of the United States from the Youth of America*. New York: Macmillan, 1970.

Rogers, Dorothy. *Psychology of Adolescence*. 3rd ed. Englewood Cliffs, New Jersey: Prentice-Hall, 1976.

Rosenberg, Morris. *Society and the Adolescent Self-Image*. Princeton: Princeton University Press, 1965.

Schoolar, Joseph, ed. *Current Issues in Adolescent Psychiatry*. New York: Brunner-Mazel, 1973.

Sebald, Hans. *Adolescence: A Sociological Analysis*. Englewood Cliffs, New Jersey: Prentice-Hall, 1968.

Seidman, Jerome M. *The Adolescent: A Book of Readings*. New York: Dryden, 1953.

Sherif, Muzafer, and Sherif, Carolyn W. *Reference Groups: Exploration into Conformity and Deviation of Adolescents*. New York: Harper & Row, 1964.

Simon, Sidney, et al. *Values Clarification: A Handbook of Practical Strategies for Teachers and Students*. New York: Hart, 1972.

Sklansky, Morris A., et al. *High School Adolescent: Understanding and Treating His Emotional Problems*. New York: Association Press, 1969.

Snyder, Ross. *Young People and Their Culture*. Nashville, Tennessee: Abingdon, 1969.

Stierlin, Helm. *Separating Parents and Adolescents: A Perspective on Running Away, Schizophrenia and Waywardness*. New York: Quadrangle, 1974.

Strang, Ruth. *The Adolescent Views Himself: A Psychology of Adolescence*. New York: McGraw-Hill, 1957.

Sugar, Max., ed. *The Adolescent in Group and Family Therapy*. New York: Brunner-Mazel, 1975.

Thompson, Charles, and Poppen, William. *For Those Who Care: Ways of Relating to Youth*. Indianapolis and New York: Bobbs-Merrill, 1972.

Wattenberg, William W. *The Adolescent Years*. New York: Harcourt, Brace, 1955.

Wheelis, Allen. *The Quest for Identity*. New York: W. W. Norton, 1958.

White, Winston. *Beyond Conformity*. New York: Free Press, 1961.

Whyte, William P. *Street Corner Society*. Chicago: University of Chicago Press, 1943.

Witham, W. Tasker. *The Adolescent in the American Novel: 1920–1960*. New York: Frederick Ungar, 1964.